Waterfowl of North America

Labrador Ducks. Watercolor by Sir Peter Scott

Waterfowl of
North America

PAUL A. JOHNSGARD

INDIANA UNIVERSITY PRESS

BLOOMINGTON & LONDON

The publisher and the author gratefully acknowledge the generous support of the International Wild Waterfowl Association.

Published in Canada by Fitzhenry & Whiteside Limited, Don Mills, Ontario

Manufactured in the United States of America

Library of Congress Cataloging in Publication Data

Johnsgard, Paul A
Waterfowl of North America.

Bibliography
Includes index.
1. Waterfowl—North America.   I. Title.
QL696.A5J62   598.2'97   74-30900
ISBN 0-253-36360-8
1 2 3 4 5 79 78 77 76 75

Dedicated to
JEAN DELACOUR AND PETER SCOTT
Whose Work Has Provided the Foundation
for My Own Efforts

Contents

vii

TABLES

BREEDING AND WINTERING DISTRIBUTION MAPS

The page numbers for the breeding and wintering distribution maps may be found in the index under the species' vernacular names.

Plates

Brant Goose
Muscovy Duck
Wood Duck

European Wigeon
American Wigeon
Falcated Duck

Following page 338

Gadwall
Baikal Teal
American Green-winged Teal
Common Mallard
Mexican Mallard
Florida Mallard
Northern Pintail
Bahama Pintail
Garganey
Blue-winged Teal

Cinnamon Teal
Northern Shoveler
Canvasback
Redhead
Ring-necked Duck
Tufted Duck
Greater Scaup
Lesser Scaup
Common Eider
King Eider

Following page 450

Spectacled Eider
Steller Eider
Oldsquaw
Harlequin Duck
Black Scoter
Surf Scoter
White-winged Scoter
Bufflehead

Barrow Goldeneye
Common Goldeneye
Smew
Hooded Merganser
Red-breasted Merganser
Common Merganser
Masked Duck
Ruddy Duck

Preface

It was with a considerable degree of hesitation that, during the winter of 1970–71, I sat down and contemplated the scope and structure of a possible book on the waterfowl of North America. On my bookshelf behind me were copies of A. C. Bent's *Life Histories of North American Wild Fowl,* F. H. Kortright's *The Ducks, Geese, and Swans of North America,* and Jean Delacour's *The Waterfowl of the World.* My task, as I saw it, was to try to develop a book that might be useful to the greatest number of people without seriously overlapping with any of these great works. Bent's classic volumes had admirably summarized the early "life history" information. Kortright's book has been the standard reference for waterfowl illustrations and plumage descriptions for the past thirty years. Delacour's multivolume monograph obviously commanded sufficient authority to render unnecessary detailed consideration of taxonomic questions. My own earlier books on waterfowl behavior (*Handbook of Waterfowl Behavior*) and waterfowl biology (*Waterfowl: Their Biology and Natural History*) made superfluous additional descriptions of sexual behavior patterns or general comparative reviews of ecology and breeding biology.

What remained to be done, I finally decided, was to provide an up-to-date series of accounts dealing with the ecology and reproductive biology of every waterfowl species presently known to breed on the North American continent. In this way, the recent field studies of three separate groups, the wildlife biologists, ecologists, and ethologists, might be integrated. I hoped to make the book understandable to nonprofessionals, but still retain sufficient specific information as to make it a useful reference for students and professional waterfowl biologists. Secondly, information on both field and in-hand identification of all waterfowl species likely to be encountered in North America seemed to me to be equally important, especially in view of the increasing requirements for hunters to recognize quite precisely what they shoot or attempt to shoot. Also, practical means of accurate identification of waterfowl, and the further determination of waterfowl as to age and sex, are of foremost importance to biologists concerned with waterfowl management. These two goals thus became the nucleus for the development of the book. Illustrative materials in the form of distribution maps and photographs of live birds were added to supplement written descriptions of ranges, plumages, and identification criteria. Except where otherwise indicated all photographs and drawings are mine.

The text of the book was subsequently prepared in two sections. First, the preliminary materials were developed for each species, including ranges, subspecies, weights, measurements, and identification aids. For this section it was usually expedient or necessary to rely on a variety of previous publications. Delacour's *Waterfowl of the World* was the primary basis for subspecies criteria and provided the major source of wing and culmen measurements. Likewise, the criteria for specific and generic limits used here are largely those of Delacour and of my own earlier publications. Where such usages differ significantly from those of the American Ornithologists' Union (1957 and supplement in *Auk,* 90:411–419, 1973), these differences are noted. A further deviation from the general practice of the A.O.U. is the use of distinctive vernacular names for subspecies, but whenever possible these names have been devised by the addition of an appropriate adjective to the basic vernacular name of the species.

The separate accounts of the distribution, ecology, and behavior of all the species known to breed in North America were written next. I tried to avoid as far as possible the earlier literature that has been repeatedly summarized by Bent, Kortright, and Delacour, and instead to emphasize information having possible application in the conservation and management of each species. Space limitations forced the adoption of a uniform format and a rather terse writing style, with little or no consideration for each species' possible esthetic values or its relative sporting importance. Thus, when the species accounts had been completed the text still seemed vaguely unsatisfying and somehow unfinished. The three preliminary chapters were then envisioned as a means of providing a cohesive overview and introduction to the individual species accounts and as an expression of my personal evaluation of the significance of our waterfowl resource to twentieth-century America.

It is impossible to acknowledge adequately all the sources of encouragement and assistance I have had during the course of gathering information and assembling materials for this book. The most significant of these is perhaps the John S. Guggenheim Foundation, whose fellowship supported me through the winter, spring, and summer of 1971, when a substantial part of the initial draft was formulated. The University of Nebraska Research Council provided me with a leave of absence during that year and also with a summer faculty fellowship during 1972. Travel expenses associated with fieldwork and manuscript preparation during the summer of 1972 were provided by a grant from the Penrose fund of the American Philosophical Society. The National Science Foundation had earlier (1964–68) provided me with a research grant that allowed several years of study and summer fieldwork that would have otherwise been impossible to accomplish. Two years of study at the Wildfowl Trust, in England, financed by fellowships from the National Science Foundation (1959) and the U.S. Public Health Service (1960), were an equally important background component. The pleasant associations I had there with the Wildfowl Trust's scientific staff greatly influenced me, and its unsurpassed collection of live waterfowl gave me a unique research opportunity at a critical stage in my professional development.

I would be remiss not to mention a few people who have individually assisted me in various ways during the preparation of this book. In particular, Sir Peter Scott most kindly provided the marvelous Labrador duck painting, which fully captures the essence of that beautiful but extinct bird. It is especially appropriate that Scott, who has personally done so much to prevent the extinction of such species as the Hawaiian goose, has contributed this interpretation of a species that no one will ever again see in life.

Although I have used my own photographs whenever possible, in a few instances I have resorted to those taken by others. For their use, I would like to thank Burr Betts, Dirk Hagemeyer, and George Moffett. I was also graciously allowed to photograph waterfowl in a number of private collections, including those of Betty Carnes, Winston Guest, Jack Kiracofe, William Lemburg, William Macy, Christopher Marler, "Mickey" Ollson, Charles Pilling, and George Searles, to all of whom I again express my appreciation. Unpublished information on certain species was provided by Robert Alison, Dale Crider, Dennis Crouch, Robert Elgas, Dirk Hagemeyer, John Lynch, Calvin Lensink, and George Schildman. I owe a special debt of thanks to the International Wild Waterfowl Association, for a substantial subsidy toward the printing costs associated with this book.

No doubt the greatest help and the strongest guiding influence of all were provided by my parents, who from my childhood encouraged me to develop my interests in birds as well as in nature in general. Through the books they gave me I was introduced to the writings of H. A. Hochbaum, F. H. Kortright, and Aldo Leopold, all of whom thus transmitted to me their own love of wildlife and enabled me to determine the kind of life I wanted to shape for myself. In a real sense, this present book is the fulfillment of a long-standing self-promise that one day, with a contribution of my own, I would try to repay these persons and the countless others who have directed their lives toward the understanding and preservation of our North American waterfowl.

Part I Introduction

The Biology of Waterfowl

The term *waterfowl,* at least as it is applied in North America, is generally restricted to the ducks, geese, and swans of the bird family Anatidae. About 140 species of this group of swimming and diving birds have survived throughout the world to the present day, and four more have become extinct during historical times. Many more species have existed in the past; the fossil record of this family extends back roughly fifty million years to very early Cenozoic times, although very little is known of the actual appearance and structure of the earliest form of waterfowl. Presumably these ancestral birds were semiaquatic, perhaps much like the modern-day species of screamers (Anhimidae), which together with the true waterfowl make up the order Anseriformes. These in turn seem to have been derived from land-adapted and fowllike birds that later diversified into such groups as pheasants, quails, partridges, turkeys, and other "gallinaceous" species.

In part because of their common evolutionary ancestry, waterfowl and the upland, or gallinaceous, birds have certain similarities in their biology that are more fundamental than the obvious differences in their adaptations to aquatic versus terrestrial habitats. One of the most significant of these common attributes is the rather advanced, or precocial, state in which the young are invariably hatched. This implies that they are well covered with down and thus can better maintain a steady body temperature than can birds hatched naked or nearly so. They also are hatched with their eyes open, and they are sufficiently coordinated so that they can begin feeding on their own in a day or less of leaving the egg. They have a variety of calls and can respond quickly and effectively to calls of their parents that may help to keep the family together and safe from danger. They typically remain together as a cohesive "brood" during the period between hatching and initial flight, or fledging, and during this time they undergo the socialization processes that may be impor-

3

tant later in pair formation at the time of sexual maturity. They also learn the local topography and, especially in the case of females, the landmarks necessary to allow the birds to "home" to their natal area at the time of initial nesting.

Unlike most upland game birds, nearly all North American waterfowl are migratory to some degree, and although the timing and general compass-direction tendencies for movement may be innately transmitted from generation to generation, a considerable part of the specific aspects of migration is dependent on a transmission of migratory "traditions" from the older birds to the younger ones by direct experience. This flexibility in migratory behavior accounts for the surprisingly rapid shifts in migratory pathways and stopover points that waterfowl are able to make when major environmental changes occur, such as the establishment of bird refuges, the filling of impoundments, and the like. On the other hand, this adaptability also may cause an area to be "burned out" of its waterfowl use, when disturbance or excessive mortality disrupts the traditional use of an area. This capability for human manipulation of usage by waterfowl in their migratory or wintering areas poses enormous problems for wildlife biologists, who must choose carefully between the desirability of providing safe and attractive areas for use by large numbers of birds and the potential dangers imposed by such congregations: disease or parasite transmission, crop depredations on nearby private lands, and the encouragement of unrestricted or uncontrolled hunting in areas adjacent to the controlled-usage areas. Interstate and international politics may even become involved, in view of the great economic significance of waterfowl hunting in certain parts of North America.

Usually during their first fall or winter of life, but in the case of swans, geese, and sea ducks in their second winter, the family bonds that promoted the brood's survival and transmission of migratory traditions are broken and are replaced by pair-bonding processes. The strength and duration of pair bonds in waterfowl differ greatly among species and are in general linked to the relative importance of the presence of the male in protecting the female, her eggs, or their offspring during their most vulnerable periods. Swans and geese exhibit a combination of the strongest pair bonds, the smallest clutch sizes, the longest periods of prefledging vulnerability of the young, and the longest deferral of sexual maturity. All of these interrelated characteristics suggest that the gambles associated with reproduction are much greater in these species than in the typical ducks, where conditions variably approach the opposite extreme.

Swans and geese are so large and generally so conspicuous that their nests may be readily apparent to predators, their incubation periods and fledging periods are so long that renesting attempts in the typically abbreviated nesting seasons of northern latitudes are fruitless, and the requirements for space and food adequate to rear a brood are so great that territorial behavior may limit the density and success of nesting birds in the best habitat. Thus, in keeping with the royalty often ascribed to swans, their social behavior is based on a nonegalitarian doctrine of differential social status and reduced probabilities of successful reproduction in an environment of limited resources and difficult survival.

In contrast, duck species such as mallards and other common "dabbling ducks" represent the ultimate in trends toward a democratic society. Sexual .maturity follows hard on the attainment of fledging, and male mallards may begin pair-forming behavior within six months of their hatching. Pair bonds, even after they are formed, are relatively weak, and shifting about of mates may occur even without the needs generated by the death of one member of a pair. The territorial behavior by males of most duck species is weak or may even be lacking, apart from a defense of the female herself, and even this terminates shortly after the female has begun to incubate her clutch of eggs. In most ducks, the males never even see their own offspring, for by the time of hatching they have begun their vulnerable flightless period associated with the postnuptial molt. This molt may be undertaken at a considerable distance from the nesting area, the male undertaking a "molt migration" as soon as he deserts his mate. Should the female in the interim suffer the loss of her clutch or even her brood, she may remate with any available male still in suitable reproductive condition to fertilize her second clutch of eggs, and she may thereby still at least attain her own reproductive success. Parent-offspring bonds in many ducks are rather weak, promoting the development of broods of mixed family origins or even mixed species broods.

Mixing of young of different species is also facilitated by the generally weak territorial defense of male ducks, particularly toward other species. The result is that females of two or more species may nest in close proximity, or one may even inadvertently "drop" one or more of her eggs in another's nest. Nests that are used by two or more females are called "dump nests," and because of frequent fighting over nest possession the eggs are often only ineffectively incubated or not incubated at all. Such dump-nesting is most prevalent in hole-nesting species where suitable nest cavities are limited, and in such species (such as goldeneyes) true territorial behavior involving the defense of the nesting area is well developed, which would help to reduce the occurrence of mixed clutches.

Certain species of duck are much more prone to dropping their eggs in the nest of other females; this is especially true of ruddy ducks and redheads.

Both species are in fact best regarded as incipient nest "parasites," since perhaps as many or more eggs are laid in other nests of their own or other species as are incubated by the females themselves. Studies to date have suggested that the hatching success of parasitically laid eggs is rather low, and virtually none of the adaptations of the highly specialized socially parasitic species of birds are to be found in these ducks. Indeed, only a single species of duck, the South American black-headed duck, is believed to be an obligate nesting parasite, since no nest of this species has yet been found. However, female black-headed ducks have been observed with flightless young, so that some doubt as to this species' dependence on parasitic nesting still remains.

It is characteristic of all species of waterfowl to delay the start of incubation until the last egg has been laid. The length of time needed to complete a clutch varies greatly and depends on the total clutch size and the time interval between successive eggs, which is usually one or two days. During the egg-laying period the female usually spends little time at the nest, leaving it exposed to possible predation or other losses. However, in geese and swans, the male is usually present to guard the nest: As the clutch nears completion the female progressively lines the nest with down and plucked feathers, although the amount used varies considerably in different species. Swans generally use very little down in their nests, geese and ducks tend to use more, and some arctic-nesting ducks use rather large quantities, as in the case of eiders. The tropical-nesting whistling ducks normally have no down in their nests. Usually the nesting down is dark-colored, even if the other underpart feathers are white, although some hole-nesting species do have white down.

In most species of North American waterfowl the actual clutch size is variable, although the "normal" size of initial clutches may be fairly predictable, especially in species having smaller clutches. There is less variation in clutch size among high-latitude nesters than among more tropical ones, and among ground-nesting forms versus hole-nesters. Clutches that are laid late in the breeding season also tend to be smaller than the ones started earlier, and likewise repeat clutches laid by a female who was unsuccessful in her first nesting attempt are appreciably smaller than initial ones. Since the size of the clutch is also a reflection of the female's tolerance for physiological drain, the health and general fat reserves of the particular female also tend to influence the total size of the clutch. In general, clutch size tends to be smallest in swans, slightly larger in geese, larger still in surface-nesting ducks, and largest in hole-nesting ducks. Clutches also tend to average larger in low-latitude species than high-latitude ones, perhaps because of the need for effective covering and warming of the entire clutch under cold conditions, the other demands on energy reserves associated with nesting in arctic environments, or even the shorter time available for nesting and brood-rearing under these adverse conditions.

In at least some species of whistling duck, one Australian species of swan, and a very few other species of waterfowl, the male actively participates in incubation, often sharing incubation time more or less equally with the female. Among the North American waterfowl, only in the whistling ducks does the male normally participate in this way. Male mute swans, and to some extent the other swans, may regularly tend the eggs in the absence of the female, and in at least the case of the mute swan the male may take over incubation duties should the female die. Active participation by the male in normal incubation duties may also occur among the other swans to a rather greater degree than is currently appreciated, because of the difficulty of distinguishing actual incubation of the eggs from simply guarding them.

Once incubation begins, the female usually becomes very reluctant to leave the nest, and in at least some arctic species of waterfowl she may fast for the entire incubation period. It is common among temperate-zone species of duck that the female takes early-morning and late-afternoon or evening breaks from incubation, so that she may forage for a while. At this time she may be joined by the drake, if he is still in attendance. As hatching approaches, the female sits more continuously, and a certain amount of effective communication between the female and the still unhatched eggs seems to occur. The process of the exit from the egg, called pipping, may require twenty-four hours or more, and although the last-laid egg is often the last to hatch, the entire clutch typically hatches in a remarkably synchronized fashion, often within a total time span of five or six hours. Several additional hours after hatching are required for the down to dry and to fluff properly, so that the brood are likely to remain in the nest for at least the first night of their lives. By the following morning the female generally leads her brood from the nest, sometimes never to return to it. However, a few waterfowl species do use the old nest as a place to brood their young; this is especially typical of swans and of such pochards as canvasbacks and redheads, which usually construct semifloating nests of reeds well away from land. The large, bulky nests of swans also provide a convenient substitute for land-brooding and may be used for a month or more by the family, especially at night.

Although among geese and swans the parental attachment for the young persists through the entire posthatching period and the following migration, the brood bond of female ducks toward their offspring is much weaker and more variable, presumably being dependent on hormonal controls. Generally it persists through most or nearly all of the prefledging period, which may be as little as about forty days in some surface-feeding ducks and arctic-breeders, or as much as sixty to seventy days in certain diving ducks. At varying times before the young are ready to fledge, the female typically begins her post-nuptial molt, which always includes the flight feathers. Then, like the male, she becomes flightless for a time and thus highly secretive in her behavior, for she is then very vulnerable to predation and, in addition, is usually weak from the stresses associated with molting and reproduction. The length of the flightless period seems to vary considerably among species and even for the same species in different regions, but in general it is probably no less than a month and no more than two months. Thus, females of many species have often just emerged from their flightless period when they are required to begin moving toward their winter quarters. In both sexes molting of the body feathers may thus continue well into the fall migratory period. Whereas among ducks it is typical for the male to begin molting considerably in advance of the female, in geese and swans the molting of the adults is more synchronized, and indeed the female typically molts in advance of the male, often starting shortly after the young are hatched.

The timing of the fall and winter prenuptial molt back into breeding plumage varies even more than that of the postnuptial molt. Geese and swans lack a prenuptial molt altogether, and thus they exhibit virtually no seasonal variation in appearance. Evidently all ducks have a rather extensive prenuptial molt; although it is most conspicuous among males it is also present in females and affects all the feathers except those of the wings and sometimes the tail. In one North American species, the oldsquaw, there is even a third molt and a partially new plumage occurring during the winter, involving some head feathers and the scapulars. For male ducks, the timing of the prenuptial molt and subsequent assumption of the nuptial plumage is closely tied to the timing of pair-forming behavior. Social displays may begin before the males are in "full" plumage, but typically there is a close relationship between the occurrence of courtship activity and the timing of maximum brilliance of feathers and unfeathered areas such as the bill and the legs, as well as iris coloration in some species.

The intensity and complexity of pair-forming or "courtship" displays vary greatly, being under the influence of a multitude of environmental factors. These include the need for stimulating and synchronizing the sexual rhythms of the other sex, the need for sexual and species specificity to avoid homosexual matings or matings between different species, and the ecological counterpressures favoring cryptic or nonconspicuous behavior and appearance in response to varying amounts of predation danger.

With the probable single exception of the muscovy duck, all the species included in this book are ones that form monogamous pair bonds, lasting either until incubation has begun (in the case of ducks) or indefinitely, and potentially as long as both members of the pair survive (in geese and swans). For such pair-forming species, there is generally a distinction to be made between the pair-forming displays that initially forge the pair bond (which require the sexual and species-specificity previously mentioned) and the pair-maintaining displays that probably serve to synchronize sexual rhythms of the pair. Lastly, displays associated specifically with the facilitation of actual mating, or copulation, are needed in all species. A promiscuous species such as the muscovy duck has no need for the first two categories of display, and thus its social displays are limited to aggressive signals used in male-to-male interactions and heterosexual displays associated directly with mating.

It is interesting to note that although aggressive and threat displays used by males toward other males are obviously functional and serve to facilitate social dominance and achieve preferential opportunities for mating among the fittest males, there is also a surprising component of aggression in the behavior of males toward females and vice versa. The reason for this aggressive component are still speculative but obviously include the fact that the male sex hormone testosterone is closely linked with aggressiveness among vertebrates, and additionally there is a clear relationship between the ability of a male to keep other competing males away from an available female and his subsequent chances of mating with her himself. Likewise, females must be able to repel males effectively if they are to avoid constant harassment and possible rape by the still unmated males, which are usually present in considerable excess over unmated females.

The social behavior of waterfowl, like other birds, is largely dependent on communication by visual, vocal, or tactile methods, with the elements of the communication system being "packaged" in relatively nonmistakable stereotyped behavior patterns, or "displays." The repertoire of displays of any species is usually unique when the displays are considered collectively, even though some components may be identical to those of other species. The recognition of such corresponding, or "homologous," display elements is thus the basis for comparative behavioral analysis, just as the recognition of homologous anatomical elements is the basis for comparative anatomy. Thus displays are usually given descriptive names that, if well chosen, will serve to provide a shorthand means of identification for persons familiar with the corresponding display in other species. Although the same motor pattern associated with a visual display may be nearly identical in two related species, it is apparent that plumage patterns or other morphological differences may confer specificity on the two species. Likewise, differences in the tracheal anatomy of two species, such as length, diameter, and configuration, may generate acoustical differences in calls made under the same circumstances and motivation. Additionally, tension variations in the sound-producing syringeal apparatus, as well as the volume of air that is passed through it, may produce varying sound frequencies and amplitudes, resulting in characteristic call patterns that are the functional equivalent of human languages.

Following its establishment, a pair bond is maintained and strengthened by various mutual activities by the members of a pair. Among geese and swans the repeated performance of a "triumph ceremony," which is performed after the eviction of a real or symbolic "enemy" from the vicinity of the pair, is the primary behavioral bond that holds the pair together. This is generally marked by excited calling and head-waving movements by the two birds, and often also by wing-shaking or wing-waving movements as well. Among ducks, ritualized drinking and preening movements, which may differ little if at all from those normally performed as functional "comfort activities," provide a corresponding means of providing a simple mate-recognition signal system. In certain species of ducks, and particularly in the pochards and sea ducks, the same or similar signals may serve as early stages of precopulatory behavior by the pair.

Copulation is performed in the water by all the North American species of ducks. Its occurrence may be largely limited to the time immediately preceding and during the egg-laying period (as in geese and swans), or it may be much more prolonged and begin several months before the time when actual fertilization of the female is needed. To what extent such behavior might play an important role in the strengthening or maintenance of pair bonds is uncertain at present. Likewise, the significance of the generally well-developed postcopulatory displays is still rather speculative.

Raping or attempted rapes of females by males is a surprisingly common feature of the social behavior of ducks, but it is either extremely rare or totally absent among geese and swans. It has been argued by some that the raping of females whose eggs have been lost and whose mates have already deserted might provide the functional advantage of assuring the fertility of a second clutch, but this, too, is difficult to state with certainty.

Adaptations associated with foraging and food-getting are another important phase of waterfowl behavior. It is instructive to compare the diversity of bill shape and leg placement that exists among the waterfowl group as compared with, for example, the remarkable similarity of beaks and legs among the upland game birds of North America. There can be little doubt that, by these structural modifications that influence the birds' capabilities for diving, underwater activities, and extracting various kinds of foods, the waterfowl have achieved a maximum degree of habitat exploitation with a minimum of interspecies competition for the same foods. Thus, with such closely related forms as the blue-winged teal, cinnamon teal, and northern shoveler, there exists a progressive gradient in bill structure involving length, width, and relative development of sievelike lamellae. These change the bill from a tool adapted basically to probing and picking up materials from below the surface to a surface-straining device of remarkable efficiency. Likewise, the bills of swans are primarily adapted for the tearing and consumption of submerged aquatic plants, whereas those of most geese are much more efficient at clipping or tearing terrestrial herbaceous vegetation close to the ground. Similarly the heavy mollusk-crushing bills of scoters and the larger eiders differ impressively from those of their relatives the harlequin and oldsquaw, which consume large quantities of soft-bodied crustaceans, insects, and much smaller bivalve mollusks.

In parallel with species differences in bill shapes and foraging adaptations, the habitats utilized by various species of North American waterfowl differ remarkably. Freshwater, brackish, and saltwater habitats are all utilized, standing-water and flowing-water communities are likewise used, and water areas of all depths from temporarily flooded meadows to lakes several hundred feet deep are exploited for feeding and resting. Closely related species of birds that have similar bill shapes and foraging methods often differ in the habitats utilized. Thus, brackish to more saline wintering habitats are favored by red-breasted mergansers and Barrow goldeneyes, while freshwater lakes and rivers are the primary wintering areas of their respective close relatives, the common merganser and the common goldeneye. Similarly, the common mallard and black duck are associated, respectively, with open-country marshes and forested swamps for breeding, and the greater and lesser scaups are effectively segregated by habitat preference differences in both breeding and wintering areas. A more comprehensive summary of such breeding habitat differences among species is to be found in the chapter dealing with distribution and migration.

Waterfowl vary appreciably in their capabilities for ready takeoff and prolonged flight; this, too, is understandable in terms of ecological adaptations. The species that are the best divers and underwater swimmers (such as the stiff-tailed ducks and the mergansers) have sacrificed aerial agility and the ease of becoming airborne for anatomical needs associated with foraging requirements. However, in such swimming "generalists" as the surface-feeding ducks that rarely have to dive for their food, the legs are placed fairly far forward and are relatively close together. This improves their walking movements on land and increases the ease of rapid takeoff from either ground or water. On land the birds simply spring into the air, while on water a combined thrusting movement of the feet and wings downward into the water instantly propels them into the air. By comparison, in order to take flight directly the masked duck must first make a shallow dive and use the associated forward propulsion of the feet and perhaps also the wings to gain the needed momentum to leave the water. Or, as in the ruddy duck, a long pattering run over fairly open water, involving both wings and feet, is required to bring the bird to "flight speed."

Speed of flight, maximum altitudes attained, and maximum duration of flight are all associated with such aerodynamic problems as "wing-loading," the configuration of the wings, and the total weight of the bird. Such heavy-bodied birds as swans are among the most slowly flying waterfowl, averaging about 35 miles per hour on short, local flights and somewhat more on long, migratory trips. On long, migratory flights swans have been found to fly as high as 10,000 feet, presumably to avoid air turbulence associated with lower altitudes. They can cover between 250 and 700 miles in a single "leg," much of which may be done in darkness. Under these conditions a star-filled sky is much more useful than a cloudy one, since overcast conditions obscure the navigational information provided by the constellations. Surprisingly, the moon is evidently of less value than the stars for nocturnal navigation, except possibly as an aid to illuminating surface landmarks.

Waterfowl Distributions and Migrations in North America

The species of waterfowl breeding in North America have distribution patterns that collectively reflect the past geologic and ecological histories of this continent. In general, our waterfowl species may be grouped into those that are limited (endemic) to North America, those that are shared between North and South America, and those that are shared with Europe and/or Asia. Of the forty-four species known to breed in continental North America, the resulting grouping of breeding distributions is as follows:

Limited to North America: Snow goose (also on Greenland and Wrangel Island), Ross goose, Canada goose (also on Greenland), wood duck, American wigeon, black duck, blue-winged teal, redhead, canvasback, ring-necked duck, lesser scaup, Labrador duck (extinct), surf scoter, bufflehead, hooded merganser.

Shared with Eurasia: Trumpeter swan (whooper swan), whistling swan (Bewick swan), white-fronted goose, brant goose, gadwall, green-winged teal, mallard, pintail, shoveler, greater scaup, common eider, king eider, harlequin duck, oldsquaw, black scoter, white-winged scoter, common goldeneye, red-breasted merganser, common merganser.

Shared with South America: Fulvous whistling duck, black-bellied whistling duck, muscovy duck, cinnamon teal, masked duck, ruddy duck.

Shared with Asia only: Emperor goose, spectacled eider, Steller eider (rarely to Norway).

Shared with Europe only: Barrow goldeneye (Iceland and Greenland).

Native to Eurasia, introduced into North America: Mute swan.

13

It is thus clear that the strongest zoogeographic affinities of our waterfowl are with Europe and Asia, since twenty-three out of the forty-four native North American species have populations shared with one or both of these areas. Only six species are shared with South America, and, of these, the fulvous whistling duck has a more general tropical distribution that includes Africa and southern Asia. Consequently, it would appear that South America has played only a minor role in providing waterfowl stock for North America, and vice versa.

Certainly the great number of waterfowl species shared between the North American and Eurasian landmasses can be largely attributed to Pleistocene and post-Pleistocene history. Ploeger (1968) analyzed the distributions of eighteen species of arctic-breeding Anatidae and concluded that both their present distributions and their described geographic variations could be attributed to the physical-geographical situation existing in the Northern Hemisphere during Late Glacial times. Only a minority (38 percent) of these species exhibit noticeable geographic variation, and most of the eighteen have breeding ranges that include both North America and Eurasia. The exceptions are three Eurasian geese (red-breasted, bean, and lesser white-fronted geese), three North American geese (Canada, Ross, and snow geese), and the North Atlantic barnacle goose. It is of interest that these are all geese, a group noted for their strongly traditional wintering and breeding grounds, as opposed to the less tradition-bound ducks.

If the remaining species of North American waterfowl that have transatlantic or transpacific ranges are considered, the following relationships may be seen:

Same subspecies throughout Northern Hemisphere: Gadwall, pintail, shoveler.
Two or more Northern Hemisphere subspecies: Trumpeter swan, green-winged teal, mallard, greater scaup, black scoter, white-winged scoter, common goldeneye, red-breasted merganser, common merganser.

It is clear that at least a majority of these less-arctic-adapted species exhibit measurable geographic variation, suggestive of a longer period of isolation between North American and non-North American populations. Of the thirteen remaining species which lack both South American affinities and transatlantic or transpacific ranges, the majority have obvious or probable ecological replacement forms in Europe or Asia:

Ecological replacement forms present: Wood duck (mandarin duck), American wigeon (European wigeon), black duck (Chinese spot-bill), blue-winged teal (garganey), canvasback (European pochard), lesser scaup (tufted duck), hooded merganser (smew).

No obvious replacement forms present: Snow goose, Ross goose, Canada goose, redhead, Labrador duck, surf scoter.

Of the last group of species, it might be mentioned that some Eurasian species with similar or overlapping habitat requirements do exist, namely the "tundra" bean geese for the snow and Ross geese, and the gray-lag goose for the larger forms of the Canada goose. However, many more ecological differences exist between these relatively distantly related species than is true of the species pairs mentioned above.

In theory at least, each North American waterfowl species should occupy habitats and exhibit behavioral niche adaptations slightly different from those of all other native species. Oftentimes it is impossible to pigeonhole these differences neatly in just a few words, but it is nevertheless of some interest to try to identify the habitat types with which each species is most closely associated during the breeding period. This has been attempted in Table 1, which lists major North American habitat types and their associated nesting waterfowl species in an arctic to tropic gradient. It suggests the following general affiliations among major climatic zones, breeding habitats, and waterfowl groups: Arctic tundra—geese, swans, and sea ducks; boreal forest—sea ducks and pochards; broadleaf temperate or tropical forests—perching ducks; temperate nonforested wetlands—dabbling ducks and pochards; tropical wetlands —whistling ducks. The great importance of the arctic tundra habitats and of breeding habitats associated with the native grassland areas of North America is further illustrated by an examination of relative continental densities of breeding waterfowl (Figure 1). This map is based on a similar one (in Linduska, 1964, p.720) illustrating duck breeding densities, with additional information on arctic goose and swan breeding areas inserted by the author. Indicated major wintering areas were derived from a variety of sources, including Linduska (1964), Leopold (1959), and others. Clearly, the importance of the "duck factories" of the Canadian Prairie Provinces cannot be overemphasized, especially for the important game species of dabbling ducks and pochards. Likewise, the Alaskan and Canadian arctic habitats are of critical importance to our goose, swan, and sea duck populations. These latter areas, although remote, are highly sensitive to ecological disruption, and their "development" could well spell disaster for some waterfowl species.

The major wintering areas of North American waterfowl are also relatively easily identified and may be fairly readily characterized. In brief, they consist of the Central Valley of California, the lower Mississippi valley, the

TABLE 1

HABITAT PREFERENCES OF NORTH AMERICAN WATERFOWL

PRIMARY FOODS BREEDING HABITATS	Whistling Ducks, Swans, and Geese MOSTLY PLANT MATERIALS	Perching and Dabbling Ducks MIXED PLANT AND ANIMAL FOODS	Diving Ducks and Stiff-tails MOSTLY ANIMAL MATERIALS (some exceptions)
High Arctic			
Grassy tundra	"Tundra" Canada Geese		Oldsquaw
Coastal sedge tundra	Brant Goose		
Upland tundra	White-fronted Goose		
Coastal deltas	Snow Goose		
Inland lakes	Ross Goose		
Inland ponds	Whistling Swan		King Eider
Low Arctic			
Grassy tundra	Emperor Goose		Spectacled Eider
Coastal deltas			Steller Eider
Rocky tundra			Common Eider
Upland tundra		Pintail[1]	
Rivers and lakes			Barrow Goldeneye
			Red-breasted Merganser
Shallow lakes			Black Scoter
Boreal Forest			
Shallow lakes	"Lesser" Canada Geese		Surf Scoter
			Greater Scaup
			Common Goldeneye
Marshes	Trumpeter Swan		
Swamps and bogs			Ring-necked Duck
Mountain streams			Harlequin Duck
Rivers and lakes			Common Merganser
Parklands			
Wooded ponds		Green-winged Teal	Bufflehead
Marshy lakes		American Wigeon	Lesser Scaup
Shallow lakes			White-winged Scoter
Deciduous Forest			
Marshes and swamps		Black Duck	Hooded Merganser
Rivers and ponds		Wood Duck	

TABLE 1 continued

Grasslands			
Prairie marshes	Giant Canada Goose		Canvasback
			Ruddy Duck
Ponds and potholes		Mallard[1]	
		Blue-winged Teal	
		Shoveler	
Alkaline sloughs	Great Basin Canada Goose	Cinnamon Teal	Redhead
		Gadwall	
Tropical Habitats			
Swamps	Black-bellied Whistling Duck	Muscovy Duck	
Marshes	Fulvous Whistling Duck		Masked Duck

1. The ecological ranges of these species are much broader than indicated here.

Gulf coasts of the United States and Mexico, the Pacific coast from southern Alaska to Baja California, and the Atlantic coast from Maine to Florida. Limited wintering also occurs in central and southern Mexico, in Central America to Panama, and even in northern South America. However, most of the North American waterfowl do not winter much beyond central Mexico, and the annual midwinter counts by the United States Fish and Wildlife Service provide at least a reasonable basis for judging the winter distribution patterns on a flyway-by-flyway basis (Table 2). A few species, such as the wood duck, which are nearly impossible to census aerially have been excluded, and in some cases the identifications are only to species groups ("eiders," "scoters"). Nevertheless, these figures do provide a rather useful indication of the continental distribution patterns of most wintering waterfowl.

The importance of Mexico as a wintering area for North American waterfowl is not apparent in Table 2, but should not be underestimated. Thus, an examination of count data from Mexican surveys is of some interest (Table 3). Comparing these figures, which are generally of earlier surveys, with the inclusive counts from more recent years in Table 2 suggests some relative values for the wintering areas of Mexico. Considering the two most numerous wintering species of waterfowl in Mexico, the pintail and the lesser scaup, it seems probable that perhaps as much as a fourth of the total North American populations of these species may winter within Mexico's borders. Similarly,

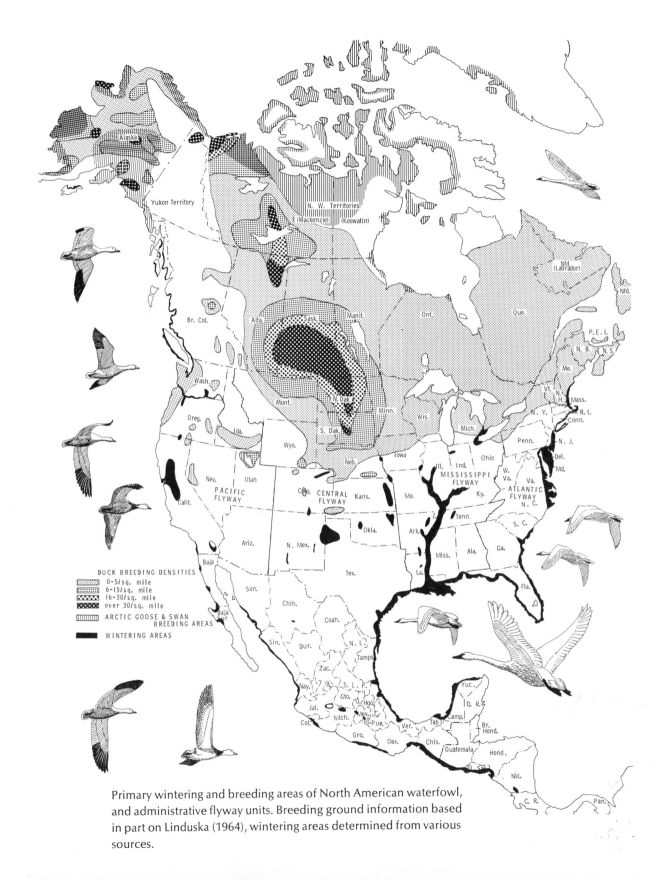

Primary wintering and breeding areas of North American waterfowl, and administrative flyway units. Breeding ground information based in part on Linduska (1964), wintering areas determined from various sources.

TABLE 2

WINTER SURVEY POPULATION DISTRIBUTION, BY FLYWAYS, 1966–1969

	Average Total U.S. (1,000s)	% Pacific (and Mexico West Coast)	% Central (and Mexico East Coast and Central)	% Mississippi	% Atlantic
Tree Ducks	3.4	—	100	—	—
Swans					
Trumpeter	6	100	—	—	—
Whistling	108	45.2	—	—	54.8
Geese					
Snow/Blue	1,198	41.2	25.0	29.2	4.6
Ross	25	100	—	—	—
White-fronted	159	68.6	9.8	21.5	—
Canada	1,652	17.8	14.7	29.7	37.8
Brant	353	44.9	—	—	55.1
Ducks					
American Wigeon	1,494	45.3	8.4	38.6	7.6
Gadwall	1,080	4.0	6.9	87.2	2.3
Green-winged Teal	1,362	23.2	11.4	60.2	5.0
Mallard	6,898	24.5	28.6	44.1	2.7
"Mottled Duck"	68	—	9.6	87.4	2.9
Black Duck	476	—	—	33.8	66.2
Pintail	3,360	53.9	12.6	29.1	4.4
Blue-winged & Cinnamon Teal	173	3.5	11.1	77.1	8.2
Shoveler	586	45.1	4.7	46.0	4.2
Canvasback	268	23.7	3.4	16.8	55.9
Redhead	568	2.4	56.5	7.5	33.6
Ring-necked Duck	243	2.1	2.5	57.9	39.7
Scaups	1,560	7.8	2.9	44.9	44.3
Eiders & Scoters	309	41.9	—	tr.	58.1
Oldsquaw	10	3	—	19	77
Bufflehead	90	35.6	4.6	6.2	53.4
Goldeneyes	164	28.8	4.7	17.4	49.0
Mergansers	193	13.3	36.7	22.7	27.2
Ruddy Duck	223	63.2	6.8	15.7	14.2

TABLE 3

SUMMARY OF MEXICAN WINTER WATERFOWL SURVEYS[1]

	Gulf Coast	Interior	Pacific Coast	Total	Abundance Index[2]
Whistling Ducks	28,700 (3)	tr. (9)	30,800 (9)	59,500	10
Whistling Swan	tr.			tr.	23
White-fronted Goose	20,600 (3)	1,200 (3)		21,800	12
Snow/Blue Goose	4,600 (3)	1,100 (9)		5,700	15
Canada Goose	7,600 (3)			7,600	14
Geese (3 species above)			10,800 (15)	10,800	—
Brant Goose			74,200 (15)	74,200	9
Wood Duck	tr.			tr.	23
American Wigeon	100,000 (17)	38,000 (14)	52,200 (17)	190,000	6
Gadwall	54,300 (17)	21,800 (17)	54,800 (17)	130,900	7
Green-winged Teal	19,200 (17)	56,400 (14)	129,200 (17)	204,800	5
Mallard	100 (3)		400 (9)	500	19
"Mottled Duck"	200 (3)			200	22
Mexican Duck		4,900 (3)		4,900	16
Pintail	171,800 (17)	212,000 (14)	470,100 (17)	853,900	1
Blue-winged Teal	130,300 (17)	41,900 (14)	62,600 (17)	234,800	4
Shoveler	18,000 (17)	67,700 (14)	235,100 (17)	320,800	3
Canvasback	8,000 (17)	13,300 (14)	500 (9)	21,800	12
Redhead	80,400 (17)	1,400 (14)	23,700 (17)	105,500	8
Ring-necked Duck	10,300 (17)	400 (9)	400 (9)	11,100	13
Lesser Scaup	209,200 (17)	5,600 (14)	172,200 (17)	387,000	2
Scoters			1,000 (9)	1,000	17
Bufflehead	100 (3)	tr. (3)	300 (9)	400	20
Common Goldeneye			300 (9)	300	21
Mergansers	500 (3)		200 (9)	700	18
Ruddy Duck	3,800 (3)	1,700 (14)	36,400 (17)	41,900	11

1. First figures indicate average counts; numbers in parentheses indicate number of years (to 1964) involved in calculation of averages.
2. Figures indicate relative rank (1 = high, 23 = low) of average counts for species.

Mexico probably supports at least half of North America's wintering shoveler population and an even higher proportion of our blue-winged and cinnamon teal. Important wintering concentrations of brant geese, white-fronted geese, redheads, and ruddy ducks also occur in Mexico, sometimes within quite restricted areas. A recognition of the importance of Mexico in the maintenance of adequate wintering grounds for North American waterfowl is absolutely essential, as is the continued cooperation of the Canadian, American, and Mexican governments in the management of these resources.

Between these wintering areas and the breeding areas of North America are a variety of traditional migratory "stopover" points or "staging areas," consisting of river valleys, major marsh systems, lakes, and some reservoirs. These too play an important role in the maintenance of our waterfowl resources, and wetland drainage, diversion of river water for irrigation or other purposes, or local water pollution and associated destruction of waterfowl food sources can have serious repercussions on migratory pathways and patterns.

It is traditional to think of the migration pathways of North America as consisting of four fairly well-defined "flyways," consisting of aerial pathways organized in roughly parallel north-south bands between the Atlantic and Pacific coasts. Using this concept, which was developed by F. C. Lincoln on the basis of waterfowl banding results, the Fish and Wildlife Service has subdivided North America into administrative flyway units (see Figure 1) that are used in establishing harvest regulations and facilitating population analyses. Such organization is a great improvement over administration on a state-by-state basis but should not obscure the fact that flyways are only convenient constructs used for visualizing the much more complex interactions of forty-odd species of waterfowl that annually traverse our continent.

The management of a resident species of game bird is difficult enough, but the management of migratory birds such as our waterfowl is complicated by their need for breeding, migratory, and wintering areas and the frequent separation of these areas by thousands of miles. Closed hunting seasons on an endangered species will do nothing to save it if its wintering grounds are fouled by pollution or if its breeding marshes are drained for agricultural purposes. Thus the oil spill off the coast of southern California may well destroy a waterfowl population breeding in western Canada, and Nebraska hunters may wait in vain for the "big flight" of birds that once wintered in polluted Gulf coast waters. Fortunately, wintering and migratory traditions seem to be more flexible than breeding ground traditions, and the *sine qua non* of effective waterfowl management is the preservation and protection of adequate breeding ground conditions.

There is an unsurpassable beauty embodied in a flock of snow geese clamoring in the sky and beating steadily toward the distant horizon, but the logistical complexities in the navigational problems, timing, and energy balances of these migrations make these esthetic considerations secondary. After enduring and surviving the fall migration southward, a female snow goose must acquire sufficient energy reserves in the form of fat during the winter to allow the 3,000-mile return flight to the breeding grounds. The arrival at the grounds must be accurately timed to within a few days. Arriving too early will mean unnecessary fasting and waiting until the nesting grounds are free of snow; arriving too late will not allow enough time for laying, incubation, and brood-rearing in the short arctic summer. The female's physical condition must allow for the energy drainage associated with a full clutch of eggs, as well as for additional fat reserves to draw on during incubation, since the presence of egg predators may not allow the female to leave the nest to eat during the entire incubation period. The female may thus lose up to a fourth of her body weight during the incubation period, and with unusually cold weather during the incubation period she may succumb to starvation or freezing only a few days prior to the hatching of her clutch. If the young do hatch successfully, the parents must tend to them as well as regain their own needed fat reserves for the energy drains associated with molting and the fall migration. Additionally, the young must be fully fledged in less than fifty days after hatching if they are to avoid perishing in the fall freeze-up. The return migration south is marked by the additional hazards of hunting and by a transmission of the traditional migratory routes to the young geese.

In short, the sight of a migrating goose flock represents far more than a simple measure of the passing seasons; it is an unwritten testimony to dogged persistence in spite of adversity, to an inherited trust in the species' long-term design for survival in the face of individual starvation and violent death. It provides a revealing insight into the workings of natural selection in a harsh and intolerant environment; the genetic blueprint for each new generation is predicated on the reproductive successes and failures of the last. It is an example that should lift the human spirit; despite individual disasters, the geese endure. Each spring they push relentlessly northward to rendezvous with fate on a distant arctic shoreline; each fall they return with the future of their species invested in a new generation of offspring. We can ask for no greater symbol of determination despite appalling hardships than is provided by waterfowl; we should be content with no less than a maximum commitment to their continued existence.

Hunting and Recreational Values
of North American Waterfowl

It is almost as difficult to find individuals opposed to waterfowl conservation as it is to hear Americans speaking out against motherhood or corn on the cob. Yet, in a real sense, it has been the American tradition of unchecked population expansion, taming the wilderness, and converting prairies and marshes into cornfields that has nearly spelled disaster for some of our native waterfowl. Of a wetland area in the United States that originally covered some 127 million acres, nearly 50 million acres have already been drained and lost as waterfowl habitat. Marshes have not only been converted to farmland but also have provided land for expanding suburbs and have been covered with cement or asphalt for roads, airports, and the other hallmarks of modern civilization. All of this has been done in the hallowed name of progress, for the benefits of a greater gross national product, and in hopes of a higher collective standard of living. Unfortunately, waterfowl have had few spokesmen to decry their changing standards of living, and their gross national product can only be measured in terms of the numbers of birds that annually fly southward toward their wintering areas. These numbers, as reflected in annual harvests and changes in season lengths and bag limits, provide a measure of the health of our waterfowl resource. In recent decades that health index has often sagged alarmingly, and a few species have scarcely been able to recover from these setbacks.

Some persons might well pose the questions: "Just how important to our economy is a healthy waterfowl population? So what if one or two species might become extinct, aren't there plenty more to take their places?" It is nothing if not traditional to measure the value of things in terms of dollars, the very lodestone of American values. Thus, there are the annual license fees and "duck stamp" costs paid by some two million hunters—and the costs of ammunition, gas, lodging, and expendable supplies that are used on every hunt. Then there are the depreciation costs on guns, clothes, vehicles, boats, decoys, and all the other special equipment on which the waterfowl hunter lavishes his care and dollars. Costs of raising and training hunting dogs, rental or lease costs for hunting areas, hunting club costs, and similar ancillary expenses all contribute to the overall economic impact of waterfowl hunting. The 1965 National Survey of Hunting and Fishing reported that the average American waterfowl hunter spends over fifty dollars per year on his sport. With more than two million waterfowl hunters in the United States and Canada, at least a hundred million dollars per year would be a minimum economic value of waterfowl hunting.

What are the immediate returns to hunters for their investments? Putting aside the esthetic aspects of hunting—the memorable sunrises, the dances of phragmites on a distant horizon, the self-satisfaction of a difficult shot and a "clean" kill—the sheer poundage of the waterfowl harvest is enormous. Close to twenty million ducks and geese are shot each year by hunters in the United States and Canada (Table 4). This harvest represents some fifty million

TABLE 4

ESTIMATED AVERAGE ANNUAL HARVESTS, CANADA AND THE UNITED STATES

(indicated in 1,000s of birds)

	Canada[1]	Alaska[2]	Rest of U.S.[3]	Estimated Total Kill	Total Kill Index[4]
Geese					
Snow and Blue Goose	27.4	tr.	319.2	345.6	13
Ross Goose	2.5	—	.6	3.1	28
White-fronted Goose	41.7	.4	102.4	144.5	17
Canada Goose	147.8	7.8	578	733.6	5
Brant Goose	1.5	.6	34.8	36.9	24
Ducks					
Wood Duck	115	—	589.6	704.6	6
American Wigeon	178	9.1	825.8	1,012.9	4
Gadwall	77	.8	483.6	561.4	8
Green-winged Teal	287	11	1,124.4	1,422.4	2
Mallard	1,030	16.3	3,360	4,406.3	1
"Mottled Duck"[5]	—	—	90.2	90.2	21
Black Duck	276	—	366.4	642.4	7

TABLE 4 continued

	Canada[1]	Alaska[2]	Rest of U.S.[3]	Estimated Total Kill	Total Kill Index[4]
Pintail	194	14.5	990.4	1,198.9	3
Blue-winged & Cinnamon Teal	109	.2	302.2	411.4	11
Shoveler	29.6	3.7	346.0	379.3	12
Canvasback	14.8	.1	123.6	138.5	18
Redhead	39.8	—	162.4	202.2	14
Ring-necked Duck	84	.1	402.6	486.7	9
Lesser Scaup	68	1.0	371.6	440.6	10
Greater Scaup	50.7	1.1	76.2	128.0	19
Eiders	10.2	—	4.9	15.1	26
Oldsquaw	6.4	.2	6.5	13.1	27
Scoters	68.5	.7	49.8	119.0	20
Bufflehead	36.4	1.3	112.6	150.3	16
Goldeneyes	70	2.6	82.8	155.4	15
Hooded Merganser	35.9	—	42.8	78.7	22
Other Mergansers	20.0	.5	15.6	36.1	25
Ruddy Duck	3.4	—	52.6	56.0	23
Total Retrieved Kill	3,025	72	11,019.5	14,116.5	—
Estimated Unretrieved Kill (38%)	1,149	27	4,187.4	5,364.2	—
Estimated Total Kill	4,174	99	15,206.9	19,480.7	—
Estimated Total Hunters	385.6	11.1	1,724.2	2,120.9	—
Estimated Kill per Hunter	10.8	8.9	8.8	9.2	—

1. Based largely on 1968 season (Tener and Loughrey, 1970), except that figures for minor species and sea ducks are estimates of author, based on data of Benson (1968, 1969) for 1967 and 1968 seasons. Excludes non-sport kill by natives.
2. Average of two seasons (1967 and 1968). Excludes non-sport kill by native Alaskans.
3. Average of four seasons (1964 through 1968).
4. Ranking according to relative estimated total kill, from 1 (high) to 28 (low).
5. Includes mottled and Florida mallards.

pounds of fresh meat, or approximately ten birds per hunter. Average season kills per hunter are of little significance, since the vast majority of persons who buy "duck stamps" take only a few birds, and perhaps as much as 80 percent of the annual kill may be accounted for by only about 20 percent of the hunting population. Regardless of the statistical problems of a "typical" season kill for an "average" hunter, it is evident that at least four species (mallard, green-winged teal, pintail, and American wigeon) have annual harvests of a million or more birds. Although these figures seem high, the species concerned are ones that can tolerate high harvest rates. They all mature rapidly, have fairly large clutch sizes, often will renest following early nest failures, and can breed in a diversity of habitats and climates.

Probably much more serious than these harvest rates are the much lower ones of such species as redheads, canvasbacks, and ruddy ducks. These birds nest in prairie marshes that exhibit rather specific vegetative characteristics and stable water levels. The females are usually ineffective breeders or even nonbreeders during their first year of life, and nest desertion rates are often high, because of water fluctuations or nest parasitism. Additionally, female redheads and canvasbacks are much more vulnerable than males to hunting mortality, a factor which tends to exaggerate a normally unbalanced sex ratio and to reduce reproductive efficiency. Hunting thus increases the population stress on species which are the first to suffer from drainage or other breeding habitat disturbances, or which winter in restricted areas that are often subjected to oil pollution or other man-made disturbances.

North America has already witnessed the irrevocable extinction of several game birds, including the passenger pigeon, the heath hen, and the Labrador duck. In the case of the Labrador duck, the species was virtually extinct before biologists even recognized that it was in serious danger and before its nests or young had even been found. Some reputed Labrador duck eggs do exist but lack sufficient documentation, and no biologist was sufficiently foresighted as to save a complete skeleton of the species. Perhaps we may excuse this case of early extinction as an apparent example of death by natural causes, or at least one in which man's tampering with the environment played no obvious role. The breeding grounds, being undiscovered, remained undisturbed, and the small numbers of birds taken during the hunting season could not have been a significant factor in extinction.

Now, nearly a century later, the breeding grounds of all the North American waterfowl have been found. More importantly, even those species breeding on the remote arctic tundra may soon feel the effects of oil or mineral exploration. There are also the possibilities of massive oil spills on restricted wintering or breeding coastlines, of reproductive failures brought on by pesticides, or of poisoning by heavy metal pollutants. The worlds of man and waterfowl are ever more closely linked with one another, and the geese that once bred in unknown lands "beyond the north wind" now carry with them the mercury that they may have swallowed with wheat on Dakota grainfields and the DDT or other pesticides that they ingested while wintering on the delta of the lower Mississippi. In some cases, the tissue levels of these poisons may even render the birds unfit for human consumption, and the hunters' hard-sought trophies then become useless piles of flesh and feathers, the ultimate degradation of animals that once flew free and wild, transient spirits, unfettered and untamed by man except in death.

If the economic values of North American waterfowl to hunters can be measured in terms of annual harvests, how then does one measure their values to bird watchers or bird photographers? There is no way of knowing exactly how many people fit those categories, but it has been estimated that there are over eight million bird watchers in the United States and over three million people who photograph birds or wildlife. Thus, perhaps five times as many people gain direct pleasures from live waterfowl as hunt them for sport, and the dollars they spend on travel, binoculars, cameras, film, lenses, and related items are no doubt at least as great as the hunters' expenditures.

Of course one need not spend money to gain esthetic pleasures and values from waterfowl. Are not the unexpected and unsought pleasures often the most memorable ones? What are the values to a youngster, who may not know a canvasback from a Canada goose, when he sees a skein of waterfowl etched against an autumn sky? And does not the flock of geese that is lost to hearing and view by one person enter the sensate world of another in the distance, thus linking the two by a common bond? What scene can so capture and stir the imagination as a flock of wild swans? What sounds are as haunting as those of wild geese overhead on a foggy night? What sight is more compelling than that of a female duck with a brood of young paddling dutifully behind her?

Perhaps the esthetic values of waterfowl must be viewed in two some-what opposing ways. Even a common species can provide an impressive spectacle if seen in large enough numbers; the massive flocks of migrating snow geese provide testimony to that opinion. Further, by virtue of its very abundance, the common species is likely to be seen by a large percentage of the bird-watching or nature-oriented population. It is, in short, a "reliable" species for the daily checklists of many people and may be looked upon as an old and close friend with whom every encounter is a renewed pleasure. Alternatively, there are the special rewards of seeing a rare species or one associated with a highly limited habitat or geographic area. The "rarity values" of these species are in inverse relation to the ease or likelihood of seeing them on a given day. Although it is unlikely that they will ever be seen in such numbers as to impress the uninformed observer, a single sighting becomes an event to be remembered for years, if not for a lifetime. This, then, is the esthetic value of a tufted duck, a European teal, or a masked duck, each of which is a species to be appreciated by the dedicated bird watcher without reference to its beauty or lack thereof.

Using these criteria—either the relative abundance as an index to the relative recreational value of a waterfowl species, or relative infrequency of occurrence as an index to a species' rarity—it is possible to establish some esthetic values of the various waterfowl species. The annual Audubon Christmas counts provide a convenient means of assessing the general relationship between the continental distribution of bird watchers and the winter distribution patterns of waterfowl. By using these winter counts, even the arctic-breeding species may potentially be included in the calculations, and most of the birds are by then in their finest plumages. During the period 1954 to 1962 these counts were annually summarized not only as to cumulative total numbers of individual birds seen per species but also as to the numbers of counting points in which each species was observed. The former figure provides a useful means of judging the relative winter abundance, or "recreation index," of each species, while the latter provides an indication of the species' winter distribution relative to the distribution of bird watchers. Thus, the fewer total stations at which a species was seen during this nine-year period, the greater the species' rarity index. The smallest total numbers of birds reported during this period provides an alternate means of judging the rarity index.

With these criteria in mind, an analysis (Table 5) of the recreational and rarity values of North American waterfowl can be made. The results indicate

TABLE 5
SUMMARY OF AUDUBON CHRISTMAS COUNTS, 1954–1962

	Average Total Count	Recreation Index	Cumulative Total Stations	Rarity Index
Fulvous Whistling Duck	10.8	42 (Tie)	16	6
Black-bellied Whistling Duck	30.3	39	8	4
Trumpeter Swan	10.8	42 (Tie)	9	5
Whistling Swan	26,575	19	302	18
Mute Swan	796.5	31	237	17
Snow and Blue Goose	110,121	7	459[1]	21
Ross Goose	334	35	19	7
White-fronted Goose	11,677	26	156	14
Emperor Goose	70	37	1	1 (Tie)
Canada Goose	298,963	3	1,600	38
Brant Goose	142,768	6	208	16
Wood Duck	1,397	30	664	24
American Wigeon	167,967	4	1,555	36
European Wigeon	12.3	41	71	9
Gadwall	15,174	24	972	29

TABLE 5 continued

	Average Total Count	Recreation Index	Cumulative Total Stations	Rarity Index
Green-winged Teal	44,682	13	1,314	34
"Common Teal"[2]	.5	43	5	3
Mallard	1,039,060	1	3,488	44
"Mottled Duck"[3]	539	13	145	13
Black Duck	159,587	5	2,326	43
Pintail	429,337	2	1,717	40
Blue-winged Teal	3,463	29	401	19
Cinnamon Teal	368	34	137	12
Shoveler	29,142	17	886	27
Canvasback	77,282	11	1,377	35
Redhead	94,475	8	897	28
Ring-necked Duck	20,807	21	1,269	32
Lesser Scaup	81,661	10	1,606	39
Greater Scaup	90,005	9	851	26
Common Eider	32,640	16	159	15
King Eider	16.5	40	53	8
Steller Eider	67	38	3	2
Harlequin Duck	179	36	93	10
Oldsquaw	17,189	22	689	25
Black Scoter	6,345	27	449	20
Surf Scoter	28,164	18	498	22
White-winged Scoter	21,386	20	596	23
Bufflehead	15,190	23	1,559	37
Barrow Goldeneye	566	32	124	11
Common Goldeneye	42,212	14	2,311	42
Hooded Merganser	3,804	28	1,185	30
Red-breasted Merganser	13,988	25	1,197	31
Common Merganser	37,248	15	1,857	41
Ruddy Duck	54,209	12	1,274	33
Masked Duck	.2	44	1	1 (Tie)

1. Tallied for "snow goose" only.
2. European green-winged teal.
3. Includes mottled and Florida mallards.

that the five most important waterfowl in terms of recreational value to bird watchers are the mallard, pintail, Canada goose, American wigeon, and black duck. All of these were seen in numbers averaging in excess of 150,000 birds per year on Christmas counts. Species that were seen at an average of at least 200 stations per year include the mallard, black duck, common goldeneye, and common merganser. Thus, by both measurements, the mallard and black duck provide great recreational value to America's winter bird watchers. On the other hand, species seen in the smallest total numbers per year were the masked duck, European or "common" teal, fulvous whistling duck, trumpeter swan, and European wigeon. Two of these, the teal and the wigeon, are accidental visitors from Europe or Asia, while the others are native species with limited wintering distributions. If a rarity index on the basis of numbers of stations reporting the species is established, the four rarest species are the masked duck, emperor goose, Steller eider, and European teal. Even rarer than these would be the spectacled eider, which has made only one appearance on the Christmas counts, and that a single individual. The tufted duck has also appeared on Christmas counts several times in recent years.

Whatever values we place on them, we must recognize the special relationship we share with our waterfowl resource. They were not created for us, but only exist with us, traversing the same continent, drinking the same water, breathing the same air. They provide an historic link with our American past, when our pioneering ancestors' survival sometimes depended on them. They also confront us with a fearful vision of the future we have shaped for us and them, as when they are caught in floating deathtraps of crude oil or succumb to pesticide paroxysms. They are uncertain refugees from another time and a different America, when smoke on the horizon meant an Indian campground rather than a factory and when the sound of distant thunder was caused by bison herds instead of bulldozers and jackhammers.

We cannot expect to learn directly from or communicate with waterfowl; they speak separate languages, hear different voices, know other sensory worlds. They transcend our own perceptions, make mockery of our national boundaries, ignore our flyway concepts. They have their own innate maps, calendars, and compasses, each older and more remarkable than our own. We can only delight in their flying skills, marvel at their regular and precise movements across our continent, take example from their persistence in the face of repeated disaster. They are a microcosm of nature, of violent death and abundant rebirth, of untrammeled beauty and instinctive grace. We should be content to ask no more of them than that they simply exist, and we can hope for no more than that our children might know and enjoy them as we do.

Part II Species Accounts

Identification Key to
North American Waterfowl

The key on the following pages provides an efficient means of identifying virtually all North American waterfowl that may be examined in the hand. The procedure for using it is comparable to that used for all such dual-choice or "dichotomous" keys. One simply chooses which of the initial descriptive couplets (A or A′) best fits the unknown bird. Having chosen one of these, the pair of descriptive couplets (a and a′) immediately below the chosen alternative is next considered, without further regard for the rejected one. Subsequent choices, which are sequentially numbered (1 and 1′, 2 and 2′, etc.) must then be considered until the name of a species has been reached. In no case will more than eleven choices be required to identify any of the 52 waterfowl species or subspecies represented in the key. After having tentatively determined the identity of the unknown bird, one should refer to the appropriate "Identification" sections of the text, to confirm or reject the initial determination. Illustrations in this book or other references should also be consulted, bearing in mind that sexual or seasonal variations in plumage may exist.

A. Legs with completely reticulated (networklike) scale pattern, iridescent colors absent from plumage (geese, swans, and whistling ducks)
  a. Smaller (folded wing under 300 mm.*), legs extended beyond the tail (whistling ducks)
    1. Bill blackish, upper wing surface lacking white patterning
      2. Buffy stripes present on flanks . . . **Fulvous Whistling Duck**
      2′. Black and white spots present on flanks . . . **Cuban Whistling Duck**

*Wing lengths are of folded, unflattened wings; culmen length is measured from tip of bill to edge of forehead feathers.

1'. Bill red (in adults), extensively white on upper wing surface . . . **Black-bellied Whistling Duck**

a'. Larger (folded wing over 300 mm.), legs not extending beyond the tail

  1. Primaries white (swans)

    2. Bill usually reddish, with variably large black knob at base, longest primaries more than 7 cm. longer than outer ones . . . **Mute Swan**

    2'. Bill usually black (flesh-colored in juveniles), longest primaries not more than 7 cm. longer than outer ones, bill never with knob at base

      3. Bill usually with yellow present in front of eyes, weight under 20 pounds, folded wing under 575 mm., less than 50 mm. from tip of bill to anterior end of nostril . . . **Whistling Swan**

      3'. Bill usually without any yellow in front of eyes, weight often over 20 pounds, folded wing at least 540 mm. in adults, usually at least 50 mm. from tip of bill to anterior end of nostril . . . **Trumpeter Swan**

  1'. Primaries not white (geese)

    2. Legs, feet, and bill black, head and neck plumage mostly black

      3. White present on cheeks

        4. White cheeks extending above eyes and across forehead, breast black . . . **Barnacle Goose**

        4'. White cheeks not extending in front of eyes, breast brown . . . **Canada Goose**

      3'. White absent from cheeks . . . **Brant Goose**

    2'. Legs, feet, and bill variously reddish, yellow, or flesh-colored, never black

      3. Under tail coverts white, throat brown or white

        4. Feet orange to yellow, white on head lacking or limited to narrow area in front of eyes . . . **White-fronted Goose**

        4'. Feet red, pink, or flesh-colored, head often entirely white

          5. Smaller (folded wing under 400 mm.), bill short and often warty at base, lacking definite black "grinning patch" . . . **Ross Goose**

          5'. Larger (wing over 400 mm.), bill longer and never warty at base, with definite black "grinning patch" at sides . . . **Snow (and "Blue") Goose**

      3'. Under tail coverts gray, throat black . . . **Emperor Goose**

A'. Legs with lower part of tarsus having scutellate (vertically aligned) scales, iridescent coloration often present on wings or body (typical ducks)

  a. Feet with weakly lobed hind toe, middle toe longer than outer toe, iridescent color usually present on wing surface (perching and dabbling ducks)

    1. Upper wing surface mostly iridescent bluish or purplish, tail long and rather square-tipped, claws relatively sharp (perching ducks)

2. White on upper wing surface lacking or limited to upper coverts, folded wing over 300 mm. long . . . **Muscovy Duck**

2'. White on upper wing surface limited to tips of secondaries, wing under 300 mm. long . . . **Wood Duck**

1'. Upper wing surface not iridescent except on secondary feathers, tail usually short and rounded (sometimes pointed), claws not especially sharp (dabbling ducks)

    2. Middle and lesser upper wing coverts white, pale gray, or light blue

        3. Feet gray, upper wing coverts gray or white

            4. Tertials greatly elongated and sickle-shaped, underwing lining white, head crested . . . **Falcated Duck**

            4'. Tertials not greatly elongated or sickle-shaped, underwing lining gray, head uncrested

                5. Axillar feathers mottled with dark gray . . . **European Wigeon**

                5'. Axillar feathers white or only slightly flecked with gray . . . **American Wigeon**

        3'. Feet yellow or orange, upper wing coverts bluish

            4. Bill spatulate (spoon-shaped) . . . **Shoveler**

            4'. Bill normally shaped or only slightly spatulate

                5. Bill uniformly narrow for most of its length (maximum 44 mm.), rusty cinnamon color absent, head with white crescent (males) or brownish with clear buffy to white spot between eye and bill . . . **Blue-winged Teal**

                5'. Bill longer (minimum 41 mm.) and slightly spatulate toward tip, rusty cinnamon or yellowish color often present on body, head uniformly cinnamon (males) or brownish with darker streaking that usually obscures the pale area between the eye and bill . . . **Cinnamon Teal**

    2'. Middle and lesser upper wing coverts grayish brown or brown

        3. Wing speculum iridescent blue, violet, or bluish green, with black (or black and white) bars in front and behind; feet yellow to reddish

            4. White present both in front of and behind the speculum

                5. Vermiculations present on tertials (males), or the tertials grayish (females); females with white or nearly white under tail coverts and white on most or all rectrices . . . **Common Mallard**

                5'. Vermiculations never present on tertials, the tertials brownish with green cast; under tail coverts dark brown with lighter edging; white, if present on rectrices, limited to three outer feathers . . . **Mexican Mallard**

            4'. White present only behind the speculum, or altogether absent from upper wing surface

                5. Tawny coloration present in front of black bar on greater secondary coverts, predominant body color tawny brown . . . **Florida and Mottled Mallards**

    5′. Tawny coloration absent from secondary coverts, predominant body color dark brown . . . **Black Duck**

3′. Wing speculum not as described above, legs and feet usually grayish

    4. Speculum iridescent green and black, lined in front with cinnamon buff or buffy white

        5. Folded wing over 220 mm., buffy white present in front of speculum, which is green on outer secondaries . . . **Falcated Duck**

        5′. Folded wing under 220 mm., cinnamon-tinted in front of speculum, which is black on outer secondaries

            6. Middle tail feathers over 75 mm., black outer secondaries widely tipped with white . . . **Baikal Teal**

            6′. Middle tail feathers under 75 mm., black outer secondaries only narrowly tipped with white . . . **Green-winged Teal**

    4′. Speculum not green and black; if green is present at all it is limited to the anterior half of the speculum

        5. Secondaries white, gray, and black, with black extending to the secondary coverts, tail rounded, underwing lining white . . . **Gadwall**

        5′. Secondaries lacking black, or black is limited to a narrow bar at rear of speculum; tail variably pointed; underwing lining dusky or brownish

            6. Speculum iridescent green anteriorly, throat and cheeks white, bill reddish at base . . . **Bahama Pintail**

            6′. Speculum bronze to copper-colored, or lacking iridescence and brownish; cheeks never white and bill never with reddish color . . . **Pintail**

a′. Feet with strongly lobed hind toe, iridescent coloration usually lacking on wings (two exceptions), length of outer toe usually greater than that of middle toe (one exception), body generally adapted for diving (pochards, sea ducks, and stiff-tailed ducks)

1. Bill narrow, cylindrical, serrated at the edges and with a hooked tip (mergansers)

    2. Smaller (folded wing under 200 mm.), bill short and gray to black, feet gray or yellowish

        3. Upper forewing and tertials white, no definite crest . . . **Smew**

        3′. Upper forewing brown or mottled grayish white, head crested . . . **Hooded Merganser**

    2′. Larger (folded wing over 200 mm.), bill long and reddish, feet orange to red

        3. Nostril nearer to base of bill than center, feathering at base of upper

mandible extending farther forward than that of lower mandible . . .
Red-breasted Merganser

3'. Nostril nearer to middle of bill than base, feathering at base of upper and lower mandible extending about equal distance forward . . .
Common Merganser

1'. Bill not as described above

2. Tail feathers unusually long and narrow, bill broad and flattened at tip, wings relatively short, and legs placed well to the rear of the body (stiff-tailed ducks)

3. White present on secondaries, nail of bill not recurved, outer toe not longer than middle toe . . . **Masked Duck**

3'. White lacking on wings, nail of bill recurved, outer toe longer than middle toe . . . **Ruddy Duck**

2'. Tail feathers not unusually long and narrow; bill variously shaped; wings not unusually short, and legs only moderately situated toward rear of body (pochards and typical sea ducks)

3. Secondaries with iridescent bluish speculum, tail somewhat pointed

4. Inner secondaries curved outwardly, underwing surface white . . . **Steller Eider**

4'. Inner secondaries not curved, underwing surface dusky . . . **Harlequin Duck**

3'. No iridescence on wing, the secondaries brown, gray, or white, tail either rounded or pointed

4. Very small (folded wing under 190 mm.), white present behind eye . . . **Bufflehead**

4'. Larger (folded wing over 200 mm.), white present or absent on head

5. Feathering present along sides or top of bill almost to nostrils or sometimes beyond

6. Tertials straight and little or no longer than secondaries

7. Feathering on sides of bill, white present on secondaries . . . **White-winged Scoter**

7'. Feathering present on top of bill, no white present on secondaries . . . **Surf Scoter**

6'. Tertials elongated and curved outwardly

7. Feathering on bill extending farther on sides than on top, extending laterally to a point below the nostrils . . . **Common Eider**

7'. Feathering on top of bill extending farther than on sides, never with feathering below the nostrils

8. Top of nostrils almost hidden by feathers, pale buffy or white area around eyes . . . **Spectacled Eider**

8'. No feathering near nostrils, unfeathered basal enlargement of bill almost reaches the eyes . . . **King Eider**

5′. No feathering present on top or sides of bill

    6. White markings present on upper wing surface

       7. White largely limited to the secondaries (sometimes extending to inner primaries); upper wing coverts gray, brown, or black; feet gray

         8. Back blackish or dusky brown, bill only slightly wider (up to 4 mm.) near tip than at base, with long or rudimentary crest present . . . **Tufted Duck**

         8′. Back grayish white or dusky brown, bill definitely wider (at least 5 mm.) near tip than at base, never distinctly crested

            9. White of wings extending to inner primaries, nail of bill at least 8 mm. wide . . . **Greater Scaup**

            9′. White of wings limited to secondaries (inner primaries may be quite pale), nail of bill under 7 mm. wide . . . **Lesser Scaup**

       7′. White or pale gray markings present on upper wing coverts, tertials, or both, feet yellow to orange

         8. Bill gradually tapering in width from base, nail of bill raised and at least 12 mm. long . . . **Barrow Goldeneye**

         8′. Bill about as wide at nostrils as at base, nail of bill relatively flattened and no more than 11 mm. long . . . **Common Goldeneye**

    6′. No white markings on upper wing surface

       7. Secondaries gray to grayish white, at least more grayish or paler than primaries, tail rounded and no more than 75 mm. long

         8. Bill with one (females) or two (males) pale rings, folded wing under 210 mm., upper forewing and back dark brown or black . . . **Ring-necked Duck**

         8′. Bill with only one pale ring or none, folded wing at least 210 mm., forewing and back gray or light brown

            9. Bill long (exposed culmen over 50 mm.), and forehead sloping; upper wing coverts with vermiculations . . . **Canvasback**

            9′. Bill shorter (exposed culmen under 50 mm.), and with a high forehead; upper wing coverts not vermiculated . . . **Redhead**

       7′. Secondaries brown or blackish, no lighter than rest of wing; tail slightly or greatly pointed and usually longer than 75 mm. centrally

         8. White or pale gray feathers present on flanks, a variable amount of white (sometimes only a narrow ring) around eye . . . **Oldsquaw**

8′. Flanks brown, reddish brown, or black; white lacking around eye or limited to areas below and in front of eye

9. Outer (10th) primaries narrower and shorter than adjacent ones, bill fairly long (over 40 mm.) and somewhat enlarged basally . . . **Black Scoter**

9′. Outer primaries not narrow and shorter than adjacent ones, bill short (under 30 mm.) and not enlarged basally . . . **Harlequin Duck**

WHISTLING DUCKS
Tribe Dendrocygnini

Whistling ducks comprise a group of nine species that are primarily of tropical and subtropical distribution. In common with the swans and true geese (which with them comprise the subfamily Anserinae), the included species have a reticulated tarsal surface pattern, lack sexual dimorphism in plumage, produce vocalizations that are similar or identical in both sexes, form relatively permanent pair bonds, and lack complex pair-forming behavior patterns. Unlike the geese and swans, whistling ducks have clear, often melodious whistling voices that are the basis for their group name. The alternative name, tree ducks, is far less appropriate, since few of the species regularly perch or nest in trees. All the species have relatively long legs and large feet that extend beyond the fairly short tail when the birds are in flight. They dive well, and some species obtain much of their food in this manner. Eight species are represented in the genus *Dendrocygna,* including all three of the species included in this book. A ninth species, the African and Madagascan white-backed duck (*Thalassornis leuconotus*), is considered by the author (Johnsgard, 1966) to be an aberrant whistling duck.

Two of the three species included in this book regularly nest in the southern United States, while the third (the Cuban whistling duck) might be regarded as North American on the basis of its occurrence in the West Indies, although it is not known to have ever reached continental North America.

FULVOUS WHISTLING DUCK

Dendrocygna bicolor (Vieillot) 1816

Other Vernacular Names: Fulvous Tree Duck, Long-legged Duck, Mexican
  Squealer.

Range: Ceylon, India, Madagascar, eastern Africa, northern and eastern South
  America, and from Central America north to the southern United States.

Subspecies: None recognized by Delacour (1954). The A.O.U. *Check-list*
  (1957) recognizes *D. b. helva* Wetmore and Peters as a distinct North
  American race breeding south to central Mexico.

Measurements (after Delacour, 1954):
  Folded wing: Both sexes 200–235 mm.
  Culmen: Both sexes 42–52 mm.

Weights: One male weighed 747.7 grams, one female 771.4 grams (Meanley
  and Meanley, 1956). John Lynch (pers. comm.) has provided November
  weights for full-winged birds in covered pens in Louisiana. Seven males
  averaged 675.5 grams (1.49 pounds) and ranged from 621 to 756 grams,
  while six females averaged 689.9 grams (1.52 pounds) and ranged from
  632 to 739 grams.

IDENTIFICATION

In the Hand: Like the other species in this genus, the presence of long legs extending beyond the short tail, an entirely reticulated tarsus, and an elongated and elevated hind toe are typical. The fulvous whistling duck is the only North American species with grayish blue bill and foot coloration and extensive tawny-fulvous color on the head and underparts. The wings are entirely dark on the upper surface, lacking any white or grayish white patterning.

In the Field: The most widespread species of whistling duck in North America, fulvous whistling ducks are likely to appear almost anywhere in the southern states. On water or land, their long and usually erect necks, duck-like heads, and short-tailed appearance are distinctive. At any distance, the fulvous whistling duck appears mostly tawny brown, darker above and brighter below, with the buffy yellow flank stripe the most conspicuous field mark. In flight, the long neck and long, often dangling legs are evident, and the head is usually held at or even below the body level. In contrast to the wing coloration of the other two species of whistling ducks that might be encountered in North America, the upper wing surface is neither white nor grayish white, but is instead dark brown like the mantle. The wings are broader and more rounded than in more typical ducks, and a distinctive slower wingbeat is characteristic. A whistled *wa-chew'* or *pa-cheea* call is frequently uttered, both in flight and at rest. The fulvous whistling duck feeds in rice fields and shallow marshes and occasionally comes into cornfields as well.

AGE AND SEX CRITERIA

Sex Determination: No obvious external sexual differences occur, so internal examination may be required. McCartney (1963) believed that females could be distinguished on the basis of being smaller, duller, and having a continuous rather than an interrupted dark line on the crown and neck.

Age Determination: Not yet well studied, but if the findings of Cain (1970) on the black-bellied whistling duck apply, notched tail feathers may persist until about the 35th week of age, and the penis of a male under ten months lacks spines. Dickey and van Rossem (1923) reported that immature birds may be distinguished from older ones by the former's concave rather than straight bill profile. The plumage of immature birds is very similar to that of adults, but the brown tips on the back feathers average slightly darker, according to these writers.

DISTRIBUTION AND HABITAT

Breeding Distribution and Habitat: During the early part of the twentieth century the fulvous whistling duck was believed to be limited as a breeding

Breeding distribution of the fulvous whistling duck in North and
Central America. Recent extralimital breeding and non-breeding
records are also indicated.

Extralimital Records

● B = Breeding
○ = Non-breeding

species to Texas and central and southern California, with possible casual breeding in central Nevada, southern Arizona, and Louisiana as well (Bent, 1925). Nesting in Louisiana was first verified in 1939 (Lynch, 1943), where it was later determined to be a common breeding bird in the rice belt (Meanley and Meanley, 1959). In the mid-1960s the first Florida breeding record was obtained at Lake Okeechobee (*Audubon Field Notes,* 19:519), where the population soon grew to about 200 birds (*ibid.,* 22:600). Following the development of large winter flocks in the vicinity of Virginia Key, Dade County, breeding was verified there in 1968, and nests or broods have been found each year thereafter (*ibid.,* 22:517; 23:581; 24:592). Moderately large winter flocks now also occur in the vicinity of Naples, and breeding has occurred there as well (*ibid.,* 24:249).

Breeding of this species in California is highly localized, with the traditional center of breeding in the vicinity of Los Baños, Merced County, although there are many other localities where breeding records were established in earlier years (Grinnell and Miller, 1944). In more recent years the birds have been nesting in small numbers in the Salton Sea area (*Audubon Field Notes,* 10:410; 23:694), where they also casually winter, but the species is virtually unknown west of the Coast Range in recent years (*ibid.,* 24:538). There is no recent information on the breeding status of this species in Nevada, where it has reportedly nested at Washoe Lake and near Fallon. The current breeding status of the species in Arizona is also uncertain, although it is sometimes seen at Imperial National Wildlife Refuge (*ibid.,* 24:526). There is one Kansas breeding record (*American Birds,* 25:873).

In south Texas the species breeds along the coast from the vicinity of San Benito (*ibid.,* 5:299), Brownsville, and the Santa Ana National Wildlife Refuge (*ibid.,* 13:442; 20:583), northward locally through the Corpus Christi area inland as far as Mathis (*ibid.,* 22:624; 18:521), although recently the species has almost been eliminated from southern Texas by the poisoning of seed rice (*ibid.,* 19:561). The species is abundant in the east Texas rice belt as far west as Colorado County according to Carrol (1932), who first related the bird's distribution in Texas to rice culture practices. Singleton (1953) reported that up to 4,000 birds have been seen in Brazoria County during the summertime.

The typical breeding habitat in California consists of freshwater marshes where tules or cattails grow interruptedly (Grinnell and Miller, 1944), while in Louisiana extensive areas of rice fields, especially those heavily infested with weeds, are the preferred nesting habitat (Meanley and Meanley, 1959).

Wintering Distribution and Habitat: Considerable seasonal movements are typical of this species, and it is thought that the majority of the Louisiana population moves to Mexico during winter. Leopold (1959) reported that in Mexico the largest winter populations occur in coastal Guerrero, although the species is not abundant even there. There is also an apparently sedentary Mexican population that occurs on the coasts of Sonora, Sinaloa, Nayarit, Guerrero, and along the Caribbean coasts of Tabasco, Veracruz, and Tamaulipas, which is probably enhanced to some degree by winter migrants.

An interesting and unexplained recent phenomenon has been the proliferation of winter records of fulvous whistling ducks in the eastern United States and, to a limited extent, in the central and western states as well. These records have been ably discussed and summarized by Hartz (1962) and Jones (1966). Jones plotted on a small-scale map the winter records he found for the period 1949–1965; these have been transferred to the accompanying range map and some additional or more recent records have also been added. It is quite apparent that much of the middle and southern Atlantic coast region must almost be considered as now within the normal winter range of the species, although the breeding origin of these birds is still unknown.

GENERAL BIOLOGY

Age at Maturity: The usual age of sexual maturity is still somewhat uncertain, but inasmuch as captive birds sometimes breed during their first year, it may be assumed that this at least occasionally occurs in the wild. Marvin Cecil has personally informed me that to his knowledge the fulvous whistling duck is the only species of the genus that often breeds in its first year of life, while the others do not breed in captivity until their second year. Meanley and Meanley (1958) observed normal copulation by a male when it was eight months old. McCartney (1963) suggested that yearlings may be relatively late nesters, judging from observations of captive birds.

Pair Bond Pattern: Whistling ducks have strong pair bonds, with the male regularly assisting in the rearing of the young. For this reason it is assumed that the normal pair bond is permanent, as in geese and swans, although actual data on this point appear to be lacking.

Nest Location: Dickey and van Rossem (1923) reported that all of "some 50" nests they located in 1921 were located in tufts of a dwarf species of *Scirpus,* while in 1922 these tules were flooded and nests occurred in dense clumps of living or dead *Scirpus* of a larger species, in knotweed (*Polygonum*), or on floating materials in open water. Lynch (1943) reported that nests were found in rice fields, on levees or along dikes, or sometimes occurred as floating nests in standing rice. Meanley and Meanley (1959) noted that nests were either on rice field levees or (in six of eight cases) over water between levees, while others were attached to growing plants. At the Welder Wildlife Foundation in Texas the nests of this species are always over water, which is usually from 3 to 7 feet deep (*Audubon Field Notes,* 22:623).

Clutch Size: Because of the prevalence of "dump-nesting" by other females, the typical clutch size is difficult to ascertain. Dickey and van Rossem (1923) estimated the normal range to be 10 to 16 eggs, Lynch (1943) estimated 10 to 15, and Meanley and Meanley (1959) judged that 13 eggs are an average clutch size. The average clutch size of nine successful nests reported by Cottam and Glazener (1959) was 12.6 eggs. The rate of egg-laying is apparently one per day (Meanley and Meanley, 1959; Dickey and van Rossem, 1923).

Incubation Period: The incubation period is apparently from 24 to 26 days, with estimates of 24 by Meanley and Meanley (1959), 25 by Dickey and van Rossem (1923), and 28 by Johnstone (1970). The longer estimates of 30 to 32 days by Delacour (1954) do not appear to be justified.

Fledging Period: Meanley and Meanley (1959) noted that initial flight occurred in a captive female at 63 days.

Nest and Egg Losses: A high incidence of nest losses by desertion or by flooding was reported by Dickey and van Rossem (1923), and likewise Meanley and Meanley (1959) suggested that initial nesting success was apparently low, with only three of ten observed nests being successfully hatched. Cottam and Glazener (1959) reported that nine of seventeen nests they studied were successful, and 94 out of a total of 164 eggs were hatched, a hatching success of 57 percent. In the nine successful nests, 94 of 113 eggs hatched, or 83.2 percent. However, renesting probably compensates for this figure and is facilitated by a prolonged breeding season. Nests have been found as late as August in both Louisiana and California, and in Texas there are egg records from May 16 to September 19 (Bent, 1925), indicating a breeding season of nearly four months.

Juvenile and Adult Mortality: There are no available estimates of mortality rates in this species, although many writers have commented on their susceptibility to hunters because of their unwary behavior and their fragile bone structure. Meanley and Meanley commented that, since they are so readily killed, it is fortunate that most of the birds have moved southward out of Louisiana prior to the start of the waterfowl hunting season.

GENERAL ECOLOGY

Food and Foraging: Few studies on the foods and feeding behavior of fulvous whistling ducks have been performed. Howard Leach (cited by Leopold, 1959) found that in the crops of five birds taken in California's Imperial Valley the seeds of water grass (*Echinochloa*) predominated, with small quantities of *Polygonum* and *Melilotus* also present. From stomach analysis Dickey and van Rossem (1923) noted that wild timothy (*Phleum*) formed the bulk of the summer food during one year, while the seeds of *Polygonum* species were important in the late summer and fall of 1922.

Meanley and Meanley (1959) reported that rice seeds comprise 78 percent of the food of fifteen birds collected in water-planted rice fields near the coast, while in dry-planted fields and in early fall samples rice was a minor part of the diet, with weed seeds forming the bulk of the food. When foraging, the birds often pull down the seed heads of emergent plants and strip them. They also often feed by tipping-up, or simply by lowering the head into the water without tipping-up. They also dive well and may remain submerged from about 9 to 15 seconds, with intervening surface periods of 10 to 18 seconds (Johnsgard, 1967b). Studies on possible depredations on rice crops have been made by Meanley and Meanley (1959), who found little evidence of significant damage to rice by this species.

Sociality, Densities, Territoriality: The extreme sociality of this species has been stressed by Dickey and van Rossem (1923), who mentioned that even during the peak of the laying season the birds continually gathered into small groups of mated pairs for feeding and resting together, separating only in the early morning hours for laying. Several larger flocks, apparently of nonbreeding birds, were also present through the summer period, reaching a minimum in early July and then being augmented by apparently unsuccessful nesters. Such sociality sometimes favors fairly high nest concentrations, at least when favored nesting habitat is restricted. Dickey and van Rossem noted about fifty nests in an area approximately half a mile long by two hundred yards wide, and felt that many more were present but remained undetected. These figures would suggest a nesting density of at least 1.4 nests per acre. Meanley and Meanley (1959) found a much lower breeding density of thirteen and twenty pairs in two five-square-mile study areas.

Interspecific Relationships: It is possible that some competition for food exists between the fulvous and black-bellied whistling ducks, but since their nest site preferences are wholly different there would seem to be little if any competition for breeding locations. Rylander and Bolen (1970) pointed out that, whereas the black-bellied whistling duck is primarily a wading and perching species, the fulvous is mainly a swimming species and mostly dabbles for food. They also related its relatively larger foot size to the fact that it is a better swimmer and to its possibly greater reliance on diving.

Nesting associates of fulvous whistling ducks in Louisiana include the red-winged blackbird, purple gallinule, king rail, least bittern, and long-billed marsh wren (Meanley and Meanley, 1959). In California, the eggs of redheads and ruddy ducks have been found in nests containing those of fulvous whistling ducks (Dickey and van Rossem, 1923), and all three species are known to be social parasites (Weller, 1959). Shields (1899) reported the eggs of this species in both redhead and ruddy duck nests.

General Activity Patterns: The nocturnal foraging activity pattern of the whistling ducks is well known. Meanley and Meanley (1959) noted that in late April, fulvous whistling ducks usually would leave the coastal marshes about 8:00 p.m. for the rice fields, often in flocks of 30 or 40 birds. Later in the summer, flocks of 150 to 200 birds were seen in rice fields, and a maximum flock size of 3,000 birds was reported for Lacassine National Wildlife Refuge in late summer. Cottam and Glazener (1959) suggested that migration may occur at night.

SOCIAL AND SEXUAL BEHAVIOR

Flocking Behavior: The strong flocking behavior of this species, even in the breeding season, has already been noted. Because of their strongly gregarious tendencies, fulvous whistling ducks decoy readily and will also be attracted to a whistled imitation of their call.

Pair-forming Behavior: Presumably because of the strong and apparently persistent pair bonds of this species, descriptions of pair formation are almost nonexistent. Meanley and Meanley (1959) noted what appeared to be courting flights in spring, when three or four ducks flew in unison in erratic flights. On one occasion a single female was observed being followed by three males on the ground. Very limited observations on captive birds suggest that the male pair-forming displays are virtually identical with those of geese, although triumph ceremonies are lacking (Johnsgard, 1965).

Copulatory Behavior: Copulatory behavior has been described by Johnsgard (1965) and also by Meanley and Meanley (1958). This species typically copulates in water of swimming depth, and precopulatory activities are scarcely separable from normal bathing movements involving head-dipping on the part of both birds. The postcopulatory "step-dance" is a highly stereotyped display in which both birds rise parallel in the water and each bird raises the folded wing on the opposite side from its partner as they both tread water rapidly.

Nesting Behavior: Although nest locations vary considerably according to local conditions, they are typically in emergent vegetation and often are roofed over so as to be nearly hidden from above. Nests in water often have ramps, sometimes several feet long, leading to the rim, and rarely if ever is any significant amount of down present in the nest. Males presumably help females construct the nest, and Delacour (1954) was of the opinion that the male may spend more time than the female at the nest.

Brooding Behavior: Both sexes attend the young and probably undergo their postnuptial molt at about the same time, during the roughly two-month fledging period. McCartney (1963) noted that most hatching dates in Louisiana were in July, while the peak flightless period was mid-September.

Postbreeding Behavior: With the fledging of the young, families gather into larger flock units and move to favorable feeding areas prior to the fall migration. Dickey and van Rossem (1923) noted that, although in 1921 all the birds had left Buena Vista Lake by the first of September, in 1922 favorable water conditions attracted "thousands" of birds, which began to move south shortly after the first of October. McCartney (1963) suggested that the eastern Texas and Louisiana population may migrate nonstop to and from their Mexican wintering grounds on Mexico's Gulf coast, an air distance of about 600 miles.

Trumpeter Swan, Adult (drinking)

Lesser Snow Goose (Blue Phase), Adult and young

Lesser Canada Goose, Adults

Atlantic Brant, Adult

Barnacle Goose, Adults

Wood Duck, Adult Male

American Wigeon, Pair

Gadwall, Pair

Green-winged Teal, Pair

Mexican Mallard, Adult Male

Florida Mallard, Pair

Northern Pintail, Pair

Blue-winged Teal, Pair

Cinnamon Teal, Pair

Shoveler, Pair

Canvasback, Pair

Redhead, Pair

Ring-necked Duck, Pair

Greater Scaup, Pair

King Eider, Pair

Steller Eider, Adults

Oldsquaw, Male in Winter Plumage

Harlequin Duck, Male

Surf Scoter, Male

Bufflehead, Pair

Barrow Goldeneye, Pair

Common Goldeneye, Pair

Hooded Merganser, Displaying Male

Red-breasted Merganser, Male

Common Merganser, Pair

Ruddy Duck, Male

CUBAN WHISTLING DUCK

Dendrocygna arborea (Linnaeus) 1758

Other Vernacular Names: Antillian Tree Duck, Black-billed Tree Duck, Cuban Tree Duck, West Indian Tree Duck.

Range: Resident in the West Indies.

Subspecies: None recognized.

Measurements (after Delacour, 1954):
   Folded wing: Both sexes 230-270 mm.
   Culmen: Both sexes 45-53 mm.

Weights: No quantitative data available. Lack (1968) reports the adult weight as 1,150 grams.

IDENTIFICATION

In the Hand: Identifiable as a whistling duck on the basis of the long legs, entirely reticulate tarsus, and the elongated hind toe, this species is the largest of all whistling ducks. Its folded wing measurements (230-270 mm.) and its long, black bill (culmen 45-53 mm.) will separate it from all other species of the genus.

In the Field: This West Indian duck is unlikely to be seen in continental North America, except as an escape from captivity. Like the others of its genus, it has long legs and neck, a short tail, and relatively rounded wings which produce a distinctive body profile. The birds swim well, but often feed in shallow waters or on dry land. This species also perches in trees to some extent. It is the only North American whistling duck that is predominantly dark brown, with a blackish bill and mottled black and white flanks. In flight, it exhibits ashy white markings on the wings in the areas where the black-bellied whistling duck appears pure white. Its call is rather infrequently uttered, but is a clear whistle sounding like *wheet-a-whew'-whe-whew'*.

AGE AND SEX CRITERIA

Sex Determination: No external plumage characteristics are available to separate the sexes.

Age Determination: Not yet studied, but no doubt the notched juvenal tail feathers are carried for much of the first fall of life.

OCCURRENCE IN NORTH AMERICA

Apparently the Cuban whistling duck has not yet been definitely reported from continental North America, but it is a resident on some of the nearby Bahama Islands (Andros, Watling, Inagua), in Cuba, the Isle of Pines, Hispaniola, Jamaica, Grand Cayman, Puerto Rico, the Virgin Islands, Barbuda, and Antigua (A.O.U., 1957). According to Bond (1971), its major range includes the Bahamas, the Greater Antilles, and the northern Lesser Antilles, while it is only of casual occurrence elsewhere in the West Indies.

BLACK-BELLIED WHISTLING DUCK

Dendrocygna autumnalis (Linnaeus) 1758

Other Vernacular Names: Black-bellied Tree Duck, Gray-breasted Tree Duck, Pichichi, Red-billed Tree Duck, Red-billed Whistling Duck.

Range: From northern Argentina northward through eastern and northern South America, Central America, Mexico, and the extreme southern United States.

North American Subspecies (recognized by Delacour, 1954):

D. a. autumnalis (L.): Northern Black-bellied Whistling Duck. North and Central America south to Panama. *D. a. fulgens* Friedmann, recognized by the A.O.U. (1957), is not considered by Delacour to be acceptable.

Measurements (after Delacour, 1954):

Folded wing: Both sexes 217-246 mm.

Culmen: Both sexes 43-53 mm.

Weights: Average of 35 males collected during May was 28.7 ounces, or 816.5 grams (range 680-907). The average weight of 37 females collected during May was 29.6 ounces, or 839.2 grams (range 652 to 1021), according to Bolen (1964). Of birds collected through the breeding season, 9 males averaged 799.5 grams (range 728 to 952) and 8 females averaged 893.4 grams (range 832 to 978). The greater average weight of the females probably reflects their breeding condition, since, in the linear measurements presented by Bolen, males averaged slightly larger in all measurements except tail length.

IDENTIFICATION

In the Hand: Like the other whistling ducks, this species has long legs that extend beyond the short tail, an entirely reticulated tarsus, and an elongated and elevated hind toe. It is the only whistling duck with a red bill, pink feet, or pure white on the upper wing surface.

In the Field: Whistling ducks stand in a rather erect posture on land, where their long necks, long legs, and ducklike body are evident. In the water they swim lightly, with the tail well out of the water and the neck usually well extended. The black-bellied whistling duck is easily recognized in both situations by its red bill and the large white lateral stripe that separates the brownish back from the black underparts. In flight, the long neck and trailing legs are apparent, and the blackish underparts and underwing surface contrast strongly with the predominantly white upper wing surface. Both in flight and at rest, the birds often utter clear whistling notes, the most typical of which is a four- to seven-note call sounding like *wha-chew'-whe-whe-whew,* or *pe-che-che-ne* (Leopold, 1959). As a cavity-nesting species, it is more often seen perching in trees than is the fulvous whistling duck. Like that species, it is quite gregarious and gathers in large flocks when not breeding.

AGE AND SEX CRITERIA

Sex Determination: There are no apparent external differences in the sexes, so internal examination is required for determination of sex.

Age Determination: According to Cain (1970), notched juvenal rectrices may persist until the bird is about thirty-five weeks old. Birds between six and eight months old have the black feathers of the rump region tipped with white and the penis of males lacks spines, while birds at least ten months old have entirely black rump feathers and males have well-developed spines on the penis. Sexual maturity probably occurs in the first year of life, although reliable data on this point are lacking.

DISTRIBUTION AND HABITAT

Breeding Distribution and Habitat: In the United States, the breeding area of the black-bellied whistling duck is almost entirely limited to southern Texas. Bolen (1962) stated that the northernmost part of its breeding range lives within a fifty-mile radius of Corpus Christi. It is also a common breeder in the lower Rio Grande valley, including Santa Ana and Laguna Atascosa refuges, and has bred recently in the vicinities of Rio Hondo, Brownsville, and Falfurrias (*Audubon Field Notes,* various issues). North of Corpus Christi there are fewer records, but broods or nests have been found at Mathis (*ibid.,* 13:442), Beeville (*ibid.,* 24:697), and in the vicinity of San Antonio (*ibid.,* 18:521, 23:673). It has been reported as far north as Eagle Lake (Peterson, 1960), and Bolen *et al.* (1964) consider it "well established" in Live Oak, San Patricio, Kleberg, and Brooks counties. In some years as many as twenty pairs nest at Santa Ana Refuge (*Audubon Field Notes,* 24:607), and several hundred young have been seen in favorable years at Laguna Atascosa Refuge (*ibid.,* 20:583, 22:624). In Texas the nesting habitat was described by Meanley and Meanley (1958), who found ten nests in a thicket of trees and shrubs near a small lake. All the nests were in hollow trees, eight being ebony (*Pithecolobium*) and two being hackberry (*Celtis*). The associated plants and breeding birds were those characteristic of a semiarid climate.

Outside of Texas, only a few breeding records have been obtained for the United States. There are two breeding records for the Miami area, which may represent escapes from the Crandon Park Zoo (*ibid.,* 23:652). The first definite record of nesting in Arizona was obtained near Phoenix in 1969 (Johnson and Barlow, 1971), although for several years the species had been seen increasingly around Phoenix, Tucson, and Nogales (*ibid.,* 22:634; 24:630). There are no nesting areas in the rice belt of Louisiana, and the species was reported for the first time in that state only recently (*ibid.,* 22:668). Likewise, the species is extremely rare in California, with only three state records (*American Birds,* 26:904).

In Mexico this species is much more common than the fulvous whistling duck. It breeds principally along the tropical coasts, but occasionally nests in the temperate uplands (Leopold, 1959). It also breeds commonly farther south in Central America to central Panama.

Wintering Distribution and Habitat: In southern Texas this species is usually present from April to early November, with only a few birds normally overwintering (Bolen, 1962). It may be presumed that the Texas population moves into the coastal regions of Mexico. Leopold mentioned large winter flocks in the mangrove swamps of Nayarit, and smaller numbers of both spe-

•B = Extralimital Breeding Records

Breeding distribution of the black-bellied whistling duck in North and
Central America. Recent extralimital breeding records in the United
States are indicated.

cies of whistling ducks were noted in the rivers and lagoons of Veracruz and Tabasco. Reportedly this species also at times occurs in large numbers on the south coast of Chiapas, as well as on the larger rivers in the northern part of that state.

GENERAL BIOLOGY

Age at Maturity: Not established with certainty, but males develop spines on the penis and acquire a fully adult plumage between 10 and 21 months of age (Cain, 1970); this suggests that breeding initially occurs at the end of the first or second year of life. Ferguson (1966) reported that two of six aviculturalists responding to a survey reported initial breeding in each of the first three years of life.

Pair Bond Pattern: Like the other species of *Dendrocygna,* this species exhibits a strong pair bond, with the male assisting in nest and brood defense. There is definite evidence (Bolen, 1967b) that the male participates in incubation. The pair bond is presumably permanent and potentially lifelong (Bolen, 1971).

Nest Location: In contrast to the fulvous whistling duck, this species preferentially nests in cavities. Of 20 natural nest sites studied by Bolen *et al.* (1964), 17 were in trees and 3 were on the ground. Ten of the tree sites were water-isolated, 5 were within fifty feet of water, but 2 were about a quarter mile from the nearest water. The occurrence of herbaceous rather than shrubby vegetation under the nest entrance may be important in nest site selection, as is the presence of a nearby perch. The height of the nest entrance averaged 270.7 centimeters for those above water and 162.5 centimeters for those over land. No down or nest materials are normally present in cavity nests, and ground nests consist of shallow baskets of woven grasses.

Clutch Size: Bolen (1962) estimated the average clutch to range from 12 to 16 eggs, which are laid one per day. Normal clutch size data are obscured by a strong tendency for dump-nesting by this species; Bolen *et al.* (1964) reported that nearly half of 428 eggs found in southern Texas in 1962 remained unhatched, apparently because of desertion related to multiple nest use. There is some evidence of double-brooding in this species (Johnson and Barlow, 1971).

Incubation Period: Bolen *et al.* (1964) reported the incubation period as 28 days, while Cain (1970) found that in an artificial incubator the eggs usually hatched between 29 and 31 days after initial incubation began. In contrast, Lack (1968) reported a 26-day incubation period. It is of interest that the incubation period in this cavity-nesting species seems to average somewhat longer than that of the fulvous whistling duck, a ground-nesting form.

Fledging Period: Cain (1970) reported that captive-reared ducklings were first observed flying between 56 and 63 days of age.

Nest and Egg Losses: Bolen *et al.* (1964) reported that, of 428 eggs studied, only 83 hatched, a hatching success of 19.4 percent. Predation losses were mainly attributed to raccoons and rat snakes, but the biggest source of nesting failure was caused by dump-nesting. In a more recent study, Bolen (1967a) compared nesting success of natural cavity nests with that of unprotected and protected nesting boxes. Of the 32 natural cavity nests, 14 (44 percent) hatched, about the same nesting success rate as he found in 13 unprotected boxes. However, 44 protected nesting boxes had a 77 percent nesting success, as compared with a total overall average nesting success of 61 percent for all three types of nesting sites.

Juvenile and Adult Mortality: There appear to be no available estimates of mortality rates in this species. Bolen (1970) reported that, although adult sex ratios favored males slightly, there was no statistical indication that females have a higher mortality rate than males.

GENERAL ECOLOGY

Food and Foraging: The only detailed study of the food intake of this species is that of Bolen and Forsyth (1967), based on an analysis of 22 stomachs and 11 crops. By volume, these foods were 92 percent plant materials, with a predominance of sorghum grain and Bermuda grass (*Cynodon*) seeds. Later in the summer the seeds of other species, such as smartweeds (*Polygonum*) and water star grass (*Heteranthera*), were utilized in minor amounts; virtually no leaves, stems, or roots of any plants were found in the samples. At least locally, rice and corn are consumed in large quantities, and the birds may cause substantial crop damage (Leopold, 1959). Animal foods are quite limited and include gastropod mollusks and various insects.

Unlike the fulvous whistling duck, this species prefers to forage while standing in shallow water, rather than swimming or diving for its food. Bolen *et al.* (1964) reported that the birds are rarely seen in water deeper than the length of their legs.

Sociality, Densities, Territoriality: Like the fulvous whistling duck, this species is highly social and may be seen in flocks almost throughout the year. It is also somewhat colonial in nesting; Leopold (1959) found a "rather large" breeding colony in oak groves at the crest of the Sierra de Tamaulipas. Bolen *et al.* (1964) estimated a resident population of 250 pairs in a 150,000-

acre area of Lake Corpus Christi, Mathis, Texas, where an abundant stand of water-killed trees was present. In 1966 some 26 broods totalling 271 young were seen on the 45,000-acre Laguna Atascosa National Wildlife Refuge (of which about 7,000 acres are water), and more recently 380 young have been counted there (*Audubon Field Notes,* 20:583, 22:624). It would seem probable that nesting density is determined by the availability of adequate nest cavities in otherwise suitable habitats.

Interspecific Relationships: No detailed information is available. This species and the fulvous whistling duck often occur in mixed flocks in coastal Mexico, but probably have little competition for food or nesting sites. In aggressive disputes, this species typically dominates the smaller fulvous whistling duck (Cottam and Glazener, 1959). Major enemies are probably those that destroy the eggs or young, such as raccoons and snakes. In spite of repeated comments to the effect, there is no real evidence that alligators are an important predator on this species. Another hole-nesting species, the muscovy, occurs in many of the same areas, and Bolen (1971) has found that female muscovy ducks sometimes displace nesting females of this species.

Daily Activities and Movements: Like other whistling ducks, these birds are distinctly nocturnal in their activities, spending the daylight hours resting or sleeping, and moving out to feeding areas at sundown. No doubt their strong vocalizations are an important means of communication when flying under nocturnal conditions, and the white upper wing markings are also highly conspicuous in flight. Leopold (1959) has mentioned how one's eyes are irresistibly drawn to the flashing wings of this species when it is seen in flight.

SOCIAL AND SEXUAL BEHAVIOR

Flocking Behavior: Flock sizes of up to 2,000 birds have been reported (Phillips, 1923), indicating the highly gregarious tendencies of this species.

Pair-forming Behavior: Virtually nothing has been learned of the details of pair formation in this or any other species of whistling duck. It must be presumed that the formation of pairs is a very gradual and inconspicuous process, since I never observed obvious courtship during two years when the species was under observation on a nearly daily basis.

Copulatory Behavior: Copulatory behavior has been described by various writers (Johnsgard, 1965; Meanley and Meanley, 1958). Unlike the fulvous whistling duck, copulation usually occurs while the pair is standing on shore or in quite shallow water. The male, and sometimes also the female, performs drinking movements scarcely different from those used in normal drinking behavior. Thereafter, mounting occurs, and after treading is completed there is a rather inconspicuous postcopulatory display involving mutual calling and a slight wing-lifting on the part of the male.

Nesting and Brooding Behavior: Both sexes apparently participate in nest site selection, and the male also assists with incubation. No down is plucked from the breast of either sex during incubation, and quite possibly the heat of summer is responsible for some embryonic development (Cain, 1970). When the young hatch, both sexes carefully tend them. Typically, one adult swims in front of, the other behind the brood. When threatened by a predator, one parent often leaves the group to decoy and harass the animal while the other leads the brood to safety. Young have also been observed riding on the backs of swimming adults (Bolen *et al.,* 1964).

Postbreeding Behavior: Little definite information is available on this, but the Texas population apparently begins its southward migration not long after the young have grown and the adults have completed their postnuptial molt.

SWANS AND TRUE GEESE
Tribe Anserini

The approximately twenty extant species of swans and true geese are, unlike the whistling ducks, primarily of temperate and arctic distribution, especially in the Northern Hemisphere. It is thus not surprising that continental North America may lay claim to at least nine breeding species, or nearly half of the known total. Additionally, sufficient records of a tenth, the barnacle goose, are known as to warrant its inclusion in the book even though there is no indication that it nests in continental North America.

Several additional Old World species of geese and swans have been reported one or more times in North America, but the likelihood of at least some of these being escapes from captivity seems so great that their inclusion seems unjustified. These species include the red-breasted goose (*Branta ruficollis*), which has been collected in California at least five times and has also been seen in recent years in Texas, Pennsylvania, and Kansas, but is not known to nest nearer than central Siberia. The bean goose (*Anser fabalis*) has been reliably reported from Alaska (Byrd *et al.*, 1974), while the smaller pink-footed goose (*A. f. brachyrhynchus*) has been collected in Massachusetts (Bent, 1925) and seen in Delaware (*Audubon Field Notes*, 8:10, 9:235). Other Old World species that have been reported, such as the lesser white-fronted goose (*Anser erythropus*) and the bar-headed goose (*Anser indicus*), appear to have represented escapes from captivity, although a specimen of the former species was recently shot in Delaware (*American Birds* 27:597).

Geese and swans are generally large waterfowl that are almost entirely vegetarian in their diets. Swans forage predominantly in water, eating surface vegetation or tipping-up to reach underwater plants, but occasionally resort to eating terrestrial plants on shorelines or even in fields. Geese, however, forage both in water and on land, with some species such as brant foraging exclusively on aquatic life while others rely largely on terrestrial herbaceous plants. In most geese the cutting edges of the upper and lower mandibles are coarsely serrated in the manner of the pinking shears, providing an effective method of clipping off vegetation close to the ground. Like whistling ducks, swans and true geese have a reticulated tarsal pattern, lack iridescent or sexually dimorphic plumage patterns, and form strong, persistent pair bonds. Indeed, the fidelity of swan and goose pairs is legendary, although in actual fact this pairing behavior falls slightly short of their supposed perfect fidelity.

Although some authorities recognize a larger number of genera and species, recent investigators have generally recommended that only two or three swan genera be recognized (*Coscoroba, Cygnus,* and perhaps *Olor*) and that the genera of typical true geese be reduced to no more than three (*Anser, Branta,* and perhaps *Nesochen*). Likewise, species limits have been enlarged in recent years, so that the Old World and New World representatives of the arctic swans are now usually considered conspecific, the "blue goose" is generally recognized to be nothing more than a color phase of the snow goose, a single species of brant goose is recognized, and although a larger number of Canada goose races have recently been designated they are clearly part of an intergrading series of population complexes.

MUTE SWAN
Cygnus olor (Gmelin) 1789

Other Vernacular Names: None in general use.

Range: Breeds through the temperate portions of Europe and western Asia, as well as eastern Siberia. Introduced and locally established in New Zealand, Australia, and North America, especially along the northeastern coast, centering on Long Island.

Subspecies: None recognized. A variant, called the "Polish swan," is known to be a color phase.

Measurements (after Delacour, 1954):

Folded wing: Both sexes 560-625 mm. Frith (1967) reports males as 560-622 and females as 535-570 mm.

Culmen: Males (from knob) 70-75 mm. Frith reports males as 70-85 and females as 73-90 mm.

Weights: Bauer and Glutz (1968) summarized available data. Males seldom weigh over 13.5 kilograms (29.7 pounds), and females should not weigh much over 10 kilograms (22 pounds). However, four old birds weighed between September and December averaged 16.225 kilograms (35.78

pounds), with a maximum of 22.4 kilograms (49.39 pounds). Fisher and Peterson (1964) reported a maximum male weight of 50.6 pounds, an apparent record weight for flying birds. Scott *et al.* (1972) presented weight data indicating that although male mute swans average slightly heavier than male trumpeters (12.2 vs. 11.9 kilograms), female mutes average slightly lighter than female trumpeters (8.9 vs. 9.4 kilograms).

IDENTIFICATION

In the Hand: Mute swans are the only white swans that have generally reddish to orange bills with an enlarged black knob at the base (lacking in immatures), outer primaries that are not emarginate near their tips, and a somewhat pointed rather than rounded tail. The trachea, unlike those of native North American swans, does not enter the sternum.

In the Field: This large swan is usually seen in city parks, but may occasionally be seen as a feral bird under natural conditions, especially in the eastern states and provinces. The neck of the mute swan is seemingly thicker than those of the trumpeter and whistling swans, and while swimming the bird holds it gracefully curved more often than straight. Further, the wings and scapulars are raised when the birds are disturbed, rather than being compressed against the body. The orange bill and its black knob are visible at some distance. In flight, the wings produce a loud "singing" noise that is much more evident than in the native North American swans, and, additionally, mute swans rarely if ever call when in flight, as is so characteristic of the native species. A snorting threat is sometimes uttered by male mute swans, which is their apparent vocal limit.

AGE AND SEX CRITERIA

Sex Determination: Males are considerably heavier and larger than females, and individuals in excess of 10 kilograms are most probably males. Males also have larger black knobs at the base of the bill and most often assume the familiar threatening posture. For immature birds, internal examination is required to determine sex.

Age Determination: Any bird still possessing feathered lores or some brownish feathers of the juvenal plumage is less than a year old. Second-year birds may have smaller knobs and less brilliant bill coloration than is typical of older birds.

DISTRIBUTION AND HABITAT

Breeding and Wintering Distribution and Habitat: In North America the mute swan occupies a sedentary breeding and wintering range that is a direct reflection of human activities. There seems to be no historical account of the spread of the species in the Hudson Valley and on Long Island after it was originally released as a park bird. Being properly considered an exotic, the species was not included in bird lists until the 1930s, when the fourth (1931) edition of the A.O.U. *Check-list* noted that it had become established on the lower Hudson Valley and the south shore of Long Island, sometimes straying to the coast of New Jersey. East Coast hurricanes, such as the one that occurred in 1939, caused additional dispersal of birds previously confined to wealthy estates on Long Island and in Rhode Island. By 1949 the species had spread through much of Long Island and had also become well established in Rhode Island (*Audubon Field Notes,* 3:5; 10:370). By the late 1950s it was nesting along the entire shore of Rhode Island (*ibid.,* 12:396), and a brood had been reported in the District of Columbia (*ibid.,* 12:403). A secondary population center was simultaneously developing on upper Lake Michigan around Grand Traverse Bay and Lake Charlevoix (Edwards, 1966). Early counts of this population were reported by Banko (1960), who noted an increase from two birds in 1948 or 1949 to forty-one by 1956. Apparently initiated by a release of two birds in 1918, the flock consisted of at least six hundred by 1973, when efforts began to transplant and establish new flocks in Illinois, Texas, Ohio, Arkansas, Oklahoma, and New Mexico (*Chicago Tribune,* August 30, 1973).

The annual Christmas counts of the Audubon Society provide a rough index to the population growth of mute swans in North America. During the years 1949 through 1969, the numbers of such counts approximately doubled from 403 to 876, while the total number of mute swans counted increased from 374 to 1,644. The average total count for the ten-year period 1950–1959 was 504 birds, with an average of fewer than twenty stations reporting the species, while during the period 1960–1969 the average total count was 1,434 birds, with an average of thirty-four stations reporting mute swans.

In recent years, pioneering birds have occupied new localities for breeding. These include nestings in Massachusetts (*Audubon Field Notes,* 17:446), Delaware (*ibid.,* 19:531; 20:557), New Hampshire (*ibid.,* 23:638), and Connecticut (*ibid.,* 24:583), plus isolated breedings in South Dakota (*ibid.,* 22:618), Saskatchewan (*ibid.,* 21:618; 23:618), Ontario (*ibid.,* 23:584),

Breeding (hatched) and wintering (shaded) distributions of the mute swan in North America. Recent extralimital breeding records by apparently feral birds are also indicated.

and Virginia (*American Birds,* 26:842). A feral flock also occurs near Victoria, British Columbia (Ronald Mackay, pers. comm.).

GENERAL BIOLOGY

Age at Maturity: The earliest known age of reproductive maturity in North America has been reported as two (Johnston, 1935) or three (Willey, 1968) years, but studies in England indicate considerable variation may occur. Perrins and Reynolds (1967) indicated that three years of age is the most common time of initial breeding for females, but a few birds may breed at two and some may not breed until they are six years old. Initial breeding by males occurred between three to seven years of age. Minton (1968) found that of forty-three mute swans, half initially nested and raised young at the age of three, while an additional third did so the following year, with a slight tendency for females to mature earlier than males. Three birds did not breed until they were at least six years old.

Pair Bond Pattern: The strong pair bond of swans is well known. Minton (1968) reported that "divorce" (the changing of partners when both are still alive) among the paired population had an incidence of about 4 percent for nonbreeding pairs and 1 percent for breeding pairs. In cases where both birds survived to following years, 82 percent of the successful breeders and 78 percent of unsuccessful breeders remained paired. Of seventy-one pairings first studied in 1961, six were still intact in 1966. During the six-year study, eleven males and nine females were known to have had at least three different mates, but in several cases (twelve males and two females) birds that had apparently lost their mates remained on their nesting territory the following year. In some cases there was a gap of two or three years before re-pairing, while in others the birds apparently gave up pairing permanently.

Nest Location: Nests are usually built on islands or in shallow water, sometimes in colonies, with one English colony in Dorset having had as many as 500 nests (Scott and Boyd, 1957). Established breeders tend to use previous nest sites. Willey (1968) estimated the average size of twelve nesting territories as 4.4 acres (range 0.5 to 11.8 in Rhode Island). Minton (1968) noted that both breeding and nonbreeding pairs were more prevalent on small (10 acres or less) water areas than on larger ones, but considering availability, larger water areas were slightly favored. Likewise, streams were favored over canals or rivers (over 20 feet wide), especially by breeding pairs. Clean, weed-filled waters were also preferred over more polluted waters.

Clutch Size: Most studies indicate that about 6 eggs constitute an average clutch size for mute swans; Perrins and Reynolds (1967) reported such an average for 92 nests. Studies summarized by Bauer and Glutz (1968) also indicate averages of between 5.8 and 6.2 eggs. Clutch sizes of up to 11 eggs laid by one female are known, and renesting attempts appear to average less, or about 4 eggs (Perrins and Reynolds, 1967).

Incubation Period: This is generally estimated as 35 to 36 days, with some estimates of up to 38 days (Bauer and Glutz, 1968). The female incubates, but the male actively protects the nest.

Fledging Period: This has been variously reported as four and a half months (Bauer and Glutz, 1968), 18 weeks (Lack, 1968), and 18 to 20 weeks (Scott and Boyd, 1967).

Nest and Egg Losses: Willey and Halla (1972) reported the loss of 87 eggs and young from a total of 236 in 47 nests after severe flooding and cold weather in Rhode Island in 1967. Minton (1968) reported a 59 percent nesting success among 352 pairs, and a 52 percent success for 11 renesting attempts, with 80 percent of the nest losses due to human disturbance or destruction.

Juvenile Mortality: Minton (1968) found that the average brood size (219 broods) at fledging over a six-year period was 3.5 birds, while the total number raised to fledging averaged 2.0 per breeding pair. Perrins and Reynolds (1967) likewise found an average brood size of 3.1 young for 83 broods, with an estimated 2.0 young raised per pair (including pairs that did not hatch any young at all) to September. They estimated that the average mortality rate between hatching and fledging was 50 percent, with an additional 23 percent mortality rate for the rest of the year. Willey (1968) estimated a prefledging mortality of 56.4 percent in 1968, with the snapping turtle apparently a primary predator of cygnets.

Adult Mortality: Perrins and Reynolds (1967) estimated that among immature birds there is a 67 to 75 percent survival (25 to 33 percent mortality) rate, while breeding adults have a survival rate of 82 percent, possibly decreasing after the sixth year of life. There is little difference in the estimated mortality rates of the two sexes. Ogilvie (1967) estimated a higher mortality rate of 40.5 percent for birds banded when under a year old and 38.5 percent for those banded when over a year old, with the possibly greater survival in the third and fourth years of life than during the first two. Overhead wires were found to be a major cause of mortality, with oiling, disease, fighting, cold weather, and shooting also accounting for some mortality.

GENERAL ECOLOGY

Food and Foraging: The food of mute swans is almost exclusively of plant origin and mainly consists of aquatic plants. Willey (1968) estimated that adults eat an average of 8.4 pounds of vegetation per day. In general, the birds feed on subsurface plants they can reach when swimming or by tipping up in the manner of dabbling ducks. In England these include algae (*Chara, Enteromorpha, Ulva, Nitella*), pondweeds *Zostera, Potamogeton, Ruppia*), grasses, and other herbaceous plants (Gilham, 1956). Some terrestrial vegetation is also consumed, and sometimes small aquatic animals, including fish and amphibians, have been reported in the diet.

Sociality, Densities, Territoriality: Minton (1968) has studied population densities in England and reported a density of one pair (about 30 percent nonbreeders) per 5.5 square miles on his study area of 550 square miles. He noted that this represented about one breeding pair per 8 square miles, compared with earlier estimates of one pair per 16 square miles reported for England and Wales as a whole. The highest reported county densities were one pair per 3 square miles for Middlesex and one per 7 square miles in Dorset. Atkinson-Willes (1963) reported that the famous mute swan colony at Abbotsbury in Dorset averaged 66 pairs of breeding swans (range 39-104) in the years 1947–1956 and had an average total population of about 700 birds. A tradition of protection and abundant food in the form of *Zostera* and *Ruppia* account for this concentration of birds. Comparable figures are not available for North America, but the highest Christmas counts have usually occurred in central Suffolk County, where the total number of birds seen in a 15-mile-diameter area (176 square miles) has averaged 452 for the 1960–1969 period, or 2.6 per square mile. If Minton's estimate that 30 to 40 percent of the population represents breeding birds, this would represent a breeding density of nearly one pair per square mile, assuming no spring dispersal. Willey (1968) estimated that between 24.5 and 54.3 percent of the Rhode Island population represented potential breeders. Thus it would seem that, at least locally, mute swan breeding populations in North America may be as high as or higher than in Great Britain.

Interspecific Relationships: In Europe the mute swan is a species that nests largely in populated areas that support few other breeding waterfowl, and there is probably little competition with other species. Dementiev and Gladkov (1967) reported it tolerant toward other birds and sometimes occurring with nesting gray-lag geese. Willey (1968) stated that nesting birds may kill other swans that intrude into their nesting territories. He also considered them a substantial threat to humans, particularly children. Stone and Masters (1971) reported that six captive mute swans killed six adult geese and two adult ducks, as well as forty ducklings and goslings, during a twenty-month period.

General Activity Patterns and Movements: Mute swans are highly sedentary birds in Great Britain. Atkinson-Willes (1963) reported that only a small number of banded mute swans had been proven to have moved more than a hundred miles, and only two had been known to cross the English Channel. More recently, Harrison and Ogilvie (1968) noted that 10 of 2,700 band recoveries exhibited overseas movement from Great Britain, with recoveries from Holland, the Baltic coasts of East and West Germany, Sweden, and France, and many of these recoveries were related to severe winter conditions that forced birds to move from the continent to Britain.

According to Minton (1968), most movements of mute swans occur before their mating and acquisition of a territory, after which they become quite sedentary. Most pairs return to their territory year after year, with only 2 percent of the surviving paired population that Minton studied moving their territories more than five miles. Nonbreeding pairs and unsuccessful breeders frequently move to the nearest flock for molting in midsummer, while unsuccessful breeders molt on their territories and move into flocks during fall. Among paired birds, movements are usually less than ten miles, and only about 5 percent of the 450 paired birds studied moved farther than this. However, unsuccessful breeders are more likely to move greater distances than successful ones.

SOCIAL AND SEXUAL BEHAVIOR

Flocking Behavior: As noted, flocking occurs among nonbreeders and unsuccessful breeders during the midsummer molting period, and later in the fall these flocks are increased by the addition of family groups forced out of their territories by cold weather. Atkinson-Willes (1963) indicated eleven locations (mostly coastal) where accumulations of more than 250 swans have regularly been reported in Great Britain. The largest flocks are generally found on a 1,240-acre reservoir at Abberton, a sumer molting area attracting up to nearly 500 birds maximally, and along the Essex coast at Mistley, where 800 to 900 birds are attracted to waste corn from a mill.

Pair-forming Behavior: Minton (1968) reported on the initial pairing behavior of 125 mute swans of known age. Nearly half of these were two-year-olds, another 30 percent were three-year-olds, and a few (one male, four females) took mates when only a year old. Most birds were paired for at least a year before they actually attempted to nest, with only 2 of 60 birds that were no more than two years old actually nesting that year. Birds tended to pair with others of about their own age, with a slight tendency for the males to be older than the females. Further, in 74 percent of the initial pairings neither partner had ever been paired before. Birds pairing for the first time with a previously paired bird were generally replacements for dead mates.

Copulatory Behavior: Copulatory displays have been described by various persons, such as Boase (1959), Johnsgard (1965), and others. Precopulatory displays involve mutual bill-dipping and preening movements, with the neck feathers ruffled. Following treading, both birds rise in the water breast-to-breast, with necks and heads extended vertically but with wings closed; then they gradually arch their necks and settle back on the water.

Nesting and Brooding Behavior: After the establishment of a breeding territory, nests are constructed on land or shallow water. The nests are usually about a meter in diameter and 0.6 to 0.8 meter in height and are constructed in the form of a large mound of vegetation consisting of rushes, reeds, other herbaceous vegetation, and sometimes also sticks. The nest cup is lined with finer materials and also with down and feathers. The female typically does most of the nest construction, but the male helps gather material from nearby, passing it back toward the nest over his shoulder. Down-plucking may begin with the start of egg-laying, the initiation of incubation, or not until the last or penultimate egg is deposited. The female does the incubation, but is closely guarded by the male. The young typically leave the nest on the day after hatching and remain closely attended by both parents. The young often ride on the backs of one or both parents. The wing molt of both parents normally occurs during the fledging period of the brood (Bauer and Glutz, 1968; Dementiev and Gladkov, 1967, etc.).

Postbreeding Behavior: Successful breeders remain with their young well past the fledging time, usually until severe weather forces the families to retire to winter quarters and to merge with larger groups of swans. Typically, the young of the past year are driven out of the territory by their parents before the latter begin to breed again. Minton (1968) reported two cases in which young remained with their parents until the following summer or until molting, and in neither case did the parents breed during that year. Two cases of pairing between parents and offspring were noted by Minton. One involved the pairing of a female with its yearling son after the male parent had died, while the other involved a female observed paired with a two-and-one-half-year-old son. In neither case did actual nesting occur.

TRUMPETER SWAN

Cygnus cygnus (Linnaeus) 1758
(*Olor buccinator* of A.O.U., 1957)

Other Vernacular Names: Wild Swan.

Range: Breeds in Iceland, Scandinavia, Russia, Central Asia, Siberia to Kamchatka, the Commander Islands, and Japan (*C. c. cygnus*); in North America, isolated breeding populations currently exist in southern Alaska, British Columbia, western Alberta, eastern Idaho, southwestern Montana, and Wyoming. Introduced and breeding at various national wildlife refuges in Oregon, Washington, Nevada, South Dakota, and elsewhere. Some movement occurs in winter, but most populations are not strongly migratory.

North American Subspecies:

C. c. buccinator Richardson: Trumpeter Swan. Considered by Delacour (1954) only subspecifically distinct from *C. c. cygnus,* the Whooper Swan. Recognized by the A.O.U. (1957) as a separate species.

Measurements (after Banko, 1960):

    Folded wing: Adult male 545-680 mm. (average 618.6), adult female 604-636 mm. (average 623.3).

    Culmen: Adult male 104-119.5 mm. (average 112.5), adult female 101.5-112-5 mm. (average 107).

Weights: Nelson and Martin (1953) indicated an average weight of seven males as 27.9 pounds (12,652 grams), with a maximum of 38 pounds; the average of four females was 22.5 pounds (10,249 grams), with a maximum of 24.5 pounds. Banko (1960) reported that the minimum weight of eight males at least two years old was 20 pounds, while the minimum weight of fourteen females of similar age was 16 pounds. Eight males at least one year old had a minimum weight of 18 pounds, and four females of this age had a minimum weight of 15 pounds. Scott *et al.* (1972) reported the average weight of ten males as 11.9 kilograms, with a range of 9.1 to 12.5; seven females averaged 9.4 kilograms, with a range of 7.3 to 10.2. Hansen *et al.* (1971) also presented weight data indicating that ten adult males averaged 11.97 kilograms (range 9.5 to 13.6), and eleven adult females averaged 9.63 kilograms (range 9.1 to 10.4).

IDENTIFICATION

In the Hand: As noted in the whistling swan account, the dorsal surface of the sternum should be examined to be absolutely certain of species identification; the presence of a dorsal protrusion near the sternum's anterior end is the best criterion of a trumpeter swan. Further, if the bird weighs more than 20 pounds (18 if less than two years old), measures at least 50 mm. from the tip of the bill to the anterior end of the nostril, and has entirely black lores or at most a pale yellow or gray mark on the lores, it is most probably a trumpeter swan.

In the Field: In the field, the absence of definite yellow coloration on the lores and a voice that is sonorous and hornlike, often sounding like *ko-hoh,* rather than higher pitched and sounding like a barking *wow, wow-wow,* are the most reliable field marks for trumpeter swans (Banko, 1960). Except within its known limited geographic range, an unknown swan should be identified as a trumpeter only with extreme care. Hansen *et al.* (1971) stated that the nearly straight culmen profile typical of this species, as compared with a concave culmen in the whistling swan, provides a useful clue for field identification.

AGE AND SEX CRITERIA

Sex Determination: Internal examination must be used for determining sex, since there are no known external sexual differences.

Age Determination: The grayish plumage of the juvenile is held during most of the first year of life, and the lores are likewise feathered for the first few months of life. At least in some cases, the birds may form pairs when twenty months old and begin nesting as early as thirty-three months after hatching (Monnie, 1966). Second-year birds thus may perhaps be distinguished from older ones on the basis of their incompletely developed sexual structures. Young birds have their forehead feathers extending forward to a point on the culmen, while in adults the feathers on the forehead have a more rounded anterior border. Although the birds are usually pure white at the age of twelve to thirteen months, a few dark feathers may persist somewhat longer (Hansen *et al.*, 1971).

DISTRIBUTION AND HABITAT

Breeding and Wintering Distribution and Habitat: Although the trumpeter swan was once strongly migratory, the remaining flocks are now relatively sedentary, with the Canadian or Alaskan population undergoing limited migrations to southeastern Alaska and the western parts of British Columbia (Banko, 1960). Mackay (1957) concluded that swans breeding in the Peace River district of Alberta migrate to the northern United States and mix with swans from the Red Rock Lakes Refuge during winter months, while the breeding areas of those wintering in western British Columbia were still unknown. Hansen *et al.* (1971) confirmed that these birds represent the Alaskan breeding population. Banko considers the presence of permanently open water with associated aquatic vegetation, a certain amount of level and open terrain, and a minimum of heavy timber near watercourses as important features of winter habitat. The breeding habitat found in Red Rock Lakes Refuge are characterized by Banko as large shallow marshes or shallow (to four feet deep) lakes, of high fertility, with a profusion of aquatic plants of submerged and emergent growth forms, and generally untimbered but well-vegetated shorelines. Within Yellowstone Park the breeding lakes are generally deeper, more heavily timbered, higher in elevation, and represent more marginal breeding habitat. During the years 1954 to 1957 an average of 13 nesting pairs occupied Upper Lake (2,880 acres), 51 occupied River Marsh (8,000 acres), and 15.5 occupied Swan Lake (400 acres), a total average population of about 80 pairs on 11,280 acres, or 4.5 pairs per square mile.

Breeding (hatched) and wintering (shaded) distributions of the trumpeter swan in North America.

Besides the Red Rock–Yellowstone–Grand Teton population, other major nesting populations occur in Canada and Alaska. Marshall (1968) reported that the nesting population at Grande Prairie, Alberta, numbers about 100 birds, and in Alaska the birds nest commonly along the southern coast from Yakutat to Cordova and in the Copper River drainage. Additional Alaskan breeding grounds are in the Kantashna, Tanana, Susitna, and Koyukak river valleys, the vast Yukon River delta, the Kenai Peninsula, and the adjacent coast west of the Cook Inlet. The total Alaska population has been estimated at 2,800 swans, which, added to the Canadian population and an estimated 800 birds in the contiguous United States, may represent 4,000 to 5,000 birds (Denson, 1970, Hansen *et al.*, 1971).

Transplants from Red Rock Refuge to other refuges have produced new breeding populations in the coterminous United States. Swans were introduced in Malheur Refuge in Oregon in 1939 and again in 1955, with the first successful breeding in 1958. That same year success occurred in Ruby Lake National Wildlife Refuge, Nevada, after releases in 1949. In 1960 birds were released in Lacreek National Wildlife Refuge in South Dakota, with the first successful nesting in 1963 (Monnie, 1966; Marshall, 1968). Later introductions were made at the Turnbull National Wildlife Refuge, Washington, and at the Hennepin County Park near Minneapolis, Minnesota. After nesting unsuccessfully in 1965 at Turnbull Refuge (*Audubon Field Notes,* 20:585), later attempts were more successful, and in 1970 a total of eight pairs nested, hatching sixteen young (*ibid.,* 24:700). Besides these refuge nestings, other localized nestings or nesting attempts have been reported, such as those near Brooks, Alberta, and north of Battleford, Saskatchewan (Ronald Mackay, pers. comm.), near Terrace, British Columbia (*Audubon Field Notes,* 20:592), in southern Montana (*ibid.,* 13:444; 24:702), and at Valentine National Wildlife Refuge in the Nebraska sandhills (as an offshoot of the Lacreek population). Marshall (1968) reported that forty-two public zoos then had at least one pair of swans, with reproduction occurring in at least four of these zoos. Because of these transplant successes and the recognition of the surprisingly large Alaskan population, the trumpeter swan was recently removed from the list of endangered species as determined by the United States Fish and Wildlife Service.

Although the trumpeter swan is not known to occur in the Aleutian Islands, the whooper swan (now generally regarded as being conspecific with the trumpeter) has been reported there several times (Byrd *et al.,* 1974). There is no proof of breeding by whooper swans on these islands, however.

GENERAL BIOLOGY

Age at Maturity: Monnie (1966) reported that some known-age trumpeter swans (two out of nine) initially formed pairs when twenty months old, and initial nesting occurred the following year. Banko (1960) summarized evidence that nesting may begin as early as the fourth year of life or as late as the sixth year, but it would seem probable that these examples are atypical, and that initial nesting in the third year of life would be characteristic. Some captive swans do not begin nesting until much older, especially if they are reared under wild conditions. A pair in the Philadelphia Zoo first nested successfully in 1965, although the female (wild caught and of unknown age) had been in the zoo since 1959. Like mute swans, two-year-old pairs may establish territories, even though actual nesting is not attempted (Monnie 1966).

Pair Bond Pattern: Like other swans, trumpeters are monogamous and have strong pair bonds. Banko (1960) reported a single case of a trio living together, although the sex of the extra bird was not learned. Griswold (1965) also reported a captive trio, in which a male was paired with two females. Banko assumed that a permanent pair bond was typical of this species, and Hansen *et al.* (1971) found one case of a female remating with another swan in the year following the loss of her mate.

Nest Location: Banko (1960) reported on 109 nests observed in four seasons in Red Rock Refuge. Over 70 percent of these were located on or very near a previous nest site, with four sites used all four years. Island sites were preferred over shorelines, and fairly straight shorelines tended to be avoided. Highest concentrations occurred where irregular shorelines combined with numerous sedge islands to produce maximum habitat interspersion, producing maximum nest densities of one nest per 70 acres. Hansen *et al.*, (1971) found that 32 of 35 Alaskan nests were in water from 12 to 36 inches deep, and 21 of 40 nests were in beaver impoundments between 6 and 14 acres in area. Stable water levels and tall, dense emergent plants apparently provide the necessary security, food supply, and nest support needed by these birds.

Clutch Size: Of 74 completed clutches observed by Banko, the average was 5.1 eggs, with a range of 3 to 9. Hansen *et al.* stated that 53 clutches from the Copper River area averaged 4.9 eggs, while 160 clutches from the Kenai region averaged 5.3 eggs. Yearly differences were noted, with small clutches typical of years having late springs and larger clutches typical of more favorable breeding seasons. The eggs are laid at two-day intervals.

Incubation Period: Estimates range from 32 to 37 days. Hansen *et al.* noted that six nests in the Copper River area had periods of 33 to 35 days. There is no good evidence that the male assists in incubation under natural conditions.

Fledging Period: Banko (1960) summarized data indicating that the fledging period is probably normally from 100 to 120 days, with known minimum and maximum periods of 91 and 122 days. A very similar range, from 90 to 105 days, has been reported for Alaskan birds (Hansen *et al.,* 1971).

Nest and Egg Losses: Banko (1960) noted that egg-hatching success varied from 51 to 66 percent during three different years. During six years at Grande Prairie, Alberta, the comparable percentages ranged from 55 to 92 percent (Mackay, 1964), and three years' data from the Kenai Peninsula, Alaska, indicate an average 82 percent hatching success (Hansen *et al.,* 1971). Infertility and embryonic deaths appear to be the major causes of hatching failure, with egg predation being insignificant. A few Alaskan nests have been found destroyed by bears and wolverines (*Gulo luscus*).

Juvenile Mortality: According to Banko (1960), considerable preflight mortality occurs, with possibly 50 percent or more of the young being lost during this period. Most of this mortality occurs early in life, from apparently varied but uncertain causes. Monnie (1966) reported cygnet losses to great horned owls, and probably also raccoons, while Banko suspected minks or skunks might play a predatory role at the Red Rock Refuge. Hansen *et al.* (1971) found a rather low (15 to 20 percent) mortality rate for the first eight weeks and practically none afterwards.

Adult Mortality: Banko (1960) suspected that trumpeter swans are virtually free of most natural enemies once they have fledged and thought that only coyotes or golden eagles might be of possible significance as predators, although firm evidence for this was lacking. Starvation during severe winters may be a significant mortality factor, at least in Canada, while disease and parasites appear to be unimportant.

GENERAL ECOLOGY

Food and Foraging: Although small cygnets rely on high-protein foods such as aquatic insects and crustaceans, they progressively shift to a vegetable diet as they grow older. Banko (1960) summarized data on trumpeter swan foods and reported use of foliage and tubers of pondweeds (*Potomogeton*), water milfoil (*Myriophyllum*) leaves and stems, pond lily (*Nuphar*) seeds and leaves, water buttercup (*Ranunculus*) leaves, and a variety of additional herbaceous foods such as *Chara, Anacharis, Lemna, Scirpus, Sparganium, Carex, Sagittaria,* and other materials. When feeding in shallow waters, trumpeters use their strong legs and large feet to excavate the tubers and rhizomes of various aquatic plants, often forming large holes on the shallow bottoms of the Red Rock Lakes marsh. They also swim with the neck and head under water, pulling rooted materials off the bottom of the ponds. They are also readily able to remove duckweed (*Lemna*) or other small foods from the water surface by straining it through the bill in the manner of dabbling ducks and may feed heavily on duckweed when it is available. Vos (1964) described as "puddling" a characteristic rapid paddling of feet during swimming, apparently serving to stir food up from the pond bottom. This he observed mostly in an adult female, occasionally in its mate, and several times in a cygnet. Female swans of various species frequently perform this behavior when leading broods, apparently thus improving the foraging efficiency of the short-necked and weak-legged youngsters.

Sociality, Densities, Territoriality: Only during the winter season are trumpeter swans appreciably social, and then the limited areas of open water force a degree of sociality upon them. Banko (1960) noted that it is seldom that more than six or eight swans fly together in local flights unless they are simultaneously flushed. He included a photo of eighty birds occupying a small spring in mid-January, but mentioned that as early as February pairs and small flocks begin to spread out over the snowfields that overlie their breeding habitat. As noted earlier, the average refuge density between 1954 and 1957 was 4.5 pairs per square mile (142 acres per pair) on three major nesting habitats, and in the most favorable nesting habitats about 70 acres per nesting pair was recorded during one year. The actual size of the defended area was not determined, but Banko indicated that birds occupying open shoreline usually defended more area than did those nesting on islands, although shoreline nesters sometimes defended only a small bay area around the nesting site. Hansen *et al.* (1971) suggested that spatial isolation, rather than food supply or size of area, was important in determining territorial boundaries.

Interspecific Relationships: Trumpeter swans have no significant contact with whistling or mute swans on their breeding or wintering areas, and Banko (1960) reports that they are highly tolerant of other bird and large mammal species. Even among pairs on their breeding territory, the presence of geese, pelicans, cranes, or herons is usually not sufficient to cause aggression, although swans leading young are less tolerant than others. However, one case was found of a nesting swan's killing a muskrat that approached a brood. Vos (1964) also noticed several threats by nesting birds.

General Activity Patterns: Vos (1964) reported on daily activity patterns of three captive swans, which may not be wholly typical of wild birds. He noted that bathing, preening, sleeping, loafing, swimming, and foraging were performed several times daily and usually in unison by the pair. Preening bouts typically follow bathing and last for varying periods up to 85 minutes. Preening was followed by resting or sleeping, and favored resting spots were also used for preening and sleeping. Some sleeping periods lasted as long as 85 minutes, and the male usually had longer sleeping bouts than did the female. In total, the adult pair slept about the same amount of time during the egg-laying period, while later in the summer a month-old cygnet slept more than the total of both parents. In general, preening most commonly occurred early in the morning, early in the afternoon, and during the evening. Feeding occurred after the morning and evening preening periods, reaching a maximum in early afternoon, with a secondary evening peak.

Daily Movements: There are few good data on daily movements, but Monnie (1966) reported that local movements of up to about a hundred miles were noted at Lacreek Refuge over a prolonged period. Banko (1960) reported that flights during local movements were usually performed at lower altitudes than were longer flights.

SOCIAL AND SEXUAL BEHAVIOR

Flocking Behavior: This has been discussed earlier under sociality. Mackay (1957) mentioned that cygnets of a family evidently remain together for at least the first year after hatching, since three broodmates that were banded in Alberta in 1955 were all shot in Nebraska the following fall.

Pair-forming Behavior: Monnie (1966) reported that courtship among 20-month-old swans began in mid-January and continued until mid-March during which time among nine birds two apparent pairs were formed, plus a trio involving two males and a female, while two females remained unpaired. Monnie did not specifically indicate whether this courtship consisted of actual copulatory behavior or of mutual triumph ceremonies. Banko (1960) described the triumph ceremonies of this species, which are typically performed following the expulsion of a territorial intruder. However, he noted that mutual display also regularly occurs in the wintering areas among birds in flocks, although he did not clearly associate this behavior with pair formation. Triumph ceremonies involving more than two birds most probably represent participation by the past season's offspring, if my observations at the Wildfowl Trust are also characteristic of wild birds.

Copulatory Behavior: Vos (1964) observed eleven copulations in captive trumpeter swans, all of which occurred in shallow water and ten of which were seen between April 16 and 26, with the first egg being laid April 21. One copulation was also seen on July 12, or more than a month after hatching occurred. Typically, both sexes rise together in the water, variably extending the wings (Johnsgard, 1965) but with the male usually fully extending his, and usually, but not always, with both calling in unison. Finally, the wings are flapped once or twice, followed by bathing and then preening.

Nesting Behavior: Most preliminary nest-building is by the female, but the male helps gather nesting material and to a limited extent may assist in nest construction. Females not only spend more time nest-building, but also are more effective in gathering materials (Vos, 1964). Vos did not observe the male actually incubating, but saw it sitting on the nest once during the egg-laying period. However, Griswold (1965) did report an instance of apparent incubation assistance by the male, inasmuch as both birds were once seen on the nest, with four eggs under one and three under the other. This is apparently the only report of possible incubation by the male. Banko (1960) reported one probable instance of renesting following nest destruction.

Brooding Behavior: Following an incubation period of 32 to 33 days (Mackay, 1964) or 33 to 37 days, (Banko, 1960), the cygnets hatch, normally all at about the same time. However, Griswold reported a staggered hatching period in one pair. He noted that the first two young to hatch were seen entering the water initially when about 48 hours old, while the third left the nest when about 24 hours old. Griswold's observations were complicated by the fact that two females were present, and both may have contributed to the clutch. Vos (1964) noted that for the first few weeks a young bird was closely guarded, with the two parents placing themselves on either side of the cygnet. However, the female was generally more closely associated with it. Normally when swimming the female led the cygnet, with the male following behind. In contrast to the mute swan, young trumpeter swans have never been seen riding on a parent's back (Johnsgard and Kear, 1968). Griswold reported that by the age of about three months a female attained a weight of 14.5 pounds, and four males weighed from 13.5 to 16 pounds, collectively averaging about 15 pounds. Banko mentioned a 19-pound cygnet of preflight age, and Hansen *et al.* (1971) stated that such a weight may be attained in only eight to ten weeks.

Postbreeding Behavior: There is no evident molt migration in trumpeter swans. In Alaska, nonbreeding birds gather in flocks on large, open lakes and begin their wing molt almost simultaneously, with nearly all of them beginning and terminating their flightless period within ten days of one another. A less regular molting pattern occurs in breeding birds. Males usually begin their wing molt early in the incubation period, or sometimes as late as after the time of hatching. Females begin molting their flight feathers from 7 to 21 days after the clutch has hatched. Since the flightless period is about 30 days long, both members of a pair are rarely flightless simultaneously, and both sexes regain their flying abilities prior to the fledging of the young. In Alaska, some young may still be unable to fly at the time of freeze-up, and the birds seem to postpone their fall migration as long as possible, with family groups being the last to leave the breeding grounds (Hansen *et al.,* 1971).

WHISTLING SWAN

Cygnus columbianus (Ord) 1815
(*Olor columbianus* of A.O.U., 1957)

Other Vernacular Names: Wild Swan, Whistler.

Range: Breeds in arctic parts of Russia and Siberia (*C. c. bewickii*), eastern
   Siberia (*C. c. jankowskii*), and in arctic North America from western
   Alaska across the northern parts of the Northwest Territories to Southampton Island, Nottingham Island, and the Belcher Islands. The North
   American population winters mostly along the Atlantic and Pacific coasts,
   but passes through the interior during migrations, and varying numbers
   overwinter in northern Utah.

North American Subspecies:

   C. c. columbianus (Ord.): Whistling Swan. Considered by Delacour
      (1954) only subspecifically distinct from *C. c. bewickii,* the Bewick
      swan. Recognized by the A.O.U. (1957) as a separate species.

Measurements (after Banko, 1960):

   Folded wing: Adult male 501-569 mm. (average 538), adult female 505-
      561 mm. (average 531.6).

   Culmen: Adult male 97-107 mm. (average 102.6), adult female 92.5-106
      mm. (average 99.9).

Weights: Nelson and Martin (1953) indicated an average weight of thirty-five
   males as 15.8 pounds (7,165 grams), with a maximum of 18.6 pounds; forty-
   two females averaged 13.6 pounds (6,167 grams), with a maximum of
   18.3 pounds. Banko (1960) reported that seven males at least two years
   old had a maximum weight of 19.5 pounds, and twenty-one females of the

same age class had a maximum weight of nineteen pounds. Sherwood (1960) mentioned a male that weighed 19⅝ pounds. Scott *et al.* (1972) reported the average weight of twenty-nine males as 7.5 kilograms (range 7.4 to 8.8) and thirty-nine females averaged 6.6 kilograms (range 5.6 to 8.6).

IDENTIFICATION

In the Hand: Whistling swans can only be confused with trumpeter swans when being handled; the absence of a fleshy knob at the base of the bill readily separates them from mute swans. To be certain of identification, the upper surface of the sternum must be examined to see if a protrusion near its anterior end is present, which would indicate a trumpeter swan. If this point cannot be checked, the bird is probably a whistling swan if it weighs under 20 pounds, measures less than 50 mm. from the tip of the bill to the anterior end of the nostril, and has bright yellow or orange yellow spots on the lores.

In the Field: Unless both trumpeter and whistling swans are seen together, a size criterion is of little value in the field. Rather, the differences in their voices are perhaps the best field mark, in association with the presence or absence of yellow coloration on the lores. If the lores are completely black, the bird may be of either species, but if a prominent yellow to orange yellow mark is present, the bird is a whistling swan. Further, if the voice is sonorous and hornlike, often sounding like *ko-hoh,* it is a trumpeter, whereas the voice of the whistling swan is more like a high-pitched barking sound, *wow, wow-wow* (Banko, 1960).

AGE AND SEX CRITERIA

Sex Determination: No external differences in the sexes exist that would allow for sex determination without internal examination.

Age Determination: Birds possessing feathered lores and/or some grayish feathers persisting from the juvenal plumage are in their first year of life. Apparently the rate of sternal penetration of the trachea is fairly constant for the first three years, and by the second winter the tracheal loop starts to rotate and begin its expansion into the carina of the sternum (Tate, 1966). Together with the length of the tracheal perimeter within the sternum, the changes in the shape of the nasal bones are good indicators of age, according to Tate. First-year birds have a well-defined "V" groove formed by the nasals and lachrymals, which gradually alters by medial fusion with age, so that the V is nearly obliterated in old birds. In young birds the feathers of the forehead extend forward to a point in the midline, while in older birds this point gradually recedes until a smooth and rounded brow is formed.

DISTRIBUTION AND HABITAT

Breeding Distribution and Habitat: In North America the whistling swan has a breeding range well to the north of the trumpeter swan's, in arctic tundra. Heaviest nesting concentrations in Canada are in the coastal strip from the west side of the Mackenzie Delta to the east side of the Anderson Delta, with sparser populations inland, especially south of the tree line (Banko and Mackay, 1964). This Northwest Territories population evidently winters on the Atlantic coast (Sladen and Cochran, 1969). In central and eastern Canada swans are usually absent from the rocky Precambrian shield, but occur wherever typical tundra occurs, north to Banks Island and south to about the Thelon River. In Alaska, major breeding areas are the north side of the Alaska Peninsula and adjoining Bristol Bay, the Yukon-Kuskokwim Delta, and, to a much lesser extent, the Kotzebue Sound area (Gabrielson and Lincoln, 1959).

Wintering Distribution and Habitat: Whistling swans winter in two widely separated areas. Approximately half the continental population winters in the Atlantic Flyway, primarily on Chesapeake Bay and Currituck Sound. The rest of the population winters in the Pacific Flyway, chiefly in the Central Valley of California. Some usually also overwinter in the Great Salt Lake valley of Utah, the numbers there being influenced by the severity of the winters (Sherwood, 1960). Normally their winter habitat includes sufficient aquatic plant life to provide adequate food, but during unusually severe winter conditions field-feeding in cornfields has been observed (Nagel, 1965).

Preferred wintering habitat in the Chesapeake Bay area consists of open and extensive areas of brackish water no more than 5 feet deep (Stewart, 1962). January counts in that region indicated the following percentage usage of available habitats: brackish estuarine bays, 76 percent; salt estuarine bays, 9 percent; fresh estuarine bays, 8 percent; slightly brackish estuarine bays, 6 percent; and other habitats, 1 percent. Freshwater areas are used primarily by early fall arrivals.

GENERAL BIOLOGY

Age at Maturity: Very little reliable information is available on the age of sexual maturity in whistling swans. They have been bred only rarely in captivity; Delacour (1954) reported a breeding by a five-year-old female with an

Breeding (hatched) and wintering (shaded) distributions of the whistling swan in North America.

older male, and Robert Elgas (pers. comm.) successfully bred a pair of hand-reared whistling swans when they were six years old. Two pairs of swans hatched from wild-taken eggs nested initially when they were four years old, according to William Carrick (pers. comm.). Scott (1972) believed that the closely related Bewick swans may normally breed initially at four years.

Pair Bond Pattern: Like the other swans, the pair bonds of this species appear to be strong and potentially permanent. Peter Scott (1972) reported that there had been no cases of "divorce" among hundreds of individually recognizable Bewick swans in seven years of observation, and up to three years have been required for bereaved swans to take a new mate. Dafila Scott (1967) reported that some swans have left in the spring with one mate and returned the next fall with a different one, suggesting that mate replacement sometimes occurs during a single breeding season. Some tentative pairing may occur during the second winter, but in six of seven cases she observed, these pairings had broken up by the following winter. Peter Scott (1972) noted, however, that some swans may remain with their parents for their second or even third winter of life.

Nest Location: Nests of whistling swans are typically well scattered over the tundra. Banko and Mackay (1964) reported that nest sites vary in location from the edge of water to the top of low hills a half mile from water, with small islands in tundra ponds being preferred locations.

Clutch Size: According to Banko and Mackay (1964), 4 eggs constitute the normal clutch, with as many as 7 being found at times. Lensick (1968, and in Scott *et al.,* 1971) reported that 5 was the normal clutch size in good springs, with only 3 or 4 eggs usually present in cold, wet springs. The average clutch size of 297 clutches was 4.3, with a mode of 5 and a range of 1 to 7.

Incubation Period: Banko and Mackay (1964) estimated the whistling swan's average incubation to be about 32 days. A slightly shorter incubation period (29 to 30 days) has been estimated for the Bewick swan (Dementiev and Gladkov, 1967). Robert Elgas (pers. comm.) noted a 30-day incubation period for Alaskan whistling swan eggs incubated under geese.

Fledging Period: Not definitely established for the whistling swan. Banko and Mackay reported that hatching occurs in late June or early July, while fledging occurs about the middle of September, suggesting an approximate 75- to 80-day fledging period. A remarkably short fledging period (40-45 days) has been suggested for the slightly smaller Bewick swan (Dementiev and Gladkov, 1967), but this hardly seems possible in view of the much longer periods reported for the other admittedly more temperate-adapted swans.

Nest, Egg, and Cygnet Losses: Virtually no quantitative information is available on hatching success, but Banko and Mackay (1964) estimated that an average of only two or three cygnets per hatched clutch survived until fledging in autumn. By counting the percentage of the distinctively plumaged juveniles during fall and winter, estimates of productivity and mortality can be attained. Chamberlain (1967) noted that the percentage of young birds in the 1964–1965 winter season on Chesapeake Bay ranged from 9.46 to 13.9 percent, while in 1965–1966 it ranged from 8.22 to 12.1 percent, with the percentage of young highest during January counts because of the relatively later arrival of family groups than of nonbreeders. Compared to average brood sizes ranging from 2.55 to 2.63 young per pair in Alaska and the Northwest Territories, winter brood counts ranged from 2.15 to 2.63, suggesting a cygnet mortality of 18.25 to 25.49 percent. During the eight-year period between 1964 and 1971, in the Atlantic coast wintering population, the percentage of juveniles ranged from 4.8 to 14.6 percent (average 11.1) and the average number of cygnets per family varied from 1.54 to 2.24 (average 1.93) birds (J. J. Lynch, unpublished progress reports of productivity and mortality among geese, swans, and brant).

Adult Mortality: Information on adult mortality rates in whistling swans is lacking, since few are banded and in general they have not been legal game. Some information on the Bewick swan relative to annual survival can be obtained from the returns of individually recognized birds to the Wildfowl Trust in later years. Evans (1970) provides a listing of such sightings for a seven-year period for birds which were adults or second-year birds when first sighted and recognized individually. Of a total of 792 birds in this category, 287 were seen the subsequent winter season, indicating a minimum survival rate of 36.2 percent. However, 27.5 percent returned a third season, 26.6 a fourth, 34.3 a fifth, 28.6 a sixth, and 33 percent (6 of 18) returned seven years after initially being sighted. This rather astonishing number of birds at least nine years old indicates that the survival rate of swans must be relatively high, and the sightings of birds returning in the third and subsequent seasons suggest an annual survival rate of nearly 87 percent.

GENERAL ECOLOGY

Food and Foraging: Like the other swans, the whistling swan feeds predominantly on vegetable materials from aquatic plants. Martin *et al.* (1951) list grasses and sago pondweed (*Potamogeton pectinatus*) as major food in both the eastern and western populations, and additionally list wild celery (*Vallisneria*), lady's thumb (*Polygonum persicaria*), horsetail (*Equisetum*), and bur reed (*Sparganium*) as important foods in one region or the other. Sherwood (1960) reported that tubers and seeds of sago pondweed were the exclusive food of twelve specimens obtained in the Great Salt Lake valley, although other aquatic foods were available. Stewart and Manning (1958) and Stewart (1962) reported on the winter foods of swans in Chesapeake Bay and found that birds foraging in the preferred brackish estuarine bay habitat relied largely on wigeon grass (*Ruppia*) and to a lesser extent on sago pond-weeds, with bivalve mollusks (*Mya* and *Macoma*) also being taken in considerable amounts. Four birds collected in fresh water estuaries had been feeding almost exclusively on wild celery, and four from estuarine marsh ponds had been eating wigeon grass, three-square (*Scirpus*), and grasses.

Sociality, Densities, Territoriality: During the nonbreeding season whistling swans are highly social, with flock sizes often numbering in the hundreds. Thompson and Lyons (1962) made observations on a flock of 1,022 swans during spring migration in Wisconsin and counted the birds in groups making local movements to and from foraging areas, mostly on fallow fields nearby. Nearly 35 percent of the flock counts were of paired birds, with units of 3, 4, or 5 birds also fairly common. This would suggest that yearling birds often remain with their parents during spring migration, although no attempt was made to distinguish young birds from adults. Apart from a small percentage of single birds, the remaining flock sizes gradually diminished in frequency up to a unit size of 13 birds. In the Bewick swans wintering at the Wildfowl Trust, up to three seasons' young have been observed consorting with their parents, making flock units of 13 to 15 birds. Thus, it is apparent that even large flocks of swans have a well-developed substructure that is probably related to family bonding.

The low densities of swans on the breeding grounds is probably a reflection of territorial tendencies. Lensick (1968) reported nesting densities of from 130 to 320 hectares per pair (0.8 to 2.0 pairs per square mile) at the Clarence Rhode National Wildlife Range in Alaska. Smith and Sutton (in United States Fish and Wildlife Service, Special Scientific Report: Wildlife, No. 25) reported on swan densities based on aerial surveys in the Northwest Territories. In the wooded delta of the Mackenzie River they reported densities indicating a six-year (1948–1953) average of 1.5 swans per square mile. In the area between the Mackenzie and Anderson rivers, the comparable averages were: coastal tundra, 1.7; upland tundra, 1.3; and transition zone (to coniferous forest), 0.3 swans per square mile. In 1950 the area from the Armak River to Kent Peninsula was also surveyed and found to have a swan density of 0.16, while southwestern and southeastern Victoria Island had a density of 0.007. It would seem that a density of about one pair per square mile might be expected in favorable lowland tundra habitats.

Interspecific Relationships: Whistling swans probably have little normal contact with either trumpeter swans or mute swans in the wintering areas and none in their breeding areas. Edwards (1966) noted the presence of wintering whistling swans in the flock of resident mute swans at Grand Traverse Bay, Michigan. Martin *et al.* (1951) and others have suggested that whistling swans may despoil the supply of duck foods in some areas, and certainly the preferred foods such as sago pondweed and wigeon grass are also used by many ducks. Wigeons and canvasbacks are species with habitat preferences and foods similar to those of whistling swans in the Chesapeake Bay region (Stewart, 1962). Sherwood (1960) mentions observing a considerable number of species of geese and swans feeding among swans without any visible intolerance on the swans' part. He passed on the view that the swans may actually increase the forage for the ducks, both by pulling up more food than they actually consume and by possibly creating new sago beds by dissemination of seeds and tubers as well as by "cultivation" of the marsh bottom.

General Activity Patterns and Movements: Since swans typically feed on or closely adjacent to their nesting areas, they normally are not forced to move about extensively in search of food. Thompson and Lyons (1964) noted that pronounced diurnal foraging flights were not characteristic of the spring flock of whistling swans they studied and noted that average midday counts were only about 200 birds fewer than average morning or evening counts (749 and 771, respectively). Sladen and Cochran (1969) observed that swans rarely reached an altitude of 1,000 feet during local movements. At the Wildfowl Trust in England, the Bewick swans typically roost on the mud flats of the nearby Severn River and fly in twice daily to the Trust grounds to eat the grain put out for them. Or, they may stay at the Trust all day, returning to the river only after the late afternoon feeding period.

SOCIAL AND SEXUAL BEHAVIOR

Flocking Behavior: As noted above, whistling swans are to be found in flocks consisting of aggregated pairs and family groups at all times except during the nesting season. Such groups often merge in "staging areas" at various points along their migration routes; these areas provide a combination of abundant food and relative safety from large predators. They often consist of temporarily flooded fields or permanent water areas no more than about five feet deep. Bent (1925) noted that on the East Coast the swans often associate with Canada geese, on which they apparently rely for warning of possible danger. Fall flocks of from 10,000 to 25,000 swans have been reported in Alberta and Utah (Banko and Mackay, 1964).

Pair-forming Behavior: Very little is known of the pair-forming behavior of whistling swans, but it is probably comparable to that of the better-studied Bewick swan. Peter Scott (1966) noted that two-year-old birds spent quite a lot of time in courtship display during the winter months. However, Dafila Scott (1967) mentioned that many of the pair bonds formed during the second winter are only temporary and usually are broken by the following winter. As with the other swans, pair formation is a gradual and inconspicuous process, with a major feature being the tendency of males to defend mates or potential mates and, after expelling intruders, to return to the female, where they join in a mutual triumph ceremony (Johnsgard, 1965). Differences in the head shape and bill patterning are apparently important bases for individual recognition among the arctic-breeding swans, and it is probable that individual differences in vocalizations may also play a role in mate recognition.

Copulatory Behavior: Like the trumpeter swan, copulation in whistling and Bewick swans is preceded by mutual head-dipping movements that closely resemble those of bathing birds. Unlike the mute swan, preening movements do not play a role in precopulatory behavior. As treading is terminated, the male releases his grip on the female's nape as both birds extend their necks strongly upward and utter loud notes, usually simultaneously extending and shaking their wings (Johnsgard, 1965).

Nesting and Brooding Behavior: The nests of whistling swans are usually mounds of moss, grasses, or sedges and are from one to two feet high (Banko and Mackay, 1964). In the Bewick swan it is typical that the pair uses an old nest site after some refurbishing, with the female lining the nest with down or sometimes feathers (Dementiev and Gladkov, 1967) The female usually assumes all the incubation duties, as with other white swans, but the male remains close by and actively guards the nest. Egg-laying begins shortly after arrival at the tundra breeding grounds in late May or early June, and hatching occurs in late June or early July (Banko and Mackay, 1964). In southeastern Victoria Island, at the northern edge of the species' range, the nests are constructed in as little as five days or less, and in one case a nest was built and three eggs were deposited in no more than eight days (Parmelee *et al.,* 1967). Hatching there begins in early July, and young are probably still about into September, although the fledging period is still not definitely known. No doubt a critical relationship exists between the time of fledging and the first freezing weather, which may greatly influence breeding success during some years.

Postbreeding Behavior: The postnuptial molt of the adults occurs while the young are still flightless, the pen becoming flightless about two weeks after the young hatch, while the cob does so about the time the female regains her flight (Banko and Mackay, 1964). Assuming each may be flightless for about a month, the adults should both have regained their powers of flight by the time the young are about eighty days old, or nearly fledged themselves. At that time, or mid-September, a fairly leisurely fall migration southward begins through the interior of Canada along the Mackenzie River valley. By early October, concentrations of up to 25,000 birds occur on Lake Clair and Richardson Lake in northeastern Alberta, after which the population splits into two groups, according to whether the birds will winter in the western or Atlantic coastal regions (Banko and Mackay, 1964).

WHITE-FRONTED GOOSE

Anser albifrons (Scopoli) 1769

Other Vernacular Names: Specklebelly Goose, Tule Goose.

Range: Circumpolar; breeding from western and northern Alaska eastward across northern Canada to Keewatin, the western coast of Greenland, and in arctic Eurasia excepting Scandinavia, Iceland, and Spitzbergen.

North American Subspecies (after Delacour, 1954):

A. a. frontalis Baird: Pacific White-fronted Goose. In North America, breeds in arctic Alaska from the Bering Sea coast east to northeastern Keewatin and winters in the western and southern United States and adjacent Mexico.

A. a. gambeli Hartlaub: Gambel White-fronted Goose. Breeding grounds uncertain, probably in the MacKenzie Basin (Elgas, 1970), with most wintering occurring on the Gulf coast. Birds wintering in central California ("Tule" white-fronted geese) have recently been proposed as a new subspecies, *elgasi* (Delacour and Ripley, 1975).

A. a. flavirostris Dalgety and Scott: Greenland White-fronted Goose. Breeds on the west coast of Greenland, wintering mainly in Ireland, but occasionally reaching the eastern United States.

Measurements:

A. a. frontalis: Folded wing: adult males 380-441, adult females 362-419 mm. Culmen: adult males 44-56.5, adult female 42-54 mm. (Elgas, 1970).

A. a. gambeli: Folded wing: adult males 441-480, females 410-441 mm. Culmen: adult males 55-62, adult females 49-59 mm. (Elgas, 1970).

A. a. flavirostris: Folded wing: males 410-455, females 392-420 mm. Culmen: males 45-57 mm. (Delacour, 1954).

Weights:

Pacific White-fronted Goose: Nelson and Martin (1953) reported that twenty-two males averaged 5.3 pounds (2,404 grams), with a maximum of 7.3 pounds; eighteen females averaged 4.9 pounds (2,222 grams), with a maximum of 6.3 pounds.

Tule White-fronted Goose: Nelson and Martin (1953) reported that twenty-one males averaged 6.6 pounds (2,993 grams), with a maximum of 7.5 pounds; thirteen females averaged 5.6 pounds (2,539 grams), with a maximum of 6.5 pounds. Swarth and Bryant (1917) reported somewhat higher weights, with six males averaging 7.25 pounds (3,288 grams) and four females averaging 6.31 pounds (2,861 grams).

IDENTIFICATION

In the Hand: This brownish goose can be recognized in the hand by its yellowish to reddish bill, which lacks a black "grinning patch," and its yellow to orange feet. The distinctive white forehead and the black blotching on the undersides are completely lacking in immature birds, which are almost uniformly brown in color. Domestic grey-lag geese (*Anser anser*) might perhaps be confused with white-fronted geese, but these usually have pinkish feet and legs and are considerably larger throughout.

In the Field: Both on land or water and in the air, white-fronts are notable for their rather uniformly brownish coloration, which is relieved by their white hindquarters and, at close range, by white foreheads on the adults. Sometimes their orange legs may be seen in flight, but usually at least a few of the birds in a flock will show black spotting underneath. They are generally extremely wary birds, and often utter a cackling *lee-leek* or *lee-lee-leek!*, resembling taunting laughter, while in flight.

AGE AND SEX CRITERIA

Sex Determination: No plumage characters are available for external sex determination.

Age Determination: Birds in their first year of life have little or no abdominal spotting and have yellowish feet and legs. Second-year birds are apparently adult in plumage and in the color of the bill and legs, although wild birds evidently do not breed before their third year (Boyd, 1962).

DISTRIBUTION AND HABITAT

Breeding Distribution and Habitat: In Alaska the white-fronted goose breeds primarily in the northern portion and nests mainly near the coast. At Barrow and to the east it is a common coastal breeder, extending in marshy areas from one to twenty miles inland, with apparent centers of abundance at Smith Bay and the Colville Delta. White-fronts are also common nesters in the Kotzebue Sound region along the Noatak and Kobuk rivers, and in the Yukon-Kuskokwim region. The southern limit of breeding appears to be the base of the Alaska Peninsula (Gabrielson and Lincoln, 1959). In Canada the species breeds from the Alaska boundary eastward to the Perry River, north at least as far as Victoria and King William islands, and south to the Hanbury and Thelon rivers. The preferred breeding habitats are the muddy borders of small tundra lakes and the floodplains and mouths of arctic streams, where there are broad flats that often have grass-covered hummocks (Snyder, 1957). Dzubin *et al.* (1964) characterize the preferred nesting habitat as middle to low arctic vegetation, in open tundra, the borders of shallow marshes and lakes, river banks and islands, deltas, dry knolls, and hillocks near rivers and ponds. Two major types of topography are used for breeding: coastal tundra with little surface relief, and gently rolling upland tundra 50 to 700 feet above sea level with lakes and ponds in the depressions. Willow- and shrub-fringed streams and ponds are used by white-fronted geese to a greater extent than by other geese. Elgas (1970) found that birds he regarded as tule white-fronted geese in the Old Crow area of the Yukon inhabited unusually heavy brush and woody vegetation, rather than coastal tundra.

Wintering Distribution and Habitat: In the United States, most wintering habitat occurs in the Central Valley of California and on the Gulf coast of Louisiana and Texas. In Mexico considerable numbers of white-fronted geese occur in northern and central areas, with a few as far south as the coasts of Tabasco and Chiapas (Leopold, 1959). There the birds prefer interior or coastal marshes or wet meadows and usually fly out to stubble to feed on fallen grain or green plant material. Alkaline flats and sandbars are not used as much as by snow geese. In California, plains, fields, and swampy lowlands are used for roosting, while foraging is done in open fields. However, the tule white-fronted goose reportedly inhabits marshes overgrown with tules (*Scirpus*), cattails (*Typha*), or willow (*Salix*), and rarely forages in grain-

Breeding (hatched) and wintering (shaded) distributions of the white-fronted goose in North America.

fields. In these marshes the birds apparently forage primarily on the tubers and rhizomes of *Scirpus,* which they pull up from the bottom in water as much as one and one-half feet deep (Longhurst, 1955).

GENERAL BIOLOGY

Age at Maturity: Dzubin *et al.* (1964) reported that most white-fronted geese do not mature until their second or even third summer. Boyd (1954, 1962) believed that they do not breed until their third year. Two aviculturalists who responded to a survey by Ferguson (1966) reported breeding by captive birds in their third year.

Pair Bond Pattern: Pair bonds are apparently permanent in these as in other true geese, but specific data appear to be lacking. Inasmuch as fall and winter flocks are obviously composed in part of family groups (Boyd, 1953; Miller and Dzubin, 1965), it seems clear that pair bonds are persistent in this species.

Nest Location: Nests are usually situated on flats or on a slight hummock, often bordering a lake or stream (Snyder, 1957). Dzubin *et al.* (1964) noted that nests are seldom far from water. Typically the nest is located on a slight incline or at the top of a hillock, so that visibility of the surrounding area is not restricted. Conover (1926) noted that all three nests he found were on small hills.

Clutch Size: Relatively little information on average clutch sizes is available. Kessel *et al.* (1964) reported an average clutch of 4.3 eggs for twelve nests in the Hooper Bay area, with a range of 3 to 6 eggs. Calvin Lensink (pers. comm.) found that 301 clutches from the Yukon-Kuskokwim Delta averaged 4.86 eggs, with yearly maximal and minimal averages of 5.32 and 3.72, respectively.

Incubation Period: The incubation length is somewhat uncertain, with estimates ranging from 22 to 28 days. Most estimates for the European race *A. a. albifrons* are for 27 or 28 days, but that of the Greenland white-fronted goose has been estimated at only 22-23 days (Fencker, 1950). This is close to the 21 to 22-day period determined by Brandt (1943) for a single nest in Alaska. According to him, seven eggs were deposited in a nest during a 10-day period. Conover (1926) also mentioned what probably was the same nest, with the clutch completed on June 1 and hatching completed on June 24.

Fledging Period: Dzubin *et al.* (1964) estimated a 6- to 7-week fledging period, while a more questionable 5-week period had been estimated for the Greenland white-fronted goose (Salomonsen, 1950).

Nest and Egg Losses: Few specific data appear to be available on nesting success for North American white-fronted geese. Dzubin *et al.* (1964) indicated that the hatching rate is usually above 80 percent in good breeding years. Calvin Lensink (pers. comm.) found that Class I broods during the late 1960s and early 1970s in the Kuskokwim delta area collectively averaged 3.94 goslings for 79 broods, suggesting that hatching success may be fairly high. Hansen (1961) noted a nesting success of 89 percent (eight of nine nests) in one year.

Juvenile Mortality: Most data on juvenile mortality are from the Greenland and European populations of white-fronted geese. Boyd (1958) estimated a first-year annual mortality of 46 percent after banding and about 43 percent for second-year birds, compared to an adult mortality rate of 34 percent. Among European white-fronted geese wintering in England, Boyd (1959) noted that between 1947 and 1959 the mean brood size ranged from 2.7 to 3.6 and the proportion of young birds in the population varied from 14 to 46 percent. He believed that the marked differences in the yearly proportions of young birds must have resulted from variations in the percentage of adults which successfully bred rather than annual brood-size differences. Miller *et al.* (1968) estimated a first-year mortality rate of 44.1 percent for Saskatchewan-banded geese and estimated that juveniles were 2.4 times more vulnerable to mortality than were adults. The percentage of immature in migrating populations ranged from 11 to 38 percent and averaged 23 percent between 1960 and 1966.

Adult Mortality: Miller *et al.* (1968) estimated an average annual adult mortality rate of 31.3 percent for Saskatchewan-banded geese. This compared fairly closely to Boyd's (1958) estimates of 34 percent for adult Greenland white-fronted geese and 28 percent for adult European white-fronts.

GENERAL ECOLOGY

Food and Foraging: Records of foods taken during winter are rather limited, and Martin *et al.* (1951) list a variety of cultivated grain plants (wheat, rice, barley) as important foods. Native plants that are taken include the vegetative parts of various grasses such as panic grass (*Panicum*), saw grass (*Cladium*), wild millet (*Echinochloa*), and the rootstocks of cattail (*Typha*), as well as sedges and rootstocks of bulrushes (*Scirpus*). Hanson *et al.* (1956) noted that of six adults collected on their breeding grounds at Perry River, four had eaten horsetail (*Equisetum*) stems and branches, two had eaten blades or stems of cotton grass (*Eriophorum*), and one had consumed horsetail rootstalks. Barry (1967) found that twelve adult birds collected between June and August on the Anderson River delta had been eating sedges and horsetail.

Sociality, Densities, Territoriality: White-fronted geese are relatively nongregarious and rarely occur in large flocks except perhaps during fall migration. Shortly after arriving at their wintering grounds they spread out and become inconspicuous (Miller *et al.*, 1968). Breeding densities are generally very low; the Pacific Flyway population of some 200,000 geese nest over an area of about 40,000 square miles in western Alaska, while the Central Flyway population of some 70,000 birds nest over 84,000 square miles of northern and eastern Alaska and 35,000 square miles of arctic Canada (Dzubin *et al.*, 1964). Although not colonial nesters, white-fronted geese do at times gather for nesting in favored locations, and Dzubin *et al.* reported that breeding densities in the best habitats of the Yukon-Kuskokwim delta area average 6 to 7 birds per square mile. In large areas of the Canadian arctic the estimated density was only 1 bird per 3 to 16 square miles. Averages for aerial surveys made during a six-year period indicate that in the Mackenzie Delta breeding populations averaged 0.4 geese per square mile, while in the upland and coastal tundra areas between the Mackenzie and Anderson rivers the average densities for the period were 1.4 and 1.2 birds per square mile. This illustrates well the tendency of white-fronted geese to favor upland nesting habitats. Bailey (1948) noted that near Barrow, Alaska, the birds often nested in small colonies, with fifteen to twenty pairs present within a quarter mile.

Interspecific Relationships: Little specific information on possible interspecific competition between white-fronted and other geese exists. During migration, white-fronts often mingle with and forage with Canada geese and seemingly consume much the same foods, but only rarely are they seen among flocks of snow geese. Nesting in the Hooper Bay area occurs in about the same habitats as are used by emperor geese, but the white-fronted geese show a distinct preference for nesting on small hills, while emperor geese nest on flatlands and closer to water (Conover, 1926). After hatching, the families move to inland tundra ponds, while emperor and cackling goose families utilize rivers and tidal sloughs. Major avian predators on nests are probably jaegers, while glaucous gulls consume considerable numbers of young goslings. Foxes, especially red foxes, also account for the loss of some nests and young, as may eagles and snowy owls (Dzubin *et al.*, 1964, Barry, 1967).

General Activity Patterns and Movements: During migration, white-fronted geese follow a very similar daily routine to that of Canada geese, and often forage with them. Miller and Dzubin (1965) noted that two feeding flights are typical; one occurs in early morning and the other in late afternoon. White-fronts tend to be more wary than either snow geese or Canada geese, and this may serve to keep the species somewhat separated.

SOCIAL AND SEXUAL BEHAVIOR

Flocking Behavior: Large flock sizes are not typical of white-fronted geese, except perhaps during fall congregation and migration. Large flocks of molting birds do evidently occur in the vicinity of the upper Selawik River, northwestern Alaska, where flocks of 2,000 to 5,000 birds have been seen on two large lakes (United States Fish and Wildlife Service, Special Scientific Report: Wildlife, No. 30). Also, during the accumulations of birds in their fall staging areas in western Canada, peak populations of 25,000 to 50,000 birds have been found spread out on eight to twenty shallow lakes (Miller and Dzubin, 1965). Shortly after reaching their wintering quarters, however, the birds tend to spread out into smaller groups and become quite inconspicuous. Likewise during spring migration the flock sizes of birds passing through the Platte River valley of Nebraska are generally not very large, usually no more than a few dozen.

In studying the behavior of wintering flocks in England, Boyd (1953) reported that the wintering flocks often numbered several hundred birds, but as flock sizes increased, their unity of behavior decreased, with the larger flocks tending to break up into smaller units that acted independently.

Pair-forming Behavior: Little has been written on pair-forming behavior, but it apparently consists of the gradual development of individual associations during the second (or possibly third) winter of life, supplemented and strengthened by repeated use of "triumph ceremonies" between the paired birds (Boyd, 1954).

Copulatory Behavior: Copulation is preceded by mutual head-dipping associated with considerable tail-cocking and exposure of the white under tail coverts. After treading, both birds again strongly cock their tails, lift their folded wings, and call, with necks vertically stretched (Johnsgard, 1965).

Nesting and Brooding Behavior: The birds typically arrive at the nesting grounds in pairs (Bailey, 1948). Nesting is initiated shortly after the arrival at the breeding grounds, usually in the second half of May. A high degree of synchronization of nest initiation and egg-laying is not as evident in white-fronted geese as in the snow, cackling Canada, and Ross geese. The female constructs a nest that is usually lined with mosses, grasses, and finally down. The male does not normally approach the nest closely, but remains several hundred yards away. In spite of the birds' large size and their tendency to nest in hilly situations, the nests are extremely difficult to locate. Unlike the Canada goose but in common with emperor geese, incubating females usually do not attempt to leave the nest and sneak away unobserved at the first sign of danger. Instead, they suddenly flush from the nest when approached too closely. Even when the location of the nest is known, the brown plumage of the female so closely matches the dead tundra vegetation that it is nearly impossible to see her until she flushes.

With the hatching of the brood, the male joins the family and, at least in the Hooper Bay area, the families then tend to move to inland tundra ponds, well separated from families of emperor and cackling geese (Conover, 1926). Unlike snow geese, the families do not flock together, and, when frightened, the goslings typically scatter and dive in the thick cover (Barry, 1967).

Postbreeding Behavior: Little is known of possible molt migrations in the white-fronted goose. Such movements would seem probable, on the basis of observations indicated in the "Flocking Behavior" section above.

SNOW GOOSE

Anser caerulescens (Linnaeus) 1758

(Until 1973, regarded by the A.O.U. as *Chen caerulescens and C. hyperborea*)

Other Vernacular Names: Blue Goose, Wavy, White Brant, White Goose.

Range: Breeds in arctic Siberia, on Wrangel Island, and along the arctic coast of Alaska and Canada and adjoining islands to northwestern Greenland. In North America, winters on the Pacific coast to California, the Gulf coast, the Atlantic coast south to North Carolina, and to a limited extent in the interior along the Mississippi and Missouri rivers.

Subspecies:

A. c. caerulescens (L.): Lesser Snow (Blue) Goose. In North America, breeds from Alaska east to Baffin Island and winters primarily in the central valley of California, the Gulf coast, and in the Mississippi Valley north to Missouri.

A. c. atlanticus (Kennard): Greater Snow Goose. Breeds in northwestern Greenland and on Baffin, Devon, and probably Grinnell islands and winters along the middle Atlantic coast south to North Carolina.

Measurements (after Delacour, 1954):

A. c. caerulescens: Folded wing: males 395-460, females 387-450 mm. Culmen: males 51-62, females 50-61 mm.

A. c. atlanticus: Folded wing: males 430-485, females 425-475 mm. Culmen: males 59-73, females 57-68 mm.

Weights:

Lesser Snow Goose: Cooch *et al.* (1960) reported that 467 adult males averaged 6.05 pounds (2,744 grams), while 522 adult females averaged 5.55 pounds (2,517 grams). Nelson and Martin (1953) report maximum weights of lesser snow (and blue) geese as 6.8 pounds for males and 6.3 pounds for females.

Greater Snow Goose: Nelson and Martin (1953) reported that twenty-one males averaged 7.3 pounds (3,310 grams), with a maximum of 10.4 pounds; thirteen females averaged 6.2 pounds (2,812 grams), with a maximum of 6.5 pounds.

IDENTIFICATION

In the Hand: Snow geese are likely to be confused in the hand only with Ross geese and perhaps with immature white-fronted geese. On examination of the bill, the presence of the black "grinning patch" and the absence of warty protuberances at the bill's base should indicate a snow goose, and additionally no goose with a folded wing longer than 400 mm., a culmen longer than 50 mm., and a weight of more than 4 pounds (or 2,000 grams) would be a Ross goose. Young blue-phase snow geese sometimes are confused with young white-fronted geese, but the yellowish legs, feet, and bill and the lack of a black grinning patch will serve to distinguish young white-fronted geese. Domestic white geese might be confused by hunters with snow geese; these birds lack black wingtips and have no black grinning patch.

In the Field: Both in the air and on the ground or water, snow geese are readily identified by the partially or extensively white plumage, contrasting with the dark flight feathers. Wild snow geese call almost constantly, and their rather shrill, repeated *"la-uk!"* notes are reminiscent of barking dogs. In flight the emperor goose might be confused with a blue-phase snow goose, but this dark phase does not occur in the range of the emperor goose, and additionally emperor geese exhibit dark rather than white tail coverts in flight. Snow geese usually travel in larger flocks than do white-fronted geese, and even at a considerable distance the under wing coverts of white-fronts appear nearly as dark as their primaries, while in "blue" geese the anterior under wing coverts are much lighter, and they also show much more white around the head.

AGE AND SEX CRITERIA

Sex Determination: No plumage characters are available for sex determination without resorting to measurements.

Age Determination: The presence of a dull-colored, usually dusky bill, and legs and feet that are brownish to dusky, is indicative of a first-year bird. Juvenile white-phase birds are generally grayish in body tone, while juvenile blue-phase birds have little or no white on the head. Snow geese may attempt to nest when two years old, but only rarely succeed under natural conditions (Cooch, 1958). In captivity, snow geese normally breed at three years of age, but sometimes breed in their second year of life (Ferguson, 1966). Thus, an open oviduct or a fully developed penis would indicate a bird two years old or older.

DISTRIBUTION AND HABITAT

Breeding Distribution and Habitat: In Alaska, the breeding evidence for the snow goose is limited to a few, mostly old, records, primarily from the vicinity of Barrow, and a recent report of nesting at Prudhoe Bay (*Birds,* 4:19 1972). Gabrielson and Lincoln (1959) also mentioned the finding of two nests near the mouth of the Kinak River in 1953. In Canada, however, the

Breeding (hatched) and wintering (shaded) distributions of the snow goose (lesser snow goose horizontal hatching, greater snow goose vertical hatching) in North America.

nesting range is extensive, from the Mackenzie River delta in the west to Ellesmere Island in the north, Baffin Island in the east, and Cape Henrietta Maria in the south. Within this range, the greater snow goose has the most northerly breeding range, including northern Baffin Island, Devon Island, Ellesmere Island, and adjacent Greenland (Snyder, 1967). Parmelee and MacDonald (1960) found the greater snow goose common on Forsheim Peninsula of Ellesmere Island and reported that it is known to nest on Bylot, Devon, Somerset, and Axel Heiberg islands, as well as northwestern Baffin Island and Thule, Greenland. The "blue" phase of the lesser snow goose has a breeding range centering from northern Hudson Bay to southwestern Baffin Island and occurring north to Victoria Island (Parmelee *et al.*, 1967). Cooch (1963) reported that Bowman Bay, Baffin Island, had a frequency of blue-phased birds of 98 percent in 1960, while the percentages were 82 at Cape Dominion and 53 at Koukdjauk, Baffin Island. On Southampton Island, the "blue" phase comprised 33 percent at Boas River, while at Eskimo Point on the mainland of Keewatin it was 15 percent. At Perry River, Northwest Territories, it was 12 percent, and 1 percent was present as far northwest as Banks Island. The breeding habitat of lesser snow geese generally consists of low, grassy tundra associated with flat limestone basins or islands in braided deltas, and is usually near salt water (Cooch, 1961, 1964). Snyder (1967) has characterized the breeding habitat as low, flat tundra, usually near lakes, ponds, or on river floodplains. The greater snow goose, however, typically nests in habitats where stony terrain meets wet and grassy tundra. On Bylot Island the greater snow goose nests where the land is flat, marshy, and protected from the north by mountains (Lemieux, 1959).

Wintering Distribution and Habitat: Winter surveys performed by the United States Fish and Wildlife Service between 1966 and 1969 indicate that of an average winter count of some 1.2 million birds, about 40 percent occurred on the Pacific Flyway and adjacent Mexico. About 25 to 30 percent occurred in the Central Flyway, the same percentage in the Mississippi Flyways, and the remaining 5 percent (consisting mostly of greater snow geese) wintered on the Atlantic Flyway. In the Chesapeake Bay region, Stewart (1962) reported that the typical habitat of greater snow geese consists of salt-marsh cordgrass (*Spartina alterniflora*), which fringes the coastal bays or occurs as islands within them, and provides both food and cover for the geese.

The traditional wintering area of lesser snow and blue geese in the Mississippi Flyway has been the coast of Louisiana. Their attraction to the mud flats along the Mississippi Delta has apparently been produced by the growth of various grasses and sedges (*Zizaniopsis, Scirpus, Spartina, Panicum,* and *Typha*) whose roots provide favored foods (Bent, 1925). Snow geese also commonly winter along the entire coast of Texas, but mainly occur on the brackish marshes and low prairies. The greatest concentrations are in Chambers and Jefferson counties, where up to 300,000 or more birds sometimes occur (Texas Game, Fish, and Oyster Commission, 1945). Sometimes considerable numbers also occur in northern Mexico, along the coast of northern Tamaulipas as well as in the interior *bolsones* of Chihuahua and Durango (Leopold, 1959).

The Pacific Flyway's wintering concentrations are centered in California, from the Tule Lake and Klamath areas in the north to the Salton Sea in the south, with massive concentrations in the Central Valley. The Puget Sound region and the adjacent Frazer River delta of British Columbia is also an important wintering area for Pacific coast birds. This diverse range, from arid desert climates below sea level to moist and humid coastlines, encompasses an equally broad range of habitats. However, the common attraction would appear to be the availability of edible natural grasses or cultivated grainfields, with the bays, lakes, and marshes providing safe resting locations.

GENERAL BIOLOGY

Age at Maturity: According to Cooch (1958), snow geese may attempt to nest when two years old, but succeed only under ideal conditions. Of 44 responses by aviculturalists to a survey by Ferguson (1966), 31 indicated initial breeding the third year, 11 the second year, and 2 the fifth year. However, Lynch and Singleton (1964) concluded from age-ratio data that at least during favorable years the two-year-old segment of the adult flock must significantly contribute to breeding production. Barry (1967) found that 17 percent of the geese he banded as goslings were on the Anderson River breeding grounds two years later.

Pair Bond Pattern: Pair bonds in snow geese are apparently strong and often permanent. Pairing between white- and blue-phased birds is common but not random, with the offspring of all types of mating equally viable (Cooch, 1961).

Nest Location: Nesting of snow geese is typically in colonies, often numbering several thousand birds. Cooch (1964) reported nesting colonies exceeding 1,200 pairs per square mile, and noted that the largest known colonies are on Baffin Island, Banks Island, and north of Siberia on Wrangel Island. On Wrangel Island two kinds of nest location are typical (Uspenski, 1966). One is the colonial type (averaging 12 to 64 nests per hectare), in which 114,200 nests occurred on 3,700 hectares (or 12 nests per acre). The other type consists of small colonies or single pairs nesting with brant geese and Pacific eiders near the nests of snowy owls (*Nyctea scandiaca*). In the case of the large colonies the nests are protected by the concerted defense of the large number of birds, while in the second case the snowy owls, in protecting their own nests, also provide protection for the geese and ducks.

Soper (1942) reported that the nest is always placed on a slight grassy swell on the tundra, where the ground is relatively firm and well grown with mosses and grass. Most nests are built with plucked and shredded tundra moss and lined with fine grasses and down, while some are built with grass and chickweed and are smaller and less bulky than those made of moss.

Clutch Size: Clutch sizes of both phases of lesser snow geese are the same, 4.42 eggs prior to any losses due to predation or other sources (Cooch, 1961). Uspenski (1966) indicated an average clutch of 3.27 eggs for 645 nests on Wrangel Island, with the highest clutch average (3.55) in areas of high nesting density, apparently reflecting predation losses. Eggs are laid in colonies over a twelve-day period, and both phases begin and end all their egg-laying within the same interval. However, white-phased birds tend to begin their nesting slightly earlier than do blue-phased ones, according to Cooch. Lemieux (1959) reported that 22 greater snow goose clutches averaged 4.8 eggs, with clutches of early nests averaging 2.5 eggs more than those begun only four days later. Attempted renesting has not been reported.

Incubation Period: Cooch (1964) reported an incubation period of 22 or 23 days for lesser snow geese. Earlier (1961), he reported that white-phased birds have an average incubation period of 23.1 days, while blue-phased birds have a 23.6-day incubation period.

Fledging Period: Cooch (1964) reported that 42 days are required for obtaining flight in lesser snow geese. Earlier (1958), Cooch had estimated a fledging period of 49 days. Lemieux (1959) estimated a six-week fledging period for the greater snow goose, while Weller (1964) reports a five and one-half to six-week fledging period.

Nest and Egg Losses: Cooch (1961) has presented data to show that in an early (unusually mild spring) season an average of 19 percent of the eggs fail to hatch, from infertility, predation, flooding, or other causes. In a normal season this rises to 36.5 percent and in a retarded breeding season to 49.0 percent of the eggs, with the major increases occurring in losses resulting from flooding, desertion, and dump-nesting. Harvey (1971) also reported egg losses of 20 percent, mostly occurring late in incubation.

Juvenile Mortality: Cooch (1961) reported that the average brood size at the time of hatching was 4.22 for thirty-three broods he studied in 1952. By the twelfth week the average size of the brood had been reduced to 3.33 for thirty-two broods, or an approximate twelve-week mortality of more than 20 percent. Lynch and Singleton (1964) presented productivity data on snow geese for the period 1949 to 1959, indicating that winter samples reported average brood sizes ranging from 1.6 to 2.7 and percentages of immatures ranging from as low as 1.8 percent to 54.9 percent. The percentage of adult-plumaged birds accompanied by young varied from 1.6 percent to as much as 75.7 percent, suggesting that in favorable years at least some two-year-old birds must successfully nest. On the basis of such figures and banding studies, a probable 60 percent first-year mortality rate has been suggested (Cooch, 1963). On the basis of band returns, Rienecker (1965) estimated a first-year mortality rate of 49.1 percent.

Adult Mortality: Cooch (1964) estimated that adult lesser snow geese have an annual mortality rate of about 30 percent, based on an analysis of banded birds. Boyd (1962) provided an independent calculation apparently based on these figures and concluded that the lesser snow goose had an adult mortality rate of 27 percent, compared with a rate of 23 percent for the greater snow goose. This compares closely with a 22.5 to 25 percent adult mortality rate for the population of lesser snow geese wintering on the West Coast (Rienecker, 1965).

GENERAL ECOLOGY

Food and Foraging: Foods of snow geese have been studied relatively little, and most available information is from the wintering areas. On the Atlantic coast, salt-marsh cordgrass (*Spartina alterniflora*) rootstocks are evidently major foods (Stewart, 1962; Martin *et al.*, 1951). On the Gulf Coast, a larger variety of foods are taken, including the rootstocks of bulrushes (*Scirpus*), cattail (*Typha*), cordgrass, salt grass (*Distichlis*), the seeds and vegetative parts of square-stem spike rush (*Eleocharis quadrangulata*), and other herbaceous materials (Martin *et al.*, 1951). Glazener (1946) noted that in the marsh areas of Texas snow geese feed on reeds (*Phragmites*), salt grass, cordgrass, cattails, smartweed (*Polygonum*), and sedges (*Carex* and *Cyperus*), while in prairie pastures they feed on a variety of grasses (*Andropogon, Paspalum, Festuca, Eragrostis, Panicum, Setaria,* and *Sporobolus*). In the rice belt of Texas snow geese also sometimes consume considerable amounts of rice. Lynch (1968) has pointed out that in recent years the lesser snow geese of the Gulf coast have deserted the coastal marshes and their traditional foods and now largely winter and forage in rice fields, cattle pastures, and other agricultural lands. This is not so true of greater snow geese, which still feed mainly on "three-square" (*Scirpus* spp.) rhizomes. Limited samples from the western states indicate that rootstocks of bulrushes, vegetative parts of cultivated wheat, and various other plants are taken. Several authors have commented that the bird's strong serrated bill is well adapted for pulling up and tearing roots. Coues (cited in Bent, 1925) mentions how the birds closely crop short grasses in the manner of domestic geese (*Anser anser*) and put to good use their toothlike bill processes while pulling up and consuming roots and culms. Glazener (1946) also said that, unlike the Canada geese, which graze, snow geese are mainly "grubbers." Uspenski (1965) noted that while on their breeding grounds on Wrangel Island, the geese ate only the plants available in their immediate nesting area, and Barry (1967) reported a fairly catholic breeding-grounds diet, including sedges, ryegrass (*Elymus*), cotton grass (*Eriophorum*), willows, and horsetail (*Equisetum*).

Sociality, Densities, Territoriality: Snow geese are among the most social of all geese, and fall and winter flock sizes numbering in the tens of thousands of birds are not at all unusual. Cooch (1961) has mentioned the strong female ties that are present, at least through the first year. Such subadult birds remain with their parents until the latter's early stages of incubation, when the subadults separate from the breeding colony and molt on its periphery.

Densities of snow geese on their breeding grounds are sometimes almost incredible. Uspenski (1965) reported approximately 300,000 birds and 114,200 nests on Wrangel Island in 1960, which he believed represented the main world nesting center for the species. As noted earlier, these 114,200 nests occurred in an area of 3,700 hectares, or a nesting density of almost 8,000 per square mile. Cooch (1964) noted that he was aware of nesting concentrations of 1,200 pairs per square mile, allowing an average territory size of only about two acres per pair. Ryder (1967) noted nest densities of up to 4.61 nests per 1,000 square feet in preferred mixed (birch and rock moss) habitats of Arlone Lake in the Perry River area, but the average for mixed and birch-dominated habitats was about one nest per 1,000 square feet, the equivalent of 45 nests per acre.

Interspecific Relationships: In general, snow geese form single-species nesting colonies, although Uspenski (1965) mentioned that on Wrangel Island the birds sometimes nest among brant geese or even close to the nests of snowy owls. Snow geese sometimes breed in close proximity to small Canada geese (Parmelee *et al.,* 1967), and Nelson (1952) described at least two probable wild hybrids between these species. MacInnes (1962) remarked that the Baffin Island Canada geese he studied at Eskimo Point which nested among the blue-phased snow geese suffered as many egg losses to jaegers as did those nesting outside the colony. Barry (1956) noted that, while the brant nested near the coastline of Southampton Island, the snow geese nested at least one-fourth mile inland from the high tide line.

Major egg predators of snow geese appear to be arctic fox (*Alopex lagopus*), as well as jaegers, gulls, and ravens. Jaegers are sometimes serious egg predators; Cooch (1961) mentioned that they destroyed all the eggs laid during the first two days of nesting at Eskimo Point in 1959, and also (1964) that they destroyed 49 percent of the eggs of brant geese and snow geese laid in poor habitat at Anderson River, Northwest Territories. Uspenski's (1965) clutch size data suggest that egg predators are most effective in colonies with low densities or at the periphery of nesting colonies and provide a possible explanation for the colonial nesting tendencies of this species. Herring gulls (*Larus argentatus*) may sometimes also be significant egg predators, as indicated by Manning's (1942) observations on Southampton Island and by Harvey's (1971) more recent studies.

General Activity Patterns and Movements: Little specific information has been written on general activity patterns, which seem to be much like those of other geese. Roberts (1932) reported that in western Minnesota the spring migrants typically spent the night on a lake, left at sunrise, and fed until about 10:00 a.m. They then returned to the lake and waited until about 4:00 p.m. to come out once again to forage in stubble fields.

Glazener (1946) similarly noted that wintering snow geese in Texas typically left to feed in the morning somewhat later than the Canada geese, and most of them left *en masse*. They fed up to thirty miles from their roosting sites and moved to watering places in midmorning. Then they made a midafternoon flight to feed again and sometimes remained feeding until after dark. While the spring migration is typically a protracted one involving short daily movements and much local foraging activity, the fall migration across the continental interior is sometimes a nonstop flight to the wintering area. Cooch (1955) reported that in 1952 the population of lesser snow geese wintering on the Gulf coast flew nonstop from James Bay to Louisiana, an air distance of 1,700 miles, in less than sixty hours.

SOCIAL AND SEXUAL BEHAVIOR

Flocking Behavior: The large average size of snow goose flocks is well known; Spinner (1948) provided accurate counts of a greater snow goose spring flock of 13,494 birds and a fall flock of 2,659 individuals. Musgrove and Musgrove (1947) noted that during the spring in Iowa, flocks of 15,000 to 20,000 are commonly seen in areas of concentration, while scattered flocks of 500 to 10,000 may be found between these concentration points. They gradually move up the river at the rate of about twenty miles a day, stopping at traditional concentration points that may at times hold nearly half a million birds.

Pair-forming Behavior: Pairs are apparently formed in snow geese, as they are in other species of geese, by the increasing association of individual birds and the development of pair bonds by the repeated performance of the triumph ceremony. This presumably occurs during the second winter of life, although the birds may not successfully nest until they are three years old. Pairing between color phases is common but does not occur randomly (Cooch, 1961), thus the incidence of intermediate ("hybrid") geese is relatively low. Sibley (1949) estimated that at least 10 percent of the migrant geese he observed in eastern Kansas consisted of such birds. Cooch (1961) suggested that intermediate, or heterozygotic, individuals have been responsible for the northward spread by genes producing blue-phased birds, rather than through pioneering by pure blue-phased birds.

Copulatory Behavior: Copulation is preceded by the usual mutual head-dipping. After treading, the tail is not so strongly cocked nor are the wings raised so high as is typical of most species of *Anser* (Johnsgard, 1965).

Nesting and Brooding Behavior: The female constructs the nest with the materials at hand, usually mosses and grasses (Soper, 1942). Little down is present when the first egg is laid, but the down mat is luxuriant by the time the clutch is complete (Sutton, 1931). Only the female incubates, but the male stands close guard, often within fifteen feet of the nest (Barry, 1956). The female rarely leaves the nest voluntarily during incubation, but will forage some if driven off the nest (Manning, 1942). Manning reported that both sexes become very wary about four days prior to hatching, but after the young hatch the male becomes quite fearless. The female usually leads the young after hatching, while the male remains behind and protects the brood from intruders. Such families gather together into flocks containing about forty adults, then leave the nesting grounds.

Postbreeding Behavior: Adult birds undergo their molt while their offspring are still flightless, and during this time they may gather in fairly large flocks. Cooch (1957) described cases in which more than 15,000 flightless birds have been caught by being driven into large enclosures. Nonbreeding adults and subadults, having molted somewhat earlier than breeders, leave the breeding grounds about the time the young birds make their first flights, while adults and their young follow about three weeks later, or early September (Cooch, 1964).

ROSS GOOSE

Anser rossii Cassin 1861
(*Chen rossii* of A.O.U., 1957)

Other Vernacular Names: None in general use.

Range: Breeds mainly in the Perry River region of the Northwest Territories eastward along the Queen Maud Gulf to at least 97°02′ W. latitude, and southward in the interior to at least 66°21′ N. longitude (Ryder, 1967), and winters mostly in central California, with vagrant birds occasionally reaching the midwestern states and rarely the eastern states. Limited breeding also occurs on Banks and Southampton islands and on the McConnell River, Keewatin District.

Subspecies: None recognized.

Measurements (after Delacour, 1954):

Folded wing: Males 360-380, females 345-360 mm.

Culmen: Males 40-46, females 37-40 mm.

Weights: Nelson and Martin (1953) reported that eighteen males averaged 2.9 pounds (1,315 grams), with a maximum of 3.6 pounds; twenty-one females averaged 2.7 pounds (1,224 grams), with a maximum of 3.4 pounds.

IDENTIFICATION

In the Hand: Although the Ross goose is normally found only within a limited winter and summer range, it occasionally strays far from its usual migratory route, and individual birds may turn up almost anywhere. If examined in the hand, Ross geese exhibit a short bill (under 47 mm.) that may be black along the edges but has no definite "grinning patch" and in adult males is usually warty near its base, which is bluish. Ross geese also never exceed 4 pounds (or 2,000 grams), and their folded wing measurements never reach 400 mm.

In the Field: Ross geese are best distinguished by direct size comparison with snow geese when they are in the same flock, or by their comparable size to large ducks, such as mallards. The bluish base of the bill may be evident at fairly close range. Some birds of intermediate size and appearance have been seen in wild flocks, indicating that natural hybridization does occur and thus adds to the difficulties of field identification of Ross geese among snow goose flocks (Trauger *et al.,* 1971).

AGE AND SEX CRITERIA

Sex Determination: No plumage characters are available for external sex determination.

Age Determination: Not yet closely studied, but apparently comparable to the snow goose. In general, immature birds are less conspicuously marked with gray than is the case with snow geese, and they are more difficult to recognize at comparable distances.

DISTRIBUTION AND HABITAT

Breeding Distribution and Habitat: The initial discovery of the breeding range of the Ross goose was in the Perry River area, and until the early 1950s the species was believed limited to that region. However, it is now known to breed also on Banks Island (Manning *et al.,* 1956), the McConnell River on the west side of Hudson Bay, and on the Boas River delta of Southampton Island (MacInnes and Cooch, 1963). Ryder (1967) found many previously unknown colonies south and east of the Perry River and noted that they were all on islands in lakes. These islands provide protection, in the form of rocks or shrubs, from wind and also to some extent from rain and snow. Flat islands lacking such protection were avoided, and the preferred lakes were not only sufficiently large to prevent predators from swimming across but also shallow enough (under five or six feet) to prevent ice bridges from being

Breeding (hatched) and wintering (shaded) distributions of the Ross
goose in North America.

present at the start of the nesting season. Barry (1964) reported that Ross geese nearly always nest on remote island-studded lakes, eight to forty miles inland, in fairly dry surrounding countryside. Less often they nest along rivers or on lake shores. Ryder (1969) judged that the availability of food in the form of sedges and grasses is of major significance in determining the distribution of nesting colonies; also important are protection from flooding during the spring breakup and a source of nest cover in the form of shrubs or rocks. Islands that rise from ten to twenty feet above water level but which have sufficient level places to allow for growth of food and nesting materials provide optimum nesting habitat.

Wintering Distribution and Habitat: The primary wintering location of Ross geese is in central California, where they mix with and occupy similar habitats of the wintering lesser snow geese in the Sacramento and San Joaquin valleys as well as nearer the coast in Ventura and Orange counties (Bent, 1925). Recent records from the Salton Sea suggest a southern extension of the wintering range in that area (O'Neill, 1954). Kozlik *et al.* (1959) noted that geese color-marked at Tule Lake wintered throughout the Central Valley, but were not seen in the Imperial Valley, suggesting a possible different migratory route for birds wintering in that area. Marshall (1958) noted that following a mid-October arrival in the Klamath Basin, Ross geese move to the northern San Joaquin Valley, where they remain until February or March.

The last few decades have resulted in a surprising number of Ross goose records from east of the Rocky Mountains, mainly between Ontario and Texas. Apart from two very early (1910 and 1916) Louisiana records, most of them date from the 1950s or later. Sutton (1967) summarized these records for Texas (three records in 1953–1954), Oklahoma (one record in 1961), Kansas (one record in 1951), Colorado (one record in 1964), and Louisiana (one record plus the two early ones). In more recent winters Ross geese have become an almost annual occurrence in Texas (*Audubon Field Notes,* 23:352, 24:381), and they are also regular visitors to the Rio Grande Valley in New Mexico (Gary Zahm, pers. comm.). Most remarkable is a late-November flock of 200 at Squaw Creek National Wildlife Refuge, Missouri (*Audubon Field Notes,* 23:324). In the fall and winter of 1970–71 Ross geese were reported in North Carolina, Missouri, Colorado, Louisiana, Nevada, Texas, and New Mexico (*American Birds,* 25:545). A total of 79 Ross geese have been trapped with about 500 wild lesser snow geese during banding operations in the mid-1960s in Nebraska, and 4 of these banded birds have since been recovered in California, Mexico, and the Keewatin District of Canada (George Schildman, pers. comm.). The occurrence of some seemingly intermediate birds among such trapped birds also opens the possibility that hybrids between lesser snow geese and Ross geese may be present in un-known numbers. Trauger *et al.* (1971) have since reported on a number of such apparent hybrids.

GENERAL BIOLOGY

Age at Maturity: Ferguson (1966) reported that, of eight respondents to a questionnaire, six reported initial breeding of Ross geese at three years, and one each reported initial breeding in the first and second years of life.

Pair Bond Pattern: Presumably pair bonds are permanent in Ross geese, although specific data on this point are lacking. Ryder (1967) mentioned the strong attachment of males to incubating females and defense of the young; he also noted that family bonds are retained by yearlings until the incubation period of the next season's eggs is begun. Thus, it is evident that individual pairs must remain together throughout the nonbreeding period.

Nest Location: Nests are built on various habitats and substrates, but Ryder (1967) established that preferred nest sites are mixed habitats of small birch stands and rocks, while pure rock or birch habitats have intermediate preference, and open habitats of low tundra have the lowest nest usage. Ryder concluded that sufficient protection from the elements and ample space for grazing determine nest density in a particular location. In the preferred mixed habitat types, nests had an average density of 9.5 per 1,000 square feet, with a maximum of 20.6 nests in this area, or only 50 square feet per nesting pair.

Clutch Size: Ryder (1970b) reported a mean clutch size of 3.6 to 4.0 eggs prior to incubation in three years of study. Average clutch sizes in early nesting seasons averaged larger than those in late-starting seasons during these years. Nests started early in the nesting season averaged larger than those initiated only three to four days later. The interval between eggs aver-aged 1.5 days. Removing a few of the eggs from a nest did not seriously affect hatching of the remainder, but adding eggs to a completed clutch resulted in very low nesting success. Ryder (1970a) has suggested that the small average clutch size of this species has evolved in relation to the food available to the female before arriving on the nesting grounds, as represented by the maxi-mum increases in body weight that she can carry during her spring migration. A small clutch size thus avoids depleting the postlaying energy reserves of the female and correspondingly increases the probability of her efficient incuba-tion and brooding of her eggs and young. Ryder found no evidence of at-tempted renesting.

Incubation Period: On the basis of forty-five last eggs laid, Ryder (1967) determined the average incubation period as 22 days, with a range of

19 to 25 days. No incubation occurs prior to the laying the last egg, and only 2 percent of the nests had down present prior to the laying of the penultimate egg. After the laying of the last egg, however, 82 percent of the observed nests had down present.

Fledging Period: Since freezing weather typically occurs between forty and forty-five days after the time of hatching, the fledging period is evidently slightly more than forty days (Ryder, 1969).

Nest and Egg Losses: Ryder (1967) reported that of 351 eggs in ninety-one nests studied in 1963, 93.7 percent hatched, while in 1964 he found a 79.2 percent hatch of 230 eggs in fifty-nine nests. The percentage of eggs destroyed was remarkably low, being 2.2 and 14.4 percent for the two years, respectively, while the remainder of egg failures resulted from infertility or embryonic deaths. Arctic foxes caused high nest losses in 1964 at one locality, but avian predators caused few egg losses. In later studies, Ryder (1970b) reported yearly hatching success rates of 60.6 and 80.3 percent.

Juvenile Mortality: Ryder (1967) noted that the average brood size of ninety-nine broods from Perry River was 2.88 for broods not more than one week old. Fall flocks in Saskatchewan had an average of 2.72 young per family, and winter counts in California indicated an average of 1.65 young per family, or a total decrease in brood size of 42 percent.

Adult Mortality: No figures on adult mortality rates are available.

GENERAL ECOLOGY

Food and Foraging: Little has been written of the foods of Ross geese. Hanson *et al.* (1956) reported that the gizzards of five birds collected on the breeding grounds included mostly sedges (*Eriophorum* and *Carex*) and some grass (*Poa*). Ryder (1967) examined twenty-six birds from the Perry River region and found some roots of grasses and sedges, leaves of grasses, sedges, and birch (*Betula*), and the stems and spikelets of grasses and sedges. Roots were consumed early in the season, while later on leaves and spikelets were utilized. No animal materials were found, even though several goslings were included in the sample.

Dzubin (1965) noted that during fall migrant geese in Alberta and Saskatchewan use large lakes for resting and fly out twice daily to wheat and barley fields, where they feed on waste grain.

Sociality, Densities, Territoriality: Sociality and associated densities on the breeding ground are even higher in the Ross goose than in the snow goose. Dzubin (1965) noted that spring flocks are much smaller and more scattered than fall groupings moving through Saskatchewan and Alberta, with fall staging areas in the Kindersley district often reaching peaks of 10,000 to 20,000 birds in the early 1960s. Dzubin (1965) noted that in 1964 about 3,000 birds occurred on five small lakes, another 4,500 occurred on four lakes, and 1,700 were on three small saline sloughs. Temporary puddles from 10 to 150 acres in size and containing spike rush (*Eleocharis*) mats were used heavily for resting and feeding. Marshall (1938) mentioned a single flock of 8,000 Ross geese in the San Joaquin Valley of California.

Breeding ground densities on preferred islands are often high; the total number of nests on five islands in Arlone Lake was 769 in 1963 and 906 in 1964. These islands had an average density of 4.26 nests per 1,000 square feet. Observations of two pairs provided territory estimates indicating maximum territory sizes of 8 and 12 feet in open and rock habitats, respectively. Nesting begins somewhat earlier in higher than in lower concentrations (Ryder, 1970b).

Interspecific Relationships: Ryder (1967) investigated possible competition with snow geese for nesting sites on Arlone Island and concluded that both species avoid open situations and prefer edge areas of birch or mixed habitats. However, he could not find any definite evidence of competition, since Ross goose densities and clutch sizes were as high in regions of high snow goose densities as they were in areas where snow goose densities were low. Food was abundant, and interspecific aggressive interactions were uncommon. Ryder believed that a future substantial increase in snow geese could, however, alter nesting space for Ross geese.

Ryder's studies indicated that, at least in his study area, avian nest predation was not a significant factor in affecting nesting success. However, arctic foxes apparently not only sometimes kill adult birds but also may cause stress by harassment during laying and sometimes cause great damage to nests. Ryder noted that 144 Ross goose nests and 122 snow goose nests were destroyed in one week during 1964; this caused the desertion of one island nesting colony.

In the wintering areas, Ross geese initially mingle with snow geese and white-fronted geese, but later tend to leave them and forage separately (Marshall, 1958). At this time they are associated mostly with cackling Canada geese, and feed mainly on green feed, whereas snow geese and white-fronted geese forage on rice fields and cereal croplands (Marshall, cited in Dzubin, 1965).

General Activity Patterns and Movements: Ross geese are apparently very similar to snow geese in their daily activities and movements. Dzubin

(1965) has documented the gradual shifting of fall migration routes in western Canada to a more easterly direction, associated with the loss of surface waters on the Canadian prairies since 1955. Kozlik *et al.* (1959) have also provided observations on wintering and spring migratory movements of color-marked birds.

SOCIAL AND SEXUAL BEHAVIOR

Flocking Behavior: Ryder (1967) noted that on their arrival at the breeding grounds, Ross geese are in small flocks of two to fifty birds. These represent family groups or their multiples, and when incubation begins, the nonbreeders flock together, leaving the nesting grounds at the time of hatching to undertake their molt migration. Shortly after hatching, units of two to fifteen families leave the nesting grounds and move to inland lakes and river courses. By three weeks after hatching, such postnuptial flocks may number as many as two hundred birds.

Pair-forming Behavior: By the time they reach their nesting grounds, the Ross geese are apparently already mated, and no copulatory or courtship behavior was noted by Ryder (1967). Copulations have been observed during spring migration in April, although it is apparent that they could not account for the fertilization of eggs laid in June. Triumph ceremonies were observed commonly by Ryder, and this behavior is known to be important in the formation and maintenance of pair bonds in geese.

Copulatory Behavior: The precopulatory behavior of Ross geese consists of the usual mutual head-dipping, which is followed by treading. Postcopulatory posturing is relatively weak (Johnsgard, 1965).

Nesting and Brooding Behavior: Ryder's (1967) study indicated that nest-building normally begins immediately after arrival at the nesting grounds and that considerable variation in nest construction occurs. During the egg-laying period the geese spend short periods at the nest site, with one bird grazing while the other defends the territory. The male usually leads the attack, with the female immediately behind. During this time territorial disputes are at a maximum, while when incubation begins the colony becomes noticeably silent. Only the female incubates, while the male remains near the nest and defends it. Females incubate with the head held up, as in snow geese, rather than with the head and neck on the ground, as in the genus *Branta*. Unless disturbed, the female covers the eggs with down when leaving the nest. After hatching, the male defends the brood, while the female leads them away from the source of danger.

Postbreeding Behavior: As mentioned earlier, families rapidly merge into flock units, which may number several hundred geese within a few weeks after hatching. Loss of the flight feathers of adults is attained about fifteen to twenty days after the peak of hatching in early July. Within three weeks of hatching, the young have sheathed tail and flight feathers emerging. By the end of August the young are capable of flight and the birds prepare to migrate south.

EMPEROR GOOSE

Anser canagicus (Sewastianov) 1802
(*Philacte canagica* of A.O.U., 1957)

Other Vernacular Names: Beach Goose.

Range: Breeds in coastal Alaska from the mouth of the Kuskokwim River to the north side of the Seward Peninsula, St. Lawrence Island, and on the northeastern coast of Siberia. Winters on the Aleutian Islands and along the Alaska Peninsula probably to Cook Inlet with vagrant birds wintering in British Columbia and the western United States south to California.

Subspecies: None recognized.

Measurements (after Delacour, 1954):

Folded wing: Males 380-400, females 350-385 mm.

Culmen: Males 40-49, females 35-40 mm.

Weights: Average of six males was 6.2 pounds (2,812 grams), with a maximum of 6.8 pounds; nine females averaged 6.1 pounds (2,766 grams), with a maximum of 6.9 pounds (Nelson and Martin, 1953).

IDENTIFICATION

In the Hand: Emperor geese can hardly be confused with any other species when in the hand; the multicolored reddish bill lacking exposed "teeth," the yellowish legs and feet, and a scalloped feather pattern of gray, black, and white are all unique.

In the Field: Along their very limited range, emperor geese are usually found along saltwater shorelines, where they occur in small flocks. The golden to orange staining on their white head feathers is conspicuous and contrasts with the otherwise grayish plumage. In flight, the lack of white feathers above or below the tail makes this species unique among geese. They also have relatively short necks and heavy bodies, associated with a rapid and strong wingbeat. In flight, the birds often utter a repeated *kla-ha* or an alarm note *u-leegh.*

AGE AND SEX CRITERIA

Sex Determination: No plumage characters are available for external sex determination.

Age Determination: Brown rather than black barring on the back and gray mottling on the head and neck indicate a bird in its first year.

DISTRIBUTION AND HABITAT

Breeding Distribution and Habitat: The emperor goose's breeding distribution in North America is the most restricted of any goose species and is limited to the west coast and adjacent islands of Alaska. Gabrielson and Lincoln (1959) described the range as extending from Kotzebue Island on the north to the Aleutian Islands on the south, with the chief breeding occurring from the mouth of the Koskokwim River to the north side of the Seward Peninsula. The most eastern breeding record is reported for Cape Barrow, where a pair was taken in 1929, and the most southerly for Amak Island. It was uncertain to Gabrielson and Lincoln whether birds on St. Lawrence Island were nesters or simply nonbreeding and molting birds, but Fay (1961) has established that both breeding and molting does occur there. Bailey (1948) found that emperor geese were common nesters on the north shore of the Seward Peninsula and thought they were probably less common nesters on the north shore of Kotzebue Sound to at least Point Hope. Williamson *et al.* (1966) indicated that, although the emperor goose possibly breeds at Cape Thompson, it was rarely seen there.

Throughout their North American range, favored nesting habitats are in low, wet tundra, usually near the coast and often near lakes or ponds. Con-

Breeding (hatched) and wintering (shaded) distributions of the
Emperor goose in North America.

over (1926) reported that nesting at Hooper Bay occurred within ten miles of the coast. Spencer *et al.* (1951) noted that, although it nested in association with cackling geese twelve to fifteen miles from the coast in this area, it also nested farther inland with white-fronted geese and "lesser" (Alaska) Canada geese. Barry (1964) noted that ponds and marshes in low, rolling hills, inland from the tidal areas favored by brant, were preferred nesting habitat, with emperors, cackling Canada geese, and brant geese overlapping somewhat in their nesting habitat zones.

In Siberia, nesting occurs over a broad area adjoining the Bering Sea, and favored nesting habitats consist of coastal flats, islands in the mouths of small rivers emptying into the sea, and to some extent of swampy marshes along the lower reaches of rivers flowing through tundra (Dementiev and Gladkov, 1967). Kistchinski (1971) also reported that coastal "lagoon" tundra and inland moss-sedge tundra represented the two main nesting habitats.

Wintering Distribution and Habitat: Virtually the entire emperor goose population of North America is believed to winter along the Aleutian Islands. Kenyon (1961) estimated a wintering population of 25,000 to 37,000 birds for the Aleutian Islands and added that, since large numbers may also winter along the Alaska Peninsula, the total winter population may be around 200,000 birds. The birds are abundant in winter around Kanaga Island, but have been reported all the way from the Sanak group to Attu (Murie, 1959). In some winters about 2,000 have been seen at Izembek Bay (*Audubon Field Notes,* 20:116, 22:114). They also winter on the Commander Islands, inhabiting stony, rubble-covered coasts (Dementiev and Gladov, 1967).

In recent winters increasing numbers of emperor geese have turned up along the West Coast, from California to British Columbia and inland Idaho. This is believed to be the result of the transferring of some emperor goose eggs to the nests of white-fronted geese by wildlife biologists, with a resultant shift in wintering movements (*Audubon Field Notes,* 24:633).

GENERAL BIOLOGY

Age at Maturity: Ferguson (1966) reported that fifteen of seventeen aviculturalists responding to a questionnaire indicated that initial breeding of captive emperor geese occurred when they were three years old, with the other two indicating two years and five years.

Pair Bond Pattern: Little documented information is available on this point, but most observers have noted strong pair bonds, which are presumably permanent.

Nest Location: Nests are typically placed near water, such as on an island, a bank, or in a large tussock (Conover, 1926). Sometimes the drift-wood debris on the high tide line is chosen for concealing the nest (Barry, 1964). In the Hooper Bay region we noted (Kessel *et al.,* 1964) that thirteen nests were all in grassy marsh habitat, mostly within a few feet of water, but sometimes from twenty to forty feet from the nearest pond. Calvin Lensink (pers. comm.) reported that emperor geese nest farther from the coast than do brant and more often are found nesting along the main shoreline than on small islets. Around Hooper Bay they often nest in upland hummocks or "pingos" several yards from water, and on other coastal flats they may nest in clumps of wild rye (*Elymus*) well away from water.

Clutch Size: Of five hundred active nests that were found on the Yukon-Kuskokwim Delta between 1963 and 1971, the clutches averaged 4.72 eggs, with yearly means ranging from 3.83 to 5.59 (Calvin Lensink, pers. comm.). This area perhaps supports as much as 90 percent of the world's emperor goose population and must represent optimum habitat; but in Siberia, clutch sizes are comparable, usually of 5 or 6 eggs (Dementiev and Gladkov, 1967). The egg-laying rate has not been reported.

Incubation Period: A 24-day incubation period has been generally reported for the emperor goose. Brandt (1943) estimated a period of approximately 25 days at Hooper Bay, the same period as Kistchinski (1971) determined for two nests in northeast Siberia.

Fledging Period: Apparently not yet definitely established.

Nest and Egg Losses: Losses to egg predators, principally jaegers, reduced the average clutch from 5.5 to 3.8 in one study (United States Department of the Interior Resource Publication 43, p.19, 1967), or an approximate 30 percent egg loss. Brood counts made in 1950 and 1954 (United States Fish and Wildlife Service, Special Scientific Report: Wildlife, Nos. 8 and 27) indicate an average brood size of 4.5 for 28 broods, suggesting a somewhat low early mortality, assuming no brood mergers occurred. Calvin Lensink (pers. comm.) reported an average of 3.85 goslings in 318 early (Class I) broods.

Juvenile Mortality: Fairly substantial losses of newly-hatched goslings to glaucous gulls have been noted by various observers (Brandt, 1943; Conover, 1926). Arctic foxes have also been reported to prey on both eggs and young where they are abundant (Barry, 1964).

Adult Mortality: No estimates of adult mortality rates are yet available for emperor geese.

Food and Foraging: The emperor goose has been aptly called the "beach goose," as a reflection of its littoral foraging tendencies. Cottam and Knappen (1939) have provided most of the available data on the foods of this species. In their sample of thirty-three stomachs, mostly from spring and summer specimens from Alaska, the contents were almost entirely (91.6 percent) vegetable material. Only two of the birds had been feeding predominantly on animal material, a finding in contrast to most earlier opinions on foraging tendencies of emperor geese. Major food sources consisted of algae (30.7 percent), eelgrass and pondweeds (13.9 percent), grasses and sedges (24.9 percent), unidentified plant fiber (22 percent), mollusks (3.7 percent), crustaceans (2.2 percent), and other animal materials (2.6 percent). Sea lettuce (*Ulva* and *Enteromorpha*) made up 17 percent of the total and occurred in twelve stomachs, while the remainder of the algae consisted of green algae. Eelgrass is apparently also a favored food, judging from its occurrence in the samples.

Murie (1959), in referring to wintering birds, commented on their use of kelp, sea lettuce, and *Elymus* shoots. Barry (1964) noted that young birds feed on aquatic insects and marsh grass at first, and later may consume berries. Dementiev and Gladkov (1967) mentioned that various invertebrates, particularly mussels and other mollusks and crustaceans collected in the tidal zone, are major sources of food. Quite possibly there are local or seasonal variations in the dependence upon animal foods by this species.

Sociality, Densities, Territoriality: Little has been written on this specific aspect of the emperor goose. During a few days in early June, I noticed a total of 400 to 500 emperor geese within a few square miles of the Hooper Bay marsh (Kessel *et al.,* 1964), but these were mostly in groups of no more than a few dozen birds.

Brandt (1943) noted that during spring migration the geese moved northward in flocks of about 15 to 40 birds and that early arrivals at the nesting grounds were in pairs or small parties.

During the summer molt, emperor geese gather in large groups in favored localities. Fay (1961) noted that about 5,000 birds were present along one of the southern lagoons of St. Lawrence Island, out of a total summer population of 10,000 to 20,000 birds. Many of these were immature nonbreeders, and Fay believed that St. Lawrence Island represents the principal summering area for the population of immatures produced in Alaska and Siberia.

Breeding densities have not been carefully estimated, but in the Hooper Bay area the emperor goose comprises about 10 percent of the breeding waterfowl population, which has been estimated at 130 birds per square mile (Spencer *et al.,* 1951), so a density of 6 or 7 pairs per square mile would be indicated. This compares well with a more recent estimate made by Mickelson (1973) of 20 pairs on a four-square-mile study area. There were also 204 cackling goose pairs, 32 black brant pairs, 19 white-fronted goose pairs, and 42 spectacled eider pairs present on the area.

Interspecific Relationships: There would appear to be little if any competition between emperor geese and any other species of geese for food because of the emperors' rather specialized diet, although in common with brant geese, they do consume substantial amounts of sea lettuce and eelgrass. Nesting is done in the same general habitat as is used by Canada geese and white-fronted geese, but suitable nest locations are never lacking in typical lowland tundra habitats.

Major egg predators would appear to be jaegers, although, following hatching, the young are taken by a variety of species, including glaucous and glaucous-winged gulls, three species of jaeger, and perhaps also the snowy owl (Brandt, 1943).

General Activity Patterns and Movements: During the long arctic summer days on the nesting grounds at Hooper Bay, there seemed to be no definite schedule of activities for the emperor geese. Nonbreeding birds or birds that were still in the process of egg-laying could be seen foraging around the edges of tundra ponds at almost any hour, usually in pairs or what appeared to be family groups of five to seven birds. They were far less wary and more "curious" than any of the other geese, and, when flushed, they would typically circle several times around the person flushing them, often almost at eye level, before flying away. Eskimos thus found them easy targets and, even with a single-shot .22-caliber rifle, could usually kill more than one bird from a flock before it finally left the area.

During early September at Izembek Bay, I have observed migrant birds foraging along the beaches in the tidal zone, and rarely if ever do they undertake daily flights to the tundra to feed on berries, as is typical of the Canada geese. Berries such as crowberries (*Empetrum*) are, however, eaten on the breeding grounds (Barry, 1964).

SOCIAL AND SEXUAL BEHAVIOR

Flocking Behavior: As noted earlier, large flocks of emperor geese are rarely encountered, except perhaps in summer molting areas (Fay, 1961).

The largest winter flock that I have found on record is 2,350 during a Christmas count at Izembek Bay, Alaska (*Audubon Field Notes,* 22:114).

Pair-forming Behavior: Pair formation probably occurs at the wintering areas, since the birds arrive at their breeding areas already in pairs (Bailey, 1948; Brandt, 1943). I observed no pair-forming behavior at Hooper Bay and saw no aggressive behavior in the small groups that moved about together, suggesting that they were family units. Observations of geese in captivity indicate that a typical triumph ceremony is present, which no doubt serves to establish and maintain bonds in emperor geese as in other goose species.

Copulatory Behavior: I have never observed a completed copulation, and the only apparent precopulatory behavior I have seen rather closely resembled normal feeding behavior on the part of both birds. Brandt (1943) noted that mating occurred in shallow water, just deep enough to allow the female to sink beneath the surface.

Nesting and Brooding Behavior: According to Brandt the female builds a nest in grasses usually close to water, first hollowing out a cup from 2.2 to 4.5 inches deep, enough to allow the female to be well concealed but also leaving an adequate accumulation of grasses and moss below. Incubation begins with the completion of the clutch, but little down is added until near the end of incubation, when it is liberally deposited. The male remains near the incubating female, but not as close as in white-fronted geese. Following hatching, the male joins the family and they move to rivers and sloughs near the coast, where the young forage for aquatic insects or may feed on sedges and tundra berries with their parents.

Post-breeding Behavior: Molting of breeding adults begins about two or three weeks after the young are hatched. It is probable that immature nonbreeders do not molt on the breeding grounds, but rather fly to St. Lawrence Island for molting, where "herds" of up to 20,000 flightless birds may accumulate during summer (Fay, 1961). Their flightless period occurs between mid-June and early August, or considerably earlier than that of breeding adults that have hatched their young in late June or July. Arrival of fall migrants at Izembek Bay may occur as early as mid-August; these early arrivals are presumably also nonbreeders. Apparently a sizable portion of the Asiatic population of emperor geese molt at Ukouge lagoon, on the northern coast of Siberia (Kistchinski, 1971).

CANADA GOOSE

Branta canadensis (Linnaeus) 1758

Other Vernacular Names: Cackling Goose, Canadian Goose, Honker, Hutchins Goose, Richardson Goose, White-cheeked Goose.

Range: Breeds across most of North America, from the Aleutian Islands across Alaska and northern Canada and south to the central United States. Resident flocks of larger subspecies are also established at many wildlife refuges, in some cases well beyond the probable original range of the subspecies. Also introduced into New Zealand, Great Britain, and Iceland.

North American Subspecies (based on Delacour, 1954):

B. c. canadensis (L.): Atlantic Canada Goose. Breeds in southeastern Baffin Island, eastern Labrador west probably to the watershed line, Newfoundland, Anticosti Island, and the Magdalen Islands.

B. c. interior Todd: Hudson Bay (Todd) Canada Goose. Breeds in northern Quebec, Ontario, and Manitoba around Hudson and James bays, south to about 52° N. latitude and north as far as Churchill and the Hudson Strait.

B. c. maxima Delacour: Giant Canada Goose. Originally bred on the Great Plains, from the Dakotas south to Kansas, Minnesota south to Missouri, western Kentucky, Tennessee, and northern Arkansas. Now largely limited to captive flocks in wildlife refuges. Hanson (1965) considers the geese that breed in southern Canada from Alberta to Manitoba to represent this race.

B. c. moffitti Aldrich: Great Basin (Moffitt) Canada Goose. Breeds in the Great Basin of North America between the Rocky Mountains and the eastern parts of the Pacific states, intergrading to the north with *parvipes* and to the east with *interior* and probably originally also with *maxima*.

B. c. parvipes (Cassin): Athabaska (Lesser) Canada Goose. An intermediate and ill-defined form that links the larger, southern subspecies with the small, northern and tundra-breeding populations. Breeds from central Alaska eastward across northern Canada and southern Victoria Island to western Melville Peninsula and eastern Keewatin southward to the northern parts of the Canadian Prairie Provinces, where it intergrades with *moffitti*.

B. c. taverneri Delacour: Alaska (Taverner) Canada Goose. Probably breeds through much of the interior of Alaska, some distance from the coast, from the base of Alaska Peninsula to the Mackenzie River delta, intergrading locally with *minima, occidentalis,* and probably also with *parvipes*. Not recognized by the A.O.U. (1957); apparently considered part of *minima* and *parvipes*.

B. c. fulva Delacour: Queen Charlotte (Vancouver) Canada Goose. Breeds along the coast and islands of British Columbia and southern Alaska, north to Glacier Bay, largely nonmigratory.

B. c. occidentalis (Baird): Dusky (Western) Canada Goose. Breeds along the Prince William Sound, Cook Inlet, and inland through the Cooper River drainage, east to Bering Glacier.

B. c. leucopareia (Brandt): Aleutian Canada Goose. Rare; limited to a few of the Aleutian Islands such as Buldir; recently (1970) released on Amchitka. The name *leucopareia* has also been applied earlier (e.g., Aldrich, 1946) to the populations here recognized as *parvipes* and *taverneri*.

B. c. asiatica Aldrich: Bering Canada Goose. Extinct; once bred on the Commander and the Kurile islands.

B. c. minima Ridgway: Cackling Canada Goose. Breeds along the coast of western Alaska from Nushagak Bay to the vicinity of Wainwright, where it probably intergrades with *taverneri*.

B. c. hutchinsii (Richardson): Baffin Island (Richardson) Canada Goose.

Breeds on the coast of the Melville Peninsula, Southampton Island, western Baffin Island, Ellesmere Island, and perhaps western Greenland. Intergrades with *parvipes* in Keewatin (MacInnes, 1966). Apparently extends west to Victoria Island (Parmelee *et al.,* 1967).

Measurements:

Because of the extreme size variation of different subspecies, average measurements are of little significance unless the subspecies is known. The extreme ranges for adults are wing length 330 mm. (*minima*) to 556 mm. (*maxima*), and culmen length 26 mm. (*minima*) to 68 mm. (*maxima*).

Weights: Like linear measurements, weights vary greatly according to age, sex, and subspecies. The following summaries provide an indication of this variability:

Cackling Canada Goose: 30 males averaged 4.4 pounds (1,005 grams), with a maximum of 5.6 pounds; 20 females averaged 3 pounds (1,360 grams), with a maximum of 5.1 pounds (Nelson and Martin, 1953).

Baffin Island ("Hutchins' ") Canada Goose: 31 males averaged 4.5 pounds (2,041 grams), with a maximum of 6.0 pounds; 37 females averaged 4.1 pounds (1,856 grams), with a maximum of 5.2 pounds (Nelson and Martin, 1953).

Alaska Canada Goose: 4 males averaged 4.95 pounds (2,241 grams), with a maximum of 5.07 pounds; 5 females (excluding one immature) averaged 4.54 pounds (2,059 grams), with a maximum of 4.96 pounds (Kessel and Cade, 1958).

Athabaska Canada Goose: 184 adult males averaged 6.10 pounds (2,766 grams), with a maximum of 7.87 pounds; 194 adult females averaged 5.45 pounds (2,471 grams), with a maximum of 7.25 pounds (Greib, 1970).

Dusky Canada Goose: 36 adult males averaged 8.28 pounds (3,754 grams), with a maximum of 9.83 pounds; 26 adult females averaged 6.9 pounds (3,131 grams), with a maximum of 8.82 pounds, in late November and early December (Chapman, 1970).

Atlantic ("Common") Canada Goose: 232 males averaged 8.4 pounds (3,809 grams), with a maximum of 13.8 pounds; 159 females averaged 7.3 pounds (3,310 grams), with a maximum of 13.0 pounds (Nelson and Martin, 1953).

Hudson Bay Canada Goose: 44 adult males averaged 9.28 pounds (4,212 grams), with a maximum of 10.4 pounds; 45 adult females averaged 8.3 pounds (3,856 grams), with a maximum of 8.5 pounds (Raveling, 1968b).

Great Basin Canada Goose: 10 adult males averaged 9.9 pounds (4,334 grams), and 9 females averaged 8.17 pounds (3,930 grams), with the maximum weight recorded for 190 geese being 15 pounds (Yocom, 1972).

Queen Charlotte ("Western") Canada Goose: 9 males averaged 10.2 pounds (4,625 grams), with a maximum of 13.8 pounds; 6 females averaged 7.8 pounds (3,537 grams), with a maximum of 9.5 pounds (Nelson and Martin, 1953).

Giant Canada Goose: 13 captive adult males averaged 14.39 pounds (6,523 grams), with a maximum of 16.5 pounds; 13 adult females averaged 12.16 pounds (5,514 grams), with a maximum of 14.19 pounds (Hanson, 1965).

IDENTIFICATION

In the Hand: Even in the juvenal plumage, the distinctive dark head and neck with the lighter cheeks and throat are evident. Because of this, the Canada goose could be confused only with the barnacle goose, from which the Canada can be distinguished by the absence of white feathers over the forehead connecting the white cheek patches. (Some large Canada geese may have a small white forehead patch that is discontinuous with the cheek markings.) Canada geese also lack the definite black and white tips on the upper wing coverts typical of barnacle geese.

In the Field: Even at great distance, Canada geese are usually readily recognized by their black heads and necks, brownish body and wings, and white hindpart coloration. This combination also applies to brant geese, but these small geese are limited to coastal waters and may be recognized by their short necks and ducklike size. The small races of Canada geese also have relatively short necks, with the neck length becoming progressively greater as the body size increases, so that the largest forms of Canada geese appear to be unusually long-necked. When in flight overhead the birds show uniformly dark under wing coverts of about the same color as the primaries and, except for their black necks, might be easily mistaken for white-fronted geese if the latter's dark abdominal spotting is not visible. The smaller races have high-pitched "cackling" calls sometimes sounding like *luk-luk,* while the larger forms have "honking" notes often sounding like *ah-onk'.*

AGE AND SEX CRITERIA

Sex Determination: Males average slightly heavier than females, but no consistent external plumage or soft-part differences appear to be present and usable for sex determination.

Age Determination: First-year Canada geese can be recognized by one or more of the following criteria: notched tail feathers, an open bursa of Fabricius averaging 27 mm. in depth (range 24-35 mm.), a pinkish red area of skin around the vent, and, in males, a penis that is pink, less than 10 mm. long, and not coiled or sheathed. Second-year birds have tail feathers lacking notches, a bursa of Fabricius that averages 20.5 mm. long (range 18-24 mm.), a pinkish red skin area around the vent, and, in males, a penis about 10 mm. long, and 4 mm. in diameter when unextended, and both coiled and sheathed. Older birds have tail feathers without notching, a bursa that is usually closed but may be open in about 40 percent of two-and-one-half-year-old geese, a naked skin area around the vent that is flesh red to purple, and, in males, a penis that is flaccid, dark red to purple, sheathed, and 50 to 100 percent larger than that of second-year birds. Females in their third year or older have open oviducts (Hanson, 1949). Higgins and Schoonover (1969) reported that Canada geese of the small arctic type can be aged with more than 90 percent accuracy by neck plumage characters. Adult geese of this type have their black neck markings sharply demarcated from the pale breast, whereas in immatures the colors gradually merge.

DISTRIBUTION AND HABITAT

Breeding Distribution and Habitat: Because of the extraordinarily great subspecific diversity in breeding habitats and the collective enormous breeding range of these races, no concise summary of distribution and habitat is possible for the Canada Goose. Virtually all of the nonmountainous portions of continental Canada and Alaska might be considered breeding range, as well as the Great Basin of the United States and, until recently, the northern prairies as well. Recent reintroduction of Canada geese into refuges and other managed areas throughout the northern states has blurred subspecific distinctions and has confused the picture as to original versus current or acquired breeding ranges.

Canada geese (*B. c. canadensis* and *B. c. interior*) using the Atlantic Flyway represent about 40 percent of the total population and breed through an extensive area in eastern Canada. This breeding area consists of two major habitat types, the forest-muskeg of the James Bay lowlands and the arctic tundra on the upper Ungava Peninsula, Cape Henrietta Maria, and on the Belcher Islands and other Hudson Bay islands (Addy and Heyland, 1968). Birds wintering in the Mississippi Flyway represent about 30 percent of the total population. They breed throughout a large area of central Canada and are largely represented by the Hudson Bay race *B. c. interior*. Their breeding

Breeding and wintering distributions of the Canada goose in North America. Approximate breeding distributions of subspecies are indicated.

habitats are generally similar to those just mentioned for Atlantic Flyway birds, and appear concentrated on the coastal strip of sedimentary deposits adjoining southern Hudson Bay (Hanson and Smith, 1950).

Canada geese using the Central Flyway consist of a complex of several breeding populations and subspecies. The larger forms include some Hudson Bay geese that breed to the west and southwest of Hudson Bay (Vaught and Kirsch, 1966), as well as some Great Basin Canada geese that breed on the prairies of western Canada and Montana. This population once included substantial numbers of giant Canada geese that bred in the tall prairies of the northern plains states, and restocking efforts have begun to develop new population nuclei in areas from Nebraska and Missouri to the Dakotas and Minnesota. Also using the Central Flyway are much smaller geese that include both the extremely small tundra-nesting Baffin Island race and the slightly larger Athabaska Canada goose, which also breeds from the arctic tundra southward through the boreal coniferous forests of Canada. MacInnes (1962) reported on the nesting habitat of tundra-nesting birds of this "tall grass prairie" population of Baffin Island Canada geese. Slightly to the west of this population, but also using the Central Flyway, is the "short grass prairie" population of small geese, which includes both the Athabaska and Baffin Island races of Canada geese that migrate through the high plains east of the Rockies. The breeding areas of this population include a broad and diffuse area of the Northwest Territories. The eastern segment of this population breeds primarily along the Arctic Ocean coast between longitudes 101° and 110° W., with a probable zone of interspersion with the tall grass population in the eastern region (Grieb, 1968). Birds breeding to the north along the coast of southeastern Victoria Island are typical *hutchinsii* and are likewise barren land breeders. The western segment, however, is composed predominantly of forest-breeding birds (presumably *parvipes*) that nest in the Mackenzie River drainage from 110° W. longitude west to the Yukon Territory and from about 58° N. latitude to the Arctic Ocean. Collection of an adult male *parvipes* from the north-central Brooks Range suggests that the western limit of this race may actually be in north-central Alaska (Campbell, 1969), although there is a good possibility that the birds seen and collected there were nonbreeders that had migrated there for molting. The remaining major contributor to the Central Flyway is the "highline" population of Great Basin Canada geese or intergrades between that race and the Hudson Bay race. Typical Great Basin geese breed on the prairie areas of southwestern Saskatchewan, southern Alberta, and eastern Montana, while birds of uncertain racial status breed from the area of Portage la Prairie, Manitoba, westward to eastern Alberta and northward possibly to tree line (Grieb, 1966).

The Pacific Flyway likewise is made up of several population complexes. Six subspecies occur typically in this flyway. The nearly extinct Aleutian Canada goose is limited to a few (Buldir and possibly Amchitka) of the treeless Aleutian Islands, and the similar cackling Canada goose breeds on coastal tundra along the mainland of Alaska. Away from the immediate coastal strip, and especially along such major rivers as the Yukon, Kuskokwim, Kobuk, and Colville, the Alaska Canada goose (or "lesser," according to Gabrielson and Lincoln, 1959) is the typical breeding bird. To the south, toward the Copper River, Prince William Sound, and Cook Inlet, it is replaced by a larger and darker form, the dusky Canada goose, which breeds along this moist coastline from Cook Inlet to Bering Glacier, with maximum abundance in the Copper River delta (Hansen, 1962). To the south, along Alaska's coastal panhandle and on the adjoining islands and mainland of British Columbia, the even larger and more sedentary Queen Charlotte Canada goose breeds in a comparable climate and similar vegetational habitats. It is isolated by about a 300-mile hiatus from the range of *occidentalis* and breeds from Cross Sound near Glacier Bay south to Dixon or possibly somewhat into British Columbia (Hansen, 1962). Finally, in the interior river valleys, reservoirs, and lakes of the Pacific Flyway states from the eastern slopes of the Cascades across the Rocky Mountains to Montana and south to California, Nevada, Utah, and Colorado, the Great Basin Canada goose breeds over a diffuse but extremely extensive area. Yocom (1965) has mapped its breeding range and estimated its 1951 breeding population as about 17,000 birds.

Wintering Distribution and Habitat: Wintering habitats vary less than breeding habitats, and it is not unusual to find representatives of three subspecies mixing on migration routes and on wintering areas. There is a general inverse relationship between the size of the bird and the distance between its breeding and wintering areas, with the smallest races (Baffin Island and cackling) migrating to the most southerly wintering areas, while the largest forms (Queen Charlotte Island, giant, and Great Basin) are often virtually nonmigratory and may winter on their breeding ranges.

Definitions of typical wintering habitats no doubt differ according to region, but one useful analysis is that of Stewart (1962), based on studies at Chesapeake Bay. The habitat there is optimal because of the presence of extensive agricultural areas adjacent to open, shallow expanses of fresh, slightly brackish, or brackish estuarine bays, providing food in grainfields as well as in the shallow estuaries and providing roosting sites in the bays. In estuarine marshes or salt marshes smaller numbers were typical, and there they fed in *Scirpus* or cordgrass (*Spartina*) communities and roosted on larger marsh ponds or impoundments as well as on adjacent estuaries or bays. In the interior United States, the increasing numbers of large reservoirs that remain ice-free all winter and are adjacent to grainfields have resulted in an increasingly delayed fall goose migration and progressively more northerly wintering areas in recent years, at least for the larger subspecies. This combination, then, of safe roosting sites and the availability of agricultural crops or other suitable foods would seem to be the prime requisites for wintering habitat. Documentation of such wintering population changes in the upper Mississippi Valley has been made by Reeves *et al.* (1968) for Illinois and Wisconsin birds. Apparently at least part of the stimulus for the development of goose overwintering at Horicon Refuge was the establishment of a resident flock and a reflooding of the marsh. Likewise, a simple combination of food and sanctuary was responsible for developing the famous flocks of geese at Horseshoe Lake, Illinois.

GENERAL BIOLOGY

Age at Maturity: There may be individual or racial variation on this point. Two-year-old females of the larger subspecies no doubt occasionally breed; Craighead and Stockstad (1964) found that between 27 and 36 percent of the wild female Great Basin Canada geese they studied bred at this age, as did all three-year olds. Brakhage (1965) indicated that a third of the two-year-old female giant Canada geese under observation nested, and Sherwood (1965) found that about three-fourth of such females produced eggs. Martin (1964) and Williams (1967) also reported breeding by two-year-old Great Basin Canadas. Evidently nearly all two-year-old male giant Canada geese are capable of breeding, and a very small portion of yearling males may attempt to breed (Brakhage, 1965). The small Canada geese breeding in the eastern arctic (*B. c. hutchinsii* in the broad sense) may exhibit incomplete nesting behavior and sometimes defend territories as two-year-olds. Williams (1967) reported that some captive Aleutian Canada geese nested and reared young at that age.

Pair Bond Pattern: Canada geese are monogamous and exhibit strong pair and family bonds. Separation from a mate, or its death, will result in the forming of a new pair bond, usually during the next breeding season (Hanson, 1965). Sherwood (1967) found that pairs can be developed in a few hours in older, experienced and "acquainted" geese, and these remained permanent as long as both remained alive. He found no polygamy, promiscuity, or pairing between broodmates. Pairing normally occurred on the nesting grounds, when the birds were two years old. Yearlings typically remained near their parents and rejoined them after the nesting season. Some yearlings formed temporary pairs, and broodmates retained their family bonds well into their second year.

Nest Location: Nest locations vary greatly according to topography and vegetation. The same nest site may be used for several years (Martin, 1964). Hanson (1965) stressed the importance of muskrat houses as nest sites for marsh-nesting giant Canada geese, while in Manitoba common reed (*Phragmites*) is preferred over prairie grasses for nest construction (Klopman, 1958). Hardstem bulrush (*Scirpus acutus*) is a highly favored nesting site in the western states (Williams, 1967). MacInnes (1962) reported that tundra-nesting birds strongly favored small islands surrounded by open water, with fairly hard, dry tops. Williams concluded that several factors contribute to favorable nest locations. These include good visibility, a firm and fairly dry nest foundation, a close proximity to water, adequate isolation, and nearness to suitable feeding grounds and brooding habitat. Dimmick (1968) noted that 72 percent of 145 Great Basin Canada goose nests he studied were on islands, apparently the nesting site safest from predators. The highest nest density occurred near feeding areas, and 74.5 percent of the nests had excellent or good visibility. Sand was preferred over cobblestone for a nest substrate, and nests built over mud were elevated to keep the bottoms dry. The average distance to water was 45.7 feet, and shrubs or driftwood provided cover for the majority of the nests.

Clutch Size: In the case of the larger races of Canada geese, the clutch size is fairly consistently centered around 5 eggs, with averages of various studies (Williams, 1967) ranging from 4.6 to 5.7. Weller (in Delacour, 1964) could find no correlation between clutch size and geographic location among nineteen studies of larger Canada geese. Fewer data are available on the arctic-nesting races. MacInnes (1962) reported an average complete clutch size of 5.1 to 5.4 eggs for *hutchinsii,* and Gillham (cited in Spencer *et al.,* 1951) reported an average clutch of 4.7 eggs for *minima.* The rate of egg-laying is slightly more than one day per egg in both the small races (MacInnes, 1962) and the larger forms (Williams, 1967).

Incubation Period: Unlike clutch size, incubation periods do apparently vary geographically. The largest forms of Canada geese require from 26 to 28.6 days (Hanson, 1965) for incubation, averaging 28 days (Williams, 1967). This compares with 25 to 28 days for the Hudson Bay Canada goose (Kossack, 1950) and 24 to 25 days for the east arctic *hutchinsii* (MacInnes, 1962). Further, although the more southerly-breeding races often attempt renesting (Atwater, 1959) if their first effort is broken up, MacInnes (1962) found no indications of renesting in his arctic study area.

Fledging Period: Like incubation periods, racial variations exist in fledging periods in relation to body size and length of the growing season. Hanson (1965) reviewed this relationship and noted that although the giant Canada goose requires from 64 to 86 days to attain flight, the cackling Canada goose has a fledging period of only 42 days. The estimated period for the Hudson Bay Canada goose was 65 days.

Nest and Egg Losses: Weller (in Delacour, 1964) has summarized published data on nesting success in the larger Canada geese. The average of nine studies was a 67 percent hatch of total nests studied, with a range of 24 to 80 percent. Hanson (1965) likewise reported an average nesting success rate of 58.6 percent based on nine studies of birds he considered to represent the giant Canada goose and a 71.1 percent average nesting success for eight studies of the Great Basin Canada goose. MacInnes (1962) reported a high nesting success rate (75 to 90 percent) for *hutchinsii* during two years of study, although it is typical of arctic-nesting waterfowl to exhibit great yearly fluctuations in productivity as an apparent result of annual weather variations.

Juvenile Mortality: Estimates of juvenile mortality based on brood size counts are not completely reliable, since brood mergers do occur. Hanson (1965) estimated an average brood size at the time of hatching, on the basis of all available data, as 4.2 young for the giant Canada goose and 4.1 for the Great Basin Canada goose. MacInnes (1962) reported that various studies indicated an 82 to 97 percent brood survival under wild conditions for the Great Basin Canada goose, and his studies on *hutchinsii* indicated an 85 to 90 percent brood survival during two years of study.

Following fledging, juvenile birds are subjected to considerably higher mortality than are adults, at least in part as a result of inexperience. MacInnes (1963) reported an annual mortality of 75 percent for juveniles as compared to 25 percent for adults in the tallgrass prairie flock, and Martin (1964) noted a 47 to 64 percent mortality rate in first-year birds compared to a 35 to 45 percent rate in adults. Vaught and Kirsch (1966) estimated a 35 to 50 percent mortality rate of immature Canada geese in the Swan Lake, Missouri, flock. Likewise, Hansen (1962) estimated a 56.9 percent annual juvenile mortality rate for the dusky Canada goose, compared with a rate of 28.9 percent for adults.

Adult Mortality: Grieb (1970) has summarized reported mortality rates for various populations of Canada geese and calculated a 38.9 percent adult mortality rate for the shortgrass prairie population (mainly Athabaska Canada geese). Annual adult mortality estimates include lows of 25 percent in adults of the tallgrass prairie flock and about 25 to 30 percent for adults in the Swan Lake flock, both of which consist predominantly of the Hudson Bay Canada goose (Vaught and Kirsch, 1966). Higher estimates of a 35 to

45 percent adult mortality rate have been made for the Great Basin Canada goose, while Hanson and Smith (1950) estimated an all-age annual mortality rate of 52 percent for the Horseshoe Lake flock. The data of Martin (1964), Williams (1967), and Hansen (1962) suggest adult mortality rates of about 30 to 40 percent for Canada geese in the western United States.

GENERAL ECOLOGY

Food and Foraging: Most studies of food habits of Canada geese are of wintering or migrating birds and may not be typical of breeding birds. Martin *et al.* (1951) summarized data from a variety of areas, indicating that the vegetative parts, particularly the rootstalks, of many marsh plants are consumed. Important plants include cordgrass (*Spartina*), salt grass (*Distichlis*), sago pondweed (*Potamogeton pectinatus*), wigeon grass (*Ruppia*), hardstem bulrush (*Scirpus acutus*), glasswort (*Salicornia*), and spike rush (*Eleocharis*). In a study of foods found in 263 gizzards and 31 crops from Lake Mattamuskeet, North Carolina, Yelverton and Quay (1959) found that sedges (mainly *Eleocharis* species and *Scirpus acutus*) made up 63 percent of the food volume, while grasses constituted nearly all the remainder, with corn grains being most important. Likewise, Stewart (1962) found that waste corn was the food of primary importance for Chesapeake Bay geese wherever it was readily available, while sprout growth of various grain crops was also consumed, together with the vegetative parts of various submerged plants. In large estuarine bay marshes and coastal salt marshes, the stems and rootstalks of such emergent plants as three-square (*Scirpus americanus* and *S. olneyi*) and cordgrass are taken in large quantities.

Sociality, Densities, Territoriality: Many recent studies, such as that of Raveling (1969a), have clearly established the fact that the basic social unit in Canada geese is the family. Raveling determined that it (adults and first-year young) remained intact all winter and always reassembled if separated. When captured and released together, initial separation occurred, but in no more than seven and one-half days the family was again intact. Rejoining of such families by yearling offspring of the past season was apparently fairly common. Although such yearlings sometimes formed temporary pair bonds during their second summer of life, these usually broke down, and either the birds returned to their parents, or the yearling siblings remained together through the fall and winter. In some cases, permanent pairing occurred in late winter or early spring between birds that had formed temporary pair bonds as yearlings. With the assumption of a permanent pair bond, the family bond is finally broken, and the potential depends both on specific preferences on the part of both sexes and on relative male dominance in the vicinity of the female, as indicated by Collias and Jahn (1959). These authors believed that sexual behavior such as copulation facilitated pair formation, and they also established that a bird could recognize the voice of its mate even when unable to see it. Pair and family bonds are maintained and strengthened by repeated use of the triumph ceremony (Raveling, 1969a).

Estimates of breeding densities are available from various areas and apparently vary greatly. MacInnes and Lieff (1968) found marked differences in nest density of *hutchinsii* in adjacent kilometer square plots during the same year, as well as considerable differences in density of the same plots in two consecutive years. The highest density they reported for the two years was 13 nests in a square kilometer plot. Earlier (1962) MacInnes reported that optimum breeding habitat at McConnell River supported up to 6 nests per square mile. In his 55-square-kilometer study area (21.2 square miles) he reported 129 nests in 1966 and 99 in 1967, or an average density of 4.7 nests per square mile. Hansen (1962) reported some remarkable nesting densities of the dusky Canada goose in the Copper River delta. In 1954 there was an overall average density of 6.4 successful nests (8.0 calculated total nests) per square mile on an 88-square-mile area, while in 1959 one small (2.08-square-mile) nesting area had an average density of 108 nests per square mile. This area of high density nesting was limited to 12 square miles of river delta adjacent to the coast. Perhaps the finest goose nesting ground in all of North America occurs over an 800-square-mile area from Igiak Bay to about the southern tip of Nelson Island, Alaska, where goose breeding populations average 130 birds per square mile. In 1950 about 60 percent of these were cackling Canada geese, or an estimated 78 birds per square mile (Spencer *et al.,* 1951). In 1951 three study plots totalling two square miles in area had an average density of 153 nests per square mile, of which about 40 percent were of cackling Canada geese (Hansen, 1961), or roughly 60 nests per square mile.

Some examples of extreme nest site proximity have been reported for the larger and more southerly breeding forms, as summarized by Williams (1967). He noted a case of 11 goose nests on a single haystack in Oregon and 31 nests on an island about one-half acre in size in California. Hansen (1965) also noted several other cases in which nest density ranged from 10 to 66 per acre. It would thus seem that basic territorial tendencies of Canada geese probably do not limit breeding densities or influence nesting distribution as much as do physical factors such as availability and distribution of suitable nesting sites.

Interspecific Relationships: Little has been specifically noted as to relationships with other species and possible competition for food or nesting sites. In some areas the birds breed in close association with black brant (Spencer *et al.,* 1951), while in other areas of eastern Canada they are found in association with snow geese. Some studies suggest that losses to predators of eggs and young are low compared to those resulting from flooding (Hansen, 1961), chilling, or other weather-related losses. Predators that have been responsible for high nesting losses include the coyote, red fox, striped skunk, raven, crow, magpie, and various gulls (Hanson, 1965). Of these, probably only the mammals are effective predators once the goslings have left the nest.

General Activity Patterns and Movements: Some studies on variations in activities according to time of day have been performed. Collias and Jahn (1959) noted that during the pre-egg stages, territorial activity is greatest early in the morning, as was also true of copulation frequency. All of the observed copulations were seen between twenty days prior to the laying of the first egg and the initiation of incubation.

Canada geese typically fly out to forage in early morning and late afternoon in areas where they cannot forage in roosting sites. Prior to taking flight, preflight intention movements, which consist of simultaneously lifting and shaking the head, are usually performed. Raveling (1969b) analyzed the occurrence of this signal and found it tended to be given least and for the shortest time by single birds. The number of signals and the length of time from the first signal to takeoff were found to increase progressively for pairs and families of three and four birds, while families of five exhibited a counter-trend. Raveling noted that, whereas a gander did not always respond to head-tossing by members of his family, they always responded almost immediately to his head-tossing. The importance of this signal in synchronizing and coordinating family activities is thus clearly apparent. Changes in vocalizations and the appearance of the distinctive upper tail covert pattern appear to be the major releasers for actual flight in these as in nearly all other geese.

A fairly complete survey of the general behavior patterns of Canada geese has been presented by Balham (1954).

SOCIAL AND SEXUAL BEHAVIOR

Flocking Behavior: Probably the first suggestion of the importance of the family in the formation of larger flocks of geese was that of Phillips (1916), whose conclusions have been fully confirmed by later investigators such as Raveling (1969a) and Sherwood (1965). Raveling (1968a) compared flock substructure at the time of takeoff, while in steady flight, and at the time of landing, and concluded that only at the time of landing, when families almost invariably appeared together, did flock subunits clearly reflect actual family units.

Pair-forming Behavior: As has been noted above, permanent pair formation typically occurs in two-year-old birds, probably in late winter or early spring. Mutual association of two birds and their coordinated performance of the triumph ceremony after aggressive encounters provide the basic means of establishing a pair bond. Collias and Jahn (1959) described this process and noted that weather played a role in the intensity of pair-forming behavior, with cold weather tending to separate incipient pairs. After the selection of a nest site and associated establishment of a nesting territory, young of the past year are driven away from the parents and the female and her nest site are defended from all intruders. The importance of male protection was illustrated by one pair in which the male died during the incubation period and the female failed to hatch her young as a result of domination and disturbance from other pairs and unmated males.

Copulatory Behavior: Copulation in Canada geese is preceded by mutual head-dipping movements resembling bathing. It is usually initiated by the male, but the female soon participates and usually continues to neck-dip until the male prepares to mount her (Klopman, 1962). Postcopulatory display is mutual and usually consists of raising the breast upward, extending the neck and pointing the bill vertically upward, and partially extending the wings away from the body. Calls may be uttered by either or both birds.

Nesting and Brooding Behavior: Nest-building is normally done by the female almost exclusively, although the male may very rarely participate to a limited extent (Collias and Jahn, 1959). In one instance noted by Collias and Jahn a female built an entirely new nest from available materials in about four hours, and 45 minutes later had deposited her first egg in it. Down is usually added only after the first few eggs have been laid, and later on some contour feathers may also be placed in the nest. To a limited extent nest-building behavior may continue throughout the incubation period, which prevents the nest from becoming flattened down. While incubating, the female usually leaves the nest only two or three times a day, to rest, forage, drink, bathe, and preen, and usually is gone for less than an hour at a time. The process of hatching requires about a day, and the young remain in the nest the first night. Females typically leave the nest with their brood the day after hatching, but may bring them back to the nest for the next several nights for brooding (Collias and Jahn, 1959). Adoption of strange goslings is most likely to occur before they are a week old and if they and the parents' brood are of about the same age, after which the adults are likely to attack strange goslings.

Postbreeding Behavior: According to Hanson (1965), females normally precede their mates in the postnuptial wing molt by a week to ten days, when the young are between thirty and fifty days old. Apparently about thirty-two days are required for Hudson Bay Canada geese to regain flight, while thirty-nine days were required for a single adult male giant Canada goose studied by Hanson. Nonbreeding Canada geese may perform substantial migrations to areas where they undergo their molt, particularly to the barren grounds of the Thelon River delta, Northwest Territories, where many large Canada geese may be seen in late summer (Sterling and Dzubin, 1967). Other subspecies probably undergo molt migrations as well. The dusky Canada goose may move to the western side of Cook Inlet, while the Queen Charlotte molts along Glacier Bay. The Alaska Canada goose perhaps molts along the arctic coast of Alaska, the Athabaska Canada goose between the Mackenzie and Anderson rivers in the Northwest Territories, and the Ungava Peninsula may be a molting area for Canada geese of the Atlantic Flyway (Sterling and Dzubin, 1967).

BARNACLE GOOSE

Branta leucopsis (Bechstein) 1803

Other Vernacular Names: None in general use.

Range: Breeds in northeastern Greenland, Spitzbergen, and southern Novaya Zemlya. Winters in Ireland, Great Britain, and northern Europe, with only rare occurrences in eastern North America.

Subspecies: None recognized.

Measurements (after Delacour, 1954):

Folded wing: Both sexes 385-420 mm.

Culmen: Both sexes 27-32 mm.

Weights: Boyd (1964) reported that twenty adult males captured in February averaged 4⅛ pounds (1,870 grams), with a maximum of 4⅝ pounds; fifteen adult females averaged 3¾ pounds (1,690 grams), with a maximum of 4⅛ pounds.

IDENTIFICATION

In the Hand: This small, dark-breasted goose may be identified by its white cheeks and forehead, its black breast, and the grayish upper wing coverts that are distinctively tipped with black and white.

In the Field: Only an occasional visitor to North America, the barnacle goose nevertheless has appeared in a surprising number of localities, mainly along the eastern coast. It is slightly larger than a brant and differs from it in having a predominantly white head and a light gray rather than dark grayish brown upper wing coloration. The underwing coloration is likewise light silvery gray and much lighter than that of the brant. The extension of the black neck color over the breast will readily separate the barnacle goose from the Canada goose, even at a great distance, and the contrast between the dark and light parts of the body is much greater as well. Its call is a barking, often repeated *gnuk;* a flock sounds something like a pack of small dogs.

AGE AND SEX CRITERIA

Sex Determination: No plumage characters are available for external sex determination.

Age Determination: The presence of gray flecking on the head and a somewhat grayish rather than entirely black neck will serve to identify first-year birds. The black and white markings on the upper surface of the wings are also less well developed in first-year birds, so that the upper wing surface appears somewhat duller and darker. The usual age of attaining sexual maturity is still not definitely established for this species, but Ferguson (1966) indicated that sixteen of twenty aviculturalists reported it as the third year, three reported it as the second year, and one as the fourth year.

OCCURRENCE IN NORTH AMERICA

Even prior to 1900 it was recognized that barnacle geese occasionally visit the eastern states. Bent (1925) summarized these early records, which were mostly for October and November and extended from Vermont through Massachusetts, Long Island, and North Carolina. Godfrey (1966) likewise summarized early and more recent records for Canada, which included specimens from Baffin Island and Quebec and sight records for Labrador and Ontario. A sight record for Nova Scotia has also been recently obtained (*Audubon Field Notes,* 24:617).

In recent years, numerous sight or specimen records of barnacle geese have been obtained in the United States. These include Atlantic coast records from New York (*Audubon Field Notes,* 21:504; 22:436), Delaware (*ibid,* 20:23; 22:19), Maryland (*ibid,* 16:67; 19:365), Connecticut (*ibid,* 22:161), and North Carolina (*ibid,* 5:95; *American Birds,* 25:563). There are also a few more interior records from Ohio (Borror, 1950), Tennessee (*Audubon Field Notes,* 24:512), Nebraska (*Nebraska Bird Review,* 37:2-3), Oklahoma (*Audubon Field Notes,* 24:617), Texas (*ibid,* 23:496; *American Birds,* 25:600), and Alabama (*Audubon Field Notes,* 24:289;

American Birds, 25:589). The only Pacific coast record would seem to be one for the Skagit Flats, Washington (*Audubon Field Notes,* 16:67). Although it is quite possible that some of these may represent escapes from captivity, there is no doubt that many of them represent wild birds that presumably originated in Greenland.

BRANT GOOSE

Branta bernicla (Linnaeus) 1758

Other Vernacular Names: American Brant, Black Brant, Brent.

Range: Circumpolar, breeding along arctic coastlines of North America and Eurasia, as well as on Greenland, Iceland, and other arctic islands. Winters on coastal areas, in North America south to northwestern Mexico and North Carolina.

North American Subspecies:

B. b. hrota (Müller): Atlantic Brant Goose. In North America, breeds on northern and western Greenland and on the mainland coast and islands of northern Canada west to about 100° W. longitude.

B. b. nigricans (Lawrence): Pacific (Black) Brant Goose. In North America, breeds in northern Canada from the Perry River and adjacent islands westward to coastal Alaska. Considered by Delacour (1954) to represent *B. b. orientalis* (Tougarinov), with *nigricans* restricted to the questionably valid "Lawrence brant goose," which is not recognized by the A.O.U. (1957). The proper application of *nigricans* to any population of brant is still questionable (Manning *et al.,* 1956; Williamson *et al.,* 1966)

Measurements (both races):

Folded wing: Both sexes 310-351 mm.

Culmen: Both sexes 29-38 mm.

Weights:

Atlantic ("American") Brant: 19 males averaged 3.4 pounds (1,542 grams), with a maximum of 4.0 pounds; 14 females averaged 2.8 pounds (1,270 grams), with a maximum of 3.9 pounds (Nelson and Martin, 1953).

Pacific ("Black") Brant: 26 males averaged 3.4 pounds (1,542 grams), with a maximum of 4.9 pounds; 15 females averaged 3.1 pounds (1,406 grams), with a maximum of 3.6 pounds (Nelson and Martin, 1953). Hansen and Nelson (1957) reported that 189 males averaged 3.19 pounds (1,447 grams), with a maximum of 4 pounds; 181 females averaged 2.87 pounds (1,302 grams), with a maximum of 3.81 pounds.

IDENTIFICATION

In the Hand: The tiny size (under 4 pounds, or 2,000 grams) will separate this species from all others except the smallest races of Canada geese, which have white on their cheeks instead of on the upper neck. Also, the central tail feathers of Canada geese extend beyond the tip of the tail coverts, which is not true of the brant goose.

In the Field: In their coastal habitat, brant are usually seen in small flocks on salt water some distance from shore, their white hindquarters higher out of the water than is typical of ducks. The head, neck, and breast of this bird appear black, the sides grayish to whitish. When in flight, the birds appear short-necked, and the white hindquarters contrast strongly with the black foreparts, while both the upper and lower wing surfaces appear grayish brown. The birds usually fly in undulating or irregular lines, rather than in V-formations like Canada geese, and have surprisingly soft and gutteral notes, *r-r-r-ruk* or *ruk-ruk*.

AGE AND SEX CRITERIA

Sex Determination: No plumage differences are available for external sex determination.

Age Determination: Yearling brant have conspicuous white edgings on their upper wing coverts, which allow for easy recognition of this age-class. At least one or more white-tipped secondary coverts will also identify yearling birds during their summer flightless period, according to Harris and Shepherd (1965), who also reported that at least some females apparently breed at two years of age. Yearling males have penile development ranging from the typical small and unsheathed juvenile condition to the full adult condition, while all older age classes of males have a fully adult penis condition.

DISTRIBUTION AND HABITAT

Breeding Distribution and Habitat: In Alaska, the Pacific brant breeds abundantly from the Kuskokwim Delta and Nelson Island northward along the coastline to the Yukon Delta and in smaller numbers northward and eastward to the Yukon border (Gabrielson and Lincoln, 1959). It also breeds uncommonly on St. Lawrence Island (Fay, 1960). In Canada it extends from the Alaskan border eastward to Perry River and north to Prince Patrick Island and probably Ellef Ringnes Island (Snyder, 1957). From Perry River and Prince Patrick Island eastward it is replaced by the Atlantic brant, which breeds north to Ellesmere Island, on Somerset Island, and on the mainland along Queen Maud Gulf, Cape Fullerton, Southampton and Coats islands, and southern Baffin Island (Snyder, 1957). The breeding locality and taxonomic validity of the Lawrence brant goose is unknown, which makes the suitable application of the trivial name *nigricans* uncertain.

The typical breeding habitat of brant geese is lowland coastal tundra, usually just above high tide line, which makes the nesting grounds highly susceptible to flooding by storm tides. Low islands of tundra lakes and dry inland slopes well covered with vegetation are used to some extent as well. In the Yukon-Kuskokwim Delta, the heart of the Pacific brant nesting habitat, nesting occurs on low, grass-covered flats dissected by numerous tidal streams in a belt two or three miles wide (Spencer *et al.,* 1951). In this area the brant prefer the short sedge cover, with the highest nest density (up to 144 per square mile reported) found three to five miles from the coast (Hansen and Nelson, 1957). However, at Prince Patrick Island, at the northern edge of the range, the brant nest on grassy mountain slopes up to three miles inland and usually at least a mile from the coast. Nest densities there are much lower, with a dozen pairs scattered over several square miles, and the nests are several hundred yards apart (Handley, 1950).

Wintering Distribution and Habitat: According to midwinter survey averages, slightly more than half of the brant population winter on the Atlantic coast, while the remainder occur on the Pacific coast from British Columbia to Mexico.

On the West Coast, the preferred wintering habitat of Pacific brant consists of large areas of shallow marine water covered with eelgrass (*Zostera marina*), usually to be found in bay situations. In 1952, a total wintering population inventory revealed about 175,000 birds, 63 percent of which occurred in Baja California, mostly in Scammon Lagoon and San Ignacio Bay (Leopold and Smith, 1953). California also accounted for 25 percent (mostly in Humboldt Bay, Morro Bay, and bays in Marin County), Washington

Breeding and wintering distributions of the brant goose in North America. Horizontal hatching indicates breeding range of Pacific brant, vertical hatching that of Atlantic brant, and diagonal hatching apparent area of intergradation.

supported 9 percent (mostly in Puget Sound), and the remaining 3 percent were distributed along the coasts of Oregon, British Columbia, and southeastern Alaska. Smith and Jensen (1970) have also reported on Mexico's wintering brant population and documented a recent major shift from traditional wintering areas to coastal Sonora and Sinaloa, where over 35,000 birds wintered in 1969.

On the Atlantic coast, shallow expanses of salt water on coastal bays also are prime habitat, with the birds in the Chesapeake Bay area being most abundant along the barrier-beach side of the bays, concentrated wherever sea lettuce (*Ulva lactuca*) is abundant. Along the eastern Chesapeake, they concentrate in Tangier Sound and adjoining estuaries, especially where eelgrass and wigeon grass (*Ruppia*) are commonly found, and sometimes also occur in shallow areas of brackish water. The Chesapeake Bay flock represents about 5 percent of the Atlantic population, which is almost entirely restricted to the coastal area from Massachusetts to North Carolina (Stewart, 1962). Brant sometimes occur during migration on the lower Great Lakes (Sheppard, 1949), but generally are restricted as wintering birds to saltwater habitats.

GENERAL BIOLOGY

Age at Maturity: Harris and Shepherd (1965) reported that six of nineteen Pacific brant that they examined had evidently nested as two-year-olds, but that no yearlings showed any signs indicating breeding. Barry (1967) estimated that possibly 10 percent of the two-year-olds may breed during favorable nesting seasons.

Pair Bond Pattern: Presumably the usual strongly monogamous pair bond pattern typical of all geese applies to brant as well; at least no observations of wild or captive birds contradict this view. Einarsen (1965) noted that when Atlantic brant pairs occur on the Pacific coast, the pairs are generally inseparable, and he suggested that the reason for the lack of interbreeding on Prince Patrick Island, where both forms occur together, is that strong pair bonds have been formed prior to arrival at the breeding grounds and thus mixed pairing is rarely if ever developed.

Nest Location: As noted earlier, nests are usually located in low herbaceous vegetation often close to the high tide line, but sometimes in upland situations. Barry (1956) mentioned that the majority of the nests he observed in a colony on Southampton Island were on small river delta islands covered with low, thick grass and were less than a mile from the coast. Later (1962) he stated that preferred nesting habitat is covered with sedge mat vegetation extending only about one-quarter mile inland from the normal high tide line and that over 90 percent of the brant nested in this zone. Einarsen (1965) stated that small islands only a few square feet in area or a small promontory extending out into a pond or lake are often selected. The nests are usually bowl-shaped, and thus a sitting goose is able to flatten out on the nest so as to be barely visible above ground level.

Clutch Size: Barry (1956) reported that clutch sizes in a colony containing 203 Atlantic brant nests varied in different areas from 3.77 to 4.41, with an overall average of 4.0 and an observed range of 1 to 7 eggs. Hansen and Nelson (1957) reported that 116 Pacific brant nests had an average clutch of 3.5 eggs, and Gillham (cited by Einarsen, 1965) noted that in 1939 a sample of 83 Pacific brant nests averaged 4.96 eggs per clutch, while in 1940 a total of 108 nests averaged 3.8 eggs per clutch. This reduction in clutch size was evidently related to a severe freeze occurring about eight days after migration had terminated. Barry (1962) found a strong relationship between weather and clutch size. In the favorable 1953 season he found an average clutch of 4.6 eggs in 13 completed nests that had not yet suffered any egg losses. In two seasons that were retarded by cold weather, not only were the average clutch sizes smaller (4.3 for 109 completed clutches and 3.9 for 33 completed clutches), but also the nests that were started late had smaller clutches than the earliest ones. The collective average clutch size for 853 nests was 3.94 eggs. The eggs are generally laid at the rate of one per day, but frequently a day may be skipped toward the end of the egg-laying period (Barry, 1956). At least one case of attempted renesting following freezing weather has been reported (Gillham, in Einarsen, 1965). Barry (1962) also mentioned that a few cases of attempted renesting occurred in the colony he studied, but the clutches were not successfully completed.

Incubation Period: Barry (1956) reported the incubation period to be 24 days for ten of twelve nests, with one case each of 23- and 25-day periods. Einarsen estimated a 25 to 28 day incubation period, but provided no basis for this.

Fledging Period: Barry (1962) indicated that from 45 to 50 days are required for young Atlantic brant to attain flight. Einarsen (1965) estimated seven weeks for the Pacific brant.

Nest and Egg Losses: Because of the vulnerability of brant nests to flooding, nest and egg losses are likely to be high in some years or in certain locations. Barry (1962) noted that predation and other losses took 27 percent of 723 eggs in marked nests during three years of study. During three years in the Kashunuk study area of Alaska, the hatching success of Pacific brant nests ranged from 81 to 85 percent (United States Fish and Wildlife

Service, Special Scientific Report: Wildlife, No. 68). Specific data on possible flooding effects are not available, but Einarsen (1965) mentioned that the Yukon-Kuskokwim Delta had severe floods and storms in 1952 and 1963, with resultant high nest and brood losses. The 1963 storm, associated with high tides, flooded nearly the entire brant nesting zone in the Clarence Rhode National Wildlife Range, destroying thousands of eggs and young brant. However, Jones (1964) found that the percentage of immature brant seen during fall counts in Izembek Bay was sufficiently high (23 percent) to indicate that production in other areas was adequate to offset this localized complete loss. Burton (1960) concluded from age-ratio counts of brant geese in Europe that the 1958 breeding season in the Soviet arctic was associated with abnormally low temperatures during the summer months and must have been nearly a complete failure.

More recent counts by Jones (1970) indicate that the annual average incidence of juveniles in fall brant populations ranged from 18 to 40 percent between 1963 and 1969. Family groups contained averages of 2.58 to 2.86 juveniles. The percentage on apparent nonbreeders ranged from 31 to 69 percent over a four-year period, averaging 56 percent. During these years the percentage of juveniles averaged 25 percent, thus apparently a nonbreeding or unsuccessfully breeding segment of about 50 percent of adult-plumaged birds is typical even during years of good reproduction.

Juvenile Mortality: Studies in Alaska (United States Fish and Wildlife Service, Special Scientific Report: Wildlife, No. 68) indicate that the average brood size of the first-week young ranged from 3.4 to 3.8 birds in three different years. By the age of three weeks, the average brood size had been reduced to 2.2 to 3.2 birds. Finally, counts of juveniles in fall flocks at Izembek Bay suggest average family sizes of 2.58 to 2.86 juveniles per successful pair (Jones, 1970). Ignoring pairs that completely lost their eggs or young, it is evident that about half of the hatched young are lost before reaching the wintering grounds. These first-year birds are more vulnerable than adults to various kinds of mortality; Hansen and Nelson (1957) estimated an average annual mortality rate of 45.4 percent for juveniles based on direct recoveries of birds banded in Alaska.

Adult Mortality: Hansen and Nelson (1957) estimated an adult annual mortality rate of 21.8 percent on the basis of direct recoveries of birds banded as adults. If indirect recoveries through the sixth year are added, the estimated annual adult mortality rate is 32.2 percent. Boyd (1962) recalculated these figures and concluded that a mean adult mortality rate of 15 percent was typical of this population, compared to a 14 percent rate of brant wintering in Britain and 17 percent for birds breeding on Spitzbergen.

GENERAL ECOLOGY

Food and Foraging: The close relationship between the distribution and abundance of eelgrass (*Zostera marina*) and the brant goose has long been recognized (Cottam *et al.,* 1944). Second in importance to eelgrass, and used by brant when eelgrass is absent or depleted by disease, is sea lettuce (*Ulva* spp., especially *U. lactuca*). In some areas wigeon grass (*Ruppia*) is used to a limited extent by Atlantic brant (Martin *et al.,* 1951). However, eelgrass is clearly the preferred food of both the Atlantic and the Pacific populations, and the most extensive eelgrass beds in the world occur in Izembek Bay, Alaska, which during the fall temporarily supports the entire Pacific coast brant population (Jones, 1964; Jones and Jones, 1966). Here, about a quarter million birds feed on about 40,260 acres of eelgrass lying just below the water surface or exposed during low tide. The leaves of the eelgrass form dense mats often arranged in windrows, along which the brant swim while feeding. The protein content of the eelgrass in this bay averages about 7 percent, while samples of eelgrass and sea lettuce from Washington and Oregon average about 15 percent (Einarsen, 1965).

Sociality, Densities, Territoriality: As might be expected in a species that nests in a colonial fashion, brant geese are relatively social and gregarious. Jones and Jones (1966) reported seeing little strife in flocks consisting of two or three family groups, but hostile encounters were common in larger fall flocks. These generally were initially related to maintaining the integrity of family groups. However, by early October hostile encounters between adults and juveniles indicated that the family bonds were being broken. This dissolution of family bonds was completed by late October, after which hostile encounters were again rarely seen, and the population consisted of a few very large groups containing all age groups. Thus, unlike most geese, family bonds are evidently not maintained through the first winter of life. Einarsen (1965) has also emphasized the gregariousness of brant geese, noting their strong tendency to "raft" and to breed in colonies.

Estimates of breeding densities have been made by Hansen and Nelson (1957), who noted that in the best nesting areas on the Yukon-Kuskokwim Delta nest densities of up to 144 per square mile occur in the short sedge zone some three to five miles from the coast. Barry (1956) reported a colony of about 700 nesting pairs in a stretch of coast about four and one-half miles long and usually less than one-quarter mile wide, or a little more than a square mile in area. Nesting density within this area varied considerably, with the highest density on the islands of the Boas River delta. The distribution of these islands, about a foot above high tide, evidently strongly affected the breeding density. Thus, territoriality probably plays only a minor or negligible role in affecting brant nesting densities. Territories were maintained by bluffing rather than fighting, according to Berry, but sometimes birds would be chased off a nesting territory and "escorted" away for some distance.

Interspecific Relationships: Barry (1956) noted that the brant colony he studied was entirely separated from the colony of blue and snow geese, which nested on higher ground at least one-fourth mile inland from the high tide line. In Alaska, the Pacific brant nests in association with cackling Canada geese on the Yukon-Kuskokwim delta, but again nesting occurs slightly closer to the coast (Spencer *et al.,* 1951). Major avian predators of eggs are gulls and jaegers, especially the parasitic jaeger, but the arctic fox often causes heavy destruction to nesting colonies and probably is primarily responsible for the brant's tendency to select coastal or delta islands for its nesting sites (Barry, 1967).

General Activity Patterns and Movements: Einarsen (1965) has commented on the brant's unusual flying ability, noting that he had clocked flying brant at a ground speed of 62 miles per hour, compared with 36 to 40 miles per hour for Canada geese. He also noted their relatively faster wingbeats (three to four per second) and more streamlined body and wing. When facing a head wind, the birds almost skim the wave tops, but even without strong head winds the birds do not fly high. Flocks usually are in long strings, undulating somewhat in flight, in marked contrast to the more highly organized flight formations of the larger geese. According to Einarsen, brant rarely reach a height of more than two or three hundred feet above the ocean and certainly rarely stray far from salt water. Lewis (1937) has, however, described the probable migration route across western Quebec between Hudson Bay and the brants' wintering grounds on the Atlantic coast. The distance from the Gulf of St. Lawrence to James Bay or Ungava Bay is nearly 600 miles, apparently made in a nonstop flight at considerable height during the nighttime hours. Birds arriving at the mouth of the St. Lawrence in late spring are typically in small flocks, with 155 such flocks averaging about 40 birds and rarely exceeding 100 birds (Lewis, 1937). However, when the brant arrive at the nesting grounds on Southampton Island the flocks seldom exceed 20, and the birds are mostly paired (Barry, 1956).

SOCIAL AND SEXUAL BEHAVIOR

Flocking Behavior: The generally gregarious nature of brant geese has already been mentioned. Even shortly after hatching their broods, families will sometimes merge. Barry (1956) mentions seeing six or eight adults with ten or fourteen young swimming in a group, and Einarsen (1965) illustrates two pairs of adults with nine or ten very recently hatched young being closely convoyed. Typically a family consists of an adult swimming ahead, the young birds, and the other adult taking up the rear, a trait that persists almost until the families break up in the fall (Jones and Jones, 1966).

Flocking by nonbreeding birds is also typical of brant; Barry (1956) noted that yearling birds remained separate from the nesting colony on Southampton Island. This group of about 200 birds flew out to feed each day in flocks of 40 to 50 birds, and during the midsummer molt, they congregated in a bay by the Boas River.

Pair-forming Behavior: Little has been written on pair-forming behavior in brant. Barry (1956) observed two instances of possible courtship flights involving three birds, but noted that nearly all the birds were mated prior to arrival at their breeding grounds. Einarsen (1965) also mentions seeing several trios of seemingly courting brant on their wintering grounds between mid-January and late March. He believed that the female took the lead in these flights and was followed by two or more competing males. Although such flights may play a role in pair formation, it is highly probable that pair bonds are formed and maintained in brant as in other geese, by the repeated performance of the triumph ceremony between two birds. Such ceremonies may be seen between paired birds in captive flocks. Jones and Jones (1966) mentioned seeing apparent hostility postures between wild birds that met and moved away together, and noted that this behavior frequently was the means by which a family member regained its own group.

Copulatory Behavior: Precopulatory behavior in brant consists of mutual head-dipping movements that resemble bathing movements, but lacks the strong tail-cocking elements present in many geese. At times this head-dipping also takes the form of up-ending and is followed by mounting. The precopulatory display consists of the male lifting his bill, stretching his neck, and calling, but neither sex exhibits wing-lifting or wing-spreading at this time (Johnsgard, 1965).

Nesting and Brooding Behavior: Observations on nesting behavior have been provided by Barry (1956). Pairs establish nesting territories as soon as the habitat is free of ice and snow. The nest is usually a simple hollow about two inches deep and nine inches across, with a sparse amount of grass pulled up from the immediate vicinity of the nest. Down is deposited with the laying of the first egg and increased with each additional one. Females cover the eggs with down whenever they leave the nest, and during the egg-laying period the male remains within 100 yards of the nest. However, once incubation is under way, the female rests low and inconspicuously on the nest, with her neck extended along the ground. When she returns to the nest after feeding, the male escorts her until he is about 15 feet from the nest, and after the female is back on the nest he returns to a distance of about 50 to 100 yards to forage and keep watch. At times the male may fly at gulls and jaegers, chasing them from the vicinity of the nest.

When the young are hatched, they do not remain on the nest long, but are soon led out to the edges of the tidal flats, where they apparently feed on larvae and small crustaceans (Barry, 1956). Einarsen (1965) reported that the young also feed on the tender parts of sedges and, when disturbed, can effectively dive within a few days of hatching. Both sexes closely attend the young, although the adults become flightless about a week or ten days after the young are hatched. The flightless period lasts about thirty days; thus the adults are again able to fly about the time the young are fledged, and sometimes only shortly before the onset of freezing weather (Barry, 1962).

Post-breeding Behavior: With the arrival of freezing weather shortly after fledging, the adults and young gradually move to more southerly areas. In the case of the Pacific coast population, this is the Izembek Bay area on the northern tip of the Alaska Peninsula. Arrival there averages about August 25, and a mass departure occurs about eight weeks later (Jones, 1964). The fall migration route of the birds wintering on the Atlantic coast has been discussed by Lewis (1937), who noted that the east side of Hudson Bay and Ungava Bay are probably important fall staging areas.

King's (1970) recent observations of large numbers of molting Pacific brant near Cape Halkett, Alaska, numbering perhaps as many as 25,000 birds, is of great interest. These congregations would suggest that birds breeding farther east or south in Canada may congregate there in nonproductive years, or that the Arctic Slope may support a greater breeding population of brant than had been previously believed.

PERCHING DUCKS
Tribe Cairinini

The perching ducks and related gooselike forms are a diverse array of some fourteen species that are largely subtropical to tropical in occurrence. Although they vary in size from as little as about a half a pound in the "pygmy geese" (*Nettapus*) to more than twenty pounds in the spur-winged geese (*Plectropterus*), all possess some common features. These include a tendency toward hole-nesting, especially in trees; sharp claws; associated perching abilities; and long tails that presumably increase braking effectiveness when landing in trees. Nearly all species exhibit extensive iridescent coloration in the body, especially on the upper wing surface; this coloration is often exhibited by females as well as males. As a result, this tribe includes some of the most beautifully arrayed species of the entire family, of which the North American wood duck is an excellent example, as is the closely related Asian mandarin duck (*Aix galericulata*). The wood duck is the only perching duck that is native to the United States or Canada, but inasmuch as Mexico must be regarded as a part of North America, the inclusion of the muscovy duck as a North American species is fully justified.

Perching ducks, together with all of the following groups of waterfowl included in this book, are representatives of the large anatid subfamily Anatinae. Unlike the whistling ducks, swans, or true geese, species of this subfamily have a tarsal scale pattern that has vertically aligned scutes (scutellate condition) above the base of the middle toe, and the sexes are usually quite different in voice, plumage, and sexual behavior. These sexual differences can be attributed to the weaker and less permanent pair bonds characteristics of true ducks, with a renewal of pair bonds typically occurring each year. As a result, pair-forming behavior tends to be more complex and elaborate in these species, as a dual reflection of the greater and more frequent competition for mates and the need for safeguards in reducing or avoiding mixed pairings between species during the rather hurried pair-forming period. In these species, the males typically assume the initiative in pair-forming activities, and

161

thus they are usually more colorful, more aggressive, and have the more elaborate pair-forming behavior patterns. On the other hand, the females retain a subdued, often concealing plumage pattern, associated with their assumption of most or all incubation and brood-rearing responsibilities. As a result, humans usually find it easy to recognize the distinctively plumaged males of most species, while the females of related species are often so similar that even experienced observers may find it difficult to identify them with certainty.

Following the initiation of incubation, the males in this subfamily typically abandon the females and begin their postnuptial molt, during which they become flightless for a time and usually also acquire a more femalelike body plumage. Thus, unlike the species in the subfamily Anserinae, typical ducks have two plumages, and thus two body molts, per year. In males this double molt is most apparent, since the "eclipse" plumage attained following the postnuptial molt is usually less colorful and often quite femalelike.

Although in all the species which have so far been studied the female also has a comparable summer molt and plumage, in most cases this plumage is so similar to the winter plumage that separate descriptions are not necessary. In most cases the "eclipse" plumage of males is held for only a few months, presumably to allow the male to regain the more brilliant plumage associated with pair formation as early as possible. In some cases, however, this "nuptial" plumage is not regained until well into winter (e.g., ruddy duck, Baikal teal, blue-winged teal), so that "summer" and "winter" plumages may be more or less recognizable. The situation is further complicated in the oldsquaw, which has a third partial molt in the fall (affecting both sexes but most apparent in the male) and which is restricted to the scapular region. Except in such special cases, the two major plumages of the male are referred to in the species accounts as "nuptial" and "eclipse" plumages, while the "adult" plumage of females refers to both of the comparable breeding and nonbreeding plumages.

The 115 species of waterfowl that belong to the subfamily Anatinae are grouped into a number of tribes, most of which include one or more native North American species. The only major tribe of Anatinae that is not represented in this continent is the shelduck tribe Tadornini, which has representatives in both South America and Eurasia. It is true that there are some old records of Atlantic coast occurrences for the ruddy shelduck (*Tadorna ferruginea*) and the common shelduck (*Tadorna tadorna*), as well as a few more recent sight records (*Audubon Field Notes*, 16:73; *American Birds*, 26:842; 27:41), but these are quite possibly the result of escapes from captivity.

MUSCOVY DUCK

Cairina moschata (Linnaeus) 1758

Other Vernacular Names: Musk Duck, Pato Real.

Range: From central and northeastern Mexico southward through the forested parts of Central and South America to Peru and Argentina. Nonmigratory and relatively sedentary.

Subspecies: None recognized.

Measurements (after Delacour, 1954):

Folded wing: Males 300-400, females 300-315 mm.

Culmen: Males 65-75, females 50-53 mm.

Weights: Leopold (1959) reported that wild males range in weight from 4.39 to 8.82 pounds (1,990-4,000 grams), and that females range from 2.43 to 3.24 pounds (1,100-1,470 grams). Domesticated muscovies are often much heavier, particularly males. Delacour (1959) reported weights of muscovies as 2.5 and 5 kilograms for females and males, respectively, which would be more typical of domesticated varieties.

IDENTIFICATION

In the Hand: Any large, predominantly blackish duck with a rather squarish tail measuring more than 100 mm. and with bare skin around the eyes is of this species. Domesticated varieties, which are sometimes mistakenly shot by hunters, may vary greatly in coloration, but usually are quite large and obviously of domestic origin.

In the Field: Within its Mexican range, the muscovy is largely confined to coastal rivers and lagoons, often in or near forests. Although sometimes feeding in open situations, the birds usually return to timbered areas to rest and roost. Either on land or in water the blackish body coloration is evident, with little or no white showing on the wing coverts. In flight, the white under wing coverts and the white that is usually also present on the upper wing surface contrasts strongly with the otherwise dark body coloration. In spite of their size, they fly swiftly and strongly, often producing considerable wing noise. Otherwise, muscovies are normally quite silent, both in flight and at rest.

AGE AND SEX CRITERIA

Sex Determination: In adults, the strong size dimorphism and caruncles on the head and bill of the male make sex determination simple. A culmen length in excess of 55 mm. and the presence of naked skin on the face are indicative of a male.

Age Determination: No definite information is available, but it is probable that the amount of white present on the upper wing surface increases with age, as does the size of the caruncles on the male's bill. Sexual maturity is attained in the first year among captive birds, but the situation in wild muscovies is not known.

DISTRIBUTION AND HABITAT

Breeding Distribution and Habitat: The natural North American breeding distribution of the muscovy duck is limited to the lowland portions of Mexico, from central Sinaloa on the west and Nuevo Leon on the east southward and eastward along both coasts with the exception of those portions of the Yucatán Peninsula that lack suitable rivers and lagoons (Leopold, 1959). There are no records of the species' natural occurrence in the United States, but unsuccessful attempts have been made to establish this species in Florida, using offspring of wild stock from South America.

The muscovy duck also extends southward through virtually all of the

Breeding distribution of the muscovy duck in North and Central America.

lowland regions of Central America, southward over much of continental South America, especially the forested areas east of the Andes Mountains. Its southern limits are reached near Tucumán, Santiago del Estero, and Santa Fe, Argentina.

The breeding habitat consists of rivers, lagoons, marshes, and similar areas of water at relatively low altitudes that are associated with forests or heavy woodland. Slowly flowing rivers associated with tropical forests, as well as backwater swamps associated with such rivers, seem to represent their preferred habitat.

Wintering Distribution and Habitat: There are no indications of migratory movements in this species, which occurs in climates affected little if at all by seasonal temperature fluctuations. During the dry seasons the birds often move into coastal swamps or lagoons.

GENERAL BIOLOGY

Age at Maturity: Not yet established for wild birds. Domesticated muscovy ducks regularly breed in their first year of life.

Pair Bond Pattern: Current evidence indicates that the muscovies virtually lack pair bonds, the matings occurring promiscuously, and, except during the limited period of female receptiveness, there is little close association between the sexes. The few observations available on wild birds indicate such a social pattern (Delacour, 1959), and this is certainly true of captive birds (Johnsgard, 1965).

Nest Location: Nests are usually located from 3 to 20 meters high, in tree hollows or among palm leaves. Nests located among rushes at ground level have, however, been reported in Argentina (Phillips, 1923). In most cases little or almost no down is present.

Clutch Size: The normal clutch size is probably eight or nine eggs, but apparent dump-nesting sometimes results in clutches twice this size or even larger (Phillips, 1921).

Incubation Period: Incubation periods under natural conditions by wild birds have still not been determined, but a 35-day period has been reported for captive birds' eggs (Delacour, 1959; Lack, 1968).

Fledging Period: Not reported.

Nest and Egg Losses: Not yet studied.

Juvenile and Adult Mortality: Not known. Once beyond their first year, it seems possible that at least males might have a rather low natural mortality, owing to their unusual size and strength.

GENERAL ECOLOGY

Food and Foraging: Phillips (1923) summarized the information on food available at that time. Items reported taken included small fish, insects, small reptiles, and water plants. Termites are said to be a favorite food, and their nests are sometimes torn open by the birds in search of them. Muscovies have also been observed chasing small crabs, and feeding on water lily seeds and on the roots of *Mandioca*. Wetmore (1965) noted that the stomachs of two birds from Panama contained various seeds, including those of pickerel-weeds (Pondeteriaceae) and sedges (*Fimbristylis*).

Captive muscovy ducks that I have seen were never observed diving and seemed to spend much time foraging on land, presumably for seeds and insects. Although fish have been reported as part of their diet, it seems unlikely that they would be able to capture them under normal conditions since muscovies are bulky and rather awkward birds.

Sociality, Densities, Territoriality: During the breeding season males are highly aggressive toward one another, and such behavior no doubt tends to disperse the breeding population. A single male is often associated with more than one female, and perhaps such females might sometimes nest in close proximity. There seem to be no estimates of breeding densities available.

Interspecific Relationships: Not enough is known of the ecology of this species to speculate on its possible competitors and enemies. The comb duck (*Sarkidiornis melanotos*) is a fairly closely related tropical forest species which also nests in cavities, but the ecological relationships between these two forms are still obscure. Comb ducks seemingly occupy more open country than do muscovy ducks and are thought to be less dependent on undisturbed forests.

General Activity Patterns and Movements: Outside the breeding season, muscovy ducks usually gather in groups ranging from a few to 50 or more birds, wandering about rather extensively (Monroe, 1968). The birds typically fly during morning and evening hours (Wetmore, 1965), often spending the warmer parts of the day resting along the shore. At night they typically retire to tree roosts, with as many as a dozen or more birds sometimes roosting in a single tree (Phillips, 1923).

SOCIAL AND SEXUAL BEHAVIOR

Flocking Behavior: Most observers report that wild muscovies are usually found in small groups of a half dozen or so birds, but occasionally in larger groups. These groups are not closely coordinated and on disturbance will often disperse in all directions. Perhaps the advantages of common roosting behavior tend to maintain flocking behavior outside the breeding season; at least pair bonds and family bonds do not seem to be sufficiently strong as to facilitate such flocking behavior.

Pair-forming Behavior: Not yet studied in wild muscovies. However, no definite pair bonds have been found among captive or domestic muscovy ducks.

The rather simple display of the male serves both as aggressive signals toward males and as sexually oriented signals toward females. At such times he utters a soft breathing or hissing note, simultaneously raising his crest, moving his head slowly forward and backward, shaking his tail, and holding his wings slightly away from the body. Females normally respond to this display by fleeing, sometimes uttering a simple quacking note. I have never observed any female behavior that could be interpreted as inciting behavior, and no other type of apparent pair-forming behavior has been observed by me (Johnsgard, 1965).

Copulatory Behavior: According to most observers, copulation in this species normally takes the form of apparent rape, with the male chasing and eventually overpowering the much smaller female. However, during the egg-laying period the female may actively solicit copulation, assuming a prone posture on the water and waiting thus as the male performs his sometimes rather lengthy precopulatory behavior, which consists of characteristic head movements and of pecking the female's back feathers. After treading, the female bathes, but no definite male postcopulatory displays have been described (Johnsgard, 1965).

Nesting and Brooding Behavior: Not yet studied in detail, but probably rather similar to that of the wood duck.

Postbreeding Behavior: Other than the fact that considerable wandering by wild birds occurs during the nonbreeding season, almost nothing is known of this stage in the life cycle of muscovy ducks.

WOOD DUCK

Aix sponsa (Linnaeus) 1758

Other Vernacular Names: Carolina Duck, Summer Duck, Woodie.

Range: Breeds in forested parts of western North America from British Columbia south to California and east to Idaho, and in eastern North America from eastern North Dakota to Nova Scotia, south to Texas and Florida. Winters in the southern and coastal parts of the breeding range and southward into central Mexico.

Subspecies: None recognized.

Measurements (after Delacour, 1959):

Folded wing: Males 250-285, females 208-230 mm.

Culmen: Males 33-35, females 30-33 mm.

Weights: Nelson and Martin (1953)) reported that 248 males averaged 1.5 pounds (680 grams), with a maximum of 2.0 pounds; 163 females averaged 1.4 pounds (635 grams), with a maximum of 2.0 pounds. Mumford (1954) also reported an average weight of 1.5 pounds for 109 males, and 1.44 pounds for 99 females. Fall weights of immature and adult birds are scarcely separable; Jahn and Hunt (1964) noted that 49 fall-shot adult males averaged $1\frac{9}{16}$ pounds, while 23 immature males averaged $1\frac{1}{2}$ pounds.

IDENTIFICATION

In the Hand: Male wood ducks, even in eclipse plumage, can be recognized in the hand by their iridescent upper wing surface and long, squarish tail, which is also somewhat glossy. Unlike all other North American duck species, both sexes have a silvery white sheen on the outer webs of the primary feathers and a bluish sheen near the tips of the inner webs.

In the Field: Wood ducks sit lightly in the water, with their longish tails well above the surface. The birds are usually not found far from wooded cover. Often they perch on overhanging branches near shore and feed in fairly heavy woody cover that is flooded. The crest is evident on both sexes at a considerable distance, as is the male's white throat. The brilliant color pattern of males in nuptial plumage is unmistakable. In the air, wood ducks fly with great ease and apparent speed, the bill tilted below the axis of the body and the head often turned, giving a "rubber-necked" appearance, while the long tail is also evident. The underwing surface is speckled with white and brownish, and the white on the trailing edge of the secondaries is usually apparent, as is the white abdomen. The male has a clear whistle with rising inflection, while the female utters a somewhat catlike and owllike sound, but no true quacking notes.

AGE AND SEX CRITERIA

Sex Determination: The tertial coverts of females are pinkish, while those of males are dark purple. Females also have large white "teardrop" tips on the secondaries, while males have narrow, evenly white tips on these feathers (Carney, 1964). In any adult plumage, the throat of the male has two white extensions up the sides of the head, the eye is somewhat reddish, and the bill is reddish at the base.

Age Determination: In males, the tertials of juveniles are pale bronze, with pointed and frayed tips, while those of adults are deep purple, with squarish tips. These adult tertials grow in during the first fall of life. In immature birds the middle and greater coverts may show a mixture of the duller juvenal feathers and the very dark purple first winter coverts. In females, juveniles may have tertials that have pointed and frayed tips, rather than rounded tips, and the tertial coverts may be the greenish yellow ones of the juvenal plumage rather than the pink ones of the first winter plumage. In immature females the iridescent coloration usually does not extend onto the second row of middle coverts, and the most proximal greater covert of immatures is greener, duller, and smaller than adjacent ones; while in older females it is greener or lighter purple than adjacent ones, but approximately the same size (Carney, 1964).

DISTRIBUTION AND HABITAT

Breeding Distribution and Habitat: To a much greater extent than would be expected from a forest-adapted species, the wood duck in Canada is largely limited to the more southern regions. Godfrey (1966) lists its breeding range as including Graham and Vancouver islands, southern British Columbia, the Midnapore area of Alberta, east-central Saskatchewan, southern Manitoba, southwestern and southeastern Ontario, extreme southern Quebec, and the Maritime Provinces. Cape Breton Island is the limit of its breeding range (*Audubon Field Notes,* 15:451), and although the wood duck regularly occurs during summer on Prince Edward Island, it is not yet known to nest there. The United States range is clearly divided into eastern and western components, with a gap in the Rocky Mountain region and western plains. The western breeding range extends from Washington to California, with the center in the western portions of Washington and Oregon and the eastern limits in northern Idaho and northwestern Montana. Except for one study in California (Naylor, 1960), this population has been investigated relatively little by comparison with the eastern population. Naylor estimated that of a total western breeding population of about 16,000 pairs in 1958, 7,500 were in Oregon, 6,000 were in Washington, 1,500 were in California, and the remaining 860 were located in Idaho, British Columbia, and Montana.

The remainder of the North American breeding wood duck populations extend from the Missouri and Mississippi valleys eastward over an area that more or less corresponds to the distribution of temperate deciduous and mixed deciduous-coniferous forests. To the west, the breeding limits occur in central North Dakota (Hibbard, 1971), eastern South Dakota (*Audubon Field Notes,* 15:420), eastern Nebraska (Rapp *et al.,* 1970), eastern Kansas (Johnston, 1965), eastern Oklahoma (Sutton, 1967), and east-central Texas (Texas Game, Fish, and Oyster Commission, 1946). Benson and Bellrose (1964) estimated that about half of a continental population of 400,000 breeding pairs in 1962 bred in the northern halves of the Atlantic and Mississippi flyways. Sincock *et al.* (1964) believed that the twelve states in the southern halves of these flyways may produce about 650,000 wood ducks annually.

The preferred summer habitat of wood ducks consists of freshwater areas such as the lower and slower-moving parts of rivers, bottomland sloughs, and ponds, especially where large willows, cottonwoods, and oaks are present (Grinnell and Miller, 1944). The presence of trees at least 16 inches in diameter (breast height), having cavities with entrances at least 3.5 inches wide and interiors at least 8 inches in diameter, appear to be minimal nesting re-

Breeding (hatched) and wintering (shaded) distributions of the wood duck in North America.

quirements (McGilvrey, 1968). Although cavities with extremely large entrances are rarely used, the height of the entrance and the depth of the cavity are not critical, nor is the direction of the entrance or its immediate proximity to water seemingly important (Grice and Rogers, 1965). The entrance should, however, be protected from weather, and the cavity must be well drained.

Besides the presence of usable nesting sites, the breeding habitat must contain adequate food sources, suitable cover, available water, and suitable brood-rearing locations. McGilvrey's summary of these requirements indicates that foods should include overwintering seeds or nuts (acorns, domestic grains, etc.), native herbaceous plants, and aquatic or aerial insect life. Breeding cover should include trees, shrubs, or both. The trees should have low branches, providing overhead and lateral cover, and preferably should be flooded. Shrubs that have strong stems rising and spreading out about two feet above the water level are highly desirable, such as buttonbush (*Cephalanthus*). The water should be no more than eighteen inches deep for best foraging, should be still or slow-moving, and should be available through the incubation period. Ideal brood-rearing habitat includes a source of available foods (such as insects and duckweeds) for ducklings, water persisting through the fledging period, and dense overhead cover such as provided by flooded shrubs or dead tree tangles. The presence of herbaceous aquatic plants is highly desirable, as are resting sites for the brood, but trees are not needed at this stage.

Wintering Distribution and Habitat: Virtually the entire North American wood duck population winters within the borders of the United States; a few winter in southwestern British Columbia and in extreme southern Ontario on Lake Erie (Godfrey, 1966), and in Mexico the wood duck is only an occasional winter vagrant (Leopold, 1959). The western population of wood ducks winters primarily in California; Naylor (1960) reported that California supported most of an estimated wintering population of about 55,000 birds.

The eastern wood duck population is many times larger than the western one, but in recent years (1966–1969) has been almost entirely overlooked during midwinter surveys. Counts made in the early 1960s indicate about 100,000 birds in the Mississippi Flyway and progressively smaller numbers in the Atlantic and Central flyways. No doubt the forest-inhabiting tendencies of this species make it relatively unsatisfactory for aerial censusing. Recoveries of wood ducks banded in Wisconsin indicate that these birds move south along the Mississippi Valley to Arkansas, Louisiana, Texas, and Mississippi, and move farther east only to a limited extent (Jahn and Hunt, 1964). On the other hand, wood ducks banded in Massachusetts evidently move south along the Atlantic coastal plain and winter primarily in the Carolinas, Georgia, and northern Florida; only a few recoveries are found as far west as Louisiana and Mississippi (Grice and Rogers, 1965). It would thus seem that the Mississippi River and its tributaries provide one migratory thoroughfare, while the Atlantic coast provides another, with uplands and mountains being avoided and providing barriers to population interchange.

Secluded freshwater swamps and marshes are the favored wintering habitats of wood ducks throughout the southern states, particularly where acorns, hickory nuts, water-lily seeds, and similar foods are readily available. Stewart (1962) noted that fall migrant wood ducks congregate where the masts of beech and oaks are available, and they also utilize interior impoundments with stands of spatterdock (*Nuphar*). Small numbers use fresh estuarine bay marshes, especially where narrowleaf cattail (*Typha augustifolia*) and white water lily (*Nymphaea odorata*) are present. Among the estuarine river marshes, the largest spring and fall populations are found in fresh or slightly brackish water, especially where arrow arum (*Peltandra*) is common.

GENERAL BIOLOGY

Age at Maturity: A one-year period to maturity is well established for wood ducks. Ferguson (1966) noted that 19 of 24 aviculturalists reported breeding by captive birds in the first year, while the remainder reported second-year breeding. Many studies, as summarized by Grice and Rogers (1965), have reported that birds marked as juveniles often returned the following year to the same area for nesting. Of an estimated 95 marked wild females believed alive as yearlings, 30 were found by Grice and Rogers to be nesting that year. Since many birds were not accounted for, the actual percentage of nesting by wild yearling birds is no doubt much higher.

Pair Bond Pattern: Apparently pair bonds are renewed yearly, since males normally desert females at the beginning of incubation and the females rear their young alone (Grice and Rogers, 1965). On occasion, however, males have been seen in company with females and broods, and there is at least one record of a male incubating (Rollin, 1957).

Nest Location: A number of studies on natural nesting cavities of wood ducks have been made, and several general characteristics of cavity requirements have emerged. McGilvrey (1968) summarized the optimum natural cavity as having a height of 20 to 50 feet, an entrance 4 inches in diameter, a cavity bottom of 100 square inches, a cavity depth of 24 inches, and a tree diameter of 24 to 36 inches. There appears to be a preference for high cavities and those with small entrances, which raccoons are unlikely to be able to enter (Bellrose *et al.,* 1964; Weier, 1966). Apparently there is also a preference for nesting in rows or clusters of large trees of similar size, rather than in isolated large trees (Grice and Rogers, 1965). Open stands are also preferred over dense woods. At least in the case of artificial cavities (nest boxes), those situated over water are greatly preferred to those on land. Cavities with entrances only slightly larger than the minimum possible (3½ x 4 inches) are preferred, as are those with cavity depths of less than 50 inches (Bellrose *et al.,* 1964).

Clutch Size: Estimates of clutch size are often confused by dump-nesting involving several females, which tends to inflate estimates of clutch size. Naylor (1960) estimated that 13.8 eggs represented a normal complete clutch, while dump nests averaged 28.5 eggs per nest. Similarly, Cunningham (1969) noted that the average clutch size of "single" nests ranged from 13.5 to 15.9 during three years, while that of dump nests averaged about 28 eggs. The incidence of dump-nesting was related to population density. Leopold (1966) reported an average clutch of 13.9 eggs for early nests. He noted that of 297 potential "egg days," only 13 were missed; thus the egg-laying rate is essentially 1.04 days per egg. Renests usually average smaller (Leopold, 1966), and as many as two renesting attempts have been noted (Grice and Rogers, 1965). A few instances of double brooding have also been found (Rogers and Hansen, 1967).

Incubation Period: The incubation period averages about 30 days, with reported extremes of 25 and 37 days (Grice and Rogers, 1965). Leopold (1966) noted that about half the clutches hatch in 30 days and two-thirds in the interval between 29 and 31 days, with pipping starting two days prior to hatching.

Fledging Period: Grice and Rogers (1965) noted that about 70 percent of the juveniles studied were capable of flight (after being thrown into the air) at sixty days of age, before their primaries were fully grown.

Nest and Egg Losses: A large number of studies of wood duck nests have been made, and most indicate fairly high success rates. Weller (1964) summarized three studies (mostly from artificial nesting boxes) that totalled 1,648 nests and averaged a 66 percent nest success. Leopold (1966) reported a 94 percent nesting success for 281 nests, and a 75 percent hatching success for 2,860 eggs. In the majority of studies, the single most important predator is the raccoon, and by the construction of relatively raccoon-proof nesting boxes, the nesting success is generally quite high (Grice and Rogers, 1965). In areas where starling populations are high 20 percent or more of the nests have sometimes been destroyed, but starlings' use of wood duck nesting boxes can be reduced by constructing boxes with cavities that are too well lighted for these light-intolerant birds (Bellrose and McGilvrey, 1966).

Juvenile Mortality: Grice and Rogers (1965) determined that of 135 broods studied over a three-year period, brood size was reduced from an average of 12.5 at hatching to 5.8 at the time of fledging, or a loss of approximately 50 percent of the young during the 70-day fledging period. They found that early-hatched broods had the lowest mortality, while late-hatched young had an average brood size of 9.9 at hatching and only 2.2 at fledging. Jahn and Hunt (1964) also calculated an average brood size of 5.8 young for birds near the flight stages, based on six different studies. Estimates of first-year mortality rates for birds banded as juveniles range from 61.7 percent to 82.5 percent, with an average of three New England studies being 76.7 percent (Grice and Rogers, 1965).

Adult Mortality: Studies of banded birds in three New England states have provided estimated annual adult mortality rates of 51.7 to 63.7 percent, with an average of 58.9 percent (Grice and Rogers, 1965).

GENERAL ECOLOGY

Food and Foraging: A considerable number of food analyses (Martin *et al.,* 1951) of wood ducks have consistently pointed toward a high usage of fruits and nuts of woody plants, such as dogwood and elm trees, including beechnuts, acorns, hickory nuts, as well as a substantial consumption of the seeds of floating-leaf aquatic plants (*Brasenia, Numphaea, Nuphar*). Additionally the seeds and vegetative parts of other aquatic plants such as wild rice (*Zizania*), pondweeds (*Potamogeton*), arrow arum (*Peltandra*), duckweeds (*Lemna* and others), and bur reed (*Sparganium*) are consumed in large quantities. Stewart (1962) found that in the Chesapeake Bay area, wood ducks feeding on river bottomlands fed mostly on beechnuts and acorns, while birds in the estuarine river marshes predominantly consumed the seeds of arrow arum. Among the oaks, species that produced fairly small acorns are used more by wood ducks than those with large acorns, particularly in bottomland soils that are occasionally flooded (Brakhage, 1966). These include such species as pin oak (*Quercus palustris*), water oak (*Q. nigra*), willow oak (*Q. phellos*), and Nuttall oak (*Q. nuttallii*). Wood ducks may search for such acorns among the forest litter, or sometimes pluck them from the branches before they have fallen. When on water, they tip-up but only rarely dive for food; indeed only female wood ducks have so far been observed performing foraging dives (Kear and Johnsgard, 1968). Preferred foraging habitat is water no more than 18 inches deep, the approximate limit a duck can reach by tipping-up.

Sociality, Densities, Territoriality: During most of the year the wood duck is found only in small flocks of a dozen birds or less, with larger aggregations occurring only during the nocturnal roosting period. Both on the wintering grounds and during migration such social roosting is typical, and roosts sometimes support hundreds of birds. Hester (1966) noted that roosts vary in size from less than an acre to several acres, and the numbers of birds using them range from less than a hundred to several thousand, with one recorded roost of 5,400 birds.

On arrival at their nesting grounds, wood ducks are usually in small groups of up to a dozen birds, and usually already in pairs. Once established on their nesting areas, pairs do not seem to restrict their movements to a particular territory or defend an area as such, but rather the males simply protect their females from attentions by other males (Grice and Rogers, 1965).

Breeding densities are apparently determined by the availability of suitable nesting cavities, which are usually fairly limited unless supplemented by artificial nesting boxes. In one study where boxes were not used, 37 of 67 cavities on 442 acres were used during one year (Bellrose *et al.*, 1964), or about 12 acres per nest. Examples of high nesting densities achieved with nesting boxes include 41 nests on an 8-acre pond, 95 nests on a 150-acre refuge, and 37 nests on 100 acres (McGilvrey, 1968).

Interspecific Relationships: Because of their specialized nesting adaptations, competition for nest sites between wood ducks and other duck species is extremely limited. The common goldeneye is the only other cavity-nesting duck species that has an overlapping breeding range, and this occurs only near the northern edge of the wood duck's range. A study in New Brunswick (Prince, 1968) indicated that competition between the two species was limited because of site- and cavity-preference differences, as well as differences in their preferred foraging and loafing areas. Wood ducks also used areas with somewhat larger trees and ones that were more varied in outer dimensions. Cavities used by the two species were similar in their entrance sizes, but goldeneyes evidently preferred cavities which were less deep and of a fairly definite inside diameter as compared with wood duck cavities.

Competition for cavities may also occur with other species. McGilvrey (1968) noted that other competitors include starlings, squirrels, bees, hornets, hooded mergansers, screech owls, and sparrow hawks. At least in some areas, squirrels may be serious competitors for nests, especially where only natural cavities are available.

Predators of eggs are numerous, but the most important is the raccoon.

In the southern states various snakes may also be important, and locally or occasionally fox squirrels, minks, opossums, or rats may also pose problems. Duckling predators include minks, turtles, fish, snakes, bullfrogs, predatory birds, and other predatory mammals (McGilvrey, 1968).

General Activity Patterns and Movements: The evening roosting behavior of wood ducks is well known and has been frequently studied as a population index technique. These flights are usually most pronounced during fall and winter. A study by Martin and Haugen (1960) indicated that the morning flights lasted for about 45 minutes and usually ended by 15 minutes after sunrise. Early evening flight activity mainly occurred during the last 50 minutes before sunset, but both morning and evening flights gradually occurred nearer the periods of darkness and were made during a shorter period of time as the fall season progressed.

Stewart (1958), using color-banded birds, studied local movements of broods and families. He found that at the age of about two weeks, broods moved away from their natal sites into new habitats and often merged with other wood ducks. Some of such brood movements were quite long, with a maximum record of 3.5 miles. When leading broods, females continued to make their morning and evening feeding flights and started gathering into small groups when the ducklings were about six weeks old. At the age of eight weeks, when the young fledged, additional congregation occurred, with some segregation of adult and young birds. In early October, the ducks moved from ponds and lakes to rivers and creeks, usually at distances of under fifteen miles, and by late October the fall migration had begun.

SOCIAL AND SEXUAL BEHAVIOR

Flocking Behavior: Judging from changes in numbers of birds at roosting sites, two periods of social flocking seem to be prevalent. Hartowicz (1965) found an early peak of numbers at roosting sites in mid-June, which he believed might represent nonbreeders, unsuccessful breeders, or males that have deserted their females prior to molting. A similar peak occurred in September, which presumably represented both young and old birds. Stewart (1958) noted that in late-summer concentrations, the morning flights away from the roosting sites consisted of larger flocks than did the evening flights back to the roost, which usually numbered from one to twenty birds.

Pair-forming Behavior: Pair formation evidently occurs on the wintering grounds, since birds arrive at their nesting areas already paired (Grice and Rogers, 1965). The pair-forming displays of wood ducks are numerous and complex (Johnsgard, 1965), but an integral feature of pair formation is the performance of inciting by a female toward a specific male. In effect, the female incites a particular male to attack other birds, usually other males. This inciting behavior is highly ritualized and rarely leads to attacks. Instead, the "preferred" male responds to inciting by swimming ahead of the female and turning the back of his head toward her. This combination of inciting and turning-of-the-back-of-the-head display seems to be a fundamental feature of pair formation in nearly all true ducks (Johnsgard, 1960).

Copulatory Behavior: Unlike other North American surface-feeding ducks, copulation in wood ducks is preceded by the female assuming a prone position well in advance of treading. I have seen no preliminary mutual displays by the pair prior to the female's assumption of this posture, in which she lies flat on the water with her head low and her tail tilted slightly upwards. The male typically swims around her, making drinking or bill-dipping movements and sometimes pecking gently at her. Mounting then occurs, and after treading is completed the male usually first swims rapidly away from her while turning-the-back-of-the-head, then he turns and faces the bathing female (Johnsgard, 1965).

Nesting and Brooding Behavior: Leopold (1966) reported that mated pairs begin to look for nests shortly after they arrive in late March, spending several mornings investigating possible sites. The male accompanies the female, but does not enter the nesting box. After five or six days of such behavior, the first egg is laid. Egg-laying occurs in early morning, while the mate waits nearby, after which the birds leave until the following morning. Down-picking begins with the fourth to eighth egg. While the last few eggs are being laid, the female may spend the night in the box, presumably picking down. Incubation begins with the last egg, and during the incubation period two rest periods are normally taken daily, during early morning and late afternoon hours. The male usually accompanies the hen on such flights, until he deserts her for his postnuptial molt. During first nestings the male usually attends the female into the fourth week of incubation. The female remains in the nest during the four- to six-hour hatching period, and the family usually spends its first night in the nest. The next morning the female usually takes her rest flight, then returns to the nest and calls the young from the cavity with a series of low *kuk* notes. The young jump from the nest in rapid succession, and the family then walks to the nearest water.

Stewart (1958) noted that newly-hatched broods went to water areas that were nearest the hatching place, provided that vegetative cover was present. For the first two weeks of life little brood congregation occurs, although lost individual ducklings may attach themselves to other broods. Because of such brood merger, age differentials among ducklings in broods are not uncommon.

Postbreeding Behavior: Following their desertion of the females, male wood ducks evidently move to secluded woodland ponds or swamps, where they are rarely seen. Females undergo their molt later than males; they probably normally leave their broods and begin to molt between six and eight weeks after the young have hatched. Like the males, they then inhabit the thickest possible cover and are almost never seen (Grice and Rogers, 1965). Shortly after regaining flight, the young and the adults begin to congregate in preparation for their fall migration.

SURFACE-FEEDING DUCKS
Tribe Anatini

The surface-feeding, dabbling, or similarly described ducks are a group of about thirty-six species of mostly freshwater ducks that occur throughout the world. Many of them are temperate or arctic-breeding species that nest on dry land near freshwater ponds, marshes, rivers, or similar rather shallow bodies of water. Associated with this breeding habitat are their adaptations for foraging by "tipping-up" rather than by diving for food, an ability to land and take off abruptly from small water areas or land, and a moderately good walking ability but reduced perching capabilities as compared with perching ducks. Also unlike perching ducks, iridescent coloration on the wing is limited to the secondary feathers, or in rare cases is lacking altogether.

The surface-feeding ducks are among the most abundant and familiar of all North American ducks and include such popular sporting species as mallards, pintails, wigeons, and various teals. They range in size from less than a pound to more than three pounds and are among the most agile of waterfowl in flight, relying on maneuverability rather than unusual speed to elude danger. The number of North American breeding species is somewhat uncertain, but is at least nine. Additionally, the European wigeon very probably nests occasionally in continental North America, the Baikal teal is possibly a very rare nester, and the Bahama pintail breeds in the West Indies. Further, the "Mexican duck" is often considered to be a separate species from the common mallard, as are the populations called the Florida duck and mottled duck, so these might also be added, bringing the possible total to fourteen. Beyond these, the falcated duck is recognized by the A.O.U. (1957) as belonging on the list of North American birds although there is no evidence for breeding, and in recent years there have been several sight records for the garganey, as well as an occurrence of the Chinese spot-billed duck (*Anas poecilorhyncha*) on Adak Island (Byrd *et al.,* 1974). Some of the records of falcated duck, Baikal teal, and garganey may well have been the result of escapes from captivity, but it seems likely that others of them represent wild birds, and thus these species are included in this book.

In most respects, the surface-feeding ducks closely resemble the perching ducks in their anatomy and biology, but differ from them in that they are nearly all ground-nesting species that are ill-adapted for perching. Although considerable diversity in bill shape exists among the surface-feeding ducks, most biologists now agree that recognition of a single genus (*Anas*) is most representative of the close relationships that exist among these species, rather than maintenance of the traditional separate genera for the shovelerlike ducks, the wigeons, and other subgroups. Similarly, it is quite clear that recognition of separate species of Old World and New World green-winged teals and species recognition for the endemic Mexican, Florida, and Gulf coast populations of mallards are not in keeping with the modern species concept of potentially interbreeding natural populations. Although such changes force some modifications of traditional vernacular names of these populations, these disadvantages seem minor compared to the distortions of natural relationships forced by the retention of traditional nomenclature.

EUROPEAN WIGEON

Anas penelope Linnaeus 1758

(Until 1973, regarded by the A.O.U. as *Mareca penelope*)

Other Vernacular Names: None in general use.

Range: Breeds in Iceland and the more temperate portions of Europe and Asia south to England, Germany, Poland, Turkistan, Altai, and northwestern Mongolia. Winters in Europe, northern and central Africa, and Asia. Regularly seen in fall, winter, and spring in North America, especially along the Atlantic and Pacific coasts, and most commonly seen in the interior during spring. Not yet determined to be a breeding species in North America, although such breeding seems probable.

Subspecies: None recognized.

Measurements (after Delacour, 1956):

Folded wing: Males 254-270, females 236-255 mm.

Culmen: Males 33-36, females 31-34 mm.

Weights: Schiøler (1925) reported that forty-two adult males averaged 819 grams (1.81 pounds), and twenty-three immature males averaged 706 grams (1.56 pounds), with a maximum male weight of 1,073 grams.

Among females, twenty-four adults averaged 724 grams (1.6 pounds), and twenty immatures averaged 632.5 grams (1.39 pounds), with a maximum female weight of 962 grams.

IDENTIFICATION

In the Hand: Either sex may be safely distinguished in the hand from the American wigeon by the presence of dark mottling on the underwing surface, particularly the axillars. It may be distinguished from other surface-feeding ducks by the white to grayish upper wing coverts and the green speculum pattern, with a black anterior border. Both sexes are more brownish on the cheeks and neck than is true of the American wigeon.

In the Field: Females are not considered safely separable from the female American wigeon in the field, but if both species are together the more brownish and less grayish tones of the European species will be evident. Males in nuptial plumage are easily recognizable, since they exhibit a creamy yellow rather than a white forehead, and a cinnamon-red head and neck color instead of a light grayish one. Since some male European wigeon exhibit a green iridescence around and behind the eye, similar to that of the American wigeon, this is not a good field mark for distinguishing the two. The call of the male European wigeon is a shrill double whistle, sounding like *whee-uw,* while that of the American species is a series of weaker repeated single notes. Calls of the females are nearly identical. In flight, the mottled under wing coverts and axillars might be visible under favorable conditions.

AGE AND SEX CRITERIA

Sex and Age Determination: Probably the same criteria as indicated for the American wigeon apply to this species.

OCCURRENCE IN NORTH AMERICA

The great number of specimen and visual records of European wigeon in North America has led several people to speculate that breeding, of at least a local or periodic nature, must occur on this continent. Hasbrouck (1944) compiled nearly 600 North American sight or specimen records for this species through the early 1940s. On this basis of these he concluded that a regular southward fall migration occurs along the Atlantic and Pacific coasts, followed by an apparent northward spring migration through the continental interior. Of the records he presented, about 60 percent are from states or provinces largely or wholly in the Atlantic Flyway. The remainder are about equally divided among the states and provinces representing the Pacific and Mississippi flyways, while only about 2 percent of the records are from Central Flyway states.

The Pacific Flyway states and provinces for which Hasbrouck listed records extended from Alaska to California. Since then, one or more records have also been obtained for Nevada (Linsdale, 1951), Idaho (*Audubon Field Notes,* 22:608), Utah (*ibid,* 10:44), and Arizona (*ibid,* 20:447). Hasbrouck listed records from the Central Flyway states of Wyoming, Nebraska, and Texas. More recent records are now available for Montana (*ibid,* 19:98; 22:608; 23:500; 24:629), South Dakota (*ibid,* 22:55, 307; 23:72), Oklahoma (Sutton, 1967), Colorado (Bailey and Niedrach, 1967), Kansas (Johnston, 1964), New Mexico (Ligon, 1961), and North Dakota (*Audubon Magazine,* sec. 2, November, December, 1942:12; *Audubon Field Notes,* 6:24). Hasbrouck reported European wigeon records for all the Mississippi Flyway states except Tennessee, Arkansas, Mississippi, and Alabama and for all the Atlantic Flyway states except Vermont and West Virginia. Imhof (1962) has since reported a sight record for Alabama. I have not encountered other records for the remaining states, but it seems only a matter of time before the European wigeon will have been reported from all of the contiguous states and provinces.

AMERICAN WIGEON

Anas americana Gmelin 1789

(Until 1973, regarded by the A.O.U. as *Mareca americana*)

Other Vernacular Names: Baldpate, Widgeon.

Range: Breeds in northwestern North America, from the Yukon and Mac-Kenzie regions east to Hudson Bay and south to California, Arizona, Colorado, Nebraska, and the Dakotas, with infrequent breeding farther east. Winters along the Pacific coast from Alaska southward to as far as Costa Rica, the southern United States, and along the Atlantic coast from southern New England south.

Subspecies: None recognized.

Measurements (after Phillips, 1924):

Folded wing: Males 252-270, females 236-258 mm.

Culmen: Males 45-48, females 33-37 mm.

Weights: Nelson and Martin (1953) indicate that the average weight of 264 males was 1.7 pounds (770 grams), with a maximum of 2.5 pounds; 108 females averaged 1.5 pounds (680 grams), with a maximum of 1.9 pounds. Jahn and Hunt (1964) reported that 29 fall-shot adult males averaged 2 pounds (907 grams), and 173 immature males averaged 1.94 pounds (879 grams); 28 adult females also averaged 1.94 pounds, and 146 immature females averaged 1.69 pounds (765 grams). The heaviest weights they recorded were 2.63 pounds for males and 2.31 pounds for females.

IDENTIFICATION

In the Hand: Apart from the European wigeon, American wigeon are the only surface-feeding ducks that have white or nearly white upper wing coverts, separated from a green speculum by a narrow black band. The rather short bluish bill and similarly colored legs and feet are also distinctive; only the pintail has comparable bill and foot coloration, and this species lacks pale gray or white on the upper wing coverts. See the European wigeon account for distinction from that species.

In the Field: American wigeon can be recognized on land or water by their grayish brown to pinkish body coloration. They often feed on land, eating green leafy vegetation, and float about buoyantly in shallow water, where they feed on aquatic leafy materials or steal it from diving ducks. The short bill and similarly short, rounded head are often evident, and when the male is in nuptial plumage his pure white forehead markings are visible for great distances, as are the large white areas on the sides of the rump, contrasting with the black tail coverts. The white upper wing coverts are usually not visible when the bird is at rest, but when in flight this is the best field mark, alternately flashing with the grayish underwing surface and with the white abdomen of both sexes. American wigeon are about the same size as gadwalls and often mix with them in flight. Both species have white underparts, but while the gadwall exhibits white at the rear of the wing only, the wigeon exhibits dark secondaries and white on the forward half. Males often call in flight or when on the water, uttering a repeated and rather weak whistle. Females are relatively silent ducks, and their infrequent, gutteral quacking notes are not repeated in long series.

AGE AND SEX CRITERIA

Sex Determination: Vermiculations on the scapulars, back, or sides indicate a male. Entirely white middle coverts indicate an adult male. Adult males also have long, sharply pointed tertials that are black on the outer web and have narrow white margin, while females have shorter tertials that are brownish gray edged with white on the outer web. The greater tertial coverts of adult males are gray; those of adult females are dark brown with white edges. Immatures may be sexed by their middle coverts, which in males vary from dirty white to dark, with light centers surrounded by poorly defined cream or gray edging, and in immature females are dark, without light centers and usually with fairly well-defined light brown edging (Carney, 1964).

Age Determination: Immatures of both sexes have small, light-edged, and brownish tertials that are often faded or frayed. The greater tertial coverts may also be frayed and faded (Carney, 1964). The tail feathers may also have notched tips.

DISTRIBUTION AND HABITAT

Breeding Distribution and Habitat: The breeding range of the American wigeon is broad, extending from the Bering coast to the Atlantic, and from the Beaufort Sea coast and Hudson Bay south to northeastern California and the northern parts of Utah, Colorado, and Nebraska. Eastward from western Minnesota the breeding distribution becomes distinctly broken, with scattered breeding records in southern Quebec, Nova Scotia, New Brunswick, and Prince Edward Island (Godfrey, 1966). Likewise, in the eastern United States there are spotty breeding records for New York (DeGraff and Bauer, 1962), southern Michigan (*Audubon Field Notes,* 21:569), Delaware (*ibid,* 16:464), and Massachusetts (*American Birds,* 26:834). There are a few early breeding records for western Pennsylvania and Indiana. This species breeds regularly at Seney National Wildlife Refuge in northern Michigan (Beard, 1964) and is a rare but regular breeder in several Wisconsin counties (Jahn and Hunt, 1964).

Studies on breeding habitat preferences are limited. Keith (1961) compared the percentage of paired ducks on three different lake areas and two areas of potholes in southeastern Alberta. He indicated that each of the three lake areas accounted for more than 20 percent usage by wigeons, while the two areas of potholes had between 10 and 20 percent usage. The highest usage (nearly 30 percent) occurred on a large 20.8-acre lake with an average depth of 3 to 3.5 feet, limited emergent vegetation, and a relatively large amount of water milfoil (*Myriophyllum*) and pondweeds (*Potamogeton*) among the submerged plants. Potholes received even less relative use by broods, while the lake just mentioned accounted for about 40 percent of the brood use. Gadwalls exhibited a similar pattern of habitat use by pairs and broods.

Munro (1949) noted that wigeon prefer to nest around certain lakes or marshy sloughs that are surrounded by dry *Carex* meadows, in which the nests are placed. Unlike most dabbling ducks, females and young frequent the open water of marshy ponds, lake bays, or marsh-edged rivers, with this preference for open water perhaps related to the commensal foraging relationship between wigeons and diving waterfowl. The closely related European wigeon likewise prefers to nest where shoreline meadow belts are present, and additionally apparently requires partly wooded shorelines, since it is absent from both open tundra and small forest ponds (Hildén, 1964). To some extent, the

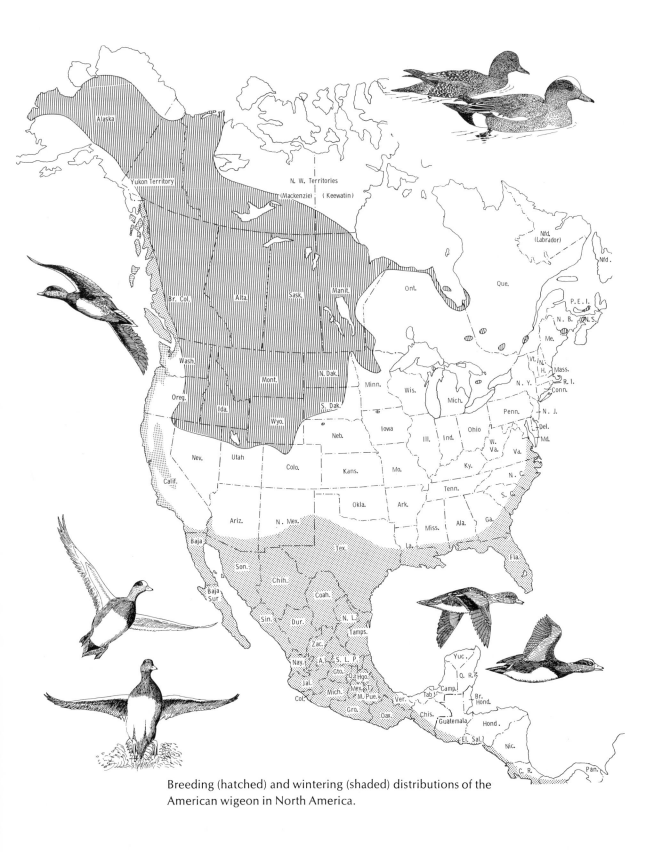

Breeding (hatched) and wintering (shaded) distributions of the
American wigeon in North America.

American wigeon also shows a preference for nesting in wooded or brushy habitats (Phillips, 1924).

Wintering Distribution and Habitat: The wintering distribution of wigeon is extensive, with nearly half of the winter population occurring in the Pacific Flyway, according to recent census figures. Large numbers of birds also winter in the Mississippi Flyway, but relatively few occur in the Central or Atlantic flyways. In the western states, wigeon occur from Puget Sound to Willamette Valley and southward to Humboldt Bay along coastal bays, rivers, and on inland valleys, pastures, and wet meadows where greens are readily available (Chattin, 1964). To the south, lettuce and alfalfa fields attract the birds to the Imperial Valley, and considerable numbers winter along the coast and interior of western Mexico, especially where pondweeds are abundant (Leopold, 1959). In the Mississippi Flyway, Louisiana represents the major wintering area for wigeon, while along the Atlantic coast they winter on fresh and brackish areas from Long Island southward, particularly in Maryland, South Carolina, and Florida.

In the Chesapeake Bay area the wigeon is an abundant migrant and common winter resident (Stewart, 1962). It is most often found on fresh or brackish estuarine bays where submerged plants such as wild celery (*Vallisneria*), naiad (*Najas*), pondweeds (*Potamogeton*), and wigeon grass (*Ruppia*) are plentiful. In more salty water the birds occur where eelgrass (*Zostera*) and wigeon grass are abundant, and in marsh habitats they prefer areas containing wigeon grass or muskgrass (*Chara*).

GENERAL BIOLOGY

Age at Maturity: Wigeon presumably normally nest in their first year of life. Ferguson (1966) indicated that fourteen of twenty-two respondents to a survey indicated first-year nesting by captive birds, while six and two reported second- and third-year nesting, respectively.

Pair Bond Pattern: Apparently renewed each year. In the closely related Chiloe wigeon (*Anas sibilatrix*) the male regularly participates in brood care and presumably has a more persistent pair bond.

Nest Location: Few analyses of nest site preferences have been made. Girard (1941) noted that of forty-five nests, the average distance from water was 98 yards and the range 2 to 350 yards. Keith (1961) noted an average distance of 72 feet and an average relative light penetration of 47 percent at the floor of the nest. He found that 81 percent of twenty-one nests were in *Juncus* cover (15 percent above the average of all species), while the rest were in mixed prairie or weeds. Phillips (1924) mentioned that the nest is often located at the base of a tree, and Munro (1949) stated that nests are frequently in sedge meadows.

Clutch Size: Girard (1941) reported an average clutch size of 9.55 eggs for forty-five nests in Montana. Keith (1961) noted an average of 8.9 eggs for twenty nests in Alberta. No data are available on renesting incidence or clutch sizes of such renests.

Incubation Period: Hochbaum (1944) reported a 23-day incubation period, based on a single clutch. Scott and Boyd (1957) reported a 22- to 25-day range for eggs of captive birds. Johnstone (1970) indicated a 24-day period.

Fledging Period: Hochbaum (1944) estimated a 45- to 58-day fledging period. Lee *et al.* (1964) estimated a 47- to 50-day fledging period.

Nest and Egg Losses: Girard (1941) reported that 4.6 percent of forty-five nests he studied were destroyed by crows and another 3.13 percent by skunks. An average of 7.15 eggs hatched in the successful nests he studied. Keith (1961) noted that the average brood size of seventy-five Class I (downy) broods he saw was 7.2 young, or a 19 percent reduction from the average clutch size that he had calculated.

Juvenile Mortality: Relatively few brood size counts on older broods seem to be available. Lee *et al.* (1965) reported an average brood size of 7.6 for 106 broods of all ages. Yocom (1951) counted 13 broods that were from two-thirds-grown to full-grown and averaged 5.6 young.

Adult Mortality: The only estimate of post fledging mortality rates I have found is that of Keith (1961), who calculated a 54 percent average annual mortality rate for all age classes based on band return data. This is somewhat higher than published estimates of adult mortality rates in European wigeon (Boyd, 1962; Wainwright, 1967).

GENERAL ECOLOGY

Food and Foraging: To a much greater extent than any other North American surface-feeding duck, the American wigeon is a grazing bird and one dependent on the vegetative parts of aquatic plants. Animal materials play a very small role in adult food consumption, although they are the prime food of ducklings (Munro, 1949). In most areas, wigeon grass and pondweed seeds and vegetative parts are prime components of the wigeon's diet (Martin *et al.,* 1951), supplemented by a large variety of other, mostly freshwater, aquatic plants. Cultivated crops such as lettuce, alfalfa, barley, and others are sometimes utilized heavily on wintering areas where they are readily available.

The tendency of American wigeon to feed on the aquatic plants brought up by diving ducks such as canvasbacks has long been recognized, and the ecological distribution of these two species on their migration routes and wintering grounds is quite similar (Stewart, 1962). Stewart noted that virtually all of more than 150 digestive tract contents he examined contained leaves, stems, and rootstalks of submerged plants, regardless of the habitats in which the birds were collected. Since wigeon are not among the species of surface-feeding ducks known to dive for food (Kear and Johnsgard, 1968), it must be imagined that such underwater plants are either reached by tipping-up or by feeding on materials brought to the surface by diving ducks or swans.

Sociality, Densities, Territoriality: American wigeon do not usually congregate in extremely large flocks, although rich sources of foods such as lettuce fields or similar truck crops may result in fairly large numbers of birds. Jahn and Hunt (1964) noted a maximum fall concentration of 67,000 birds on Horicon National Wildlife Refuge and noted the birds' attraction to large open-water lakes with extensive beds of submerged plants.

During spring migration, wigeon usually move north in small groups. Munro (1949) mentioned that spring flocks often numbered ten or fewer birds. Wigeon often mingle with gadwalls at this time, as well as with coots and diving ducks.

Little information is available on breeding densities. Keith (1961) reported a five-year average of 5 wigeon pairs using a 680-acre study area in Alberta, or almost 5 pairs per square mile. If only water acreage is considered, this density would represent about 3.6 pairs per one hundred acres. A maximum brood density of 0.45 broods per acre has been reported for a 20-acre marsh in northern Michigan (Beard, 1964). Estimates of home ranges and territory sizes are apparently not yet available.

Interspecific Relationships: Because of its relatively unique foraging adaptations, there is probably little if any food competition between wigeon and other surface-feeding ducks, and certainly the availability of nest sites is not a limiting factor for wigeon. The wigeon's most important relationships with other waterfowl are with canvasbacks, redheads, whistling swans, and coots, all of which bring to the surface submerged plant materials. The ability of the wigeon to steal such materials from other birds has earned it the name "poacher," although it is questionable whether the other species suffer seriously as a result.

Perhaps because their nests are usually so well hidden, wigeon are little affected by social parasitism or parasitic egg-laying by other species. Weller (1959) noted only two cases (involving the shoveler and the white-winged scoter) of other species depositing their eggs in wigeon nests.

Predators of eggs and young are probably much the same as for other surface-feeding ducks, but too few wigeon nests have been studied for definite statements on this point. Evidently crows and skunks do take some eggs (Girard, 1941).

General Activity Patterns and Movements: Few specific data are available on daily activity rhythms of wigeon. During fall migration, there appears to be a differential sex movement. Male wigeon leave the Delta, Manitoba, area shortly after completing their molt, and early arrivals in Wisconsin are mostly adult males (Jahn and Hunt, 1864). On the other hand, concentrations of immature males and females have been found in other areas, suggesting possible different fall migration routes.

Spring counts in Washington (Johnsgard and Buss, 1956) indicated that early migrants had more nearly equal sex ratios than did later ones, suggesting that paired birds move north faster than unpaired ones. Likewise, Beer (1945) observed that paired wigeon were the first to depart from their wintering grounds in southwestern Washington.

SOCIAL AND SEXUAL BEHAVIOR

Flocking Behavior: See sociality section above.

Pair-forming Behavior: Most pairing occurs on the wintering grounds, prior to the start of northward migration. However, there is probably some separation of pair members, and the remaining unpaired males continue to vie for the available females through the migration period. Aquatic courtship is marked by ritualized aggression in the form of gaping and raising of the folded wings, and an important aspect of pair formation is the combination of inciting by females and turning-the-back-of-the-head by males (Johnsgard, 1960, 1965). Inciting may also occur during aerial chases; Hochbaum (1944) mentions wigeon hens reaching back laterally to "bill" one of the chasing males. Many such aerial chases originate as, or develop into, attempted rape chases, and their role in pair formation is probably limited.

Copulatory Behavior: Copulation is preceded by mutual head-pumping, and in the single instance of observing a completed copulation, I noted that the male turned and faced the female while remaining in an erect posture for several seconds (Johnsgard, 1965).

Nesting and Brooding Behavior: Incubation begins with the laying of the last egg and is undertaken by the female alone. After hatching, the female leads her young into open-water areas such as marsh-lined ponds. For the first several weeks the young are entirely surface-gleaners and dabblers, slowly and deliberately moving through the marsh. When about four weeks old, they begin to tip-up for food. Brooding female wigeon are among the noisiest of ducks, and when their brood is threatened, females typically remain behind, quacking loudly while the young escape to cover. This distraction behavior may last fifteen minutes or more. Only when the young are nearly grown is the female usually silent (Beard, 1964). Beard also reported that female wigeon were highly aggressive toward strange ducklings, even of their own species. Of sixteen cases of young being driven away by female wigeon, fifteen involved wigeon ducklings. If the young duckling survived the first three or four attacks and persisted in following the brood, it was frequently accepted.

Postbreeding Behavior: Adult males leave their breeding grounds in southern Manitoba in late August and early September, and soon thereafter wigeon begin to concentrate in such northern states as Wisconsin, where they gather on areas that provide a combination of protection from disturbance and a supply of submerged aquatic foods. Apparently in certain localities there is a differential migration of immature male and female wigeon (Jahn and Hunt, 1964).

FALCATED DUCK

Anas falcata Georgi 1775

Other Vernacular Names: Bronze-capped Teal, Falcated Teal.

Range: Breeds in central and eastern Siberia, probably west to the Yenisei River, and southeast to Hokkaido in Japan. Winters in China, Japan, and southeastern Asia south to Vietnam and upper Burma, with occasional stragglers wintering in western North America, especially Alaska.

Subspecies: None recognized.

Measurements (after Delacour, 1954):

Folded wing: Males 230-242, females 225-235 mm.

Culmen: Males 40-42, females 38-40 mm.

Weights: Few weights are available. Dementiev and Gladkov (1967) reported that males weigh about 750 grams, females 640 to 660 grams. Bauer and Glutz (1968) reported the weight of a male in September as 640 grams. Chen Tso-hsin (1963) indicated that ten males averaged 713 grams (1.57 pounds), with a range of 590 to 770 grams, while five females averaged 585 grams (1.29 pounds), with a range of 422 to 700 grams.

IDENTIFICATION

In the Hand: Both sexes of this rare dabbling duck are similar to wigeon and also have a greenish speculum. But there is no black anterior border on the greater coverts, and the coverts are never pure white, only grayish to grayish brown. The elongated sickle-shaped tertials on the male are unique, and by themselves will identify that species, but females lack these ornamental specializations. The brownish underparts of females, their longer culmen length (over 36 mm.), and the presence of a rudimentary crest will serve to separate them from female wigeon.

In the Field: Males in nuptial plumage, with their long, bronze- to green-glossed crest, "scaly" breast pattern, and long sickle-shaped tertials that nearly reach the water, are distinctive. The species is so rare in North America that lone females should not be identified in the field, since they closely resemble female wigeon and gadwalls.

AGE AND SEX CRITERIA

Sex Determination: Except when in eclipse plumage, the presence of sickle-shaped tertial feathers will serve to distinguish adult males from females. In eclipse, a brighter speculum pattern and a slight iridescence on the head may identify males.

Age Determination: Not yet established, but no doubt the notched tail criterion will serve to identify immature birds through much of their first fall of life.

OCCURRENCE IN NORTH AMERICA

Like the Baikal teal, most records of this Asian species have come from Alaska. Gabrielson and Lincoln (1959) have mentioned two of these, a male that was collected on St. George Island and a pair seen at Attu Island. More recently, two males have been collected and several more birds seen at Adak Island (Byrd *et al.,* 1974).

The only Canadian record to date is that of a male that was observed near Vernon, British Columbia, in 1932 (Godfrey, 1966). Records from farther south must be regarded with great caution because of the probability of their being escapes from captivity. They include a sight record from San Francisco, California (*Audubon Field Notes,* 7:289), and one from Roaches Run, Virginia (*ibid,* 21:402).

GADWALL
Anas strepera Linnaeus 1758

Other Vernacular Names: Gray Duck.

Range: Breeds throughout much of the Northern Hemisphere, in North America from Alaska south to California and from Quebec south to North Carolina; also breeds in Iceland, the British Isles, Europe, and Asia. Winters in North America from coastal Alaska south to southern Mexico, the Gulf coast, and along the Atlantic coast to southern New England.

North American Subspecies:

A. s. strepera L.: Common Gadwall. Range as indicated above.

Measurements (after Delacour, 1956):

Folded wing: Males 260-282, females 235-260 mm.

Culmen: Males 38-45, females 36-42 mm.

Weights: Bellrose and Hawkins (1947) reported that 16 adult males averaged 2.18 pounds (989 grams) and 68 immatures averaged 2 pounds (907 grams), while 14 adult females averaged 1.87 pounds (848 grams) and 66 immatures averaged 1.78 pounds (807 grams). Nelson and Martin (1953) found the average of 104 males to be 2 pounds, and of 89 females to be 1.8 pounds. Maximum weights reported for males appear to be 2.5 pounds (Jahn and Hunt, 1964) to 2.6 pounds (Nelson and Martin), and 2.31 pounds for females (Jahn and Hunt), with a reported female maximum of 3 pounds (Nelson and Martin) seeming dubious.

IDENTIFICATION

In the Hand: Positive identification of gadwalls in the hand is simple; they are the only dabbling ducks with several secondaries entirely white on the exposed webs, the remaining secondaries being black or grayish. Confirming criteria are the yellow legs and slate gray (males) or gray and yellowish (females) bill color, a white abdomen, and the usual presence of some chestnut coloration on the upper wing coverts.

In the Field: Although one of the easiest species of ducks to identify in the hand, gadwalls are perhaps the waterfowl most commonly misidentified or unidentified by hunters because of the species' lack of brilliant coloration. On the water, the male appears to have an almost entirely gray body, except for the black hindquarters, which are apparent at great distances. In spring, the upper half of the head appears to be a considerably darker shade of brown than the lower part of the head and neck, but during fall this difference is not so apparent. The female is best recognized by her association with the male, but at fairly close range the yellowish sides of her otherwise gray bill can be seen, and the bill is clearly shorter and weaker than that of a female mallard, which she closely resembles. The white secondaries are usually not visible when the birds are at rest. However, the white secondary pattern is highly conspicuous during flight, with white also appearing on the underparts of the body and on the under wing coverts, the rest of the bird appearing brownish. From early fall until spring the courting calls of the males can be heard, either when in flight or on the water, a combination of low-pitched *raeb* notes interspersed with *zee* whistles, often in a distinctive *raeb-zee-zee-raeb-raeb* cadence (on the water only). The female has various mallardlike quacking notes, including a series of paced *quack* notes when alarmed, or a decrescendo series of notes that are somewhat more rapid and higher pitched than occurs in mallards.

AGE AND SEX CRITERIA

Sex Determination: The presence of vermiculations anywhere on the body indicates a male, as do chestnut-tipped longer scapulars. The tertials of adult males are long, pointed, and silver gray; those of adult females are shorter, more bluntly pointed, and silver brown with cream-colored tips. Juveniles of both sexes may have short, bluntly pointed and frayed tertials. The greater tertial coverts of adult males rarely have any white tipping, while those of females do. Adult males have some black or chestnut middle coverts that are not edged, while females have only a few black or chestnut coverts; they are limited to the last few rows and are edged or barred. Immature females usually lack chestnut on their middle coverts, while immature males usually have some chestnut present (Carney, 1964).

Age Determination: The juvenal tertials of both sexes are short, bluntly pointed, and usually frayed at their tips. The greater tertial coverts of both sexes in immatures are partly black and partly gray and, as in adult females, are usually tipped with white. However, immature males have narrower coverts with less white tipping than those of adult females, while the posthumeral feathers of adult females are wider than those of young males and are more heavily edged with cream (Carney, 1964). The tips of some of the tail feathers may be notched in immatures; Oring (1968) reported that these are lost in an asymmetric fashion between September and February, but females may retain some juvenal tail feathers until spring.

DISTRIBUTION AND HABITAT

Breeding Distribution and Habitat: The gadwall is distinctly westerly and southerly in its primary breeding distribution, with only scattered and uncertain nesting records from Alaska (Gabrielson and Lincoln, 1959) and with Canadian breeding largely limited to southern British Columbia, the grassland areas of Alberta, Saskatchewan, and Manitoba, and two restricted areas in southern Ontario (Godfrey, 1966). There is also a record of a young bird presumed to be a gadwall collected on Anicosti Island. There has also been suggestive evidence of breeding along the St. Lawrence River near Trois Rivieres (*Audubon Field Notes,* 22:591).

In the United States, breeding extends from Washington south to central California and eastward through Nevada, Arizona, New Mexico, Texas, Kansas, Nebraska, Iowa, and Minnesota, with scattered breeding to the east. The southwesternmost breeding may be near Topock, Arizona (*Audubon Field Notes,* 3:247; 5:303) Presently, gadwall breeding in Wisconsin is rare and limited to two counties (Jahn and Hunt, 1964). There are three breeding records for Michigan (Zimmerman and Van Tyne, 1959).

Beginning in the mid-1940s, gadwalls began nesting at Jones Beach, Long Island (*Audubon Field Notes,* 1:172; 2:199; 3:229), and substantial populations soon developed there (Sedwitz, 1958). Additional breeding populations developed at Pea Island National Wildlife Refuge, North Carolina (*Audubon Field Notes,* 3:233; 8:339; 9:372; 10:377), and later at Brigantine National Wildlife Refuge, New Jersey (*ibid,* 14:439; 23:647). There are also breeding records from Pennsylvania, New Jersey, Delaware, and Maryland, and new ones from Virginia (*ibid,* 22:595), Massachusetts (*ibid,* 24:661), and, most recently, Connecticut (*American Birds,* 26:834).

Breeding (hatched) and wintering (shaded) distributions of the gadwall in North America.

Some of these may have resulted from "seeding" of gadwalls in New England (Borden and Hochbaum, 1966), and this is certainly true of recent nesting records in Florida (Emmons, 1970). Whether this eastern invasion will persist indefinitely remains to be seen, but the original New York population has evidently recently declined (Foley, 1970). Henny and Holgersen (1974) have recently documented this eastern range expansion.

Breeding habitat of gadwalls is typically made up of marshes or small lakes in grassland. In particular, the presence of grassy islands is of considerable significance in determining nest distribution and density. Alkaline marshes seem to be preferred over those with low salt concentrations. Drewien and Springer (1969) noted that during two years of study, gadwall pairs were consistently more numerous on shallow prairie marshes than on temporary water areas, shallow to deep marshes, or deep and open-water marshes. Preferred nesting cover consists of dense, coarse vegetation, and the presence of herbaceous weeds interspersed with shorter vegetation on islands surrounded by open water may facilitate colonial nesting (Duebbert, 1966). Heavy grass or brush, such as provided by shrubby willows, is also an important nesting cover.

Wintering Distribution and Habitat: Wintering occurs over much of the United States north to coastal British Columbia and southward through Mexico, where it is abundant on both coasts and the interior, with the largest concentrations on the Nayarit coast (Leopold, 1959). It ranks about seventh in abundance among the species of waterfowl wintering in Mexico, with the average totals of recent wintering surveys in excess of 130,000 birds.

By flyways, the largest concentration of wintering gadwalls occurs in the Mississippi Flyway, in spite of the fact that most breeding occurs within the limits of the Central Flyway. Louisiana often supports a large percentage of the birds wintering in the Mississippi Flyway, although the numbers vary with the conditions of the habitat (Hawkins, 1964). Many of the Central Flyway gadwalls also winter on the Texas coast or move on into Mexico.

In the Chesapeake Bay area, migrant and wintering gadwalls usually are found on slightly brackish estuarine bays, where there are such submerged plants as wigeon grass (*Ruppia*), clasping-leaf pondweed (*Potamogeton perfoliatus*), and water milfoil (*Myriophyllum*). They also occur on natural ponds and marsh impoundments where wigeon grass and muskgrass (*Chara*) are the most common submerged plants (Stewart, 1962).

Age at Maturity: Of twenty-two respondents to a survey, thirteen reported breeding by captive gadwalls at one year of age, with seven and two indicating second- and third-year breeding, respectively (Ferguson, 1966). Apparently some wild first-year males never become sexually active (Oring, 1969).

Pair Bond Pattern: Gadwalls renew their pair bonds every year, and these are terminated early in the incubation period, when males desert their mates and begin their postnuptial molt.

Nest Location: In a study involving 660 nests, Williams and Marshall (1938) noted that the three most preferred cover types, in sequence of decreasing importance, were hardstem bulrush (*Scirpus acutus*), brushy willows (*Salix* spp.), and various herbaceous weeds. In a sample of 381 nests studied by Miller and Collins (1954), nettle was a highly preferred nest site. They found that about 84 percent of the nests were in vegetative cover between 13 and 36 inches high, and about 44 percent of the nests were on islands. Nest concealment was very high, with over 90 percent of the nests concealed on all four sides and about 70 percent concealed from above as well. About 85 percent were located from 3 to 50 yards from water. In some studies (Keith, 1961; Hunt and Naylor, 1955), the use of weeds as nest cover is of equal or lesser importance than that provided by Baltic rush (*Juncus balticus*), which often occurs as a shoreline belt around prairie marshes. However, Gates' (1962) study in Utah showed a clear preference for dry over wet sites and upland vegetation over lowland cover types, with the densest and driest cover types generally being selected.

Clutch Size: A variety of clutch size samples from North American gadwalls indicate an average between 9 and 11 eggs. Miller and Collins (1954) reported an average clutch of 11.0 eggs in 344 nests, similar to Gates' (1962) estimate of 11.1 eggs in 141 early nests. Similarly, Sowls (1955) noted an average clutch of 10.5 eggs for 17 early nests. Keith (1961) noted a decrease in clutch size from about 10 to 9 eggs as the breeding season progressed in Alberta. Williams and Marshall (1938) indicated a modal clutch size of 10 eggs in Utah, but the average of 660 nests was 9.09 eggs, probably reflecting renesting influences. The renesting incidence has been estimated to be 82 percent in Alberta and 96 percent in Utah. Duebbert (1966) noted an average clutch of 9.6 for 140 clutches in a colonial nesting situation in North Dakota, but his indicated clutch range of 5 to 20 eggs and comment on egg variability suggest that parasitic egg-laying probably influenced his data. Eggs are laid at a daily rate (Gates, 1962). Gates reported that renests, up to three of which were found, averaged 7.8 eggs, as compared with 10.7 eggs in initial nesting attempts by the same birds.

Incubation Period: Normally 26 days represent the incubation period, although there are records of 25-day and 27-day incubation periods (Bauer and Glutz, 1968), as well as a case of a nest hatching after 29 days, during which incubation was abnormally disturbed (Duebbert, 1966). Vermeer (1968) calculated an average period of 25.1 days based on a sample of ten clutches, with a range of 22 to 27 days. Oring (1969) reported a 24-day average period for incubator-hatched gadwalls, and a 25.7-day average for clutches hatched under natural conditions.

Fledging Period: Hochbaum (1944) estimated a 49- to 63-day fledging period. Most other published estimates are for seven weeks. Oring (1968) reported the first-flight in 47 of 50 hand-reared gadwalls between 50 and 56 days of age.

Nest and Egg Losses: Nesting success no doubt varies greatly with time and locality, but some high nesting success rates have been reported. Duebbert (1966) noted a nesting success averaging nearly 90 percent during two years for an island-nesting population. A similar 90 percent nesting success was noted for 381 nests in California (Miller and Collins, 1954). In Utah, Williams and Marshall (1938) reported an 85 percent hatching success for a sample of 6,000 eggs. Keith (1961) found a much lower nest success in Alberta, but estimated that, with renesting included, 45 percent of the females in his study area eventually successfully hatched a brood. Vermeer (1970) reported a nest success of only 33.3 percent for one group of island-nesting gadwalls in Alberta, as compared with an earlier (1968) nesting success of 90.0 on a different island. He found (1970) that gadwalls nested in higher densities in the presence of terns (*Sterna*) and probably also gulls (*Larus*), although some species of gull may cause heavy egg and chick mortality. Oring (1969) found an overall nesting success of 46 percent for 30 nests, with losses to ground squirrels, raccoons, and skunks.

Juvenile Mortality: Fledging success from 26 gadwall broods studied by Vermeer (1968) was nil, because of high predation on ducklings by California gulls (*L. californicus*). Gates (1962) estimated an average prefledging duckling mortality of 23 percent, with most losses occurring in the first eighteen days of life. The most important duckling predators in this area were also California gulls. Gates (1962) calculated a first-year mortality rate of 67 percent for birds banded as juveniles.

Adult Mortality: Gates (1962) estimated an annual adult mortality rate of 52 percent for birds banded as adults or unaged. This is identical to results obtained from banded gadwalls in England (Wainwright, 1967).

Food and Foraging: In the several studies that have been done on gadwall foods, there has been a consistently low percentage of animal materials present and a high incidence of the vegetative parts of submerged plants. Martin *et al.* (1951) reported high use of wigeon grass, algae such as muskgrass (*Chara*), pondweeds, and other aquatic plants. In a fall sample of nearly 200 stomachs from Utah, Gates (1957) noted that the foods found were mostly the vegetative parts of wigeon grass, pondweeds, horned pondweeds (*Zannichellia*), and the seeds of hardstem bulrush (*Scirpus acutus*) and salt grass (*Distichlis*). Stewart (1962) found that among gadwalls shot in brackish and freshwater estuaries of the Chesapeake Bay, vegetative parts of plants such as wigeon grass, muskgrass, eelgrass (*Zostera*), pondweeds, and naiad (*Najas*) were the principal foods.

Gadwalls are almost exclusively surface-feeders, although they have been observed diving for food on a few occasions (Kear and Johnsgard, 1968). Thus, they are largely dependent on food that they can reach by tipping-up and tend to feed in rather shallow marshes with abundant submerged plant life growing close to the surface.

Sociality, Densities, Territoriality: Gadwalls are relatively social on the nesting grounds, at least in island-nesting situations. Gates (1962), studying in an area where no island-nesting was possible, noted a definite spacing-out of pairs and moderately large home ranges (average of five pairs per 67 acres). These home ranges overlapped considerably and shared common areas for foraging or loafing, although not simultaneously. Established males attempted to discourage new pairs from breeding in the same area but were often unsuccessful.

In island-nesting situations, territoriality is virtually nil, and Duebbert (1966) believed that gadwalls have evolved behavior patterns that enable many pairs to nest in a very restricted area. He noted nest densities of 78 and 121 nests on a seven-acre island at Lower Souris National Wildlife Refuge during two summers, and there is an earlier record of 106 nests on a one-half-acre island (*Audubon Field Notes*, 1:172).

Interspecific Relationships: Nest site competition with other ducks is probably not significant for gadwalls. Gates (1962) noted that other species of surface-feeding ducks seem less dependent than the gadwall on dry and/or dense cover for nesting. Vermeer (1968) noted a fairly low rate of nest parasitism in gadwall nests, with 11 of 54 nests being affected. These were mostly by lesser scaup and white-winged scoters. There is also a reported case of nest parasitism by redheads (Weller, 1959).

Gadwalls have been shown to exhibit a preference for nesting among tern colonies (Vermeer, 1970) in Alberta. Likewise, in Russia, nesting has been noticed among gulls, terns, plovers, and other shorebirds (Dementiev and Gladkov, 1967). Bengtson (1972) found that predation by ravens was the greatest single cause of nesting failure, while minks, parasitic jaegers, and great black-backed gulls also accounted for some losses. Egg predation by California gulls on gadwall nests is sometimes extremely high, and they may also be responsible for duckling losses (Odin, 1957).

General Activity Patterns and Movements: In contrast to mallards and pintails, gadwalls typically exhibit a considerable delay between the arrival at their nesting grounds and the beginning of nesting. Gates (1962) noted an average postarrival period of seventeen days prior to establishment on a breeding home range and another prenesting period of eleven days before the beginning of egg-laying. This delay is apparently related to the gadwall's dry and dense nesting cover. During this prenesting period, paired birds remain gregarious until the home range area is established, and pairs may forage and loaf together. Gates found that home ranges of gadwalls in Utah ranged from 34 to 87 acres, with nests well scattered, whereas Duebbert (1966) found that much larger home ranges occurred among a group of colony-nesting gadwalls. There, incubating females sometimes flew more than a mile to rest and feed unmolested by strange drakes.

SOCIAL AND SEXUAL BEHAVIOR

Flocking Behavior: Although gadwalls nest relatively late, an early reestablishment of bisexual flocks in fall is typical. This seems to be related to the fact that gadwalls begin pair formation activities unusually early, even while males are still in eclipse plumage. In Austria this activity begins in August, and within a month 50 to 70 percent of the females appear to be paired. Thus, the fall migration of this species does not show sexual segregation, at least by comparison with many other surface-feeding ducks (Bezzel, 1959). Sex ratio counts made during early and later stages of migration also do not show changes suggestive of differential sex migration or earlier migration of paired birds (Johnsgard and Buss, 1956).

Pair-forming Behavior: Although pair-forming behavior in gadwalls begins unusually early, and most aquatic courtship has occurred prior to the acquisition of the males' nuptial plumage, there is a secondary spring peak of social courtship (Bezzel, 1959). Also, aerial chases progressively increase toward spring, with a peak (in Austria) in May, or just prior to the onset of incubation. Duebbert (1966) also noted a high intensity of aerial chases in late May and early June in North Dakota, when many paired birds moved to the nesting island and egg-laying began. Flights continued through most of the incubation period of July. Duebbert interpreted the earlier pursuit flights as a reflection of individual intolerance, and the later ones as increasingly sexual. It is unlikely that such aerial chases play any functional role in normal pair formation, but rather pairs seem to be formed by the combination of female inciting and male turning-the-back-of-the-head displays, as in other ducks that have been studied (Johnsgard, 1965).

Copulatory Behavior: As in other surface-feeding ducks, copulation is preceded by mutual head-pumping behavior. Following treading, the male utters a whistle-grunt call, then turns and faces the female in a motionless and erect posture (Johnsgard, 1965).

Nesting and Brooding Behavior: When looking for nest sites the pair may fly out to grassy areas and land together. While the male waits, the female walks into the weedy growth. This phase may precede actual egg-laying by five to seven days (Duebbert, 1966). When laying, females go to their nest sites between 5:00 and 7:00 a.m., either flying to a point up to 25 feet away and walking the remaining distance to the nest or, in the case of nests in tall cover, landing within a few inches of the nest's location. Duebbert found that the male may desert the female as early as the seventh day of egg-laying, or remain until the day prior to the hatching of the eggs. Gates (1962) indicated that the desertion usually occurred before the midpoint of incubation.

Following hatching, females with broods move to deep-water marshes and edges of large impoundments, sometimes traveling in excess of a mile, and in one study averaging about half a mile (Gates, 1962). Gates found no evidence of brood mergers in the broods of marked hens that he studied.

Postbreeding Behavior: Shortly after or even before leaving their mates, males begin to molt. Gates found that such males retained some sexual interest nevertheless, and that some even participated in attempted rapes of other nesting females. Oring (1969) confirmed Gates' observations as to the variations in times at which males deserted their mates, and believed that the sight of postbreeding groups might hasten the breakup of pairs. He also believed that some yearling males never participate in courtship display and are the first to undergo postnuptial molt of their flight feathers. They are then followed in sequence by early breeding males, later breeding males, sexually active but nonbreeding drakes, early breeding females, and finally late breeding females. Some late breeding hens may migrate to their winter quarters before undergoing their flightless period. Maximum molting congregations of males occurred at the end of June, and by early August about half of the adult males were flightless. At this time, captive males were not yet flightless but were exhibiting dawn and dusk periods of nervousness that seemed to be indicative of premigratory restlessness. As the wild birds regained their powers of flight they formed large, wary flocks, which fed during the entire day if undisturbed. Most of them had left the area by the end of September.

BAIKAL TEAL

Anas formosa Georgi 1775

Other Vernacular Names: Clucking Teal, Formosa Teal, Spectacled Teal.

Range: Breeds in eastern Siberia and northern Ussuriland, possibly also in Kamchatka. Some summer records from St. Lawrence Island, King Island, and mainland Alaska, but no established records of breeding. In winter found mainly in central China, with smaller numbers in Japan, Taiwan, and southeast Asia rarely as far as India, and with rare stragglers along the Pacific coast of North America to California.

Subspecies: None recognized.

Measurements (after Phillips, 1924):

Folded wing: Males 200-216, females 190-198 mm.

Culmen: Males 35-38, females 33-36 mm.

Weights: Few weights are available. Dementiev and Gladkov (1967) reported the species ranges from 500 to 600 grams; Bauer and Glutz (1958) noted a weight of 480 grams for a male in December. Chen Tso-hsin (1963) stated that twelve males averaged 437 grams (0.96 pounds), with a range of 360 to 520 grams, while eight females averaged 431 grams (0.95 pounds), with a range of 402 to 505 grams.

AGE AND SEX CRITERIA

Sex Determination: Among adult birds, females can probably be recognized by their relatively dull speculum pattern, the absence of ornamental tertials or iridescent head-patterning, and a paler throat than occurs in eclipse-plumage males.

Age Determination: Not yet established, but first-year birds probably retain notched tail feathers through their first fall of life.

IDENTIFICATION

In the Hand: Because of its very similar speculum patterns, the Baikal teal is most readily confused with the green-winged teal, from which it can be readily separated by its longer tail (minimum 75 mm.) and larger size (over 14 ounces, or more than 400 grams). The male's distinctive head pattern is usually not attained until late winter, but the ornamental chestnut-striped scapulars and tertials are present earlier. Females should be carefully compared with the female green-winged teal, which they closely resemble, but differ in their definite white (rather than buffy and faintly striped) cheek spot at the base of the upper mandible, their clearer white throat with an extension up the sides of the cheeks, and the dark area above the eye that interrupts the pale superciliary stripe.

In the Field: The male in nuptial plumage is unmistakable at close range. The bird sits in the water with its colorful head low on the breast, its tail well out of the water, the ornamental scapulars hanging down over the flanks, and vertical white bars visible in front of the black under tail coverts and on the sides of the breast. Its distinctive clucking call, *ruk-ruk'*, or *ruk,* is uttered only during spring display. The quacking notes of the female are rather infrequent. In the air it resembles a green-winged teal, but has brownish gray rather than white under wing coverts. Lone females should not be identified as Baikal teal except under extremely favorable conditions, when their distinctive facial markings noted above can be clearly seen.

OCCURRENCE IN NORTH AMERICA

Not surprisingly, most of the records of this beautiful Asian species of duck have originated from Alaska. Gabrielson and Lincoln (1959) summarized the majority of these, which include a male collected at Wainwright, two males collected on King Island, a pair collected on St. Lawrence Island, a pair collected at Wales, and a male that was also collected at Wales. In May of 1959 a pair was seen at Cape Sabine, and an unverified report of possible nesting at Hooper Bay was made during 1959 (Maher, 1960). The Baikal teal was also reported seen on Amchitka Island in 1971.

There is apparently only one Canadian record, that of an immature male at Ladner, British Columbia (Hatter, 1960). Records from south of Canada are also few and perhaps are best regarded as probable escapes from captivity. These include a record from California (*Condor*, 34:257), a sight record from Ohio (Borrer, 1950), a bird shot in Washington (Jewett *et al.*, 1953), a sighting in Pennsylvania (*Audubon Field Notes*, 14:296), and two sightings in New Jersey (*ibid.*, 15:315). Most recently, birds have been shot in California and Oregon (*American Birds*, 28:679, 692).

Fulvous Whistling Duck, Pair

Cuban Whistling Duck, Pair

Black-bellied Whistling Duck, Pair

Mute Swan, Subadult

Mute Swan, Adults

Trumpeter Swan, Pair

Whistling Swan, Adult

White-fronted Goose, Adult

White-fronted Goose, Adult

Lesser Snow Goose, Adult

Lesser Snow Goose, Adults

Ross Goose, Adults

Emperor Goose, Adult

Aleutian Canada Goose, Adult

Cackling Canada Goose, Adult

Atlantic Canada Goose, Pair

Baffin Island Canada Goose, Pair

Barnacle Goose, Female and brood

Pacific Brant Goose, Pair at nest

Pacific Brant Goose, Adult

Muscovy Duck, Adult male

Wood Duck, Adult male

Wood Duck, Pair resting

European Wigeon, Adult males

European Wigeon, Pair

American Wigeon, Adult male

American Wigeon, Pair

Falcated Duck, Adult male

Falcated Duck, Pair

GREEN-WINGED TEAL

Anas crecca Linnaeus 1758

(Until 1973, regarded by the A.O.U. as *Anas carolinensis*)

Other Vernacular Names: Common Teal, Greenwing, Northern Green-
winged Teal, Teal.

Range: Breeds throughout much of northern Europe and Asia, the Aleutian
Islands, temperate North America, and Iceland. In North America, winters
from southern Canada (along both coasts) through the central and southern states to Mexico and Central America.

North American Subspecies (recognized by Delacour, 1956):

A. c. crecca L.: European Green-winged (Common) Teal. Breeds in Iceland, Europe, and Asia. In North America, seen occasionally during winter, especially along the Atlantic coast.

A. c. nimia Friedmann: Aleutian Green-winged Teal. Resident in the Aleutian Islands, from Akutan westward.

A. c. carolinensis Gmelin: American Green-winged Teal. Breeds on the continent of North America, from north-central Alaska to New Brunswick and Nova Scotia.

Measurements (of *carolinensis,* after Delacour, 1956):

Folded wing: Males 179-191, females 172-183 mm.

Culmen: Males 34-37, females 33-36 mm.

Weights: Nelson and Martin (1953) reported the average weight of 199 males to be 0.8 pounds (362 grams), and 81 females averaged 0.7 pounds (317 grams). Jahn and Hunt (1964) reported the average weight of 45 adult and 149 immature fall-shot males to be the same, 12 ounces (340 grams); 33 adult and 114 immature females averaged 11 ounces (312 grams). Maximum reported weights for males appear to be one pound, reported by Nelson and Martin (the 1 pound 5 ounce record cited by Jahn and Hunt for an immature male is presumed to be a misprint). The maximum weight reported for females is 1 pound 2 ounces, reported by Jahn and Hunt for an adult, while Nelson and Martin reported 0.9 pound as a maximum female weight.

IDENTIFICATION

In the Hand: This species is the smallest of the North American dabbling ducks, rarely if ever exceeding a pound (450 grams) in weight and having a tail of less than three inches (75 mm.). The bill is relatively long but unusually narrow (12-14 mm.). Besides this small size, the presence of a speculum that is green inwardly, black outwardly, narrowly edged behind with white, and with a brownish anterior border, is relatively diagnostic. A similar speculum pattern occurs only in the rare Baikal teal.

In the Field: Green-winged teal float lightly in the water, the tail usually well above the water, and males exhibit buffy yellow triangular patches on the black under tail coverts. The only white marking shown by males is the vertical bar in front of the gray sides (usually) or (in the rare European and Aleutian races) a horizontal white stripe between the back and flanks. In good light, the iridescent green head patch may be distinguished from the otherwise chestnut head, the two areas separated by a narrow and often faint (brighter in the European and Aleutian forms) buffy white stripe. Field recognition of the Aleutian and European races must be based on males; females can scarcely be distinguished in the hand. In the field, female green-winged teal may be identified by their small size, dark-colored bill, and brownish color, with the head showing a darker eye-stripe and a paler area near the base of the bill. In flight, green-winged teal are the essence of agility, twisting and turning like shorebirds, and alternately flashing their white under wing coverts and dark brownish upper wing. The dark upper wing color is perhaps the best way to separate green-winged teal from blue-winged or cinnamon teal, although green-winged teal also appear to have shorter necks and both sexes have pure white abdomens. During winter and spring the whistled *krick'-et* calls of the males can be heard almost as far away as the birds can be seen and often provide the first clue as to their presence in an area. The female has a variety of weak quacking notes and a decrescendo call of about four notes.

AGE AND SEX CRITERIA

Sex Determination: External characters that indicate a male are vermiculations anywhere, usually on the sides, scapulars, or back. The most distal tertial (adjacent to first iridescent secondary) in males has a black stripe which is sharply delineated, while in females the stripe is blackish to brownish, grading into the basic feather color (Carney, 1964). Internal examination should be used if these criteria fail.

Age Determination: Notched tail feathers indicate an immature bird, as do tertials that are small, narrow, and rather delicate, with frayed tips. In immatures, middle coverts just anterior to the tertial coverts are often rough and show wear at their edges, and they are usually narrower and more trapezoidal than those of adults (Carney, 1964).

DISTRIBUTION AND HABITAT

Breeding Distribution and Habitat: The North American breeding range of the green-winged teal is similar to that of the American wigeon. On the Aleutian Islands the race *nimia* is a common resident throughout (Murie, 1959; Kenyon, 1961) and is replaced by *carolinensis* on the Alaska Peninsula. The latter form breeds throughout Alaska, except perhaps on the treeless tundra of the Arctic coast, where there are few records of occurrence (Gabrielson and Lincoln, 1959). In Canada the species has an extensive range, from British Columbia and the Yukon on the west to Labrador and Newfoundland on the east and northward at least to the tree line. In Newfoundland it is second only to the black duck as a common breeder, and it is also common in Nova Scotia and New Brunswick (Moisan *et al.*, 1967).

In the United States, green-winged teal are common breeders in eastern Washington, are rare in Idaho and Oregon, but are common in extreme northern and northeastern California. Only a few pairs are recorded each year in Utah and Nevada, and they are generally uncommon in the Great Plains states except for the Dakotas (Moisan *et al.*, 1967). They are occasional breeders in

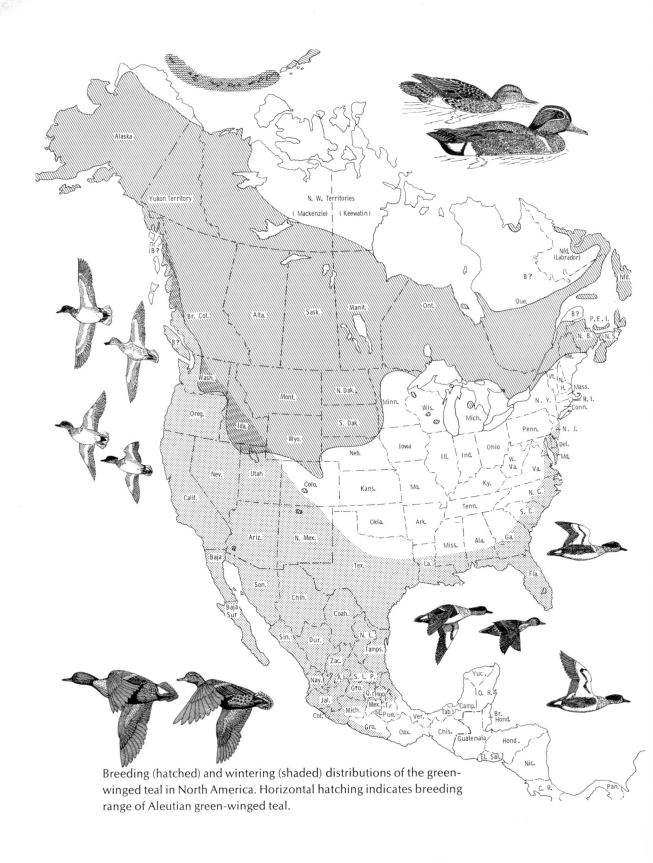

Breeding (hatched) and wintering (shaded) distributions of the green-winged teal in North America. Horizontal hatching indicates breeding range of Aleutian green-winged teal.

western and northeastern Minnesota (Lee *et al.,* 1964a), are infrequent in Wisconsin (Jahn and Hunt, 1964), are local breeders in Michigan (Zimmerman and Van Tyne, 1959), and are relatively rare in New York (Foley, 1960). Although they are regular breeders in Maine, there are only scattered breeding records in other eastern states, including Ohio (*Audubon Field Notes,* 7:308), Pennsylvania (*ibid.,* 7:302; 20:557), Massachusetts (*ibid.,* 8:333), and New Jersey (*ibid.,* 14:439; 16:464).

Judging from aerial surveys, the highest continental breeding densities occur in the Athabaska Delta, the Slave River parklands, and east of Great Slave Lake. The aspen parklands area of Canada is next highest in density. This would indicate that green-winged teal prefer the wooden ponds of parklands for breeding rather than prairie potholes (Moisan *et al.,* 1967). Munro (1949) characterized the typical nesting habitat as grassland, sedge meadows or dry hillsides with aspen or brush thickets, or open woods adjacent to a slough or pond. Hildén (1964) pointed out that the European race also prefers to breed on small waters surrounded by woodland, generally does not breed on the eutrophic grassy lakes of open farming country, and avoids open tundra habitats.

Wintering Distribution and Habitat: The green-winged teal winters along the Aleutian chain (*nimia*) along the coast of southeastern Alaska, south through coastal British Columbia, in the western coastal United States including particularly the Central and Imperial valleys of California, and southward to central Mexico. In Mexico it is common on both coasts and in the interior, but is particularly abundant in Sinaloa and Nayarit (Leopold, 1959). Along the coasts of Texas and Louisiana the species is an abundant winter resident, with an average of 60 percent of the continental wintering population in recent midwinter surveys occurring in the Mississippi Flyway. Since most of these birds are produced in western Canada, they evidently migrate down the Central Flyway and then shift eastward into the coastal marshes of Louisiana (Moisan *et al.,* 1967). It is also thought that whereas the Central Valley of California obtains most of its wintering teal from Alaska, those using the Imperial Valley originate in the Northwest Territories and the Prairie Provinces of Canada. The harvest rate of teal in California is very high, with nearly a third of the total continental kill occurring in that state (Moisan *et al.,* 1967).

The preferred wintering habitat consists of coastal marshes, especially those near rice fields in Louisiana and Texas. Open salt water is apparently avoided (Moisan *et al.,* 1967). Stewart (1962) reported that teal prefer creeks and ponds that are bordered by mud flats at low tide. Tidal creeks and marshes of estuarine locations are seemingly preferred over salt marshes. Late fall counts on estuarine bay marshes showed higher usage of fresh or brackish waters, while winter and spring counts indicated a higher use of saltwater marshes.

GENERAL BIOLOGY

Age at Maturity: Green-winged teal probably normally breed at one year of age. Ferguson (1966) stated that thirteen of twenty-two aviculturalists reported first-year breeding in American green-wings. The nine reports of from two to four years prior to breeding are probably a reflection of this species' general reluctance to breed under captive conditions.

Pair Bond Pattern: Pair bonds are reestablished yearly, as in other surface-feeding ducks. I have seen only one report of a male in full eclipse remaining with a female and its brood (Munro, 1949).

Nest Location: Keith (1961) noted that 22 nests of this species that he found averaged 65 feet from the nearest water and had an average light penetration at the floor of the nest of only 32 percent, the smallest average figure he reported. He noted that this species and the blue-winged teal had the best-concealed nests of the twelve species studied. The vast majority (86 percent) of the nests were found in Baltic rush (*Juncus balticus*) cover, with the rest in mixed prairie and cattails (*Typha*). In an Iceland study involving the European green-winged teal, Bengtson (1970) reported that among 207 nest sites, 173 were under shrubs, most of which were less than half a meter high. Girard (1941), reporting on 15 nests, indicated that the average distance to water was 34.2 yards, with a range of 4 to 100 yards.

Clutch Size: Keith (1961) reported an average clutch size of 8.7 eggs for eighteen nests. Girard (1941) found that fifteen nests had an average clutch of 7.53 eggs. In reviewing European records, Bauer and Glutz (1968) concluded that 8 to 10 eggs are typical, with normal limits of 5 to 12. Information on renesting clutch sizes and incidence of renesting are not yet available.

Incubation Period: Probably normally 21 to 23 days, with an exceptional case of 25 days reported (Bauer and Glutz, 1968).

Fledging Period: Apparently 44 days (Bauer and Glutz, 1968), although shorter estimates have been made (Lack, 1968).

Nest and Egg Losses: Although his sample size was small, Girard (1941) found that 75.2 percent of the eggs in fifteen total nests hatched, and that an average of 5.66 eggs per successful nest hatched. Crows were responsible for some egg losses. Keith (1961) did not calculate a hatching rate for the twenty-one nests he found, but noted that four nests were deserted, eight were taken by skunks, one by an unknown mammal, and at least three hatched. He noted that mammalian predation levels were highest in the *Juncus* zone, the preferred nesting cover of green-winged teal.

Juvenile Mortality: Little specific information is available on prefledging mortality, but it is seemingly low. Munro (1949) believed that the high brood survival he observed in green-winged teal was related to the intense brood defense exhibited by females. Moisan *et al.* (1967) estimated that brood sizes at the time of fledging average from 5 to 7 young. Yocom (1951) found an average brood size of 5.5 young for twenty-seven broods between two-thirds and fully grown, and Munro (1949) indicated an average brood size of 6.2 young for August broods. However, brood mergers are not uncommon in this species, and may influence such counts.

Moisan *et al.* (1967) estimated a 70 percent first-year mortality rate for green-winged teal banded as immature birds.

Adult Mortality: An annual adult mortality rate of 50 percent has been estimated for North American green-winged teal (Moisan *et al.,* 1967). This is close to an estimate of 45 percent for European green-winged teal banded in England (Wainwright, 1967).

GENERAL ECOLOGY

Food and Foraging: The small bill of the green-winged teal limits the size of materials it can consume, and plant seeds are apparently an important part of its diet. Martin *et al.* (1951) list panic grass (*Panicum*), bulrush (*Scirpus*), and pondweeds (*Potamogeton*) as primary foods, with both seeds and vegetative parts taken in pondweeds. The oogonia of muskgrass (*Chara*) are evidently preferred by green-winged teal, but not the "leafy" portions (Munro, 1949). Stewart (1962) noted that the seeds of Olney three-square (*Scirpus olneyi*) and wigeon grass (*Ruppia*), as well as amphipods and gastropods, were the principal foods of 34 birds taken on estuarine bay marshes of Chesapeake Bay, while 8 birds from river marshes had consumed seeds of a variety of plants including bulrushes, smartweeds (*Polygonum*), and other aquatics. In a Texas study, Rolle and Bolen (1969) found that, in comparison with blue-winged teal from the same playa lake, green-winged teal samples showed a higher volume of smartweed (*Polygonum*) seeds and lower amounts of wild millet (*Echinochloa*) and grain sorghum (*Sorghum*).

In a detailed study of teal food consumption in England, Olney (1963) found that at least during the fall months seeds occurred in nearly all 456 birds examined and represented 76.2 percent of the total food volume. Most of the seeds ranged from 1 to 2.5 mm. in size, with an overall range of 0.5 to 11 mm. Likewise, the mollusks that he found were no larger than 6 mm.

Sociality, Densities, Territoriality: Green-winged teals are relatively social birds, usually occurring in moderate-sized flocks during both fall and spring.

For the most part, however, they do not occur in large flocks. Jahn and Hunt (1964) noted that, since teal do not concentrate in refuges but rather remain scattered widely in small flocks, a relatively high hunter kill of this species occurs in Wisconsin.

Estimates of breeding densities are few. In the grassland area of southeastern Alberta, Keith (1961) found a five-year average of three pairs (range two to five) using 183 acres of water on his study area, or a density of one pair per 60 acres. Detailed ground surveys in the preferred parkland habitats are not available, but no doubt would show higher breeding densities. Atkinson-Willes (1963), speaking of the European race, has commented on the fact that this species is extremely difficult to study during the breeding season and that it apparently does not occur in high densities anywhere throughout its vast breeding range.

Territoriality or home range information is likewise lacking.

Interspecific Relationships: Because of its extremely small size and unusually high dependence on seeds, it is unlikely that the green-winged teal directly competes with any other surface-feeding ducks for food. Rollo and Bolen (1969) noted apparently significant differences in food consumption between green-winged and blue-winged teal during fall in Texas. The two species also show considerable differences in wintering areas, migration timing, and preferred nesting habitats. Yocom (1951) noted that green-winged teal nest more frequently in the yellow pine (*Pinus ponderosa*) zone of Washington than do the other two species of teals.

Competition for nesting sites is likewise probably negligible, and the green-winged teal is not included in the list of species Weller (1959) found as parasitizing or being parasitized by other species. Crows (Girard, 1941) and skunks (Keith, 1961) have been noted as nest predators, although teal nests are usually very well concealed. Bengtson (1972) observed a very low incidence of nest parasitism and listed only minks and ravens as nest predators.

General Activity Patterns and Movements: No specific information on daily activity rhythms or on local movements appear to be available. Migratory movements have been summarized by Moisan *et al.* (1967), Low (1949), and Munro (1949).

SOCIAL AND SEXUAL BEHAVIOR

Flocking Behavior: During the fall, there is apparently an early southward movement of adult males, while adult females and immatures remain north somewhat longer (Moisan *et al.,* 1967). Jahn and Hunt (1964) found a consistent disproportion of immature males among hunters' kills in Wisconsin, leading them to believe that differential sex migration may occur, with females moving farther south than males. An early spring preponderance of males in sex ratio counts in Washington (Johnsgard and Buss, 1956), as well as in the Netherlands (Lebret, 1950), suggests that females indeed may winter farther south than males. Spring flocks are usually small in size, often consisting of a dozen birds or less.

Pair-forming Behavior: Pair formation in the wild probably begins, as it does in the European race, in early fall and continues through the winter and spring. McKinney (1965) noted that teal he observed in mid-March in Louisiana were virtually all paired. In Austria, about 50 percent of the birds are paired by the end of January and over 90 percent are paired by the end of March (Bezzel, 1959). However, aquatic social courtship, which begins during September in Austria, does not reach a peak until about the middle of March.

The social pair-forming displays of green-winged teal are well known (Johnsgard, 1965; McKinney, 1965) and are too numerous and complex for description here. However, the female's inciting display is frequent during pair formation and serves to indicate the female's preference for or pair bond with a specific male, while the turning-of-the-back-of-the-head (or "turn-back-of-head," in McKinney's terminology) display is the typical response of a preferred male to such inciting. Aerial flights are not of special significance in pair formation; McKinney believed that they simply serve to change the location of a courting group.

Copulatory Behavior: Mutual head-pumping is the precopulatory display of the green-winged teal. Following copulation the male draws his head backward along the back in a "bridling" display posture (Johnsgard, 1965).

Nesting and Brooding Behavior: Female teal usually line their nests with a considerable quantity of down and, when leaving, will cover the eggs with the down or other nest lining (Munro, 1949). Females defend their young with remarkable intensity and, if disturbed with a brood on land, will perform distractive movements while dragging one or both wings. When defending a brood on the water, they fly or rush about on the water in front of the intruder, often continuing this activity for several minutes while their broods hide in the nearby weeds. Munro (1949) illustrated two females thus jointly defending a merged brood, and he believed that, because of the mother's strong brood defense, there is relatively little mortality of these tiny ducklings.

Postbreeding Behavior: Males usually desert their mates about the time incubation begins and may gather in small groups prior to molting. They may move to special molting areas; Hochbaum (1944) notes that, although green-winged teal are uncommon breeders in the Delta, Manitoba, area, they pour into the marshes in mid-June and early July. By mid-September migrant teal have become common as far south as southern Wisconsin, and populations peak there in mid-October (Jahn and Hunt, 1964).

COMMON MALLARD

Anas platyrhynchos Linnaeus 1758

Other Vernacular Names: Greenhead, Green-headed Mallard, Northern Mallard.

Range: Breeds throughout much of the Northern Hemisphere, in North America from Alaska to northern California and east to Ontario and the Great Lakes, with recent breeding extensions into New England. Also breeds in Greenland, Iceland, Europe, and Asia. Winters through much of the breeding range and south to extreme northern Mexico.

North American Subspecies (see also accounts of Mexican mallard, Florida mallard, and mottled mallard):

A. p. platyrhynchos L.: Common Mallard. Range as indicated above, except for Greenland.

A. p. conboschas Brehm: Greenland Mallard. Resident on coastal Greenland, with vagrant birds probably sometimes reaching continental North America.

Measurements (of *p. platyrhynchos,* after Delacour, 1956):
Folded wing: Males 260-270, females 240-270 mm.
Culmen: Males 50-56, females 43-52 mm.
Weights: Bellrose and Hawkins (1947) reported the average weight of 631 adult males as 2.78 pounds (1,261 grams) and 730 immatures as 2.59 pounds (1,174 grams); 402 adult females averaged 2.39 pounds (1,084 grams), and 671 immatures averaged 2.28 pounds (1,034 grams). Maximum male weights were reported by Nelson and Martin (1953) to be 4 pounds and by Jahn and Hunt (1964) as 3.81 pounds; maximum female weights were reported by these authors as 3.6 and 3.81 pounds, respectively. Additional weight data are presented by Mumford (1954) for 3,092 males and 2,300 females.

IDENTIFICATION

In the Hand: The familiar green-headed and white-collared male in nuptial plumage needs no special attention, but females or immature males may perhaps be confused with other species. Except for the rare Mexican mallard, the presence of a bluish speculum bordered both in front and behind with black and white will serve to distinguish common mallards from all other North American ducks, with additional criteria being orange-colored legs and feet, a white underwing coloration, and a yellow to orange bill with varying amounts of black present. See the Mexican mallard account for distinction from that species, and the black duck account for recognition of hybrids.

In the Field: Mallards are large, surface-feeding ducks that exceed in size all dabbling ducks except the black duck. On the water, the dark, often apparently black, head color of the male is evident, as are the reddish brown chest and the grayish white sides and mantle, contrasting with the black hindquarters. More than any other dabbling duck, male mallards are dark at both ends and light in the middle. Females may be recognized by the combination of their fairly large size and their orange yellow bill, which is distinctly heavier and more orange than that of a female gadwall. Females also show a definitely striped head, with a dark crown and eye-stripe, contrasting with pale cheeks and a light superciliary stripe. The familiar, loud *quack* of the female is frequently heard, and her call consisting of a series of notes of diminishing volume is also commonly uttered. During aquatic display males utter a sharp whistled note, usually single but sometimes double, that can be heard for several hundred yards. Unlike many other dabblers, this courtship note is not uttered in flight. In flight, the male's immaculate white under wing coverts contrast with the female's brownish abdomen and upperparts. In the male the white of the under wing coverts is continuous with the whitish sides and abdomen and is terminated in front by chestnut and behind by black. The two white stripes associated with the speculum are also evident in flight.

AGE AND SEX CRITERIA

Sex Identification: Apart from internal examination or cloacal characters, males older than juveniles usually have some vermiculated feathers present. Wing characters useful for sexing mallards include the vermiculated scapulars, which indicate males. If vermiculations are lacking and the white barring on the greater secondary coverts extends at least to the thirteenth proximal covert, the bird is a female; in males the white does not extend beyond the twelfth secondary covert (Carney and Geis, 1960).

Age Determination, Males: Juvenal tertials are present until late November. They lack the pearly color of adult tertials and are often frayed and faded. Likewise, juvenal tertial coverts are often frayed, faded, and narrow. Immatures may have light edging on the inner webs of the four most distal primary coverts, and their middle coverts are often frayed, are somewhat trapezoidal, and are smaller and narrower than those of adults (Carney, 1964).

Age Determination, Females: Frayed or faded tertials or tertial coverts indicate an immature bird, and the two most proximal tertial coverts may lack the white of the anterior speculum bar. Immatures may also have conspicuous light edging on the inner webs of the four most distal coverts, which is lacking or minute in adults, and the middle coverts are narrow and trapezoidal (Carney, 1964). The presence of notched tail feathers indicates an immature bird for either sex.

DISTRIBUTION AND HABITAT

Breeding Distribution and Habitat: The breeding range of the mallard in North America is extremely broad. It breeds throughout Alaska, including the Aleutian Islands (Gabrielson and Lincoln, 1959), although the number of definite records from the coastal tundra areas of western and northern Alaska indicate that it is uncommon to rare as a breeding bird in these areas. In Canada it breeds from British Columbia and the Yukon Territory eastward to southern Quebec and north to James Bay, the Hudson Bay coast of Manitoba, and in the Northwest Territories approximately to tree line. Although not yet

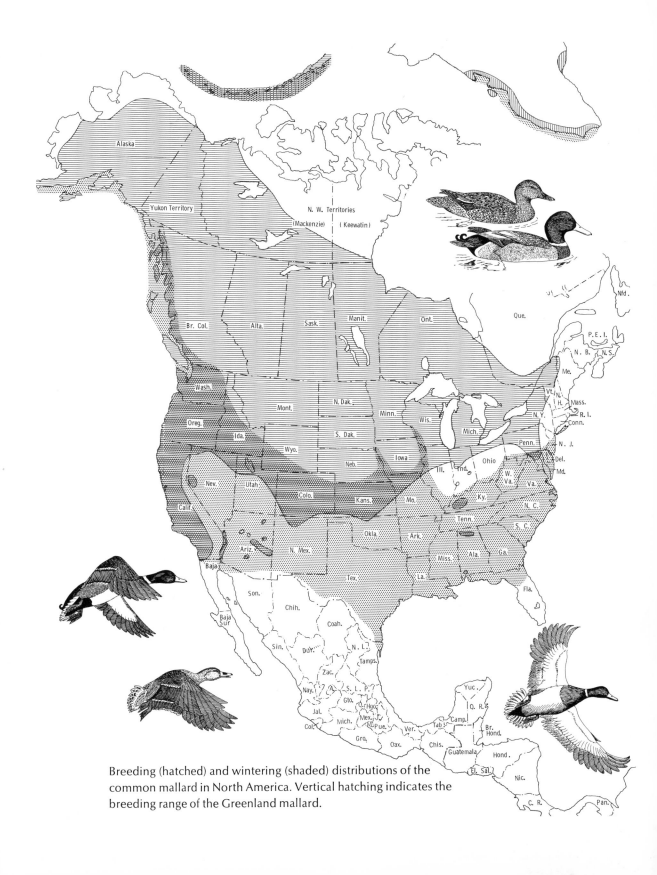

Breeding (hatched) and wintering (shaded) distributions of the
common mallard in North America. Vertical hatching indicates the
breeding range of the Greenland mallard.

reported as a breeding bird in the Maritime Provinces, the species' eventual occurrence there would seem highly likely.

South of Canada, the mallard's breeding range extends broadly across the United States, south to southern California, Arizona, northern New Mexico, eastward across the Great Plains to the Great Lakes and New England. The mallard's invasion of the eastern states and New England as a breeding and wintering bird has been a gradual process that may be traced back to the beginning of the twentieth century (Johnsgard, 1961, 1967) and has not yet become stabilized. It finally reached Maine in the early 1950s (Coulter, 1953, 1954) and now is a relatively common nesting species there. South of New York and western Pennsylvania the mallard is distinctly an uncommon breeder. It is a rare breeder near Warren, Pennsylvania (*Audubon Field Notes*, 18:506), has bred a few times in Maryland (*ibid.*, 8:338; Stewart 1962), has nested at least once in South Carolina (*Audubon Field Notes*, 13:425), Arkansas (*ibid.*, 24:692), and Mississippi (*ibid.*, 20:576). There are also some Louisiana breeding records (*ibid.*, 15:474; 23:668).

Since the species breeds over such a broad range, it is difficult to separate preferred from acceptable breeding habitats. However, some trends are evident. Hildén (1964) noted that mallards accept waters of almost any kind for breeding, and they will breed in dense woods or on rocky shores as well as around open lakes or on the meadows of grassy lakes. The presence of shallow-water feeding areas and the availability of suitable nest sites appear to be the only critical features. Mallards prefer to nest in fairly dry sites with rather tall vegetation, such as among upland weeds, dry marshes, or in hay-fields (Lee *et al.*, 1964a). In forested situations they will sometimes nest in trees or in stumps (Cowardin *et al.*, 1967), but this habitat is not highly preferred by mallards. Hildén (1964) found mallards breeding on coastal islets covered by grassy or herbaceous growth, but not on wooded ones.

Wintering Distribution and Habitat: Because of their large body size and associated hardiness, mallards are likely to be found wintering anywhere food is available and open water can be found. This includes the Aleutian Islands and the southern coast of Alaska, coastal British Columbia, the coastal states south of Canada, south to extreme northeastern Mexico, and many of the interior states in the southern parts of the United States. Along the Atlantic coast the mallard winters as far north as the New England states, extending locally to southwestern Quebec and rarely to Newfoundland and Nova Scotia.

Stewart (1962) judged that shallow, brackish bays with adjacent extensive agricultural areas represent the optimum habitat for migrant and winter resident mallards in the Chesapeake Bay region. From 50 to 86 percent of the fall, winter, and spring population during 1958–1959 occurred in this combination of habitats, while estuarine river and bay marshes, coastal salt marshes, and other miscellaneous habitats supported the remainder. Almost no birds were seen on bay marshes having salt water.

GENERAL BIOLOGY

Age at Maturity: Mallards regularly breed at one year of age. This was the opinion of twenty out of twenty-four aviculturalists contacted by Ferguson (1966), and there are many records of wild mallards breeding in their first year of life. First-year females may have somewhat smaller clutch sizes and are less prone to renest than older females (Coulter and Miller, 1968).

Pair Bond Pattern: Mallard pairs are broken and re-formed every year. Once the original mate has left his incubating female, she may re-pair with another mate if renesting is attempted (Sowls, 1955). Lebret (1961) noted several instances of males joining other females after their original mate had begun nesting activities. However, he also mentions a case in which two birds were known to be paired in each of five seasons.

Nest Location: Mallards prefer to place their nests in fairly high vegetations; in one Minnesota study the average vegetation height at 47 nests was 24 inches, with a range of 10 to 50 inches (Lee *et al.,* 1964b). In a California study (Miller and Collins, 1954), nearly half the nests were located in vegetation between 13 and 24 inches tall, with nettle (*Urtica*) and saltbrush (*Atriplex*) apparently being preferred nesting cover. About two-thirds of the mallard nests in this study were concealed on all four sides, and about half were also concealed from above. The same percentage of nests were located between 3 and 50 yards from water. In a Vermont study, early-nesting mallards often used live conifers or fallen trees for nesting sites, but most later-nesting mallards nested in new or old growth of raspberry or nettle (Coulter and Miller, 1968). In a study of mallards in Montana, Girard (1941) found that, of 267 nests, a third were in tall grasses and over a fourth were in short grasses. Thistles (*Salsola* and *Cirsium*) were in third place for nest cover usage, with 13 percent of the total being found in such cover.

Clutch Size: Clutch size data show a surprising amount of variability among different studies, perhaps reflecting the effects of renesting or other influences. Average clutches of about 9.5 eggs have been reported by Lee *et al.* (1964a), Coulter and Miller (1966), Anderson (1965), and (for early nests) Keith (1961). Clutches averaging 8.5 to 9.0 eggs have been reported by Miller and Collins (1954), Duebbert (1970), Earl (1950), and Hunt and Naylor (1955). Clutches averaging fewer than 8 eggs were reported by Girard (1941) and also by Hickey (1952), who used data from various studies. Bauer and Glutz (1968) noted similar variation in European studies. They established a clear relationship between season and clutch size, with early (March) clutches averaging 10 or more eggs, while clutches laid in late May or June averaged from 6.8 to 8.8 eggs. Ogilvie (1964) reported that eggs are laid daily, often with a day's gap during the first 7 eggs.

Incubation Period: Incubation under natural conditions averages 28 days, with a 2- or 3-day variation on each side of this mean (Girard, 1941). Ogilvie (1964) reported an average of 27.6 days for fifty-one clutches, with a range of 24 to 32 days.

Fledging Period: Oring (1968) reported a range of 55 to 59 days in the fledging periods of ten captive mallards, with an average of 56.6 days. This is generally in agreement with Hochbaum's (1944) early estimate of 49 to 60 days.

Nest and Egg Losses: A large number of studies have been made on nest success in mallards; Weller (1964) reported that the average of nine studies was 47 percent nesting success, with a range of 13 to 85 percent. Similarly, Jahn and Hunt (1964), in a variety of studies, estimated that 43 percent of the females succeeded in hatching broods and that the brood size near fledging was 6.3 young. Renesting by hens losing their first clutch is not uncommon; Coulter and Miller (1968) reported that 53 percent of thirty-two marked hens were known to renest following nest losses, including females in all stages of incubation at the time of nest loss. In sixteen cases, the renesting interval varied from 8 to 18 days from the time of nest loss, with no clear relationship between this interval and the stage of incubation at the time of nest loss. The clutch size of fifteen renests averaged one egg fewer (9.6 vs. 10.6) than the first nests of these females.

Juvenile Mortality: Bellrose and Chase (1950) estimated a 55 percent annual mortality rate for juvenile males during their first year after banding. Other estimates as high as 75 percent have also been made (Keith, 1961).

Adult Mortality: The annual adult mortality rate for mallards has been estimated at 47 to 48 percent by Hickey (1952) and Gollop (1966); 40 percent (for males) by Bellrose and Chase (1950); and 43 percent (for mallards wintering in England) by Wainwright (1967). Other estimates have ranged from 38 percent to 58 percent (Keith, 1961).

GENERAL ECOLOGY

Food and Foraging: One of the mallard's significant foraging characteristics is its ability to utilize agricultural grain crops as well as natural aquatic foods, depending on their relative availability. Important natural foods include wild rice (*Zizania*), pondweeds (*Potamogeton*), smartweeds (*Polygonum*), bulrushes (*Scirpus*), and a large variety of other emergent or submerged plants (Martin *et al.,* 1951). The proportion of animal materials in their diet is usually under 10 percent and is probably highest during summer. Farm crops that are often heavily utilized include corn, sorghum, barley, wheat, oats, and almost any other grains that might be available.

Girard (1941) noted that in Montana field-feeding by mallards begins in mid-August. The birds begin to congregate in groups about 2:30 p.m. and leave their water areas between 3:00 and 6:00 p.m. They often feed all night, and return to water about 7:30 to 8:30 a.m. During the hunting season their feeding schedule is somewhat modified, and the birds both leave to feed later in the afternoon and return earlier in the morning, thus avoiding exposure to hunters. During winter in Montana the birds usually remain on the water all night. There their chief food is wheat, although they also consume barley, oats, and rye.

Winner (1959) made a similar study of field-feeding in mallards and black ducks. He found that afternoon feeding flights of mixed mallard and black duck flocks began from 9 to 205 minutes before sunset, with flights being initiated early as the flock size and/or percentage of mallards in the population increased. He found no clear relationship between flight initiation and temperature, absolute light intensity, or the time at which legal shooting terminated. Bossenmaier and Marshall (1958) noted that mallards and pintails left on their morning feeding flights just at daybreak, or about 30 minutes before the geese left on their flights, and sometimes would be back on the lake before the geese had left. They observed no overnight foraging and noted that feeding flights occurred in all types of unfavorable weather, including fog and blizzards.

Stewart's (1962) study of the foods of 85 mallards from the Chesapeake Bay region indicated the foods varied locally among birds collected in estuarine bays, estuarine river marshes, estuarine bay marshes, and river bottomlands. In the estuarine areas, seeds of shoreline, emergent, or submerged plants (*Scirpus, Polygonum, Sparganium, Potamogeton, etc.*) were prevalent, as were the leafy portions and rootstalks of submerged species.

In Louisiana, mallards have made increasing use of rice or plants associated with the culture of rice in recent years, and in one study over 90 percent of the wintering mallards were located in or near the rice-growing area (Dillon, 1959).

Like most other surface-feeding ducks, mallards will sometimes dive in order to obtain their food (Kurtz, 1940; Kear and Johnsgard, 1968), although tipping-up is the usual manner of foraging. When foraging in grain fields, mallards can consume surprising amounts of grain, which in one study averaged about seven ounces per bird per day, assuming two feedings each day (Bossenmaier and Marshall, 1958).

Sociality, Densities, Territoriality: Shortly after mallards have completed their prenuptial molt into their winter plumage, social courtship begins and flocks of both sexes begin to be formed. Large flocks are facilitated where field-feeding in grainfields occurs, since mallards tend to move back and forth between their resting and foraging areas in fairly large flocks. Winner (1959) noted that mixed winter populations of mallards and black ducks on a 940-acre reservoir ranged in size up to about 8,000 birds, with up to several thousand feeding in a single cornfield.

Flock sizes remain fairly large throughout winter and gradually tend to break up as paired birds separate from flocks containing unmated males likely to harass females.

Breeding densities vary greatly in different habitats, but are generally not extremely high. Drewien and Springer (1969) noted an average density over a sixteen-year period of 6.7 pairs per square mile in prairie pothole habitat in South Dakota. Stoudt (1969) reported a fifteen-year average density of 28 pairs and 9 broods per square mile in a Saskatchewan study area, and noted that four other study areas have had peak mallard densities of 9 to 54 pairs per square mile. Duebbert (1969) reported a nest density of 24 nests on a 125-acre field, although only 17 pairs were observed on the 4-square-mile study area. He suggested that some female mallards may have flown 3 to 5 miles to this area of prime nesting cover. Drewien and Fredrickson (1970) estimated that there were 78 mallard nests on a 19-acre South Dakota island in 1967, and 60 nests in 1968. In 1967 they found an average distance between nests of 34 feet, with a range of 7 to 150 feet. Favored nesting cover in the form of tall nettles and protection from predators evidently had been responsible for this unusual density.

The existence of true territoriality in mallards, as well as in most other surface-feeding ducks, is highly doubtful. Dzubin (1955) noted that mallards do not defend a rigid area and that apparent territories may overlap with those of other pairs of mallards. Additionally, the female is defended outside the limit of the "territory." This and other studies make it clear that the female, rather than a specific area, is the male's focus of defense, and a territory in the classic sense of a defended area does not exist (Raitasuo, 1964). Hori (1963) suggested that aerial chases in mallards are more a reflection of a tendency toward polygamy than evidence for territoriality, and McKinney (1965) believed that such chases served as a mechanism for dispersion of pairs. Thus the term "home range" is more properly applied to the area within which a breeding pair of ducks remains and which is not defended *per se*.

Interspecific Relationships: The close evolutionary relationships existing between the mallard and the black duck (Johnsgard, 1959) suggest that interspecific competition between them may be significant in their considerable area of present overlap. Mixed courtship groups of these two species indicate that some interspecific competition for mates does exist, although the rate of mixed pairing and subsequent hybridization is quite low (Johnsgard, 1967a).

Coulter and Miller (1968) found that nest sites selected by mallards and black ducks were quite similar, although they did not analyze the relative attraction of these two species to different habitat types. On islands in Lake Champlain, mallards showed a higher rate of use of dead herbaceous plants, such as nettle, and tree boles, crotches, and stubs for nest sites, while black ducks had a higher usage rate of fallen limbs or logs and dead treetops. They believed that such use of wooded islands by black ducks was common only where sedge-meadow bogs, their preferred habitat, were not nearby. In contrast, the mallard prefers nesting on typical grassland marsh habitats and likewise is not attracted to wooded habitats (Johnsgard, 1959). However, both species can and will use stumps and trees for nesting in special situations (Cowardin *et al.*, 1967).

Besides competition with other ducks, mallards have the usual number of egg and duckling predators with which to contend. These include crows, skunks, coyotes, and similar enemies.

General Activity Patterns and Movements: Like other surface-feeding ducks, the mallard is largely diurnal and has a polyphasic pattern of activity patterns recurring through the day that is in part related to temperature, wind, light, and other environmental variables (Raitasuo, 1964). Some overall patterns can, however, be detected in the birds' behavior patterns. Girard (1941) noted that during April observations most resting occurred in midmorning and midafternoon hours, mating and fighting activities were mostly seen in the morning, foraging in water was seen both during morning and afternoon, and foraging adjacent to the shore or on land near shore was mostly seen in late afternoon. Field-foraging flights typically occur close to sunrise and sunset.

Winner (1960) studied movements of marked mallards and black ducks during late fall and winter on O'Shaughnessy Reservoir, in central Ohio. Of 62 individually marked mallards, he found that their stopover period on the reservoir ranged from 0 to 18 days, with an average of 3.4 days. Ducks left the reservoir under all weather conditions, but the two largest decreases he observed occurred during weather conditions characterized by an overcast sky, falling barometric pressure, relatively constant temperature, and southerly winds.

SOCIAL AND SEXUAL BEHAVIOR

Flocking Behavior: The mallard's adaptability to field-feeding in grainfields and its large size and associated hardiness are in large measure responsible for its ability to winter relatively far north in the grain-growing belt of North America, spending the night on large lakes or reservoirs and feeding in adjacent grainfields. Jahn and Hunt (1964) noted that during October mallards will readily fly 15 to 25 miles from an aquatic concentration site to feed on corn and will remain in agricultural areas of Wisconsin on into winter. Even as far north as North Dakota, mallards in substantial numbers have recently begun to winter on Garrison Reservoir and similar large reservoirs.

Pair-forming Behavior: In September, as juvenile mallards begin to assume their first winter plumage and as adult birds are regaining their nuptial plumages, pair-forming behavior is initiated. It is apparent that if members of previous pairings locate one another they will reestablish their pair bonds without any special ceremonies, and this accounts for the moderate number of paired birds seen in early fall before social display begins in earnest (Lebret, 1961). Shortly after about 90 percent of the males have assumed their nuptial plumages, social display reaches a peak of activity and continues at a relatively high level through winter and spring (Bezzel, 1959; Johnsgard, 1959). Before the end of the year, at least 90 percent of the females are already paired; thus it is apparent that a substantial amount of "courtship" display must go on among birds that are already apparently paired. This display may help serve to strengthen pair bonds, but more probably it channels aggressive tendencies toward other males into a ritualized pattern of behavior that reduces actual fighting and facilitates the maintenance of the flock (Lebret, 1961).

Although the complex aquatic courtship displays of males must, in ways still uncertain, influence mate choice among females, the actual pattern of pair formation between individual birds is much less conspicuous. In large part it consists of females inciting "chosen" males against others and of the associated responses of such males, which may include hostile responses toward the indicated "enemy" as well as a ritualized turning-of-the-back-of-the-head display toward the female. Mutual drinking behavior and ritualized preening by the male toward the female are other important aspects of pair formation in mallards (Johnsgard, 1959, 1965).

Copulatory Behavior: Copulation in mallards is preceded by mutual head-pumping, which may be initiated by either sex. As treading is completed, the male releases his grip on the female's neck, draws his head backwards along the back in a "bridling" movement as a whistle is uttered, and then swims rapidly around the female in a "nod-swimming" display (Johnsgard, 1965).

During late spring, especially as females are beginning to nest and are no longer so closely guarded by their mates, a great deal of raping behavior is characteristic of mallards. These rapes are largely performed by unmated males, but males that have recently deserted their incubating mates may also participate in such behavior to some extent.

Nesting and Brooding Behavior: McKinney's (1953) study of incubation behavior in mallards is quite complete, and others have made less intensive observations. Once the female begins incubation, she normally leaves the nest only twice a day to feed. Girard (1941) noted that about two hours are taken each day for foraging, usually between 6:30 and 8:30 a.m. and again in the late afternoon. Coulter and Miller (1968) noted, however, that considerable variation in the feeding period occurred, and McKinney (1953) reported that feeding periods usually lasted only thirty to sixty minutes.

When on the nest, the female may change her position at a rate averaging once every thirty-five minutes (McKinney, 1953). The bird then typically rises, preens or tugs at her breast feathers, turns a varying amount, and settles back down on the eggs. Then she "paddles" with her feet in a manner that helps to turn the eggs. Finally, she pats in the nest edge with the underside of her bill and pulls nesting material in toward the nest. Down gradually accumulates in the nest by the preening and tugging action of the female and may be quite abundant by the time of hatching.

Mallard eggs require about thirty hours to complete pipping (Girard, 1941), and most of the eggs hatch during daylight hours (Bjärvall, 1968). The first night after hatching is typically spent in the nest, and the family leaves the nest the next morning, usually before 10:00 a.m. (Bjärvall, 1968).

The female normally looks after her brood for most of the eight-week period required for the young to attain flight. However, several instances are known in which a female has laid a second clutch after successfully hatching an earlier one, and in at least two of these cases part of the original brood were still alive at the time the female started her second clutch (Bjärval, 1969).

Postbreeding Behavior: Male mallards desert their incubating females at varying times, from as early as the start of incubation until as late as the third or fourth week of incubation. However, there is a still undetermined period following desertion of the female during which sexual vigor is retained (Johnson, 1961), and such males may for a time be of significance in facilitating renesting or in mating with other females.

Males about to lose their flight feathers may gather in flocks of several hundred to several thousand birds, loafing on beaches and feeding in marshes, sloughs, meadows, and the like. However, with the loss of flight ability, the males become extremely secretive and are rarely seen (Hochbaum, 1944). Following a flightless period of about 24 to 26 days (Boyd, 1961), the males again begin to gather in conspicuous places. Females usually do not begin their wing molt until they have abandoned their well-grown broods, and thus the peak of their flightless period occurs more than a month after that of males.

SOUTHERN MALLARDS
(Mexican, Florida, and Mottled Ducks)
(Anas diazi and *A. fulvigula* of A.O.U., 1957)*

Other Vernacular Names: Dusky Mallard, New Mexican Duck, Summer
Black Duck, Summer Mallard.

Range: Currently exists as three separate populations. One is resident in peninsular Florida from about Tampa on the west coast to the vicinity of
Gainesville in the interior and Indian River on the east. Another breeds
along the Gulf coast from the Mississippi Delta to central Veracruz (Johnsgard, 1961c), wintering over most of the breeding range but probably undergoing some seasonal movements. The third is currently limited to a
breeding range in the Rio Grande valley of southern New Mexico, extreme
southwestern New Mexico, and adjacent Arizona, and also occurs locally
in Chihuahua, Durango, northern Jalisco, and the central highlands of
Mexico south to the Trans-Mexican volcanic belt (Aldrich and Baer,
1970). Wintering occurs through much of the breeding range, but there is
probably a partial movement out of the northernmost breeding areas in the
United States (Johnsgard, 1961c).

Subspecies:

A. platyrhynchos diazi Ridgway: Mexican Mallard. Range in New Mexico,

Arizona, and Mexico as indicated above. The form *novimexicana* Huber is not recognized by Delacour (1956), Johnsgard (1961c), or Aldrich and Baer (1970).

A. p. fulvigula Ridgway: Florida Mallard. Range in Florida as indicated above.

A. p. maculosa Sennett: Mottled Mallard. Range in the Gulf coast as indicated above. This form is not recognized by Delacour (1956), although Johnsgard (1959, 1961c) concluded that it is probably a valid subspecies. The uncertainty of its validity makes a consistent method of providing suitable vernacular names for these populations impossible. If *maculosa* is eventually deemed invalid, the vernacular name "southern mallard" might best be applied to the populations now included in *fulvigula* and *maculosa*. Currently, neither the technical nor the vernacular names used by the A.O.U. (1975) provide a clear indication of the relative relationships of these forms to one another or to *platyrhynchos,* and the A.O.U. decision not to recognize vernacular names for subspecies tends to maintain an unwarranted degree of taxonomic separation of these populations.

Measurements:

Folded wing: males 241-289, females 223-271 mm.

Culmen: males 50.4-59, females 45.5-55.1 mm.

Weights: Leopold (1959) indicated that *diazi* males range from 2.13 to 2.36 pounds (960 to 1,060 grams) and females from 1.8 to 2.17 pounds (815 to 990 grams). Beckwith and Hosford (1955) stated that thirty adult males of *fulvigula* averaged 2.19 pounds (994 grams), with a maximum of 2.81 pounds. Eleven females averaged exactly the same, but had a maximum of 2.5 pounds. Hoffpauir (1964) found that twenty-six males of *maculosa* averaged 2.27 pounds (1,028 grams), while ten females averaged 2.04 pounds (927 grams).

IDENTIFICATION

In the Hand: Adult males are generally similar to females of the common mallard, especially *diazi,* which however are more heavily streaked and spotted with brown on the underparts and have unspotted yellow bills with (usually) black nails. Males of *maculosa* and *fulvigula* are generally darker and more tawny, with yellow to yellowish orange bills, black nails and a black mark near the base of the upper mandible. They also lack a definite white bar on the greater secondary coverts, since this area is suffused with tawny.

Females of all the populations are virtually identical to the males except for bill coloration. Females of *diazi* can be distinguished from female common mallards by one or more of the following traits: (1) the upper tail coverts are darker, with no patterning along the quill and with narrower light margins; (2) the outer tail feathers are darker, with little or no white present; (3) the under tail coverts are dark brown, with a lighter edging, instead of white with a central brownish stripe; (4) the small under wing coverts are barred with brown; (5) the bill is darker, shading anteriorly to olive green with very little orange near the base; (6) the tertials are overlaid with a greenish cast; (7) the speculum is more greenish and has a reduced white border; and (8) the breast feathers usually are a darker brown, varying in pattern from three separate spots to a merged *fleur-de-lis* (Huey, 1961). Females of *fulvigula* and *maculosa* tend to be even darker than those of *diazi* and may have a more purplish speculum without a definite white anterior border.

In the Field: Birds of all three populations look very much like female common mallards in the field, but average variably darker in their plumage tones. The major difference is that *both* sexes have a yellow or olive bill color, with little or no dark spotting present, and when in flight the birds exhibit little or no white on their outer tail feathers. The body tones of *diazi* are sometimes only slightly darker than those of female common mallards, but females of *fulvigula* and *maculosa* are distinctly more tawny. These latter types also lack a definite white bar in front of the speculum. Female hybrids between common mallards and black ducks are very similar to females of these populations and are essentially impossible to distinguish in the field. Such hybrids do retain a small but distinctive white or grayish white bar on the greater secondary coverts, which would help to separate them from either Florida or mottled mallards, the only forms likely to be encountered where hybridization between common mallards and black ducks is most prevalent.

AGE AND SEX CRITERIA

Sex Determination: Adult males have a bill that is entirely yellow, except for a black nail (sometimes yellow in *diazi*) and a black spot near the back of the upper mandible (lacking in *diazi*). Females have a more olive-colored bill (sometimes orange basally in *diazi*) that grades to olive green toward the culmen or has limited black spotting on the sides and culmen (usually absent in *diazi*). Internal examination may be required in the case of immature birds.

Age Determination: Not yet reported, but very probably the criteria mentioned in the account of the black duck may be applied to these populations as well.

Breeding distributions of the Florida (diagonal hatching), mottled
(vertical hatching), and Mexican (horizontal hatching) mallards in
North America.

DISTRIBUTION AND HABITAT

Breeding and Wintering Distribution and Habitat: Relatively few migratory movements seem to be typical of these southern populations of mallard-like ducks, and thus breeding and wintering distributions can be dealt with simultaneously.

The Florida population ("Florida duck") is confined to the peninsular portion of Florida, with the population's northern limits at about Cedar Key, Gainesville, and Daytona Beach. The population is centered west of Lake Okeechobee, with the majority of the birds found in Hendry, Lee, Charlotte, and Glades counties (Chamberlain, 1960). Chamberlain estimated that during ten years of study the Florida population ranged from 5,000 to 30,000 birds. However, a more recent estimate was of 50,000 birds during the fall of 1966 (Stieglitz and Wilson, 1968).

Several sight records have been obtained along the coast of Alabama for "mottled ducks," and the state's first specimen was collected in 1955 (Imhof, 1958). A nest was later found on Dauphin Island. There have been sight records of as many as eighteen birds seen in Mississippi, but apparently no specimens have been collected in the state (*Audubon Field Notes,* 14:455).

In Louisiana the birds are fairly common in coastal areas, and in the late 1960s the total average winter population has been estimated at 40,000 to 70,000 birds. These occur fairly evenly over the marshes of southeast and southwest Louisiana, especially in the salt and brackish marshes along the coast. This population is continuous with the Texas population, which extends from the Louisiana border to the Mexican border. Summer populations over a 26,000-square-mile area in Texas were estimated at 20,000 birds in 1952, which occurred from the coastline inland for 50 to possibly as far as 100 miles (Singleton, 1953). The Mexican population is of unknown size, but extends from the Texas border south to central Veracruz. The resident Mexican population may be no larger than a few thousand birds, although there may be some southward movement along the coast during the fall and winter, so that seasonally the population could be somewhat larger than this.

Besides this normal breeding range, there is also an extralimital record of *fulvigula* breeding at the Cheyenne Bottoms Waterfowl Refuge in Kansas, where the birds have been seen regularly for several years (McHenry, 1968). There is also a recent nesting record for *diazi* in Texas (Ohlendorf and Patton, 1971) and some recent sight records of this form for Arizona (*Audubon Field Notes,* 24:418, 630), where definite nesting records are lacking. There is only a single record of *maculosa* for Oklahoma (*American Birds,* 25:597), and there are two records of *diazi* from Nebraska (*Nebraska Bird Review,* 38:89).

In addition to this Gulf coast population, there is also an interior population ("Mexican duck") that once had a breeding range extending from southeastern Arizona and central northern New Mexico southward along the Rio Grande valley and the interior highlands of Mexico to the Valley of Mexico (Johnsgard, 1959; Aldrich and Baer, 1970). Its current breeding range is now considerably reduced, and the center of the remaining population seems to be in northern Jalisco and east-central Chihuahua. During winter months some concentrations of up to 1,000 birds have been seen in the lakes of central Mexico, but these are probably at least in part migrant birds from farther north. The breeding range in Texas is apparently greater than has been previously believed (*American Birds,* 28:71).

Breeding habitat preferences for the mostly coastal-dwelling populations have not been carefully analyzed. Beckwith and Hosford (1957) found birds nesting near Lake Okeechobee, Florida, on a relatively flat habitat having about 65 percent of the surface area in wet prairies, seasonal marshes, and sloughs; 13 percent in ponds, most of which were shallow; 1.3 percent in sawgrass (*Mariscus*) marsh; and the rest in terrestrial vegetation of various types. Engeling (1949) described the preferred habitat of Texas birds as salt marshes, coastal prairies, bluestem meadows, and fallow rice fields. Nesting is usually in open prairies, and later birds move to rice fields and marshes. The only study to date of the New Mexico population is by Lindsey (1946). He located four nests, all in meadows or lowlands containing three-square (*Scirpus americanus*), salt grass (*Distichlis*), rush (*Juncus balticus*), sedge (*Carex*), or barley (*Hordeum*). Leopold (1959) noted that nearly all the habitats in which he observed "Mexican ducks" contained some cattail (*Typha*) or tule (*Scirpus*) marsh, and that this seemed to represent their preferred habitat.

GENERAL BIOLOGY

Age at Maturity: Six of seven aviculturalists responding to a questionnaire by Ferguson (1966) said that "Florida ducks" mature their first year. Beckwith and Hosford (1967) also noted that reproductive maturity occurred during the first year of life.

Pair Bond Pattern: Observations on social display are relatively few, but indicate that the period of pair formation and the type of pair bond formed differ in no substantial way from that of mallards or black ducks (Johnsgard,

1959). Singleton (1953) noted that the maximum number of paired birds seen was during March and the minimum was during August, when only 4 percent appeared to be paired. Stieglitz and Wilson (1968) raised the possibility that, in the Florida population at least, the pair bond may be virtually permanent, since mated pairs were seen all year and males seemed to be absent only during the brood-rearing period. Engeling (1951) mentioned that two birds banded as a pair in January of 1949 were shot together in January of 1950, indicating the maintenance of a pair bond through one brooding season.

Nest Location: Lindsey (1946) found the only four nests so far described for *diazi.* One was in a low *Scirpus-Distichlis* meadow, one was in a moist *Distichlis* meadow, one was in a *Juncus* meadow, and one was located in a growth of *Carex* and scattered *Hordeum.* They ranged from being placed almost immediately beside water to being placed a distance of 0.1 mile from the nearest water. Beckwith and Hosford (1957) noted that most of the five nests they found in Florida were placed near water and that three were situated in tomato fields.

In a Florida study (Stieglitz and Wilson, 1968) it was found that a species of paspalum (*Paspalum*) was the dominant plant at 55.6 percent of eighty-eight nests, and broom sedge (*Andropogon*) dominated at 18.1 percent. Cover height at nest sites averaged 34 inches and ranged from 6 to 96 inches. The nests averaged 27.8 feet from water, and almost 80 percent were between 10 and 40 feet from water.

Clutch Size: Good clutch size information is available only from the Florida population. Stieglitz and Wilson (1968) reported that the average clutch of 117 nests was 9.4 eggs, and the range was 5 to 13. Clutch sizes decreased through the breeding season, with early nests averaging 10.1 eggs and later ones averaging 8.9 eggs. Ten was the modal number of eggs in completed clutches. Eggs were apparently laid at the rate of one a day, although critical data on this point were not obtained. Renesting is apparently prevalent, at least in the Texas population. Engeling (1949) reported a case in which one female made five nesting attempts, laying a total of 34 eggs, before she finally successfully hatched a brood of nine ducklings. Singleton (1953) reported that 108 nests of *maculosa* in Texas averaged 10.4 eggs per clutch.

Incubation Period: In a Florida study two wild nests hatched after 25 to 26 days of incubation, while two clutches that were hatched in an incubator had an incubation period of 26 days. From 21 to 30 hours elapsed between initial pipping and the hatching of the last egg (Stieglitz and Wilson, 1968).

Fledging Period: Not yet accurately measured but probably similar to the eight-week period in mallards. Engeling (1949) noted that by the age of six weeks the young were fully feathered except for their wing feathers.

Nest and Egg Losses: In a Florida study 76.7 percent of ninety island nests hatched (Stieglitz and Wilson, 1968), with an average of nine ducklings hatching from successful nests. However, in a Texas study, only ten of forty-six nests were known to hatch. Of the remainder, twenty were destroyed by predators, five were flooded, one was trampled by cattle, nine were deserted, and the fate of two was unknown. Direct or indirect destruction by dogs was the major source of predation in this study (Engeling, 1949), while in the Florida study avian predators, probably crows, destroyed six nests. In another Texas study, a 96.2 percent hatching success was reported (Singleton, 1953).

Juvenile and Adult Mortality: No specific estimates of juvenile or adult mortality rates are available. Engeling (1949) estimated that an average brood of eight or nine ducklings at hatching is normally reduced to five or six young at the time of fledging.

GENERAL ECOLOGY

Food and Foraging: The only detailed study of food consumption is that of Beckwith and Hosford, who analyzed the food contents of nearly 150 birds collected in all seasons. The yearly average for food intake was 87 percent of vegetable origin. The highest incidence of consumption of animal material was from summer samples, when almost 40 percent, mostly water beetles, was of such origin. Panic grass (*Panicum*) was the most important summer plant food, with smartweeds (*Persicaria*) in second place. Fall foods included seeds of ragweed (*Ambrosia*), paspalum, bristle grass (*Setaria*), panic grass, and smartweeds. Winter foods included spike sedge (*Eleocharis*), beak rush (*Rynchospora*), bulrush (*Scirpus*), fanwort (*Cabomba*), and ragweed. Major spring foods were smartweeds, cockspur (*Echinochloa*), bristle grass, and wax myrtle (*Cerothamnus*).

Sociality, Densities, Territoriality: Probably the southern mallards do not differ greatly from common mallards or black ducks in these respects, although little information is available. There is one record of a high nesting density on a small island in Indian River, Florida, that represents a maximum density of 23.3 nests per acre. The largest actual number of nests on a single island was 7, representing a density of 1.2 nests per acre (Stieglitz and Wilson, 1968).

Stieglitz and Wilson did not detect any territorial defense behavior in the dense nesting population they studied. Three nests were once found in a fifteen-foot-diameter circle, two of which were within five feet of each other.

Engeling (1950) noted that the "territory," more probably a home range, of one pair was 0.5 mile in diameter.

Interspecific Relationships: The degree of interaction among these southern populations with the mallard and black duck is still incompletely known. Such contacts occur only during winter and are apparently limited. However, interaction in the form of hybridization with mallards has been found in New Mexico (Lindsey, 1946), and there is also at least one similar record of natural hybridization on the Texas coast (*Audubon Field Notes,* 19:561). Quite possibly the relatively continuous pair bonds that seem to be present in the southern mallard populations prevent more frequent mixed pairing.

General Activity Patterns and Movements: The small amount of information so far available on these southern populations indicates that they are relatively sedentary. Engeling (1951) reported on forty-nine returns from birds banded in coastal Texas. None of the returns was from south of Aransas County, suggesting little or no southward movement during winter. The maximum movement was one of about 100 miles to the northeast. Similarly, Hyde (1958) noted that of thirteen recoveries of birds banded in Florida, the distance of movement ranged from 0 to 130 miles and averaged only 45 miles.

SOCIAL AND SEXUAL BEHAVIOR

Flocking Behavior: Apparently flock sizes in southern mallards are not normally very large, although observations are limited. Beckwith and Hosford (1957) noted that in Florida flocks of up to 50 birds may be seen in August. By November they are usually in groups of 6 to 20 birds. Flocks of up to 13 birds are seen until late February, when the birds break up into units of pairs, trios, and single birds. Aldrich and Baer (1970) reported that a wintering flock of at least 1,000 birds was seen during January in Mexico, but counts made during May resulted in a total count of 120 ducks on 14 different areas, or fewer than 10 birds per observation site.

Pair-forming Behavior: Almost no observations on pair-forming behavior have been seen in wild birds, a further indication that pair bonds may be relatively continuous under natural conditions. Among captive specimens of *fulvigula* the normal mallard repertoire of social displays has been observed (Johnsgard, 1959).

Copulatory Behavior: Copulatory behavior takes the same form in these southern populations as is typical of common mallards and black ducks (Johnsgard, 1965).

Nesting and Brooding Behavior: During the incubation period, the female probably normally leaves the nest once or twice a day, for periods of about two hours. The time at which the male deserts his female to begin the postnuptial molt probably varies considerably, but Engeling (1950) believed that males may remain with their mates until about the time of hatching. The young remain in the nest from 12 to 24 hours, and the female leads them away from the area of the nest between 24 and 48 hours after hatching (Stieglitz and Wilson, 1968).

Postbreeding Behavior: Little specific information is available on late summer activities. In Texas, the birds move from open prairie areas to rice fields and marshes at this time (Engeling, 1951). A postnuptial molt involving a flightless period is present (Beckwith and Hosford, 1957), but details on its length and timing are lacking.

BLACK DUCK
Anas rubripes Brewster 1902

Other Vernacular Names: Black Mallard, Red-legged Black Duck.

Range: Breeds from Manitoba and Ontario eastward to Labrador and New-foundland, south to Minnesota, and through the Great Lakes states to the Atlantic coast, where breeding occurs south to coastal North Carolina. Winters through the southern parts of the breeding range and south to the Gulf coast.

Subspecies: None recognized. Perhaps *rubripes* should itself be regarded as a subspecies of *platyrhynchos* (Johnsgard, 1959, 1961c), in which case the vernacular name "black mallard" would be most appropriate.

Measurements (after Delacour, 1954):

Folded wing: Males 265-292, females 245-275 mm.

Culmen: Males 52-58, females 45-53 mm.

Weights: Nelson and Martin (1953) reported that the average weight of 366 males was 2.7 pounds (1,224 grams), while the average weight of 297 females was 2.4 pounds (1,088 grams). Jahn and Hunt (1964) found that 86 adult males averaged 2.94 pounds (1,332 grams), while 185 immatures averaged 2.69 pounds (1,219 grams); 80 adult females averaged 2.56 pounds (1,162 grams), and 172 immatures averaged 2.44 pounds (1,106 grams). Maximum weights reported for males are 3.8 pounds, reported by Nelson and Martin, and 3.88 pounds for females, as reported by Jahn and Hunt.

IDENTIFICATION

In the Hand: Black ducks may be readily identified in the hand by their mallardlike shape and size, an almost entirely brownish black body color, and the absence of any white anterior to the speculum. Little or no white is normally present on the trailing edge of the secondaries, but hybridization with mallards has gradually diluted the purity of most black duck populations, so this criterion is not absolute. Female hybrids between mallards and black ducks most resemble mottled ducks, but usually show some white on the greater secondary coverts, especially on the outer web (Johnsgard, 1959). Male hybrids usually show some green iridescence behind the eyes, often forming a fairly distinctive green patch.

In the Field: The dark body with only slightly lighter head color makes black ducks conspicuous in any gathering of ducks. They are mallardlike in every respect except their coloration, including their vocalizations. In flight, the white under wing coverts contrast more strongly with the dark body and upper wing coloration than is true of mallards, and this flashing wing pattern of dusky and white makes black ducks recognizable for as far away as they can be seen. When in breeding condition, the brilliant yellow bill of the male is very conspicuous and allows for ready sexual identification.

AGE AND SEX CRITERIA

Sex Identification: External features that indicate a male are a bright yellow bill that lacks spotting, breast feathers with rounded light markings centrally (instead of V-shaped markings) or no light central markings at all, and bright reddish rather than brownish feet. Cloacal or internal examination is the most reliable sexing method.

Age Determination: Immature birds may have small, frayed, or faded tertials and tertial coverts, compared to larger and freshly grown feathers in adults. The middle coverts of immatures may be narrow and somewhat trapezoidal, especially just anterior to the tertial coverts (Carney, 1964). Immatures may also exhibit notched tail feathers.

DISTRIBUTION AND HABITAT

Breeding Distribution and Habitat: To a degree greater than any other North American waterfowl species, the black duck is largely limited to the eastern, forested portion of the continent. In Canada its summer range extends westward only to eastern Manitoba, where it is generally scarce (Godfrey, 1966). There is a definite breeding record for Oak Lake, Manitoba

(*Audubon Field Notes,* 19:555). In Saskatchewan there are a few scattered records (Murray, 1959), and also a few from Alberta, where it has been reported to nest (Godfrey, 1966). From Ontario eastward to Newfoundland it is the commonest breeding duck species in most areas, at least as far north as the tree line.

In the United States the black duck is largely a breeding bird of the eastern forests and coastal marshes, as Stewart (1958) has pointed out. He listed two areas of high breeding population densities, the hemlock–white pine–northern hardwood forest region east of longitude 85° W., and the tidewater areas of Delaware Bay and the eastern shore of Chesapeake Bay, Maryland. Boreal coniferous forests and tidewater areas to the north of Maryland support medium breeding densities, while low breeding densities occur in tidewater areas south to North Carolina and in several forest associations. These are the boreal coniferous and hemlock–white pine–northern hardwood regions west of longitude 85° W., the maple–basswood forest region, and northern parts of the beech–maple, mixed mesophytic, and oak–chestnut forest regions as defined by Braun (1950).

Although Minnesota represents the normal western limit of black duck breeding habitat in the United States, there have been a few isolated records of nesting in North Dakota (*Audubon Field Notes,* 2:209; 5:296). In spite of the regular occurrence of black ducks in hunter kills along the Central Flyway states from North Dakota to Oklahoma, there is no indication that the black duck is now significantly extending its breeding range to the west (Johnsgard, 1961b).

Stewart stated that typical interior breeding habitats include alkaline marshes, acid bogs and muskegs, lakes and ponds, and the margins of streams, while in tidewater areas the birds breed in salt, brackish, and fresh marshes, as well as in the margins of bays and estuaries. Stotts and Davis (1960) noted that of 731 nests found, almost 60 percent were in wooded habitats, versus 17 percent in marshes.

Wintering Distribution and Habitat: Wintering black ducks may be found over a wide geographic range from Minnesota and coastal Texas on the west to the Atlantic coast from northern Florida to Nova Scotia on the east (Johnsgard, 1959). Stewart (1958) indicated that wintering black ducks are characteristically found within the eastern deciduous forest formation and tend to concentrate on coastal tidewaters and on the larger streams, lakes, and reservoirs of the interior. The heaviest coastal concentrations occur from North Carolina to Massachusetts, but large numbers also occur on the rivers of Tennessee, Kentucky, Ohio, Indiana, and Illinois (Johnsgard, 1959). Geis *et al.* (1971) noted a similar pattern of wintering concentrations and

Breeding (hatched) and wintering (shaded) distributions of the black duck in North America.

also indicated the western end of Lake Erie and the Atlantic coastline north to Nova Scotia as areas of winter concentrations.

Stewart (1962) noted that migrant and wintering black ducks in the Chesapeake Bay area occupy a greater variety of habitats than any other waterfowl species, but brackish estuary bays with extensive adjacent agricultural lands were strongly favored. Estuarine bay marshes, especially those with salt water, also received high usage, as did coastal salt marshes and adjacent impoundments. In general, black ducks showed a higher usage of saltwater habitats than did mallards, which concentrated on fresh to brackish water areas.

GENERAL BIOLOGY

Age at Maturity: Like mallards, black ducks are known to be sexually mature their first year. Coulter and Miller (1968) found that first-year female black ducks had clutch sizes that were below the average they found for the species (8.4 vs. 9.5), and that only one of seven yearling hens renested when their nests were removed.

Pair Bond Pattern: Pair bonds are broken during the incubation period and reestablish in the fall during social courtship. The incidence of older adults re-pairing with their earlier mates seems to be fairly low (Stotts, 1968).

Nest Location: Stotts (1955) reported that of 356 nests found in the Kent Island area of Maryland, about 80 percent were near the margins of wooded areas, with marshes and cultivated fields being second in frequency of usage. Coulter and Miller (1968) noted that among nests found in sedge-meadow bogs over a fourteen-year period at Goose River, Maine, over 80 percent were associated with leatherleaf (*Chamaedaphne*) and sweet gale (*Myrica*) as principal cover plants. Leatherleaf's preferential use for overhead cover is apparently related to its characteristic low-growing densely branched growth form and its nearly persistent leaves. Additionally, its extensive roots form small hummocks that are elevated above the damp floor of the marsh, making it an excellent nest site. On wooded islands, cover usage was quite different, with sites being selected that offered the best concealment in places where ground litter was also available. These sites included live conifers, blueberry (*Vaccinium*) bushes, dead or fallen woody growth, and live or dead herbaceous plants, especially nettle (*Urtica*). Coulter and Miller found that island-nesting by black ducks was common only where sedge-meadow covers or other marsh nesting covers are not available.

The study by Stotts and David (1960) indicated that honeysuckle (*Lonicera*) and poison ivy (*Rhus radicans*) were favored covers, accounting for 43.3 percent of 593 nests, while brush or tree cover accounted for 32.1 percent and marsh grasses 14.0 percent.

Clutch Size: Clutch sizes reported in the literature generally range from 9.1 to 9.5 eggs, with the former reported by Stotts and Davis (1960) and the latter by Coulter and Miller (1968). Coulter and Miller's study, based on 620 clutches, indicated a range in clutch sizes from 4 to 15 eggs, with nearly 50 percent of the clutches having either 9 or 10 eggs. They found a decrease in average clutch size as the season progressed, a larger average clutch size produced by females known to be at least two years old compared with birds of mixed ages, and a slightly larger average size for first nests over renests by the same birds. In two of twenty-two cases the rate of egg-laying deviated from one per day, and disturbance may have caused these deviations.

Incubation Period: Apparently the incubation period of black ducks is very similar to that of mallards, about 27 days. Stotts and Davis (1960) estimated the average incubation period to be 26.2 days, with a range of 23 to 33 days. The incubation period was shorter in artificially incubated eggs than in naturally incubated ones.

Fledging Period: Reported as seven and one-half weeks by Wright (1954) and as eight and one-half weeks by Lee *et al.* (1964a).

Nest and Egg Losses: In a study by Stotts and Davis (1960), only 38 percent of 574 nests were terminated by hatching one or more eggs, and 15 percent of the eggs in successful nests were not brought to hatching. Fully half of the nests studied were destroyed by predators, 34 percent by crows alone, while raccoons also destroyed a considerable number. Besides destroying whole clutches, crows (principally fish crows) also removed almost 10 percent of the eggs from nests that later were successfully terminated. Wright (1954) estimated that an average of eight eggs are normally hatched per successful nest, based on his studies in Canada. Summarizing various studies, Jahn and Hunt (1964) judged that an average of 64 percent of the hens succeed in hatching broods.

Coulter and Miller (1968) estimated a 31 percent renesting rate in black ducks, compared with an earlier estimate of 16 percent by Stotts and Davis. The former authors reported a surprisingly high (77 percent) hatching success in renesting attempts, but did not indicate the hatching success of initial nesting attempts.

Juvenile Mortality: Wright (1954) estimated that black duck broods average about 8 ducklings for broods under two weeks of age, and that an additional average of 1.7 ducklings are lost during the first six weeks of life, so that about 6 ducklings per successful brood may be expected to reach flight stage. Jahn and Hunt (1964) summarized several studies and estimated that 6.9 young per female are reared to the age of flight. Later mortality rates of juvenile birds are substantially higher than adults; Geis *et al.* (1971) estimated a 64.9 percent first-year mortality rate for birds banded as immatures.

Adult Mortality: Geis *et al.* (1971) estimated that the annual adult mortality rate for banded black ducks was about 40 percent for adults of both sexes, with females having a considerably higher mortality rate than males. Thus adult males have an approximate 38 percent annual mortality rate, compared to 47 percent for females.

GENERAL ECOLOGY

Food and Foraging: Perhaps because it tends to inhabit more distinctly salty water on its coastal wintering grounds, the black duck consumes a higher proportion of food of animal origin than does the mallard. In coastal bays about half the total food intake may be of mollusks, especially univalves (Martin *et al.,* 1951). However, even in brackish estuaries the black duck sometimes feeds heavily on the leaves, stems, and rootstalks of submerged aquatic plants, the seeds of submerged and emergent plants, and the rootstalks of emergent marsh plants (Stewart, 1962). Stewart found the univalve *Melampus* commonly represented in birds taken in salt or brackish water; the bivalve *Macoma* was found in somewhat fewer samples. Hartman's (1963) study of fall and winter foods of black ducks shot on the Penobscot estuary, Maine, has emphasized the importance of *Macoma* and *Mya* clams as food of this species; these two genera of mollusks accounted for nearly half of the identified food materials by volume. Important plant foods included acorns, the stems and leaves of cordgrass (*Spartina*), and the seeds of various sedges (*Carex*) and bulrushes (*Scirpus*). Mendall's (1949) study of Maine black duck foods showed a similar high incidence of mollusk consumption during winter, while foods taken at other seasons were predominantly of vegetable origin.

Although the black duck obtains most of its food from the surface or from what it can reach by tipping-up, it has been known to dive for food on several occasions (Kear and Johnsgard, 1968). Likewise, field-feeding in grainfields is almost as common among black ducks as among mallards, at least where both species occur together. Winner (1959) described the field-feeding periodicities of both mallard and black duck in Ohio and found that mixed foraging flocks of the two species were prevalent.

Sociality, Densities, Territoriality: Like the mallard, black ducks congregate in extremely large numbers during fall and winter wherever the combination of open water and sufficient food supplies can be found. By spring, the flock sizes begin to decrease as paired birds start to avoid unpaired males.

Although Stotts (1957) reported some unusually high nesting densities on certain islands of Chesapeake Bay (up to 21.4 nests per acre), these were clearly artifacts of island nesting. Coulter and Miller (1968) also reported maximum densities of about 5 nests per acre on an island in Lake Champlain. However, in the preferred bog-nesting habitats of Maine, densities were never higher than one nest per twenty to forty acres, and similarly Stewart (1962) found a breeding density of 5.3 pairs per hundred acres on a thousand-acre area of brackish estuarine bay marsh in Maryland. Jahn and Hunt (1964) reported similar breeding densities in Wisconsin. Thus a nesting density of about one pair per twenty acres would seem typical of high-quality, nonisland breeding habitat.

Divergent opinions as to the existence of territorial behavior in black ducks have appeared in the literature (Stotts and Davis, 1960), and the evidence favoring such behavior in this species is not convincing. Stotts and Davis described several instances of aggression, which they attributed to territoriality, but noted that it was most evident in late April and May, when most renesting was in progress. This would clearly indicate that typical territoriality was not involved and that aggressive or sexual behavior associated with attempted renesting was responsible for much of the apparent territoriality.

Interspecific Relationships: The close evolutionary relationships between mallards and black ducks have been previously studied (Johnsgard, 1959; 1961c), and a low but significant rate of natural hybridization has been established. This interaction has apparently risen in recent years, as mallards have moved increasingly eastward as wintering and breeding birds, and at least locally may be of genetic significance. In one study (Goodwin, 1956) it was found that, in spite of fairly frequent hybridization, mallards increased rapidly in proportion to black ducks in the population. This may be brought about by nonselective mating or by tendencies toward cross-matings in the case of female black ducks. On the other hand, ecological differences in the form of habitat breeding preferences tend to keep the two forms separated on their breeding grounds and probably operate against the maintenance of mixed pairings (Johnsgard, 1959). The primary zone of contact between mallards and black ducks has moved considerably eastward during the past half century, and current evidence indicates that hybridization between them will continue to increase (Johnsgard, 1967a).

General Activity Patterns and Movements: Winner's (1959) study on field-feeding behavior of mallards and black ducks indicated that mallards tend to leave for the evening feeding flight earlier than black ducks, although mixed flocks were often seen. Field-feeding behavior by black ducks may be relatively less common than in mallards; Mendall (1949) found that only a small proportion of black ducks in Maine's grain-growing district actually consume grain, and noted that crop damage by black ducks is very rare. Little preference is shown there among black ducks for fields containing oats, buckwheat, or barley. However, development of a grain-feeding "tradition" among black ducks may become increasingly likely as mallards become more abundant in the eastern states and mixed flocks become more frequent.

SOCIAL AND SEXUAL BEHAVIOR

Flocking Behavior: Black ducks are seemingly almost identical to mallards in their flocking behavior, congregating during fall and winter wherever the combination of water and safe foraging areas exists, sometimes massing in flocks of several thousand birds. In spite of the flock size, the basic unit composition is that of individual pairs of birds and generally small groups of unpaired males and females. As the percentage of obviously paired birds increases during the winter, the flock sizes tend to decrease.

Pair-forming Behavior: Pair-forming behavior in black ducks has a seasonal pattern very similar to that of mallards. Adult birds that had been previously paired and meet again after molting probably re-pair without any ceremonies, thus accounting for the low percentage of paired birds seen in August (Stotts, 1958). Other adults begin social display in September or October, but it is probable that immature females do not begin pair-forming activity until they are six or seven months old, and young males when slightly older (Stotts and Davis, 1960). This would account for the sharp increase in apparently paired birds seen between November and January (Johnsgard, 1960b). The highest incidence of apparently paired birds is in April, when virtually all females appear to be paired. Although Stotts (1958) noted a maximum pair incidence of about 90 percent, the excess of males in wild populations prevents all males from obtaining mates.

Actual pair-forming mechanisms, as well as the motor patterns and vocalizations associated with social display, appear to be virtually identical in mallards and black ducks (Johnsgard, 1960b). Mixed courting groups frequently occur in areas where the two species have overlapping ranges, and mixed pairs involving both of the two possible pairing combinations have been seen.

Copulatory Behavior: Precopulatory and postcopulatory behavior patterns of black ducks are identical to those of mallards (Johnsgard, 1965).

Nesting and Brooding Behavior: Females deposit eggs in the nest at the rate of about one per day, with most laying occurring fairly early in the morning and often within two hours after sunrise. Males rarely accompany their mates to the nest during egg-laying, but rather typically wait at a customary loafing site that is often the point of water nearest the nest. A down lining usually begins to appear when the clutch is about half complete and typically becomes profuse just before incubation begins. Unlike their behavior early in incubation, females rarely leave their nests during the last few days prior to hatching. Pipping usually takes about twenty-four to thirty hours from the time cracks first appear on the egg, and at that time the female typically begins to perform "broken-wing" behavior if disturbed on the nest (Stotts and Davis, 1960). Stotts and Davis also determined that the average attendance period of males with females following the start of incubation was 14.3 days, with a range of 7 to 22. In the case of renesting females, the average period of male attendance was 9.1 days. Thus, in many cases, the original mate was present long enough to fertilize the female for an attempted renest.

Postbreeding Behavior: Following the male's desertion of his mate, he begins to undergo his postnuptial molt and enters a flightless period that probably lasts about four weeks. At this time the birds are usually wary and are rarely seen. There is no clear evidence of any substantial molt migration of male black ducks to specific molting areas. However, Hochbaum (1944) mentioned that a few male black ducks molt in the Delta, Manitoba, marshes, and the birds summering near Churchill, Manitoba, may also be mostly postbreeding males (Godfrey, 1966). Likewise, the female deserts her brood at about the time they become fledged, or at some stage prior to this time, and also begins her postnuptial molt. By August both sexes are again flying and starting to gather with immature birds in favored foraging areas.

BAHAMA PINTAIL

Anas bahamensis Linnaeus 1758

Other Vernacular Names: Bahama Duck, Bahama Teal, White-cheeked Pintail.

Range: The Bahama Islands, the West Indies, Colombia, eastern South America from Curacao to Argentina, central Chile, and the Galapagos Islands, with rare stragglers reaching the southeastern United States.

North American Subspecies:

A. b. bahamensis L.: Lesser Bahama Pintail. The Bahama Islands, the West Indies, and northern and northeastern South America.

Measurements (after Delacour, 1956):

Folded wing: Males 211-217, females 201-207 mm.

Culmen: Males 42-44, females 40-43 mm.

Weights: Weller (1968) reported on the weights of the somewhat larger race *A. b. rubrirostris*. Seven adult males averaged 710.4 grams (1.57 pounds), and four adult females averaged 670.5 grams (1.48 pounds). Haverschmidt (1968) reported that males of *A. b. bahamensis* range in weight from 474 to 533 grams, and females from 505 to 633 grams.

IDENTIFICATION

In the Hand: This dabbling duck could only be easily confused with the more common species of pintail, since both have elongated central tail feathers. However, the Bahama pintail's central feathers are of the same reddish buff color as the more lateral ones, and no other North American species of duck has white cheeks and throat, sharply contrasting with dark brown on the rest of the head. Likewise, the red marks at the base of the bluish bill are unique.

In the Field: The field marks for this rare but distinctive species are simple: a generally reddish brown duck with white extending from the cheeks to the base of the neck, red spots on the side of the bill, and a pointed tail. It is considerably smaller than the more common northern pintail, but has the same general body profile. In flight, it also exhibits a similar pattern of white, gray, and dark brown on the under wing coverts, but is otherwise much more reddish buff than the northern pintail. The male utters a weak *geeee* sound during courtship display, and the female's calls are scarcely distinct from those of the northern pintail.

AGE AND SEX CRITERIA

Sex Determination: Adult males have a distinctly more brilliant red color at the base of the bill and more immaculate white cheeks and throat than females. The tail is also longer (female maximum 85 mm., male minimum 85 mm.).

Age Determination: Not yet determined, but first-year birds no doubt exhibit notched tail feathers. In the related species *A. georgica,* Weller (1963) noted that the juvenal plumage is held until midwinter and, although the juvenal tail feathers are shed earlier, worn juvenal tertials are carried through midwinter. Weller believed that the same molt pattern may apply to this species.

OCCURRENCE IN NORTH AMERICA

In spite of the large number of recent records of this species in North America, there are very few old records. Bent (1923) listed only a single record for Florida in 1912, and more recently there was a Virginia record (*Auk,* 56:471) and one from Wisconsin (A.O.U., 1957). However, since the 1960s a remarkable number of sightings were made in a variety of Florida locations, including Pasco County, Fort Lauderdale, Lantana, West Palm Beach, Everglades National Park, and Loxahatchee National Wildlife Refuge

(*Audubon Field Notes,* 16:23; 19:372; 21:409; 23:470; 24:495; *American Birds,* 25:300, 568; 28:42, 629).

Beyond these Florida records, there have also been recent sightings or specimen records from Alabama (*Audubon Field Notes,* 24:617), Delaware (*ibid.,* 22:19), and Illinois (*ibid.,* 24:511). It is of course possible that some of these recent records represent escapes from captivity.

PINTAIL

Anas acuta Linnaeus 1758

Other Vernacular Names: American Pintail, Common Pintail, Sprig, Sprigtail.

Range: Breeds through much of the Northern Hemisphere, in North America from Alaska south to California and east to the Great Lakes and eastern Canada, in Greenland, Iceland, Europe, and Asia, as well as in the Kerguelen and the Crozet islands. Winters in the southern parts of its breeding range in North America, south to Central America and northern South America.

North American Subspecies:

A. a. acuta L.: Northern Pintail. Range as indicated above, except for the Kerguelen and the Crozet islands.

Measurements (after Delacour, 1956):

Folded Wing: Males 254-287, females 242-266 mm.

Culmen: Males 48-59, females 45-50 mm.

Weights: Nelson and Martin (1953) reported that 937 males averaged 2.2 pounds (997 grams), while 498 females averaged 1.8 pounds (815 grams), with maximums of 3.4 and 2.4 pounds, respectively. Bellrose and Hawkins (1947) indicated that 237 adult males averaged 2.28 pounds (1,034 grams), compared to 403 immatures that averaged 2.15 pounds (975 grams); sixty adult females averaged 1.96 pounds (888 grams), and 219 immatures averaged 1.84 pounds (834 grams). Maximum weights of 2.63 pounds (1,190 grams) have been reported for both males and females by Jahn and Hunt (1964).

IDENTIFICATION

In the Hand: A pintail of either sex may be recognized in the hand by its slim-bodied and long-necked profile, sharply pointed rather than rounded tail, gray feet, gray to grayish blue bill, and a speculum that varies from brownish or bronze to coppery green, with a pale cinnamon anterior border and a white trailing edge. Another long-tailed species, the oldsquaw, has a large lobe on the hind toe, the outer toe as long or longer than the middle toe, and secondaries that lack iridescence or a white trailing edge.

In the Field: The streamlined, sleek body profile of pintails is apparent on the water or in the air. When on the water, males show more white than any other dabbling duck; their white breasts and necks can be seen for a half mile or more. When closer, the dark brown head, often appearing almost blackish, is apparent, as are the grayish flanks, separated from the black under tail coverts by a white patch on the sides of the rump. Females are somewhat smaller, mostly brownish ducks, with a dark bill that shows no trace of yellow or orange, and they show no conspicuous dark eye-stripe or pale spot on the lores as in some other female dabbling ducks. During winter and early spring, males spend much time in courtship display, and one of their distinctive courtship calls, a fluty *pfüh,* can often be heard before the birds are seen either in flight or on the water. The quacking notes of female pintails are not as loud as those of female mallards, and the decrescendo series of notes is usually rather abbreviated.

AGE AND SEX CRITERIA

Sex Determination: An iridescent bronzy speculum with a black bar in front of a white tip indicates a male, as does the presence of tertials that are long and gray with a wide black stripe. Vermiculations on the scapulars or elsewhere also indicate a male, but juvenile males may lack both vermiculations and the speculum characteristics mentioned above. Thus, juvenile birds may have to be examined internally to be certain of their sex (Carney, 1964).

Age Determination: In males, the tertial coverts of juveniles are edged with a light yellowish brown, while those of older males are without such light edges. In immature males, the middle coverts are also similarly edged and may appear narrow, rough, and frayed. In females, the tertial coverts of immature birds are also narrow and frayed, and the middle coverts are narrow and somewhat trapezoidal with barring near the feather edges, rather than being rounded with barring between the edge and the feather shaft (Carney, 1964).

DISTRIBUTION AND HABITAT

Breeding Distribution and Habitat: One of the most widely distributed of all North American ducks, the pintail breeds from the Aleutian Islands on the west to the Ungava Peninsula on the east, and from northern Texas and New Mexico on the south to at least as far north as Victoria Island, Northwest Territories. There is even a record of a brood at 82° N. latitude on Ellesmere Island, some seven hundred miles north of the previous known breeding limits (Maher and Nettleship, 1968).

In Alaska the pintail breeds virtually throughout the state, wherever suitable habitats occur, and it is both the most abundant and most widely distributed of Alaska's surface-feeding ducks (Gabrielson and Lincoln, 1959). In Canada it likewise has a nearly cosmopolitan breeding distribution, perhaps being absent only from the high arctic islands of the District of Franklin, the interior of Ontario and Quebec, Newfoundland, and parts of the Maritime Provinces (Godfrey, 1966).

In the United States south of Canada, the pintail is most abundant as a breeding species in the Great Plains and western states, from Washington south to California and eastward to Iowa and Minnesota, where it is an uncommon to occasional nester. In Wisconsin it is an infrequent nester (Jahn and Hunt, 1964). There are a few nesting records for Michigan (Zimmerman and Van Tyne, 1959), as well as for northwestern Ohio and northwestern Pennsylvania. There is at least one nesting record for Indiana (*Audubon Field Notes,* 11:416). It is a rare breeding species in New York (Foley, 1960; *Audubon Field Notes,* 16:462), is also rare in Massachusetts (*Audubon Field Notes,* 17:446), and has bred at least as far south as southeastern Pennsylvania (*ibid.,* 20:557) and North Carolina (*ibid,* 14:434).

The breeding habitat of the pintail obviously varies greatly throughout its enormous geographic range. In the arctic it is found in marshy, low country where shallow freshwater lakes occur, especially those with a dense vegetational growth near shore. It also occurs in brackish estuaries and along sluggish streams which have marshy borders (Snyder, 1957). Hildén (1964) concluded that the pintail has a psychological dependence on open landscape and thrives best in wide, open terrain with shallow waters, swamps, bog lakes, and quiet rivers. Ponds surrounded by trees appear to be avoided, but Hildén

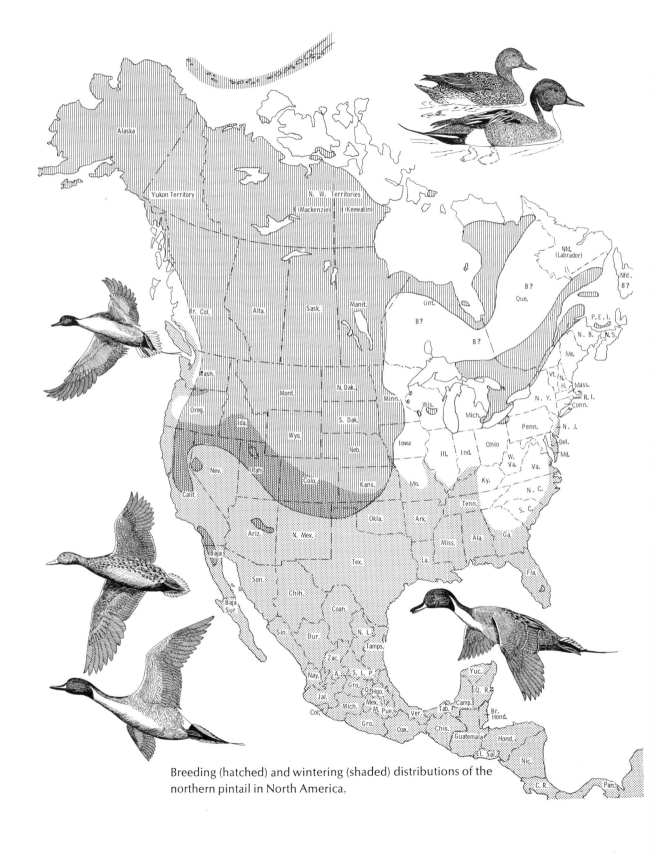

Breeding (hatched) and wintering (shaded) distributions of the
northern pintail in North America.

noted that either herbaceous or grassy islets are used for nesting. Munro (1944) noted that the favored breeding habitat in British Columbia is open, rolling grassland with brushy thickets and aspen copses, and adjacent sloughs or ponds. Lee *et al.* (1964a) has stated that in Minnesota the pintail is a bird of the prairies and is rarely found in wooded country. Keith (1961) found the highest abundance per unit of shoreline of pintail pairs on a large (21-acre) lake with a maximum depth of five feet, low shoreline vegetation, and an abundance of submerged plants.

Wintering Distribution and Habitat: To an extent only slightly less than that of the mallard, the pintail is able to winter almost anywhere that a combination of open water and available food may be found. In Canada it winters north to Queen Charlotte Island on the Pacific coast and to the Maritime Provinces on the Atlantic coast (Godfrey, 1966). South of Canada it winters in varying numbers in most states, but is particularly abundant in California, where about 75 percent of the pintails in the Pacific Flyway winter (Chattin, 1964). In Mexico the pintail is the most abundant species of wintering waterfowl, with the largest concentrations on the west coast and progressively smaller numbers in the interior and Gulf coast regions. Leopold (1959) found that the largest concentration of wintering pintails is in the delta of the Río Yaqui in Sonora, where the birds are attracted to rice stubble. Some, however, continue on into Central America and even at times reach Colombia, South America.

Stewart (1962) described the optimum wintering habitats for pintails in the Upper Chesapeake region to be shallow, fresh or brackish estuarine waters having adjacent agricultural areas with scattered impoundments. He noted that pintails also locally use estuarine bay marshes and estuarine river marshes of fresh or brackish, as well as saltwater estuarine bay marshes.

GENERAL BIOLOGY

Age at Maturity: There is general agreement that pintails breed in their first year of life. Seventeen of twenty-five aviculturalists contacted by Ferguson (1966) indicated that this was true of captive birds, and it likewise seems to be generally true of wild pintails. Sowls (1955) found that 13 of 115 females banded as juveniles returned to nest at Delta, Manitoba, the next year.

Pair Bond Pattern: Pair bonds in pintails are renewed yearly, during a prolonged period of social display, which begins after the unisexual flocks typical of the fall period begin to merge in December (Smith, 1968).

Nest Location: In one California study (Hunt and Naylor, 1955), plants that were frequently used for nesting cover were ryegrass (*Elymus*), saltbush (*Atriplex*), and Baltic rush (*Juncus balticus*), although all cover types received some usage. Two other California studies (Miller and Collins, 1954; Rienecker and Anderson, 1960) indicated a preference for nesting in upland situations in relatively low plant cover. In the former study, almost 70 percent of the nests found were in plant cover no more than twelve inches high and 16 percent were in upland situations. Over half the nests lacked concealment on at least one side, and nearly 10 percent were almost without concealment. The average distance to water was as great or greater than in any other duck species, with almost 30 percent of the nests at least fifty yards from water. Herbaceous annual weeds such as saltbush, mustard (*Brassica*), and nettle (*Urtica*) were heavily used for nest cover. Sowls (1955) reported that about 30 percent of the pintail nests he found were more than a hundred yards from water, and some nests were farther from water than those he found of any other duck species. Keith (1961) likewise noted a high average distance of pintail nests to water (164 feet), the frequent placing of nests in sparse cover, and a tendency for pintails to use the past year's dead growth for cover. This last point is largely a reflection of the early date of nest initiation in pintails, which are among the earliest of waterfowl breeders. Pintails also frequently make their nests in shallow depressions, rendering them vulnerable to flooding by heavy rains (Sowls, 1955).

Hildén (1964) and Vermeer (1968, 1970) have investigated the tendency of pintails and other ducks to nest in the vicinity of gulls and terns.

Clutch Size: Pintails exhibit the same kind of variations in reported average clutch sizes as occur for mallards and, as with the mallards, this is probably a reflection of their early nest initiation and opportunities for renesting. The largest reported average clutch sizes are 9.0 for forty-five "early" nests (Sowls, 1955) and 9.2 reported by Miller and Collins (1954) for forty-one successful nests. Average clutch sizes of slightly more than 8 eggs have been reported by Anderson (1965) and Hildén (1964). Clutch sizes of 7 eggs or fewer have been reported by several authors. Sowls (1955) and Keith (1961) found such clutch sizes typical of late-nesting birds and considered them renests. Sowls found that, among marked females, about 30 percent (nineteen of sixty-two) attempted to renest following initial nest losses.

Incubation Period: Hochbaum (1944) reported a 21- to 22-day incubation period for incubator-hatched pintail eggs. Sowls (1955) reported it as 21 days. The shorter incubation and fledging period of pintails as compared with mallards may in large measure account for their ability to nest in more northerly latitudes.

Fledging Period: Oring (1968) reported that five male pintails required an average of 45.8 days to attain flight, while five females averaged 40.8 days. A somewhat shorter fledging period (five to six weeks) has also been estimated for pintails in the northern part of their breeding range (Maher and Nettleship, 1968).

Nest and Egg Losses: Estimates of nesting success vary greatly, with some studies indicating a success in excess of 90 percent (Miller and Collins, 1954) and others as low as about 40 percent (Hunt and Naylor, 1955). Sowls (1955) found that the pintail was the most persistent renester among five species of surface-feeding ducks that he studied. He estimated that perhaps 44 percent of the total pintail nests he found were the result of renesting efforts.

Miller and Collins (1954) estimated that the average hatch per successful clutch was 8.5 young, while Rienecker and Anderson (1960) found an average hatch of 7.2 eggs per successful nest. The average brood size for seventy recently hatched broods counted by the latter authors was 5.2 young. This is nearly identical (5.3) to the average of seventy broods of comparable age reported by Ellig (1955). In his study, skunks proved to be a major predator of nests of pintails as well as of other ground-nesting duck species. The generally poor concealment of pintail nests probably makes them unusually vulnerable to predators that locate nests visually, such as crows and other birds.

Juvenile Mortality: Because of the tendency for brood merging, counts of broods near the time of fledging fail to provide an indication of prefledging losses. Thus Rienecker and Anderson (1960) noted an average brood size of 5.2 for week-old pintail broods and 7.3 young per brood among broods estimated to be five to six weeks old. They estimated, however, that an average of 5.0 young survived to fledging, compared with an average of 7.2 hatched young per successful clutch, representing a prefledging mortality of about 30 percent.

Adult Mortality: Sowls (1955) estimated an annual mortality rate for pintails of about 50 percent, based on banding recoveries reported by Munro (1944). Boyd (1962) estimated a 48 percent mortality rate for pintails banded in Russia, and Wainwright (1967) estimated a lower (37 percent) mortality rate, based on a quite limited sample.

GENERAL ECOLOGY

Food and Foraging: The most complete analysis of pintail foods is that of Martin *et al.* (1951), who noted a high incidence of plant foods taken by a sample of over 750 birds killed during fall and winter. Seeds of bulrushes

(*Scirpus*), smartweeds(*Polygonum*), the seeds and vegetative parts of pond-weeds (*Potamogeton*), wigeon grass, (*Ruppia*), and a variety of other native and cultivated plants were present in these samples. Bulrushes and pondweeds are also important summer foods for flightless birds, judging from a study by Keith and Stanislawski (1960). Stewart (1962) noted that 32 pintails shot in the Chesapeake Bay region had eaten foods that varied with the habitats utilized. Birds taken near agricultural fields showed corn and weed seeds associated with cornfields; those shot in estuarine bay marshes had a variety of seeds of submerged, emergent, and terrestial plants and only a limited amount of corn; and those from estuarine river marshes and estuarine bays had no corn present at all. Munro (1944) believed that, unlike mallards, pintails would not feed in cornfields where water was not immediately available in the field, and thus field-feeding opportunities for pintails were relatively limited. Bossenmaier and Marshall (1958) noted that pintails in Manitoba did not field-feed as zealously as mallards, and a large percentage of this species usually remained on the lake. They did, however, report that dry cut grainfields were sometimes heavily used during fall by both mallards and pintails. Unlike mallards, pintails seem to show a greater preference for small grains than for corn and often migrate out of northerly areas when waters are still open and waste corn is still available in fields (Jahn and Hunt, 1964).

Perhaps to a greater extent than most surface-feeding ducks, pintails are able to dive for their food (Kear and Johnsgard, 1968). The depth they are able to reach is still unknown. Sugden (1973) reported that pintail ducklings preferred feeding in shallow water near shore, and 38 percent of the food in 144 samples was vegetable matter.

Sociality, Densities, Territoriality: Perhaps because of the pintail's tendency for breeding in dry, upland situations, its population concentration on the breeding ground never seems to be extremely high. Drewien and Springer (1969) reported that, over a sixteen-year period, pintails had an average density of 5.6 pairs per square mile in a South Dakota study area. This is close to a figure of 29 pairs seen on a four-square-mile study area in South Dakota reported by Duebbert (1969), or about 7 pairs per square mile. When calculated according to available water area, pair density per unit area of water ranged as high as 12.6 pairs per 100 acres in Drewien and Springer's study, with these high densities occurring on temporary water areas and shallow marshes. Deeper marshes had a considerably lower pair density. Keith (1961) noted a five-year average of 22 pairs of pintails on 183 acres of impoundments in Alberta, or about 12 pairs per 100 acres of water.

Little evidence favoring the existence of territoriality is available for pintails. Munro (1944) noted that there was little hostility among male pintails sharing the same nesting area. Sowls (1955) found that pintails, as well as other surface-feeding ducks he studied, lacked definite territorial boundaries, exhibited defensive behavior in various parts of their home ranges, and commonly shared loafing sites with other pairs of their species. He noted that "defensive flights" of pintails reached a peak about the time of most early egg-laying, which would represent the time that females were relatively unguarded by their mates and subject to harassment by other drakes. Sowls also noted that at least six hens nested within 200 yards of a single pond, but there was almost no evidence of aggression among these pairs. Smith (1968) likewise observed little aggression among pintails during the breeding season and confirmed that aerial pursuit behavior is closely related to the period of egg-laying. Mated males also pursued other females most strongly during the time that their own mates were laying eggs. In fact, mated males were more likely than unmated ones to chase females, since unmated males more commonly responded with courtship behavior. Smith questioned a territorial interpretation of these flights and instead suggested that they tend to disperse nesting females and perhaps also insure the fertilization of females during the egg-laying period.

Interspecific Relationships: There is no definite evidence of competition between pintails and other duck species for nest sites or other habitat requirements. Pintails do exhibit a strong tendency to nest in the presence of gulls or terns (Hildén, 1964; Vermeer, 1968, 1970). Anderson (1965) also reported on ducks nesting in the vicinity of gulls, and indicated that 33 of 107 such nests found were pintail nests.

Pintails have the usual array of egg and duckling predators, and at times seem to suffer fairly high nest losses to them (Ellig, 1955; Anderson, 1956).

General Activity Patterns and Movements: The pintail follows a daily activity pattern that is quite similar to that described for the mallard, and indeed the two species often migrate and forage together. Pintails are exceptionally strong fliers and sometimes undertake movements of remarkable length. Chattin (1964) noted that pintails which were banded in Alaska or elsewhere in North America have been sometimes recovered in the drainages of the Anadyr, Kolyma, and Lena rivers of the Soviet Union, 2,000 miles or more from continental North America. Low (in Aldrich *et al.,* 1949) described an apparent counterclockwise migration route of pintails, which sometimes move southward out of Canada through the Dakotas, westward to California, south into Mexico, and make a return spring flight through the Central and Mississippi flyways of interior North America.

SOCIAL AND SEXUAL BEHAVIOR

Flocking Behavior: During the fall migration flight there is a surprising separation of ages and sexes in migratory flocks arriving at wintering areas, and apparently a certain degree of sexual separation persists into early winter. Smith (1968) noted large flocks of males and smaller flocks of hens in Texas during early December, followed by mixed flocks later in the month. Pair formation evidently proceeds relatively rapidly. Smith did not indicate the rate of pair formation, but at least in Bavaria about 90 percent of the females are mated by the end of February. Early flocks arriving at the breeding grounds of southern Manitoba are of paired birds, and Sowls (1955) noted that such early arrivals contained a mixture of mallards and pintails and averaged about twelve birds per flock.

Following the breeding season, and particularly after the postnuptial molt, pintails again begin to gather in fairly large flocks in preparation for the flight southward. Where they raft on large lakes during the hunting season, they may resort to feeding in shallow waters or on land either at night or after legal shooting hours.

Pair-forming Behavior: As noted, pair-forming behavior begins on the wintering ground and is virtually completed by the time the birds have completed their spring migration. Pintails seem to have a moderately disproportionate sex ratio favoring males, suggesting a higher mortality rate among females. Thus, during spring migration only a few females, but many males, remain unpaired, and intense aquatic and aerial courtship activity is a prominent feature of spring pintail flights.

Male pintails exhibit a diverse array of aquatic courtship displays (Smith, 1968; Johnsgard, 1965), but their actual significance in the formation of pairs remains obscure. Smith noted that during aerial courtship a female sometimes indicates her preference among males by shifting in his direction, and when on water the combination of female inciting and the preferred male turning-the-back-of-the-head appears to be a critical factor in the formation of individual pair bonds (Johnsgard, 1960, 1965). Smith likewise noted that when a preferred male turned the back of his head toward the female, she often responded with inciting and following him.

Copulatory Behavior: Copulation is preceded by the mutual head-pumping behavior typical of surface-feeding ducks. After treading is completed, the male normally performs a single "bridling" movement similar to that of mallards, but does not follow it with the usual nod-swimming. Turning-the-back-of-the-head and "burping" have also been observed following copulation (Johnsgard, 1965).

Nesting and Brooding Behavior: Female pintails normally lay their eggs shortly after sunrise (Sowls, 1955). They are laid at the rate of one per day, and incubation begins with the last egg. The nests are often so poorly concealed that the eggs may be hidden only by the usually plentiful down lining. The male may perhaps normally desert his mate only a few days after incubation begins (Sowls, 1955), but Bent (1923) reported that males may sometimes assist somewhat in the care of the young. An indication of the length of the pair bond after incubation begins is provided by Smith, who noted that five of six renesting pintails remained with their original mates during renesting attempts which resulted from initial nests being destroyed between the fourth and twentieth days of incubation.

Following hatching, the female typically has to move her brood a considerable distance to water, and pintail broods appear to be among the most mobile of surface-feeding ducks. Sowls (1955) reported that one female pintail moved her brood 800 yards within the first 24 hours after hatching. Female pintails are among the most persistent of all surface-feeding ducks in the defense of their broods (Bent, 1923), and the seemingly low brood mortality rate of this species is perhaps a reflection of this fact.

Postbreeding Behavior: By the time most females are incubating, groups of male pintails begin to gather in favored molting areas, such as around shallow tule-lined sloughs and marshes. Sowls (1955) determined the flightless period for male pintails to be from 27 to 29 days. Males are usually flying again by early August, and females are probably able to fly by the end of that month or early September. It seems probable that tundra-breeding pintails might migrate some distance southward before undergoing their postnuptial molt, since the frost-free season would not otherwise allow the female to rear a brood before beginning her flightless period.

GARGANEY

Anas querquedula Linnaeus 1758

Other Vernacular Names: None in North America.

Range: Breeds from Iceland (rarely) to the British Isles, and from temperate portions of Europe and Asia to Kamchatka and the Commander Islands. In winter, found in southern Europe, northern and tropical Africa, southern Asia, and the East Indies, with stragglers very rarely occurring in Australia and North America.

Subspecies: None recognized.

Measurements (after Delacour, 1956):

Folded wing: Males 187-198, females 165-194 mm.

Culmen: Males 35-40, females 34-39 mm.

Weights: Bauer and Glutz (1968) reported weights during various months; 37 males averaged 402 grams in September, and 47 females averaged 381 grams during the same month. The heaviest male weight recorded was 542 grams (in September), and the heaviest female weighed 445 grams (in August).

IDENTIFICATION

In the Hand: This rare Eurasian duck is most safely identified in the hand, especially in the case of females. The garganey is a small dabbling duck with grayish upper wing coverts, a green speculum bordered narrowly behind and more broadly in front with white, and bluish gray bill and feet. Additionally, males not in eclipse exhibit a whitish superciliary line extending down the back of the neck, elongated scapulars ornamented with glossy black and white stripes, and blackish spots or bars on the brown breast and tail coverts. Females have a longer (at least 34 mm.) and wider bill than the green-winged teal, and show a more definite pale superciliary stripe and whitish cheek mark than either green-winged or blue-winged teal females.

In the Field: Females cannot safely be identified in the field, and the few North American records would demand specimen identification of females. Males in nuptial plumage are so distinctive, with their rich brownish head and white head-stripe, their scaly brown breast, gray sides, ornamental scapulars, and spotted brownish hindquarters, that field identification may be possible. In flight they most resemble blue-winged teal, having similar underwing coloration but grayish rather than bluish upper wing coverts. The voice of the male is a mechanical wooden rattling note, like that of a fishing reel. The female has an infrequent, weak, quacking voice.

AGE AND SEX CRITERIA

Sex Determination: The somewhat brighter speculum pattern of the male, and the pale bluish gray forewing color, in contrast to the female's more brownish upper wing surface, should serve to distinguish males even when in eclipse plumage. At that time the males also reportedly have purer white throats and underparts (Delacour, 1956).

Age Determination: Not yet studied, but the notched juvenal tail feathers are probably carried for much of the first fall of life. In their absence, worn tertials from the juvenal plumage should be searched for to recognize first-year birds.

OCCURRENCE IN NORTH AMERICA

The inclusion of the garganey on the list of North American waterfowl has rested on the somewhat questionable evidence of several sight records in recent years. These include sightings of individual birds in North Carolina (*Audubon Field Notes,* 11:334), Alberta (Sugden, 1963), and Manitoba (*American Birds,* 25:759), and of three separate sightings in the Aleutian Islands during recent years (*Audubon Field Notes,* 24:634; *American Birds,* 25:785). It was not until May 1974 that the first North American specimen was obtained, on Buldir Island in the Aleutian chain (*American Birds,* 29: 936).

BLUE-WINGED TEAL

Anas discors Linnaeus 1766

Other Vernacular Names: Bluewing, Teal.

Range: Breeds from British Columbia east to southern Ontario and Quebec, south to California and the Gulf coast, and along the Atlantic coast from New Brunswick to North Carolina. Winters from the Gulf coast south through Mexico, Central America, and South America, sometimes to central Chile and central Argentina.

Subspecies:

A. d. discors L.: Western Blue-winged Teal. Breeding range as above except for the Atlantic coast.

A. d. orphna Stewart and Aldrich: Atlantic Blue-winged Teal. Breeds along the Atlantic coast from southern Canada to North Carolina. Of uncertain validity; not recognized by Delacour (1956).

Measurements (after Delacour, 1956):

Folded wing: Males 180-196, females 175-192 mm.

Culmen: Males 38-44, females 38-40 mm.

Weights: Nelson and Martin (1953) reported that 105 males averaged 0.9

pounds (408 grams), while 101 females averaged 0.8 pounds (362 grams). Jahn and Hunt (1964) indicated that 10 adult and 77 immature fall-shot males averaged 1.0 pound (453 grams); 77 adult females averaged 0.88 pound (397 grams), and 216 immatures averaged 0.94 pound (425 grams). Maximum weights for males of 1.3 pounds (589 grams) were reported by Nelson and Martin and 1.31 pounds (595 grams) by Jahn and Hunt. The latter authors report the same maximum weight for females, while Nelson and Martin indicate a maximum female weight of 1.2 pounds (543 grams).

IDENTIFICATION

In the Hand: Blue-winged teal can be easily distinguished in the hand from all other North American ducks except perhaps the cinnamon teal. Any teallike dabbling duck with light blue upper wing coverts, a bill that widens only slightly toward the tip, and an adult culmen length of less than 40 mm. is probably a blue-winged teal. Males in nuptial plumage exhibit a white crescent on the face and white on the sides of the rump, but no cinnamon red body color. The females of blue-winged and cinnamon teal have overlapping measurements for both bill length and bill width, but the cinnamon has slightly longer soft flaps over the side of the mandible near the tip, producing a semi-spatulate profile when viewed from the side. Additionally, female blue-winged teal almost always have an oval area at the base of the upper mandible that is free of tiny dark spotting and thus appears light buffy to whitish, compared with the rest of the more brownish face. The same is true of the chin and throat, although the contrast is not quite so apparent. Spencer (1953) found that mandible length, but not its width, serves to separate these two species fairly well, as do differences in the shape of the lachrymal bone.

In the Field: On the water, blue-winged teal appear as small dabbling ducks with dark bills and generally brownish body coloration, the white facial crescent and lateral rump spot of the male being the only conspicuous field marks. Females have rather uniformly brown heads, without strongly blackish crowns or eye-stripes, but with a whitish or buffy mark just behind the bill. The bluish upper wing coverts are normally invisible on the water, but in flight these show up well and alternately flash with the under wing coverts, which are pure white except for a narrow anterior margin of brown. The call of the male is a weak, whistling *tsee* note, infrequently heard except during spring. The female has a high-pitched quacking voice and a poorly developed decrescendo call of about three or four notes, muffled at the end.

AGE AND SEX CRITERIA

Sex Determination: The presence of pale cinnamon body feathers with black spotting indicates a male except during eclipse plumage. At any time, a strongly iridescent green speculum indicates a male, whereas females have a dull green speculum. Males have white-tipped greater coverts, while in females these coverts are heavily spotted with dark (Carney, 1964).

Age Determination: The presence of any notched tail feathers indicates an immature bird of either sex. In males, the tips of the greater secondary coverts of immatures often have dark spots, which are usually lacking in adults. The tertial coverts of immature males are narrow, pointed, and often edged with light brown, while in adults this is not the case. Indications of an immature female are frayed or wispy tips in the tertials, narrow greater tertial coverts which are sepia rather than greenish black, and more rounded feathers with tan edges (Carney, 1964). Dane (1968) has provided additional age criteria.

DISTRIBUTION AND HABITAT

Breeding Distribution and Habitat: The breeding range of the blue-winged teal is surprisingly extensive, considering its unusual sensitivity to cold weather. In Alaska it was reported as an "uncommon summer resident" by Gabrielson and Lincoln (1959), who thought that it probably breeds in the Copper River area but knew of only one Alaskan breeding record, a brood seen in the Matanuska Valley. However, Hansen (1960) noted that the species is a regular breeder in the Tetlin area and perhaps is locally quite common as a breeding species in Alaska.

The species breeds across most of the southern part of Canada (Godfrey, 1966) from Victoria, British Columbia, and the southern Yukon eastward to the Maritime Provinces and western Newfoundland (Tuck, 1968). Except in the Prairie Provinces, however, the blue-winged teal is not an abundant breeder anywhere in Canada. Probably the vicinity of Great Slave Lake represents the northern limit of common breeding in Canada, and east of Manitoba breeding also becomes increasingly infrequent (Bennett, 1938).

In the United States south of Canada, the blue-winged teal breeds from the Pacific to the Atlantic coasts, but has its distributional center in the marshes of the original prairies. Besides being one of the most abundant breeding species in North and South Dakota, it constitutes nearly half of the breeding duck populations of Minnesota (Lee *et al.,* 1964a) as well as Wisconsin (Jahn and Hunt, 1964) and is the commonest of Iowa's breeding ducks (Musgrove and Musgrove, 1947). Although the blue-winged teal is outnumbered by the closely related and similar cinnamon teal in the western states, it has recently pioneered new breeding areas from British Columbia to California (Wheeler, 1965). It also breeds locally in central Arizona, New Mexico, and Oklahoma. In Texas it is a local breeder along the Gulf coast (*Audubon Field Notes,* 13:442; 14:455; 20:583; 22:625). It is locally common in Louisiana (*ibid.,* 13:435) and has occasionally bred in Alabama (*ibid.,* 14:455). On the Atlantic coast it regularly breeds from coastal Maine southward through Massachusetts, New York, New Jersey, Delaware, and Maryland. In Virginia it has bred at Chincoteague and Back Bay Refuge and inland as far as Waverly (*ibid.,* 6:277); in North Carolina it breeds regularly at Pea Island National Wildlife Refuge; and there are occasional breedings as far south as central Florida (*ibid.,* 22:601).

The preferred nesting habitats of blue-winged teal are marshes in native prairie grassland, with true or tallgrass prairies of greater importance than the drier mixed prairies to the west (Bennett, 1938). Other grassland habitats used are the bunchgrass prairies of the Pacific Northwest, locally wet areas on the dry western plains, and, to a more limited extent, coastal prairies or marshes. Stewart (1962) noted that in the Chesapeake Bay area, breeding populations are mostly restricted to areas having fairly extensive salt-marsh cordgrass (*Spartina*) meadows with adjoining tidal ponds or creeks. Drewien and Springer (1969) reported that although larger ponds received heavy use by pairs prior to nesting, small and shallow marshes had the highest use by blue-winged teal during the nesting season. However, Sowls (1955) and Keith (1961) found that a variety of lake, pothole, and flooded ditch types were used by breeding birds. Glover (1956) found high nesting densities in bluegrass (*Poa*) and sedge (*Carex*) meadows with interspersed shallow sloughs having little open water.

Wintering Distribution and Habitat: To a greater extent than any other North American duck species, the blue-winged teal migrates out of the colder portions of North America and moves to both Central and South America. Only a few hundred thousand teal are counted during winter surveys within the limits of the United States. Nearly 80 percent of these are in the Mississippi Flyway, primarily in coastal Louisiana, where they have been abundant since a 1957 hurricane greatly increased their food supply (Hawkins, 1964). Several hundred thousand winter each year in Mexico, where they are the fourth most abundant wintering species of waterfowl and are especially prevalent along the Gulf coast. Leopold (1959) noted that the largest single concentration of teal in Mexico is on the *lagunas* of northwestern Yucatán, where over 80,000 birds were counted in 1952. The species also winters throughout

Breeding (hatched) and wintering (shaded) distributions of the blue-winged teal in North America.

the Central American countries, and as far south as Panama it is the most common of the wintering North American waterfowl (Bennett, 1938). The blue-winged teal also has been recorded in the winter months over most of South America, with records extending as far south as the vicinity of Buenos Aires, Argentina, and the Coquino Province of Chile.

Although relatively few birds winter there, Stewart (1962) noted that the preferred wintering habitat in Chesapeake Bay consists of brackish estuarine bay marshes. In Puerto Rico, blue-winged teal inhabit freshwater lagoons with cattail and sedge cover, and small, open pools in the midst of dense mangrove swamps in salt or brackish water (Bennett, 1938).

GENERAL BIOLOGY

Age at Maturity: Fourteen of twenty aviculturalists contacted reported that captive blue-winged teal bred when a year old (Ferguson, 1966). Dane (1966) noted that almost all first-year females initiated their first clutches before June 4 (at Delta, Manitoba), or not significantly later than did older females.

Pair Bond Pattern: Pair bonds are renewed each year during winter and early spring. The percent of females that may remate with males of the past year is still unknown but probably low, considering the long migratory routes, fairly high mortality rates, and a probable differential sex migration during fall involving an early departure of males (Jahn and Hunt, 1964).

Nest Location: Bennett (1938) noted that in a sample of over 300 nests, bluegrass (*Poa*), slough grass (*Spartina*), and alfalfa (*Medicago*) were of descending importance as sources of nest cover and that pure stands of bluegrass received the highest nesting use. Burgess *et al.* (1965) found that bluegrass cover accounted for 40 percent of 111 nests, with alfalfa and mixed native grasses being second and third in importance, respectively. Glover (1956) also reported a high usage of bluegrass or sedge meadows for nesting cover in Iowa. In Minnesota, alfalfa is used less for nesting than in Iowa, apparently because of its delayed growth. Dry sites in undisturbed grasses or lightly grazed pastures are preferred, with the average vegetation heights about 12 inches (Lee *et al.,* 1964a). Teal seem to accept nesting cover that ranges from about 8 to 24 inches high at the time of nest initiation. They avoid unusually tall cover (Bennett, 1938) and steep slopes. Depending on the topography, the nests may be situated within a foot or two of the water level (Glover, 1956), or may average as much as 10 feet above the water level (Burgess *et al.,* 1965). However, nests are usually within a quarter mile of water, and in one study (Glover, 1956) they tended to be about halfway between water and the highest surrounding point of land.

Clutch Size: The highest reported average clutch sizes are 10.97 eggs for 100 Manitoba nests initiated before June 4 (Dane, 1966), 10.6 eggs for 54 Manitoba nests completed by June 15 (Sowls, 1955), and 10.3 eggs for 126 nests in Minnesota (Lee *et al.*, 1964a). Eggs are laid at the rate of one per day. There is a decline in clutch size among later nests, with Sowls (1955) reporting an average clutch of 8.8 eggs in late nests, Glover (1956) noting an average clutch of 6.4 eggs in 48 apparent renests, and Bennett (1938) finding an average of only 4.3 eggs in 27 renesting attempts.

Although Sowls (1955) found the incidence of renesting fairly low among blue-winged teal in Manitoba, a more recent study by Strohmeyer (1968) indicated that 35 to 40 percent of the unsuccessful females attempted to renest, and in certain years or situations the renesting rate may exceed 50 percent. None of the individually marked first-year females renested, but 50 percent of the older ones did so. The hatching success and brood survival rate were similar among initial nests and renests, although the clutch sizes of renests were appreciably smaller than the original clutches, especially those which were not begun immediately after the loss of the first nest.

Incubation Period: Glover (1955) and Bennett (1938) reported the incubation period to be 21 to 23 days, based on their observations in Iowa. Dane found a slightly longer average incubation period of 23 to 27 days for wild females in Manitoba. For fifteen clutches that were incubated artificially, the average period was 24.3 days.

Fledging Period: Hochbaum (1944) reported a fledging period of 38 to 49 days, or about the same as the six-week period reported by Bennett (1938). Weller (1964) reported a 39- to 40-day fledging period.

Nest and Egg Losses: Bennett (1938) noted a 60 percent hatching success for 223 Iowa nests, compared with a 21 percent success for 173 nests studied in the same area by Glover (1956). Lee *et al.* (1964b) reported a 35 percent hatching success for 257 nests in Minnesota. He noted that the average size of twenty-eight hatched clutches was 9.4 eggs, and the average size of newly hatched broods was 7.6 young. Jahn and Hunt (1964), summarizing nine studies, found that an estimated average of 49 percent of the females succeeded in producing broods. A large number of predators or scavengers are responsible for nest and egg destruction, including crows, skunks, ground squirrels, badgers, mink, and probably others (Bennett, 1938). Egg destruction by weasels was reported by Teer (1964). Mowing and flooding also contributed to nest losses, and mowing in hayfields is sometimes a serious source of nest losses.

Juvenile Mortality: Brood counts of older broods are poor estimates of prefledging brood mortality, because of brood mergers and the occasional loss of an entire brood. Bennett (1938), counting adult female-to-young ratios, concluded that an average of about 5.1 young (of an initial successful hatch of 9.24 young) survived to reach the migratory stage by late August. These figures are close to those of Glover (1956), who estimated that 9.3 hatched per successful nest and that broods about eight to ten weeks old averaged 5.16 young per female. A prefledging mortality of about 45 percent would thus seem to represent a reasonable estimate of brood losses.

Postfledging mortality of immatures is probably high, but few estimates are available. Geis *et al.* (cited by Jahn and Hunt, 1964) estimated a 77 percent annual mortality rate for immature birds. Lee *et al.* (1964b) estimated a 62 percent mortality for mixed age birds in the first year after banding.

Adult Mortality: Bellrose and Chase (1950) estimated an annual mortality rate of 57 percent. Boyd (1962) calculated a 45 percent mortality rate for adults.

GENERAL ECOLOGY

Food and Foraging: The adult food intake of blue-winged teal is approximately three-fourths vegetable material, with a somewhat higher rate of animal materials taken during spring. Seeds are especially prominent among the plant materials, although the vegetative parts of such plants as duckweeds (*Lemnaceae*), naiads (*Najas*), pondweeds (*Potamogeton*), wigeon grass (*Ruppia*), and similar aquatic plants are also consumed (Martin *et al.*, 1951). Bennett (1938) found that, on a volume basis, the sedge, naiad, and grass families contributed over half of the total food intake of 385 teal samples, while insects, mollusks, and crustaceans comprised about 25 percent. The apparently high use of seeds by blue-winged teal, as well as by other waterfowl, may in part be a reflection of sampling bias, resulting from the slower rate of digestion of hard seeds as compared with soft foods when both are ingested simultaneously (Swanson and Bartonek, 1970).

Blue-winged teal feed almost entirely from the surface or by tipping-up; only one observation of them diving for food seems to have been made (Kear and Johnsgard, 1968). Their small body size and restriction to foraging at or near the surface probably accounts for their strong tendency to inhabit shallow and small water areas.

Sociality, Densities, Territoriality: The social bonds of blue-winged teal persist through spring migration, even though the majority of the birds are paired at that time (Glover, 1956). After their arrival at the breeding grounds, the males become increasingly intolerant of one another and direct their attacks primarily toward the females of other pairs (McKinney, 1970). Mc-

Kinney interprets this as territorial defense, although most other workers have not detected the presence of true territoriality in this species. Glover (1956) obtained no data during his study to support the idea of territorial defense. Bennett (1938) described "nesting territories" and "male waiting territories," but observed no defense by males of the latter, nor did he see any females defending their nesting areas. Drewien and Springer (1969) noted that during the start of nesting activities, pairs of blue-winged teal showed an intolerance for other breeding birds of their species and thus tended to disperse over the available habitat. There seems, however, to be no evidence that blue-winged teal exhibit defensive behavior relative to any area *per se,* but rather only defense of the female.

Nesting densities of blue-winged teal in favorable habitats seem to be among the highest of all dabbling ducks. Keith (1961) found a four-year average of 31 pairs on 183 acres of impoundments in Alberta, or an average density of 18 pairs per 100 acres. Drewien and Springer reported pair densities of 17.4 to 63.6 pairs per 100 acres on various pond types during two years of study in South Dakota. Jahn and Hunt (1964) reported six-year average densities of 4 to 22 pairs per 100 wetland acres in four geographic areas in Wisconsin. Bennett found nest densities ranging from as low as 1 per 100 acres to as high as 1 per 0.1 acre within 220 yards of a water area. Glover (1956), working in the same area, reported an average nest density of 1 nest per 12.5 acres of total cover, with a maximum of 1 per 1.3 acres on a 30-acre island.

Interspecific Relationships: Among the other surface-feeding ducks, only the cinnamon teal is sufficiently closely related and similar in its habitat requirements as to be a possible serious competitor for mates, food, or nesting sites. Mixed courting groups involving these two species may sometimes be seen among wild birds, and several wild hybrids have been reported, although the incidence is surprisingly low considering the similarity of the females of these species. In captivity, at least, males of each species regularly perform courtship displays to females of the other, so evidently the primary responsibility for proper species recognition resides with the female. Studies of possible differences in habitat requirements of the two species in areas where they both breed have not been undertaken, partly, no doubt, because of the difficulties of recognition of females and summer-plumaged males.

Predators causing nest losses in blue-winged teal are numerous and include crows, skunks, ground-squirrels, minks, badgers, foxes, weasels, and, no doubt, others (Bennett, 1938; Glover, 1956). Ducklings may be taken by some of these same predators, as well as by snapping turtles, large predatory fish, and probably some avian predators.

General Activity Patterns and Movements: No specific information on daily activity patterns seems to be available. Likewise the distances of daily movements both on the breeding grounds and during migration have not received critical attention.

SOCIAL AND SEXUAL BEHAVIOR

Flocking Behavior: Except immediately prior to and during the nesting season, blue-winged teal are distinctly flocking birds. Broods of several families typically join together during late summer, and flocks usually consist of several hundred birds during the start of the migration period (Bennett, 1938). There is apparently an early fall departure of adult males prior to that of females and immatures (Jahn and Hunt, 1964). With the start of the hunting season, the flocks of 100 to 500 birds break up and reconstitute themselves into groups usually containing fewer than 30 birds. During the spring migration the flocks usually number fewer than 30 birds and often consist of only a pair or two (Bennett, 1938). Glover (1956) noted that about 60 percent of the early spring migrants reaching northern Iowa were already paired.

Pair-forming Behavior: McKinney (1970) noted that most blue-winged teal wintering in Louisiana are firmly mated by mid-March. The male displays occurring during pair formation are numerous (Johnsgard, 1965; McKinney, 1970). Aerial displays are few and apparently limited to short "jump-flights" by the male toward the female apparently to attract the female's attention. Aquatic displays consist mostly of ritualized forms of foraging ("mock-feeding," tipping-up, or "head-up and up-end") and comfort movements (shaking, preening, bathing, wing-flapping). The primary display of the female is inciting, and the male's response to it is frequently turning-the-back-of-the-head. As McKinney noted, this is one of the most frequent of male displays and, I believe, perhaps the most important single display in the establishment of pair bonds.

A number of observers (e.g., Bent, 1925; Bennett, 1938) reported that much of the courtship of blue-winged teal occurred in the air. Glover (1956) made the interesting observation that most of the early flights he observed were led by a male, while the later ones were typically led by females. It is highly probable that the earlier ones he observed were indeed flights associated with pair formation, while the later ones were aerial chases of the attempted rape or "expulsion flight" type, in which males that were already paired were chasing females from the pair's vicinity or were attempting to rape them.

Copulatory Behavior: As in other surface-feeding ducks, copulation is preceded by a mutual head-pumping behavior that has often been confused by earlier observers with the hostile chin-lifting or pumping movements occurring during aggressive encounters. During copulation the male firmly grasps the female's nape, and McKinney (1970) once recorded a male uttering calls softly during treading. Typically the male utters a single loud whistled *peew* or nasal *paaay* note immediately after releasing the female and assumes a rather stiff and erect body posture, with his bill pointing sharply downward (Johnsgard, 1965; McKinney, 1970).

Nesting and Brooding Behavior: During the egg-laying phase, females visit the nest on a daily basis to lay their eggs, usually shortly after sunrise. Egg-laying may begin a few days to more than a week after the beginning of nest construction (Glover, 1956). The nest is lined with available materials, usually a mixture of bluegrass and down. In about 80 percent of 134 nests studied by Glover, the down was not added until four or more eggs were present.

Incubation begins within 24 hours of the laying of the last egg, and usually the nest is left once or twice a day for resting and foraging. The pair bond of the male typically begins to wane after about three days of incubation, and he begins to associate with other such males in groups of from 3 to 35 individuals (Bennett, 1938). Females probably do not leave the nest during the last 48 hours of incubation, or at least after the process of pipping begins. Within 24 hours of hatching, the female typically leads her brood from the nest and takes them into fairly heavy brooding cover. A favorite cover is a mixture of bulrushes in water one to two feet deep. Cover containing bur reed (*Sparganium*), reeds (*Phragmites*), or cattail (*Typha*) is used much less, apparently because the plant density is too great and the tall, rank plant growth crowds out important food plants and shuts out sunshine (Bennett, 1938).

Postbreeding Behavior: After deserting his mate, the male moves into suitable molting cover and soon begins his postnuptial molt. Hochbaum (1944) noted that some birds may renew their wing feathers within two and one-half weeks after dropping them, but he believed that a three- or four-week flightless period was more typical. Shortly after regaining their flight, adult males begin to leave the breeding grounds, to be followed later by females and young.

CINNAMON TEAL

Anas cyanoptera Vieillot 1816

Other Vernacular Names: None in general use.

Range: In North America, breeds from British Columbia and Alberta southward through the western states as far east as Montana, Wyoming, western Nebraska, western Texas, and into northern and western Mexico. Also breeds in northern and southern South America. The North American population winters in the southwestern states southward through Mexico, Central America, and northwestern South America.

North American Subspecies:

A. c. septentrionalium Snyder and Lumsden: Northern Cinnamon Teal. Breeds in North America as indicated above.

Measurements (after Delacour, 1956):

Folded wing: Males 176-194, females 167-185 mm.

Culmen: Males 39-47, females 39-45 mm.

Weights: Nelson and Martin (1953) reported that twenty-six males averaged 0.9 pounds (408 grams), while nineteen females averaged 0.8 pounds (362 grams), with maximum weights of 1.2 pounds (543 grams) and 1.1 pounds (498 grams), respectively.

IDENTIFICATION

In the Hand: The rich cinnamon red color, the reddish eyes, and the lack of white on the body distinguish the male cinnamon teal from the only other teallike duck with blue upper wing coverts, the blue-winged teal. Females are much more difficult to identify, but if the bill is fairly long (culmen length of 40 mm. or more), somewhat wider toward the tip, and the soft lateral margins of the upper mandible distinctly droop over the lower mandible toward the tip, the bird is most probably a cinnamon teal. Unlike female blue-winged teal, female cinnamons have yellowish rather than whitish cheeks with fine dark spotting extending to or nearly to the base of the bill, eliminating the pale mark or at least making it smaller than the size of the eyes. Likewise, fine dark spotting on the cinnamon teal extends farther down the chin and throat, restricting the size of the clear throat patch. Duvall (cited by Spencer, 1953) found that twenty-six female blue-winged teal had a maximum exposed culmen length of 41 mm., while seventeen female cinnamon teal had a minimum exposed culmen length of 41 mm., with means of 38.7 and 43 mm., respectively.

In the Field: Female cinnamon teal cannot be safely distinguished from female blue-winged teal except under the best conditions and by experienced observers. Their smaller cheek spot, more rusty body tone, and longer, somewhat spatulate bill are most evident when both species are side by side. However, males can be recognized, even when in full eclipse, by their reddish to yellowish eyes, and when in full nuptial plumage their coppery red body color is unique among North American ducks. The vocalizations of the females of the two species are nearly identical, but male cinnamon teal have a low, gutteral, and shovelerlike rattling voice, which is uttered during courtship display. In flight, the male's reddish underpart and upperpart coloration, relieved by the light blue upper wing covert pattern, is easily recognized, but the females cannot be distinguished from female blue-winged teal. Normally, females closely associated with males of either species can be safely assumed to be of the same species.

AGE AND SEX CRITERIA

Sex Determination: The presence of reddish eyes or dark cinnamon red feathers anywhere on the head or body indicates a male. In the eclipse plumage, males can be recognized by their brighter green speculum, their yellowish red eyes, their white-tipped greater secondary coverts, or their ornamental tertials, which are pointed and blackish with buffy stripes. Immature males may lack many of these traits, but are likely to exhibit at least one of them. Males acquire a reddish iris color at about eight weeks of age (Spencer, 1953).

Age Determination: Notched tail feathers indicate an immature bird of either sex. Frayed or faded tertials or their coverts, which are narrow and edged with light brown, also indicate immaturity, and immature males lack the ornamental pointed and buffy-striped tertials of adults.

DISTRIBUTION AND HABITAT

Breeding Distribution and Habitat: Unlike all other North American waterfowl excepting the whistling ducks and stiff-tailed ducks, the cinnamon teal has an extralimital breeding distribution in South America. In North America the northern limit of its breeding range is in western Canada, where the cinnamon occurs and apparently breeds in southern British Columbia, southern Alberta, and perhaps southern Saskatchewan (Godfrey, 1966).

In Washington it is common east of the Cascades and occurs casually to the west; evidently it is about equally abundant with the blue-winged teal in the eastern half of the state (Yocom, 1951). In Oregon both species breed, but the cinnamon teal probably extends somewhat farther west and at least in the Malheur area is the more common species. In California the cinnamon teal nests commonly in the Tule Lake and Lower Klamath areas (Miller and Collins, 1954), in Lassen County (Hunt and Anderson, 1966), in the Sacramento Valley (Anderson, 1957), in the Merced County grasslands (Anderson, 1956), and in the Suisun marshes (Anderson, 1960). Blue-winged teal were not reported as nesting in any of these studies, but in the Lake Earl area of Del Norte County both species evidently nest and the blue-winged teal may be the more common (Johnson and Yocom, 1966). The cinnamon teal breeds as far south as Baja California, and also breeds locally in Tamaulipas and as far south in central Mexico as Jalisco (Leopold, 1959). In Arizona, New Mexico, and western Texas its breeding is probably regular but localized. The center of its breeding abundance is perhaps in Utah, where the Bear River marshes seemingly provide optimum habitat (Williams and Marshall, 1938). It breeds east to the La Poudre Valley of north-central Colorado, but is greatly outnumbered there by blue-winged teal, and it is a very rare breeder in Nebraska. To the north, it breeds as far east as eastern Wyoming and eastern Montana. There are extralimital breeding records for North Dakota (Phillips, 1924) and Oklahoma (Sutton, 1967), as well as a remarkable instance of attempted breeding near Ocean City, Maryland (*Audubon Field Notes,* 16:464).

An analysis of breeding habitat requirements and preferences for cinna-

CINNAMON TEAL   283

Breeding (hatched) and wintering (shaded) distributions of the
cinnamon teal in North America.

mon teal has not yet been made, but some points are evident. Like the blue-winged teal, cinnamon teal nest preferentially in fairly low herbaceous cover under 24 inches high, preferably in grasses but with herbaceous weeds and bulrushes also locally utilized. They seem, like the gadwall, to be particularly attracted to alkaline waters, and in this respect evidently differ from blue-winged teal. Small and shallow water areas seem to have preference over larger and deeper bodies of water. In the potholes area of Washington state, blue-winged and cinnamon teal pairs utilized ponds that had a surrounding grassy zone of salt grass (*Distichlis*), brome (*Bromus*), and sedges (*Carex*). Such ponds were used for nesting, while those having both open water zones and considerable emergent vegetation (mainly *Scirpus and Typha*) received the highest brood use (Johnsgard, 1955).

Wintering Distribution and Habitat: Since cinnamon teal are not distinguished from blue-winged teal during winter surveys by the United States Fish and Wildlife Service, such counts are almost useless for estimating winter populations. Leopold (1959) judged that of the total teal seen during the 1952 counts in Mexico, about 75 percent or more were blue-winged teal. However, cinnamon teal were noted to be prevalent among birds counted in Sinaloa and Nayarit. Areas of winter concentration were found in coastal Sinaloa and Nayarit, the southern uplands from Jalisco to Puebla, and the coast of northern Veracruz. Probably most of the cinnamon teal of North America winter in western Mexico, since the birds are apparently rare in Guatemala and are virtually unknown elsewhere in Central America. Cinnamon teal winter sparingly along the Gulf coast of southern Texas and presumably along much of the Gulf coast of Mexico, where they probably occupy habitats similar to those of blue-winged teal.

GENERAL BIOLOGY

Age at Maturity: Eleven of nineteen aviculturalists informed Ferguson (1965) that cinnamon teal bred in captivity in their first year of life, while seven reported second-year breeding and one third-year. Comparable data from wild birds are not available, but it may be assumed that most females initially nest when a year old.

Pair Bond Pattern: Cinnamon teal renew their pair bonds each year, probably while still in their wintering areas (McKinney, 1970). In the few sex ratio counts which have been made for this species, either males have been a surprising minority relative to females (Spencer, 1953; Johnsgard and Buss, 1956) or have constituted a slight excess (Evendon, 1952).

Nest Location: In a study involving 524 nests in Utah, Williams and Marshall (1938) reported that half of the total were found in salt grass, with hardstem bulrush (*Scirpus acutus*) providing cover for another 23 percent, and most of the rest being placed in other grasses, sedges, or broadleaf weeds. In a California study, Miller and Collins (1954) reported that of forty nests found, cinnamon teal exhibited a preference for nesting on islands, using nettle (*Urtica*) cover less than twelve inches high. The nests were usually well concealed, with 70 percent being hidden from all four sides and above; all of them were within fifty yards of water, and 40 percent were within three yards of water. In another California study (Hunt and Naylor, 1955) involving 147 nests, ryegrass (*Elymus*) and Baltic rush (*Juncus balticus*) were primary types of nest cover, with salt grass having the next highest use.

Spencer (1953) has emphasized that specific nest cover plants may not be as important as other factors related to nest site selection. His studies at Ogden Bay and Farmington Bay indicated a predominant use of salt grass as cover for 396 nests, whereas at Knudsen's Marsh it is present in only small quantities and did not serve as cover for any of 145 nests. On the basis of cover "preference" calculations (usage relative to cover availability), salt grass scored much lower than many plant species occurring in trace quantities. Vegetation providing a cover height of twelve to fifteen inches and good to excellent concealment was seemingly preferred, especially when such cover was close to stands of tall vegetation such as cattails, bulrushes, or various forbs.

Clutch Size: Clutch sizes for initial nests of cinnamon teal average about 9 or 10 eggs; Hunt and Naylor (1955) reported that the average size of 76 clutches from successful nests was 9.3 eggs. In a renesting study, Hunt and Anderson (1965) noted that 6 initial nestings averaged 10.0 eggs, 6 second nestings averaged 8.3 eggs, and a single third nesting attempt had 9 eggs. Spencer (1953) reported an average clutch of 8.9 eggs in 104 successfully hatched nests, with very early and very late clutches tending to be smaller than those in midseason.

Incubation Period: Reported as 24 to 25 days by Delacour (1956). Spencer (1953) observed a range of 21 to 25 days in wild cinnamon teal nests.

Fledging Period: Apparently not yet definitely determined. Lack (1968) reported six weeks, but the reference given (Hochbaum, 1944) does not include this information. Spencer (1953) reported that captive-reared birds were fully feathered and probably capable of flight when seven weeks old.

Nest and Egg Losses: One of the highest reported nest successes was that of Williams and Marshall (1938), who found that 84 percent of 2,655 eggs in 524 nests hatched. Hunt and Naylor (1955) found an even higher hatching success, 93 percent of 125 eggs in 1951 and 85.5 percent of 583 eggs in 1953.

Girard (1941) reported a 72 percent hatching success for 22 nests in Montana. However, Anderson (1956) found that only 20 percent of 70 nests studied in Merced County, California, hatched in 1953 and only 1.9 percent of 56 nests hatched in 1954. Most of these losses were attributed to predatory mammals, including dogs, cats, raccoons, skunks, and opossums. Spencer (1953) noted that skunks and California gulls destroyed a total of 777 of 1,870 teal eggs during two years of study at Ogden Bay, Utah. Nesting and hatching successes were 45 and 43 percent, respectively. Parasitism by redheads was fairly frequent and resulted in a slight decrease in hatching success through increased nest desertion rates and in a slight decrease in average sizes of teal clutches.

Juvenile Mortality: Reinecker and Anderson (1960) estimated that an average of 9.2 ducklings hatched from successful nests and that prefledging mortality reduced this number to an average terminal brood size of 6.2 young. Spencer (1953) reported average brood size reductions from about 9 young shortly after hatching to 4.5 or 4.7 young (two years' data) for broods about ready to fledge, or approximately 50 percent prefledging mortality.

No estimates of postfledging mortality rates of immature birds are available.

Adult Mortality: Estimates of adult mortality rates are apparently unavailable.

GENERAL ECOLOGY

Food and Foraging: Few food analysis studies have been performed on cinnamon teal, although it seems probable that dietary differences from the blue-winged teal would be very few. Martin *et al.* (1951) noted the seeds of bulrushes, salt grass, and sedges, and the seeds and vegetative parts of pondweeds (*Potamogeton*) and horned pondweeds (*Zannichellia*) in summer and fall food samples. The small amount of animal materials present included mollusks, beetles, bugs, fly larvae, and the naiads of dragonflies and damselflies.

Sociality, Densities, Territoriality: Williams and Marshall (1938) estimated the cinnamon teal breeding density on 3,000 acres of potential nesting cover to average 0.17 nests per acre, or nearly 110 nests per square mile. Hunt and Naylor (1955) estimated that 266 pairs of cinnamon teal were present in Honey Lake valley in California and mostly nested in the 2,000-acre Fleming Unit of that management area, representing an approximate density of 90 pairs per square mile. Spencer (1953) calculated a nesting density of 0.18 nests per acre for 357 acres on a Utah study area, or about 120 per square mile. All of these studies suggest that breeding densities of 100 or more pairs per square mile of habitat are possible in cinnamon teal, which is considerably greater than figures available for blue-winged teal. Quite possibly the effects of crowding produced by the relatively fewer areas of marsh habitat available in the arid western states account for this apparently higher nesting density. McKinney (1970) noted that paired cinnamon teal, like blue-winged teal, restrict their activities to relatively small areas, although the home ranges of neighboring pairs tend to overlap and territorial boundaries are difficult to define. Spencer (1953) reported that most territories he observed were under 30 square yards in area, with the nest site inside these limits or no more than 100 yards from it.

Interspecific Relationships: The extent to which cinnamon teal and blue-winged teal might compete for food or other aspects of their habitat in areas of joint breeding is still unknown. In central and eastern Washington both species are about equally common and appear to occupy virtually identical habitats (Yocom, 1951; Johnsgard, 1955).

As with other surface-feeding ducks, a variety of mammalian and avian predators probably take eggs and ducklings, but in no case has this been proven a serious limiting factor controlling teal populations.

General Activity Patterns and Movements: Nothing specific on these points is available. Spencer (1953) noted that this species is diurnal and that migrating flocks were often seen during the daytime, but not at night. He also noted that social display could occur at any time during the day, but was most intense before 10:00 a.m. and after 4:00 p.m. Cool and cloudy weather increased the frequency of midday display activities.

SOCIAL AND SEXUAL BEHAVIOR

Flocking Behavior: Most observers report that cinnamon teal generally are to be found in small flocks, usually consisting of paired birds (Phillips, 1924). However, this would not apply to fall flocks, since pairing has not occurred by that time. Spencer (1953) reported that the spring migrant flocks he observed were often in groups of 10 to 20 birds, while during fall the early flocks of migrating males were usually in groups of fewer than 150 birds.

Pair-forming Behavior: Displays associated with pair formation probably begin on the wintering grounds when the males have regained their nuptial plumage, or roughly the end of the calendar year. Spencer (1953) observed captive birds displaying as early as late February, but by the time the wild cinnamon teal migrants arrived in Utah during March a large percentage already appeared to be paired. The displays associated with the formation of pairs are extremely similar to those of shovelers and blue-winged teal, with ritualized forms of foraging behavior being the most highly developed displays. As in the other two species of "blue-winged ducks," short "jump-flights" are also more prevalent than is true of the other surface-feeding ducks. McKinney (1970) is probably correct in pointing out that the presence of light blue upper wing coverts on this group of species is evidently related to their exposure during such display flights. Inciting by females takes on a strong vertical head-pumping component, which is somewhat similar to that occurring in a precopulatory situation. The male's usual response is to perform the turning-of-the-back-of-the-head display while swimming in front of her. Very probably this display plays a major role in the formation of pairs.

Copulatory Behavior: Copulation is preceded by mutual head-pumping movements, with the tip of the bill tilted slightly downwards rather than upwards as in hostile encounters. After treading is completed, the male may utter a single soft rattling note; he assumes a lateral posture with bill pointed downward, hindquarters and wings somewhat raised, and shakes his tail while paddling his feet (McKinney, 1970).

Nesting and Brooding Behavior: Females usually construct a rather simple nest of dead grasses and plant stems, with fresh green material rarely being used. They are usually shallow bowl-shaped depressions, which are lined with more plant materials and down as the clutch nears completion. The first few eggs may be deposited at intervals of one to three days, while the later ones are usually at the rate of one per day, with most laying done between the hours of 8:00 and 10:00 a.m. Incubation begins within twenty-four hours of the laying of the last egg, and during the incubation period the female may feed for a maximum of two hours a day, usually during late afternoon. As little as seven hours may elapse between the start of pipping and the evacuation of the nest.

After hatching, the female moves her brood to rearing cover that provides adequate foraging opportunities, such as small ditches or ponds, and suitable escape cover, such as surrounding emergent vegetation. If suitable waterways are present, the broods may move as far as a mile in three or four days, but are more likely to remain in a small area (Spencer, 1953).

Postbreeding Behavior: Male cinnamon teal probably desert their mates during the early stages of incubation. Spencer (1953) did not observe any sizable groups of males during the postbreeding molting period, but by early August adult males were already beginning their southward migration. Adult males were rarely encountered after mid-September, and, after mid-October, the majority of the total cinnamon teal population had moved southward out of northern Utah. The rate of the southward movement is apparently rather fast, even for immature birds. One immature female, banded at Ogden Bay on July 31, was shot near Mexico City on August 15, suggesting an average minimum movement of 114 miles per day.

NORTHERN SHOVELER

Anas clypeata Linnaeus 1758

(Until 1973, regarded by the A.O.U. as *Spatula clypeata*)

Other Vernacular Names: Shoveller, Spoonbill, Spoonbilled Duck.

Range: Breeds through much of the Northern Hemisphere, including the British Isles, Europe except for northern Scandinavia, most of Asia except for the high arctic, and in North America from western and interior Alaska southward to California and eastward to the Great Lakes, with some breeding along the middle Atlantic coast.

Subspecies: None recognized.

Measurements (after Delacour, 1956):

Folded wing: Males 225-245, females 220-225 mm.

Culmen: Males 62-64, females 60-62 mm.

Weights: Nelson and Martin (1953) reported that 90 males averaged 1.4 pounds (634 grams), and 71 females averaged 1.3 pounds (589 grams). Combining the data of Bellrose and Hawkins (1947) and that of Jahn and Hunt (1964) for fall-shot birds, 21 adult males averaged 1.53 pounds (694 grams), and 65 immature males averaged 1.49 pounds (676 grams); fifteen adult females averaged 1.41 pounds (639 grams), and 68 immatures averaged 1.34 pounds (608 grams). Maximum weights reported for males are 2.0 pounds by Nelson and Martin and 1.94 pounds by Jahn and Hunt, while for females the maximum weights are 1.6 and 2.12 pounds, respectively.

IDENTIFICATION

In the Hand: The strongly spatulate bill, which has soft lateral margins near the tip that hang over the sides and obscure the long lamellae, is unique to the shoveler among North American species of waterfowl. Additionally, the light blue upper wing coverts and the orange legs and feet are distinctive.

In the Field: Whether on the water or in the air, the long, spoonlike bill of both sexes is easily apparent, being distinctly longer than the head and destroying the otherwise fairly sleek lines of the duck. Males do not acquire their striking nuptial plumage until rather late in the winter, so that during fall most shovelers are femalelike in appearance, with the enlarged bill and bluish upper wing coverts being the primary field marks, the latter normally visible only when the bird is flying. In flight, the underwing surface is entirely white, and the underparts of females or dull-plumaged males are brownish, so that from underneath the birds distinctly resemble female mallards except for the more prominent bill. During late winter and spring the males acquire a white breast, a large white area between the black tail coverts and the reddish brown sides, and an iridescent green head. At this time they are reminiscent of male mallards, except that the breast is white and the sides reddish brown, instead of vice versa. Males are quite silent except during aquatic courtship, when low-pitched rattling notes are uttered. The female has a quacking voice similar to those of cinnamon and blue-winged teal, and her decrescendo call is usually about five notes long, with the last one or two rather muffled.

AGE AND SEX CRITERIA

Sex Determination: The presence of iridescent green on the head or of any pure white or chestnut brown feathers on the body indicates a male. All birds with completely noniridescent secondaries are females, but some females do show iridescence on the secondaries. Most females exhibit cream edging on the lesser and middle coverts, while males lack this or have only a few cream-edged feathers near the wrist (Carney, 1964).

Age Determination: The presence of notched tail feathers indicates an immature bird, and most immatures also have small dusky spots on their greater coverts, which are lacking in adults. The presence of fading and fraying on the tertials or their coverts indicates immaturity. In immatures these are brownish or brownish black, while in adults the tertials are greenish black (males) or heavily washed with white at the tips (females), according to Carney (1964).

DISTRIBUTION AND HABITAT

Breeding Distribution and Habitat: Like the other Holarctic surface-feeding ducks, the gadwall, pintail, mallard, and green-winged teal, the shoveler occupies a broad breeding range across most of North America. In Alaska it is generally uncommon, but is most abundant on the Copper River delta and the lakes of the Minto area. It apparently breeds as far west as Norton Sound, since ducklings have been collected near St. Michael (Gabrielson and Lincoln, 1959).

In Canada the shoveler as a breeding species is largely limited to the area west of Ontario and extending northward to tree line as well as westward to the coastal range of mountains in British Columbia. In Ontario and to the east it is only a very localized breeder, with most of the records from near the eastern Great Lakes and the St. Lawrence valley. It has also bred in eastern New Brunswick and on Prince Edward Island (Godfrey, 1966).

In the United States south of Canada the shoveler breeds from central Washington southward through Oregon to south-central California and eastward across the Great Plains to Nebraska, with localized breeding localities in New Mexico, Kansas, and Oklahoma. Occasional nestings in Texas have been reported (*Audubon Field Notes,* 15:485). Northern Iowa and Minnesota apparently represent the eastern limit of regular breeding by shovelers. In Wisconsin the species now breeds only occasionally and in a few localities (Jahn and Hunt, 1964), and in Michigan the records likewise are limited to a few counties (Zimmerman and Van Tyne, 1959). Shovelers have not been known to breed in Indiana since 1935 (Mumford, 1954), but have occasionally nested in Ohio (Stewart, 1957). In New York they have nested on Long Island and in the Montezuma marshes north of Lake Cayuga (*Audubon Field Notes,* 10:372; 11:391; 13:410). They have also nested in New Jersey (*ibid,* 13:410), Delaware (*ibid,* 15:456), and at least as far south as Pea Island National Wildlife Refuge, North Carolina (A.O.U., 1957).

Shallow prairie marshes represent the preferred breeding habitat of shovelers, particularly those with abundant plant and animal life floating on the surface, such as duckweeds and associated biota. Drewien and Springer (1969) reported the highest density of pairs during the nesting period on shallow marshes, with somewhat lower usage of shallow to deep marshes. Keith (1961) indicated that the highest shoveler usage in his study areas occurred

Breeding (hatched) and wintering (shaded) distributions of the
shoveler in North America.

on a fairly large shallow lake with a maximum depth of 5 feet and with water milfoil (*Myriophyllum*) and pondweeds (*Potamogeton*) as principal submerged aquatic plants. Female shovelers leading broods seem to favor especially water areas having an abundance of pondweeds as well as waterweeds (*Anacharis*); the latter also usually supports an unusually rich associated animal life (Girard, 1939).

Hildén (1964) concluded that the nesting habitat of shovelers must include waters with open rather than wooded shores, the waters preferably being shallow, eutrophic, and with a mud bottom. Coastal shorelines that offer freshwater pools or shallow shores for feeding are acceptable, and nesting sometimes occurs on islets with gravel or polished rock shorelines. There is apparently a moderately strong attraction of shovelers to nesting gulls or terns.

Wintering Distribution and Habitat: According to winter survey data of recent years, approximately 90 percent of the total North American wintering shoveler population of 586,000 birds occurs in the Pacific and Mississippi flyways, with about equal abundance in each, and the remainder in the Central and Atlantic flyways. Since 1957 increasing numbers have wintered in Louisiana, and along the Pacific coast they are abundant winter visitors as far north as Puget Sound. There the shoveler occurs in moderately large flocks, keeping to the freshwater meadows and avoiding the saltwater habitats (Jewett *et al.,* 1953). In Oregon it at least occasionally winters on the Columbia River and along the coastal bays, and in California it is an abundant winter resident in the Central Valley and to a lesser extent along the coast. In Mexico it is outnumbered only by the pintail and lesser scaup among wintering waterfowl; it is especially abundant on the Pacific coast, where more than 200,000 birds usually may be found. Leopold (1959) reported that the largest winter concentrations are at Laguna de Joya, in southern Chiapas. It becomes progressively less common on the Pacific coast through Guatemala and El Salvador and occurs irregularly in Panama. It is fairly common on the Caribbean slope at least as far south as Honduras, but apparently has not been recorded in British Honduras. It is common on the Caribbean coast of Mexico during winter, and extends northward and eastward along the Gulf coast states at least as far north as Chesapeake Bay, where small wintering groups are usually present (Stewart, 1962).

In the Chesapeake Bay area, transient and wintering shovelers are usually well distributed on fresh and brackish estuarine bay marshes and are generally commonest on stillwater ponds subject to slight tidal variations. In saltwater situations shovelers are usually more localized and apparently prefer artificial impoundments along drainage systems (Stewart, 1962).

GENERAL BIOLOGY

Age at Maturity: Eleven of twenty aviculturalists reported shovelers breeding under conditions of captivity at the age of one year (Ferguson, 1965).

Pair Bond Pattern: Pair bonds are lacking in shovelers between late June and the time they again acquire their nuptial plumage, about November to December (McKinney, 1970). The incidence of remating with mates of the previous breeding season among wild birds is still unreported, but McKinney (1965) noted that among captive shovelers some birds re-paired while others deliberately chose new mates. As McKinney (1970) has emphasized, there is no evidence that polyandry is characteristic of shovelers.

Nest Location: In one Montana study (Girard, 1939), it was found that over half of 132 nests utilized short grasses, 23 percent were hidden in tall grasses, 13 percent in thistles (*Salsola* and *Cirsium*), and the rest were under various other herbaceous or shrub covers. In a Utah study, salt grass (*Distichlis*) provided cover for 65 percent of 37 nests, with bulrushes (*Scirpus*) and various herbaceous weeds making up most of the remainder. Since the favored salt grass typically grows adjacent to water, most of the nests were located fairly near water. However, Keith (1961) found that the only other surface-feeding ducks with nest locations averaging farther from water than the shoveler were the gadwall and pintail, both of which are noted for their upland nesting tendencies. Miller and Collins (1954) verified a tendency for upland nesting by shovelers, as well as a preference for nesting in grasses usually under 12 inches high and almost never more than 24 inches high. They found that almost 30 percent of the total nests located were more than fifty yards from water, and more nests were over one hundred yards from water than was true of any other species.

Clutch Size: The largest average clutch size reported for shovelers is 10.7 for early nests, compared with an average of 10.1 for all forty-five nests of this species that were located (Keith, 1961). Hildén (1964) reported an overall average clutch size of 9.19 for forty-three nests. It seems likely that the relatively low average clutch size (8.2) reported by Williams and Marshall (1938) must have reflected considerable renesting effort, which has been established in shovelers (Sowls, 1955) but apparently occurs at a rather low incidence.

Incubation Period: Girard (1939) estimated the incubation period of wild shovelers to be about 28 days. This is substantially longer than the 21- to 22-day period reported by Hochbaum (1944) or the 22- to 25-day period estimated by Bauer and Glutz (1968), and these shorter estimates are more probably correct.

Fledging Period: Reportedly fledging may occur as early as 39 to 40 days after hatching (Weller, 1964), but probably six or seven weeks is more usual (Bauer and Glutz, 1968). Hochbaum's (1944) estimate of 52 to 60 days is almost certainly too high.

Nest and Egg Losses: Girard (1939) estimated that on two Montana wildlife refuges where predator control was practiced 69.69 percent of 1,135 eggs successfully hatched. In a Utah study, 90 percent of 189 eggs hatched, with predation playing a minor role in nest failures. Keith (1961) estimated that 42 percent of sixty nests he found in Alberta hatched successfully, and judged that about 75 percent of the unsuccessful females attempted to renest, so that a total of 62 percent of the females eventually brought off broods.

Juvenile Mortality: Girard (1939) believed that about 6 eggs per successful nest hatched in his study, and of these, 5 young survived to reach the "flapper" stage. McKinney (1967) noticed that female shovelers often killed ducklings from other broods, but the birds in his study were unusually crowded. It is clear from brood counts such as those made by Rienecker and Anderson (1960) that under natural conditions some brood mergers do occur and terminal brood sizes may be substantially larger than brood sizes at hatching. These authors estimated that about 7 young per brood represented the actual terminal brood size in their study, compared to an observed average of 10.3 young.

Postfledging mortality rates are not yet well established. Keith (1961) estimated an all-age mortality of 58 percent annually.

Adult Mortality: Boyd (1962) calculated a 44 percent annual adult mortality rate for shovelers banded in Britain. Wainwright (1967) calculated a somewhat lower (37 percent) mortality rate for this species.

GENERAL ECOLOGY

Food and Foraging: Perhaps to a greater extent than any other North American surface-feeding duck, the shoveler consumes a considerable amount of small aquatic animal life, especially forms such as ostracods, copepods, and similar crustaceans that it is able to "sieve" from the water with the long, closely spaced lamellae of its bill. Insects such as aquatic beetles, water boatmen, caddis fly larvae, naiads of damselflies and dragonflies, and small mollusks also may represent important foods at various seasons or locations. Duckweeds (*Lemnaceae*) and the vegetative parts of pondweeds (*Potamoge-*

ton), wigeon grass (*Ruppia*), and other aquatic plants are also taken, as are the seeds of bulrushes (*Scirpus*), pondweeds, and the like (Martin *et al.,* 1951). A limited sample of shovelers taken in the Chesapeake Bay area had consumed seeds of three-square (*Scirpus*), wigeon grass, salt grass (*Distichlis*), the vegetative parts of wigeon grass and muskgrass (*Chara*), and a variety of mollusks, crustaceans, and small fish (Stewart, 1962). During spring and summer, at least, the seeds of spike rush (*Eleocharis*) appear to be a favored food for shovelers as well as blue-winged teal and other surface-feeding ducks (Keith, 1961).

Shovelers have been observed diving for food on only a few occasions (Kear and Johnsgard, 1968), and they usually are found on waters so shallow that diving is not required. McKinney (1970) observed shovelers diving for food occasionally, but noted that they predominantly feed at the surface, and to a lesser extent by tipping-up.

Sociality, Densities, Territoriality: McKinney (1970) has stressed the high degree of hostile behavior that he observed among captive shovelers and agreed with Sowls (1955) that shovelers are the most territorial of all the North American dabbling ducks. McKinney believed that several of the shoveler's display patterns had their origins in the territorial system of shovelers. However, Hori (1963) found strong mate defense but no evidence of territoriality among wild shovelers. Poston (1969) observed little territorial behavior among wild shovelers in a fairly dense population, and it seems possible that the apparently strong territoriality noted by McKinney was an artifact of maintaining a large number of pairs (four to seven) in pens of less than 1 acre in area. Poston (1969) found that ponds under 1.25 acres were used by only a single pair of wild shovelers, while five ponds ranging from 1.25 to 2.0 acres were each occupied by two breeding pairs. He also found that the home ranges of six pairs averaged 49.7 acres and ranged from 15 to 90 acres. On a study area of three square miles, he reported breeding densities of 11.3 and 12.7 pairs per square mile during two years of study. Stoudt (1969), reviewing breeding density figures from five prairie study areas, noted shoveler densities of two to ten pairs per square mile. It is possible that not only the rather small body size of shovelers (Goodman and Fisher, 1962) but also their strong dispersal tendencies, compared with most other dabbling ducks, are reflections of the fact that shovelers probably have to "work harder" for their food and must be able to forage over a larger area than do other surface-feeders.

Interspecific Relationships: Because of their highly specialized bill form, shovelers probably compete very little with other *Anas* species for food. The cinnamon teal's bill form exhibits an incipient degree of spatulate development.

A study of food intake among shovelers, cinnamon teal, and blue-winged teal in areas of geographic overlap would be of considerable interest but has not yet been undertaken.

In their nest site preferences and tendency to breed along open shorelines, shovelers are similar to pintails and, to a more limited extent, gadwalls. Weller (1959) reported that the shoveler has been reported to be socially parasitized by the redhead and lesser scaup, and its eggs have been found in the nests of mallards, American wigeons, cinnamon teal, and redheads.

A variety of egg predators has been reported for shovelers, including skunks and crows (Sowls, 1955; Girard, 1939). Weasels have sometimes been noted to take shoveler ducklings.

General Activity Patterns and Movements: One of the few studies of general activity patterns of shovelers is that of McKinney (1967), who reported on the breeding phase of the life cycle. He noted that during the prelaying period females inspected possible nesting cover during the morning hours, especially near dawn. Likewise, egg-laying was performed during the same hourly schedule. During incubation, females always spent the early morning hours on the nest and exhibited a peak in periods away from the nest during late afternoon. Copulations were seen at nearly all times of the day. Copulations were observed as early as 23 days before the laying of the first egg, but diminished during the egg-laying period and were rarely seen during incubation. Male chasing activities were seen throughout the prelaying through incubation period, but only infrequently did males attempt to rape strange females, and they were rarely successful. There seemed to be no correlation between time of day and frequency of chases by males.

SOCIAL AND SEXUAL BEHAVIOR

Flocking Behavior: Regrettably, little has been written on flock sizes of shovelers, which are of interest because they would shed light on the question of possible intraspecific food competition as related to the specialized foraging adaptations of this species. In the closely related Australian shoveler, the typical situation is for the birds to be in small groups or pairs, widely dispersed (Frith, 1967). Since all the species of shovelers often forage in small groups, with each bird dabbling in the wake of the one in front (Johnsgard, 1965), the maintenance of relatively small flock sizes would be advantageous from this respect as well.

Pair-forming Behavior: Pair-forming in wild shovelers begins on the wintering grounds in mid-December and continues until the birds depart for their breeding grounds (McKinney, 1970). The pair bond is strong and may persist until about hatching or even somewhat afterward. During pair-forming behavior, a variety of male courtship displays are performed, most of which are derived from motor patterns associated with foraging, such as dabbling, head-dipping, and tipping-up (Johnsgard, 1965; McKinney, 1970). The primary female display is inciting, and the typical male response to this display is to swim ahead of the inciting female and turn the back of his head toward her. This turning-the-back-of-the-head is one of the commonest displays observed during pair formation and may persist for a few days or weeks after a pair bond has been formed (McKinney, 1970). Although unpaired males may attempt to perform the display toward paired females, they never approach the female closely while performing the display.

Copulatory Behavior: Copulation is preceded by the usual mutual head-pumping, which is easily distinguished from that associated with aggressive behavior by the lower angle at which the bill is held. Male shovelers may utter a series of soft notes during treading, and immediately after releasing the female they utter a single loud, nasal note followed by a series of repeated wooden sounds while remaining in a rigid posture beside the female, with the body fairly erect and the bill pointed downward (McKinney, 1970).

Nesting and Brooding Behavior: Females may begin to look for suitable nest sites as early as twenty-seven days before laying begins (McKinney, 1957). Typically, six to eight days are spent in nest construction, and eggs are then laid at the rate of one per day (Girard, 1939). During the egg-laying period the female may initially spend only a hour or two at the nest, but later may be there for the entire morning. The male does not accompany the female to her nest, but she returns to her mate when away from the nest for foraging, resting, or other activities (McKinney, 1957). During later stages of incubation the female is increasingly reluctant to leave the nest, even when disturbed, and probably remains on it for the last day or so of incubation. About twelve hours elapse between the pipping and hatching of individual eggs, and the female usually leaves the nest within twenty-four hours of hatching her brood (Girard, 1939). Frequently the male remains with the female and young for a short time after hatching occurs, although it is questionable whether they ever "help" rear the brood.

Postbreeding Behavior: Shortly before they begin their flightless period, males may begin to gather in small groups along favored feeding areas. This usually occurs by the end of June in southern Canada, and most of the males are flightless between mid-July and mid-August. Unpaired males may become flightless before those which have bred, and females that have reared families become flightless after rearing their brood, or about the latter part of August (McKinney, 1967).

POCHARDS (Fresh Water Diving Ducks) Tribe Aythyini

Until recent classifications by Jean Delacour and others, the pochard group was not taxonomically distinguished from the more marine-adapted sea ducks, here included in the following tribe Mergini. Nevertheless, the pochards are a readily definable group of mostly medium-sized ducks that differ from their close relatives, the surface-feeding ducks, in several respects. Their legs are situated somewhat farther back on the body, so that they are less adept at walking on land; their feet and associated webs are larger, increasing diving effectiveness (reflected by the increased length of the outer toes); and their bills are generally broad, heavy, and adapted for underwater foraging. Depending on the species, the predominant food may be of animal or vegetable origin. Internally, the males have tracheal tubes that are variably enlarged, and in contrast to the typically rounded and entirely bony structure of the tracheal bulla, this feature is angular and partially membranaceous. No iridescent speculum is present on the wings, but in many species the secondaries are conspicuously white or at least paler than the rest of the wing. The birds nest closely adjacent to water and sometimes even above the water surface, on reed mats or similar vegetation.

North America has five well-distributed species of pochards, one of which (the greater scaup) also extends to the Old World. Additionally, North American tufted duck records have become so numerous in recent years that the inclusion of that species has seemed necessary. One other Old World species, the common pochard (*Aythya ferina*), has rarely occurred in Alaska, with several Aleutian Islands records in recent years (Byrd *et al.,* 1974).

301

CANVASBACK

Aythya valisineria (Wilson) 1814

Other Vernacular Names: Canvas-backed Duck, Can.

Range: Breeds from central Alaska south to northern California and east to Nebraska and Minnesota. Winters from southern Canada south along the Atlantic and Pacific coasts to central and southern Mexico.

Subspecies: None recognized.

Measurements (after Delacour, 1959):

Folded wing: Males 225-242, females 220-230 mm.

Culmen: Males 55-63, females 54-60 mm.

Weights: Nelson and Martin (1953) reported that sixty-two males averaged 2.8 pounds (1,268 grams), and seventy-nine females averaged 2.6 pounds (1,178 grams). Combining the data of Bellrose and Hawkins (1947) and that of Jahn and Hunt (1964) for fall-shot birds, eight adult males averaged 2.99 pounds (1,356 grams), while fourteen immatures averaged 2.83 pounds (1,283 grams). Five adult females averaged 2.49 pounds (1,129 grams), and nine immatures averaged 2.47 pounds (1,120 grams). Nelson and Martin reported a maximum male weight of 3.5 pounds (1,577 grams) and a maximum female weight of 3.4 pounds (1,542 grams). Dzubin (1959) has provided weight data for various age classes, including some spring weights.

IDENTIFICATION

In the Hand: Canvasbacks are the only North American pochards that have a culmen length in excess of 50 mm. (or two inches); additionally the bill is uniquely sloping from its base to the tip and lacks a pale band near the tip. Supplementary criteria include the presence of vermiculated upper wing coverts, with the white predominating over the dark, rather than the darker tones predominating.

In the Field: When on the water, male canvasbacks appear to be nearly white on the mantle and sides, whereas male redheads are distinctly medium gray, and the longer, more sloping head of the canvasback is usually evident. Compared to the redhead, the head is a duller chestnut brown, darker above and in front of the red eyes; in redheads the head is a more coppery red and little if at all darker in front of the yellow eyes. Female canvasbacks are distinctly longer-bodied than female redheads and lighter in brownish tones, with brown breast usually distinctly darker than the more grayish sides, whereas in redheads the difference in color between the breast and the flanks is not very apparent. Both sexes appear longer-necked than redheads; in males this is accentuated by the extension of the reddish brown color beyond the base of the neck. In flight, this difference is also apparent; the black breast of the male canvasback is more restricted and does not reach the leading edge of the wings, whereas in redheads the black breast extends to the front of the wings. In females the brownish breast appears sharply separated from the pale grayish sides, while in female redheads the brown breast color is continuous with the brown of the sides and flanks. Except during courtship, canvasbacks are relatively quiet, but the male's cooing courtship call (uttered only on the water) may be heard frequently during spring.

AGE AND SEX CRITERIA

Sex Determination: A reddish eye color indicates a male in any adult plumage, as does the presence of rusty brown on the head or black feathers on the breast or tail coverts. However, since females are extensively vermiculated, this trait is not diagnostic for sex. Even in full eclipse the head of the male is relatively dark and lacks the pale areas around the eyes and the pale throat typical of females. Dzubin (1959) reported that by thirty days of age males begin to exhibit lighter scapular feathers than do females.

Age Determination: Immature birds of both sexes may still carry juvenal tertials, which are usually frayed to a pointed tip and are iron gray with or without white flecking, whereas in adults they are rounded and always have some vermiculations of flecking. The presence of any juvenal tertial coverts, middle coverts, or greater coverts, which can be easily recognized by their more uniformly grayish and unflecked or lightly flecked pattern, compared with the vermiculated first-winter or adult feathers, indicates immaturity (Carney, 1964).

DISTRIBUTION AND HABITAT

Breeding Distribution and Habitat: The canvasback occupies a breeding range and habitat comparable to that of its close European and Asian relative, the common pochard. It tends to have a somewhat more northerly distribution than that of the redhead, although the habitat requirements of these two species are quite similar. In Alaska the canvasback has a relatively wide breeding distribution and is a common summer resident in much of that state (Hanson, 1960). Its northernmost known occurrence is north of the Arctic Circle, but south of tree line (Campbell, 1969).

In Canada the canvasback ranges from the Old Crow area of the Yukon and the Anderson River of the Northwest Territories southeastward to central and southern British Columbia, and especially through the prairie areas of Alberta, Saskatchewan, and Manitoba. There is also a very local breeding area on Walpole Island, southern Ontario (Godfrey, 1966).

The breeding range in the United States south of Canada is disrupted and probably declining because of the extensive marsh destruction and drainage that has occurred in the prime areas of the canvasback's range. In eastern Washington the canvasback is a rare nesting bird in Adams and Lincoln counties (Yocom, 1951). In Oregon it nests at Malheur National Wildlife Refuge (Erickson, 1948), as well as in the Klamath Lake–Tule Lake area of southern Oregon and adjacent California. It also nests locally in the Ruby Lake area of Nevada, in northern Utah, northern Arizona, southern Idaho, northern Colorado, and Wyoming. The heart of its United States nesting range is probably in the prairie pothole area of eastern Montana and the Dakotas and the sandhills lakes of Nebraska. The southern limit of breeding in the prairie states is apparently Kansas (Johnstone, 1964). To the east, the canvasback nests locally in northern Minnesota (Lee *et al.,* 1964), has rarely nested in Wisconsin (Jahn and Hunt, 1964), and has evidently bred on the Montezuma marshes of New York (*Audubon Field Notes,* 19:540). There is a single breeding record for Michigan (Zimmerman and Van Tyne, 1959) and apparently only one for Illinois (*Audubon Field Notes,* 19:519).

The preferred breeding habitat of canvasbacks consists of shallow prairie marshes surrounded by cattails, bulrushes, and similar emergent vegetation, large enough and with enough open water for easy takeoffs and landings, and with little if any wooded vegetation around the shoreline. Dwyer (1970) noted a much higher breeding canvasback population outside than inside Riding Mountain National Park in Manitoba, apparently because of the reduced numbers of trees around the breeding ponds. Keith (1961) found the highest use of canvasback pairs per unit of shoreline on a shallow lake with a maximum depth of eight feet, having scattered strands of bulrushes, shorelines dominated by rushes (*Juncus*), sedges (*Carex*), and spike rush (*Eleocharis*), and with several cattail-covered islands. Brood use per acre of water was also highest on this lake; apparently female canvasbacks moved from smaller nesting marshes to larger impoundments following hatching. Hochbaum (1944) noted that canvasbacks tend to use larger bays in the Delta, Manitoba, marsh than do other resident diving ducks, which frequent sloughs and potholes to a greater extent.

Wintering Distribution and Habitat: To a rather surprising degree, the interior-nesting canvasback tends to move to coastal areas for the winter months. On the Pacific coast some wintering occurs as far north as southern British Columbia and the Puget Sound area of Washington, and some occurs in western Oregon, but the center of the canvasback wintering habitat is the San Pablo Bay of central California.

Recent winter surveys by the United States Fish and Wildlife Service indicate that about one-fourth of the continental canvasback population winters in the Pacific Flyway, most of it north of the Mexican border. In Mexico, the canvasback is a relatively minor component of the wintering waterfowl, with the largest numbers found on the Pacific coast and in the interior. Leopold (1959) noted that, during 1952 surveys, most of the canvasbacks seen were on Lakes Chapala and Pátzcuaro, with the remainder primarily found near Tampico.

In the Atlantic Flyway, which harbors the majority of the North American canvasback population, wintering birds commonly occur from as far south as central Florida (Chamberlain, 1960) to coastal New England, but concentrate in the Chesapeake Bay area. This area typically supports nearly three-fourths of the Atlantic Flyway canvasback population, or almost half

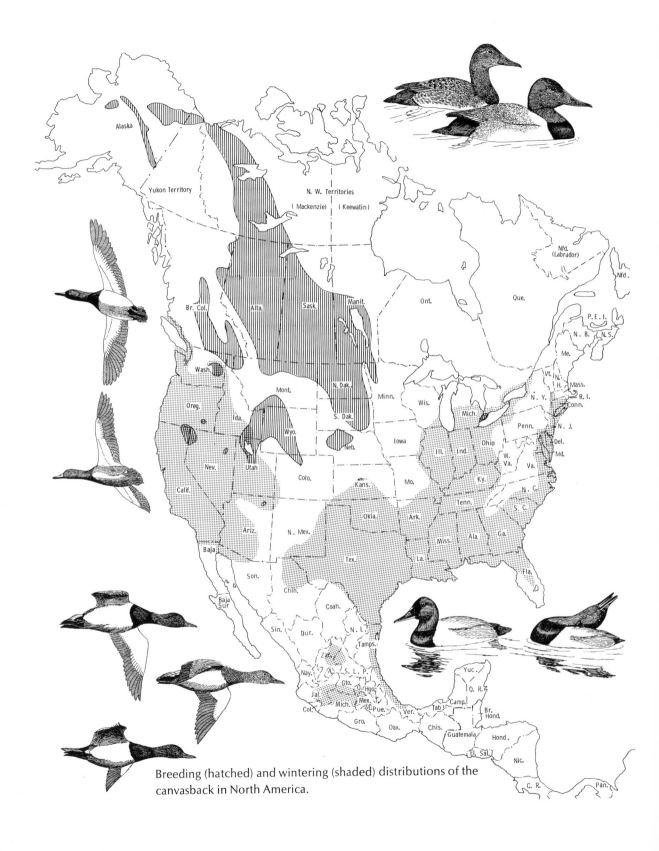

Breeding (hatched) and wintering (shaded) distributions of the canvasback in North America.

of the entire continental population (Stewart *et al.,* 1958). The Detroit River–Lake St. Claire area and the coastal area of the Mississippi Valley represent other major wintering locations in eastern United States.

Stewart (1962) reported that the optimum canvasback habitat in the Chesapeake Bay area consists of fresh and brackish estuarine bays containing extensive beds of submerged plants or abundant invertebrates, especially certain thin-shelled clams and small crabs. Beds of wild celery (*Vallisneria*) in freshwater estuarine bays are heavily utilized by canvasbacks, as are pondweed (*Potamogeton*), wigeon grass (*Ruppia*), and eelgrass (*Zostera*) in the brackish bays. Brackish estuarine bays are the principal wintering habitats, with both saltwater and freshwater estuarine bays being used relatively little.

GENERAL BIOLOGY

Age at Maturity: Canvasbacks probably normally reproduce when a year old, but in captivity are particularly difficult to breed successfully. Ferguson (1966) noted that only one of fourteen aviculturalists reported breeding by yearling canvasbacks, and most reported initial breeding in the second or third year. Hochbaum (1944) also noted that captive canvasbacks that bred at Delta, Manitoba, were all more than a year old, but he believed that wild canvasback females commonly nest when a year old and that males were also physically able to reproduce at that age.

Pair Bond Pattern: Pairs are re-formed each winter and spring during a prolonged courtship period. Weller (1965) found that up to 10 percent of the female canvasbacks he observed between December and March were paired, while 41 percent were paired during March and April counts. Hochbaum (1944) noted that most canvasbacks were not paired on their arrival in southern Canada, but pair formation reaches a peak in late April and early May, and most birds are paired after the middle of May. Smith (1946) also observed intense pair-forming activities in mid-April.

Nest Location: Lee *et al.* (1964b) noted that canvasbacks nested over water in emergent vegetation that ranged from 14 to 48 inches high and averaged 34 inches, higher than the averages found for both ring-necked duck and redhead. Seventeen nest sites averaged 11.0 yards from open water, and ranged from 0 to 55 yards. Preference was shown among canvasbacks for nesting in smaller bulrush marshes with some open water present. Stoudt (1971) found that 80 percent of the 172 canvasback nests he found were in cattail cover, and similar preferences for cattail have been reported by Smith (1971) and Keith (1971). Hochbaum (1944) noted a strong preference for nesting in hardstem bulrush (*Scirpus acutus*), with cattails and reed (*Phrag-*

mites) also being accepted, but softstem bulrush (*Scirpus validus*) has not been found as a nest cover. Townsend (1966) found a high usage of reed and a low usage of sedge for canvasback, just the opposite of the situation for ring-necked duck and lesser scaup. Further, canvasbacks placed their nests closer to large areas (over 50 by 50 feet) of open water than did those species, and all the canvasback nests found were within 40 feet of such areas of water.

Clutch Size: Hochbaum (1944) reported that thirty-eight nests had an average of 10 canvasback eggs present, but twenty-two of these nests also had redhead eggs. Erickson (1948) found that fifteen nonparasitized nests had 9.9 eggs initially present, compared to an average clutch of 8.6 eggs in nonparasitized renesting attempts. Among seventy-four parasitized nests, there were an average of 7.0 host eggs and 6.1 intruder eggs. Smith (1971) noted an average clutch size of 7.4 eggs for 118 nests, while Stoudt (1971) found that 172 nests averaged 8.2 eggs.

Incubation Period: Hochbaum (1944) noted that, although ranges in incubation of 23 to 29 days had been recorded, most eggs hatch in 24 days under artificial incubation conditions.

Fledging Period: Fledging reportedly occurs 56 to 68 days after hatching (Dzubin, 1959).

Nest and Egg Losses: Sowls (1948) noted a 48 percent hatching success for twenty-four nests, and Lee *et al.* (1964b) a 25 percent hatching rate for sixteen nests, with predators accounting for half the losses and the striped skunk being the primary egg predator. Smith (1971) and Stoudt (1971) reported hatching rates of 48 and 65 percent, respectively, with skunks, crows, and magpies apparent predators. Crows accounted for many of the nest losses in Sowls's (1948) study. Erickson (1948) found that parasitism affected nesting success, with 91 percent of the eggs hatching in unparasitized nests that he found, compared to 77 percent of the eggs in parasitized ones. Likewise, a lower percentage of nests hatched when parasitically laid eggs were present, and a smaller average number of canvasback young per nest hatched. Weller (1959) reported comparable results in his studies.

Juvenile Mortality: Although frequent brood disruption and mergers of unrelated broods make brood size counts of older ducklings unreliable as estimates of duckling mortality, Smith (1971) and Stoudt (1971) estimated rearing success rates of about 80 percent. Geis (1959) judged that an average of 77.4 percent of canvasback pairs are successful in raising broods, and that an average of 5.8 ducklings per brood fledged.

From banding of flightless young canvasbacks, a first-year mortality rate of 77 percent has been estimated (Geis, 1959). This high juvenile mortality rate and the specialized nesting requirements of canvasbacks are major reasons for the recent serious population declines of the species.

Adult Mortality: Geis (1959) estimated that an annual mortality rate of 35 to 50 percent is typical of canvasbacks after their first year of life. Boyd (1962) calculated a 41 percent mortality rate based on these figures. Females have considerably higher mortality rates than do males, which at least in part accounts for the seriously unbalanced sex ratios that have generally been reported for canvasbacks (Olson, 1965).

GENERAL ECOLOGY

Food and Foraging: The attraction of canvasbacks to wild celery beds in the northeastern states is very well known, and in that area they utilize both the seeds and vegetative parts of this plant extensively. Pondweeds play a secondary role there, but in the western states and the southeast their vegetative parts and seeds largely replace wild celery as the primary food. The vegetative parts of arrowhead (*Sagittaria*) and banana water lily (*Nymphaea flava*) are also of importance in the southeastern states (Martin *et al.,* 1951). Stewart's (1962) study of canvasbacks shot in the Chesapeake Bay area indicated that various mollusks and crustaceans, especially macoma bivalves (*Macoma*) and mud crabs (*Xanthidae*), are important foods for wintering birds in brackish estuaries and the Patuxent River. In Minnesota, canvasbacks have traditionally been attracted to Lake Christina, which is large and shallow and has abundant growths of sago pondweed, wigeon grass, and naiad (*Najas*), of which the sago pondweed is selectively consumed by canvasbacks (Smith, 1946). Cottam (1939) also determined that pondweeds are the most important food for both canvasbacks and redheads.

A group of immature canvasbacks were found to consume from 2 to 3 percent of their body weight per day in natural foods, or an average of 0.78 pounds of wet-weight materials per day (Longcore and Cornwell, 1964).

Sociality, Densities, Territoriality: Few figures on canvasback breeding densities are available. Lee *et al.* (1964b) noted that in a 2.5-square mile study area in Mahnomen County, Minnesota, 2.5 to 7.0 pairs were present per square mile over a four-year period. Keith (1961) found an average of 2 pairs occupying 183 acres of impoundments during five years of study in Alberta, or about 7 pairs per square mile of wetlands. Dzubin (1955) noted that canvasbacks made up 10 percent of the breeding ducks in an area of southern Manitoba having 97.8 pairs per square mile, or about 10 per square mile. Stoudt (1969) noted that the peak densities of canvasbacks on five prairie study areas in Saskatchewan, Manitoba, and South Dakota ranged from less than 1 to 11 pairs per square mile.

Hochbaum (1944) believed that territorial boundaries in canvasbacks and other pochards are less rigid than in surface-feeding ducks, and he never observed direct attacks associated with apparent territoriality. He did, however, believe that spacing of breeding pairs does exist in this species. However, Dzubin (1955) noted that canvasbacks were highly mobile during the pre-laying and incubation phases of reproduction and that certain areas had overlapping usage by different pairs, so that the concept of a home range, rather than a classic territory, seemed more appropriate.

Interspecific Relationships: Perhaps because of the similarities in nest site preferences, the canvasback is conspicuously affected by the parasitic nesting tendencies of redheads (Weller, 1959). Canvasbacks also socially parasitize other females of their own species (Erickson, 1948) and have been known to lay their eggs in the nests of both redheads and ruddy ducks.

Skunks, crows, raccoons, and no doubt a large number of other predators and scavengers have been found to be responsible for losses of eggs and ducklings, but the present unfavorable status of canvasback populations is more directly related to human activities: the destruction of breeding habitat, the pollution or other degradation of critical wintering areas, and the possible overshooting of females. Female losses are serious since females are much more vulnerable than males to shooting and since they represent a limiting factor in potential production, because of the distorted sex ratio among adults.

General Activity Patterns and Movements: Hochbaum (1944) has provided an excellent account of the daily and seasonal activities of canvasbacks on their nesting grounds.

Dzubin (1955) reported that a male canvasback occupied a home range with a maximum length of 3,900 yards during the breeding season, and that the female was somewhat less mobile, so that an overall home range of about 1,300 acres was estimated. Male canvasbacks apparently did not defend any of their home range, but did show aggression when other males approached their mates.

To a greater extent than is apparent with most ducks, canvasbacks appear to migrate in "waves," with the dates of arrival both in spring and fall being fairly predictable (Smith, 1946; Jahn and Hunt, 1964). In spring, paired birds reach the breeding grounds first, followed later by unpaired flocks. There apparently is a differential migration of ages and sexes during the fall flights, but differential sex and age vulnerability to hunting confuses the picture in interpreting fall movements.

SOCIAL AND SEXUAL BEHAVIOR

Flocking Behavior: Hochbaum (1944) noted that during spring, arriving migrant canvasbacks are in small flocks that usually number four to a dozen birds, and rarely exceed twenty. On the other hand, fall groups are typically quite large and gain in size as they move southward. Concentrations are facilitated by the restricted number of favored feeding areas. Smith (1946) reported that on the 4,000-acre Lake Christina in Minnesota maximum concentrations of about thirty thousand birds were counted during the spring migration period. He noted that it was not unusual to see a flock of several thousand birds in close association about a hundred yards off shore engaged in courtship activities.

Pair-forming Behavior: The pair-forming behavior of canvasbacks has been well described by Hochbaum (1944). His account, as well as observations by Smith (1946) and Weller (1965), indicate that pair-forming activities begin in late winter and reach their peak in mid-April, during late stages of spring migration and arrival on the breeding areas.

Pair-forming displays of the canvasback, as described by Hochbaum, have provided the basic terminology for the displays of all pochard species. A courtship call, uttered with or without a head-throw; neck-stretching; a "sneak" posture; and a threatlike posture are the major male calls and postures of canvasbacks. Females perform inciting displays with strong neck-stretching, and inciting occurs in the same situations as with surface-feeding ducks. Wing-preening displays have not been observed in canvasbacks, but preening of the dorsal region is a major precopulatory display of all pochard species (Johnsgard, 1965). Aerial chases, as described by Hochbaum, do occur frequently in canvasbacks, but whether the tail-pulling he described is a typical aspect of pair formation or rather is related to attempted rape behavior is still somewhat uncertain.

Copulatory Behavior: In canvasbacks, copulation is normally initiated by the male performing alternate bill-dipping and dorsal-preening movements. These are not highly stereotyped displays and are often overlooked by the casual observer. The female may perform the same displays, but commonly assumes a prone posture on the water without prior response. Treading lasts several seconds, and as the male releases the female's nape, he typically utters a single courtship call, then swims away in a rather rigid posture with the bill pointed nearly vertically downward. The female usually begins to bathe immediately (Johnsgard, 1965).

Nesting and Brooding Behavior: Female canvasbacks typically spend a considerable period searching for suitable nest sites and may abandon one or two nests before settling on a final location. The first eggs may be laid before the nest is completed and may be "dropped" in various places, sometimes in other nests. Eggs are laid in the morning, usually shortly after sunrise, at the rate of one per day. Down is often initially placed in the nest after the third or fourth egg, and is usually quite abundant by the time the clutch is completed. The female may be on the nest nearly continuously while the last two eggs are being deposited, and apparently begins incubation with the laying of the last egg. During incubation the female may take short rest periods off the nest during morning and evening hours, but these are reduced as incubation proceeds. The period between initial pipping and hatching varies from 18 to 48 hours (Hochbaum, 1944).

Following hatching, the female takes her brood from the nest site to the open water of larger ponds and shallow lakes, feeding heavily in morning and evening, but sometimes also at midday. The hen typically does not defend her young as intensively as do female surface-feeding ducks, but usually abandons them before they have fledged and begins to undergo her postnuptial molt (Hochbaum, 1944).

Postbreeding Behavior: Although the male accompanies the hen while she is searching for nest sites, he spends much of his time at a regular loafing site once the nest site is chosen. As soon as the clutch is completed, he typically deserts his mate (Hochbaum, 1944), although he may also remain associated with her until about mid-incubation (Dzubin, 1955). Thereafter he starts to associate with other males in similar reproductive condition and begins his postnuptial molt.

REDHEAD

Aythya americana (Eyton) 1838

Other Vernacular Names: Red-headed Duck, Red-headed Pochard.

Range: Breeds from central Canada southward to southern California, New Mexico, Nebraska, and Minnesota, with local or occasional breeding farther east. Winters from the southern part of its breeding range from Washington eastward to the middle Atlantic states and south to the Gulf coast of Mexico and Guatemala.

Subspecies: None recognized.

Measurements (after Delacour, 1959):

Folded Wing: Males 230-242, females 210-230 mm.

Culmen: Males 45-50, females 44-47 mm.

Weights: Nelson and Martin (1953) reported that eighty-two males averaged 2.5 pounds (1,133 grams), and forty females averaged 2.2 pounds (997 grams). Combining the data of Bellrose and Hawkins (1947) with that of Jahn and Hunt (1964) for fall-shot birds, four adult males averaged 2.39 pounds (1,084 grams), while fourteen immatures averaged 2.22 pounds

(1,006 grams); six adult females averaged 2.28 pounds (1,034 grams), while five immatures averaged 2.17 pounds (984 grams). Maximum weights reported by Nelson and Martin are 3 pounds (1,361 grams) for males and 2.9 pounds (1,314 grams) for females.

IDENTIFICATION

In the Hand: Easily recognized as a pochard by its lobed hind toe and generally broad, flattened bill; redheads are typical of this genus of diving ducks. Males in nuptial plumage may be identified by their uniformly coppery red head and yellow eyes and by their flattened bluish bills with a pale subterminal band and a blackish tip. The black breast and the uniformly gray speculum, of nearly the same color as the upper wing coverts, are similar to those of the canvasback, but the black breast extends from the wings to the foreneck, and the upper wing coverts are slightly darker rather than lighter than the secondaries. Females may be separated from female canvasbacks by their shorter bills and more rounded head profile (see canvasback account) and from female ring-necked ducks by their longer wings, black margined inner secondaries, less definite eyerings and eye-stripes, and the usual white flecking on their scapulars (see ring-necked duck account).

In the Field: On the water, redheads appear to be shorter-bodied and shorter-necked than canvasbacks, and have a shorter and more rounded head profile. Males have a brighter, more coppery head color, and the backs and sides of the body are medium gray rather than whitish, while female redheads are more uniformly brownish on the head, breast, sides, and back, lacking the two-toned effect of female canvasbacks. During late winter and spring, the male courtship call of redheads is frequent and audible for long distances; it is a unique catlike *meow* sound that few would attribute to a duck. Like most pochards, females rarely utter loud calls that are useful for field identification. In flight, male redheads appear mostly grayish to white from underneath, except for the black breast (which extends back to the leading edge of the wings) and brownish head. Their shorter necks and greater amounts of black on the breast are the best means of distinction from male canvasbacks. Females likewise exhibit white on the abdomen and the underwing surface, and the brown color of the head and breast extends back in an unbroken manner under the wings along the sides. Redheads fly with strong rapid wing-beats, in a swift flight with relatively little dodging or flaring such as occurs in dabbling ducks, and they are more agile in flight than canvasbacks.

AGE AND SEX CRITERIA

Sex Determination: A pale, yellowish eye indicates a male in any adult plumage, as do vermiculations anywhere except on the scapulars, where females sometimes also exhibit slight vermiculations. However, only males are vermiculated near the tips of the tertials (Carney, 1964).

Age Determination: The greater secondary and tertial coverts of adults are broad and rounded; those of males are heavily flecked with white, and those of females are unflecked or faintly flecked near their edges. Juvenal greater coverts are narrower, squared, often somewhat frayed, and may have pale edges, the males' being faintly flecked and the females' unflecked. Juvenal tertials, until molted, indicate immaturity by their frayed, pointed tips and brownish gray coloration (Carney, 1964). The blunt-tipped juvenal tail feathers are dropped between three and one-half and seven months of age, in no apparent sequence, according to Weller (1957). Weller also reports that young males can be recognized by the reduced area of black in the breast region as compared with older birds, and young females usually exhibit speckled buffy brown on their under tail coverts, whereas older females show brownish olive patches.

DISTRIBUTION AND HABITAT

Breeding Distribution and Habitat: Weller's (1964) review of the breeding distribution of the redhead is both recent and authoritative and has provided the basis for the present summary.

In Alaska redheads are now known to breed in the area of Tetlin and Minto, along the Tanana River, and in the Fort Yukon area of the Yukon and Porcupine rivers.

In Canada redheads breed in the intermontane region of British Columbia and are particularly prevalent in the Prairie Provinces of Alberta, Saskatchewan, and Manitoba, extending locally northward as far as Great Slave Lake, Northwest Territories. There are several small breeding localities in the southern part of Ontario, including Lake St. Clair, Charter Island, Luther Marsh, and Toronto Island (Godfrey, 1966; *Audubon Field Notes,* 19:538; 20:565). In Quebec redheads have bred at Lake St. Francis and perhaps also on the St. Lawrence River near Trois Rivieres (*Audubon Field Notes,* 22:590); the latter may be the result of releasing captive birds (Weller, 1964). Breeding has also been recorded in New Brunswick, which evidently is the eastern limit of the breeding range of this species.

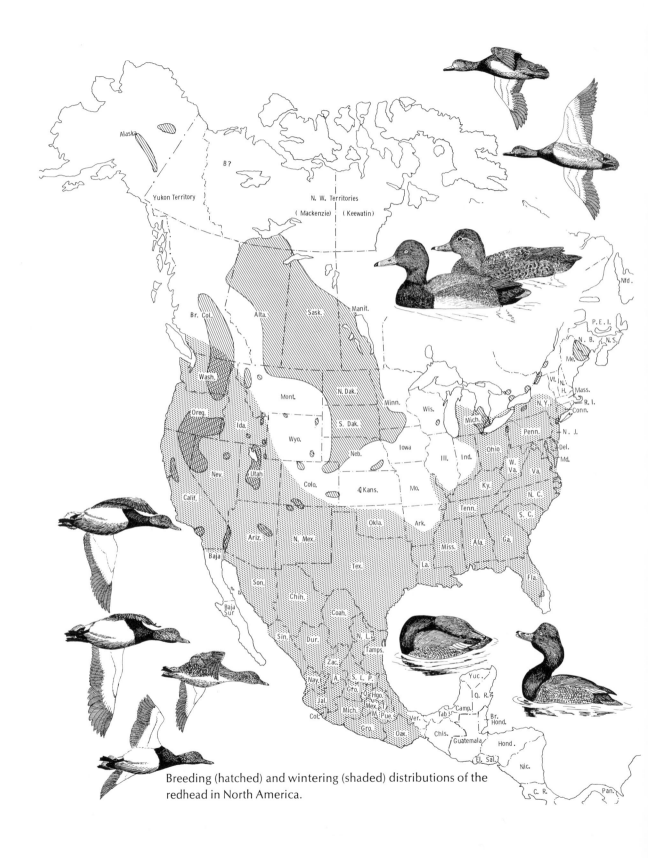

Breeding (hatched) and wintering (shaded) distributions of the
redhead in North America.

In the United States south of Canada, the breeding range of the redhead is discontinuous and declining, but is centered in the prairie potholes area of the Dakotas. Small, local breeding populations probably occur in all of the western states eastward as far as Kansas, Nebraska, Iowa, and Minnesota (Weller, 1964). The southernmost breeding record may be for a lagoon south of Carlsbad, New Mexico (*Audubon Field Notes,* 13:455). In Minnesota the species reaches the eastern limit of its major breeding range and is about the fifth most common breeding duck (Lee *et al.,* 1964a). In Iowa it is still common in a few northwestern counties (Weller, 1964), but in Wisconsin it is now a regular breeder only in one county (Jahn *et al.,* 1964). It has bred at Lake St. Clair, Michigan, as well as at several other localities (Zimmerman and Van Tyne, 1959). Additionally, there are breeding records for Ohio and Pennsylvania, and in New York nestings have occurred recently in the central part of the state as an apparent result of releasing hand-reared birds (Weller, 1964). There are also a few records of redheads breeding at Jamaica Bay, Long Island (*Audubon Field Notes,* 15:453; 19:528).

Weller (1964) described the redhead's breeding habitat as nonforested country with water areas sufficiently deep to provide permanent, fairly dense emergent vegetation for nesting cover. Weller believes that this species evolved in the alkaline water areas of the American Southwest and attains highest breeding densities in alkaline water areas.

In Minnesota redheads usually nest in wet emergent vegetation from 20 to 40 inches tall, typically among cattails or similarly high vegetation around deep potholes that have some open water present (Lee *et al.,* 1964a). Lokemoen (1966) found that redheads preferred to nest in potholes at least one acre in size, and that potholes most suitable for brood rearing were of this size or larger and were also deeper than those used for nesting. Low (1945) reported that the highest nesting densities in Iowa occurred where about 10 to 25 percent of the habitat consisted of open water; the areas of open water used for landing and taking off were at least a square rod in size, and usually 3 to 4 rods square. Water depth in nesting areas appeared to be more important than the presence of specific plant species, with a water depth of about 9 inches at the nest site seemingly favored. Water areas used for brood rearing were larger, deeper, and more open than those used for nesting.

Wintering Distribution and Habitat: Weller has provided an excellent summary of the distribution and relative abundance of redheads in their major North American wintering areas. He reported that 78 percent of the wintering birds, based on 1951 to 1956 winter inventory surveys, were concentrated along the Laguna Madre of coastal Texas and adjacent Tamaulipas. Another 11.9 percent occurred from the Chesapeake Bay area south to Pamlico

Sound, and coastal Forida supported about 5 percent. The remaining 5 percent occurred on the western coast of Mexico, in California, along the southern Great Lakes, and in other minor wintering areas. Weller characterized typical wintering areas as large bodies of water along the coast that are well protected from heavy wave action. They are often fairly shallow, and they may be brackish or highly saline, as in the case of the Laguna Madre. Stewart (1962) indicated that in the Chesapeake Bay area redheads are most numerous during winter in brackish estuarine bays containing extensive beds of clasping-leaf and sago pondweeds (*Potamogeton perfoliatus* and *P. pectinatus*), wigeon grass (*Ruppia*), and eelgrass (*Zostera*). During spring and fall migration they evidently prefer fresh and slightly brackish estuarine bays and concentrate in areas having an abundance of submerged plants such as wild celery (*Vallisneria*) and naiad (*Najas*). They also use more brackish areas like those typical of wintering birds, but concentrate on freshwater areas. Stewart suggested that seasonal shifts of habitat might be related to weather severity and resulting ice conditions in different areas during winter.

GENERAL BIOLOGY

Age at Maturity: Ferguson (1966) noted that only six of nineteen aviculturalists reported breeding by captive redheads in their first year of life, but in part this apparent delayed maturity may reflect the difficulties of breeding this species under captive conditions. Since Weller (1965) noted that all the wild females he observed had established pair bonds by the time of their arrival at breeding areas, it seems probable that many of them at least attempt to nest during their first year. Quite possibly the yearling birds are responsible for much of the parasitic egg-laying found in this species, as a result of incompletely matured nest-building and brooding tendencies.

Pair Bond Pattern: Pair bonds are established yearly, after a rather prolonged period of social courtship (Weller, 1965; 1967). Pair formation begins as early as late December or January and normally persists until about the beginning of incubation (Oring, 1964), although Hochbaum (1944) recorded a single case of the pair bond apparently persisting until after hatching.

Nest Location: Nests are typically found over standing water in emergent vegetation or on a mass of plant material surrounded by water. In Minnesota wet cattail stands are the most common nest sites of redheads, although other emergent species are also used (Lee *et al.*, 1964a, 1964b). The average height of vegetation above the water surface in a sample of Minnesota nests was 29 inches, with a range of 20 to 40 inches. This average was slightly less than that of canvasback nests and more than that of ring-necked ducks. Nine redhead nests averaged 9.7 yards from open water, with almost half within 5 yards of open water and none beyond 50 yards. Canvasback and ring-necked duck nests were very similar to those of redheads in this regard. Miller and Collins (1954) also reported that hardstem bulrush from 2 to 10 feet high was preferred nesting cover.

Lokemoen (1966) analyzed nesting preferences of redheads in Montana and found that hardstem bulrush (*Scirpus acutus*) was the most highly preferred cover but that, because of its greater abundance, cattail was most commonly used by redheads. Baltic rush (*Juncus balticus*) and spike rush (*Eleocharis*) were third and fourth place in the preference scale. Large stands and wide bands of emergent vegetation were preferred over smaller or more disrupted stands for nesting, and water depth at the nest site averaged 10 inches. Potholes larger than one acre in size were preferred over smaller ones for nesting sites, and none under one-fourth acre in size were utilized. Williams and Marshall (1938) also found hardstem bulrush to be the most highly preferred nesting cover, with alkali bulrush (*S. paludosus*) scarcely utilized and both cattail and phragmites having only limited usage.

Clutch size: Weller (1959) reported that a total of 1,380 redhead nests reported in eight different studies had an overall average clutch size of 10.8 eggs, with averages of individual studies ranging from 8.9 to 13.8 eggs. However, Weller found that of 17 nests that were laid by only a single hen, none exceeded 9 eggs and the average clutch size was only slightly over 7 eggs. Weller considered that renesting was absent or unlikely to be important in redheads because of the lateness of the peak of initial nesting attempts. Lokemoen (1966) estimated an average clutch of 7.9 eggs for nonparasitized nests, and reported finding 23 probable renesting attempts.

Incubation Period: Reported as 24 days by Hochbaum (1944). Weller (1957) reported that the incubation period ranges from 24 to 28 days, and Low (1945) stated that five nests he studied had an average incubation period of 24 days, while one other nest required 28 days.

Fledging Period: Weller (1957) reported that hand-reared birds fledged at ages of 56 to 73 days.

Nest and Egg Losses: Weller (1964) reported an average nesting success of 53 percent for 503 nests found during six different studies. He also (1959) calculated an average hatching success of 32 percent for 10,802 eggs observed in six studies. He believed that only 50 to 60 percent of the female population build nests and he found that eggs laid by nonnesting (parasitic) females had a low hatching success. More recently, Lokemoen (1966) reported 15.2 percent nesting success and 9.9 percent hatching success for the eggs in 138 nests with desertion and communal nesting attempts accounting for more than half of the failures. Mammals (mostly skunks) and birds (magpies and crows) also accounted for some nest losses.

In total, Weller (1964) believed that the 60 percent or so of the female redhead population attempting to nest hatch an average of 3.4 young per nest and that about one egg laid by each parasitic female hatches, assuming a 10 to 15 percent hatching success of such eggs.

Juvenile Mortality: Prefledging mortality of ducklings is still not well known, but Low (1945) estimated that there may be a 30 percent loss of young during the first six weeks of life. Weller (1964) provided brood size data for well-grown broods that suggest an even higher survival rate, but brood mergers very probably reduce the reliability of such data.

First-year mortality of redheads is extremely high and may average about 75 percent for the year following banding (Hickey, 1952). Rienecker (1968) calculated an even higher mortality rate (78.7 percent) for first-year birds, as Brakhage (1953) did for wild-trapped (80 percent) and hand-reared (94 percent) birds. Females of both the immature and mature age classes are considerably more vulnerable than males to gunning mortality (Benson and DeGraff, 1968) and additionally are more greatly exposed to dangers of predation during nesting.

Adult Mortality: Adult annual mortality rates of redheads have been estimated by Hickey (1952) at about 55 percent and by Rienecker (1968) at 41 percent. Longwell and Stotts (1959) estimated a 44 percent mortality for Chesapeake Bay redheads. Lee *et al.* (1964b) estimated a 62 percent adult mortality, as compared with an estimated 80 percent rate for first-year birds. These figures, although not in extremely close agreement, all suggest a dangerously high rate for adults as well. In contrast to Rienecker's conclusion, Geis and Crissey (1969) reported that highly restrictive hunting regulations resulted in significant reductions in the mortality rates of redheads and canvasbacks.

GENERAL ECOLOGY

Food and Foraging: The summaries by Martin *et al.* (1951) and Cottam (1939) of redhead foods indicate that the vegetative parts and seeds of pondweeds (*Potamogeton*), wild rice (*Zizania*), wild celery (*Vallisneria*), and wigeon grass (*Ruppia*), the seeds of bulrushes (*Scirpus*), and the vegetative parts of muskgrass (*Chara*) are major foods in various parts of the country. In the important wintering area Laguna Madre, McMahan (1970) reported that over 90 percent of the volume of food materials in 104 redhead samples consisted of wigeon grass and shoalgrass (*Diplantera*), with the latter occurring in 83 percent of the samples and alone constituting 84.2 percent of the food volume. Small gastropod and pelecypod mollusks made up the relatively insignificant proportion of animal materials that were found. Lynch (1968) noted the importance of shoalgrass to wintering redheads throughout the Gulf coast. Stewart (1962) reported on the foods of redheads from the Chesapeake Bay area, based on a sample of 99 birds. There, the leaves, stems, rootstalks, and seeds of submerged plants were also the principal foods, but the food species differed considerably. In freshwater estuaries various pond-weeds and naiad (*Najas*) were major foods, in brackish estuaries eelgrass (*Zostera*) and clasping-leaf pondweed (*P. perfoliatus*) were most important, and in samples from saltwater estuaries these two species plus wigeon grass had been taken, as well as bait corn and sorghum.

The findings of Bartonek and Hickey (1969) on summer-collected red-heads on their breeding grounds in Manitoba indicate a higher usage of animal materials by both adult and young birds than had been generally appreciated. Aquatic invertebrates form the bulk of spring and summer foods, especially cladocerans, gastropod mollusks, and the larvae of Trichoptera (caddis flies) and Tendipedidae (midges).

Sociality, Densities, Territoriality: To a degree that seems stronger than in the canvasback, the redhead appears to exhibit a sociality on the breeding grounds that may in part be related to its semiparasitic nesting tendencies. These tendencies may partly result from the redhead's specialized require-ments for nesting sites, which cause a concentration of nests in the limited suitable habitat. Williams and Marshall (1938) reported an average nesting density of 0.11 redhead nests per acre in 3,000 acres of total nesting cover, but up to 11 nests per acre in a 2-acre area of alkali and hardstem bulrushes. Vermeer (1970) noted redheads to be among the species of ducks he found nesting in higher densities among tern colonies than in areas where larids were absent, and he reported an average redhead nesting density of 0.11 nests per acre.

Densities over larger areas of breeding habitat are of course much lower. Stoudt (1969) reported that in five prairie study areas of Canada and South Dakota the peak density of redheads varied from 1 to 6 pairs per square mile. Lokemoen (1966) reported an unusually high density of 25 pairs per square mile on a 2,600-acre study area of western Montana. How-ever, a high incidence of attempted communal nesting and nest desertion were associated with this breeding density.

There is no evidence that redheads defend a territory or even part of their home range. Lokemoen (1966) noted that males did not defend any part of their home range. Hochbaum (1944) mentioned that redheads appeared to him to be the most tolerant of the diving ducks in the Delta, Manitoba, area relative to close association of pairs, with as many as three pairs occupying a half-acre slough simultaneously.

Interspecific Relationships: The significant role that social parasitism of redheads plays in the breeding biology of other marsh-nesting species has been documented by Weller (1959), who noted that eight other species of ducks, as well as bitterns and coots, have been reported parasitized, and both Weller's and Erickson's (1948) studies indicated that social parasitism by redheads reduced the hatching success of canvasback eggs. Erickson also found a reduced nesting success for canvasback nests when comparing parasitized versus nonparasitized nests.

Weller (1959) also noted that a number of other species of duck, including the ruddy duck, mallard, lesser scaup, canvasback, fulvous whistling duck, pintail, cinnamon teal, shoveler, and gadwall, have occasionally been found to drop their eggs in redhead nests.

Redheads have the usual array of egg and duckling predators, although the fact that they normally nest well away from shoreline probably reduces their losses to those by strictly terrestrial scavengers and predators. Keith (1961) did report that half the redhead nests he found in southeastern Alberta were on land, and many of these were very poorly concealed. He noted that skunks destroyed a number of redhead nests, and Lokemoen (1966) also found that skunks were the major mammalian predators of redhead nests in Montana. Low (1945) reported that minks and crows were responsible for nest losses in Iowa, and both crows and magpies were noted by Lokemoen (1966) as avian egg predators.

General Activity Patterns and Movements: Home range estimates for redheads on their breeding grounds are still generally not available. Lokemoen (1966) stated that pairs moved an average of 180 yards (variation among eleven pairs was 50 to 670 yards) from their "breeding-pair potholes" to nesting potholes.

Long-distance movements of redheads have been analyzed by Weller (1964). He documented the occurrence of a postseason adult molt migration in a northerly and somewhat easterly direction, as well as similar movements by juvenile birds. He also established the directions and relative magnitudes of spring and fall migratory movements, pointing out that the flyway concept is relatively meaningless in interpreting this species' movements. In contrast to the canvasback, which predominantly moves to the Atlantic coast or the Pacific coast for wintering, the vast majority of redheads undertake the relatively long flight over dry country to the Gulf coast. Weller attributes this difference in part to the hypothesized differences in areas of evolutionary origin of these two species.

SOCIAL AND SEXUAL BEHAVIOR

Flocking Behavior: Like canvasbacks, redheads often gather in fairly large flocks on lakes that provide protection and food, forming large "rafts" that may number in the hundreds or even thousands. During the winter and spring migration periods these large groupings tend to fragment as pair bonds are formed, and the unpaired birds congregate in courting party units. Low (1945) noted that spring migrant flocks usually did not exceed 25 individuals, and Weller (1967) mentioned that sometimes as many as 14 males were seen following a single unmated female. Shortly after arrival at the breeding grounds, the paired birds separate and disperse, and flocking behavior ceases until after the breeding season.

Pair-forming Behavior: The pair-forming behavior of redheads is similar to that of canvasbacks and other pochard species (Johnsgard, 1965; Weller, 1967) and differs in quantitative rather than qualitative characteristics. The commonest male courtship call is a catlike note, uttered during neck-kinking or a head-throw display. A softer call resembling coughing is also uttered, and aggressive neck-stretching by both sexes is frequent. Females perform inciting calls with alternate lateral and chin-lifting movements of the head, and a frequent male response to such inciting is to swim ahead and turn-the-back-of-the-head toward the inciting female. Weller (1967) noted that males on wintering areas were observed to "lead" females, and the latters' action in following them seemed to indicate a willingness to pair. This same combination of leading and following has been reported in captive birds (Johnsgard, 1965) and seems to represent a significant aspect of pair formation among both dabbling ducks and pochards. Aerial chases, involving tail-pulling, are characteristic of birds on the breeding grounds but are rare during migration, suggesting that they do not play a role in the pair-formation process, which is virtually completed by the time of the birds' arrival at their nesting grounds. More probably, they are associated with chases of the female by strange drakes, and represent attempted rapes.

Copulatory Behavior: Copulation is normally preceded by alternate bill-dipping and dorsal-preening behavior on the part of the male or, at times, by both male and female. The female then assumes a receptive posture and is immediately mounted by the male. Following treading, the male normally utters a single note as he releases his grip on the female's nape, and he swims away in a stereotyped bill-down posture. This same posture may be assumed for a short time by the female before she begins to bathe (Johnsgard, 1965).

Nesting and Brooding Behavior: Low (1945) reported on nesting and incubating behavior of redheads. He found that nest-building began two days to a week before egg-laying began. Eggs were deposited in the nest at any time of the day, as Weller (1959) later confirmed, although most eggs are apparently laid before noon. One to two more days are required to lay a clutch than there are eggs present, indicating an egg-laying rate of slightly more than one day per egg. Incubation may begin as late as 24 to 48 hours after the last egg is laid. During incubation the females that Low studied left the nest an average of six times a day. Renesting females not only left their nests more often, but also spent less total time on the nest than those making initial nesting attempts. Pipping requires from 16 to 18 hours, and Weller (1959) noted that during this period the female begins to utter low notes that probably serve to "imprint" the ducklings on their mother. Weller watched one brood that left its nest when the young were no more than 47 hours old. Redhead females are well known to be relatively poor parents, relatively rarely feigning injury when a family is approached and often deserting their brood while they are still fairly young. Low (1945) said that the young were usually abandoned by the time they were 7 or 8 weeks old, before they were able to fly.

Postbreeding Behavior: Male redheads usually abandon their females fairly early in the incubation period and soon begin to gather in groups prior to their postnuptial molt. At least in some areas a fairly long molt migration may be undertaken by such birds to more northerly areas to certain large, shallow lakes such as Lake Winnipegosis (Weller, 1964). Young redheads may also move considerably during late summer and autumn following fledging and also often range far to the north of the place where they were reared. There is no strong evidence favoring a major differential migration of the sexes during fall, but the greater vulnerability of females to gunning results in a high proportion of this sex being shot during fall migration. Rienecker (1968) noted, however, that males range farther than females in their migratory movements.

RING-NECKED DUCK

Aythya collaris (Donovan) 1809

Other Vernacular Names: Blackjack, Ring-billed Duck, Ringbill, Ringneck.

Range: Breeds from Mackenzie District through the forested regions of southern Canada, south locally to California, Colorado, Nebraska, Iowa, Pennsylvania, and New York, and from New England to Nova Scotia, Cape
Breton Island, and Newfoundland. Winters along the Pacific coast from
British Columbia to Baja, California, in most of Mexico and adjoining
Central America, in the southeastern states and along the Atlantic coast
north to Massachusetts, and in the West Indies.

Subspecies: None recognized.

Measurements (after Delacour, 1959):
Folded wing: Males 195-206, females 185-195 mm.
Culmen: Males 45-50, females 43-46 mm.

Weights: Nelson and Martin reported that 285 males averaged 1.6 pounds
(725 grams), and 151 females averaged 1.5 pounds (679 grams). Combining the data of Bellrose and Hawkins (1947) with that from fall-shot

birds reported by Jahn and Hunt (1964), 17 adult males averaged 1.74 pounds (789 grams), while 33 immatures averaged 1.53 pounds (694 grams); 15 adult females averaged 1.51 pounds (685 grams), while 29 immatures averaged 1.49 pounds (676 grams). The maximum weights reported by Nelson are 2.4 pounds (1,087 grams) for males and 2.6 pounds (1,178 grams) for females. Mendall (1958) provides additional weight data from winter, spring, and summer seasons.

IDENTIFICATION

In the Hand: Ring-necked ducks are often misidentified by hunters, the males usually being confused with scaup and the females with scaup or redheads. The pale whitish ring near the tip of the bill will separate both sexes from scaup, as will the absence of predominantly white secondary feathers. The male ring-necked duck may be readily distinguished from redheads or canvasbacks by its darker, rather glossy greenish black upper wing coverts and tertials, which lack any light gray vermiculations. Females, however, are much more difficult to separate, for although ring-necks lack the long, sloping bill of female canvasbacks, redheads also have a whitish band near the tip of the bill. Nevertheless, unlike female redheads, female ring-necked ducks have secondaries that are more distinctly grayish than are the relatively brown coverts, and a white eye-stripe and eyering are more evident. The wings are shorter (folded wing less than 200 mm. vs. at least 210 mm. in female redheads), and the scapulars are never flecked or vermiculated with whitish.

In the Field: When in nuptial plumage, the male ring-necked duck on the water is the only North American diving duck that has a black back and breast pattern, with a vertical white bar extending upward in front of the folded wing. The rare tufted duck also has a black back and breast, but lacks the white bar and has a much longer and thinner crest than does the ringneck. The ring-neck's white ring near the tip of the bill is often apparent at close range, but the chestnut ring at the base of the neck is rarely visible. Females on the water are probably best identified by their association with males, but usually exhibit a white eyering and posterior eye-stripe, as well as the white ring near the tip of the bill. Females lack the scaup's white facial mark, but they do have distinctly pale areas near the base of the bill. In flight, ringnecked ducks resemble scaup but lack white wing-stripes, and their darker back and upper wing coloration serves to separate them from redheads or canvasbacks, even before the head coloration is apparent. Ring-necks are relatively quiet ducks, and the courting calls of the male include a soft breathing note and a louder whistling sound difficult to characterize, both of which are only uttered on the water.

AGE AND SEX CRITERIA

Sex Determination: Males have yellowish rather than brownish eyes, and a pale area at the base of the bill. Vermiculated flanks or black feathers on the head, breast, or back also indicate a male. Sex determination by wing characters is difficult, but the tertials of males are more shiny greenish black and more pointed than those of females, and the secondary coverts are darker and may be slightly glossy.

Age Determination: Juvenal tertials are pointed, straight, and usually badly frayed, whereas those of adults are more rounded and usually are slightly curved. Likewise the greater and middle coverts of juveniles are relatively narrow, frayed, and rough (Carney, 1964). The tail should also be examined for notched tips.

DISTRIBUTION AND HABITAT

Breeding Distribution and Habitat: The breeding range of this strictly North American species has been documented by Mendall (1958), whose work may be consulted for details of distribution.

The ring-necked duck did not until recently breed in Alaska, but has been reported from the Bering Sea to the Canadian border (Hansen, 1960). In the past few years the species has been increasing in Alaska, and there are now several breeding records (White and Haugh, 1969). In Canada it is for the most part restricted to the area south of latitude 60° N., with its northernmost limits near Fort Simpson and lower Slave River (Godfrey, 1966). Otherwise, it breeds in the Cariboo Parklands of British Columbia, over much of Alberta, Saskatchewan, and Manitoba north of the prairie "pothole" country, in Ontario from Hudson Bay south to the Great Lakes, in southern Quebec, in the Maritime Provinces, and on Newfoundland.

To the south of Canada, the species is primarily found in the Great Lakes and New England regions, but isolated breeding does occur elsewhere. In northeastern Washington there are several breeding records (Yocom, 1951), and in Oregon there is a breeding record for the lower Klamath region (Mendall, 1958; *Audubon Field Notes,* 8:355). Limited breeding has also been reported for Nevada, Montana, and Colorado (Mendall, 1958). In Nebraska ring-necks breed locally in the sandhills lakes (Rapp *et al.,* 1950); breeding in South Dakota is rare (*American Birds,* 25:869); and in North Dakota they breed locally in the eastern and northeastern portions of the state (Stewart, 1968). In Minnesota the ring-neck ranks third, behind the blue-winged teal and the mallard, among breeding birds for the state as a whole (Lee *et al.,* 1964a). In Wisconsin it likewise ranks third (also behind the blue-winged teal

Breeding (hatched) and wintering (shaded) distributions of the
ring-necked duck in North America.

and the mallard) in abundance of breeding ducks (Jahn and Hunt, 1964), and in Michigan it is a common breeder (Zimmerman and Van Tyne, 1959). It has been recorded breeding in Illinois, Indiana, and Pennsylvania, and in New York it breeds over a 500-square-mile area of the Adirondacks (Foley, 1960). Vermont, New Hampshire, and Maine probably represent its southern limit of regular breeding in New England, but it has bred a few times in Massachusetts (Mendall, 1958), and there is even a recent record of a brood sighted in Florida (*Audubon Field Notes,* 23:644).

Mendall has characterized the favored breeding habitat as sedge-meadow marshes and bogs, ranging in size from an acre to nearly 2,000 acres. Shallow freshwater marshes, swamps, and bogs are all used by ring-necks, and bogs are especially favored, particularly those with sweet gale (*Myrica*) or leatherleaf (*Chamaedaphne*) cover. Further, white water lily (*Nymphaea odorata*) and water shield (*Brasenia schreberi*) are frequent associate plants of nesting birds in Maine, as are yellow water lilies (*Nuphar*) in Washington. Fresh water or acidic areas are apparently preferred over brackish or saline waters; a pH range of 5.5 to 6.8 is typical of breeding habitats.

Wintering Distribution and Habitat: In Canada, ring-necked ducks regularly winter in southwestern British Columbia, occasionally occur in southern Ontario, and rarely winter in Nova Scotia (Godfrey, 1966).

In recent midwinter surveys, nearly 60 percent of the wintering ring-neck population have been seen in the Mississippi Flyway, almost 40 percent in the Atlantic Flyway, and only insignificant numbers in the western states. In Mexico they are mostly limited to the Gulf coast region, with major concentrations from Tamaulipas to northern Yucatán, and especially in the Laguna de Alvarado, Veracruz (Leopold, 1959). They also winter along the Caribbean lowlands through Honduras at least as far as Panama, although in small numbers.

The Gulf coast of Texas supports some wintering ring-necks, but far fewer than does the corresponding area of Louisiana, which, with Tennessee, probably has the largest numbers of wintering birds in the Mississippi Flyway. In the Atlantic Flyway, the species is widely dispersed during winter on marshes, lakes, ponds, and reservoirs throughout the south, but peak concentrations probably occur in South Carolina, Georgia, Florida, and Alabama (Mendall, 1958; Addy, 1964). Some birds winter as far north as Chesapeake Bay, and very limited numbers occur locally even farther north.

In the Chesapeake Bay area, the preferred habitats of migrant and wintering ring-necks consist of fresh or slightly brackish estuarine bays and interior impoundments, with movement to moderately brackish waters during colder periods (Stewart, 1962). Mendall reported that on wintering areas the birds remain partial to shallow, acid marshes. They do also use coastal lagoons, where they often associate with scaup, but they generally select less brackish conditions than do scaup.

GENERAL BIOLOGY

Age at Maturity: Ferguson (1966) noted that only one of eleven aviculturalists reported breeding by captive ring-necked ducks in their first year of life, but nevertheless it is generally assumed that wild birds attain sexual maturity within a year of hatching.

Pair Bond Pattern: Pair bonds evidently begin to be formed on wintering grounds, probably starting in January or February (Weller, 1965). The pair bond typically breaks during the last week of incubation, or at the latest very shortly after hatching (Mendall, 1958). The association of apparently paired birds during fall migration may indicate the re-forming of bonds of previously paired birds, but this point has not been established.

Nest Location: Mendall (1958) reported that of 518 nest sites found, almost half were on floating islands, nearly 40 percent were on hummocks or clumps in open marsh, 9 percent were on solid islands, and the remaining few were on floating logs, in woodland swale, or in dry meadow. Only a single nest was on a dry site, and only two were in emergent vegetation, but the distance to open, permanent water averaged only 27 yards and ranged up to 400 yards. About 70 percent were within 15 yards of water sufficiently open for birds to land and take off. Perhaps the most important site criterion is the presence of a reasonably dry site with suitable cover and fairly close to water of swimming depth. About 70 percent of the nests were in a mixture of sedge (*Carex*), sweet gale, and leatherleaf vegetation, and another 10 percent were in a mixture of sedges and other plants. More nests were found under sedge than under any other growth of a single plant species, but most nests were placed in mixed cover types. There was no evident relationship to distance from shoreline or woods, but small clumps of nesting cover seemed to support more nests than did larger ones.

Clutch Size: Mendall (1958) reported that the average size of 423 completed clutches was 9.0 eggs, with an observed range of 6 to 14. Renest clutches averaged about 2 eggs fewer (6.96), with nearly half of the observed cases having 7 eggs present. Eggs are apparently laid at the rate of one per day.

Hunt and Anderson (1965) noted a reduction in average clutch size from 7.9 eggs in eight initial nests, to 7.8 eggs in eight second nests, and 7 eggs in one third nesting attempt. They found that eight of ten marked females attempted to renest following nest loss, and one attempted a second renest.

Incubation Period: Observed incubation periods on naturally incubated eggs have ranged from 25 to 29 days, with most clutches hatching after 26 or 27 days (Mendall, 1959).

Fledging Period: Mendall reported a fledging period of 49 to 56 days for wild ring-necked ducks, which is a surprisingly short fledging period for any pochard species.

Nest and Egg Losses: Mendall reported that 70 percent of 485 first nests under study hatched, while 61 percent of 52 renesting attempts hatched. This relatively high nest success was associated with a very low nest desertion rate, and most of the losses were attributed to predation. Major mammalian egg predators were minks, raccoons, and foxes, while crows, ravens, and marsh hawks were primary avian predators. Minks, crows, ravens, and raccoons alone accounted for over 70 percent of the predation losses and probably also contributed to the 19 percent loss by unknown predators.

Juvenile Mortality: Mendall found that the average brood size at hatching was 8.4 young, while that of well-grown (class III) broods was 5.2 young. Evidently the highest brood losses occur in the first 48 hours of life, and thereafter the mortality is fairly low. Some losses were definitely attributed to snapping turtles, and this species was believed responsible for considerable brood mortality in some areas. Jahn and Hunt (1964) summarized data from a variety of studies that indicated an average of about 6 ducklings per brood surviving to near the flight state. They also judged that about half the females succeeded in producing broods.

Mortality rates of birds banded as juveniles and recovered in their first year after banding are apparently high. Lee *et al.* (1964b) calculated a 75.7 percent mortality rate for such birds, and Jahn and Hunt (1964) estimated a 70 percent annual immature mortality rate.

Adult Mortality: Lee *et al.* (1964b) calculated a 66 percent annual mortality rate for ring-necked ducks recovered one to five years after banding, while Jahn and Hunt (1964) estimated a 50 percent annual adult mortality rate.

GENERAL ECOLOGY

Food and Foraging: Martin *et al.* (1951) and Cottam (1939) reported that the seeds of water shield, the seeds and vegetative parts of pondweeds, and the seeds or vegetative parts of various other submerged or emergent aquatic plants are consumed by ring-necked ducks in considerable quantities. Additionally, animal materials such as insects, mollusks, and other aquatic animal life are taken in substantial amounts, averaging about a quarter of the total diet.

Mendall (1958) made a detailed study of food intake of ring-necked ducks in Maine, and found that the tubers and seeds of two species of bulrush, seeds and vegetative parts of various pondweeds, and seeds of bur reeds (*Sparganium*) were major foods of adults, especially in spring and fall. Samples obtained during summer had a higher incidence of pondweeds and grasses, specifically wild rice (*Vallisneria*), followed by the seeds of spike rush (*Eleocharis*) and water lilies. Although nearly 90 percent of the adult food was of plant origin, samples from downy young contained about half animal matter, mostly aquatic insects. Plant materials included many of the same items taken by adults, even including the tubers of bulrushes. Mendall reported that ring-necked ducks generally feed in shallower waters than do other diving ducks in Maine, and preferred those less than five feet deep for foraging. They also tip-up at times, and generally remain submerged for relatively short periods of about 8 to 25 seconds.

Sociality, Densities, Territoriality: Mendall (1958) reported that ring-necked ducks are not averse to nesting in close proximity to one another, sometimes nesting only 5 or 6 feet apart. One quarter-acre island was found to support 6 ring-neck nests and 1 black duck nest. This would suggest the possibility of fairly high nesting densities in favorable habitats. Jahn and Hunt (1964) indicated that a six-year average density of ring-neck pairs per 100 acres of wetlands in Wisconsin was 9 for the northern highland and 6 for the central plain. Perhaps a more realistic measure of ring-neck densities is that provided by Lee *et al.* (1964b) for a 2.5-square-mile study area in Mahnomen County, Minnesota. In four years, the estimated population of ring-necked ducks ranged from 4.5 to 12 pairs per square mile and averaged 8.8, or almost twice as high as either the redhead or the canvasback populations. Mendall (1958) reported maximum densities of various study areas as ranging from a pair per 23 acres to one per 6 acres, with the latter density apparently close to the maximum possible. He believed that the unusual small home range and low level of intraspecific aggressiveness accounted for this remarkably high potential breeding density.

Mendall (1958) has discussed the possible role of territoriality in ring-necked ducks and noted that defense of the female had often been seen, but defense of specific areas had been noted only a few times, and then only prior to or during nest site selection. He nevertheless accepted the concept of territoriality as applying to this species, assuming that a condition of mutual respect served to avoid friction between pairs. Yet, little or no evidence of territorial boundaries could be found, and Mendall was unable to explain how concepts of classic territoriality might be applied to this species.

Interspecific Relationships: The rather specialized habitat preferences of the ring-necked duck largely place it out of direct contact with other pochards on the breeding grounds, and probably only the black duck regularly breeds in its preferred nesting habitats. On wintering grounds it most often associates with scaup, but tends to occupy less brackish waters.

Predators of eggs include minks, crows, ravens, raccoons, foxes, skunks, and perhaps other species, but the first four probably account for the largest number of losses (Mendall, 1958). Ducklings have reportedly been taken by snapping turtles, minks, and foxes, and no doubt other predators also account for some losses.

General Activity Patterns and Movements: Little specific information on daily activity rhythms and local movements are available. Mendall (1958) noted that ring-necks have a regular daily feeding pattern, except during courtship and the early stages of nesting. He mentioned that their morning foraging flights are seldom as early as those of black ducks and goldeneyes, but the evening feeding period is at about the same time.

Mendall also reported that on a seventy-acre study area (Barn Meadow), the first pairs to arrive in spring initially had rather large home ranges ("territories"), which decreased in size as other pairs moved in. Up to seven pairs were found to occupy the marsh, and additional pairs may have had their nests within it, but established waiting sites and/or "territories" elsewhere. Thus, it would seem that home ranges of this species may vary in size during the breeding season, but in general are probably relatively small and localized.

SOCIAL AND SEXUAL BEHAVIOR

Flocking Behavior: Mendall (1958) stated that fall migrant flocks of ring-necks are generally larger than those in spring, but groups of 10 to 25 birds are frequent. During periods of mass migration large flocks may sometimes occur, but the usual flock size of groups arriving at the wintering grounds is 5 to 25 birds. Apparently there is a substantial segregation of the sexes during fall migration, although the details of this are still obscure.

Spring migrant flocks are usually rather small, with groups of about 6 to 30 being typical. The earliest migrants are usually pairs and courting groups, followed by many unpaired birds having a large excess of males (Mendall, 1958).

Pair-forming Behavior: The pair-forming behavior of ring-necked ducks begins on the wintering grounds and probably reaches a peak during spring migration in March and April (Weller, 1965). By mid-May, when nesting is under way, it is seen very little, although scattered occurrences may take place until mid-June (Mendall, 1958).

The male pair-forming display of ring-necked ducks includes the usual pochard head-throw and "kinked-neck" calls, both of which are associated with a soft whistling note, neck-stretching, a rudimentary head-forward or "sneak" posture, and a few other less conspicuous displays (Johnsgard, 1965; Mendall, 1958). The female's inciting movements and calls are much like those of other pochards and serve the same function. Marquardt (cited in Mendall, 1958) noted the importance of the female's inciting in stimulating and maintaining male display activity, and it is certainly true that inciting behavior seems to play a major role in pair formation. The response of the preferred male to such behavior is usually to swim beside or ahead of the female and turn-the-back-of-the-head toward her. Ripley (1963) described an unusual lateral threat display in males that has not been reported by other observers, but evidently failed to observe some of the more typical ring-neck displays.

Copulatory Behavior: Ring-necked ducks normally precede copulation with mutual bill-dipping and dorsal-preening behavior. The postcopulatory display is reportedly the usual male call and bill-down posture typical of all pochards so far observed (Johnsgard, 1965).

Nesting and Brooding Behavior: Mendall (1958) has provided a large amount of information on nesting behavior, part of which may be summarized here. Females apparently select the nest site, but are accompanied by males. In early-nesting birds as much as a week or ten days may elapse between site selection and the laying of the first egg, while late-nesting birds may begin to lay almost immediately. Sometimes little or no actual nest is evident at the time the first egg or two are deposited, and until about the sixth egg there is still usually little nest shape evident. However, down is then usually added as the clutch is completed, and the vegetation overhead may be woven together to form an overhead arch. Ramps may be built to nests elevated above the ground surface, and runways to the nearest water are established. Eggs are usually laid in the forenoon, during visits lasting fifteen minutes to three hours. Incubation apparently begins on the day that the last egg is laid. During early stages of incubation the female may spend considerable time away from the nest, especially on cool days, and the period of strongest incubation behavior is between 9:00 a.m. and 3:00 p.m. During the last two weeks of incubation the females incubate more closely, and during this period the male usually abandons his mate.

Pipping of the egg occurs 24 to 48 hours prior to hatching, and most eggs hatch within a 6 to 8-hour period. The female then normally broods her young for at least 12 hours, and the family leaves the nest in late afternoon or, more frequently, shortly after sunrise on the day following hatching. In contrast to most other waterfowl, the female ring-neck may bring her young back to the nest for brooding purposes for 2 to 4 days after hatching, or even longer. Further, few females abandon their broods prior to the time of fledging, even when they themselves have become flightless. There are apparently few if any brood mergers in this species and no apparent friction between the parents of broods feeding in close proximity.

Postbreeding Behavior: Males begin their postnuptial molt even before they have abandoned their mates and soon begin to gather with other males that never attained mates or have abandoned theirs. There is probably a northward molt migration of birds that breed in Maine, but the distance and location of molting areas are still only poorly known. One such area, the St. John Estuary of New Brunswick, regularly supports several hundred molting birds in August and early September. The duration of the flightless period is probably three or four weeks, with the females having their flightless stage about a month later than the males. As young birds attain the power of flight, they begin to wander about, forming loose flocks that seem to disperse in a haphazard fashion. Before long, however, cooling weather in fall brings on initial gatherings in preparation for the southward migration.

TUFTED DUCK

Aythya fuligula (Linnaeus) 1758

Other Vernacular Names: None in North America.

Range: Breeds in Iceland, the British Isles, and through most of northern Europe and Asia to Kamchatka and the Commander Islands. Winters in central and southern Europe, northern Africa, southern Asia, the Philippines, and Japan, with stragglers regularly appearing on both the Pacific and Atlantic coasts of North America and rarely inland.

Subspecies: None recognized.

Measurements (after Delacour, 1959):

Folded wing: Males 198-208, females 189-202 mm.

Culmen: Males 38-42, females 38-41 mm.

Weights: Bauer and Glutz (1969) have summarized weight data on this species, and considerable data are also provided by Dementiev and Gladkov (1967). January weights of twenty-one males reported by Bauer and Glutz averaged 872 grams, while eleven females weighed during the same period averaged 759 grams. Maximum weights mentioned were 1,020 grams for males and 955 grams for females.

IDENTIFICATION

In the Hand: This rare Eurasian duck has been seen frequently enough in North America to warrant a knowledge of its identifying marks. The bill is slightly narrower and shorter than that of a scaup (maximum culmen length

42 mm.; maximum width under 24 mm.) and is only slightly wider toward the tip than at the base, while both the nail and adjacent tip are black in color. Whitish vermiculations are lacking on the back and upper wing coverts of both sexes. Males have a thin, drooping crest, which is rudimentary in females, but females lack a white cheek mark large enough to be continuous across the forehead (some females have a whitish mark at the sides of the mandible).

In the Field: Females may not safely be distinguished from female scaup in the field, but males may be safely recognized by the presence of a black back and chest with no white vertical bar between them (eliminating ring-necked ducks) and a thin, drooping crest on a purplish head (eliminating scaups). In flight, both sexes are very similar to scaup and cannot be safely distinguished from them by inexperienced persons. The calls of both sexes are virtually the same as those of scaup.

AGE AND SEX CRITERIA

Sex Determination: The presence of a definite, elongated crest or of definite vermiculations on the scapulars, sides, or flanks indicates a male. In eclipse plumage the sexes may be difficult to distinguish, but some vermiculations are present on the male's grayish sides and flanks, while in females the sides and flanks are more uniformly brownish. According to Veselovsky (1951) juvenile males can be distinguished from females by their darker brown head and neck color and bluish gray, rather than dark brown, bill. Kear (1970) found that by the thirty-fifth day of age males have a brighter yellow eye color than do females.

Age Determination: Although the adult plumage is attained by the end of December, individuals carrying notched tail feathers have been taken as late as April (Kear, 1970). Bauer and Glutz (1969) noted that the axillars and greater and middle upper wing coverts of immature birds are shorter and have more frayed edges than those of adults.

OCCURRENCE IN NORTH AMERICA

Either the tufted duck has become much more frequent in North America during recent years or earlier it was confused with the somewhat similar ring-necked duck. The earliest known North American records are from St. Paul and Attu islands, Alaska, as reported by Gabrielson and Lincoln (1959). Tufted ducks have also been seen several times at Adak Island (*Audubon Field Notes,* 24:634, 706; *American Birds,* 25:543, 894). There is also an unverified report that they have bred on Amchitka Island, and several have been seen there (*American Birds,* 26:891).

In Canada tufted ducks seem only to have been reported from British Columbia, the first sight record being obtained in 1961 (Godfrey, 1966). In recent years they have been reported from a variety of points in that province (*Audubon Field Notes,* 24,531; *American Birds,* 25:616).

Pacific coast records from south of Canada are largely from Washington. In the Seattle area the species has been seen almost every winter in recent years (*Audubon Field Notes,* 22:369; 469; 23:399; 24:426, 531; *American Birds,* 25:543). There is at least one winter record from Oregon (Gochfield, 1968) and several from California (*Audubon Field Notes,* 22:572; 23:101; *American Birds,* 25:621). There is also one record from the continental interior, of a male in Wyoming (Gochfield, 1968).

Atlantic coast records have recently become so numerous as to make a complete listing impossible. The largest number of state records are from Massachusetts, where the species was first reported in the 1950s (*Audubon Field Notes,* 9:9; 13:276). In the Falmouth area the tufted duck has been seen yearly since 1963 (*ibid,* 23:449, 569). New York has also reported tufted ducks in most recent winters (*ibid,* 20:204; 22:173, 422; 23:183; 24:487; *American Birds,* 25:555). Likewise, they have appeared during several winters in New Jersey (*Audubon Field Notes,* 22:158; 23:173) and also have been reported twice from Connecticut (Austin, 1969; *American Birds,* 25:548).

Gadwall, Pair

Gadwall, Adult male

Baikal Teal, Pair

Baikal Teal, Adult male

American Green-winged Teal, Pair

American Green-winged Teal, Adult male

Common Mallard, Adult male

Common Mallard, Brooding female

Mexican Mallard, Pair

Florida Mallard, Pair

Northern Pintail, Adult male

Bahama Pintail, Adult male

Garganey, Adult male

Garganey, Pair

Blue-winged Teal, Pair

Cinnamon Teal, Pair

Northern Shoveler, Adult male

Northern Shoveler, Pair

Canvasback, Adult female

Canvasback, Pair

Redhead, Adult male

Redhead, Adult female

Ring-necked Duck, Pair

Ring-necked Duck, Pair

Tufted Duck, Pair

Greater Scaup, Pair

Greater Scaup, Adult male

Lesser Scaup, Pair

American Common Eider, Adult males

American Common Eider, Group of adults

King Eider, Adult male

King Eider, Adult female

GREATER SCAUP

Aythya marila (Linnaeus) 1761

Other Vernacular Names: Big Bluebill, Bluebill, Broadbill.

Range: Breeds in Iceland, in northern Europe and Asia to northern Siberia, and in North America from arctic Alaska and arctic Canada east to the eastern shore of Hudson Bay, to northern Labrador, Anticosti Island, and Newfoundland. In North America winters on the Pacific coast from the Aleutian Islands to California, on the Gulf coast almost to Mexico, on the Atlantic coast from Florida to southern Canada, and on the eastern Great Lakes.

North American Subspecies:

A. m. mariloides (Vigors): Pacific Greater Scaup. Breeds in North America as indicated above, as well as in eastern Asia. Includes *nearctica,* which is recognized by the A.O.U. (1957) as the North American breeding form.

Measurements (after Delacour, 1959, and including *A. m. marila*):

Folded wing: Males 215-233, females 210-220 mm.

Culmen: Males 43-47, females 41-46 mm.) Godfrey, 1966, reported males to range from 41.5 to 48 mm., as compared to 39 to 43 mm. for lesser scaup males.)

Weights: Nelson and Martin (1953) reported that sixty males averaged 2.2 pounds (997 grams), while forty-three females averaged 2.0 pounds (907 grams), with maximum weights of 2.9 pounds (1,314 grams) for both sexes. Winter weights of the comparably sized European race were reported by Schiøler (1926) to average 1,256 grams for twelve adult males and 1,131 grams for eight immature males; twelve adult females averaged 1,182 grams and seven immatures averaged 1,024 grams.

IDENTIFICATION

In the Hand: As with the lesser scaup, the presence of a white speculum, a bluish bill which widens toward the tip, yellowish eyes, and vermiculated gray to brownish upperparts will eliminate all other species of ducks. For separation from lesser scaup, see the account of that species.

In the Field: In good light, male greater scaup exhibit a greenish, rather than purplish, gloss on the head and have a relatively low, uncrested head profile. Additionally their back appears more grayish, since it has a more finely vermiculated pattern. In flight, the extension of the white speculum to several of the inner primary feathers may be apparent. Female greater scaup are difficult to distinguish from female lesser scaup unless they are together. They are slightly larger and have more white on the face, especially on the forehead. The calls of the females of both species are similar, the most frequent one a low, growling *arrr* that is somewhat weaker in the lesser scaup. The courtship calls of the male greater scaup are a very soft, cooing *wa'hoooo* and a weak and very fast whistle *week-week-week,* compared with the lesser's faint *whee-ooo* and a single-noted *whew* whistle (Johnsgard, 1963). In both species these calls may only be heard at fairly close range during courtship activity.

AGE AND SEX CRITERIA

Sex Determination: Although both sexes may have vermiculated scapulars, those of males are predominantly white while those of females are predominantly dark. Females always lack flecking on the tertials and usually also on the greater and middle coverts, whereas males usually exhibit this (Carney, 1964). Most males older than juveniles will have black or blackish feathers on the head, breast, or rump, and may exhibit vermiculations on the flanks. Flank vermiculations are lacking in females.

Age Determination: Juvenal tertials are usually frayed to a pointed tip, whereas those of adults have more rounded tips. Additionally, juvenal tertials are rough, often narrower, and duller than those of adults. The tail should also be examined for squarish and notched-tipped feathers.

DISTRIBUTION AND HABITAT

Breeding Distribution and Habitat: In North America the greater scaup is primarily confined to areas north of 60° N. latitude as a breeding species, considerably farther north than is the case with the lesser scaup. However, in their choice of breeding habitats, the two species appear to be very similar.

In Alaska the principal breeding range extends from the Alaska Peninsula northward along the coast of the Bering Sea to the valley of the Kobuk River (Gabrielson and Lincoln, 1959). It also breeds to some extent along the northern coast of Alaska. It is common on the Aleutian Islands during spring and summer months, and on Amchitka Island it has at least been reported to nest (Kenyon, 1961). Breeding no doubt occurs over much of the interior of Alaska also, since scaup made up over a third of the ducks identified on aerial breeding-ground surveys made by the United States Fish and Wildlife Service between 1960 and 1969. However, at least in eastern Alaska the lesser scaup also breeds, and the relative occurrence of the two species in the state is still rather uncertain. Irving (1960) found the greater scaup to be about ten times more common than the lesser scaup around Anaktuvuk Pass, while at Old Crow near the Alaska-Canada border the reverse situation seemed to apply. Likewise King (1963) reported that in the upper Yukon River area only 52 of more than 12,000 scaup banded while molting were greater scaup, and evidently only a few nest in that area.

In Canada the breeding range extends from the Yukon eastward through the districts of Mackenzie and Keewatin and southward to extreme northwestern British Columbia, northern Manitoba, the Hudson Bay coast of Ontario and Quebec, the Ungava Bay coast, Anacosti Island, and eastern Newfoundland (Godfrey, 1965). It is probably a fairly common breeder on the Avalon Peninsula of Newfoundland (Tuck, 1968).

The breeding habitat of the greater scaup is evidently that of tundra or low forest closely adjacent to tundra. Hildén (1964) reported that this species requires relatively open landscape, cool temperatures, and shallow waters of

Breeding (hatched) and wintering (shaded) distributions of the
greater scaup in North America.

high trophic quality with open, preferably grassy, shores. He noted a strong social attraction toward nesting gulls or terns, and he found highest nesting abundance on islets with grassy or herbaceous cover, lower use of islets dominated by boulders or rocks, and little or no use of gravel-covered or wooded islets.

Wintering Distribution and Habitat: In Alaska greater scaup winter commonly along the Aleutian Islands, Kodiak Island, and along the coastline of southeastern Alaska (Gabrielson and Lincoln, 1959). In Canada they regularly winter on the coast of British Columbia, on some of the Great Lakes, and along the Atlantic coast from southern Quebec eastward through the Maritime Provinces and Newfoundland (Godfrey, 1965).

South of Canada, greater scaup may be found in winter along the coasts of Washington, Oregon, and California southward to central California. There are occasional wintering birds farther south, but only rarely do they range as far as Mexico (Leopold, 1959).

On the Atlantic coast the greater scaup is most abundant along the coast of New England. Maximum numbers seen during the annual Audubon Christmas counts generally occur along coastal New York. To the south of New York, the relative abundance of greater scaup depends largely on the severity of the winter, with southern movements greatest in years of severest winters, so that in the Chesapeake Bay area either species may be more common during a particular year (Stewart, 1962). As far south as South Carolina and Georgia the greater scaup is quite rare (Sprunt and Chamberlain, 1949; Burleigh, 1958), but apparently is fairly common in Louisiana (Lowery, 1960) and coastal Alabama (Imhof, 1962). However, Burleigh (1944) reported finding only a single definite specimen from the Gulf coast of Mississippi. Considering both the long migratory distance and the cold-weather tendencies of this species, it would seem that the Gulf coast must not be a part of its regular wintering range.

Stewart (1962) stated that in the Chesapeake Bay region the greater scaup are generally largely restricted to brackish and salt estuarine bays and coastal bays during winter, although some migrant birds use fresh and slightly brackish waters for brief periods.

GENERAL BIOLOGY

Age at Maturity: Ferguson (1966) reported that seven of twelve aviculturalists found initial breeding of greater scaup in their second year of life, and only three reported first-year breeding. Comparable data on wild birds is not available, but a delayed sexual maturity has been suggested for this species by Munro (1941).

Pair Bond Pattern: Greater scaup renew their pair bonds on a yearly basis. In captivity, pair-forming behavior may be seen from late fall through winter and early spring, and probably the same applies to wild birds.

Nest Location: Weller *et al.* (1969) reported that on the West Mirage Islands of Great Slave Lake greater scaup typically place their nests in the grass of the previous year, often in rock cracks or near water. Of 29 nests that they found, the average height above water level was 7 feet, while 28 nests averaged 19 feet away from the nearest water.

In a nesting study on Iceland, Bengtson (1970) reported on the locations of 2,016 greater scaup nests. He found nearly twice as many nests per unit area on islands versus mainland habitats (331 versus 180 nests per square kilometer). Favored nest sites were under the perennial herbaceous angelicas (*Angelica* and *Archangelica*) and shrubs, especially those under 0.5 meters high. Other herbaceous cover and sedges were used to a much lesser extent, and only one nest was found in a hole. Bengtson found that scaup exhibited a tendency for nesting in aggregated or clumped patterns and, in general, nested fairly close to water.

Clutch Size: Weller *et al.* (1969) noted that 49 nests averaged 7.8 eggs, but ranged up to 22 in number. Including only the 39 warm (currently incubated) clutches and excluding those numbering in excess of 12 eggs, as assumed multiple efforts, the average clutch was 8.5 eggs. Hildén (1964) reported an average of 9.68 eggs in 360 clutches, with a modal clutch size of 10 eggs and a maximum of 17. He also found nest parasitism to be prevalent, with both intraspecific and interspecific (in tufted duck and shoveler nests) cases being noted. Bengtson (1971) found that 1,409 clutches of greater scaup in Iceland had an overall average of 9.73 eggs, although significant yearly differences in average clutch size (9.01 to 9.83 eggs) were present.

Incubation Period: Generally reported as 24 or 25 days, but with some estimates up to 28 days (Bauer and Glutz, 1969; Lack, 1968).

Fledging Period: Not yet established, but probably similar to that of the lesser scaup.

Nest and Egg Losses: Hildén (1964) reported on egg losses in 137 greater scaup nests in the Gulf of Bothnia. Of these, 87 percent hatched, with crows and ravens accounting for most losses and flooding causing a few. This relatively low loss to species such as crows might be the result of the high social attraction of greater scaup to nesting larids, which tends to reduce crow depredations. The effectiveness of larids in reducing such predations is also greater late in their nesting season, when they are defending young, which may be advantageous to the late-nesting scaup. A more recent study by Bengtson (1972) has confirmed the higher hatching success of scaup nests in gull or tern colonies than of nests not associated with larids.

Juvenile Mortality: Hildén (1964) found that there was a tendency for scaup broods to intermix temporarily with those of tufted ducks, but he observed no indication of regular mergers of scaup broods. He did note one case of a female with fifteen young, which he thought might represent a merged brood. During three years of study he found that the rate of juvenile mortality ranged from 91 to 98 percent and that much of the mortality was attributable to gull predation and to bad weather. Since the young ducklings moved out into the open water of bays at an unusually early age, they were subjected to higher predation rates than were young tufted ducks and were also more likely to be caught in fishing nets.

Adult Mortality: Boyd (1962) estimated an annual adult mortality rate of the Icelandic population of greater scaup as 48 percent.

GENERAL ECOLOGY

Food and Foraging: The summary of Martin *et al.* (1951) indicated that during winter and spring a variety of animal materials (mollusks, insects, and crustaceans) seems to predominate in the diet, while thirty-five fall samples were predominantly made up of vegetable materials. The seeds and vegetative parts of pondweeds (*Potamogeton*), wild celery (*Vallisneria*), and wigeon grass (*Ruppia*) and the vegetative parts of muskgrass (*Chara*) were among the more prevalent plant materials found.

In a more recent study, Cronan (1957) analyzed the food contents of 119 greater scaup collected along the Connecticut coast of Long Island Sound between October and May. In this sample animal materials constituted over 90 percent of the total food volume, more than was found in earlier studies. Cronan attributed this to the fact that all the birds were taken in coastal waters. He found that the blue mussel (*Mytilus edulis*) was the most important single food by volume, while the dwarf surf clam (*Mulinia lateralis*) was of secondary importance both in volume and frequency of occurrence. Mollusks, most of which were bivalves, collectively made up nearly 90 percent of the total food contents. The only important plant food found was sea lettuce (*Ulva*), which is rapidly digested and probably was more important than the 3.6 percent of food volume that it constituted would indicate. Cronan concluded that in different areas different mollusks serve as the primary foods, but the particular species utilized are evidently determined by their relative availability.

Cronan observed scaup of both species feeding during all daylight hours, with tidal stages being significant only where mollusk beds were exposed during low tide. Since the birds normally will not feed out of water, such low tides reduce foraging. Most foraging was in depths of less than 5 feet of water, but in one case diving in water 23 feet deep was seen. Temperature, water current, normal weather variations, wind, and cloud cover all had little or no effect on foraging, but human activities did strongly affect usage of local areas by scaup. Cottam (1939) noted that under conditions of human persecution, greater scaup often go to sea and return at night to the foraging areas, especially under moonlight conditions.

Sociality, Densities, Territoriality: Bengtson (1970) reported that greater scaup exhibit a definite pattern of aggregation in their nesting distribution, but did not know whether this was produced by social attraction or by some other environmental cause. On thirteen areas he found an overall nesting density of 273 nests per square kilometer, or about 1 nest per acre. In island areas the nesting density per square kilometer averaged 331 nests, and on the mainland 180 nests.

No specific information on home ranges of the greater scaup is available, but it is apparent that nothing like classic territoriality can be present in this species.

Interspecific Relationships: In North America the lesser scaup is the nearest ecological counterpart of the greater scaup, and in Europe and Asia the tufted duck also occupies a similar ecological niche. Weller *et al.* (1969) found a considerable amount of nest parasitism between greater and lesser scaup, and Hildén (1964) likewise observed reciprocal nest parasitism between the greater scaup and the tufted duck in Finland. However, because of the rather generalized nest site requirements of these species, there appears to be little if any actual competition for nesting locations.

There is a good deal of similarity in the foods taken by lesser and greater scaup (Cronan, 1957; Stewart, 1962), at least when both are feeding in the same areas. Yet a sufficient degree of ecological segregation, apparently related to water salinity preferences and temperature tolerances, reduces such interactions to a fairly low level.

Although the presence of nesting gulls is highly attractive to scaup in providing nesting associates, at least certain species of gulls can be extremely destructive to ducklings during their first few weeks of life.

General Activity Patterns and Movements: The observations of Cronan (1957) suggest that little obvious periodicity in foraging behavior can be detected in greater scaup, and since the birds are strictly open-water feeders, they do not undertake regular foraging flights to and from feeding grounds.

Millais (1913) reported foraging movements from the open sea to mussel beds at night, as well as at dawn and sunset. Dawson (1909) also noted there was a fall evening flight starting about half an hour before sunset from Drayton Harbor on the Washington coast, where the birds feed in shallow water, back out to sea.

SOCIAL AND SEXUAL BEHAVIOR

Flocking Behavior: The "rafting" behavior of migrant and wintering scaup is well known and is indicated by their vernacular names—"raft duck," "flock duck," and "troop duck." Scaup in such rafts do not all forage at the same time, but rather feeding and nonfeeding birds may be interspersed. When feeding in a current, they often "drift feed," diving as they drift past a feeding area and eventually flying back to the other end of the raft to begin drifting toward the feeding area again (Cronan, 1957). Sizes of such rafts have not been extensively counted, but Audubon Christmas counts in the Long Island area often show an excess of 10,000 birds within a fifteen-mile diameter.

Pair-forming Behavior: The pair-forming behavior of the greater scaup is extremely similar to that of the lesser scaup, differing only in certain qualitative characteristics (Johnsgard, 1965). The inciting movements and calls of the females of these two species are virtually identical, and it is probable that some mixed courting groups may occur on common wintering grounds. However, wild hybrids between the two species are unknown, although their recognition would prove to be extremely difficult.

Male pair-forming calls and postures include soft whistled "coughing" notes, uttered with an inconspicuous jerk of the wings and tail, and a very weak *wa'-hooo* note that is produced during a head-throw display or during slight neck-stretching. Turning-the-back-of-the-head toward inciting females is very frequently performed and usually is associated with lowering of the crown feathers. Likewise, both sexes frequently perform a stereotyped preening behind the wing toward the other, especially if the birds are paired or in the process of forming pairs (Johnsgard, 1965).

Copulatory Behavior: Copulation in greater scaup is usually preceded by the male bill-dipping, preening dorsally, and preening behind the wing. The female often responds with these same displays, which closely resemble normal comfort movements, then assumes a prone posture. Following treading, the male typically releases the female's nape, utters a single call, and swims away from her in a rigid bill-down posture. The female may also assume this posture for a few seconds before she begins to bathe (Johnsgard, 1965).

Nesting and Brooding Behavior: Relatively little has been written on the nesting behavior of the greater scaup in North America. Hildén's (1964) study on the Gulf of Bothnia provides a good source of information. He found that the pair bonds of this species last longer than in tufted duck, on the average at least until the middle of the incubation period. The male remains near the nesting place and joins the female whenever she leaves the nest. In one case the male remained with his mate until hatching and was seen with the newly hatched brood.

Following hatching, the young scaup ducklings feed mainly on the surface, catching floating insects or those flying just above the surface. Thus the weather shortly after hatching, its effect on insect abundance, as well as chilling effects on the young are critical to their survival. This is especially true of this species, which quickly leaves the shelter of the bulrushes and moves into the deeper water of the bays. There they are more directly exposed to the elements, as well as to possible predation by gulls and perhaps also predatory fish. Additionally, they must feed to a greater extent by diving because of the relative rarity of insect life. This demands more energy than does obtaining food from the surface or just above it.

Postbreeding Behavior: Hildén (1964) reported seeing flocks of males as early as late June, about the time that the first scaup broods were appearing. Most males were flocked by early July, when up to 50 were seen in a group. Except for a few that remained with apparently renesting females, the males then left the area and evidently molted elsewhere. Major molting areas in North America are still unknown, but Gabrielson and Lincoln (1959) mentioned that nonbreeders are sometimes fairly numerous in southeastern Alaska during summer. Very possibly the coastal regions of the Northwest Territories also support molting scaup, although this is mere speculation.

LESSER SCAUP
Aythya affinis (Eyton) 1838

Other Vernacular Names: Bluebill, Broadbill, Little Bluebill.

Range: Breeds from central Alaska eastward to western Hudson Bay and southward locally to Idaho, Colorado, Nebraska, and the Dakotas. Winters from British Columbia southward along the Pacific coast to Mexico, Central America, and Colombia, and on the Atlantic coast from Colombia north to the mid-Atlantic states, as well as in the West Indies.

Subspecies: None recognized.

Measurements (after Delacour, 1959):
Folded wing: Males 190-201, females 185-198 mm.
Culmen: Males 38-42, females 36-40 mm.

Weights: Nelson and Martin (1953) reported that 130 males averaged 1.9 pounds (861 grams), while 144 females averaged 1.7 pounds (770 grams). Combining the data of Bellrose and Hawkins (1947) and that of Jahn and Hunt (1964) for fall-shot birds, 11 adult males averaged 1.84 pounds (834 grams), while 36 immatures averaged 1.74 pounds (789 grams); 8 adult females averaged 1.65 pounds (748 grams), while 36 immatures averaged 1.76 pounds (798 grams). Nelson and Martin reported a maximum male weight of 2.5 pounds (1,087 grams), the same maximum weight that Jahn and Hunt reported for females, while the maximum female weight indicated by Nelson and Martin was 2.1 pounds.

IDENTIFICATION

In the Hand: Lesser scaup are best separated from greater scaup in the hand, and even then some specimens may remain doubtful. In the case of females, the presence of a white facial mark and white on the outer webs of the secondaries will exclude all species but the greater scaup. Female lesser scaup usually have no white on the inner webs of any primaries, although some may be quite pale. The length of the culmen in female lesser scaup is 36 to 40 mm., while female greater scaup have culmen lengths of 41 to 46 mm. Female lesser scaup rarely exceed 2 pounds, but female greater scaup average more than 2 pounds. Males can usually be distinguished from greater scaup by a purplish rather than greenish gloss on the head, a more extensive area of grayish vermiculations on the back, no definite white on the vanes of the primaries (although the inner ones may be quite pale), culmen length of 38 to 42 mm. (vs. 43 to 47 mm.), a nail width of less than 7 mm. (vs. 8 or more), maximum bill widths of 20 to 24 mm. (vs. 22 to 26 mm.), and a maximum weight of 2.5 pounds (vs. an average weight of about 2.5 pounds). The bill of the lesser scaup also tends to have a more concave culmen profile and to be relatively narrower at the base than that of the greater scaup.

In the Field: Male lesser scaup, when seen in good light, show a purplish gloss on the head and have a higher head profile, with a rudimentary crest usually evident, rather than a green-glossed head and a low head profile. The back of the male lesser scaup also appears more speckled, since the vermiculations in these areas are coarser. In flight, the restricted amount of white on the wings may be evident. Females cannot be safely separated in the field, but those of the lesser scaup do tend to show less white in front of the eyes than do female greater scaup.

AGE AND SEX CRITERIA

Sex Determination: Although the scapulars of both sexes may be vermiculated, those of females are predominantly dark, whereas those of males are predominantly white. Females have unflecked or only slightly flecked tertials, whereas males usually exhibit considerable flecking. The greater and middle coverts are usually unflecked in females and heavily flecked in males (Carney, 1964). The presence of blackish feathers on the breast or rump, or vermiculations on the flanks, or head iridescence indicates a male.

Age Determination: Juvenal tertials are usually frayed to a pointed tip, rather than being round-tipped, and the greater coverts tend to be narrower and duller than those of older birds. The tertials of immature birds usually lack flecking, while those of older males are flecked and of females are unflecked (Carney, 1964). Squarish tail feathers with notched tips indicate an immature bird.

DISTRIBUTION AND HABITAT

Breeding Distribution and Habitat: This strictly North American species of pochard has a fairly wide breeding range in both forest and grassland habitats. In Alaska it breeds commonly in the upper Yukon Valley, and there are also two old breeding records for Glacier Bay (Gabrielson and Lincoln, 1959).

In Canada it breeds southward from the treeline of the Yukon and the Northwest Territories across the forested portions of British Columbia, Alberta, Saskatchewan, and Manitoba east to Hudson Bay and western Ontario. Farther east there are only spotty breeding records, mainly for southeastern Ontario and the eastern shoreline of James Bay (Godfrey, 1966).

South of Canada, localized breeding occurs in eastern Washington (Yocom, 1951), northern California (Reinecker and Anderson, 1960; Hunt and Anderson, 1966), central Arizona (Fleming, 1959), and northern Colorado. More widespread or common breeding occurs on the northern Great Plains, in northern and eastern Montana and the Dakotas, with the eastern limits of regular breeding occurring in northwestern Minnesota (Lee *et al.,* 1964a). There are also scattered records of breeding for Wisconsin (Jahn and Hunt, 1964), Ohio (*Audubon Field Notes,* 8:345), Indiana (Mumford, 1954), and Michigan (Zimmerman and Van Tyne, 1959).

The preferred breeding habitat of lesser scaup consists of prairie marshes or potholes and partially wooded "parklands" (Lee *et al.,* 1964a). Godfrey (1966) characterized the breeding habitat as the vicinity of interior lakes and ponds, low islands, and moist sedge meadows. Munro (1941) stated that nesting usually occurs around lakes of moderate depth with bulrushes on shore and with brushy coves. Lakes with abundant amphipods and insect larvae support the best breeding populations.

Wintering Distribution and Habitat: To a greater degree than any other pochard species in North America, the lesser scaup undertakes a surprisingly

Breeding (hatched) and wintering (shaded) distributions of the lesser scaup in North America.

long southward movement. A few lesser scaup winter in coastal British Columbia and on Lake Erie, but there is a general movement to saltwater areas of the southern United States and Mexico.

Midwinter inventories by the United States Fish and Wildlife Service during the late 1960s indicate that nearly 90 percent of the scaup (both greater and lesser) winter in the Mississippi and Atantic flyway states. In Mexico, lesser scaup are second only to pintails in estimated numbers of wintering ducks and are abundant along both coasts. There have been particularly large concentrations seen on deep coastal lagoons of Nayarit, Chiapas, Veracruz, and Yucatán, although yearly variations in numbers and distribution are considerable (Leopold, 1959). Lesser scaup are also regular winter residents in Central America as far south as Panama (Wetmore, 1965), and some birds occasionally reach South America.

Along the Atlantic coast, scaup winter from Newfoundland southward, but most of those occurring north of New Jersey consist of greater scaup. To the south the lesser scaup gradually increases proportionally, so that in Florida it makes up nearly the entire wintering population (Addy, 1964). In that state lesser scaup winter mainly along the coast, but also use some of the larger inland lakes (Chamberlain, 1960). In Louisiana the wintering scaup population is normally very high; usually more than a million can be found on Lake Borgne, Lake Pontchartrain, and other lakes near New Orleans (Hawkins, 1964).

Stewart (1962) described the lesser scaup's habitat in Chesapeake Bay as consisting of fresh, slightly brackish, and brackish estuarine bays during migration, while brackish estuarine bays are the chief wintering habitat in most years. During severe weather they may move to salt estuarine bays as well. Unlike other ducks, their distribution was apparently not closely related to the distribution of aquatic food plants, a probable reflection of their greater dependence on foods of animal origin.

GENERAL BIOLOGY

Age at Maturity: In captivity lesser scaup do not breed until they are two years old, according to eight of eleven aviculturalists responding to a survey by Ferguson (1966). There has been some speculation that a two-year period to maturity may also be typical of wild individuals as well (Munro, 1941), but evidence of breeding by at least some female yearlings was found by McKnight and Buss (1962). It is probable, however, that only a small proportion of yearling birds successfully nest, as suggested earlier for the redhead and as recently reported for lesser scaup by Trauger (1971).

Pair Bond Pattern: Pairs are renewed each winter in lesser scaup, with pair-forming behavior beginning in January or February and in general being more retarded than that of the redhead, canvasback, or ring-necked ducks (Weller, 1965). Pair bonds are broken by the middle of the incubation period (Hochbaum, 1944).

Nest Location: Munro (1941) reported that nests are in dry situations under various kinds of cover, usually close to a lakeshore. Rienecker and Anderson (1960) stated that there is a preference for nesting in dry uplands, with a slight tendency to choose islands with nettle (*Urtica*) cover. Vermeer (1968; 1970) noted that there is a strong association in the nesting of lesser scaup and terns. Miller and Collins (1954) found lesser scaup to nest principally on islands, with grasses, nettles, and saltbush (*Atriplex*) accounting for 50, 40, and 10 percent of the cover types, respectively. Nests were never found over water, but all were within 3 to 50 yards of water, usually in cover from 13 to 24 inches high. Townsend (1966) noted that nearly 80 percent of the lesser scaup nests he found were in sedge cover, many of which were on floating sedge mats. Keith (1961) found that 198 lesser scaup nests in Alberta averaged closer to water (39 feet) than those of any of the surface-feeding ducks, and Townsend found that lesser scaup and ring-necked ducks were very similar in their placement of nests relative to water. Over half of the forty nests that Gehrmann (1951) found were within 15 feet of water.

Clutch Size: Keith (1961) reported that the clutch sizes of lesser scaup decreased from 10.6 early in the nesting season to 8.5 for late nests, with an overall average of 10.0 for 131 nests. Likewise, Townsend (1966) found that ninety-four lesser scaup nests averaged 9.0 eggs, with an average reduction of one egg for every 10.3 days of the nesting season. Hunt and Anderson (1966) noted that five initial clutches averaged 10.6 eggs, five second attempts averaged 8.8 eggs, two third attempts averaged 7.5 eggs, and one fourth nesting attempt had 7 eggs present.

Incubation Period: Hochbaum (1944) reported a 22- to 23-day incubation period for lesser scaup eggs hatched in an artificial incubator, with a maximum of 26 days recorded. Vermeer (1968) reported a 24.8-day average period for eighteen clutches incubated by wild females.

Fledging Period: Hochbaum (1944) indicated that captive-reared lesser scaup attained flight in 56 to 73 days. This may be a little longer than typical; Lee *et al.* (1964a) reported a 7-week fledging period.

Nest and Egg Losses: Nesting success rates seem to vary greatly by locality and year. High nesting success rates (60 percent or more) were reported by Miller and Collins (1954), Rienecker and Anderson (1960), and Townsend (1966). Townsend found that lesser scaup nesting on islands had a higher hatching success than those nesting on the mainland. Much lower nesting success was reported by Keith (1961), who found an overall 25 percent hatching success (higher on islands) in Alberta, and Rogers (1959), who noted a high incidence of nest losses to ground predators during a year of relative drought in Manitoba. Quite possibly the local availability of suitable nesting islands has a large effect on average hatching success of this species. Vermeer (1968) noted that island-nesting lesser scaup had a high nesting success, whether or not nesting gulls were present.

Juvenile Mortality: Townsend (1966) reported that the average hatch per nest of fifty-five scaup nests was 8.7 ducklings. Miller and Collins (1954) estimated an average hatch per clutch of 9.3 ducklings. Because of the prevalence of brood merger in this species (Munro, 1941), counts of older-aged broods are not reliable indications of juvenile mortality. Vermeer (1968) found a 100 percent duckling mortality in Alberta, mainly because of California gull predation.

Postfledging mortality rates for immature lesser scaup do not seem to be available, but they are presumably as high as in related species of pochards.

Adult Mortality: Longwell and Stotts (1959) calculated a 41.8 percent annual adult mortality rate for lesser scaup in the first six years following banding, or approximately the same as the rates they calculated for redheads and canvasbacks.

GENERAL ECOLOGY

Food and Foraging: In contrast to the three preceding pochard species, both species of scaup have high rates of consumption of animal materials. Plant foods are similar to those of other pochards, including the seeds and vegetative parts of wild celery (*Vallisneria*), pondweeds (*Potamogeton*), wigeon grass (*Ruppia*), and various other submerged or emergent plants (Martin *et al.,* 1951). Cottam (1939) found that animal foods, of which mollusks made up over half, constituted only 40 percent by volume of samples from 1,051 lesser scaup taken throughout the year. Insects were of secondary importance, and other animal foods constituted only about 3.5 percent.

The most comprehensive recent study of lesser scaup foods is that of Rogers and Korschgen (1966), who analyzed 164 samples from adults on the breeding grounds, migration routes, and wintering grounds. Animal foods totalled 91.1 percent of breeding-ground food samples, 93.5 percent of fall samples, and 63.7 percent of winter samples. The most important foods were amphipod crustaceans on breeding areas, mollusks on fall concentration areas, and fishes on wintering grounds. Harmon (1962) also noted the importance of animal foods, specifically mollusks, on Louisiana wintering areas of lesser scaup.

Spring and summer foods of scaup have been studied by several people, and most have commented on the importance of amphipods ("scuds") at this time of year. Munro (1941) noted this in British Columbia, as did Dirschl (1969) in Saskatchewan, Bartonek and Hickey (1969) in Manitoba, and Bartonek and Murdy (1970) in the Northwest Territories. In the last-named study amphipods averaged more than half the total food volume among 35 scaup sampled that had eaten them. Juvenile birds had consumed almost no plant materials, but utilized free-swimming and bottom-dwelling organisms in water averaging 3.5 to 4.0 feet in depth. Adult birds also usually forage in water that is fairly shallow, but at times feed in areas some 15 to 20 feet deep. At such depths they may remain under water about one minute during each dive, but in shallower waters, 8 to 10 feet deep, they usually are submerged for less than half that duration (Cottam, 1939).

Sociality, Densities, Territoriality: Perhaps because of their dry-land nesting preferences and their tendencies to nest on islands where these are available, lesser scaup often exhibit fairly high breeding densities and may develop considerable sociality in nesting. Rogers (1959) reported that, on a square-mile study area in Manitoba, the breeding population of lesser scaup was 51 and 65 pairs during two consecutive years. Stoudt (1969) reported lower peak densities of 1 to 17 pairs per square mile for five prairie study areas in southern Canada and South Dakota. Vermeer (1970) reported a nest density of 0.08 nests per acre (51 per square mile) on islands in Lake Newell, Alberta. He also (1968) found that lesser scaup initiated 67 and 66 nests during two years on two islands on Lake Miquelon, Alberta, totalling eleven acres, or about 6 nests per acre. It is thus clear that territoriality cannot play any significant role in producing nest dispersion in this species.

Interspecific Relationships: The close relationship of lesser and greater scaup opens the possibility of interspecific competition between these species. Their nesting areas overlap widely, and there is some evidence of interspecific conflict over nesting sites and egg-laying in the nests of the other species (Weller *et al.,* 1969). Various surface-feeding ducks are sometimes also socially parasitized by lesser scaup (Weller, 1959).

The extent to which there may be food competition among the two scaup species is uncertain, but differences in migration routes and major wintering grounds tend to reduce contact between them. Stewart (1962) noted that in the Chesapeake Bay area, where both species winter, greater scaup are mostly restricted to brackish and salt estuarine bays and coastal bays, while lesser scaup range farther toward the upper limits of the adjoining estuaries and only move out into salt estuarine bays during unusually severe weather. Among birds collected in brackish and salt estuarine bays, both species had consumed the same gastropod mollusks (*Mulina lateralis, Brachiodontes recurvus*), in quantity, while samples of both species from salt estuaries included quantities of eelgrass (*Zostera*) and other gastropods (*Bittium, Mitrella lunata*). Thus, it appears that potential food competition between the two species is present, and probably the stronger tendencies of lesser scaup to use less salty or brackish waters, interior lakes, and more southerly wintering areas are the prime bases for reducing actual interspecific food competition.

General Activity Patterns and Movements: Little specific information on daily activity rhythms is available. Phillips (1925) mentioned that lesser scaup are primarily daytime feeders but do forage to some extent at night. They prefer to forage in shallow waters some 3 to 8 feet deep and probably are less affected in their feeding rhythms by tidal fluctuation than are more marine species such as the greater scaup.

Studies of local movements and home ranges on the breeding grounds have not yet been performed on this species. Hochbaum (1944) commented that the size of a lesser scaup's "territory" (home range) may be as much as an acre of open bay or only forty yards of a narrow roadside ditch. He noted that paired birds sometimes make leisurely flights beyond the limits of their territory during evening hours, apparently for exercise. Migratory movements based on banding results have been summarized by Aldrich (1949).

SOCIAL AND SEXUAL BEHAVIOR

Flocking Behavior: The "rafting" behavior of scaup on their foraging areas is well known and often results in the concentration of large numbers of birds in localized areas. A photograph in *Waterfowl Tomorrow* (p. 214) of thousands of lesser scaup in a small arroyo near Aransas Pass, Texas, provides an example of the degree of flocking behavior that occurs on the wintering grounds of this species. In Florida, where the lesser scaup is perhaps the most abundant wintering duck, extremely large flocks usually occur around such areas as St. Petersburg, Fort Meyers, and Cocoa. In Cocoa at least 200,000 were counted during the 1963 Christmas count (*Audubon Field Notes,* 18:171). If these birds were limited to the tidal estuaries that made up 15 percent of the survey area, they were spread out over no more than 25 square miles, or averaged about 8,000 birds per square mile.

Pair-forming Behavior: Pair formation evidently begins fairly late on the wintering grounds (Weller, 1965), but during spring migration becomes relatively prevalent. In eastern and central Washington it may be seen from the time the birds first arrive in March to late April, by which time most females are paired (Johnsgard, 1955; Gehrmann, 1951). Pair-forming displays of lesser scaup are very much like those of greater scaup and the other pochard species. The most elaborate posture is an extremely rapid head-throw, associated with a soft *whee-ooo* call. A sharper whistled note is also uttered during a convulsive coughlike movement, and a rudimentary form of the canvasback's "sneaking" display is sometimes performed. During female inciting, which serves as the focal point of male courtship activity, the male often swims rapidly ahead and turns-the-back-of-the-head toward the female, simultaneously lowering the crown feathers to produce a distinctive low-headed appearance. To a larger extent than the other North American pochards (excepting the greater scaup), a ritualized preening of the wing feathers that exposes the white speculum is prevalent during pair-forming display. Chases of the female, either in the air or under water, are fairly frequent (Gehrmann, 1951), and it is often difficult to determine whether these are courting chases or attempted rape chases.

Copulatory Behavior: The precopulatory displays of the male consist of bill-dipping, dorsal-preening, and preening behind the wing, which are sometimes reciprocated by the female. After treading is completed the male releases the female from his grasp, probably calls, and then swims away from his mate in a rigid posture with the bill pointed sharply downward (Johnsgard, 1965).

Nesting and Brooding Behavior: The lesser scaup is one of the latest of the prairie-nesting ducks to begin nest-building and egg-laying, although the possible advantage of such late nesting remains obscure. Not only does predation intensity tend to increase late in the season, but also renesting opportunities are reduced (Rogers, 1964).

The length of time required for nest-building apparently has not been reported, but it is probable that eggs are laid on a daily basis. The male normally deserts the female when incubation begins (Oring, 1964), although he sometimes remains as late as the middle of incubation (Hochbaum, 1944).

Following hatching, the brood is led to water and brood rearing occurs in the relatively open water of large marshes. Females normally take good care of their young and usually feign injury when their broods are endangered. Frequently two females will jointly care for their merged broods, and, when threatened, one will remain behind to threaten or feign injury while the other leads the combined brood to safety (Munro, 1941). Feigning injury and other defensive behavior decreases as the season progresses, and late in the season the females may simply attempt avoidance rather than defend their young (Hochbaum, 1944).

Postbreeding Behavior: In lesser scaup and related pochard species a relatively long period may elapse between the time the male abandons his mate and when he finally becomes flightless. Oring (1964) reported that this period may be as much as six weeks in the lesser scaup and the redhead. During this time the males gather in groups in favored areas. Hochbaum (1944) noted that male lesser scaup and redheads gather in bands, moving from the Delta, Manitoba, marsh to the adjacent lake every morning and evening from mid-June through July. As July advances they spend more of the daylight hours on the lake and finally remain there permanently, to undergo their wing molt in late July and August.

SEA DUCKS
Tribe Mergini

The sea ducks are a group of mostly arctic-adapted diving ducks that usually winter in coastal waters and typically breed in tundra situations or in northern forests. All twenty species (two of which are now extinct) depend predominantly on animal sources of food, and some feed exclusively on such materials. These foods include shellfish, mollusks, other invertebrates, and aquatic vertebrates such as fish. In general the sea ducks are thus not regarded as highly as table birds as are the surface-feeding ducks and some of the more vegetarian pochard species. Like the pochards, their legs are placed well to the rear and their feet are unusually large; thus the birds have sacrificed the ability to walk easily for their diving adaptations. Also in common with pochards, their generally heavier bodies relative to wing surface area prevent them from taking flight without running some distance over the water prior to reaching minimum flight speed. In the air they often make up in speed for their limited maneuverability, although some of the largest sea ducks are rather ponderous in flight. Some species exhibit a good deal of white on the wings while in flight, and, unlike the pochards, two species have iridescent speculum patterns. The arctic-breeding and tundra-nesting forms typically build open-cup nests in low vegetation, while the forest-nesting species often use hollow trees or other natural cavities for their nest sites. Some of these tree-nesting species have moderately long tails and can perch fairly well, but the larger eiders and scoters rarely stray far from the water's edge and are rather helpless on land.

Of the total of twenty species of sea ducks, North America is well endowed with fifteen extant breeding species, as well as the extinct Labrador duck. Further, the Old World smew has been reported several times in recent years, so that the only species not reported from North America are two Southern Hemisphere mergansers and an Asian species of merganser. Most of the North American species also occur extensively in the Old World, with the bufflehead, surf scoter, Barrow goldeneye, and hooded merganser being the exceptions.

361

COMMON EIDER

Somateria mollissima (Linnaeus) 1758

Other Vernacular Names: American Eider, Northern Eider, Pacific Eider.

Range: Breeds in a circumpolar distribution on Greenland, Iceland, the British Isles, Scandinavia, Novaya Zemlya, northeastern Siberia, and Kamchatka; and in North America from the Aleutian Islands and the Alaska Peninsula to western and northern coastal Alaska, the arctic coast of the Yukon and the Northwest Territories and offshore islands; Hudson Bay, Labrador, Newfoundland, the Gulf of St. Lawrence, New Brunswick, Nova Scotia, and coastal Maine. In North America, winters in coastal areas of the Pacific south to Washington and along the Atlantic coast south to the middle Atlantic states, with casual occurrences inland.

Subspecies (based on Delacour, 1959):

S. m. borealis (Brehm): Northern Common Eider. In North America breeds from Greenland and northeastern Canada to northern Hudson Bay, where it intergrades with *dresseri*.

S. m. dresseri Sharpe: American Common Eider. Breeds in southern Labrador, Newfoundland, the Gulf of St. Lawrence, Nova Scotia, and Maine. Also breeds in southern Hudson Bay and James Bay, a population recognized by the A.O.U. as *S. m. sedentaria* Snyder and probably a valid race, but not recognized by Delacour.

S. m. v-nigra Bonaparte: Pacific Common Eider. In North America, breeds from northern Alaska east to Coronation Gulf and the Northwest Territories, and south to the Aleutian Islands, Kodiak Island, and the south side of the Alaska Peninsula to Cook Inlet and Glacier Bay.

Measurements (after Phillips, 1926):
  Folded wing: Males 269-328, females 266-295 mm.
  Culmen: Males 49-61, females 44-57 mm.
Weights: Nelson and Martin (1953) reported that eight American eider males averaged 4.4 pounds (1,995 grams), and eight females averaged 3.4 pounds (1,542 grams), with maximums of 4.6 pounds and 3.8 pounds, respectively. One male northern eider weighed 3.4 pounds (1,542 grams), while nine females also averaged 3.4 pounds, with a maximum of 4.3 pounds. Eight male Pacific eiders averaged 5.7 pounds (2,585 grams), and four females averaged 5.4 pounds (2,449 grams), with respective maximums of 6.2 and 6.4 pounds.

IDENTIFICATION

In the Hand: In the hand, specimens may be immediately recognized as eiders by the somewhat sickle-shaped tertials and the irregular basal feathering of the bill, plus the rather large body that usually weighs in excess of three pounds. The common eider differs from all other eiders in having a lateral extension of feathering on the side of the bill that tapers to a point below the rear tip of the nostrils and an unfeathered extension of the bill that extends nearly to the eyes; these are present in both sexes and all ages. The bill color and the width of this unfeathered extension toward the eyes varies with different subspecies. Should the bill and head characteristics not be available for observation, the combination of brown barring on the sides or mantle and a folded wing length greater than 250 mm. will separate female common eiders from spectacled eiders. For adult males, the presence of white or mostly white tertials and a folded wing length in excess of 270 mm. will separate common eiders from spectacled eiders and king eiders.

In the Field: On the water, common eiders may be recognized at great distances by the male's white mantle color, which extends downward on the breast to the anterior base of the wings. King eiders have a black mantle, and spectacled eiders have blackish color extending partway up the breast toward the front of the neck. Female common eiders are less rusty-toned and paler than female king eiders and are vertically barred with dark brown rather than having crescentic brown markings. In flight, common eiders fly in a straight course with strong wing strokes; the males exhibit a continuous white mantle between their white upper wing coverts and have a black crown-stripe that is lacking in the other eiders. Male common eiders utter rather loud cooing sounds during courtship similar to those of mourning doves, but lack the tremulous quality of king eider calls. Female calls are loud and hoarse, often sounding like *gog-gog-gog,* and lack the wooden tone of king eider calls.

AGE AND SEX CRITERIA

Sex Determination: By the first spring of life, male eiders will have acquired at least some white feathers on their breasts, which together with the white upper wing coverts should be evident in any plumage. Even in the juvenal plumage the male has a lighter chest than the female.

Age Determination: Age criteria for females have not been worked out, but juveniles of either sex should be recognizable by the notched tail feather criterion. Older females should be examined internally as to the state of their reproductive organs, while males can probably be aged according to the distinctions mentioned for first-year and second-year king eider males. Reproductive maturity probably occurs in the second spring of life, although such males still retain gray coloration on their upper wing coverts.

DISTRIBUTION AND HABITAT

Breeding Distribution and Habitat: In North America the common eider has the most extensive breeding range of any of the four eider species, from the Aleutian Islands on the west to Newfoundland on the east, and from about 43° to 80° N. latitude (Maine to Ellesmere Island).

In Alaska, Pacific common eiders nest on the Aleutian Islands, Kodiak Islands, the adjacent Alaska Peninsula eastward to Cook Inlet, northward in coastal tundra along the Bering coast, and on Nunivak and St. Lawrence islands. They also breed from Tigara and Wainwright along the arctic coast westward to Demarcation Point (Gabrielson and Lincoln, 1959).

In Canada the species breeds along the Yukon and Mackenzie coastline eastward to at least Bathurst Inlet, from the Melville Peninsula southward along the coastline of Hudson Bay to James Bay, along the eastern shores of Hudson Bay, and on the Atlantic coastline of eastern Canada to the mouth of the St. Lawrence River. It also breeds in Newfoundland and the Maritime Provinces with the possible exception of Prince Edward Island. In the Franklin District its breeding range includes the coastlines of Baffin and Southampton islands, the smaller Hudson Bay islands, and at least parts of Banks, Victoria, Somerset, Cornwallis, Devon, and Ellesmere islands (Godfrey, 1966). Victoria Island and Bathurst Inlet evidently represent the eastern limits of the Pacific race, and there is seemingly a hiatus between the breeding range of this form and the more easterly races.

South of Canada, the only state having any breeding eiders is Maine, which has long had nesting eiders (Gross, 1944), but which has also had

Breeding (hatched) and wintering (shaded) distributions of the common eider in North America. Horizontal hatching indicates breeding range of Pacific, vertical hatching northern, and diagonal hatching American common eiders.

remarkable population increases in recent years. Thus, the Muscongus Bay population rose from an estimated 800 birds in 1949 to over 6,000 in 1959, and by 1965 had probably reached 7,000 (*Audubon Field Notes,* 19:523). The southwestern breeding limits in Maine are at Mark Island, Casco Bay (A.O.U., 1957).

The preferred breeding habitat of common eiders consists of low-lying rocky marine shores having numerous islands; there is also rare utilization of sandy islands and coastal freshwater lakes or rivers (Snyder, 1957). Hildén (1964) found the highest nesting abundance on boulder-covered islands, with very little use of gravel- or rock-covered ones. He also reported that grassy islands have highest usage, followed by those covered with herbaceous and, lastly, wooded vegetation. Most eiders selected central parts of islets, rather than the shoreline area, for nesting, perhaps as a reflection of their adaptation to tidal changes and also the scarcity of fine soil between the rocks to serve as nest substrates. Open terrain with extensive water areas, sparsely wooded islands with barren shores, as well as a proximity to marine foods, are basic aspects of its habitat requirements.

Wintering Distribution and Habitat: The Pacific common eider winters throughout the Aleutian Islands and in the Bering Sea, where they are sometimes abundant around the Pribilof Islands and occasionally at St. Lawrence Island (Gabrielson and Lincoln, 1959). Fay (1960) stated that upwards of 50,000 eiders (both Pacific common and king eiders) winter about St. Lawrence Island, although the king eider is much commoner and the Pacific eider is most prevalent during spring and summer months. There is probably also a western movement of birds from northwestern Canada around northern Alaska to wintering areas in the Bering Sea (Godfrey, 1965).

The remaining North American races of the common eider all winter in eastern Canada and along the Atlantic coast of the United States. In Canada wintering birds occur from southern Baffin Island and the islands north of Hudson Bay southward into Hudson and James bays and eastward to the Maritime Provinces (Godfrey, 1965). Probably most Canadian eiders winter in the waters off southern Greenland and the Labrador coast (Snyder, 1957). Regular wintering south of Canada occurs only along the coast of Maine, although birds sometimes occur as far south as New York and New Jersey, with casual occurrences as far south as North Carolina (A.O.U., 1957).

In winter common eiders are almost strictly marine birds, usually remaining well off shore and generally out of sight from land. No doubt the availability of their winter foods (mollusks and some crustaceans), as determined by their abundance and water depth, are primary aspects of wintering habitat.

GENERAL BIOLOGY

Age at Maturity: Although it has been suggested that eiders do not mature before their third year (Delacour, 1959:19), Lack (1968) cited unpublished data by H. Milne indicating that female common eiders probably first breed when two years old and males possibly not until a year later.

Pair Bond Pattern: Pair bonds are renewed annually during the winter or spring months. Males desert their mates early in the incubation period and often then directly migrate out to sea (Cooch, 1965). Since many, but not all, birds are paired on their arrival, it would seem that pair formation may occur during migration or on the breeding grounds, according to Cooch. Kenyon (1961) noted that in the Pacific common eider pairing occurred in early or mid-May, about a month prior to the start of egg-laying. Thus, the pair bond of at least some eiders may last no more than a month or two.

Nest Location: Cooch (1965) reported that at Cape Dorset the northern common eiders favored nesting areas sheltered by rocks over flat, open and grassy areas by a factor of about 9 to 1. They also often placed their nests under rock overhangs, and they tended to select ridges that were well drained and normally were snow-free early in the season. About 40 percent of the nests found were within 100 feet of water, but at least 10 percent were more than 900 feet from water, so that immediate proximity to water is not necessary. Hildén (1964) similarly found that the birds were about ten times as abundant on boulder-covered islets than on either gravelly or rocky islets, and favored those dominated by grassy rather than herbaceous or wooded vegetation. In his area the eiders were not socially attracted to gulls or terns, but in a Spitsbergen study it was reported that nesting in association with arctic terns (*Sterna paradisaea*) increased nesting success (Ahlén and Andersson, 1970).

Clutch Size: Although average clutch sizes between 4.5 and 5.5 eggs appear to be typical of common eiders in both Scotland (Marshall, 1967) and Finland (Hildén, 1964), the populations of eastern North America average between 3.25 and 4.04 eggs (Paynter, 1951). The modal clutch size of the Pacific common eider also appears to be 4 eggs (Kenyon, 1961), with a maximum of 6. Cooch (1965) similarly reported an average clutch size of 4.06 eggs for 188 first nestings of the northern common eider, as compared with 2.33 eggs in 12 renesting attempts. Eggs are normally laid at the rate of one per day, according to Cooch. Guignion (1969) reported an average of 4.3 eggs for completed clutches of the American common eider, and Freeman (1970) found that in the Hudson Bay population 536 nests averaged 4.5 eggs.

Incubation Period: Cooch (1965) estimated a 28- to 30-day incubation period for wild northern common eiders. Guignion (1969) established that the American common eider had a 25- to 26-incubation period under natural conditions, with nests in less disturbed areas hatching in a day less than those subject to some disturbance. Under artificial conditions incubation requires 24 to 25 days (Rolnik, 1943).

Fledging Period: Cooch (1965) estimated a 60-day fledging period for northern common eiders. Other estimates by workers in Europe and Asia have ranged from 60 to 75 days (Bauer and Glutz, 1969).

Nest and Egg Losses: Cooch (1965) reported that at Cape Dorset, predation and other losses accounted for 25 percent of all eggs laid during one season and 15 percent the following one. However, there was some renesting, which tended to offset these losses. Three avian predators, the raven, the herring gull, and the parasitic jaeger, were present on the area, but the losses caused by jaegers were believed negligible. Hildén (1964) reported a similar nesting success of 78 percent in Finland, which was lower than that of any other species in his study area. He attributed the high rate of nest failure, which was primarily caused by crows, ravens, and human interference, to the eiders' exposed nests, their failure to return rapidly after being flushed from the nest, their tendency to desert nests, and their early initiation of nesting. Choate (1967) reported that nest predation caused losses of 58 percent of 448 nests in Maine, over half of these losses occurring on incompleted nests. He found that larger clutches had a greater chance than smaller ones of success, which was considered to be possibly related to the age of the nesting female or her relative attachment to the clutch. Nests under cow parsnip (*Heracleum*), which provided cover for 426 of 963 nests, or under shrubs had higher hatching success than those placed in grasses or nightshade (*Solanum*). Gulls, including great black-backed and herring, that had caused partial predation on a clutch were often found to return and complete its destruction. An overall hatching success of 39 percent was found during each of two years of study. On Spitsbergen, arctic foxes and glaucous gulls were responsible for very high rates of nest and egg destruction (Ahlén and Andersson, 1970).

Juvenile Mortality: Little information is available on prefledging mortality of young, largely because of brood merger, which is so prevalent in this species. Cooch (1965) believed that adverse weather, disease, and predation by various avian and mammalian predators might all play roles in determining juvenile mortality rates. Gulls (herring and glaucous) and ravens were observed chasing or attacking ducklings, especially during the first week after hatching. Hildén (1964) estimated that over a three-year period and from a total of 1026 eggs, 773 ducklings hatched and only 208 young survived to the end of the brood season. Single broods seemingly suffered fewer losses than did combined broods, although such brood merger has generally been considered an adaptation against gull predation. The great black-backed gull is evidently the worst duckling predator in Finland, but other causes of duckling mortality appeared to be disease, parasites, and, to a limited extent, weather. Hildén found that the number of young surviving until late in the brood season ranged in different years from 0.1 to 2.5 young per pair, or from 1.3 to 3.0 per female he observed escorting ducklings.

Estimates of postfledging mortality of juveniles are still unavailable.

Adult Mortality: Boyd (1962) estimated the annual adult mortality rate of the European common eider as 39 percent.

GENERAL ECOLOGY

Food and Foraging: The importance of bivalve mollusks, especially the common blue mussel (*Mytilus edulis*), has long been recognized as a fundamental feature of the diet of common eiders. Dementiev and Gladkov (1967) reported that this species of *Mytilus* occurred in a sample of stomachs from Russian (eastern Murman) birds at a frequency of 70.3 percent, compared with 40.5 percent for *Balanus* barnacles and 24.3 percent for *Littorina* mollusks. In these and other samples various crustaceans (amphipods), echinoderms (seastars and sea urchins), and fish (sticklebacks) occurred. Summer samples of juveniles and females showed amphipods, univalve mollusks, and ripening crowberries (*Empetrum*) present. Apparently periwinkles (*Littorina*) are a prime source of foods for young ducklings.

A large sample of eiders taken between October and February in Danish waters supports the general view that mollusks (such as the bivalve *Mytilus* and the univalve periwinkle *Littorina*), crustaceans (especially the crabs *Carcinus* and *Balanus*), and sea stars (*Asterias*) are predominant parts of the winter diet of common eiders (Madsen, 1954). In an Alaskan sample of 61 Pacific common eiders, mollusks constituted 46 percent, crustaceans 30.7 percent, and echinoderms 14.4 percent of the food volumes found. A sample of 96 American common eiders showed the same relative importance of these three food sources, but a higher total consumption (81.7 percent) of mollusks (Cottam, 1939).

Cottam (1939) described the usual foraging behavior of common eiders as diving from a point usually just beyond the surf, detaching mussels from rocky bottoms, and taking relatively few species of animal foods each meal. The birds dive to moderate depths, forage particularly at low tide, and at least during fall and winter apparently feed only during daylight. At night they move to the open ocean, sometimes many miles from their foraging areas.

Sociality, Densities, Territoriality: The high degree of sociality exhibited by nesting eiders is well established and perhaps reflects their island-nesting tendencies and the gradual buildup of nesting groups in local areas protected from avian and mammalian predators. Thus Choate (1967) reported overall nesting densities of 3.8 to 8.9 nests per 1,000 square feet on various islands in Penobscot Bay. On smaller study areas within these islands higher densities (4.3 to 136.4 nests per 1,000 square feet) were found. However, he found no relationship between nesting densities and nesting success. Guignion (1969) reported an even higher average nesting density (16 nests per 1,000 square feet) on one islet that he studied. These densities are apparently well above those found by Cooch (1965), who noted that one ridge 8 acres in size supported over 100 nests (or about 0.3 per 1,000 square feet), or Marshall (1967), who reported up to 100 breeding birds per acre (or about 2 per 1,000 square feet). Manning *et al.* (1956) noted that there were an estimated 250 Pacific common eider nests on a sandy, sparsely vegetated island measuring 150 by 70 yards, or a maximum of about 2 acres.

Thus it would appear that nesting "territories" of 100 to 300 square feet are not uncommon in dense eider colonies. Prior to the start of incubation the pair may spend a good deal of time resting on communal loafing areas, but Cooch (1965) did not observe the male actively defending his mate on such areas. Since males also only visit the nest site when the female is in the process of egg-laying, it is apparent that there can be no effective male defense of the nest site either.

Interspecific Relationships: The obviously close relationship of the common and king eiders would suggest possible competition for food, nests, or other aspects of their biology. Pettingill (1959, 1962) observed mixed pairing and reported a presumed hybrid that apparently resulted from male king eiders mating with female common eiders nesting in Iceland, which is outside the king eider's breeding range. In areas where both species nest, their differences in preferred nesting habitats and substrates would probably tend to reduce such contacts.

The preferred foods of common eiders, such as *Mytilus* mussels and crabs, are virtually identical to those of king eiders, scoters, and, to lesser extent, some of the other sea ducks (Cottam, 1939). However, the usual abundance of such foods makes it unlikely that significant competition normally occurs.

Perhaps the most important relationships with other birds are those with ravens and large gulls, such as the great black-backed and glaucous. Nearly all nesting studies have indicated considerable losses to such egg and young duckling predators, as noted earlier. Diseases and parasitic infections have also been reported as possible causes of juvenile mortality by some investigators.

General Activity Patterns and Movements: That eiders exhibit marked daily periodicities in their behavior was established by Gorman (1970), who determined the frequencies of male displays throughout the daylight hours. He determined a dawn and dusk peak of display, with the one associated with sunrise higher than the one at sunset, and several bursts of activity throughout the day, interspersed with resting periods. There was also a tidal periodicity, with display being higher during periods of floods and ebb tides and lower during times of high and low tides, when eiders are roosting and foraging, respectively.

Virtually no information is available on the local or migratory movements of eiders. Atkinson-Willes (1963) considered the eider population in Great Britain to be as sedentary as any species of duck can be, and perhaps the same applies to the birds breeding in New England. The Hudson Bay population may also be fairly sedentary, but this cannot be true of the northern common eider or the Pacific common eider populations. Cooch noted that the order of fall migration of the northern common eider from Cape Dorset was the reverse of that seen in spring, with the males and subadults of both sexes apparently leaving first, followed by adult females and their offspring. In spring the males are first to arrive.

SOCIAL AND SEXUAL BEHAVIOR

Flocking Behavior: The flock sizes of migrant birds arriving at Cape Dorset in spring was studied by Cooch (1965), who noted that the earliest flocks consisted of about 10 to 17 birds, but flock sizes progressively diminished as the sex ratio equalized, so that the latest arrivals were in groups of about 2 to 4 birds, with the sexes equally represented.

During the fall migration flock sizes are considerably larger. The data of Thompson and Person (1963) for Point Barrow illustrate this nicely. Between mid-July and early September they estimated that a million eiders (king and Pacific common) fly over this point on the way to molting and/or wintering areas. The usual sequence for both species is for adult males to arrive first, followed by flocks of mixed sexes, and lastly juveniles. The mean flock size for both species was 105 birds, and the modal flock size was 26 to 50 birds. The largest flock seen was estimated at 1,100 birds.

Pair-forming Behavior: In captive birds pair-forming behavior in common eiders begins in winter shortly after the birds have attained their nuptial plumage, and it is probable that some winter courting activities also occur in wild birds (Hoogerheide, 1950). McKinney (1961) thought that pair formation in European common eiders might occur at any time from March to May. Kenyon (1961) reported May pairing in the Pacific common eider, and Cooch (1965) reported a high incidence of courtship behavior in late May.

The pair-forming patterns of the European and Pacific races of the common eider were described and compared by McKinney (1961) and limited observations on the northern and American races indicate that these forms have male display patterns nearly identical to those of the European race (Johnsgard, 1965; Cooch, 1965). Male pair-forming displays consist of a variety of relatively ritualized comfort movements such as preening, bathing, wing-flapping and wing-shaking, and several differing "cooing movements" associated with dovelike calls. McKinney recognized three individual types of cooing movements, as well as two compound combinations of these movements that occurred in the European but not in the Pacific race. Although a turning-of-the-back-of-the-head toward the female does not occur, a conspicuous lateral swinging movement of the head is present ("head-turning") and often precedes or follows other displays. McKinney regarded preening and neck-stretching as predominantly sexually motivated, while the cooing movement displays appeared to be largely associated with attack or escape tendencies. McKinney believed that the overall function of social courtship in eiders is to allow individual pair formation to occur, but did not observe specific instances of mate selection by females. He suggested that the more aggressive male which swims closer to the female, might tend to intimidate other males, and, if he is accepted by the female, would be effective in keeping other males away from her.

Copulatory Behavior: McKinney (1961) observed copulations in the European common eider from late February until early May, or more than two months before the first eggs were laid. The female assumes a prone posture early in the precopulatory situation, although it is at least often true that the male initiates the copulatory sequence. His displays include virtually all of those that may be seen in social courtship situations, but include relatively few cooing movements. Instead there is a high incidence (in the European race) of preening, bathing, neck-stretching, and shaking. The order of these displays is not rigid, but mounting is usually immediately preceded by head-turning or a cooing movement. In the Pacific race, bill-dipping, bathing, preening, and shaking are the most common precopulatory displays, and the last display prior to mounting is usually shaking or head-turning. During treading the male holds the female's nape, and in both races the male typically performs a single cooing movement display and swims away from the female while head-turning. The female's postcopulatory behavior is variable, but usually includes bathing (McKinney, 1961).

Nesting and Brooding Behavior: Cooch's (1965) study of the northern common eider at Cape Dorset provides a useful summary of nesting behavior. Female eiders evidently often return to nest sites used in prior years and prepare them for reuse by churning up the old detritus with the bill, to permit air to circulate and dry out the site. New sites are usually prepared on the same day that the first egg is laid. Most females visit their nests only at high tide during the egg-laying period and may begin to deposit down with the first egg or later. Most females begin incubation after laying their third egg, according to Cooch, even though a fourth may be laid. They may drink and bathe during the early part of incubation, but evidently little or no food is consumed during the entire period prior to hatching.

The first egg laid is the first to hatch, and up to an additional 24 hours may be required before all of the eggs have hatched. One or two additional days may be needed to dry the young thoroughly and prepare them to leave the nest. The brood is then led to tidal pools, sometimes as far as 1,000 feet from the nest. At first the ducklings feed almost entirely on the surface, but gradually gain in diving efficiency. They begin to feed on mosquito larvae a few days after hatching and later shift to other invertebrate food. As they develop, a tendency for brood merger becomes increasingly evident, and large creches of eider ducklings typically form.

Studies by Gorman and Milne (1972) on creche behavior of common eiders in Scotland indicate that the adult females guarding creches were mainly birds that had recently hatched young and that they remained with the creche only a few days before leaving it, presumably to forage and recover the body weight lost during incubation. Creche behavior is thus not typical of eider populations in areas where food sources suitable for both adults and ducklings are present in the same habitats.

Postbreeding Behavior: Males typically desert their mates when incubation starts or very early in the incubation period. The males then move back out to sea and probably begin the postbreeding migration to molting areas. Little is known of the distance of these migrations or the locations of molting areas, which are presumably well out from shore. Cooch believed that females molt while their broods are still flightless and that both the young and the females attain flight at about the same time. However, he noted only a few flightless adults in his study area, and it is probable that at least some of the females also undertake a molt migration to other areas.

KING EIDER

Somateria spectabilis (Linnaeus) 1758

Other Vernacular Names: None in general use.

Range: Breeds in a circumpolar distribution on Greenland, northern Russia,
Siberia, northern Alaska, and the arctic coasts of Canada including most
of the arctic islands, and perhaps the northern coast of Labrador. Winters
on the north Pacific, especially along the Aleutian Islands, sometimes south
as far as California; on the Atlantic coast from southern Greenland to Newfoundland, with occasional records to Georgia; and sometimes strays inland,
especially on the Great Lakes.

Subspecies: None recognized.

Measurements (after Delacour, 1959):

Folded wing: Males 275-290, females 260-282 mm.

Culmen: Males 28-34, females 35-35 mm.

Weights: Nelson and Martin (1953) reported that 14 males averaged 4.0 pounds (1,814 grams), while 9 females averaged 3.6 pounds (1,633 grams), with maximum weights of 4.4 pounds (1,995 grams) and 4.1 pounds (1,859 grams), respectively. Thompson and Person (1963) reported that 41 adult males averaged 3.68 pounds (1,668 grams) in August, while 140 adult females from the same period averaged 3.46 pounds (1,567 grams), or considerably less than the averages of Nelson and Martin. Most of these birds are apparently spring specimens, taken during the Brandt expedition to Hooper Bay, and reported on by both Conover (1926) and Brandt (1943).

IDENTIFICATION

In the Hand: Easily recognized as an eider on the basis of its sickle-shaped tertials and the extension of feathering along the sides and top of the bill, the king eider is the only eider (see also surf scoter) in which the feathering on the culmen extends farther forward than the lateral extension near the base of the bill. The unfeathered area between these two extensions is generally wider than in common eiders, particularly in males, where it is greatly enlarged. Females are the only large eiders (folded wing 260-282 mm.) that exhibit crescent-shaped dark markings on the mantle and sides of the body.

In the Field: On the water, male king eiders show more black color than any of the other eiders, with the rear half of the body appearing black except for a narrow white line where the wings insert in the flanks and a white patch on the sides of the rump. The black "thorn feathers" among the rear scapulars protrude above the back conspicuously; in the common eider these either are not evident or are white (Pacific race). The enlarged reddish base of the bill is evident at great distances, even when the birds are in flight. Females are distinctly more reddish than female common eiders; they have crescentic body markings and a definite decumbent crest, which corresponds to the unique bluish feather area on the male. In flight, king eiders are slightly less bulky and ponderous than common eiders, and in a flock containing males the discontinuity of the white on their breasts and upper wing coverts caused by the black back color is plainly evident. Calls of the female king eider include loud *gog-gog-gog* notes, like the noise produced by a hammer hitting a hollow wooden wall, while males utter tremulous cooing sounds during their aquatic courtship.

AGE AND SEX CRITERIA

Sex Determination: After the loss of the juvenal plumage, males exhibit some white on the breast or back, and even while in eclipse they retain some grayish or white feathers among the upper wing coverts.

Age Determination: Young females are probably not readily separable from adults after losing their juvenal notched tail feathers. First-year males have a generally limited amount of white in the breast and rump, in second-year males the median wing coverts are margined or shaded with dusky, and in older males these feathers are entirely white.

DISTRIBUTION AND HABITAT

Breeding Distribution and Habitat: The North American breeding distribution of the king eider is not quite as extensive as that of the common eider, and in general it is more typically arctic, with the southernmost breeding occurring at about 55° N. latitude.

In Alaska the king eider apparently breeds at only a few locations, with most of the records from near Barrow. To the west it breeds regularly but sparingly to Point Hope, Tigara, and Cape Thompson, and to the east it evidently breeds at Cambden Bay, Barter Island, and Humphrey Point (Gabrielson and Lincoln, 1959).

The Canadian breeding range is extensive but seemingly disruptive, occurring along the arctic coastlines of the Yukon and the Mackenzie and Keewatin districts, and locally on the west coast of Hudson Bay southward as far as Cape Henrietta Maria and South Twin Island. There are a few known areas of breeding records from the arctic coast of Quebec, but Labrador breeding is uncertain. Breeding apparently also occurs on most of the islands in the Franklin District, northward to northern Ellesmere Island and adjacent Greenland (Godfrey, 1965). The breeding population of Victoria Island may be as high as 800,000 birds (Parmelee *et al.,* 1967).

The preferred breeding habitat consists of freshwater ponds on arctic tundra or amid lakes and streams not far from the coast. In a few instances they have been found nesting just above the high tide lines of seacoasts, but more commonly they may be found in the vicinity of fresh water (Godfrey, 1965; Snyder, 1957).

Wintering Distribution and Habitat: Wintering in Alaska occurs on at least the eastern Aleutian Islands east to Kodiak Island and the adjacent coast of the Alaska Peninsula (Gabrielson and Lincoln, 1959). The birds also winter in large numbers around St. Lawrence Island, making up the majority of the 50,000 or so eiders that occur there (Fay, 1961).

Breeding (hatched) and wintering (shaded) distributions of the
king eider in North America.

The population of eastern North America mainly winters from southern Greenland to Newfoundland, in the Gulf of St. Lawrence, and along the Maritime Provinces, with smaller numbers reaching the New England states. According to the records of king eiders seen in the New England states during the winter of 1970–71, most of the flocks occurring that far south contain 10 to 20 birds and consist of females and immature males (*American Birds,* 25:549). The dividing line between those king eiders wintering in the Bering Sea and those that move eastward toward Greenland and the North Atlantic is not known, but some individuals from as far west as King William and Southampton islands have been found in later summer off west Greenland (Godfrey, 1965). Parmelee *et al.* (1967) judged that part of the population breeding on Victoria Island probably migrated west and part to the east.

Wintering habitats consist of the open sea or coastlines that have sources of food (mussels, etc.) at depths sufficiently shallow to permit easy diving. The birds tend to forage farther from shore than do oldsquaws and scoters, although they are seemingly less-efficient divers than the oldsquaws. Cottam (1939) summarized evidence favoring the view that king eiders forage in deeper waters than do common eiders, and indeed deeper than any other duck with the possible exception of the oldsquaw. There is in fact one record of a bird apparently diving to a depth of 180 feet and returning with mollusks in its gullet.

GENERAL BIOLOGY

Age at Maturity: There is no good evidence on this point. The eiders that bred at the Wildfowl Trust were several years old when they initially nested (Johnstone, 1961). On the basis of plumage succession, Bent (1925) and Dementiev and Gladkov (1967) judged that maturity is probably reached during the third year of life.

Pair Bond Pattern: Pair bonds are renewed yearly during social courtship. This process has not been studied in wild birds, but at least in captivity the period of courtship display occurs over several winter and spring months.

Nest Location: Manning *et al.* (1956) noted that on Banks Island the king eiders usually nested beside lakes, on small islands in lakes, or in low marshy country, but sometimes utilized almost bare hillsides. Siberian observers report nesting on low mossy tundra near small lakes or rivers at varying distances from the sea, on dry grassy tundra, and occasionally also on high-growing tundra with knotweed (*Polygonum*) present. Nests are usually well scattered, but where predation by foxes is prevalent dense nesting groups sometimes occur on river islands (Dementiev and Gladkov, 1967).

Parmelee *et al.* (1967) found about twenty-five nests on dry, often rocky, slopes in Victoria Island, none of which were near water and one of which was about a quarter mile from water. The closest nests they noted were 200 yards apart.

Clutch Size: Parmelee *et al.* (1967) reported clutch sizes for twenty-seven nests, which averaged 5.04 eggs. The normal clutch range appears to be 3 to 6 eggs, although larger and apparently multiple clutches of up to 16 eggs have been reported (Bailey, 1948).

Incubation Period: Parmelee *et al.* (1967) found that the incubation period of naturally incubated eggs was between 22 and 24 days. This is close to the 22- to 23-day period reported for artificially incubated eggs (Johnstone, 1961, 1970).

Fledging Period: Not yet reported.

Nest and Egg Losses: No specific studies on nesting losses have been done, but earlier writers have reported egg losses to both foxes and gulls (Phillips, 1926).

Juvenile Mortality: No doubt gulls and jaegers consume some newly hatched king eider ducklings; the large "nurseries" of ducklings of both this species and the common eider have usually been regarded as a means of reducing the magnitude of such losses. However, estimates of mortality for both unfledged and fledged juveniles do not appear to be available.

Adult Mortality: No estimates of adult mortality rates are available. The oldest known ages attained by wild birds are in excess of ten and fifteen years (Salomonsen, 1965).

GENERAL ECOLOGY

Food and Foraging: Foods much like those taken by the common eider appear to make up the diet of adult king eiders, with an emphasis on bivalve mollusks (especially *Mytilis* mussels), crabs (especially *Cancer* and *Dermaturus*), and echinoderms (especially sand dollars and sea urchins). Probably no other duck consumes such a high incidence of echinoderms as the king eider, nor are such a wide variety of echinoderm types usually consumed. Sand dollars and sea urchins are favored foods, but sea stars, brittle stars, and sea cucumbers have also been found in king eider digestive tracts (Cottam, 1939). Evidently eelgrass (*Zostera*) is one of the few plant foods of notable importance to king eiders, although relatively few specimens collected on the summer nesting grounds have yet been analyzed.

Because the king eider forages so far from shore, in even deeper water than related species, virtually nothing can be said of its foraging periodicities or behavior.

Sociality, Densities, Territoriality: Apparently king eiders normally are not social nesters, and only in areas where small river islands provide protection from arctic foxes do dense nesting colonies develop (Dementiev and Gladkov, 1967). More typically the nests are well scattered and several hundred yards from others of the species (Parmelee *et al.* 1967). Breeding densities are thus probably rather low in most areas, but no detailed estimates are available. If the estimate of 800,000 king eiders mentioned earlier for Victoria Island is at all close to correct, the density would be at least 10 birds per square mile for the island as a whole, and much of its interior is obviously unsuited for eiders. Banks Island, with a total land area of about 25,000 square miles, has an estimated king eider population of some 150,000 birds, or about 6 per square mile for the island as a whole (Manning *et al.*, 1956).

Interspecific Relationships: King eiders do not normally nest among common eiders, but in a few instances male king eiders have been seen intruding in common eider colonies. This has led to some instances of mixed pairing and possible hybridization (Pettingill, 1959, 1962).

The relationship of king eiders to gulls, ravens, foxes, and other possible predators of eggs and young is not yet established but is probably comparable to that indicated for the common eider. Parmelee *et al.* (1967) noted probable egg losses to jaegers and losses of both ducklings and adults caused by Eskimos.

General Activity Patterns and Movements: At least during the summer months, this high-arctic species is probably active at all hours. At Point Barrow spring migration predominantly occurs during day, with a midday pause and with midmorning and midafternoon peaks. In late summer the return migration is more continuous, starting about daybreak (or between 3 and 4 a.m.) and continuing virtually without interruption until sunset, or about 9 p.m. (Bent, 1925).

The late summer migration of king eiders past Barrow is justifiably famous, and has been mentioned by several writers. Thompson and Person (1963) have provided the most recent account of this migration. They reported that migrating eiders may be seen at almost any time during a twenty-four-hour period, but counts made during morning and evening averaged about twice as high as those made during midday. They estimated that at least a million eiders went over Barrow between mid-July and early September, including both common and king eiders. Reports of up to 75,000 king eiders per day crossing the Bering Strait in early to mid-May have also been made (Dementiev and Gladkov, 1967).

SOCIAL AND SEXUAL BEHAVIOR

Flocking Behavior: Mass assemblages of immature and molting birds are known to occur around Kolguev Island, and to a lesser extent at Vaigach Island and the west coast of Novaya Zemlya. The vicinity of Kolguev Island is a major molting area for adults, and immatures remain there throughout the year in the tens of thousands. Another area of congregation of immatures is along the coasts of the Chukot Peninsula and coastal Alaska from Point Barrow to the vicinity of Nunivak Island (Dementiev and Gladkov, 1967). In eastern North America the waters off the coast of west-central Greenland likewise attract vast numbers of molting birds (Salomonsen, 1968).

Pair-forming Behavior: The distinctive pair-forming displays of this species have been described by Johnsgard (1964a, 1965) and Sherman (1965). The male displays include several ritualized comfort movements (bathing, wing-flapping, head-rolling, and general body-shaking, or upwards-stretch) as well as two displays that are obvious homologues of the common eider's "cooing movements" and head-turning. Some of these displays have a remarkable uniformity in time-duration characteristics of the displays themselves as well as the intervals between displays occurring in sequence. Sherman (1965) reported a strong tendency for successional "linkage" between certain displays, such as an association between wing-flapping and the upwards-stretch, the upwards-stretch and pushing, and bathing and wing-flapping. Wing-flapping is more highly stereotyped in the king eider than in any of the other eider species and conspicuously exhibits the male's underparts and throat markings during its performance (Johnsgard, 1964a, 1965).

Female pair-forming activities are virtually identical to those of common eiders, although the vocalizations produced are slightly different in the two species. Inciting appears to form a fundamental feature of social display and seems to be a primary means by which associations between individual males and females is achieved (Johnsgard, 1965).

Copulatory Behavior: Like the situation in the common eider, female king eiders indicate a readiness for copulation by gradually assuming a prone posture as the male performs a nearly continuous series of displays, including the two major courtship postures (pushing and reaching) and, more typically, the four ritualized comfort movements. Of these, bathing occurs most frequently, followed in sequence by the upwards-stretch, head-rolling, and wing-flapping. Bill-dipping and preening dorsally have also been seen. In at least two of four cases the display performed just prior to mounting was wing-flapping, and in a third it was the upwards-stretch. After each completed copulation the male released the female, performed a single reaching display, and then swam rapidly away from her while performing lateral head-turning movements (Johnsgard, 1964a).

Nesting and Brooding Behavior: Parmelee *et al.* (1967) have provided the most recent and most complete observations of nesting behavior by wild king eiders. During the egg-laying period the male closely attends his mate and follows her to the nest site for her egg-laying visits. Eggs are apparently laid at the rate of one per day. However, shortly after incubation begins the males desert their mates and rapidly move toward the coast to begin their molt migration. As in the common eider, it is likely that the female spends very little time off the nest during the 22- to 24-day incubation period. In at least one case, all of six eggs in one nest hatched within a 24-hour period. Brood merging is extremely common in this species and begins shortly after hatching. The numbers of females attending such "nurseries" varies, but up to a hundred or more young have been seen together, with up to nine females in attendance. Apparently many of the females which are displaced from their broods flock together and migrate out of the region before molting. The remaining females continue to attend the growing ducklings and may remain in the breeding areas until as late as September.

Postbreeding Behavior: Salomonsen (1968) reported that at the peak of the late-summer molt migration to western Greenland, some hundred thousand king eiders congregate in the waters off western Greenland. This total includes immature birds, some of which move directly into the area from their wintering quarters. Other immatures may approach the breeding range, but fail to complete their migration and return to the molting area in June. Few adult females move to Greenland to molt, but instead perform a later, shorter migration, probably to the vicinity of Clyde Inlet, Baffin Island. In September and October this population moves southward toward the ice-free areas of southwestern Greenland and to Labrador and Newfoundland.

According to Phillips (1926), the king eider is less predictable than the common eider in its migratory behavior, with individuals more frequently appearing in large lakes in the interior parts of the continent than is the case with common eiders. However, most of the stragglers that appear during fall and winter on inland waters are immature birds (Bent, 1925).

SPECTACLED EIDER

Somateria fischeri (Brandt) 1847

(Until 1973, regarded by the A.O.U. as *Lampronetta fischeri*)

Other Vernacular Names: None in general use.

Range: Breeds in eastern Siberia, and in North America along the west coast of Alaska, from Point Barrow or beyond south to St. Lawrence Island and the lower Kuskokwim River. Wintering area unknown, presumably in the north Pacific, but never observed in large numbers on the Aleutian Islands, where often presumed to winter.

Subspecies: None recognized.

Measurements (after Delacour, 1959):

Folded wing: Males 255-267, females 240-250 mm.

Culmen: Males 21-26, females 20-25 mm.

Weights: Nelson and Martin (1953) reported that eight males averaged 3.6 pounds (1,633 grams) and four females averaged the same, with maximum weights of 3.8 pounds (1,723 grams) and 3.9 pounds (1,769 grams), respectively.

IDENTIFICATION

In the Hand: Once determined to be an eider on the basis of its sickle-shaped tertials and partially feathered bill, spectacled eiders are easily recognized by the distinctive "spectacles" around the eyes or by the fact that the lateral surface of the bill from its base to a point above the nostrils is wholly feathered with short, velvety feathers. Females have brownish bodies with darker bars on the mantle and sides as in common eiders, but their smaller body size (maximum folded wing length 250 mm.) readily distinguishes them from that species if the head and bill characters cannot be examined.

In the Field: Male spectacled eiders are unmistakable in the field; the white eye-ring surrounded by green is visible for several hundred yards. Otherwise the top half of the bird appears white, while the bottom half is a dark silvery gray, including the lower breast. Females are generally tawny brown, with pale "spectacles" and a dark brown triangular area between the eye and the bill. Indeed, when females are crouching on nests these dark brown cheek markings are highly conspicuous and often reveal the female's presence. In flight, spectacled eiders fly with considerable agility, and the extension of the blackish underparts to a point well in front of the leading edge of the wings will serve to separate males from common eiders, while their white backs distinguish them from king eiders. Male spectacled eiders are unusually quiet, and their courtship calls are inaudible beyond about 20 yards. Female calls are very similar to those of the larger eiders.

AGE AND SEX CRITERIA

Sex Determination: During the first fall and winter, the upperparts of young males are darker than those of females, and the underparts are only faintly barred with dusky. In second-year and older males the upper wing coverts and tertials are grayish or white.

Age Determination: First-year males have buffy-edged upper wing coverts. The scapulars and probably also the upper coverts of second-year males are light gray, and those of older males are white. Juvenile females have spotted rather than barred underparts, and may still carry some notched tail feathers during the first fall, but somewhat older females are probably not distinguishable from adults on the basis of external features.

DISTRIBUTION AND HABITAT

Breeding Distribution and Habitat: The North American breeding distribution of the spectacled eider is limited to a few areas along coastal Alaska. There it apparently breeds locally from Baird Inlet north and east to Demarcation Point, and is probably most common in the vicinity of Igiak Bay and the adjacent coastal lowland tundra. Farther north, it evidently also nests near Point Hope, in the vicinity of Point Barrow, and eastward in the general region of capes Halkett and Simpson (Gabrielson and Lincoln, 1959). There is occasional nesting on St. Lawrence Island (Fay, 1961). It is uncommon but a probable breeder in the Cape Thompson area (Williamson *et al.,* 1966).

There are no indications of nesting in Canada, and indeed the only report of spectacled eiders there are visual records of males on Banks and Vancouver islands (Godfrey, 1966).

The preferred breeding habitat, judging from my observations at Igiak Bay, would seem to be rather luxuriant lowland tundra with small ponds and reasonable proximity to salt water. Fairly high grass of the past season's growth seemed to provide the basic nesting cover, and nearly all nests were placed fairly close to tundra ponds (Johnsgard, 1964b). Small lakelets in coastal tundra are also used for nesting in Siberia (Dementiev and Gladkov, 1967). How far inland the birds ever move for nesting is still uncertain, but they evidently extend up the Kashunuk River some 25 miles to the vicinity of Chevak (Harris, 1966). Calvin Lensink (pers. comm.) has observed that, whereas Pacific and Steller eiders are mostly limited to the coastal fringe, spectacled eiders often nest 5 to 10 miles up estuaries. He estimated the Yukon-Kuskokwim Delta population at nearly 100,000.

Wintering Distribution and Habitat: Almost entirely unknown, but presumably in the Bering Sea. Dementiev and Gladkov (1967) believe that most wintering occurs at the southern edge of the ice of the Bering Sea. Although a few records do exist for the Aleutian Islands (Murie, 1959), there is no strong indication that these islands are within the primary wintering area. Fay (1961) reported that a few spectacled eiders may be seen moving north past St. Lawrence Island during spring migration, but they are evidently not present in the numbers that might be expected if the Bering Sea were the wintering ground for the species' entire population.

GENERAL BIOLOGY

Age at Maturity: Not certain, but generally thought to require two or three years (Bent, 1925; Dementiev and Gladkov, 1967). Males nearly two years old still retain light grayish scapulars and inner flight feathers (Johnsgard, 1964) but do exhibit male courtship behavior, suggesting that at least this sex is capable of breeding at the end of the second year of life.

Pair Bond Pattern: I have observed pair-forming behavior among wild birds during early June and among captive birds during April (Pennsylvania) and May (England). It would thus seem that pairs are formed each spring and broken after the female begins incubation.

Nest Location: According to observations at Igiak Bay, nearly all nests are placed within 3 or 4 feet of water, usually in dead marsh grasses surround-

Breeding (hatched) and presumptive wintering (shaded)
distributions of the spectacled eider in North America.

ing small tundra ponds (Johnsgard, 1964b; Kessel *et al.,* 1964). Of the thirteen nests I have seen, the farthest from water were some 60 feet away, and the average of the remaining ones was 3.3 feet. There appears to be a slight tendency toward colonialism, with nests being found as close as 12 feet apart but generally averaging within 50 feet of one another (Johnsgard, 1964b). Dau (1972) reported that nests are usually placed on sedge-dominated lowland areas, often on a shoreline (20 of 35 nests), a peninsula (8 of 35 nests), or on islands (7 of 35 nests). The greatest distance a nest was found from water was 240 feet, and the mean distance between nests was 389 feet.

Clutch Size: Our observations (Johnsgard, 1964b, Kessel *et al.,* 1964) in the Igiak Bay area indicated average clutch size of somewhat over 4 eggs. Among 232 active nests observed in the Yukon-Kuskokwim Delta, the collective average clutch size was 4.57 eggs, with annual averages ranging from 4.0 to 5.2 (Calvin Lensink, pers. comm.). The eggs are probably deposited every other day (Brandt, 1943). Dau (1972), found no definite cases of renesting, but Michael Lubbock (pers. comm.) observed several apparent renests.

Incubation Period: Dau (1972) stated that, for three nests observed under natural conditions, the incubation period lasted 24 days from the laying of the last egg. Johnstone (1970) also reported a 24-day incubation period, but did not indicate the source of his information.

Fledging Period: Dau (1972) estimated that fledging by birds reared in the wild requires about 50 days, with one marked individual attaining flight in no more than 53 days following hatching.

Nest and Egg Losses: Dau (1972) reported a nesting success of 90.9 percent for thirty-three nests in his study area, and a hatching success of 83 percent for 147 eggs in twenty-nine nests. The most important egg predators are probably the three species of jaegers that occur in western Alaska. Brandt (1943), who worked at Hooper Bay, believed that glaucous and glaucous-winged gulls were the primary predators of young ducklings and observed a pomarine jaeger attempting to rob a nest. We found the parasitic and long-tailed jaegers more common than the pomarine, and on several occasions we observed them swooping down on eider nests shortly after the female had been flushed from it.

Juvenile Mortality: Brandt (1943) believed that fairly high losses of ducklings occurred shortly after hatching, judging from brood sizes (2 to 5) he observed in the Hooper Bay–Igiak Bay area. Counts made in that region in 1950 (United States Fish and Wildlife Service, Special Scientific Report: Wildlife, No. 8) between July 1 and August 6 included a total of thirty-three spectacled eider broods, which averaged 5.2 young per brood. Between 1964 and

1971, seventy-two recently hatched (Class I) broods averaged 3.9 young per brood, according to Calvin Lensink (pers. comm.).

Adult Mortality: No information on this point is available.

GENERAL ECOLOGY

Food and Foraging: Cottam (1939) has summarized the little that is known of the foods of the spectacled eider, based on a sample of sixteen adults collected between May and July. Animal foods, particularly mollusks, made up over three-fourths of the food volume, while terrestrial and freshwater plant materials made up the remainder of the identified materials. Razor clams (*Siliqua*) constituted the majority of foods of eight birds collected in May, and it seems probable that these and other bivalves are even more important on migration and wintering areas. Seemingly, the spectacled eider consumes a lower proportion of crustaceans than does the Steller eider, and there were virtually no echinoderm remains among the samples analyzed by Cottam.

An analysis of the stomachs of five juvenile spectacled eiders by Cottam indicated that insects made up the majority of food intake for such birds, with caddis fly larvae and their cases alone constituting more than a third of the total. A variety of other insects made up most of the remaining animal materials, while the seeds and plant fiber of mare's tail (*Hippurus*) were the largest single component of the plant materials found. Pondweeds (*Potamogeton*) and crowberries (*Empetrum*) are also apparently important plant foods for immature birds.

Sociality, Densities, Territoriality: Since no large concentration of molting or wintering birds has ever been located, the degree of sociality during the nonbreeding season is unknown. In the nesting grounds, however, a surprising degree of sociality does seem to be present. A slight clustering tendency for nests was indicated by my observations (Johnsgard, 1964b), although this could not be related to island-nesting or concentrations of nests in other unusually secure locations. Brandt (1943) mentioned finding seven nests in a very restricted area, also suggestive of a colonial tendency.

Calvin Lensink (pers. comm.) found that in 1971 there were 23 nests per square mile in the Magak flats behind Hooper Bay, which he considered to represent about half the normal density for the area. In a 231-acre study area of the lower Kashunuk River, from 8 to 34 spectacled eider nests were found per year in a three-year period, and the three-year average was 23, or 64 nests per square mile (United States Fish and Wildlife Service, Special Scientific Report: Wildlife, No. 68).

I could find no evidence of a defended area, or territory, in my observations of nesting eiders at Igiak Bay, and I frequently saw a breeding pair swim within a few feet of another such pair (Johnsgard, 1964b).

Interspecific Relationships: Although Pacific common eiders have been seen in the company of spectacled eiders and have even been seen displaying among them (Johnsgard, 1964b), there is still no good evidence of marked interactions between the spectacled eider and any other species. Pacific common eiders and Steller eiders do nest in the same general habitats as spectacled eiders.

Probably the large gulls and the jaegers, and perhaps such other predators as gyrfalcons, foxes, and the like are the most important vertebrates in the breeding ecology of spectacled eiders.

General Activity Patterns and Movements: During the long summer days of June while we were at Igiak Bay, the spectacled eiders seemed to be active at all hours. Most display activities seemed to occur in early morning and late afternoon, while several copulations were seen near midday. Males and females that had completed their clutches or had lost their clutches early in incubation seemingly spent the entire day on one of the rivers, resting along the shore or diving for food in the middle. Immature birds evidently largely remained at sea, since we saw only one obviously immature male, and Conover (1926) reported that, except for a single immature female, only fully adult birds were seen by their party. We collected two nonbreeding females that may have been immature birds.

SOCIAL AND SEXUAL BEHAVIOR

Flocking Behavior: Brandt (1943) noted that spring migrant arrivals in the Hooper Bay region in May were generally seen in groups of 10 to 30 birds with a maximum of 40. By the time I arrived in the area in early June most of the spectacled eiders were already in pairs and had initiated nests. Surplus adult males were still to be found on the rivers in groups of up to 14 birds, which seemed to be constantly on the watch for lone females (Johnsgard, 1964b).

Pair-forming Behavior: Since most pairs had already been formed when I arrived at Igiak Bay in early June, it seems likely that the majority of the pair-forming behavior occurs while the birds are still in migration or just after arrival at the breeding grounds. The pair-forming behavior I observed was primarily confined to unmated males whenever they encountered a lone female.

Pair-forming displays of this species were first described on the basis of my observations of these wild birds (Johnsgard, 1964a) and were later substantiated by observations of display in captive individuals. Like the other eiders, females perform inciting movements and calls, which provide the basis for social courtship. The males respond with displays that include the usual ritualized comfort movements of eiders (wing-flapping, preening, bathing, shaking, and head-rolling), and two more specialized displays. One of these is a rapid backward rearing movement that exposes the blackish chest, or the same movement preceded by a preliminary movement of the head forward and slightly downward. This latter form approaches the reaching display of the king eider, while the former is clearly closer to the rearing display of the Steller eider. The male spectacled eider also performs a pushing display very much like that of the king eider, and a backward bill-toss followed (and sometimes also preceded) by a forward neck-jerk that is equivalent to the combination of two cooing movements of the common eider. In general, the spectacled eider has a display repertoire that merges elements of the genera *Polysticta* and *Somateria* and seems to provide a behavioral "link" between these types.

Copulatory Behavior: Only four copulation sequences have been observed (Johnsgard, 1964a), but the general pattern seems to be much like that of other eiders. After the female assumes a prone posture, the male performs a nearly continuous sequence of movements; in order of observed decreasing frequency they are preening behind the wing, preening dorsally, pushing, bathing, head-rolling, bill-dipping, and wing-flapping. In at least three cases the male performed only a single shaking (upward-stretch) display, and always immediately prior to mounting. After treading, the male released the female, performed a single head-forward-rearing display, and then produced a few lateral head-turning movements while the female began to bathe.

Nesting and Brooding Behavior: The female spectacled eider constructs her nest in grassy flats on the islands or along the periphery of tundra ponds, making a slight depression that is scantily lined with grass stems. Invariably a substantial amount of down is present (Brandt, 1943). Once incubation begins the female is extremely reluctant to leave her clutch and can often be approached to within a few feet, if not actually touched. Males evidently remain in attendance until incubation is well under way; Brandt believed that they remained until the eggs are about to hatch. However, there is typically a mass exodus of males from the breeding areas late in June, when they fly back out to sea and presumably undertake a molt migration (Johnsgard, 1964b).

Relatively little is known of the brooding behavior, but individual families seemingly remain relatively intact and there is no early movement of young to open water. Dau (1972) stated that mixed broods are not common and that the young are reared to fledging on fresh to slightly brackish water areas that are probably within a mile or two of the nest. Crowberries (*Empetrum nigrum*) are preferred foods for both the female and the young, and some salmonberries (*Rubus arcticus*) are also eaten. Grasses and sedges, as well as some insects, are apparently consumed in quantities.

Postbreeding Behavior: Regrettably, the movement of adults and young are largely unknown once they leave their breeding grounds. Movements away from mainland Alaska may occur in late July, in August, or in early September (Gabrielson and Lincoln, 1959). Williamson *et al.* (1966) reported seeing birds in the Cape Thompson area until as late as September 26. The only molting area thus far reported in Alaska is near Stuart Island, Norton Sound (Dau, 1972).

STELLER EIDER
Polysticta stelleri (Pallas) 1769

Other Vernacular Names: None in general use.

Range: Breeds in arctic Siberia and in North America from at least St. Law-rence Island and the Kuskokwim Delta northward and eastward probably to Barter Island and Humphrey Point, with no definite nesting records for Canada. In North America, winters along the Aleutian Islands, Kodiak Island, and the Alaska Peninsula, rarely as far south as the Queen Charlotte Islands.

Subspecies: None recognized.

Measurements (after Delacour, 1959):
Folded wing: Males 209-217, females 208-215 mm.
Culmen: Males 36-40, females 35-40 mm.

Weights: Nelson and Martin (1953) reported that six males averaged 1.9 pounds (861 grams), with a maximum of 2.1 pounds (951 grams), and six females also averaged 1.9 pounds, but with a maximum of 2.0 pounds (907 grams). Bauer and Glutz (1969) summarized weight data, including Rus-sian literature, indicating that during the breeding season males average about 794 grams and females about 853 grams, with maximums of 900 and 853 grams, respectively. The maximum reported male weight, 1,000 grams, was for November.

IDENTIFICATION

In the Hand: Quite different from the larger eiders, the Steller lacks feathering along the side and top of the bill, but does possess sickle-shaped tertials. Unlike those of any other species of diving duck, these tertials are iridescent blue on their outer webs, as are the secondaries. Other distinctive features are the narrow blackish bill, with soft marginal flaps near the tip, and a relatively long (up to 90 mm.), pointed tail.

In the Field: Because of their small size and agility, Steller eiders are more likely to be confused with dabbling ducks than with other eiders. The male's cinnamon-colored sides and breast are visible for long distances, as are the mostly white head and scapulars. The black markings around the eye and the rounded black spot between the breast and the sides are also unique. Females are best identified by their association with males. Their size and uniformly dark brown color is somewhat reminiscent of abnormally dark female mallards, and in flight they also exhibit a contrasting white underwing surface and two white wing bars. However, in taking off they run along the water like other diving ducks. The most conspicuous female call is a loud *qua-haaa',* while males apparently produce only soft growling notes that are not audible over long distances.

AGE AND SEX CRITERIA

Sex Determination: Following the juvenal plumage, male Steller eiders can probably be distinguished from females on the basis of their tawny chest color and the presence of white feathers on the head, mantle, or upper wing coverts.

Age Determination: After the juvenal tail feathers have been lost, females are probably difficult to age, but first-year males are presumably recognizable by the absence of white on the middle or lesser wing coverts. The age of reproductive maturity in this species is unknown. Immature males also exhibit a dull blue rather than a bright blue speculum, and their secondaries are tipped with dusky rather than white, while immature females have a dusky rather than dull blue speculum (Taber, in Mosby, 1963).

DISTRIBUTION AND HABITAT

Breeding Distribution and Habitat: The North American breeding range of this species is perhaps even more restricted than that of the spectacled eider. Conover (1926) and Brandt (1943) found the Steller eider nesting commonly in the vicinity of Igiak and Hooper bays, although in recent years it has seem-

Breeding (hatched) and wintering (shaded) distributions of the
Steller eider in North America.

ingly declined there and no nests were found in 1964 (Johnsgard, 1964b, Kessel *et al.*, 1964). However, it still breeds uncommonly on the salt tundra flats near the mouth of the Kashunuk River not far to the south of Hooper Bay (Harris, 1966). It evidently does not breed in the Norton Sound area, and Williamson *et al.* (1966) found no evidence of breeding near Cape Thompson. Some nonbreeders evidently are found near Wales through the summer, and eggs have been collected at Wainwright and Barrow. From Barrow eastward it is evidently a rather common nester in suitable habitats, with egg records from Admiralty Bay and Pitt Point (Gabrielson and Lincoln, 1959). Reportedly there is occasional nesting of this species on St. Lawrence Island (Fay, 1961), but most of the summering birds are immatures. Although the Steller eider is a common winter visitor on the Aleutian Islands, there are no recent nesting records (Murie, 1959).

The breeding habitat of the Steller eider is lowland tundra closely adjacent to the coast. Brandt (1943) noted that this species nested closer to Hooper Bay than did either the Pacific common or the spectacled eider, using the tidewater flats having small eminences near a body of water for nesting sites. In Siberia it typically nests in lacustrine basins on mossy tundra (Dementiev and Gladkov, 1967).

Wintering Distribution and Habitat: The wintering distribution of the Steller eider includes the vicinity of Kodiak Island, the south side of the Alaska Peninsula, and the eastern Aleutian Islands (Gabrielson and Lincoln, 1959). Jones (1965) reported that much of this wintering population, which totals about 200,000 birds at its peak, concentrates on Nelson Lagoon, Izembek Bay, and Becheven Bay. In some years these birds arrive prior to their postnuptial molt, while in others they may arrive as late as November. At Nelson Lagoon, which supports the largest populations, the birds feed in fairly shallow waters, apparently on crustaceans (McKinney, 1965). In Izembek Bay, another shallow bay, they forage around the extensive beds of eelgrass which almost choke the bay. Although Izembek Bay is but a short distance overland from Cold Bay, this deeper, more rocky bay is used little if at all by Steller eiders, but is commonly utilized by king eiders (McKinney, 1959).

GENERAL BIOLOGY

Age at Maturity: Not yet established. The adult male plumage is probably attained during the second fall of life (Bent, 1925), and sexual maturity probably occurs during the second or third year (Dementiev and Gladkov, 1967).

Pair Bond Pattern: McKinney (1965) observed a high incidence of pair-forming behavior among wild Steller eiders between March 31 and April 28, although many birds had already become paired by that time. Brandt (1943) believed that the male remains near his incubating mate until the clutch is about ready to hatch and then leaves the area.

Nest Location: Brandt (1943) reported that small elevations near water on tidewater flats are the preferred nesting sites of the Steller eider. Other nests have been reportedly built in flat, mossy tundra, with a single instance of a nest having been found among rocks (Bent, 1925). According to Blair (in Bannerman, 1958), this species has nested a few times in Norway among dwarf birch and scrub willow.

Clutch Size: Bent (1925) mentioned five clutches that ranged from 6 to 10 eggs and averaged 7.2 eggs. A. M. Bailey (pers. comm.) reported seven clutches from Barrow, Wainwright, and Cape Simpson that ranged from 3 (probably incomplete) to 7 eggs and averaged 6.1. Brandt (1943) noted one clutch of 7, three of 8, and one of 9 eggs. If all seventeen of these clutches are considered, the modal clutch size would be 7 eggs and the average would be 7.2 eggs.

Incubation and Fledging Periods: Still unreported.

Nest and Egg Losses: No specific information available. Phillips (1926) judged that glaucous, glaucous-winged, and perhaps mew gulls were probably serious egg predators, as well as jaegers and possibly snowy owls. Percy (in Bannerman, 1968) mentioned that dogs sometimes caused high losses to nesting waterfowl, including eiders, in Siberia.

Juvenile Mortality: No specific information available. Brandt (1943) noted that the sizes of half-grown broods usually numbered about 3 or 4 young, and he thus believed that the mortality rate for the ducklings must be fairly high.

Adult Mortality: No specific information available. Jones (1965) reported that 17 band returns had resulted from banding 833 adult eiders in 1961 and 1962.

GENERAL ECOLOGY

Food and Foraging: Cottam's (1939) summary of Steller eider foods is still almost the only source of information on this topic. Among 66 eiders taken between May and July, crustaceans (primarily amphipods) and mollusks (primarily pelecypods) constituted over 60 percent of the identified foods. Soft-bodied crustaceans such as amphipods, isopods, and barnacles appear to be a favorite food of the Steller eider. Among the bivalve mollusks, a number of species of clams and mussels were found. Insects of quiet tundra pools were also found in quantity, such as the larvae of midges, caddis flies, and other insect foods. Sand dollars and polychaete worms were also found in some stomachs and perhaps represent important foods for the birds while on salt water. Plant foods made up only about 13 percent of the stomach contents by volume. (McKinney, 1965) observed wild Steller eiders feeding on an accumulation of deal shrimps in Nelson Lagoon during early spring. Two winter samples mentioned by Cottam had eaten little other than amphipods and univalve mollusks. Other samples from birds obtained during winter and summarized by Bauer and Glutz (1969) also suggest the importance of small univalve mollusks, amphipod crustaceans, and, to a lesser extent, bivalve mollusks and isopod crustaceans. The soft-edged bill of this species also supports the idea that soft-bodied animals probably make up the primary food supply.

Although Phillips (1926) reported that while at sea the birds tend to frequent the roughest, deepest, and rockiest coastlines, there is little current evidence to support this view. Rather, they seem to prefer shallow bays with muddy or sandy bottoms, such as Izembek Bay and Nelson Lagoon (McKinney, 1965). In this respect they differ from the harlequin duck, which forages to a greater extent on hard-shelled crustaceans, such as crabs, and among the mollusks specializes in chitons, which are typical of rocky shores. When foraging, all the birds in a flock commonly dive simultaneously, sometimes in flocks of a thousand or so (McKinney, 1965).

Sociality, Densities, Territoriality: Although highly social on wintering areas, with flocks often numbering in the thousands of birds, the Steller eider seemingly shows little or no tendencies for social nesting. Nests are evidently not clustered, and overall nesting densities seem to be low, on the basis of available information. On a 231-acre study area of the lower Kashunuk River in Alaska, there were three Steller eider nests in 1951, one in 1961, and five in 1962 (United States Fish and Wildlife Service, Special Scientific Report: Wildlife, No. 68). In 1963 only one nest was found on this area (Harris, 1966). Thus, an average yearly density of 2.5 nests was typical, or about 1 nest per 100 acres.

Interspecific Relationships: Phillips (1926) noted that the most common reported association of Steller eiders has been with king eiders, but they have also been observed with Pacific common eiders and harlequin ducks. He believed their major enemies to include glaucous and glaucous-winged gulls, jaegers, snowy owls, and perhaps also mew gulls. McKinney (1965) noted that both bald eagles and gyrfalcons are obviously feared by wild Steller eiders, and he thought that these eiders might be more vulnerable than the larger species to such aerial predators, since the larger birds feed in deeper waters and farther from shore.

General Activity Patterns and Movements: Percy (in Bannerman, 1958) reported that during June and July in Siberia, the daily movements of the Steller eider seemed primarily influenced by wind and ice conditions rather than time of day. McKinney (1965) observed birds feeding in areas exposed by the receding tide at Nelson Lagoon. A similar situation obtains at Izembek Bay in my own experience; the birds follow the rising tide as it encroaches on the shallow bay, and as the tide retreats they gradually move back out to deeper waters, where they rest.

Jones (1965) reported on some migratory movements of Steller eiders banded as flightless adults at Izembek Bay during the early 1960s. All but one of the seventeen nonlocal recoveries he had obtained at that time were from Siberia, from points as distant as the Lena River, some 3,200 kilometers away. The remaining recovery came from Point Barrow, suggesting that birds from both sides of the Bering Strait move to this region to undergo their molt at least in some years. Far more birds appear at Izembek Bay for molting in some years than in others, suggesting that the distance the birds travel prior to undergoing their molt must vary from year to year.

SOCIAL AND SEXUAL BEHAVIOR

Flocking Behavior: The strong gregarious nature of this species during winter and on migration has been mentioned by a number of observers. McKinney (1965) noted fifteen flocks in early April that ranged in size from about a thousand to several thousand birds. He reported on the unusual degree of behavioral synchrony of these tightly packed rafts, particularly in their foraging behavior. Evidently the vernacular name "soldier duck" refers to their notable trait of synchronized behavior. McKinney believed that many of the differences in the social behavior and displays of the Steller eider as compared with the common eider could be attributed to its stronger social tendencies and greater readiness to fly.

Pair-forming Behavior: The social behavior and pair-forming displays of this species have been described by Johnsgard (1964a) and McKinney (1965). Like the larger eiders, several comfort movements have been ritualized and incorporated into the display repertoire, including shaking (upward-stretch), preening the dorsal region, bathing, and head-rolling. Additionally, a lateral head-turning and two types of vertical head movements are present. One is a rapid and rather limited upward chin-lifting (head-tossing) movement, while the other is a much more extreme backward movement of the head and neck in a rapid "rearing" motion. A very frequent sequence of behavior is for the male to perform a single shake, swim toward a female while performing lateral head-turning, perform a single rearing display when close to the female, and then swim rapidly away again while performing head-turning.

Females enter into social display by their performance of strong inciting gestures and calls, which seem to be equivalent in function to inciting in the larger eider species. McKinney noted that aerial display is often interspersed with flights of various lengths, with a maximum observed duration of about three minutes. Males also perform short display flights of a few feet, in which they alight near the female with a conspicuous splash.

Copulatory Behavior: I have observed two completed copulations (Johns-gard, 1964a), and McKinney (1965) reported on a much larger number of completed copulation sequences. We both noted that bill-dipping, dorsal-preening, and bathing movements were the three most typical male precopula-tory displays and were performed in a relatively constant sequence. Thus, a preening display would usually alternate with either bill-dipping or bathing. McKinney also observed a few instances of head-shaking, head-rolling, and head-turning in precopulatory situations. In all observed cases, the male per-formed a single shaking movement immediately before he rushed toward the female and mounted her. Following treading the male performs a single rear-ing display, then (in my observations) swims rapidly away while performing lateral head-turning movements. McKinney apparently observed some varia-tions in postcopulatory behavior.

Nesting and Brooding Behavior: Judging from Brandt's comments (1943), male Steller eiders normally remain in the vicinity of the nesting female for some time after incubation is under way and perhaps until the time of hatching. However, they apparently do not immediately begin their migra-tion from the area; Percy (in Bannerman, 1958) observed coastal rafts of 400 to 1,000 birds, mostly male eiders, adjacent to the nesting grounds in late June. Since fewer than 5 percent of these were females, he believed that nesting success was apparently high in spite of the dogs and other nest predators in the area. Like the other eiders, females are very strong brooders and are extremely reluctant to leave their nests once incubation is under way. They tend to nest somewhat later than the other eiders and have a larger average clutch size, so that the period of hatching is likewise later than that of the other eiders. According to Blair (in Bannerman, 1958), when the ducklings are still quite young, the females move their broods to the sea, where they often form "herds" and forage in the litter of tidal areas.

Postbreeding Behavior: As Percy (in Bannerman, 1958) has pointed out, the unusually late molt of the flight feathers of this species allows it to undertake a fairly long migration to wintering areas prior to undergoing its wing molt and becoming flightless. Both sexes are represented among the flightless birds, although the sexes tend to segregate and occupy different parts of the bay. Evidently in some instances this molt migration is in excess of 3,000 kilometers (Jones, 1965), but there seem to be yearly differences in the distances flown before molting. Thus, in some years the Steller eiders arrive at Izembek Bay as early as August, while in others they have arrived as much as three months later, in early November. Peak numbers, however, usually do not occur until the eve of the spring migration.

LABRADOR DUCK

Camptorhynchus labradorius (Gmelin) 1789

Other Vernacular Names: Pied Duck.

Range: Originally occurred along the Atlantic coast of North America, probably mainly wintering along Long Island, but recorded from Labrador to Chesapeake Bay. Possibly bred in Labrador or farther north, but no definite breeding records were ever obtained. Todd (1963) reviewed the Labrador records and questioned the authenticity of some possible Labrador duck eggs, one of which is labeled "Labrador" (Glegg, 1951). Last recorded in the fall of 1875.

Subspecies: None recognized.

Measurements (after Delacour, 1959):

Folded wing: Males 210-220, females 206-209 mm.

Culmen: Males 43-45, females 40-42 mm.

Weights: Audubon (1840–1844) reported the weight of a male as 1 pound 14.5 ounces and of a female as 1 pound 1 ounce.

EPILOGUE

The Labrador duck is now extinct, vanished forever along with the heath hen, Carolina parakeet, passenger pigeon, and an earlier America. It disappeared so swiftly and so quietly that it is not only difficult to compose a suitable epitaph, but also impossible to write a complete obituary. We do not know for certain where it nested or exactly what it consumed, nor do we even have a record of the appearance of its downy young. Interred within the few skins, mounts, and bones that are scattered throughout the world's museums like the deteriorating leaves of a now-dead oak are the genes and chromosomes that represented the species' strategy for survival in a hostile world. That strategy failed, and in its failure the Labrador duck became the first of four waterfowl species doomed to extinction in historical times.

It may be fruitless to mourn for a bird that has been gone longer than the memory of any living man, but it would be folly to ignore this lesson of history. Uncounted millions of years of evolution failed to prepare the Labrador duck for survival in a world dominated by men with the ability to kill from great distances, to pollute the seas, and to ravage the wilderness. It is approximately a century since the Labrador ducks made their last ill-fated flights from their breeding grounds along the North Atlantic coast to the vicinity of Long Island; in that period our concern has gradually changed from the problems of how birds can survive modern men to the question of whether mankind can survive modern men. The next century will no doubt provide that answer.

HARLEQUIN DUCK

Histrionicus histrionicus (Linnaeus) 1758

Other Vernacular Names: None in general use.

Range: Breeds in northern and eastern Asia, the islands of the Bering Sea, and in continental North America from Alaska and the Yukon south through the western mountains to central California and Colorado, and in northeastern North America from Baffin Island and Labrador to the Gaspé Peninsula and perhaps Newfoundland. Also breeds on Greenland and Iceland. Winters in North America from the Aleutian Islands south along the Pacific coast to California, and on the Atlantic coast from southern Canada to the New England states.

Subspecies: None recognized here. The supposed Pacific race *pacificus* is not acceptable (Dickinson, 1953; Todd, 1963).

Measurements (after Delacour, 1959):

Folded wing: Males 200-210, females 190-197 mm.

Culmen: Males 25-28, females 24-26 mm.

Weights: Nelson and Martin (1953) reported that five males averaged 1.5

pounds (679 grams), while four females averaged 1.2 pounds (543 grams), with maximum weights of 1.6 pounds (725 grams) and 1.3 pounds (589 grams), respectively. Bauer and Glutz (1969) have summarized additional weight data from North America, Iceland, and Asia, with the heaviest male reported as 750 grams and the heaviest female as 562 grams.

IDENTIFICATION

In the Hand: Recognizable as a diving duck on the basis of its large feet with lobed hind toes and lengthened outer toes. The combination of an extremely short, narrow bill (culmen length 24-28 mm.) and moderately long wings (folded wing 190-210 mm.) that are at least slightly glossed with purplish on the secondaries will eliminate all other species. Males in nuptial plumage are unmistakable; no other duck is predominantly slate blue with white spots and stripes. Females and dull-colored males, however, are not so easily recognized, having facial markings similar to those of female surf and white-winged scoters, both of which are larger and have much heavier bills.

In the Field: Normally found only along rocky coastal shorelines or on timbered and rapid mountain streams, harlequins are small diving ducks that appear quite dark on the water. Both males and females have white to grayish white areas on the cheeks, white between the eye and the forehead (continuous with the white cheeks in males, usually separate in females), and a rounded white spot halfway behind the eyes and the back of the head. Males may have additional white spotting, especially as they acquire their nuptial plumage, but these facial areas remain white to grayish white in all plumages. In flight, both sexes appear relatively dark, both above and below, exhibiting dusky brown under wing coverts. When flying along mountain streams they remain quite low, following the course of the stream. When in coastal waters they forage in small flocks, often moving their heads in an elliptical fashion as they swim. Relatively silent birds, the male has a high-pitched, mouselike squeal, and females have a harsh croaking call.

AGE AND SEX CRITERIA

Sex Determination: Sexing criteria based on feather characteristics have not been worked out, and apparently some first-year males are scarcely if at all separable externally from females. Older males have a more iridescent speculum, and the white feathers present on the head are bordered with black. When in full eclipse, males have considerably darker underparts than do females.

Age Determination: Juveniles can be recognized for a time by their notched tail feathers, as well as by their more spotted underparts and paler upperparts. After that, females cannot be obviously aged, but first-year males may be femalelike, while second-year or older males apparently have the adult pattern. Examination of the oviduct or penis structure should serve to distinguish birds in their second fall of life from older, breeding birds.

DISTRIBUTION AND HABITAT

Breeding Distribution and Habitat: The North American breeding distribution of the harlequin duck is a curiously disruptive one, with the primary center in the forested mountains of western North America and a much smaller, more poorly defined secondary center in northeastern North America.

In Alaska, harlequins probably nest throughout the Aleutian Islands (Murie, 1959). They are also common and are known to breed along the Alaska Peninsula, on Kodiak Island, on Kenai Peninsula, in the Copper River valley, and along the coast of southeastern Alaska (Gabrielson and Lincoln, 1959). Although this essentially coastal section is no doubt their primary range, they do extend into the interior of Alaska and along the Bering Sea coast. There are relatively few interior or northern records of breeding, however, with one record for the lower Yukon River valley, about fifty miles below Kaltag (Gabrielson and Lincoln, 1959), and another for the Pitmegea River, near Cape Sabine (Childs, 1969). Harlequin broods have been seen regularly at Mount McKinley National Park, and eggs have been found at Loon Lake in the Brooks Range (Dennis Crouch, pers. comm.). It is common during summer, and possibly breeds on St. Lawrence Island (Fay, 1961).

In western Canada, harlequins reportedly nest in the Yukon, over much of British Columbia, and along the western edge of Alberta. They also occur in summer in the Mackenzie River valley eastward to Great Slave Lake, although breeding there is apparently unsubstantiated. In eastern Canada there are sparse breeding populations on southeastern Baffin Island (Snyder, 1957), probably around the Ungava Bay coastline of Quebec, on Labrador, perhaps on the outer north shore of the Gulf of St. Lawrence, and on the Gaspé Peninsula (Godfrey, 1965). Todd (1963) pointed out that although harlequins are fairly common during summer on the coast of northern Labrador, no definite breeding records exist. He did, however, provide a recent breeding record for the False River area of Ungava Bay. There is no definite indication that harlequins breed on Newfoundland.

South of Canada, harlequins are confined as breeding birds to the western mountains. They are probably commonest in Washington, breeding in the

Breeding (hatched) and wintering (shaded) distributions of the harlequin duck in North America.

Olympic Mountains, on both sides of the Cascades, and in the Blue and the Selkirk mountains as well (Dennis Crouch, pers. comm). In Oregon the harlequin has been found breeding in both the Wallowa and the Cascade mountains (Gabrielson and Jewett, 1940). In California there are old records of breeding on a number of mountain streams, including the Merced, Cherry, Stanislaus, and Tuolumne rivers, as well as at the headwaters of the San Joaquín River (Grinnell and Miller, 1944). A breeding population also extends into the interior along the northern Rocky Mountains, along the Idaho-Montana border as far as Yellowstone Park, where it is locally common below Fishing Bridge on the Yellowstone River. However, the harlequin's range evidently does not extend to Colorado, where it is presently considered a rare straggler (Bailey and Neidrach, 1967).

The preferred breeding habitat appears to be cold, rapidly flowing streams, often but not always surrounded by forests. There is apparently a limited attraction to tundralike habitats, as indicated by the presence of breeding birds on Greenland and Baffin Island. Bengtson (1966) stated that no other European or North American duck is so closely bound to fast-running streams during the breeding season as the harlequin. He considered that the availability of suitable food, especially simuliid flies, largely regulates the density and distribution of harlequins in Iceland, with nest site availability of secondary importance.

Wintering Distribution and Habitat: Large numbers of harlequins winter in the Aleutian Islands (Murie, 1959), and the birds are also common to abundant during winter along the bays of the Alaska Peninsula, the coastal waters of southeastern Alaska, Prince William Sound, Cook Inlet, and the Pribilof Islands (Gabrielson and Lincoln, 1959).

In Canada the harlequin winters along the coast of British Columbia, and also along the Atlantic coast in southern Labrador, Newfoundland, and the Maritime Provinces (Godfrey, 1966).

In Washington, northern Puget Sound and the San Juan Islands probably harbor the largest number of wintering harlequins. In past years wintering flocks of 200 or even 500 birds were reported (Jewett *et al.*, 1953). Along the open coastlines of Washington, Oregon, and northern California, harlequins may also be found during winter, particularly near rocky promontories and around low-lying reefs and outer islets (Hoffmann, 1927).

Along the Atlantic coastline, harlequins winter from the Canadian border southward along the rocky coastlines of Maine and beyond in diminishing numbers as these deep, rock-bound coasts give way to shallower, sandy or mud-bottomed shores.

The favorite wintering habitat of harlequins in Iceland has been described by Bengtson (1966) as those places where the surf breaks directly against the rocks, such as around the outermost peninsulas. They are usually found in waters 3 to 4 meters deep, 100 to 300 meters from shore. They evidently prefer island points or other areas providing seclusion and protection from bad weather and the roughest water (Dennis Crouch, pers. comm.).

GENERAL BIOLOGY

Age at Maturity: Not definitely established, but plumage sequences indicate that the birds are mature in their second year of life (Bent, 1925). Hand-reared birds attained full plumage and began sexual display in their second winter (Charles Pilling, pers. comm.).

Pair Bond Pattern: Bengtson (1966) reported that only about twelve pairs were noted in a flock of two hundred birds in late December, and that males desert their mates very shortly after incubation begins, indicating a yearly renewal of pair bonds.

Nest Location: Bengtson (1966) reported that in Iceland harlequins prefer to nest on inaccessible islands, depositing their eggs in caves or holes in the lava, under dense bushes, or sometimes in rather open situations. No large trees presently occur in Iceland, and Bengtson partly attributed the species' use of other holes or crevices to the lack of hollow trees. According to Dennis Crouch (pers. comm.), hole-nesting is not typical of North American harlequins; of the twenty to twenty-five nest records he has obtained, all have been ground sites except for one involving an overturned stump in the middle of a stream. Bengtson (1966) noted that the nests are always located very close to water, and the most prominent feature of the nest is that it is mostly protected from above by dense vegetation.

Clutch Size: Bengtson (1966) reported that eleven nests he had examined ranged from 3 to 7 eggs, averaging 5.5, but that some of these clutches might have been depleted by egg collectors. Records of nineteen nests from North America indicate a mean clutch of 6.2 eggs, a mode of 6, and a range of 4 to 8 (Dennis Crouch, per. comm.). According to Bengtson, the egg-laying interval is from 2 to 4 days, with 3 probably normal.

Incubation Period: Not definite, with some literature estimates of 31 to 34 days, but recent field observations indicate only 28 to 29 days (Bengtson, 1966).

Fledging Period: Not yet definitely established, but there is one early estimate of 40 days (Bengtson, 1966).

Nest and Egg Losses: Bengtson (1966) reported that in his study area the arctic fox was absent and the mink was the only major mammalian predator. Egg-collecting activities by humans were then also a serious menace to harlequins, but have since been prohibited. Avian predators of possible importance were parasitic jaegers, great black-backed gulls, and ravens, but Bengtson did not estimate their relative importance as predators. The nests of this species are usually so well hidden that predators hunting visually would have difficulty locating nests, and mammals unable to reach nesting islands would also have limited effectiveness. Bengtson (1972) estimated a high hatching success (87 percent) in Iceland.

Juvenile Mortality: Brood counts by Bengtson on early-age broods indicated an average brood size of 5.7 young, with an observed range of 4 to 10 ducklings. Duckling survival varied from 40 to 76 percent in different years (averaging 55 percent), and in four different study areas the mean number of young reared per female varied from 1.5 to 2.2, with food availability an important factor affecting reproductive success (Bengtson, 1972). Evidently minks and bad weather are the primary mortality factors for young ducklings.

Adult Mortality: There are no estimates of annual mortality rates.

GENERAL ECOLOGY

Food and Foraging: Cottam's (1939) summary of the foods found in sixty-three adults collected between January and September is the most complete analysis available. Virtually all of this food was of animal origin, with most of the volume consisting of crustaceans (57 percent), mollusks (25 percent), and insects (10 percent). Decapods, such as smaller crabs, and soft-bodied crustaceans, such as amphipods and isopods, appeared to be the favored types of foods and together made up about half the total volume. The mollusks included a surprising number of chitons, which are no doubt obtained from rocky shorelines in wintering areas, and a variety of gastropods probably found in similar habitats. Insect foods were more prevalent in summer samples and included species typical of rapidly flowing streams (stone flies, water boatmen, midge larvae). Apparently the only echinoderm of possible importance as a harlequin food is the spiny sea urchin (*Strongylocentrotus*), remnants of which occurred in nearly half the stomachs, but in only very small quantities.

As mentioned earlier, Bengtson (1966) considered the availability of midges (*Chironomida*), blackflies (*Simulium*), and caddis flies (Trichoptera) a determining factor in the abundance of harlequins on Icelandic streams, and noted that the simuliids constituted the bulk of their nutrition on the breeding grounds. Siberian birds collected in June contained large numbers of caddis fly larvae, as well as stone fly larvae and other insects plus small fish remains

(Dementiev and Gladkov, 1967). In analyses of nine birds collected on coastal Maine in December, the amphipod *Gammerellus,* the gastropod *Nucella,* and the pelecypod *Lucinia* occurred in the largest numbers (Palmer, 1949).

On their wintering grounds in coastal waters, harlequins often forage in heavy surf over shallow waters (Bengtson, 1966). Their dives there are thus usually of short duration and probably rarely exceed 20 or 30 seconds. On rivers they forage by skimming materials from the surface, by diving, and by up-ending, the last-named method apparently less often (Bengtson, 1966). Bengtson reported that dives timed on the River Laxá usually lasted 15 to 18 seconds, while Pool (1962) noted a range of 5 to 25 seconds for the same river. Bengtson calculated a dive:pause time ratio of 4:1 for the harlequin, as opposed to 2.2:1 for the oldsquaw and 1.9:1 for the red-breasted merganser and the Barrow goldeneye on the same stream. Thus he concluded that the harlequin duck is the most efficient diving species using rushing streams in Iceland. Pool also noted that harlequins dove with greater vigor and persistence than did other species seen and foraged in much stronger currents than did the others.

Sociality, Densities, Territoriality: Bengtson noted that even on their breeding grounds the birds are relatively sociable, and territorial boundaries on the Laxá River in Iceland were very indistinct or sometimes seemingly lacking. He noted that possessive behavior of the male seemed to be related to his mate, rather than to a specific area. He also estimated (1972) that breeding densities averaged 1.3 pairs per kilometer of river (or 2.1 pairs per mile), being highest near lake outlets. This is a considerably higher breeding density than seems to be typical of the South American torrent duck (*Merganetta*), which occupies a similar ecological niche in torrential Andean streams. Dennis Crouch (pers. comm.) observed harlequin densities in Washington state of 1 pair per two to four river miles, a figure much closer to the situation typical of torrent ducks.

Interspecific Relationships: As Bengtson (1966) has pointed out, no other North American species of duck can effectively compete for food with the harlequin in its preferred habitats, fast-flowing streams. On wintering areas it consumes a variety of foods somewhat similar to those of the oldsquaw, but the harlequin typically forages in areas with heavier surf and shallower waters than does the oldsquaw. Apparently there is little if any competition with other species of waterfowl for nest sites; Bengtson reported only that eggs of common mergansers have sometimes been found in the nests of harlequins.

To what extent predators and parasites may play a role in the ecology of harlequin ducks is still rather uncertain. The harlequin's breeding populations are never so high nor are their nest sites so closely spaced or conspicuous as to attract predators in any numbers.

General Activity Patterns and Movements: For the most part, harlequins appear to be daylight foragers, coming in each morning to favored ledges and rocky coves for foraging, and sometimes roosting on rocks in the evening (Cottam, 1939). Bengtson (1966), in summer counts on the River Laxá, found the highest incidence of foraging between 5:00 and 6:00 p.m., with a secondary peak in early morning. Based on July observations in Iceland, Pool (1962) reported harlequins to forage most heavily just prior to sunset. He also noted them to fly most actively at this time, as the birds flew up and down the river in small groups. Dennis Crouch (pers. comm.) observed foraging periods lasting from 6:00 to about 10:30 a.m., and from about 4:00 p.m. until dark.

SOCIAL AND SEXUAL BEHAVIOR

Flocking Behavior: Harlequins tend to fly in dense flocks, and they are highly sociable outside the breeding season (Bengtson, 1966). During winter they typically forage in groups of 5 to 25 birds, according to Bengtson. Other observers have estimated flock sizes of as high as 500 individuals, but Dennis Crouch (pers. comm.) reported that groups of 5 to 6 are now typical of western Washington.

Pair-forming Behavior: Relatively few observations of pair-forming behavior in harlequin ducks have been made, and the descriptions have often not been in close agreement. Myres (1959a) observed only head-nodding as a social display, and was not certain whether it was agonistic or sexual in function. He observed this movement in both sexes and sometimes heard a high-pitched note accompanying the movement. Bengtson (1966) considered head-nodding to be the fundamental display movement and considered it basically an aggressive display, which is often followed by a threat posture. He also observed a bill-dipping and associated lateral bill-shaking in males, a wing-flapping that might represent a display, and both dorsal-preening and wing-preening movements that likewise were of uncertain display function. The only female display that he recognized in situations other than copulation was inciting. In this posture the female lowers her head and performs alternate head-turning movements, sometimes uttering a harsh call. Inciting has been seen much more rarely than one would predict if it plays an important role in pair formation. Bengtson further noted that no "flight-display" evidently is present in this species, unless it occurs during winter and early spring when the birds are still at sea.

Copulatory Behavior: Bengtson's (1966) observations on five completed copulation sequences and seventeen interrupted sequences provide the best description of this behavior. He stated that the precopulatory behavior may be initiated by either sex, but usually the male, by commencing mutual head-nodding. In most of the sequences that Bengtson observed, mutual bill-dipping was also noted, and it seems probable that this element separates precopulatory head-nodding behavior from that seen in other situations. Finally, there is a precopulatory "rush" of the male toward the female, which may be repeated several times before mounting is achieved. Evidently the female usually does not become prone until shortly before treading occurs. The postcopulatory behavior of both sexes is relatively simple and lacks specific posturing. Pearse (1945) provided an account of a single copulation sequence that likewise involved jerking movements of the head on the part of the male, but no other definite displays before or after copulation. Neil Smith (in Johnsgard, 1965) has also observed attempted copulatory behavior in this species, which included rapid rushes toward the female.

Unpublished notes of Jay S. Gashwiler of the United States Bureau of Sport Fisheries and Wildlife describe several observations of copulation or attempted copulation during April and May in Oregon. One copulation sequence was preceded by a number of rushes toward the male by the female and energetic "head-throwing" movements of the head back toward the shoulders. In a second instance, both sexes performed "head-throwing" and simulated pecking of the other's head or neck prior to copulation, and following treading the male chased the female over the water for a short distance a couple of times. Presumably these "head-throwing" movements are the same as the nodding movements seen by others.

Nesting and Brooding Behavior: Bengtson's (1966) account of nesting behavior in this species is the most complete one available. He stated that females choose the nest site alone, although males closely follow them and stand "guard." The nest is simple, consisting of a thin layer of grass, with occasional twigs and leaves, and lined with white down having reddish tips. Such white, rather than dark-colored, down would favor the view that harlequins are basically hole- or crevice-nesters rather than surface-nesters. The female begins to incubate before the set is completed, and at that time begins to line the nest. She sits very tightly during incubation and probably leaves the nest for only very short periods at intervals of about 48 hours. Males leave their mates when incubation gets under way and begin to congregate in favored foraging areas. Following hatching, the female takes her brood to a secluded part of the river, moving about very little. The young of different broods sometimes merge, and in such cases are guarded by both females. Unsuccessful female breeders sometimes participate in brood care also. Apparently the young are not taken to the sea until they are fledged.

Postbreeding Behavior: Bengtson (1966) stated that males remain at their areas of congregation for only a few days after deserting their mates, and then depart for the sea. He mentioned, however, that observations of eclipse-plumage males on the River Laxá have been made. Thus, the degree of molt migration in this Icelandic population is uncertain. In the Alaska population there are also apparently certain areas favored by molting birds. Summer flocks, either of males or mixed sexes, have been reported around St. Matthew and St. Lawrence islands and at Captains Bay, Unalaska Island (Gabrielson and Lincoln, 1959). Assemblages of drakes and immatures have also been reported at the Commander Islands, along the Siberian coast, and at various other points (Dementiev and Gladkov, 1967).

OLDSQUAW

Clangula hyemalis (Linnaeus) 1758

Other Vernacular Names: Long-tailed Duck.

Range: Breeds in a circumpolar belt including arctic North America, Green-land, Iceland, northern Europe and Asia, and the islands of the Bering Sea. Winters in saltwater and deep freshwater habitats; in North America, from Alaska south to Washington and infrequently beyond on the Pacific coast, on the Great Lakes, and on the Atlantic coast south to South Carolina and rarely to Florida.

Subspecies: None recognized.

Measurements (after Delacour, 1959):

Folded wing: Males 219-236, females 202-210 mm.

Culmen: Males 26-29, females 23-28 mm.

Weights: Nelson and Martin (1953) reported that thirty-one males averaged 1.8 pounds (815 grams) and fourteen females averaged 1.4 pounds (634 grams), with maximum weights of 2.3 (1,042 grams) and 1.8 pounds (8.5 grams), respectively. Schiøler (1926) reported that among wintering birds, nine adult males averaged 750.5 grams and ten juvenile males averaged 741 grams; eleven adult females averaged 686 grams, nine year-old females averaged 728.1 grams, and fifteen juveniles averaged 627.2 grams.

IDENTIFICATION

In the Hand: Probably the most seasonally variable in appearance of all North American waterfowl, oldsquaws may be recognized as diving ducks by their lobed hind toe and long outer toe, and separated from other diving ducks by their short (culmen length 23-29 mm.) flattened bill with a raised nail, rather uniformly brownish upper wing coloration, and white or grayish sides and underparts. White is always present around the eye and may vary from a very narrow eyering to an extreme where almost the entire head is white.

In the Field: Found only on deep lakes, large rivers, or along the coast, oldsquaws are fairly small diving ducks at home in the heaviest surf or the most bitterly cold weather conditions. On the water the birds appear to be an almost random mixing of white, brown, and blackish markings, but invariably the flanks and sides are white, or no darker than light gray, and some white is present on the head, either around the eye or on the sides of the neck in both areas. Except during the summer molt, the elongated tail of males is also a good field mark, as are their black breasts. Lone females might be confused with female harlequin ducks, but they always have whitish rather than dark brown sides, and they may thus also be distinguished from immature or female scoters. In flight, oldsquaws exhibit white underparts that contrast with their dark upper and lower wing surfaces. The courtship calls of male oldsquaws are famous for their carrying power and rhythmic quality, the commonest two sounding like *ugh, ugh, ah-oo-gah'* and *a-oo, a-oo, a-oo'-gah.*

AGE AND SEX CRITERIA

Sex Determination: Sex and age criteria are still not clear, although adult males can be separated from adult females by their shiny black upper wing coverts (vs. blackish brown in females and immatures) and their rufous tertials and secondaries (vs. gray to rufous in females and immatures). Adult males also always have black breasts and (except during summer molt) greatly elongated tail feathers, plus pinkish color near the tip of the bill. Criteria for separating first-winter males from females include the presence of pink color on the bill, some blackish feathers on the breast, and some grayish white scapular feathers.

Age Determination: Juvenile females are probably best recognized by the presence of notched tail feathers, while first-year males lack elongated tail feathers, have a mottled and imperfectly black breast, and have white scapulars that are not as long as in adults. Separation of second-year birds from adults may require examination of the reproductive tracts.

DISTRIBUTION AND HABITAT

Breeding Distribution and Habitat: The oldsquaw is probably the most arctic-adapted of all ducks and has an associated breeding range in North America that extends from the northernmost parts of Ellesmere Island to the southern coastline of Hudson Bay.

In Alaska the oldsquaw breeds from the base of the Alaska Peninsula in the vicinity of Ugashik, northward along the coastal tundra of the Bering Sea and Arctic Ocean, and into the interior along the valleys of the Nushagak, Kuskokwim, Yukon, and Kobuk rivers, as well as at McKinley National Park. It is probably the commonest breeding duck in such northern areas as Anak-tuvuk Pass and the Colville Delta. It is questionable whether oldsquaws breed on the Aleutian Islands, but there are breeding records for St. Paul and St. Matthew islands (Gabrielson and Lincoln, 1959). Breeding also commonly occurs on St. Lawrence Island (Fay, 1961).

In Canada the oldsquaw is the most widely distributed duck throughout the arctic regions (Snyder,1957), occurring along the coastlines of the Yukon, the Northwest Territories, Manitoba, Quebec, and Labrador. It also breeds on most if not all of the islands in the Franklin District, as well as adjacent parts of Greenland. There is also apparently an isolated breeding locality in northwestern British Columbia about fifty miles west of Atlin (Godfrey, 1966).

The breeding habitat throughout this entire range is arctic tundra in the vicinity of lakes or ponds, coastlines, or islands. Where shrubs are available for nesting cover, they are preferentially utilized, but grasses and sedges like-wise may be used. Wooded country, however, is apparently avoided.

Wintering Distribution and Habitat: As might be expected, the winter distribution of this species is about as widespread as its breeding distribution. It is common in the Aleutian Islands during winter (Murie, 1959), and it has been estimated that about 500,000 oldsquaws may annually winter around St. Lawrence Island (Fay, 1961). Along the southern coastline of mainland Alaska they are locally abundant, with great numbers occurring along the island channels of southeastern Alaska (Gabrielson and Lincoln, 1959).

In Canada, oldsquaws winter along the coastline of British Columbia, on the open waters of the Great Lakes, and along the Atlantic coast from southern Labrador and northern Newfoundland southward through the Maritime Provinces (Godfrey, 1966). They extend southward on the Pacific coast through Puget Sound and along the open coastline of Washington, becoming uncommon in Oregon and relatively rare in California. Along the Atlantic coast they occur throughout New England and southward through

Breeding (hatched) and wintering (shaded) distributions of the
oldsquaw in North America.

the Chesapeake Bay region, where they are common residents, to about as far as the Carolinas, where they are uncommon (Pearson, 1919; Sprunt and Chamberlain, 1949).

In the Chesapeake Bay region they are fairly evenly distributed along the open ocean and coastal bays, the salt estuarine bays, and some of the brackish estuarine bays. A few are also seen on some of the fresh and slightly brackish estuarine bays (Stewart, 1962). The rather great abundance of this species on Lake Michigan and some of the other Great Lakes indicates a stronger propensity for wintering on fresh water than is true of most eiders and scoters.

GENERAL BIOLOGY

Age at Maturity: Oldsquaws probably mature at two years of age, according to Ellarson (1956). Alison (1972) confirmed this with captive birds.

Pair Bond Pattern: Not yet well studied, but the frequency of social display throughout the winter and spring suggests an annual renewal of pair bonds. Alison (1972) reported that in a population of 95 pairs at least 4 re-formed their pair bonds in successive years.

Nest Location: Bengtson (1970) reported on the locations of 348 oldsquaw nests found in Iceland. He noted that this species tends to nest in pothole areas and also exhibits a distinct tendency to nest on islands when these are available. Of the total nests found, 202 were under low shrubs, 44 under high shrubs, 49 under sedge cover, 35 under angelica (*Angelica* and *Archangelica*) herbs, and 18 in herb and grass meadows. Nests were usually quite close to water; the modal distance from water was 3 to 10 meters. Evans (1970) reported that oldsquaw nests around Churchill, Manitoba, varied in their average distance from water according to areas utilized for nesting. Those on islands in fresh water averaged about 2 meters, those placed on mainland beaches averaged 9 meters, and those on mainland tundra averaged nearly 30 meters. Alison (1972), working in the same area, did not find any significant island-nesting tendencies but did confirm Evans' observations that oldsquaws often nest in association with Arctic tern colonies.

Clutch Size: Probably 6 or 7 eggs normally constitute the clutch. Jehl and Smith (1970) found an average clutch size of 6.3 for 17 completed first clutches at Churchill, Manitoba, while Alison (1972) reported an average of 6.8 eggs for 95 clutches. Bengtson (1971) reported that the average of 212 clutches from Iceland was 7.9 eggs, with significant yearly differences in mean clutch sizes that ranged from 7.0 to 8.4 eggs. Twenty renest clutches averaged 6.0 eggs (Bengtson, 1972). The average egg-laying interval is 26 hours (Alison, 1972).

Incubation Period: Reportedly 24 days, or 24 to 25 days under bantam hens (Bauer and Glutz, 1969). Alison (1972) reported a 26-day incubation period under incubator conditions.

Fledging Period: About 5 weeks (Bauer and Glutz, 1969). Alison (1972) noted that nineteen captive-reared young fledged in 35 days.

Nest and Egg Losses: Among a sample of 148 nests observed during the egg-laying period, 48 percent of the nests were lost, with predation the most frequent cause. Among 55 normal-sized clutches that failed, desertion and predation by ravens and minks were the most frequent causes (Bengtson, 1972). Alison (1972) reported a 41 percent nest loss among 95 nests, with foxes and parasitic jaegers the primary nest predators.

Juvenile and Adult Mortality: Brood mergers prevent the use of brood size counts as a measure of prefledging losses. Postfledging losses are also still unknown. Boyd (1962) estimated an annual adult mortality rate of 38 percent for Icelandic oldsquaws. The hunting mortality is probably quite low for this species. Alison (1972) reported that the brooding period mortality of adults at Churchill was nil for marked females and only 1.5 percent for males during the period 1968–1971.

GENERAL ECOLOGY

Food and Foraging: Cottam's (1939) study on oldsquaw foods and foraging behavior is the only complete one available for North America. He reported on the foods of 190 adults taken throughout most of the year and of 36 juvenile birds collected during July. Both adult and juvenile birds had a predominance of crustaceans in the digestive tracts, with mollusks, insects, and fish in decreasing order of identified foods of adults. Amphipod crustaceans (*Gammarus, Caprella,* etc.) alone constituted over 15 percent of the adult foods, while phyllopod crustaceans (especially *Branchinecta*) totalled over 30 percent of the food volume of the juvenile birds examined. Adults also had consumed a substantial number of various crabs, shrimps, and other crustaceans, which group totalled nearly half of the food volume. Among the mollusks, bivalves, univalves, and chitons were all consumed, but generally in rather small quantities. Insects were a fairly important source of food among birds collected during summer months, and most of the fish eaten were of little or no commercial value. Ellarson (1956) reported that on Lake Michigan the oldsquaw and whitefish populations are both closely dependent on amphipods (*Pontoporeia*), thus accounting for the high gill net mortality found there. Lagler and Wienert (1948) had earlier reported on the predominance of these amphipods and a small bivalve (*Pisidium*) in a sample of 36 birds from Lake

Michigan. Apparently the oldsquaws wintering in Danish waters have a higher dependency on mollusks; Madsen (1954) reported that the volumetric analysis of 110 birds revealed 65 percent bivalve mollusks, 8 percent univalve mollusks, 27 percent crustaceans, and a small amount of other animal foods.

The oldsquaw is famous for the depths it sometimes reaches during foraging, with many reports of birds foraging between 50 and 100 feet and a few records of individuals apparently exceeding 150 feet in their dives (Cottam, 1939). Probably the normal foraging depth is no more than 25 feet, at least in coastal areas where the birds are foraging on mollusks and other invertebrates of the subtidal zones. Lagler and Weinert noted that most of the birds caught in gill nets on Lake Michigan are taken at depths of 8 to 16 fathoms and that the greatest abundance of their two primary food species (*Pisidium* and *Pontoporeia*) occurs at depths of less than 60 meters (33 fathoms).

Sociality, Densities, Territoriality: Oldsquaws are not considered social nesters, and Bengtson (1970) reported that this species, like most other waterfowl he studied, showed an essentially random distribution of its nest sites. He observed a tendency to select islands for nest sites, but the overall average density of oldsquaw nests per square kilometer on thirteen study areas was 44 nests (6.9 acres per nest). In contrast, Alison (1972) found a breeding density of 4.5 pairs per square mile during four different years; he also noted positive male territoriality. Yet, although the males held territories of varying sizes and sometimes the same territory in different years, the females were nonterritorial and rarely nested in their mate's territory. Instead, they nested in a colonial manner, with nearly two-thirds of the nests within 100 feet of at least one other active nest.

Interspecific Relationships: In their seeming concentration on soft-bodied crustaceans, such as amphipods, and their secondary utilization of mollusks, oldsquaws probably only actively compete for food with harlequin ducks and, perhaps locally, Steller eiders. Considering the differences in the geographic distributions and preferred habitats of these species, it seems likely that there is little actual competition among them. Phillips (1925) noted that oldsquaws rarely associate with other ducks, and Mackay (1892) mentions seeing them a few times in the company of eiders. Hull (1914) mentioned that in Jackson Park, Chicago, oldsquaws avoided and were avoided by the other common wintering ducks, scaup and goldeneyes.

Oldsquaws build well-concealed nests that are notoriously difficult to locate. Even so, mammalian predators such as foxes are responsible for some nest losses, as are jaegers, and larger arctic gulls no doubt account for the loss of some young as well. Evans (1970) studied the nesting association of oldsquaws and arctic terns at Churchill, Manitoba, and summarized evidence that ravens and parasitic jaegers sometimes are important egg predators, and the latter may also consume ducklings. Evans reported that the oldsquaws he studied apparently gained protection from nesting near arctic terns, and he suggested means by which positive nesting associations between the two species might gradually develop. However, Alison (1972) questioned whether this relationship is actually beneficial to the oldsquaws, since he did not find any lowered nest predation rates in tern colonies.

General Activity Patterns and Movements: As with the other marine ducks, the general pattern of activity is one of foraging during the daylight hours in fairly shallow waters and moving to deeper bays or the open ocean for nocturnal resting. Mackay (1892) described this pattern in New England. He noted that in the Nantucket area the birds forage during the day in waters some 3 or 4 fathoms deep and start to leave about 3:00 p.m. for deeper waters. The flight continues until after dark. Apparently they sometimes remain on their feeding grounds after dark on clear, calm nights, but most birds shot during early morning hours have empty stomachs. In the rare cases where they have been seen foraging on freshwater ponds near the coast, they fly in to these ponds early in the morning and return to the coast about sunset. Alison (1970) observed a similar nighttime movement to deep water on Lake Ontario.

SOCIAL AND SEXUAL BEHAVIOR

Flocking Behavior: Although oldsquaws rarely associate with other species, they do form large single-species flocks, especially during fall. Mackay (1892) mentioned that flocks arriving in New England during fall usually were in groups of 75 to 100 birds, but sometimes flocks of more than 1,000 could be seen on these wintering areas. This would seem to represent an unusually large flock, however. Dementiev and Gladkov (1952) reported that fall flocks of up to 1,500 birds have been reported, that most wintering birds are found in small bands of up to 15 birds, and that spring migrant groups may number 300 to 400 individuals. The fact that these birds often feed in unusually deep waters, well out from the shore, makes it relatively difficult to obtain counts of flocks.

Pair-forming Behavior: Pair-forming behavior begins on the wintering areas, sometimes as early as December (Alison, 1970). By early May, about 70 percent of the adult males Alison observed near Toronto were already paired. The loud calls of the males, associated with social display, make courtship activity highly conspicuous. Myres (1959a) was the first to provide a partial description of oldsquaw sexual behavior patterns, and my observations (1965) and those of Alison (1970) have supplemented his observations.

Myres recognized two displays associated with these calls, the "bill-toss" and the "rear-end" displays. During the former call, which sounds like *ugh, ugh, ah-oo-gah'*, the head may be quickly tossed backward beyond the vertical while the hindquarters are maintained in a normal position. In the rear-end display, the neck and head are extended downward and forward toward the water, while the tail is raised to a nearly vertical position. Although not noted by Myres, Alison (1970) and I have observed neck-stretching and a turning-of-the-back-of-the-head by males as apparent displays, and a wing-flapping that possibly also represents a form of display behavior. Alison has observed a number of additional male displays, including lateral head-shaking, "porpoising," "steaming," "breast display," a short flight or "parachute display," and others. The most common female display is a chin-lifting that is probably a type of inciting, but Alison has observed some additional postures as well.

Copulatory Behavior: Myres (1959a) observed three instances of copulatory behavior but saw no specific associated displays. Alison (1970) has since reported that in six precopulatory situations the males invariably performed bill-tossing and lateral head-shaking, while bill-dipping, neck-stretching, and porpoising were also observed in some cases. In all cases the females performed lateral head-shaking and neck-stretching; a prone or soliciting posture was also sometimes observed. A variety of male postcopulatory displays were observed, including bill-tossing, neck-stretching, head-shaking, turning-the-back-of-the-head, and a sequence of porpoising, head-shaking, and wing-flapping.

Nesting and Brooding Behavior: According to the observations of Alison, the female hollows out her nest site immediately prior to the laying of the first egg. She normally sits very tightly, but typically feeds twice a day and on warm days may leave the nest for several hours. The males abandon their mates when the hens begin incubation, and either remain in the general area to undergo their molt or completely leave the area. After hatching, the ducklings are often reared on freshwater ponds or lakes, but at least at times they are taken to salt water when they are only a few days old (Phillips, 1925). The female typically leads the brood to open water rather than to shore when the young are threatened, and as they grow older they gradually move from smaller sedge-lined lakelets to larger reservoirs and marine waters (Dementiev and Gladkov, 1967).

Postbreeding Behavior: Throughout most of its breeding range, the breeding oldsquaws undergo their postnuptial molt in the breeding area, either as solitary birds or in small flocks. However, in eastern Siberia the breeding males and immatures evidently undertake an extensive molt migration to Wrangell Island prior to molting (Salomonsen, 1968). Fay (1961) mentions seeing considerable numbers of flightless oldsquaws on the lagoons and lakes of St. Lawrence Island, in flocks of fewer than 10 to more than 100. Whether these are immature nonbreeders that never left their wintering grounds or are birds that have moved in from other areas is apparently unknown. Probably the latter is the case, since Alison (1970) observed that the migration of the sizable wintering population in the Toronto areas is always total.

BLACK SCOTER

Melanitta nigra (Linnaeus) 1758

(Until 1973, regarded by the A.O.U. as *Oidemia nigra*)

Other Vernacular Names: American Scoter, Common Scoter, Coot.

Range: Breeds in Iceland, the British Isles, northern Europe, northern Asia, and islands of the Bering Sea; and in North America from northern Alaska probably across northern Canada, although specific breeding records are few and scattered. In North America, winters on the Pacific coast from the Pribilof and the Aleutian islands to southern California, on the Atlantic coast from Newfoundland south to about South Carolina, and to some extent in the interior, especially on the Great Lakes.

North American Subspecies:

M. m. nigra (L.): European Black Scoter. Breeds from Iceland eastward through Europe and Asia. Accidental in Greenland during winter.

M. m. americana (Swainson): American Black Scoter. Breeds and winters in North America as indicated above.

Measurements (after Delacour, 1959; for *M. m. nigra*):

Folded wing: Males 228-242, females 220-229 mm.

Culmen: Males 45-49, females 42-46 mm.

Weights: Nelson and Martin (1953) reported that eight males averaged 2.4 pounds (1,087 grams), while four females averaged 1.8 pounds (815 grams), with maximum weights being 2.8 pounds (1,268 grams) and 2.4 pounds (1,087 grams), respectively. Schiøler (1926) reported on winter

424   SEA DUCKS

weights of Danish birds representing the European race. Five adult males averaged 1,164 grams, seven second-year males averaged 1,101 grams, and eleven juveniles averaged 1,084 grams. Six adult females averaged 1,055 grams, seven second-year females averaged 1,070 grams, and four juveniles averaged 876 grams.

IDENTIFICATION

In the Hand: Recognizable in the hand as a diving duck by its enlarged hind toe and lengthened outer toe. The unusually narrow outermost primary (less evident in juveniles) and the relatively long (80-100 mm.), pointed tail will identify both sexes as black scoters. The bill is not feathered on the lateral surface or culmen, and no white feathers appear anywhere on the body except in juveniles, which have whitish underparts. The black is the smallest of the scoters, with a maximum folded wing length of 242 mm. in males and 230 mm. in females.

In the Field: Black scoter males are the blackest of all North American ducks, and females are the most uniformly dark brown of all these species. The best field mark for mature males, other than their black color, is a yellowish enlargement at the base of the bill, while females may be identified by the two-toned head and neck, which is dark brown above and grayish white on the cheeks, throat, and foreneck. Juveniles are similar, with an even sharper contrast to their head pattern. The birds take flight by running over the water, and they fly rather low but swiftly over the water. They appear dark brown or blackish on both upper and lower surfaces and have no white on the head or wings. The call of the courting male is a mellow whistle, while that of the female is grating and reminiscent of a door swinging on rusty hinges. The wings also produce a strong whistling noise in flight.

AGE AND SEX CRITERIA

Sex Determination: Adult males may be readily separated from females and immatures by their entirely black plumage. The tenth primary (outermost, excluding the vestigial eleventh primary) has its inner vane strongly narrowed for about six centimeters, or nearly the entire exposed length, while the corresponding feather of females is less strongly narrowed for only about the distal four centimeters. In first-year males this feather gradually tapers in width toward the tip or is slightly narrowed toward the tip.

Age Determination: Probably first-year females can be distinguished from older ones by the gradually tapered inner vane on their tenth primary and by their more whitish cheeks; in older females the distal half of the inner vane is only about half as wide as the proximal half and the cheeks and throat are a darker shade. First-year males are quite femalelike, and their tenth primary gradually tapers toward the tip. Some black feathers are acquired on the upperparts, but the abdomen and wings remain brownish (Dwight, 1914). By the second year, males are apparently indistinguishable from older birds.

DISTRIBUTION AND HABITAT

Breeding Distribution and Habitat: The North American breeding distribution of the black scoter is still rather obscure. Without doubt it is centered in Alaska, apparently on the Bering coast. It is doubtful whether it breeds on the Aleutian Islands (Murie, 1959), but there is an observation of a brood on Kodiak Island. It has been reported breeding in the Bristol Bay region along the Kvichak River, on Nelson Island, around Hooper and Igiak bays, and along the mouth of the Yukon, where it sometimes has constituted up to 25 percent of the observed waterfowl. Farther north, it nests at Cape Prince of Wales and the Shishmaref region of the Seward Peninsula, and probably also in the vicinity of Kotzebue Sound (Gabrielson and Lincoln, 1959). This area is perhaps the northern breeding limit for the species; at Cape Thompson the species is only a rare summer visitant (Williamson *et al.,* 1968). In the interior of Alaska the black scoter has been reported nesting in McKinley National Park and in the vicinity of Lake Louise, which is located on a tributary of the Susitna River (Gabrielson and Lincoln, 1959). It is questionable whether the arctic coast of Alaska is even occasionally used for breeding; although scoters have been seen on the lower Colville River, there is no indication of their breeding there (Kessel and Cade, 1958).

In Canada the records of definite breeding are even more limited. They include the Windy River area of southern Keewatin District, Leaf Bay in northern Quebec, and various localities in Newfoundland (Godfrey, 1966). There are other areas where summering populations can regularly be found, but these are not definitely established as representing breeding birds.

The breeding habitat consists of freshwater ponds, lakes, or rivers in tundra or wooded country. In Iceland, the species prefers to nest in pothole areas where shrubs are present (Bengtson, 1970). Since shrubs are a favored type of scoter nest cover, it would seem that true lowland tundra probably does not represent ideal habitat. Further, the extremely late nesting of scoters would tend to prevent them from extending far into arctic tundra habitats.

Wintering Distribution and Habitat: Black scoters winter commonly along the Aleutian Islands and the Alaska Peninsula from Kodiak Island to Atka Island (Murie, 1959). They have been reported as abundant at Attu Island, but Kenyon (1961) did not list them for Amchitka. They also winter among

Breeding (hatched) and wintering (shaded) distributions of the
black scoter in North America.

the islands and channels of southeastern Alaska (Gabrielson and Lincoln, 1959) and along coastal British Columbia southward to Puget Sound, where they are the least common of the scoters (Yocom, 1951). Additionally, they extend in winter along the open coast southward into Oregon and occasionally to California.

On the Atlantic coast black scoters winter from Newfoundland southward, with a few occurring irregularly on the Great Lakes (Godfrey, 1966). They are frequently quite common as far south as Chesapeake Bay, where they are generally found in the littoral zone of the ocean, with a few occurring on coastal bays and occasionally on salt and brackish estuaries of the Bay itself (Stewart, 1962). Farther south they are generally the least common of the three scoter species, and perhaps normally range as far south in winter as Beaufort County, South Carolina (Sprunt and Chamberlain, 1949).

As Stewart has mentioned, optimum winter habitat for this and the other scoters is the littoral zone of the ocean, usually within a mile of shore and in the area just beyond the breakers. There they both forage and rest, relatively independent of tidal action and human disturbance. Generally the black scoter seems to prefer areas where the water depth does not exceed 25 feet and where mussels can be found in large quantities (Cottam, 1939).

GENERAL BIOLOGY

Age at Maturity: No definite information, except that the fully adult plumage of the male is not attained until its second fall of life, and perhaps the bill coloration and enlargement may not be fully developed until even later (Dwight, 1914). Thus, pending evidence to the contrary, breeding at the end of the second year of life would seem most probable.

Pair Bond Pattern: Pair bonds are evidently renewed yearly. Bengtson (1966) noted that many females are already apparently paired on their arrival at Icelandic breeding grounds, but courtship activities are frequent during May and June, and some active, unpaired females may be seen as late as mid-June. Evidently the males desert their mates and quickly leave the area as soon as the females begin to incubate.

Nest Location: In Iceland, nests are usually placed under a dense cover of birch and willow-scrub (Bengtson, 1966). Of 308 nests found by Bengtson (1970), 199 were under low shrubs, 78 under high shrubs, 12 were in holes, 11 under angelica (*Angelica* and *Archangelica*), 5 were in meadows, and 3 among sedges. Nests more frequently were situated in locations between 10 and 30 meters from the nearest water. There was no tendency toward nesting on islands, and indeed the relative nest density was somewhat lower on islands than on the mainland.

Clutch Size: So few clutches of North American black scoters have been found that it is difficult to know what is a typical clutch size for this population. However, the European population tends to have clutch sizes of 6 to 9 eggs, with occasional records of 5 and 10, and one (probably multiple) clutch of 13 eggs reported (Bauer and Glutz, 1969). A sample of 187 first clutches averaged 8.74 eggs, with significant yearly differences in mean clutch sizes that ranged from 7.56 to 9.04 (Bengtson, 1971). Thirty renests averaged 6.1 eggs (Bengtson, 1972).

Incubation Period: Reported by Delacour (1959) as 27 to 28 days. Also estimated as 31 days (Dementiev and Gladkov, 1967).

Fledging Period: Estimated by Lack (1968) as six and one-half weeks.

Nest and Egg Losses: Seventeen percent of 109 nests were lost during the egg-laying period, primarily through predation. Of 23 normal-sized clutches that failed to hatch, desertion and raven predation were major factors (Bengtson, 1972).

Juvenile and Adult Mortality: Both prefledging and postfledging mortality losses of juveniles are little studied. Boyd (1962) estimated the annual adult mortality of the Iceland population of black scoters as 33 percent.

GENERAL ECOLOGY

Food and Foraging: Cottam's (1939) study of the foods taken by 124 adult scoters collected during ten months of the year is the most comprehensive available for North America, while Madsen's (1954) study of 219 samples from Danish coastal waters provides comparable information for the European population. Cottam reported that nearly 90 percent of the volume of food present was of animal origin, with mollusks constituting most of the animal foods. The most important of these were blue mussels (*Mytilus edulis*) and related forms, with short razor clams (*Siliqua*) of secondary importance. A larger consumption of barnacles was indicated than appears typical of other scoter species, which seem to consume a greater quantity of crabs. Madsen similarly found that mollusks constituted 77 percent of the food by volume, of which bivalves (especially *Mytilus edulis*) account for the majority, while polychaete worms, crustaceans, and echinoderms made up the remainder. The four most important foods were apparently blue mussels, cockles (*Cardium*), univalve mollusks (*Nassa*), and tubeworms (*Pectinaria*). Thus, although birds in both populations primarily consumed mussels and other mollusks, the consumption of crustaceans, annelids, and other invertebrates seemingly varied with availability or other factors. Plant materials play a small role in the diet of scoters, and even among summer samples Cottam reported that only about 13 percent of the identified food materials were of this source.

Cottam reported that black scoters usually forage in water less than 25 feet deep, but they have been known to reach 40 feet. He also noted that the European race has been reported to forage primarily in waters between 6 and 12 feet deep. Salomonsen (1968) mentioned that molting birds in the North Sea mostly occur in waters less than 5 meters deep.

Sociality, Densities, Territoriality: According to the data of Bengtson (1970), the nests of this species are essentially distributed at random, with no tendencies toward aggregation in nesting colonies. The average nesting density that he reported on thirteen different study areas in Iceland was 53 nests per square kilometer (5 acres per nest). There seems to be no evidence relating to the possible existence of territoriality in this species.

Interspecific Relationships: To what extent competition for food may exist between the black scoter and the other two species of this genus is unknown. All three forage predominantly on mollusks, but the size differences of adults (surf scoter smallest, white-winged largest) may bring about differences in effective foraging depths. The black and surf scoter seemingly both rely heavily on blue mussels and related species, but the surf scoter generally forages closer to the coastline than does the black scoter (Cottam, 1939). Phillips (1926) noted that, although the black scoter is most often seen in single-species flocks, it more commonly associates with surf scoters than with white-winged scoters.

General Activity Patterns and Movements: Phillips reported that this species is relatively active throughout the day and that migratory or local movements can occur at almost any time of day. According to him, the birds normally move into shallower waters for foraging early in the morning, often coming from some distance.

SOCIAL AND SEXUAL BEHAVIOR

Flocking Behavior: Apart from the obvious fact that migrant and wintering flocks of black scoters are often extremely large, there seems to be little specific information on flock sizes of this species. Atkinson-Willes (1963) mentioned that, although this species is gregarious, it is difficult to count, since the birds are often in rough water far from shore. In Great Britain, fairly large flocks of molting males may be seen in late summer, while the largest flocks of wintering birds include females and young birds as well.

Pair-forming Behavior: McKinney (1959) observed pair-forming behavior of black scoters in Alaska during April and May, and Bengtson (1966) described comparable display patterns that he observed in Iceland during May and June. It is possible that racial variation in these behavior patterns exist, but McKinney's and Myres's (1959a) observations on the American race closely agree with those of Bengtson and myself (1965) on European black scoters. Social courtship usually occurs in small flocks that typically contain a single female and 5 to 8 males, in McKinney's observation. Bengtson noted that as the spring progressed, the number of males in courting groups with single females increased from an average of about 4 in late May to more than 10 in late June, no doubt reflecting the gradual reduction of available females. He found that paired males performed many of the same postures as those seen in courting groups, but in markedly different relative frequencies. Paired males exhibited the highest incidence of lateral head-shaking, general shaking (upward-stretch), and wing-flapping, while the incidences of the body-up (neck-stretching of Myres), tail-snap, low-rush, short flight, and steaming were all slightly or distinctly more frequent among males in courting parties. Preening movements appeared to be most frequent in nonaggressive unpaired and paired males and least frequent in aggressive unpaired males. Definite inciting behavior by females has not been described, although threatlike bill-pointing movements have been seen (McKinney), as well as slight chin-lifting movements (Myres).

Copulatory Behavior: To judge from available observations, the precopulatory behavior of black scoters is simple and usually very short. The female seemingly adopts a prone position after both sexes have performed preening movements in various places. The male then typically performs a shake (upward-stretch) and mounts immediately. After treading, he usually swims away from the hen in a neck-stretching posture, while uttering his typical whistled notes. Some variations in postcopulatory behavior have also been reported (Johnsgard, 1965).

Nesting and Brooding Behavior: Bengtson (1970) reported that the female scoter "sits very tight" during incubation and is normally abandoned by the drake shortly after incubation begins, with some males remaining in the vicinity of the nest for as long as a week. Males typically then move out of the nesting areas and migrate to traditional molting areas. The limited brood counts that are available do not suggest that brood mergers, as in white-winged scoters and eiders, are characteristic of this species.

Postbreeding Behavior: Postbreeding movements of the North American population of black scoters are still little understood, but those in northern Europe have been well studied. Salomonsen (1968) described the molt migration of birds to the west coast of Jutland, in the North Sea. There, up to 150,000 birds congregate in August and September, in waters less than 10 meters deep. Birds from much of the Scandinavian and north Russian breeding populations occur there and probably constitute the majority of these populations. These include immatures, which may arrive there in spring, as well as adult males and possibly also some females.

SURF SCOTER

Melanitta perspicillata (Linnaeus) 1758

Other Vernacular Names: Coot, Skunk-head Coot.

Range: Breeds in North America from western Alaska eastward through the Yukon and the Northwest Territories to southern Hudson Bay, and in the interior of Quebec and Labrador. Winters on the Pacific coast from the Aleutian Islands south to the Gulf of California, and on the Atlantic coast from the Bay of Fundy south to Florida, with smaller numbers in the interior, especially on the Great Lakes.

Subspecies: None recognized.

Measurements (after Delacour, 1959):

Folded wing: Males 240-256, females 223-235 mm.

Culmen: Males 34-38, females 33-37 mm.

Weights: Nelson and Martin (1953) reported that twelve males averaged 2.2 pounds (997 grams), while ten females averaged 2.0 pounds (907 grams), and both sexes had a maximum weight of 2.5 pounds (1,133 grams).

IDENTIFICATION

In the Hand: Obviously a diving duck, on the basis of its enlarged hind toe and the outer toe as long or longer than the middle toe. Specimens can be verified as surf scoters if the outermost primary is longer than the adjacent one and feathering extends forward on the culmen almost to the rear edge of the nostrils. Additionally, there is a rounded or squarish black mark on the side of the bill near its base. Intermediate in size between the black and the white-winged scoters, surf scoters have a folded wing measurement of 240-256 mm. in males and 223-235 mm. in females.

In the Field: A maritime species that sometimes is found on large lakes or deep rivers during fall and winter, surf scoters may be distinguished on the water by the white markings on the male's forehead and nape, and the whitish cheek, ear, and nape markings of females. The white eye of adult males is often visible, but both sexes lack white on the wings. When landing, males frequently hold their wings upward and skid to a stop in the water, and when swimming, they usually hold the level of the bill slightly below horizontal. The male reportedly has a liquid, gurgling call uttered during courtship, and the female has a more crowlike note. In flight, the wings produce a humming sound, and the birds usually fly in irregular lines fairly low over the water.

AGE AND SEX CRITERIA

Sex Determination: The presence of black feathers anywhere on the body is indicative of a male, but may not serve to separate all first-year males from females, at least prior to October, when the first blackish feathers begin to appear on the head, scapulars, and flanks of first-year birds (Bent, 1925). The male's eyes change from brown to yellow during the winter, and then to white by the end of the first year (Dwight, 1914).

Age Determination: First-year females can apparently be distinguished from older birds by their conspicuous white patches on the lores and ear region. Males less than one year old lack the white forehead patch and have a less-colorful bill than full adults. Their iris color is probably also still brownish at this age. However, adult plumage changes are not well known in scoters, and there may be some reduction of the white forehead markings among adult males during late summer or fall (Bent, 1925). Some adult females develop a malelike whitish nape patch, but there is much individual variation in this (Dwight, 1914).

DISTRIBUTION AND HABITAT

Breeding Distribution and Habitat: In contrast to the other two scoter species, the surf scoter is entirely limited to North America as a breeding bird. This is rather surprising, in view of its widespread occurrence on this continent, and its marine wintering tendencies. Its failure to colonize eastern Asia is thus difficult to understand.

In Alaska, the surf scoter is widespread in summer, but many appear to be nonbreeding birds. Positive breeding records are mostly from the Bering Sea and Arctic Ocean coasts and from the upper Yukon Valley. Clutches have been found or ducklings seen at Lynx Lake (north of Bristol Bay), Kotzebue

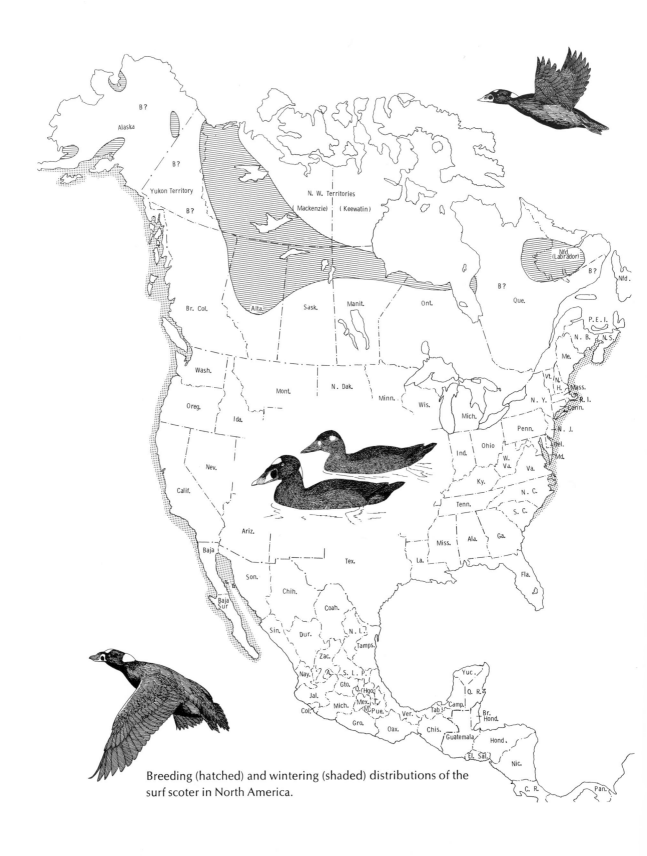

Breeding (hatched) and wintering (shaded) distributions of the
surf scoter in North America.

Sound, Mount McKinley National Park, Fort Yukon, and on the Porcupine River (Gabrielson and Lincoln, 1959).

In Canada, the species likewise is of widespread occurrence, although few actual breeding records exist. Godfrey (1966) includes within the breeding range the Yukon (probably), western McKenzie, Alberta (Elk Island Park), northern Saskatchewan (Lake Athabasca), James Bay (Charlton and Sheppard islands), northern Ontario, Quebec (Wakuach Lake and near Otelnuk Lake), and Labrador (Grand Falls and Petitsikapau Lake).

The breeding habitat requirements are little known, but probably are like those of the other scoters. Thus, freshwater ponds, lakes, or rivers, with shrubby cover or woodland in the vicinity, are probably required.

Wintering Distribution and Habitat: The wintering distribution of this species is much better known than its breeding distribution. Although stragglers do occur along the coastlines of Asia and Scandinavia, the overwhelming majority of birds evidently winter along North American coastlines. They winter abundantly in the waters of southeastern Alaska, especially along the Alexander Archipelago, with lesser numbers extending along the south coast of the Alaska Peninsula and to some extent into the Aleutian Islands (Gabrielson and Lincoln, 1959).

In western Canada, surf scoters winter in large numbers along the coast of British Columbia, and they, together with white-winged scoters, are perhaps the most numerous of the wintering ducks of the Puget Sound region of Washington (Jewett *et al.,* 1953). Phillips (1926) suggested that from Puget Sound northward, surf scoters tend to be outnumbered by white-winged scoters, while farther south the reverse presumably applies. Aerial counts in the late 1950s and early 1960s indicated that scoters constituted nearly half of the wintering diving ducks of this area (Wick and Jeffrey, 1966). Surf scoters also winter commonly along the Pacific coastlines of Oregon and California and are the commonest scoter species of northwestern Mexico. Leopold (1959) noted over 24,000 of these birds during winter inventory counts, with the largest population in San Ignacio Bay of the Baja Peninsula.

On the Atlantic coast, surf scoters winter from Newfoundland and the Gulf of St. Lawrence southward (Godfrey, 1966), with occasional birds appearing on lakes Erie and Ontario. Atlantic coast populations are seemingly not so large as those on the Pacific coast. In the Chesapeake Bay area the surf scoters are usually the commonest scoter species in the coastal sections, while white-wings are much more common in the Bay proper (Stewart, 1962). As far south as South Carolina, the surf scoter is still a fairly common winter visitor (Sprunt and Chamberlain, 1949).

Preferred wintering habitats include the littoral zone of the ocean and adjoining coastal bays, with a few utilizing salt or brackish estuarine bays in the Chesapeake region (Stewart, 1962).

GENERAL BIOLOGY

Age at Maturity: Not definitely established, but judging from their molting sequence the birds probably breed at the end of their second year, although the fully mature plumage and bill coloration may not be attained until the following fall (Bent, 1925).

Pair Bond Pattern: Apparently reestablished each winter and spring, during a prolonged period of social display (Myres, 1959a).

Nest Location: Too few nests have been found to allow many conclusions on this point. McFarlane (quoted by Bent, 1925) reported that the nests are usually located at a considerable distance from water and always well concealed under the low-spreading branches of a pine or spruce tree. Bent further said that in Labrador the ducks reportedly nest about the inland ponds and lakes, placing their nests in grass or under bushes close to the edge of the water.

Clutch Size: Probably normally from 5 to 7 eggs constitute a clutch, with larger clutches unusual (Bent, 1925).

Incubation and Fledging Period: Not yet established.

Nest and Egg Losses: No specific information.

Juvenile and Adult Mortality: No specific information. One male lived for nearly ten years at the San Diego Zoo (Delacour, 1959).

GENERAL ECOLOGY

Food and Foraging: Cottam's (1939) analysis of food samples from 168 adult scoters taken throughout the year is the only major source of information on this point. He reported that mollusks (especially blue mussels and related species) constituted 60 percent of the food volume, with crustaceans and insects another 10 percent each, and plant materials totalling about 12 percent. As with the other two scoters, bivalve mollusks make up at least half of the surf scoter's food, although clams, oysters, and scallops apparently are utilized relatively little. Cottam also reported that 7 juvenile birds had fed largely on various insects and, to a lesser extent, on mollusks and freshwater or terrestrial plants.

Cottam judged that most foraging was done in early morning, since many birds shot in midmorning hours already had empty stomachs. They often forage in water just beyond the breakers, usually in depths from 6 to 30 feet. During observations in Vancouver harbor, I noted that the surf scoters were foraging in shallower waters and closer to shore than were the much less common white-winged scoters. However, they apparently regularly are associated with that species in wintering areas, even though white-winged scoters seemingly depend to a greater extent on oysters, clams, periwinkles, and mollusks other than mussels (Cottam, 1939; McGilvrey, 1967).

Sociality, Densities, Territoriality: No specific information is available on these points. The few available observations indicate that the nests are well scattered over wide areas.

Interspecific Relationships: All three species of scoters utilize much the same habitats where they occur together, and perhaps some foraging competition does exist among them. Surf scoters apparently are closest to the black scoter in the kinds of foods utilized, but surf scoters seemingly winter in more southerly locations and forage closer to the coasts. Cottam noted that they eat less of the heavier-shelled mollusks than do the larger scoter species and also are possibly more partial to foods of vegetable origin.

Too little is known of the nesting biology of surf scoters to judge the possible importance of nest and duckling predators or to judge other important interspecific relationships occurring at this stage in the life cycle.

General Activity Patterns and Movements: Jewett *et al.* (1953) reported that the surf scoter is extremely active during the morning and evening hours, coming inshore as far as it possibly can and diving for food in the shallows, where animal life is the most abundant.

Like the other scoters, it probably retires to deeper waters to spend the night, although it is possible that some nocturnal foraging activity occurs under favorable conditions.

SOCIAL AND SEXUAL BEHAVIOR

Flocking Behavior: During migration and on wintering areas, flocks of hundreds or even thousands of scoters are not uncommon and may be of single-species groups or of mixed composition. In the Puget Sound area, white-winged and surf scoters occur in flocks of 50 to 2,000 or more birds, the two species often about equal in numbers. Large flocks have been recorded until about April, and in May groups of 40 or 50 are more usual. During the northern movement in spring, migrant flocks are often of larger size and tend to be "rafted up" in compact groups (Jewett *et al.,* 1953).

Pair-forming Behavior: Most of the available information on surf scoter pair-formation activities derives from the work of Myres (1959a) in the Vancouver area. There during late winter and spring social display may be readily seen; in late March I have observed several small groups of courting birds displaying simultaneously, while the majority of the visible birds were apparently already paired and were engaged in foraging behavior. A good deal of overt or ritualized threatening behavior is evident in these groups, with the males often attacking one another and with the female threatening any male that approaches too closely. Myres mentioned observing the females performing chin-lifting movements and uttering a crowlike note; on the basis of my observations, I regard this as functionally equivalent to the inciting behavior of eiders or goldeneyes.

Male postures and movements are several, including aggressive crouched and threat postures much like those of male goldeneyes. A common male posture is the "sentinel," in which the bird vertically stretches his neck to the utmost, with the tail either raised vertically or in the water. From this posture the male may begin "breast-scooping," which appears to be a ritualized version of breast-preening movements. A liquid, gurgling call accompanies the movements. A short flight, or "fly-away" display, is also common, and on landing the male holds his wings in an upward V posture as he skids to a stop in the water. Probably the most elaborately ritualized display is "chest-lifting," a sudden and energetic vertical chest-lifting movement, usually performed close to the female and seemingly directed toward her. I did not hear any calls associated with this display, but was greatly impressed by its similarity in form and apparent function to the "rearing" display of the male Steller eider.

Copulatory Behavior: Myres (1959a; 1959b) has provided the only detailed observations on copulation in the surf scoter. He observed four instances between late December and early January, and in no case did the birds appear to be permanently paired. The female assumed a prone posture and remained in it, in one case up to about two minutes. The male performed water-twitching (dipping and shaking the bill in the water), preening-behind-the-wing, and also "false" drinking. During treading the male flicked his wings, and on each of the occasions he performed a single chest-lifting display as he released his grip on the female. No other specific postcopulatory displays by either sex were noted.

Nesting and Brooding Behavior: No studies on the nesting behavior of this species have been performed, but in all likelihood it is very similar to that of the white-winged scoter, which has been well studied.

Postbreeding Behavior: Since well-developed molt migrations are known to occur in both black and white-winged scoters (Salomonsen, 1968), it seems probable that a comparable movement occurs in this species. Many immature birds spend their summers along the Pacific coastlines and especially along coastal Alaska. Gabrielson and Lincoln (1959) noted that summer flocks sometimes occur along the south shore of the Alaska Peninsula and around some of the Aleutians. They reportedly become plentiful at Sitka about August 15, suggestive of an early premolting arrival of adult birds.

WHITE-WINGED SCOTER

Melanitta fusca (Linnaeus) 1758

(Melanitta deglandi of A.O.U., 1957)

Other Vernacular Names: Velvet Scoter, White-winged Coot.

Range: Breeds in Scandinavia, Estonia, northern Russia, and northeastern Siberia; and in North America from northwestern Alaska, the Yukon, the Northwest Territories east to Hudson Bay, and south through western Canada to southern Manitoba and rarely to north-central North Dakota. Winters on both coasts of North America, from Alaska to Baja California and from the Gulf of St. Lawrence to South Carolina.

North American Subspecies:

M. f. deglandi (Bonaparte): American White-winged Scoter. Breeds in North America as indicated above. Delacour (1959) rejects the validity of the Pacific coastal race *dixoni.*

M. f. fusca (L.): European White-winged (Velvet) Scoter. Breeds in Europe and Asia; in North America occurs casually in Greenland.

Measurements (after Delacour, 1959):

Folded wing: Males 269-293, females 251-266 mm.

Culmen: Males 37-50, females 38-43 mm.

Weights: Nelson and Martin (1953) reported that thirteen males averaged 3.4 pounds (1,542 grams), while nineteen females averaged 2.7 pounds (1,223 grams), with maximum weights of 4 pounds (1,814 grams) and 3.4 pounds (1,542 grams), respectively. Schiøler (1926) reported on winter weights of the European race. Six juvenile males averaged 1,670 grams, while nine older males averaged 1,727 grams, with a maximum male weight of 2,104 grams. Four juvenile females averaged 1,214 grams, while eleven older females averaged 1,658 grams.

IDENTIFICATION

In the Hand: As in other diving ducks, the enlarged hind toe and lengthened outer toe is present, and specimens may be recognized as a scoter by the heavy bill and rather uniformly dark body. Unlike the other scoters, it has a bill that is feathered laterally to a point near the posterior edge of the .nostrils, its outermost primary is shorter but not appreciably narrower than the adjoining one, and its speculum is white. The white-winged is the largest of the scoters, with folded wing measuring from 269 to 293 mm. in males and from 251 to 266 mm. in females.

In the Field: White-winged scoters are usually found on the coast, but are more likely than the other scoters to be found on large interior lakes during winter. On the water the white wing markings are sometimes not visible, and a white eye-patch on the male may be the only apparent part of the bird that is not dark brown or black. Adult females very closely resemble female surf scoters on the water, but never exhibit whitish nape markings. The blackish crown of the former contrasts less sharply with the sides of the head, and the pale cheek and ear markings are generally less apparent than in the latter. As soon as the birds flap their wings or fly, the white secondary markings become apparent and provide the best field marks. In flight, white-winged scoters are the most ponderous of the scoters, usually flying low over the water in loose flocks or long lines. Males possess a bell-like, repeated whistled note, and females are said to also utter a very thin whistle.

AGE AND SEX CRITERIA

Sex Determination: By December or a little later, first-year males will begin to acquire the black feathers by which all older males can be readily separated from females, with the first such feathers appearing on the head. For younger birds, internal examination will be necessary to determine sex.

Age Determination: Males less than one year old have brownish underparts and a less colorful and swollen bill than do adults, and until fourteen or fifteen months old have a brown iris (Bent, 1925). A fully black body and wing plumage are attained during the second winter, but maximal bill size is evidently not attained until about another year has passed. First-year females have more conspicuous whitish markings on the lores and ear region than do older females, which may exhibit almost no pale marks on the sides of the head (Dwight, 1914). Some young females have a very much reduced white speculum, and additionally the outer side of the tarsus is blackish, while the inner side of the tarsus and toes are dull purplish brown (Kortright, 1943). Immatures of both sexes exhibit light, frayed tips on their tertials and the tertial coverts, and the greater coverts often are entirely brown or have less white on their tips than occurs in adults (Carney, 1964).

DISTRIBUTION AND HABITAT

Breeding Distribution and Habitat: The North American breeding distribution of this most widespread species of scoter is almost entirely limited to Alaska and Canada. In Alaska all definite records of breeding are from the interior, chiefly in the vicinity of Fort Yukon. From this area the birds also breed eastward along the Porcupine River drainage, northward at least as far as Anaktuvuk Pass, south to the Minto Lakes, and west to the Innoko watershed and the vicinity of Koyukuk (Gabrielson and Lincoln, 1959).

In Canada, the white-winged scoter is generally the commonest breeding scoter species. It ranges from the mouth of the Mackenzie River southward through the Yukon and western Mackenzie District to central British Columbia, and across the forested portions of Alberta, Saskatchewan, and Manitoba, with the eastern breeding limits in the vicinity of Churchill, Manitoba, and Ney Lake, Ontario. Breeding also occurs in the Cypress Hills area of southwestern Saskatchewan and as far south as Shoal Lake, Manitoba (Godfrey, 1966).

South of Canada, white-winged scoters often summer in coastal areas and sometimes occur in the interior states as nonbreeders during the summer months, but apparently only in North Dakota has any breeding occurred. At one time the birds regularly bred in the vicinity of Devils Lake, but they apparently became rare in North Dakota between 1900 and 1920. Since then, broods have been seen in 1936 in McHenry County, and in 1952, 1953, and 1955 at Des Lacs and Lostwood refuges, Burke County (Duebberts, 1961).

Habitat requirements of white-winged scoters have not been well analyzed in North America, but studies on the European race probably are applicable to this region as well. There, nesting on open tundra is rare, and the coastal archipelagos and lakes of the northern coniferous forest zone seem to represent the original breeding habitats of the species. Hildén (1964) found nesting to occur in open scrub heaths and birch woods of larger islands of the Valassaaret group, as well as on small islets. Boulder islets dominated by herbaceous vegetation and with shrubs and trees present seemed to represent the ideal habitat

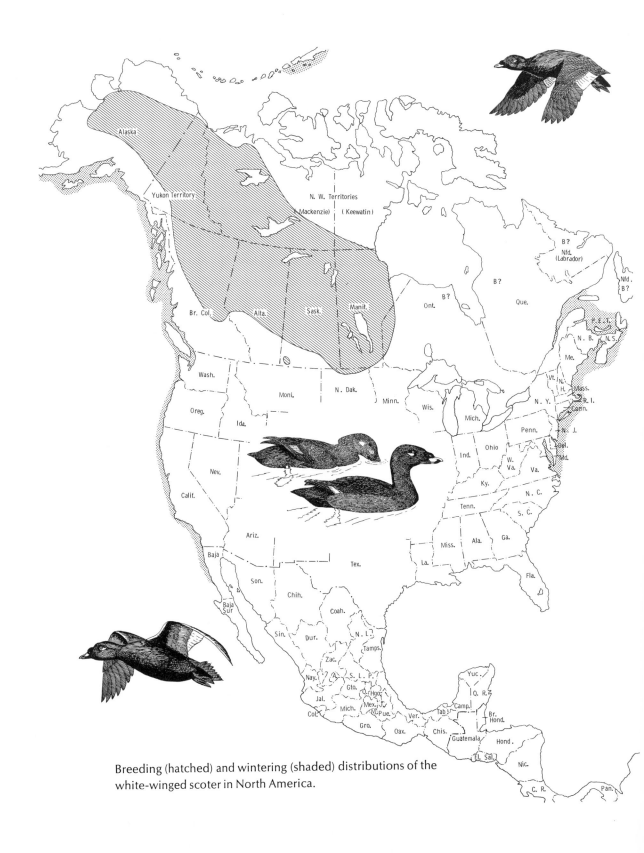

Breeding (hatched) and wintering (shaded) distributions of the
white-winged scoter in North America.

type and to provide suitable shrubby nesting cover as well as associated larid nesting colonies, to which this species is attracted. Islets richly overgrown with bushes or partially wooded sometimes had scoters nesting even in the absence of larids, indicating that these vegetational features are an important aspect of breeding habitat selection. Unlike the common eiders of the same area, the scoters nest all the way to the central parts of the larger islands. Favored brood habitats are those with extensive shoals and shallow, narrow water areas sheltered from heavy wave action.

Wintering Distribution and Habitat: In Alaska, the bays and channels of the Alexander Archipelago of southeastern Alaska seem to be the center of abundance of wintering white-winged scoters, but the species extends in smaller numbers westward to the eastern Aleutian Islands and is regularly seen around the Pribilof Islands (Gabrielson and Lincoln, 1959).

In western Canada, this species winters commonly along the coastline of British Columbia (Godfrey, 1966) and together with the surf scoter is among the commonest wintering ducks of the Washington coast and Puget Sound area (Jewett *et al.,* 1953). It is a common to abundant winter resident along the coasts of Oregon and California and is of regular occurrence as far south as San Quintin Bay (Leopold, 1959).

In eastern Canada, white-winged scoters winter from Newfoundland and the Gulf of St. Lawrence southward to the United States border and, in limited numbers, also occur on the Great Lakes (Godfrey, 1966). From Maine southward, they are relatively abundant along the New England coastline. In the Chesapeake Bay area they are the commonest of the three scoter species (Stewart, 1962), but in South Carolina they are the least common of the scoters (Sprunt and Chamberlain, 1949). White-winged scoters are rare in Florida and Louisiana waters. They are also rare through most of the interior of the United States south of Canada, although stragglers sometimes winter on reservoirs and rivers.

Like the other two scoters, it prefers for its wintering habitat the littoral zone of the ocean, just beyond the breakers and within a mile of shore. In the Chesapeake Bay area this species is common in coastal bays and in salt or brackish estuarine bays, with some birds extending into slightly brackish estuarine bays (Stewart, 1962).

GENERAL BIOLOGY

Age at Maturity: Sexual maturity reportedly occurs in the second year of life (Dementiev and Gladkov, 1967).

Pair Bond Patterns: Pair bonds are renewed each year, with pair-forming behavior beginning on wintering areas. Males desert their mates before hatching of the clutches occurs, but specific details on the timing seem to be lacking. Rawls (1949) noted that males began to band together at Delta, Manitoba, in mid-July, or about a month before the first broods were seen. This would indicate a desertion of females at the time incubation begins.

Nest Location: Hildén (1964) reported on 254 nest sites he observed on the Valassaaret Islands of the Gulf of Bothnia. About three-fourths of these were well concealed, in most instances underneath junipers (29.4 percent) or *Hippophae* bushes (24.2 percent). Cover provided by forbs accounted for 17.1 percent, and the remainder were in mixed shrub-forb cover, in other cover types, under boulders, or were exposed. Exposed nests were only typical on islets having a moderate to high density of nesting larids. Koskimies and Routamo (1953) reported an even higher usage of juniper bushes (82 percent) on the relatively large and partly wooded islands of their study area. The height and density of the surrounding bushes are apparently not important, but the nests are most often placed under stones projecting from the earth, in a cavity, or among stones that are well covered by the stems and branches of juniper. The shoreline zone is generally avoided for nesting, although dense grasses sometimes occur there. Instead, nests are generally among woodland far from shore, and on small islets lacking such cover the species does not nest at all (Hildén, 1964). Relatively few nests from the North American population have been described, but roses (*Rosa*), willows (*Salix*), raspberries (*Rubus*), and gooseberries (*Ribes*) are apparently favored cover plants (Rawls, 1949).

Clutch Size: Hildén (1964) reported an average clutch size of 8.43 eggs for 187 clutches, with a modal clutch of 9 eggs and a range from 6 to 12. Koskimies and Routamo (1953) also found an overall average of 8.43 for 90 Finnish clutches, with earlier clutches averaging slightly larger than later ones. Comparable samples from North America are not available, but Vermeer (1969) found an average clutch size of 10.2 eggs in 12 clutches, and a range of 6 to 16 eggs per clutch. The average egg-laying interval is about 40 hours.

Incubation Period: The average of 29 instances was 27.52 days, with an observed range of 26 to 29 days (Paavolainen, cited in Bauer and Glutz, 1969).

Fledging Period: Not reported.

Nest and Egg Losses: Hildén (1964) provided hatching data for 76 nests that were studied during two years, with an overall average nesting success of 91 percent. Compared with eider nests on the same study area, the rate of nesting success was higher and seemingly attributable to the white-winged scoters' more-sheltered nest locations and a lesser tendency toward nest desertion. Evidently most egg losses to crows and ravens occur during the egg-laying period, when the eggs are poorly covered and are not defended by the female. Even so, the total egg losses (15.7 percent) found for this species were less than those of the other ducks nesting in the area. Koskimies and Routamo (1953) likewise found a high loss to crows during the egg-laying period, but no incidents of predation were found after incubation had begun.

Juvenile Mortality: Because of the strong tendencies of this species to form mixed broods and for the females to abandon their young, brood size counts provide no useful estimate of prefledging mortality. At least in marine environments such as the Gulf of Finland, duckling mortality is often extremely high and usually exceeds 90 percent (Koskimies, 1955). Hildén (1964) likewise reported comparable brood losses for the Gulf of Bothnia during three years of study. In these years the loss of individual young was estimated at 92 to 100 percent and the rate of brood losses at 83 to 99 percent. These losses seem related to the low tolerance of scoter ducklings to severe weather conditions. Apparently this species is basically adapted to breeding on relatively small inland waters, and only during years of unusually fine weather is brood success high in the marine habitats. In local areas of reed bays, where the water temperature is fairly high and there is protection against rough seas, survival may be fairly high, although such sheltered areas may develop overly congested brood populations. Losses of ducklings to gulls seem to be related to variations in weather, with predation rates much higher during bad weather. Herring gulls and great black-backed gulls are evidently by far the worst of these predators (Hildén, 1964).

Rawls's (1949) studies at Delta, Manitoba, indicated that brood mergers are not typical in this sparse population. Twelve broods up to one week of age averaged 4.75 young, four broods two weeks old averaged 4.0 young, and three broods three weeks old averaged 3.0 young. Brood survival in this inland habitat is thus seemingly higher than is characteristic of marine environments.

Adult Mortality: Koskimies (1957), by marking females and observing them on nest sites in later years, calculated an annual adult mortality of only about 5 percent. Probably a more realistic estimate is Grenquist's (1965) 43 percent annual mortality rate, which was based on recoveries of banded birds.

GENERAL ECOLOGY

Food and Foraging: The survey by Cottam (1939) is still the most comprehensive study of the foods of this species. He analyzed the foods found in 819 adults and 4 juveniles, most of which were taken along the coasts of Massachusetts and Washington. Among the adults, 75 percent of the foods by volume were found to be mollusks, of which rock clams (*Protothaca*), oysters (*Ostrea*), and mussels (especially *Mytilus*) were the most prevalent, and bivalves collectively constituted 63 percent of the total. Seemingly, availability rather than specific preference determined the types of foods taken. Crustaceans were as a group second in importance and included various decapods (crabs, crayfishes, etc.), amphipods, and barnacles. Other foods found in adults included insects, fishes, plant foods, and miscellaneous materials, all in quantities of less than 3 percent by volume. The few juveniles that Cottam examined had primarily consumed various crustaceans. Rawls (1949) noted that four of five juveniles he collected at Delta, Manitoba, had been consuming *Hyalella* amphipods, as had two adult females.

McGilvrey (1967), reporting on 124 white-winged scoters collected from Maine to Long Island Sound, found substantial differences in food taken according to area of collection. In birds from Maine, over half the food volume consisted of dog winkles (*Thais*). Among Massachusetts birds, blue mussels (*Mytilus*) and yoldia (*Yoldia*) constituted over 60 percent of the volume. Birds from the Long Island area had taken a wider variety of mollusks, including periwinkle (*Littorina*), yoldia, and nassa (*Nassarius*), plus a fish, the sand launce (*Ammodytes*). A similar array of mollusk foods, including blue mussels, periwinkles, whelks (*Nassa*), and cockles (*Cardium*), have been reported to be consumed by European white-winged scoters by Madsen (1954).

Most observers report that white-winged scoters usually forage in water less than 25 feet deep, although dives to depths as great as 60 feet have been reported. Mackay (1891) stated that this species prefers to forage in water less than 20 feet deep, but can forage in waters as deep as 40 feet. This species seems to have unusually great endurance in remaining submerged. Breckenridge (in Roberts, 1932) found that a male remained submerged an average of 57.5 seconds, with intervening average rests of 12 seconds; a female had average diving and resting durations of 62 and 11 seconds respectively. Rawls (1949) reported that when adults foraged in water less than 10 feet deep, they had dive durations averaging 30 seconds and average intervening rest periods of 15 seconds. However, one three-day-old duckling that was being chased dove repeatedly for about fifteen minutes, with each dive lasting about 30 seconds and the periods between dives averaging only 10 seconds. Koskimies and Routamo (1958) noted maximum diving times of 46 and 56 seconds for females and males, respectively.

Sociality, Densities, Territoriality: Probably in most areas the nesting densities are rather low, but on favored nesting islands the densities are sometimes considerable. Robert Smith (quoted by Rawls, 1949) found 20 nests in an area of less than half an acre on a small willow island at Chip Lake, Alberta. Comparably high nesting densities have been found in southwestern Finland, where Koskimies and Routamo (1953) observed a maximum nesting density of 9 pairs /0.5 hectare (1.2 acres) of juniper on a small island. Hildén (1964) estimated that in 1962 there were 294 breeding pairs of white-winged scoters on his refuge study area, which included six square kilometers of land area, or 49 pairs per square kilometer.

Territoriality is only doubtfully present in this species. Rawls (1949) noted that territorial behavior seemed to be almost nil at Delta, Manitoba, and never observed defense of any areas. He did observe two cases of males defending their mates. Koskimies and Routamo (1953) also reported that after migratory flocks break up, the males begin to maintain small "mated female distances," which gradually become larger as the breeding period approaches. Each pair also occupies a fixed water area of varying size away from the nest site.

Interspecific Relationships: White-winged scoters probably compete to some extent for food with surf and black scoters, since these species have very similar diets and often intermingle on wintering areas. White-wings do, however, tend to winter in more northerly areas than do the smaller scoter species.

Mixed clutches presumably result for similar nest site requirements; those found in Finland involved the red-breasted merganser, tufted duck, and greater scaup (Hildén, 1964), those in North America involved the American wigeon, gadwall, and lesser scaup (Weller, 1959). In most cases the scoters deposited eggs in the other species' nests, rather than the reverse. Dump-nesting by female scoters in nests of their own species is also fairly prevalent in areas where the birds nest in close proximity.

Crows and ravens are seemingly responsible for most of the egg losses in white-winged scoters, while various large species of gulls (herring and great black-backed, particularly) have been reported to be serious duckling predators (Hildén, 1964).

General Activity Patterns and Movements: Like the other scoters, white-wings are daytime foragers. However, they may migrate either by day or by night (Cottam, 1939). Rawls (1949) indicated that a surprisingly regular daily periodicity may also occur on the breeding grounds; during seven mornings between June 26 and July 3 he observed a pair regularly fly from Lake Manitoba to an adjacent marshy bay within two minutes of 4:50 a.m., and always over the same tree. Rawls also noted that the birds usually foraged for periods up to about 25 minutes, followed by intervening rest periods of about 30 minutes. Most of the foraging he observed on Clandeboye Bay of Lake Manitoba seemed to occur during morning and late afternoon or early evening hours. On the basis of the early morning flights he observed, the nocturnal hours were probably spent on the deeper parts of the lake.

SOCIAL AND SEXUAL BEHAVIOR

Flocking Behavior: Scoter flock sizes on wintering grounds are sometimes fairly large, especially as they congregate prior to migrations. Bent (1925) mentions noting several thousand of these birds gathered in large flocks off the coast of Rhode Island in early May. Mackay (1891) stated that such migrant flocks often number 500 to 600 birds, which typically depart during afternoon hours. On their arrival at breeding grounds, these flocks evidently break up rather rapidly into paired adults and nonbreeders. Rawls (1949) noted that immature birds were usually seen in groups of about 5 to 30 birds on Lake Manitoba during the summer months, but that most of the adults seemed to be paired on arrival. Koskimies and Routamo (1953) noted that groups of males seldom have more than 20 individuals and that summer assemblies of immatures are usually not over 30 and only exceptionally reach 60 birds.

Pair-forming Behavior: Social displays of the white-winged scoter have been described by Koskimies and Routamo (1953) and by Myres (1959a). Primarily agonistic postures of the male include the "crouch," in which the body is low in the water and the head is tilted forward and downward at a 45° angle. In the "alarm" posture the neck is more elongated and sloped forward. An attack or threat posture is also present and greatly resembles the corresponding posture of male goldeneyes, in which the head and neck are stretched forward in the water as the opponent is faced. Male pair-forming displays include a "neck-erect-forwards" posture, perhaps derived from the alarm posture, but differing in that the neck is greatly thickened. A "false-drinking" is frequently performed by males; this display as well as "water-twitching" and preening movements are probably more closely associated with copulatory behavior than with pair-forming behavior. Other movements also occur, such as stretching, bathing, and wing-flapping, but it is uncertain whether these represent actual displays or are simply "displacement activities." Although some persons such as Rawls (1949) have heard adult males uttering vocal sounds, they were thought by Myres (1959a) to be silent during pair-forming display. Alex Linski (pers. comm.) reported hearing a captive male calling during courtship displays but could not describe the call.

Female displays include a chin-lifting movement that strongly resembles the inciting movements of scaup. A very thin whistled note is associated with this movement, and the posture is directed toward particular males. Threats or actual attacks on other males are also typical, thus the chin-lifting would seem to represent a functional inciting display (Myres, 1959a).

Copulatory Behavior: Myres (1959b) has described the copulatory behavior of this species, based on five observed copulations. The female apparently assumes the prone position only immediately prior to the male's mounting. Prior to copulation, false-drinking was performed by the male alone or by both sexes mutually. Additionally, the male performs preening behind the wing, preening of the dorsal region, or preening along the flanks, either on the side toward the female or the opposite side. Preening movements were seen more frequently than "water-twitching" movements of the bill, but whenever water-twitching was seen, it was always followed by preening. After mounting occurs, the male may perform a flicking movement of the wings, but postcopulatory behavior is quite simple. Myres noted that on two occasions a partial rotation of the two birds occurred before the male released his grip, and in no case was a specific posturing of the male observed at this time.

Nesting and Brooding Behavior: In spite of their late arrival at the breeding grounds, there does not appear to be a rapid transition to nesting behavior. Vermeer (1969) estimated that in Alberta during 1965, a period of 36 days elapsed between spring arrival and the laying of the first egg. Rawls (1949) likewise found that in the Delta, Manitoba, region, scoters usually arrive in the first half of May, but nests are evidently not started until the first half of June. This late nesting initiation, and the fairly long incubation and fledging periods of the species, would seemingly place a restriction on the northward breeding limits of the species.

Females do not cover their eggs with down or other materials during the egg-laying phase, and the highest nest mortality rates occur at this time (Hildén, 1964). During the egg-laying period the male remains with the female, except during the times that she is on the nest. During the incubation period small groups of males become progressively more frequent, and they have usually left the breeding area by the time the young have hatched. In a few isolated instances males have been seen participating in brood care and in protecting the young from gull attacks (Bauer and Glutz, 1969).

After hatching, females take their broods to suitable habitats, which in coastal environments consist of shallow and narrow water areas well sheltered from rough seas. However, the young often do not stay long in the sheltered bays; perhaps as their food requirements change to larger animals they move to areas where kelp beds provide ample habitat for mollusks and crustaceans. Where populations are dense and suitable brood habitats are limited, massive merging of broods often occurs, with aggregations of 100 or more young not uncommon. The loose female-young bond and the tendency of females to leave their young for prolonged periods also facilitate such brood mergers. However, reseparation of such large broods also commonly occurs, sometimes caused by strange hens swimming nearby and stimulating a "following" response on the part of some of the ducklings (Hildén, 1964).

Postbreeding Behavior: Rawls (1949) observed that by mid-July in the Delta, Manitoba, area the males were beginning to band together on Lake Manitoba. These flocks contained from 8 to 20 birds, while a month later in mid-August many individual and apparently flightless males were seen. The first flightless females were seen at the end of August, although some females were still leading broods at that time. The absence of immatures in the area at this time suggested that they may have molted earlier and had already begun their fall migration. However, Mackay (1891) reported that adults of all three species of scoter arrive in fall along the coast of New England several weeks prior to the arrival of young birds.

Steller Eider, Pair

Spectacled Eider, Adult female

Spectacled Eider, Adult male

Oldsquaw, Male in Summer

Oldsquaw, Male in Winter

Oldsquaw, Female in late Spring

Harlequin Duck, Adult male

Harlequin Duck, Pair

European Black Scoter, Pair

American Black Scoter, Male
(*Courtesy Felix Neck Wildlife Trust*)

Surf Scoter, Male (*San Diego Zoo Photo*)

Surf Scoter, Pair

White-winged Scoter, Male
(*Courtesy Felix Neck Wildlife Trust*)

White-winged Scoter, Adult female

Bufflehead, Adult males

Bufflehead, Pair

Barrow Goldeneye, Adult male

Barrow Goldeneye, Group of adults

Common Goldeneye, Pair

Common Goldeneye, Courting pair

Smew, Pair

Smew, Adult male

Hooded Merganser, Adult female

Hooded Merganser, Adult male

Red-breasted Merganser, Adult male

Red-breasted Merganser, Male in eclipse

Common Merganser, Adult male

Common Merganser, Adult female

Masked Duck, Males in eclipse and nuptial plumage (*Courtesy Dale Crider*)

Masked Duck, Juvenile (*Courtesy Dirk Hagemeyer*)

Ruddy Duck, Displaying pair

Ruddy Duck, Displaying male

BUFFLEHEAD

Bucephala albeola (Linnaeus) 1758

Other Vernacular Names: Butterball.

Range: Breeds from southern Alaska and northern Mackenzie District through the forested portions of Canada east to James Bay and south into the western United States to northern California and Montana. Winters along the Pacific coast from the Aleutian Islands to central Mexico, along the Gulf and Atlantic coasts from Texas to southern Canada, and in the interior where open water occurs.

Subspecies: None recognized.

Measurements (after Delacour, 1959):

Folded wing: Males 163-180, females 150-163 mm.

Culmen: Males 25-29, females 23-26 mm.

Weights: Nelson and Martin (1953) reported the average weight of twenty-three males to be 1.0 pounds (453 grams) and of twenty-six females to be 0.7 pound (317 grams), with both sexes having maximum weights of 1.3 pounds (589 grams). Yocom (1970) reported the average August weights of sixty-two males as 14.34 ounces (406.5 grams) and of ten females as 10.4 ounces (294.8 grams). Erskine (1972) stated that over the course of the year males average about 450 grams and females about 330 grams, with both sexes attaining their heaviest weights during the fall migration period and their lightest weights during winter.

IDENTIFICATION

In the Hand: The smallest of all the North American diving ducks, this is the only species that has a lobed hind toe, an adult folded wing measurement of 180 mm. or less, and a tail of less than 80 mm. The very short (culmen length 23-29 mm.), narrow bill is also distinctive, and there is always some white present behind the eye.

In the Field: In spite of their small size, male buffleheads in nuptial plumage can be seen for great distances; their predominantly white plumage sets them apart from all other small ducks except the extremely rare smew. The disproportionately large head with its white crest is also apparent, especially when the crest is maximally spread. The tiny female is much less conspicuous and is usually only seen after sighting the male, when its small size and white teardrop or oval marking behind the eye provide identifying field marks. In flight, buffleheads are more agile than most other diving ducks, and their small wings, which are dusky below, beat rapidly and flash the white speculum and upper wing covert coloration. Both sexes are relatively silent, even during courtship display. They are likely to be confused only with hooded mergansers when in flight, but the shorter, rounded head as well as the shorter bill set them apart from this species quite easily.

AGE AND SEX CRITERIA

Sex Determination: During their first year, male buffleheads are difficult to distinguish externally from females, but by late winter the white head markings are larger than those of a female and the male's head is generally darker. After the end of the first year of life, the presence of white in the middle coverts will separate males from females, even during the eclipse plumage. Possibly immature males can be distinguished from females during their first fall and winter by their *flattened* wing measurement (from notch in bend of wing to tip of longest primary) of 160 mm. or more (Carney, 1964).

Age Determination: By their second fall, males will have acquired white feathers in the middle coverts, while first-year males are black or brownish black in this area. Adult females have tertials which are long and have slightly drooping to rounded tips, while immature birds have shorter, straighter ones that are usually frayed and pointed (Carney, 1964).

DISTRIBUTION AND HABITAT

Breeding Distribution and Habitat: The breeding distribution of this North American hole-nesting species is associated with temperate forests. In

Alaska it is apparently rather widespread through the interior, with its greatest abundance in the upper Kuskokwim Valley, the Yukon flats, and the Porcupine River. Breeding also extends south to the Gulf of Alaska and west perhaps as far as the Bering Sea coast (Gabrielson and Lincoln, 1959).

In Canada the bufflehead breeds in the southern Yukon, western Mackenzie District, east of the Cascades in British Columbia, and across the forested portions of Alberta, Saskatchewan, and Manitoba to northwestern Ontario, where it is local and sparse. Its easternmost breeding would seem to be in eastern Ontario or central Quebec, although records are lacking (Erskine, 1972).

South of Canada there are only a few states that support breeding buffleheads. Although regular breeding in Washington would seem possible, there is so far only one definite record, for Hanson Lake (Larrison and Sonnenburg, 1968). In Oregon there seem to be only two breeding records, one for Red Butte Lake, in Linn County (Evenden, 1947), and one for the eastern slope of the Cascade Mountains (Erskine, 1960). Buffleheads have also bred at Eagle and Feather lakes, Lassen County, California (Grinnell and Miller, 1944). In the Rocky Mountains, buffleheads nest at least as far south as northern Montana and have bred as far south as Yellowstone Park (Rosche, 1954). In North Dakota buffleheads are apparently regular breeding birds in the Turtle Mountains (Stewart, 1968). Early or extralimital breeding records have also been reported for South Dakota, Wisconsin, Iowa, and Maine (Erskine, 1960).

During the breeding season the favored habitat consists of ponds and lakes in or near open woodland (Godfrey, 1966). The presence of nest cavities, often made by flickers (*Colaptes*), no doubt contributes substantially to the suitability of an area for nesting. An availability of summer foods in the form of water boatmen, aquatic beetles and their larvae, and similar insect life may also be of special importance. Alkaline ponds, sloughs, and small lakes, which are often rich in invertebrate life, are favored over large lakes and high mountain ponds, and trees having suitable nesting cavities should be either surrounded by water or very close to its shore (Munro, 1942). Erskine (1960) reported that eutrophic lakes of moderate depth, having sparse reedbeds, generally open shores, and available nest sites in the form of flicker cavities, are favored for nesting.

Wintering Distribution and Habitat: In Alaska, buffleheads winter abundantly in the inland bays of southern and southeastern Alaska, westward to the tip of the Alaska Peninsula, and in smaller numbers throughout the Aleutian Islands (Gabrielson and Lincoln, 1959). They are likewise abundant along the coast of British Columbia and inland in the southern parts of that province

Breeding (hatched) and wintering (shaded) distributions of the bufflehead in North America.

to the vicinity of Okanagan Lake (Godfrey, 1966), southward through Washington, Oregon, and California, and moderate numbers of birds reach Baja California, Sonora, and northern Sinaloa (Leopold, 1959). In the interior of Mexico and the southern United States they are present in relatively small numbers. Buffleheads wintering in the Central and Mississippi flyways have constituted only about 10 percent of the continental population inventoried during recent years, while the Pacific and Atlantic flyways have supported about a third and a half, respectively.

On the Atlantic coast the birds become progressively more common from Florida northward toward the middle and north Atlantic states, with some birds wintering as far north as coastal Maine. In the Chesapeake Bay area they occur on the various types of open estuaries, with brackish estuarine bays providing the optimum habitat. Interior impoundments are also used to some extent, and the birds seem to move farther up small tributaries and inlets than do common goldeneyes (Stewart, 1962).

GENERAL BIOLOGY

Age at Maturity: In captivity, hand-reared buffleheads breed when two years old (Charles Pilling, pers. comm.). Erskine (1961) mentions three females that were banded as flightless young birds and recaptured on nests two years later. He also has stated (pers. comm.) that wild males regularly breed when two years old.

Pair Bond Pattern: Pair bonds are renewed yearly, after a period of social display that begins as early as late January (Munro, 1942). Erskine (1961) believed that pair formation may be delayed until the breeding areas are reached. Males leave the breeding area before the young have been hatched (Munro, 1942).

Nest Location: Typically, buffleheads nest in tree cavities that have been excavated by woodpeckers, particularly flickers (Erskine, 1960; 1961). Preferred trees are those that are dead and either are situated very close to water or are standing in water (Munro, 1942). As a reflection of the flicker's preference for excavating in soft woods, nests are most often placed in aspens or, less frequently, rotted Douglas firs. Erskine found that about half of the nest sites used during one year are used again the following year, although at least in some cases different females were involved in subsequent-year use. Of 35 females retrapped on nests in later years, 23 were using the same nest site as previously. Brooks (1903) mentioned that cavities in aspen trees used by buffleheads ranged from 5 to 20 feet above the ground, while Erskine (1960) found that most nest cavities were from 1 to 3 meters above the ground or water level. In a few instances nests have been reported as high as 40 feet above the ground; reports of nesting in gopher burrows have also been made, but are not now considered reliable.

The entrance sizes suitable for buffleheads are remarkably small; Erskine (1960) reported that the modal entrance diameter range for natural bufflehead nests was 5.7 to 7.6 cm. The modal cavity depth range was 25 to 37 cm., and the modal cavity diameter range was 11.4 to 16.5 cm. Artificial nesting boxes devised by Charles Pilling (pers. comm.) for captive buffleheads are similar, with entrances 2⅞ inches wide, an internal diameter of about 7 inches, and a cavity depth of 16 inches. These boxes are made by splitting logs and hollowing them with a chain saw, followed by wiring them back together. A sawdust bed about 4 inches deep is also provided, and the box is situated with its lower end a few inches above water.

Clutch Size: According to Erskine (1960), the average clutch size for initial nests is 8.6 eggs. The observed range for British Columbia nests was 5 to 16 eggs, but clutches in excess of 12 eggs may be the result of dump-nesting (Godfrey, 1966). Eggs are laid at varying intervals, which average about 38 hours per egg. The average clutch size of five possible renests was 6.8 eggs (Erskine, 1960).

Incubation Period: Reported as ranging under natural conditions from 29 to 31 days, with a modal period of 30 days (Erskine, 1960).

Fledging Period: Estimated by Erskine (1960) to be between 50 and 55 days for wild birds.

Nest and Egg Losses: Erskine (1960) reported that in his observations about 80 percent of 106 nests were successful in hatching one or more young, and that about 92 percent of the eggs in 76 successful nests were hatched. Desertion accounted for most of the nest losses, and infertility or embryonic death were responsible for most egg failures. Erskine (1964) also reported on nest site competition among buffleheads, mountain bluebirds, and tree swallows. In one case a bufflehead nest was temporarily used by a mountain bluebird, reclaimed by a female bufflehead, and, finally, after the bufflehead was caught and banded, taken over by a tree swallow.

Juvenile Mortality: Specific information is still unavailable. Brood size counts are doubtful indexes to prefledging mortality rates because of the apparent frequency of brood abandonment and brood mergers (Munro, 1942). Erskine (1960) presented data suggesting that the average size of newly hatched bufflehead broods was 8.0 young, as compared with 4.8 young in broods nearly ready to fledge. His data indicated that large yearly variations in brood survival may occur, with predation, parasites, and drowning all apparently playing potentially significant roles.

Adult Mortality: On the basis of recoveries of banded birds, Erskine (1972) calculated an annual survival rate of 46.6 percent for adults of both sexes combined, whereas the calculated survival rate for immature birds was 27.8 percent. On the basis of recaptures of banded females on nests in subsequent years, an adult female survival rate of 50 percent was indicated. Two instances were found of birds surviving for as long as nine years after banding.

GENERAL ECOLOGY

Food and Foraging: The recent study by Erskine (1972) is the most complete analysis available for this species. Samples obtained during spring from birds on fresh waters indicated that the larvae of midges and mayflies are commonly eaten, and insects collectively represented two-thirds of the food by volume. In summer, insects constituted over 70 percent of the total food by adults and virtually all of the food found in thirty-five downy young. The larvae of dragonflies and damselflies are important foods of downies, as are aquatic beetles, while water boatmen and the larvae of dragonflies and damselflies were most prevalent in adult samples. Only in autumn and winter did plant materials attain a significant proportion of the food samples taken from birds on fresh to moderately brackish waters, when they constituted about 30 percent of total food contents. These plant materials were predominantly made up of the seeds of pondweeds (*Potamogeton* and *Najas*) and bulrushes (*Scirpus*). Insect materials still made up the bulk of the diet in autumn samples, including the sources already mentioned as well as the larvae of mayflies and caddis flies.

Winter samples were taken on both freshwater and saltwater areas, and some differences in foods taken in these two habitats were found. On freshwater wintering habitats, insect foods made up about one-third of the sample volumes, while mollusks increased accordingly and constituted about one-fourth of the total. Both gastropod snails and small bivalves such as *Sphaerium* apparently are important winter foods, at least in some areas. On saltwater habitats, insects are largely replaced by crustaceans as major food sources, while mollusks also remain important. Small crustaceans, including decapods, amphipods, and isopods, are apparently the favored source of winter foods and are supplemented by bivalve and univalve mollusks.

Wienmeyer (1967) examined 102 bufflehead stomachs in California and noted that bivalve mollusks, fish eggs, fish, snails, insects, seeds, and vegetative matter all might be locally important foods, depending on the area in which the birds had been foraging.

In general, buffleheads seem to prefer foraging in water from 4 to 15 feet in depth and, like the goldeneyes, tend to inhabit larger and more open bodies of water (Cottam, 1939; Phillips, 1925). Munro (1942) noted that buffle-heads usually forage in small groups, and they generally remain submerged from 15 to 35 seconds during foraging dives. Cronan (1957) noted that seven dives averaged 24.1 seconds, as compared with 30.3 seconds for three dives by common goldeneyes, and Erskine (1972) reported similar diving times for buffleheads.

Sociality, Densities, Territoriality: Erskine (1960) reviewed the concept of territoriality as it might be applied to buffleheads and concluded that a de-fense of the female seemed more probable than the defense of a territory. The nest location was often well removed from the "territory" occupied by the pair, which is usually on ponds or larger bodies of water, the smallest of which was found to be an acre. Nests are usually well spread out, although three cases of trees having two simultaneously occupied nests were found. Excluding such cases, the minimum distances between nests was found to be approximately 100 meters. In 1958, Watson Lake was found by Erskine to support eighteen bufflehead nests, while in 1959 a total of nineteen nests or broods were deter-mined to be present. The approximate surface area of this lake is about 450 acres; thus a density of about one breeding pair per 25 acres of water was pres-ent during these years. Not all of the lake's shoreline was actually used by buf-fleheads, and counts of both females and males on the lake never tallied with the known nesting population.

Interspecific Relationships: The small size and insect-eating tendencies of this species rather effectively remove it from competition with other diving ducks for food or nesting sites. There is, however, a dependence on wood-peckers for providing adequate nesting sites, and varying degrees of competi-tion for these sites exist with various hole-nesting bird species. Besides the common starling, mountain bluebird, and tree swallow, the larger sparrow hawk, hawk owl, and saw-whet owl may also compete with buffleheads for nest sites. Since it nests earlier than do these species, the bufflehead has an ad-vantage over them. The Barrow goldeneye nests in the same areas as the buf-flehead, but selects cavities with larger entrances (usually over 7.6 cm.) and wider cavity diameters (usually over 16.5 cm.), according to Erskine (1960).

General Activity Patterns and Movements: Like the other diving ducks, buffleheads are daytime foragers. Probably there are only quite limited daily movements associated with such foraging activities, although specific data are lacking.

Erskine (1961) reported a rather surprising degree of homing to pre-viously used nesting areas on the part of females, and to previously used win-tering areas on the part of both sexes. Of twelve determinations of nesting location changes in renests or nestings in subsequent years, the average distance between the nesting sites was less than 800 meters. Similarly, among buffleheads banded on wintering areas in Oregon, New York, and Maryland and shot in subsequent winters, forty-five were recovered less than 15 kilometers away, nine were recovered at distances of 15 to 50 kilometers, and ten from 50 to 80 kilometers away.

SOCIAL AND SEXUAL BEHAVIOR

Flocking Behavior: Like the goldeneyes, buffleheads are not highly social, and while on migration, as well as on wintering areas, tend to remain in quite small groups. The males are surprisingly pugnacious toward one another, and this general level of aggressiveness probably accounts for the rather small flock sizes typical of buffleheads.

Pair-forming Behavior: Pair-forming displays have recently been described by Myres (1959a) and Johnsgard (1965). The male displays associated with pair formation are obviously derived from attack and escape species. Male buffleheads also assume an aggressive "head-forward" posture that has an identical counterpart in the goldeneye species. Likewise, an "oblique-pumping" movement of the head is very frequent and is the comparable display to bowspring-pumping and rotary pumping in the goldeneyes. Males often chase one another while performing this display, or it may be directed toward females. At times it is interrupted by a sudden lifting of the folded wings, retraction of the head toward the back, and a down-tilting of the tail, a possible evolutionary homologue of the goldeneye head-throw-kick display. When near a female, the male will often erect his bushy crest, making his head seem even larger than normal. While in this posture the male often "leads" a female, which typically follows the male while calling and alternately stretching and retracting her neck. During this display the male may also perform quick, inconspicuous head-turning movements and sometimes suddenly turn his head backward toward the female in an inciting-like movement.

Bufflehead pair-forming activities are highly animated, with the jerky and quick movements of the males adding a mechanical or toylike quality to the proceedings. Often a male will take off, fly a short distance toward a female, and come to a skidding stop near her. This flight display is terminated by a wing-flapping accompanied by a single slapping sound, and as a final stage the male raises his folded wings above the body in the manner described earlier. Males also sometimes attack one another by submerging and approach the other bird under water, which often produces amusing and exciting results.

Female displays consist of the previously mentioned "following" movement, which is functionally equivalent to inciting, and of a "head display," which is comparable to the crest erection of the males and seemingly stimulates them to begin social courtship.

Copulatory Behavior: The most complete observations on copulation in this species are those of Myres (1959b). Unlike the goldeneyes, female buffleheads rarely remain in the receptive prone posture for more than a few moments. Myres evidently observed no specific mutual behavior prior to the assumption of this posture. However, prior to mounting, the male performs two main precopulatory displays, a lateral movement of the bill in the water ("water-twitching") and a preening movement of the dorsal region ("preen-dorsally"). The first is more frequent, but both are extremely similar to the normal bill-dipping, dorsal-preening movements observed as nondisplay comfort movements of the species. In three of eight copulations, Myres observed "wing-flicking" by the male while it was mounted, and after treading was completed the two birds typically rotated a full turn or more before the male released his grip. Postcopulatory behavior by the male was quite varied, consisting of vigorous bathing, shallow diving, or a deep dive under the surface.

Nesting and Brooding Behavior: Little information on nesting behavior is available, other than the fact that several observers have commented on the female's strong incubation tendency and her frequent reluctance to leave the nest when it is being examined. Quite possibly the small entrance prevents most avian and mammalian predators from gaining entrance, and thus there is normally little need for rapid escapes. Erskine (1960) reported that most egg-laying apparently occurred during morning hours, and that after incubation begins the highest degree of nest attentiveness is apparently during morning hours, gradually declining through the day. No tendency for a morning break in incubation was found, but birds were often found away from the nest during evening hours.

Following hatching, the female typically broods the young for 24 to 36 hours before leaving the nest. Departure from the nest usually occurs before noon, and in one case observed by Erskine about twelve minutes elapsed between the exit of the first and last duckling in the brood. The female was extremely active both before and during the nest exodus, but no vocal signals were detected. After the brood has left the nest, brood territories are established and may be occupied for four weeks or longer. They are not defended against other bufflehead broods, although female Barrow goldeneyes sometimes attack and kill young buffleheads. Brood transfers are not uncommon, and sometimes single broods have been seen accompanied by two females (Munro, 1942).

The timing of the breakdown of pair bonds is seemingly still poorly documented. There are no indications that pair bonds are ever still intact at the time of hatching, and Erskine (1972) stated that the males leave their territories as soon as the females begin incubation.

Postbreeding Behavior: It is probable but still not proven that buffleheads move to molting areas well away from their breeding grounds in western Canada. Erskine (1961) reported that thirteen females that were banded while molting and five banded as juveniles were later taken as molting adults. Fifteen of these were recaptured on the same lake at which they were banded or within 5 kilometers of that point, while the other four were recaptured at points between 25 and 65 kilometers from the point of banding. Two of the birds in the latter group were those that had been banded as juveniles. Erskine thus suggested that adult female buffleheads tend to return to the same molting area. In one instance a female was found to have molted 155 kilometers from a later nesting area, suggesting that a substantial migration to molting areas may occur. Erskine later (1972) reported that flocks of buffleheads, including males in very faded plumage but still able to fly, have been seen on Alberta lakes in areas where no breeding by this species occurred, a further indication of a molt migration. These movements probably normally involve not only adult males but also immature birds, unsuccessful females, and those that have abandoned their broods.

BARROW GOLDENEYE

Bucephala islandica (Gmelin) 1789

Other Vernacular Names: Whistler.

Range: Breeds in Iceland, southwestern Greenland, northern Labrador, and from southern Alaska and Mackenzie District southward through the western states and provinces to California and Colorado. Winters primarily along the Pacific coast from Alaska to central California, and on the Atlantic coast from southern Canada to the mid-Atlantic states.

Subspecies: None recognized.

Measurements (after Delacour, 1959):

Folded wing: Males 232-248, females 205-224 mm.

Culmen: Males 31-36, females 28-31 mm.

Weights: Nelson and Martin (1953) reported that three males averaged 2.4 pounds (1,087 grams), with a maximum of 2.9 pounds (1,314 grams). Palmer (1949) found an average weight of three males to be 1,162 grams, with a maximum of 1,219. Nelson and Martin indicated an average female weight of 1.6 pounds (725 grams), with a maximum of 1.9 pounds (861 grams). Palmer indicated a range of weights in females from 793.8 to 907.2 grams. Yocom (1970) reported the August weights of fifty-three males as averaging 2.125 pounds (1,021 grams), while fourteen females averaged 1.31 pounds (595.35 grams).

IDENTIFICATION

In the Hand: The presence of white markings on the middle secondaries and their adjoining coverts, yellow feet with a lobed hind toe, and yellowish eyes will serve to separate this species from all others except the common goldeneye. Adult male Barrow goldeneyes are very much like male common goldeneyes, but differ in the following characters: (1) The head iridescence is glossy purple, and the white cheek marking is crescentic in shape; (2) the head has a fairly flat crown, and the nail is distinctly raised above the contour of the gradually tapering bill; and (3) the body is more extensively black, especially on the flanks, which are heavily margined (at least ⅔ inch) with black, and on the scapulars, which are margined with black on an elongated outer web or both webs, producing a pattern of oval white spots separated by a black background. The upper wing surface is also more extensively black, with the exposed bases of the greater secondary coverts black and the marginal, the lesser, and most of the middle coverts also blackish. Only about five secondaries have their exposed webs entirely white, while the more distal ones may be white-tipped. The length of the bill's nail is at least 12 mm. in this species, as compared with a maximum of 11 mm. in the common goldeneye (Brooks, 1920).

Females are closely similar to female common goldeneyes, but may be separable by (1) the somewhat darker brown head, which is relatively flat-crowned in shape; (2) the brighter and more extensively yellow bill during the spring, especially in western populations, where it is usually entirely yellow; (3) the sooty middle and lesser wing coverts, which are only narrowly tipped with grayish white; and (4) the broader and more pronounced ashy brown breast band. Brooks (1920) reported that the shape of the bill and the length of the nail provide the best criteria, with the common goldeneye having a nail length that never exceeds 10 mm. (average 9.4) and the Barrow goldeneye having a nail length greater than 10 mm. (average 10.9).

In the Field: A lone female can be separated from common goldeneye females in the field only by the most experienced observers, but its somewhat darker head with its flatter crown is usually apparent, and any female with a completely yellow bill is most likely to be a Barrow goldeneye, although Brooks (1920) noted one possible exception to this rule. A male in nuptial plumage appears to be predominantly black in the upperparts to a point below the insertion of the wing, with a row of neatly spaced white spots extending from the midback forward toward the breast, where an extension of black continues down in front of the "shoulder" to the sides of the breast. Its head is distinctly "flat-topped," with a long nape and a purplish head gloss, and there is a crescentic white mark in front of the eye. In flight, females of the two goldeneyes appear almost identical (the yellow bill is often quite apparent in the Barrow during spring), but the white marking on the upper wing surface of the male is interrupted by a black line on the greater secondary coverts. Male Barrow goldeneyes have no loud whistled notes during courtship; the commonest sounds are clicking noises and soft grunting notes. Head-pumping movements of the female are of a rotary rather than elliptical form, and lateral head-turning or inciting movements are much more frequent in the Barrow goldeneye. As in the common goldeneye, a whistling noise is produced by the wings during flight.

AGE AND SEX CRITERIA

Sex Determination: Young males can be distinguished from females as early as the first November of life, with the appearance of new inner scapulars that are white with extended black edges; at about the same time white feathers begin to appear between the bill and the eyes. Thereafter, the sexes can be distinguished either by the white back or head markings or, when the bird is in eclipse, by the pure white middle coverts of the male.

Age Determination: Adult males can be distinguished from first-year males by their entirely white rather than gray or dusky middle coverts. The middle coverts of adult females are grayish, tipped with white, while those of first-year birds are grayish, with dusky bases. The presence of a largely or entirely yellow bill is indicative of a mature female, but mature females may not show this trait during fall and early winter. Some first-year females have a "more or less" orange bill by late April or early May (Brooks, 1920). First-year females also have the chest band and flanks more fawn than gray, and the neck is not white as in adults but is almost as dark brown as the head. Additionally, the iris is greenish yellow, rather than clear yellow as in adults (Munro, 1939).

DISTRIBUTION AND HABITAT

Breeding Distribution and Habitat: The North American distribution of the Barrow goldeneye is rather similar to that of the harlequin duck, consisting of a large western population associated with montane rivers and lakes and a much smaller northeastern population in tundra or subtundra habitats.

In Alaska the breeding distribution of the Barrow goldeneye is rather uncertain. It apparently breeds as far west as the base of the Alaska Peninsula (Murie, 1959) around the upper part of the Nushagak River, and extends into the interior northeastwardly through McKinley National Park to the Porcupine River. It also breeds on the Kenai Peninsula and in the upper Copper River (Gabrielson and Lincoln, 1959).

In western Canada the species breeds in the southern Yukon, southwestern Alberta, and much of British Columbia, with the densest populations in the relatively dry and sparsely wooded belt between the Okanagan and Cariboo districts. In eastern Canada it probably nests in Labrador and has been reported during summer at McCormick Island, eastern Hudson Bay, but breeding records for this general area are extremely limited (Godfrey, 1966). Todd (1963) believed that the Barrow goldeneye is restricted as a breeding bird to the treeless area of the Labrador Peninsula, while the common goldeneye has a much more extensive breeding distribution in the forested areas to the south. The Barrow goldeneye also breeds over a rather wide area in southwestern Greenland, northward to about 70° N. latitude (A.O.U., 1957).

In Washington, breeding has been reported from the Selkirk and the Cascade mountains, the Okanogan Highlands, and the Grand Coulee area in the center of the state (Yocom, 1951; Harris *et al.*, 1954). Breeding occurs sparingly in the mountains of central Oregon on certain lakes (Sparks, Diamond), and possibly also in the Wallowa Mountains (Gabrielson and Jewett, 1940). In California it breeds on various lakes (Butte, Smedberg, Table, etc.) in the mountains southward as far as Yosemite Park (Grinnell and Miller, 1944). There is also an interior breeding population that extends down the Rocky Mountains of Montana and Idaho at least as far as Yellowstone Park (Skinner, 1937). Breeding once also occurred in Colorado, but does not at present (Bailey and Niedrach, 1967).

The breeding habitat of this species consists of lakes or ponds often in the vicinity of wooded country; where large trees lack natural cavities, rocks may serve for nest sites. In Iceland the species' breeding distribution is largely related to nesting hole availability, but it favors running water over nonflowing water (Bengtson, 1970). Munro (1939) believed that a local abundance of food rather than availability of nest sites determined distribution patterns of this species in British Columbia. Thus, lakes lacking tree-nesting sites but having high populations of amphipods and other foods sometimes supported large breeding populations of goldeneyes. These lakes are often rather alkaline and sometimes have relatively little shoreline vegetation.

Wintering Distribution and Habitat: Probably the great majority of the continental population of Barrow goldeneyes winter along the Pacific coast. From Juneau southward along coastal Alaska the species is common to abundant, and small numbers winter around Kodiak Island as well (Gabrielson and Lincoln, 1959). It also winters abundantly along the coast of British Columbia

Breeding (hatched) and wintering (shaded) distributions of the
Barrow goldeneye in North America.

and more rarely occurs in the interior (Godfrey, 1966). It is common in the Puget Sound region of Washington, where it and the common goldeneye constitute about 9 percent of the wintering diving ducks (Wick and Jeffrey, 1966), and it occurs with decreasing abundance southward along the open coasts of Washington, Oregon, and northern California. The birds of the interior Rocky Mountain population probably do not migrate to salt water, but winter near their breeding areas on available open water. Thus, at Red Rock Lakes Refuge, both Barrow and common goldeneyes are common in winter and feed on grain put out for the trumpeter swans (Banko, 1960).

The wintering population of eastern North America is relatively small, with birds occurring from the north shore of the Gulf of St. Lawrence southward through the Maritime Provinces and the St. Lawrence Valley, sometimes to the Great Lakes (Godfrey, 1966). Perhaps some of these represent Greenland-bred birds. Elliot (1961) has summarized the history of records of this species in New York, and Hasbrouck (1944) provided an earlier summary of its more general distribution during winter in eastern North America.

The wintering habitats used by Barrow goldeneyes include both fresh and salt waters, with the greatest numbers no doubt occurring in freshwater or brackish habitats. Although specific figures are not available, the birds evidently prefer brackish estuaries and calm waters to open coastlines and heavy surf. Munro (1939) noted a preference for fresh or brackish rather than highly saline waters, and reported higher numbers on coastal lakes, rivers, and river mouths than on more saline waters.

GENERAL BIOLOGY

Age at Maturity: Ferguson (1966) reported that four aviculturalists reported breeding by captive Barrow goldeneyes at two years, four at three years, and one at five years. It seems probable that under wild conditions the birds regularly breed in their second year.

Pair Bond Pattern: Pairs are renewed each year during a prolonged period of social display during winter and spring, with a peak in courting activity in April (Munro, 1939).

Nest Location: Bengtson (1970) reported that of a total of 426 nests found in Iceland, 401 were in holes or cavities, 19 were under high shrubs, 5 were under low shrubs, and 1 was under tall herbs (*Angelica* or *Archangelica*). The modal distance from water of the nests he found was the 0- to 10-meter category. In British Columbia, cavities in live trees, tree stumps, or tall dead stubs are the usual nest sites (Munro, 1939). Sugden (1963) reported that 1 of 13 nests he found in the Cariboo Parklands was in a crow nest, while all the others were in holes of Douglas firs or aspens. He suggested that crow nests might be more important at higher elevations, where trees suitable for hole-nesting are less numerous.

Among Barrow goldeneye tree cavity nests in British Columbia, Erskine (1960) reported that 16 of 30 nests had entrances between 7.6 and 10.0 cm. in diameter, 11 of 19 had cavity depths between 25 and 134 cm., and 8 of 14 had cavity diameters of 16.5 to 22.8 cm. In contrast to cavities used by buffle-heads, those with top entrances are often used, and such entrances may be preferred to lateral ones.

Clutch Size: Godfrey (1966) reported an average clutch size of 9, with a range of 4 to 15 eggs, for nests in British Columbia and Alberta. Bengtson (1971) indicated an average of 10.37 eggs for 293 first clutches in Iceland. He found (1972) an average of 7.5 eggs in 39 renests.

Incubation Period: Under natural conditions incubation lasts an average of 32.5 days, with an observed range of 30 to 34 days (Godfrey, 1966). A 30-day period has been reported for captive birds, presumably with artificial incubation (Delacour, 1959; Johnstone, 1970).

Nest and Egg Losses: Slightly over half of 196 Icelandic nests failed during the egg-laying period, with desertion the major cause. Among 246 normal-sized clutches observed over a ten-year period, the estimated hatching success was 75 percent (Bengtson, 1972).

Juvenile Mortality: Munro (1939) reported that his studies on one lake in 1936 indicated a reduction of brood sizes of 33 percent (from 9 to 6) among nine broods during the first month after hatching, while in 1937 fourteen broods had a reduction in numbers of 66.5 percent during about two months after hatching. He believed that crows might account for some duckling losses and that horned owls also might contribute to losses. Exposure to rough water on some of the larger lakes was also considered a probable mortality factor. Bengtson (1972) observed that female goldeneyes often attacked and killed strange young of their own species, as well as those of other species, and were so aggressive that they often abandoned their own broods.

Adult Mortality: No estimates of natural mortality rates are available. Delacour (1959) mentioned two males surviving at least sixteen years in captivity.

GENERAL ECOLOGY

Food and Foraging: Cottam (1939) analyzed the foods taken by seventy-one adults, most of which were from British Columbia, during eleven months of the year. In these birds, insects constituted 36 percent of the food by volume, mollusks 19 percent, crustaceans 18 percent, other animal foods 4 percent, and plant materials 22 percent. The insect category included large quantities of dragonfly and damselfly naiads, caddis fly larvae, midge larvae, and various other aquatic insects. The major mollusk food was the blue mussel (*Mytilus*) and related forms, while the crustacean category was dominated by amphipods, isopods, and crayfish. The primary plant foods appeared to be pondweeds (*Potamogeton*) and wild celery (*Vallisneria*).

Munro (1939) also reported on the foods of this species, using some of the same data included in Cottam's analysis, as well as additional material, bringing the total to 116 stomachs. Salmon eggs were found to be an important food source for coastal birds, along with mollusks, crustaceans, and marine algae. Birds taken in interior regions contained a variety of insects, especially caddis fly, damselfly and dragonfly naiads, crustaceans such as amphipods and crayfish, and various plant materials. Several young birds had eaten chiefly insects, especially surface-dwelling and terrestrial species. Munro concluded that the winter foods of the Barrow and common goldeneyes are substantially the same, under the same conditions of time and space.

Sociality, Densities, Territoriality: Bengtson (1972) has provided evidence that this species was the only one among the ten duck species he studied that exhibited density-dependent relationships in hatching success and duckling mortality. He reported that breeding densities varied from 30 pairs per square kilometer in "scattered" concentrations to 100 to 600 pairs per square kilometer in "very dense" concentrations. He also observed that this species was unique in its defense of a territory prior to and during egg-laying and in females' holding brood territories after their clutches had been hatched. Evidently the strong aggressive tendencies among female goldeneyes result in high rates of nest desertion where breeding concentrations are high, and similarly tend to reduce brood survival as a result of attacks on broods sharing the same brooding areas. Dense goldeneye concentrations also tended to reduce brood survival of other duck species.

Interspecific Relationships: It seems possible that local competition for food between the Barrow and common goldeneyes may occur on wintering areas, since there appear to be no significant differences in foods consumed. There also appear to be no major habitat differences that tend to keep the two species separated on wintering areas, although Munro (1939) noted that common goldeneyes are true sea ducks during winter, frequenting the most saline waters, while Barrow goldeneyes favor fresh or brackish waters then. Their breeding areas are for the most part well isolated from one another.

Phillips (1925) mentioned that in Iceland the eggs of the red-breasted merganser are often found among those of the Barrow goldeneye, and that the parasitic jaeger is the most important predator in that area. Since the nests of goldeneyes are normally well hidden, predators such as jaegers would no doubt primarily affect the ducklings rather than the eggs.

General Activity Patterns and Movements: Like the other sea ducks, Barrow goldeneyes are daytime foragers, but little specific information on daily activity patterns or movements is available.

SOCIAL AND SEXUAL BEHAVIOR

Flocking Behavior: On the wintering grounds and during spring migration there is a free association of adults and yearlings of both sexes, producing flocks of moderate to large size. Migrant flocks mentioned by Munro (1929) generally range from 10 to 40 birds. Within a month after arrival, the adults have paired and scattered. The yearling males gradually disappear during this time, followed by the adult males as soon as the females begin incubation. Many or all of the yearling females remain on the nesting areas, leaving about the time the adult females do, followed finally by the young of the year. At this time there is again a general association of the total population on coastal waters (Munro, 1929).

Pair-forming Behavior: Pair-forming behavior begins on coastal waters in late winter, but reaches its peak on the lakes of the interior where migrant birds concentrate. The male displays of this species are quite varied and complex (Myres, 1959a; Johnsgard, 1965), differing both in postures and vocalizations from those of male common goldeneyes. These male differences in behavior and appearance, rather than female differences, probably serve to maintain species isolation and prevent hybridization (which has rarely been reported). Goldeneyes typically perform social display in small groups of several males and one or two females. The male displays, although highly ritualized, are apparently largely derived from hostile gestures of threat of attack. The female's primary display, inciting, is also a highly ritualized side-to-side movement of the head, frequently performed as she follows a displaying male. She also performs rotary pumping movements of the head, similar to those of the male, and a neck-stretching or "head-up" display. The female displays of the Barrow and common goldeneyes differ in that the Barrow females lack or very rarely perform "neck-dipping," but much more frequently perform inciting. Major male display differences include only a single type of head-throw display by the Barrow goldeneye (which is always associated with a backward kick), a "crouch" posture that is lacking in the common goldeneye, a "neck-withdrawing" movement that is the usual male response to inciting, and the absence of a "masthead" or "bowsprit" posture (Myres, 1959a; Johnsgard, 1965).

Copulatory Behavior: Myres (1959a, 1959b) and Johnsgard (1965) have described the behavior associated with copulation. Copulation is normally preceded by mutual drinking movements, after which the female becomes prone. The male then begins a long sequence of comfort movements (wing-and-leg-stretch, dipping the bill in the water and shaking it, bathing), in no apparent order. Finally, the bill-dipping and shaking becomes more vigorous ("jabbing"), is terminated by a single rapid preening movement, and the male rushes toward the female to mount her. During treading the folded wings are shaken one or more times, and before the male releases the female's nape the two birds typically rotate in the water. The male then swims rapidly away ("steaming") while uttering grunting sounds and making lateral head-turning movements. The copulatory behavior of the two species of goldeneye is much more similar than is their pair-forming behavior.

Nesting and Brooding Behavior: Few observations of nesting behavior by this species are available. Munro (1939) noted that the female begins to lose down while laying is in progress, but the amount varies considerably in different nests. Males apparently leave their mates very shortly after incubation begins. Often yearling females become attached to paired adults, and after the nesting female emerges with her brood, the young female may resume her association. At times, the yearling may even take forcible possession of the brood, driving the mother away and capturing at least some of her young. Broods usually but not always remain relatively intact, often following the parent bird in a flank-to-flank "bunch," but more commonly following head-to-tail. Carrying of the young on the back while swimming has apparently not been described in this species, although it has for the common goldeneye. Females typically abandon their brood when they are well grown but still unfledged. They may then fly some distance and join other females prior to molting, or they may molt on their breeding lakes.

Postbreeding Behavior: According to Munro (1939), there is an early, massive movement of males from the breeding grounds almost as soon as the females begin incubation. The distance and direction of this molt migration is unknown, but the males presumably move toward the coast. In Iceland, however, there is apparently no molt migration, and the adult males molt near their breeding areas (Phillips, 1925).

COMMON GOLDENEYE
Bucephala clangula (Linnaeus) 1758

Other Vernacular Names: Golden-eye Duck, Whistler.

Range: Breeds in Iceland, northern Europe and Asia from Norway to Kamchatka, and in North America from Alaska to southern Labrador and
Newfoundland, and southward through the forested portions of the northern
and northeastern United States. Winters in North America from the southern Alaska coast south through the western states to California, the interior
states wherever open water is present, and the Atlantic coast from Florida
to Newfoundland.

North American Subspecies:

B. c. americana (Bonaparte): American Common Goldeneye. Breeds in
North America as indicated above.

Measurements (after Godfrey, 1966, and Delacour, 1959):

Folded wing: Males 215-235, females 188-220 mm.

Culmen: Males 35-43.5, females 28-35 mm.

Weights: Nelson and Martin (1953) reported that fifty-eight males averaged
2.2 pounds (997 grams), and fifty-three females averaged 1.8 pounds (815
grams), with maximums of 3.1 pounds (1,406 grams) and 2.5 pounds
(1,133 grams), respectively. Schiøler (1926) provides some weights of
the European race, which is considered to be slightly smaller than the North
American form. Six adult males averaged 2.55 pounds (1,158.5 grams) in

December, and nine first-year immatures averaged 2.29 pounds (1,037 grams); five adult females averaged 1.76 pounds (799 grams) in December and January, and five first-year birds averaged 1.63 pounds (747 grams) in December.

IDENTIFICATION

In the Hand: Males in nuptial plumage or those in their first spring of life have a characteristic oval white mark between the yellowish eye and the bill. Mature males, even when in eclipse plumage, are the only North American ducks that have the combination of a folded wing length of at least 215 mm. and an uninterrupted white wing patch extending from the middle secondaries forward over the adjoining greater, middle, and lesser coverts. Females can be distinguished from all other species except the Barrow goldeneye by their lobed hind toe, a folded wing length of 190 mm. or more, the white on the middle secondaries, and their greater coverts (which are tipped with dusky) and at least the adjoining middle coverts more grayish or whitish than the tertials or lesser coverts. See the Barrow goldeneye account for characteristics that will serve to separate females of these two species.

In the Field: Along with the larger and more streamlined common merganser, goldeneyes are the only large diving ducks that appear to be mostly white-bodied, with blackish backs and heads. The oval white mark on the male can be seen for considerable distances, and even if this mark is not definitely visible, the common goldeneye male differs from the Barrow goldeneye male in several other apparent ways. The former's head is more triangular in shape, with the top almost pointed rather than flattened, the nape is not extended into a long crest, and a greenish gloss is apparent in good light. The upper half of the body appears predominantly white, with parallel black lines extending diagonally backward above the folded wing, and no black is evident on the side of the breast. In flight, both species of goldeneye exhibit dusky under wing coverts, but the common goldeneye exhibits a relatively continuous white upper wing patch, at least in males. The male's calls are varied, but the loudest and most conspicuous is a shrill *zeee-at* note that is associated with aquatic head-throw displays. Females of both species are relatively silent. The wings of males produce a strong whistling noise during flight.

AGE AND SEX CRITERIA

Sex Determination: If the middle secondary coverts are white, the bird is an adult male, and additionally first-year males have less gray on the breast than do females, have a darker back, and have a darker head, which may show a white loral spot by late winter (Bent, 1925). First-year males may also exhibit longitudinal white stripes or white edging on some of their scapulars, and if the *flattened* wing (measured from notch in bend of wing to tip of longest primary) is longer than 215 mm. the bird is a male, while if it is less than 210 mm. it is a female (Carney, 1964).

Age Determination: Adult males have scapulars with white center stripes and dark edges and have middle coverts that are entirely white, rather than partly white and partly gray as in immatures. The greater secondary coverts of adult females are heavily tipped with black and their greater tertial coverts are rounded and unfrayed over the tertials, while in immature females they are usually both frayed and faded (Carney, 1964). The middle and lesser coverts in immature females are also apparently darker than in adult females. A yellow bill-tip is indicative of sexual maturity in females, but this trait may not be apparent during fall and early winter. As in the Barrow goldeneye, first-year females have greenish yellow rather than clear yellow iris coloration, brownish rather than white necks, and fawn rather than gray flanks and chestbands (Munro, 1939).

DISTRIBUTION AND HABITAT

Breeding Distribution and Habitat: Unlike the Barrow goldeneye, this species has a breeding distribution extending over much of the cold temperate portions of the Northern Hemisphere. In North America its breeding range is nearly transcontinental, generally following the distribution of boreal coniferous forest.

In Alaska the common goldeneye probably breeds over a wide area of the interior, although confusion over the two goldeneye species makes the distribution of each rather uncertain. Gabrielson and Lincoln (1959) believe that breeding is mostly confined to the Yukon and Koskokwim river valleys, excepting the lower portions of these rivers. They are apparently most numerous from Tanana eastward toward the Canadian boundary. Broods attributed to this species have also been seen on Kodiak Island, but there seems a greater likelihood that these were of Barrow goldeneyes. It is also questionable that a brood from extreme southeastern Alaska (Chickamin River) represented this species. Both species occur on the upper Porcupine River in the vicinity of Old Crow, but their relative breeding abundance is unknown (Irving, 1960). Campbell (1969) suggested that the common goldeneye may breed as far north as the central Brooks range.

In northern Canada this species probably breeds over much of the Yukon north to treeline, over the forested portions of the Northwest Territories, and in the forested areas of all of the provinces, with breeding questionable along coastal British Columbia and in Nova Scotia except for Cape Breton Island (Godfrey, 1966). Munro (1939) questioned its widespread occurrence as a nesting species in British Columbia and could find only four possible nesting records for the province. Thus, there may be less geographic overlap of breeding ranges of the goldeneyes than is indicated on most range maps.

In central Canada the breeding range includes much of Manitoba, virtually all of Ontario except the southeasternmost portion and Hudson Bay coastline, the forested portions of Quebec, and comparable portions of Labrador, Newfoundland, and the Maritimes. These eastern populations are seemingly larger than those in the western provinces; breeding population counts in Quebec and Labrador made by waterfowl biologists in the early 1950s indicated that goldeneyes constituted over 20 percent of the nesting waterfowl, surpassed in abundance only by mergansers and black ducks. Doubtless these were mostly common rather than Barrow goldeneyes, considering the areas surveyed.

South of Canada, the common goldeneye has a restricted breeding distribution. They breed in the Turtle Mountain area of North Dakota (Stewart, 1968), over much of northern Minnesota (Lee *et al.,* 1964a), in northern Michigan (Zimmerman and Van Tyne, 1959), in New York (Foley, 1960), Maine (Gibbs, 1961), and the northern portions of Vermont and New Hampshire (Bent, 1925).

The preferred breeding habitat of common goldeneyes was described by Carter (1958) as water areas having marshy shores with adjacent stands of old hardwoods to provide nesting sites. To a much greater degree than the Barrow goldeneye, this species is limited in its breeding to water areas with trees having adequate cavities for nesting. The depth of the water and whether it is a river or a slough were judged by Carter to be of no importance. In northern coniferous forest areas, aspens are apparently important for nesting, but farther south a greater variety of trees are utilized (Dementiev and Gladkov, 1967).

Wintering Distribution and Habitat: In Alaska, common goldeneyes are frequent winter residents of the Aleutian Islands (Murie, 1959), as well as around Kodiak Island, the Alaska Peninsula, and the entire coast of southern and southeastern Alaska. They are especially abundant in the vicinity of Wrangell and around the northern tip of Admiralty Island (Gabrielson and Lincoln, 1959).

In Canada, they winter on the coast of British Columbia, as well as around Newfoundland and the Maritime Provinces, with smaller numbers occurring through the interior where open water is available.

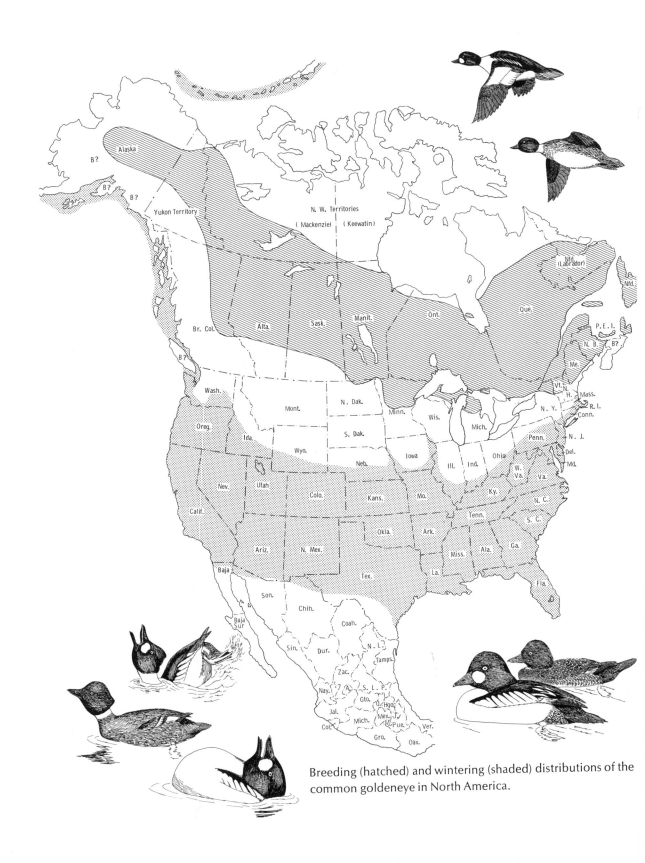

Breeding (hatched) and wintering (shaded) distributions of the common goldeneye in North America.

South of Canada, they extend in winter down the Pacific coast to the Mexican border and even beyond, although only relatively few birds move this far south. Winter surveys during the late 1960s indicated that about 29 percent of the wintering goldeneye population (both species) were found in the Pacific Flyway, and many of these would be Barrow goldeneyes.

The Atlantic coast apparently represents the primary wintering area; almost half of the continental wintering goldeneyes surveyed in the late 1960s were found in the Atlantic Flyway, and very few of these would represent Barrow goldeneyes. Common goldeneyes are common along the Atlantic coastline as far south as Florida. They also occur on the Gulf coast, but in relatively low numbers. Further, birds winter in the interior of the United States on rivers, large lakes, and reservoirs for about as far north as open water can be found.

In the Chesapeake Bay region, wintering common goldeneyes are widely distributed in coastal estuaries, but optimum habitats are apparently brackish estuarine bays, with large numbers also using salt estuarine bays. Fresh estuarine bays are primarily used by fall migrants. Munro (1939) believed that whereas the Barrow goldeneye favored fresh or slightly brackish waters in its winter habitats, the common goldeneye was prone to frequent more saline waters.

GENERAL BIOLOGY

Age at Maturity: Aviculturalists contacted by Ferguson (1966) reported reproduction by captive common goldeneyes at two years (two cases), three years (four cases), and four years (one case). Most investigators believe that nesting normally occurs among wild birds in their second year of life, and some yearling females may even attempt to nest occasionally (Grenquist, 1963).

Pair Bond Pattern: Pair bonds are renewed each winter and spring, during a period of active social display that lasts several months. In Sweden this begins in December and extends into May, but has an average peak of activity in March (Nilsson, 1969). Pair bonds are broken shortly after the female begins incubation.

Nest Location: Carter (1958) stated that all but one of the nests he found (total apparently seventeen) were in trees, and 89 percent were in maple (*Acer* spp.) cavities with a diameter at breast height of at least 8 inches. Sixteen nests averaged 18 feet from the ground or water level. Most cavities had lateral openings, but the height and entrance size seemingly mattered very little. Prince (1968) reported on sixteen goldeneye nesting sites, also in New Brunswick, of which nine were in silver maple (*Acer saccharinum*), six were in elm (*Ulmus americanus*), and one was in a butternut (*Juglans cinerea*). These were in trees with an average diameter at breast height of 67 centimeters and an average height of 7 meters. Ten of the cavities were of "bucket" type, while six were enclosed. Trees used by goldeneyes tended to be on open stands near the edges of fields or marshes, and cavities selected by them tended to vary less in cavity diameter than did those used by wood ducks. This small observed range of cavity diameter (15 to 26 centimeters) was considered to be possibly important in nest site choice. Similarly, Sirén (1951) recommended nesting boxes with internal diameters of 18 to 22 centimeters for goldeneyes.

Clutch Size: Lee *et al.,* (1964a) reported that the average clutch size of thirty-nine Minnesota nests was 10.2 eggs. Grenquist (1963) reported an average of 10.3 eggs in fifty-three clutches. Carter (1958) reported a range of 7 to 12 eggs in nine New Brunswick nests, with an average of 9. The egg-laying interval is about one and one-half days (Bauer and Glutz, 1969).

Incubation Period: Probably 27 to 32 days, with a report of 30 days in one case (Bauer and Glutz, 1969).

Fledging Period: Reported by Sirén (1952) as 61 to 66 days. Lee *et al.* (1964a) estimated a 56- to 57-day fledging period.

Nest and Egg Losses: Prince (1968) reported a nesting success of 60 percent for six enclosed nests versus only 16 percent for ten "bucket" nests in New Brunswick. Carter (1958) noted a hatching success of 96.2 percent for seventy-nine eggs, excluding one flooded clutch.

Sources of egg losses are not well known, but predation levels of enclosed nests are probably low, with rare losses to martens. However, in rainy years, soaking of the nest may cause nest abandonment by a large percentage of the females (Dementiev and Gladkov, 1967).

A study by Grenquist (1963) in Finland provides the best information on prehatching losses. Of 1,554 eggs, 50.6 percent hatched, 40.4 percent were unincubated, 6.2 percent had dead embryos, and 1.9 percent were infertile. This low hatching success was attributed to competition for nest sites and particularly to the disruptive effects caused by females that were laying for the first time and entering previously occupied nests. These were probably two-year-old females or perhaps one-year-olds that had come into reproductive condition later than the older birds. In clutches that were incubated to completion, an average of 9.6 ducklings hatched.

Juvenile Mortality: Gibbs (1962) reported that, of an original population of seventy-seven young, only twenty-two ducklings reached the age of fledging, or a 71.5 percent prefledging mortality. However, specific mortality factors could not be determined. Carter (1958) estimated a 47 percent mortality loss prior to fledging, based on reductions in average brood sizes he observed over a six-year period, resulting in a brood size of 4.8 young in broods approaching the flight stage. Predation, disease, and accidents were assumed responsible for these losses, but specific mortality factors were not identified.

Adult Mortality: Nilsson (1971) judged that adult goldeneyes in Sweden have an annual mortality rate of about 37 percent. Johnson (1967) estimated a 36 percent loss of first-year birds as a result of hunting, but a considerably lower adult mortality due to hunting was estimated, resulting from the adults using large lakes that offered some protection.

GENERAL ECOLOGY

Food and Foraging: Cottam (1939) reported on the foods found in 395 common goldeneye stomachs obtained during every month except June and August. Crustaceans (32 percent by volume), insects (28 percent), and mollusks (10 percent) constituted the primary animal foods, while a variety of plant foods totalled 26 percent. Favored foods appear to include crabs, crayfish, and amphipods among the crustaceans, the larvae of caddis flies, water boatman adults, and the naiads of dragonflies, damselflies, and mayflies among the insect foods, and various bivalve and univalve mollusks. Thirteen juvenile birds had been foraging primarily on insects, of which beetles and immature stages of caddis flies, dragonflies, and damselflies were the most important. Reporting on birds obtained in Danish waters between October and February, Madsen (1954) found that crustaceans, bivalves, and univalve crustaceans were the three most important categories of foods present, with insects playing a very minor role in these marine and brackish-water samples. A similar indication of the relative importance of these food sources was given by Stewart (1962), on the basis of twenty-three birds obtained in the Chesapeake Bay region. Olney and Mills (1963) found comparable differences between birds collected in freshwater and marine habitats, noting the wide range of foods and habitats that are utilized by this species.

Cottam (1939) also commented on the diversity of foods consumed by this species and mentioned that it seemed able to survive on almost any type of available food. He observed these birds foraging in depths of 4 to 20 feet. Nilsson (1969) noted that goldeneyes preferred foraging in waters less than 1.5 meters deep and only fed in deeper waters when the shallow areas were frozen. He found no difference in diving abilities in the sexes, with the longest observed dive (47 seconds) made by a female. Olney and Mills (1963) stated that most foraging occurs at depths less than 4 meters, and rarely do the birds exceed 9 meters in their dives. They noted that goldeneyes often turn over stones with their bills while under water, searching for aquatic insects or other organisms.

Sociality, Densities, Territoriality: Carter (1958) estimated that about 150 pairs (five-year average) of goldeneyes nested yearly on a New Brunswick study area containing 16,000 acres of hardwood swamp, or about one pair per hundred acres of swamp. Usually the available nest sites in the form of natural cavities are well scattered and result in a rather sparse, randomly distributed breeding pattern for this species. Grenquist (1963) reported how the goldeneye population in Finland underwent a rapid increase in the 1950s following a program of setting out artificial nesting boxes, but that as the population increased and the availability of nesting boxes became limited, there was increased conflict among females for the boxes, resulting in a high incidence of unhatched eggs as well as serious fighting among the females. If nest sites are available, females will sometimes nest very close to one another (Sirén, 1957a).

Interspecific Relationships: In North America, the wood duck is the only hole-nesting species that extensively overlaps in breeding range and nesting requirements with the common goldeneye. Prince (1968) has analyzed their differences in nest site characteristics and noted several criteria that might contribute to a reduction in competition for such sites. Hooded mergansers possibly compete locally with goldeneyes for available nests. Common mergansers sometimes also nest in cavities, and Grenquist (1963) reported that when females of both species used the same nesting box, it was deserted by the goldeneye. Red-breasted mergansers are either surface- or cavity-nesters, but cavities used are generally at ground level.

General Activity Patterns and Movements: Goldeneyes are well known to be daytime feeders, often "rafting" in deeper waters at night. Breckenridge (1953) studied one such raft of wintering birds on the Mississippi River near Minneapolis, Minnesota. He found that the evening flight to the rafting area began about an hour before sunset and lasted until about an hour after sunset, or when it was virtually dark. Birds were found to move into this area from as far as twenty-seven miles upstream and ten miles downstream. The maximum size of the raft was found to be somewhat over six hundred birds.

Carter (1958) noted that spring migrant goldeneye flocks were usually found in fairly large flocks that remained rafted on deeper waters, while the resident birds occurred in pairs or small groups well apart from these flocks until later in the day, when they foraged on the outskirts of the transient flocks. He found little foraging to occur during the earliest hours of daylight, and after the midday foraging period the paired birds once again separated from the others shortly before dusk.

SOCIAL AND SEXUAL BEHAVIOR

Flocking Behavior: Breckenridge (1953) found that the average flock size of the wintering goldeneyes he studied on the Mississippi River dropped from 32 to 2.7 birds between December and the end of March, apparently reflecting the gradual pairing of birds. However, active courtship was seen throughout the entire period, without any definite peak. Probably some display continues among paired birds, since Carter (1958) mentions seeing "courtship" among both paired and unpaired groups. Evidently there is a tendency for the older and the paired birds to migrate northward more rapidly than the younger ones or the unpaired adults. Carter reported this to be the case in New Brunswick, and observations in central Washington (Johnsgard and Buss, 1956) support this. A locational segregation of paired and unpaired birds was also supported by the latter study.

Pair-forming Behavior: The social displays of male common goldeneyes are probably more diverse and complex than those of any other North American waterfowl, and cannot be adequately summarized here. Several studies (e.g., Myres, 1959a; Dane and Van der Kloot, 1964) have dealt with these complexities in considerable detail.

As mentioned earlier, social display lasts over a period of several months, from early winter through spring with a probable peak in March. Carter (1958) reported that by the time the goldeneyes arrive in New Brunswick in late March, nearly 80 percent of the adult birds are already paired. A later arrival of immature birds causes a reduction in this percentage.

Social display usually involves a small group of birds; Nilsson (1969) reported a typical group as consisting of two females and three to five males, and a maximum of five females and twenty males. Aggressive situations stimulate display, and probably most of the male display postures and calls are products of ritualized aggression. These include a simple head-throw, a fast and slow form of head-throw-kick, a "bowsprit" and "masthead" posture, and a number of other less complex movements. Most of these are performed in a stereotyped manner having remarkable time-constancy characteristics (Dane and Van der Kloot, 1964; Dane *et al.* 1959). Primary female postures and calls involve a highly ritualized inciting movement (also called "head-forward" and "jiving") and a distinctive neck-dipping movement that seemingly is a strong sexual stimulus to males. A weak screeching note accompanies this movement, whereas inciting is performed silently. The female will often follow a favored male while performing inciting movements, to which the male usually responds with lateral head-turning, while swimming ahead of her (Johnsgard, 1965).

Copulatory Behavior: Behavior patterns associated with copulation are nearly as complex as those associated with social courtship. The female typically assumes a prone position, often after mutual drinking movements by the pair, and remains in it for a prolonged period as the male performs his precopulatory displays. These include a large number of seemingly unritualized comfort movements. The most common of these is display-drinking (Nilsson, 1969; Lind, 1959), with a stretching of the wing and leg of secondary frequency, and a number of other movements such as bathing, dipping and shaking the bill in the water ("water-twitching"), and rolling the cheeks on the shoulders. Just prior to mounting, the male performs a vigorous series of water-twitching ("jabbing") movements, preens suddenly and momentarily, and immediately approaches the female in a "steaming" fashion. During treading the male normally shakes his wings one or more times, and before releasing the female he pulls her around in a partial or complete circle ("rotations"). He then swims directly away, with his head feathers fluffed, performing lateral head-turning movements while uttering low grunting sounds (Johnsgard, 1965).

Nesting and Brooding Behavior: In New Brunswick, Carter (1958) found that females begin looking for nesting sites about two or three weeks after their arrival, and the first eggs are laid about a week after that. If previously used nest sites are still available from past years, these are often used, sometimes up to five years in succession, but this is not invariable (Sirén, 1957a). No down is deposited prior to the first egg, but by the time the clutch is complete the eggs are usually well surrounded by down. More is added during the first week or two of incubation (Carter, 1958).

Normally on the morning following hatching, the female calls the young from the nest, and they typically jump out of the cavity in rapid succession. The complete evacuation of the nest by the brood may occur very rapidly; in five cases the range was 40 to 150 seconds. After all the young have left the nest, the family usually rests a few minutes, then begins to move toward water (Bauer and Glutz, 1969). At times, the newly hatched young must walk a mile or more before reaching water (Carter, 1958). Swimming females have been seen letting the young climb up on their backs to rest, but the carrying of young on the back while in flight is still unproven and controversial.

Studies in Finland indicate that, after hatching, the adult female usually takes her young to small forested pools, often abandoning one or more of her ducklings in such pools and moving to another, so that by the time the young are fledged she may be caring for only a single offspring (Sirén, 1957b). Carter (1958) reported seeing untended young quite often, such birds constituting about 14 percent of the total ducklings seen. He also noted that females seem to abandon their entire brood at a much earlier age than do most species of duck.

Postbreeding Behavior: In New Brunswick, males remain in the general breeding area for a time after abandoning their mates and congregate in small groups. Most of them evidently do move to river mouths and coastal inlets before becoming flightless. Females are by then abandoning their broods and begin to molt about the time the young are nearly fledged. Females evidently remain in the general area of breeding to complete their molt. There is a gradual movement of juveniles toward the coast as they fledge, and there they gather with older birds in small groups on deep water, foraging in shallower waters during early morning and evening hours (Carter, 1958).

HOODED MERGANSER

Mergus cucullatus (Linnaeus) 1758

(*Lophodytes cucullatus* of A.O.U., 1957)

Other Vernacular Names: Fish Duck, Hairyhead, Sawbill.

Range: Breeds from southeastern Alaska and adjacent Canada eastward through the southern and middle wooded portions of the border provinces to New Brunswick and Nova Scotia; southward to Oregon and Idaho, in a southeasterly direction across the wooded parts of the northern Great Plains to the Mississippi Valley, and from there to the Atlantic coast and sporadically as far south as the Gulf coast states. Winters along the Pacific coast from southern British Columbia south to Mexico, along the Gulf coast, along the Atlantic coast north to the New England states, and to some extent in the interior, especially on the Great Lakes.

Subspecies: None recognized.

Measurements (after Delacour, 1959):

Folded wing: Males 195-201, females 184-198 mm.

Culmen: Males 38-41, females 35-39 mm.

Weights: Nelson and Martin (1953) reported that twenty-four males averaged 1.5 pounds (679 grams), and twenty females averaged 1.2 pounds (543 grams), with maximum weights of 2.0 pounds (907 grams) and 1.5 pounds (679 grams), respectively.

IDENTIFICATION

In the Hand: Apart from the very rare smew, this is the only species with a merganserlike bill (narrow, serrated, with a large, curved nail), a culmen length less than 45 mm., and a folded wing measurement less than 205 mm. Additionally, the rounded crest, yellowish legs, and ornamental black or brownish tertials with narrow white or ashy stripes are all distinctive.

In the Field: On the water, both sexes appear as small ducks with long, thin bills and fanlike crests that are usually only partially opened. Only the bufflehead has a comparable white crest, and that species lacks reddish brown flanks, has no black margin on the crest, and has a much shorter bill. Immature males or females appear as slim grayish brown birds with a brownish head and a cinnamon-tinted crest. In flight, hooded mergansers lower the crest and hold the head at the same level as the body, making a streamlined profile, and exhibit their distinctive black and white upper wing pattern, while their underwing coloration is mostly silvery gray and whitish. Females are not highly vocal, but during courtship activities the distinctive male call, a rolling, froglike *crrrooooo,* may be heard for some distance.

AGE AND SEX CRITERIA

Sex Determination: The presence of mostly pale gray middle and lesser coverts indicates an adult male, but either sex can have brownish black or brownish gray coverts. Some immature males may be recognized by having one or more pale gray feathers among the surrounding dark coverts, but other wing criteria are apparently unsuited for sexing young birds (Carney, 1964). Until the appearance of white crest markings, which normally occurs before the male is a year old, young males cannot be readily distinguished from females.

Age Determination: Males can be readily aged by the fact that first-year males lack pale gray middle and lesser upper wing coverts, or at most may have only a few feathers of such coloration. Females in their first year can be distinguished from older birds by their duller, browner overall coloration and their undeveloped crests (Bent, 1925).

DISTRIBUTION AND HABITAT

Breeding Distribution and Habitat: This strictly North American species has a breeding range somewhat similar to that of the wood duck, with eastern and western segments that are seemingly well isolated from one another.

In western North America the hooded merganser breeds as far north as southeastern Alaska, with young having been seen on the Stikine, Chilkat, and Innoko rivers (Gabrielson and Lincoln, 1959). The range continues into British Columbia, including the Queen Charlotte Islands, and the mountains of western Alberta (Godfrey, 1966). In Washington it breeds at least in the northern part of the state (Yocom, 1951), and its western breeding range apparently extends to southwestern Oregon (A.O.U., 1957). Only one nesting record exists for California (*Audubon Field Notes,* 18:483). Along the Rocky Mountains the hooded merganser extends southward through Idaho (*ibid.,* 23:680) and western Montana (*ibid.,* 20:586; 21:588). It once also bred in Wyoming and Colorado (Phillips, 1926), and a single recent nesting record for Colorado is known (*American Birds,* 25:883).

It is rather uncertain whether any breeding occurs in Saskatchewan, but breeding birds have been found in the southern and middle wooded portions of Manitoba, as well as eastward through the comparable portions of Ontario, Quebec, and New Brunswick. Rare breeding in Nova Scotia evidently marks the eastern limits of the Canadian range (Godfrey, 1966). South of Canada, recent breeding has been reported for North Dakota (*American Birds,* 25:869), Minnesota (Lee *et al.,* 1964a), Wisconsin (Jahn and Hunt, 1964), Michigan (Zimmerman and Van Tyne, 1959), Indiana (Mumford, 1952), New York (Foley, 1960; *Audubon Field Notes,* 15:465; 24:680), Vermont (*Audubon Field Notes,* 11:391; 21:551), New Hampshire (*ibid.,* 11:391), and Maine (Spencer, 1963). Breeding also occurs along much of the length of the Mississippi and its larger tributaries as far south in Louisiana as McIntosh (*Audubon Field Notes,* 10:389). Local or sporadic breeding also extends south along the Atlantic coastal states some distance, including Massachusetts (*ibid.,* 9:365, 367), New Jersey (*ibid.,* 3:239; 16:462, 464), Maryland (*ibid.,* 15:456; 20:557), South Carolina (*ibid.,* 21:556), Georgia (*ibid.,* 21:556), and Florida (Sprunt, 1954).

The preferred breeding habitat of the hooded merganser consists of wooded, clear-water streams and, to a lesser degree, the wooded shorelines of lakes. The combination of food in the form of small fish and invertebrates in

Breeding (hatched) and wintering (shaded) distributions of the hooded merganser in North America.

water sufficiently clear for foraging and suitable nest sites in the form of tree cavities is probably a major factor influencing its breeding distribution. Like the wood duck, it seems rather sensitive to cold, and its breeding range is considerably more southerly than are those of the two other mergansers.

Wintering Distribution and Habitat: The western segment of the hooded merganser population primarily winters along the Pacific coast, from as far north as southern British Columbia (Godfrey, 1966) to southern California and occasionally reaching Baja California (Leopold, 1959). Small numbers are sometimes found on the southern Great Lakes during winter, but most of the eastern wintering population may be found from Massachusetts southward along the Atlantic coast to northern Florida, and along the Gulf coast, with occasional birds reaching Tamaulipas and Veracruz (Leopold, 1959).

In the Chesapeake Bay region, only small numbers regularly winter, and these are mostly in the fresh and brackish estuarine bay marshes, with some usage of river bottomlands and fresh estuarine bays or interior impoundments. Salt estuarines and open ocean are evidently avoided (Stewart, 1962).

GENERAL BIOLOGY

Age at Maturity: Females are evidently sexually mature after their third spring of life, or when two years old (Morse *et al.,* 1969).

Pair Bond Pattern: Pair bonds are renewed yearly, with an associated period of social display (Johnsgard, 1961a). Pair bonds are broken when the female begins incubation (Morse *et al.,* 1969).

Nest Location: McGilvrey (1966) reported that six of eight nesting boxes used by hooded mergansers were in open impoundments rather than in impoundments with dead timber present. Morse *et al.* (1969) found that boxes closely adjacent to water were much more heavily used than those some distance from it.

Minimum and optimum size criteria for natural cavities have not yet been reported, but probably would tend to be smaller than those used by wood ducks. If the same habitat characteristics apply to nesting as to brooding, then the findings of Kitchen and Hunt (1969) may be of importance. They found greatest brood usage on rivers with high food resources, rivers with relatively fast currents, wide rather than narrow rivers, and those with moderately deep channels. Of 65 brood observations cited in the literature, 46 (71 percent) were on rivers or river-related habitats, 12 were on beaver ponds, and the remainder were in standing-water habitats.

Clutch Size: Morse *et al.* (1969) reported an average clutch size of 10.2 eggs for fifty-five nests, with a range of 6 to 15. Clutch sizes tended to decrease with the season and were smaller (average 9.4) for eight initial breeders than for ten older breeders (average 10.8). The egg-laying rate averaged one per 48 hours.

Incubation Period: The mean incubation period was 32.6 days for naturally incubated nests, with an observed range of 29 to 37 days (Morse *et al.,* 1969).

Fledging Period: Estimated by McGilvrey (1966) to be 71 days.

Nest and Egg Losses: Morse *et al.* (1969) found that eggs laid in forty-four of fifty-five nests were successfully hatched, a nesting success of 80 percent. In these successful nests, 92.2 percent of the eggs hatched, and the average brood size at the time of hatching was 9.6 ducklings. McGilvrey (1966) reported that a raccoon destroyed one of eight clutches under observation by him. Dump-nesting caused some losses in the study of Morse *et al.;* in 1968 there were six dump nests among a total of twenty-four clutches, three of which were unsuccessful.

Juvenile Mortality: Duckling losses sometimes appear to be quite high in this species (McGilvrey, 1966), although the sources of such mortality can only be guessed at. Postfledging mortality rates of juveniles are still unreported.

Adult Mortality: No detailed estimates, but Morse *et al.* (1969) noted that eleven of eighteen adult females banded in 1966 and 1967 returned to nest the following year, representing a minimum annual survival rate of about 60 percent. Of the eleven returning females, 64 percent used the same box the following year, and all nested within three miles of their previous site. Thus, like other hole-nesting species that have been studied, there is considerable nest site fidelity, and the numbers of returning females should provide a reasonable basis for estimating adult mortality rates.

GENERAL ECOLOGY

Food and Foraging: Surprisingly little is known of the foods of this species. Bent (1923) indicated that insects make up a large part of the food, together with small fish, frogs, tadpoles, snails, other mollusks, crayfish, and other small crustaceans. It forages on both muddy and stony bottoms and consumes a rather small amount of plant materials. Stewart (1962) reported that all of the ten hooded mergansers obtained in the Chesapeake Bay area had been feeding on various fish. Crustaceans (mud crabs and crayfish) and insects (caddis fly larvae and dragonfly naiads) were also found in some of these birds.

Relatively clear waters with sandy or cobble bottoms are preferred over mud-bottom habitats for foraging. Kitchen and Hunt (1969) found a preference among females and broods for foraging in fairly fast-moving waters, in waters having an average depth of only 20 inches, and for using cobble-bottom stream areas rather than mucky areas in most cases. Such areas tended to be rich in fish, crustaceans, and aquatic insects, although the specific foods taken were not determined.

Sociality, Densities, Territoriality: Except where nesting boxes are established, the relative rarity of suitable nesting cavities possibly places a limit on maximum breeding densities in an area. However, Kitchen and Hunt found no lack of suitable cavities in their study. Instead they correlated breeding density (broods observed) with river characteristics related to food availability. The highest brood use figure they obtained was 2.14 broods per mile of river. Additionally, heavily wooded rivers were favored over brush-lined rivers, and marshy rivers had the lowest brood densities.

Interspecific Relationships: The relationships of nesting hooded mergansers and wood ducks in their overlapping areas of breeding have not yet been analyzed, but would be of considerable interest. The fact that hooded mergansers prefer habitats with rapidly flowing water over standing-water ones, while wood ducks prefer slow-moving rivers and ponds, would tend to reduce competition for nest sites. Additionally, different food sources would certainly influence the local distribution of pairs and families. Phillips (1926) mentioned one case of wood duck and hooded merganser eggs being found in the same nest, and noted that in Maine both common goldeneye and barred owl eggs have been found with those of hooded mergansers.

Phillips indicated that the hooded merganser rarely mixes with the larger species of merganser and forages in different habitats from them. Also, it is less dependent than the other two mergansers on fish, relying to a greater extent on insects and crustaceans. It sometimes forages in the company of buffleheads, and no doubt the two species feed to some extent on the same kinds of invertebrates.

General Activity Patterns and Movements: Hooded mergansers are daylight foragers; indeed they probably require both good light and clear water to catch such active prey as fish. How much time per day is spent in foraging has not yet been reported, but incubating females normally leave their nests three times a day for this purpose (Morse *et al.,* 1969), in early morning, midday, and late afternoon.

SOCIAL AND SEXUAL BEHAVIOR

Flocking Behavior: Large flocks are not typical of this species; most writers (such as those cited by Bent, 1923) report that from five to fifteen birds typically constitute a flock. Flocks as large as a hundred birds have been seen (Harper, in Phillips, 1926), but are most unusual.

Pair-forming Behavior: Pair-forming displays by wild birds have been reported by so few observers that it is difficult to judge when most pair formation does occur. Harper (in Phillips, 1926) observed active display in early February among wild birds, and I have seen it among captive individuals (Johnsgard, 1961a) throughout the winter and spring months. Harper noted that courting flocks contained from three to ten birds, including one to three females.

Male displays of the hooded merganser are in large measure related to the ornamental crest. Crest-raising, either independently or in conjunction with other displays, is very frequent. The head and erect crest are often shaken laterally, as the bird rises slightly in the water; such shaking often precedes a head-throwing movement that includes a rolling froglike note. A silent, elliptical neck-stretching, or "pumping," movement is also frequent and is seemingly hostile in function. A turning of the depressed crest toward a female, diagonal tail-cocking, body-shaking ("upward-stretch"), and wing-flapping are all relatively frequent during pair-formation activities and all appear to represent displays (Johnsgard, 1961a). The female's movements include a pumping movement, similar to the male's and often performed simultaneously with the male's display, and a variation of inciting ("bobbing") that is apparently rather rare in this species. As in other ducks, the usual response of the male to inciting is to swim ahead of the female and turn the back of his head toward her.

Copulatory Behavior: As with the goldeneyes and the other mergansers, the female hooded merganser assumes an outstretched prone posture on the water well in advance of mounting and often after the pair has performed ritualized drinking movements. At this time the male begins to perform almost continuous and rather jerky back-and-forth head movements with lowered crest and intersperses these with drinking movements and body shakes. Suddenly he begins a number of vigorous head-shakes with his bill in the water, stops, and performs a body-shake or a few wing-flaps, preens once in the region of his back, and starts toward the female. He approaches her in a somewhat zigzag fashion, presenting first one side, then the other, of his raised or nearly raised crest toward her. He then mounts the female, and during treading flicks his folded wings. Before releasing the female's nape he pulls her around in a partial rotary movement. After treading, he swims rapidly away with an erect crest, terminating this swim either with a quick dive or with bathing (Johnsgard, 1961a).

Nesting and Brooding Behavior: After locating suitable nest sites, females begin to deposit their eggs at the rate of one every other day. Unlike many ducks, this species evidently does not normally deposit down in the nest until the initiation of incubation. Males desert their mates at about this time, and after incubation is under way the female usually leaves her nest only three times a day, in early morning, midday, and late afternoon. Several writers have commented on the secretive manner of the hen when returning to her nest. After a surprisingly long incubation period of nearly 32 days, the ducklings hatch. They usually remain in the nest a full day, leaving the cavity early the following morning (Morse *et al.,* 1969). The female may keep her brood near the hatching area or move them into other water areas, but evidently seeks out waters less than 20 inches deep that are quite close to timber (McGilvrey, 1966). At what age the female usually abandons her brood to begin her post-nuptial molt apparently has not been determined.

Postbreeding Behavior: The males probably begin to molt fairly soon after deserting their mates, but few observations on the behavior and movements of males in the postnesting season are available. They evidently become quite secretive and probably move into heavily timbered streams to complete their flightless period. Phillips (1926) noted that adult males are extremely rare along the Massachusetts coast during fall, leading him to believe that they perhaps migrate by a different route than do females and immatures.

SMEW

Mergus albellus (Linnaeus) 1758

Other Vernacular Names: None in North America.

Range: Breeds in northern Europe and Asia from Scandinavia to Kamchatka and Anadyr. Winters in southern Europe and Asia south to the Indian Ocean; accidental in North America.

Subspecies: None recognized.

Measurements (after Delacour, 1959):
Folded wing: Males 192-205, females 178-186 mm.
Culmen: Males 28-30, females 25-28 mm.

Weights: Weights of smews presented by Dementiev and Gladkov (1967) indicate that during fall adult males range from 550 to 935 grams, and in November average 814 grams. Adult females weighed during the same period ranged from 515 to 650 grams, and averaged 572 grams in November.

IDENTIFICATION

In the Hand: This rare Eurasian merganser is best identified in the hand, where it can be recognized as a merganser by its narrow, tapering bill with serrated edges and a prominent nail. It is the only merganser with a short bill (culmen length 25-30 mm.), white upper wing coverts, and grayish legs.

In the Field: The predominantly white male is not much larger than a bufflehead, but the smew's head is mostly white, rather than blackish, and has a narrow black stripe behind the eyes instead of a large white patch behind the eyes. Otherwise, the body patterns of the two species are quite similar, but the bufflehead lacks the two black stripes extending from the foreback down the sides of the breast. Females cannot safely be identified by persons lacking experience with the species, but apart from the merganserlike bill, they have a sharply bicolored head, with a chocolate brown cap extending through the eyes, and with white cheeks, throat, and foreneck. The rest of the body is a rather uniform gray. In flight, both sexes exhibit a great deal of white on the inner half of the upper wing surface, with two black stripes toward the rear of the wing. Like other mergansers, they fly with the neck and head held at the same level as the body.

AGE AND SEX CRITERIA

Sex Determination: In males, the white upper wing surface extends medially to include the scapulars, and the tertials are silvery gray. In females the tertials are brownish, and the scapulars are mostly light gray. The sexes are very similar when the male is in eclipse plumage, at which time the male's darker mantle color may serve to separate the sexes. First-year males closely resemble adult females, but are cinnamon brown rather than blackish brown in the facial region, or at most have only a few scattered blackish brown feathers, and the scapulars have clear gray brown centers (Bauer and Glutz, 1969).

Age Determination: The notched tail feathers will serve to identify juveniles for much of their first fall of life, as will the brownish edges of the central wing coverts. Year-old males can be distinguished from adult males and females as noted above.

OCCURRENCE IN NORTH AMERICA

Early records of the smew in North America are very few and have been summarized by Bent (1923). In the last decade, however, several sightings have been made and seem to justify including the species on the list of North

American waterfowl. These include a female or immature male seen on the Niagara River, southern Ontario, in 1960 (Godfrey, 1966) and a male observed at Montreal, Quebec, in 1967 (*Audubon Field Notes,* 21:400). Several records have been obtained for Alaska, one being of a female collected at Adak Island in 1970 (*ibid.,* 24:528). In 1971 another female was observed at Adak in June (*American Birds,* 25:894), and a smew was seen on Amchitka during the same year. Two male smews were observed on Attu in June 1972 (*ibid,* 26:795). An adult male was also repeatedly sighted at Vancouver, British Columbia, during November 1970 (*Syesis,* 5:147). Considering that there have been at least ten Alaskan records since 1960, the smew is probably a rare but regular visitor to the central and western Aleutian Islands, mainly during the fall months (*American Birds,* 27:103). It also is apparently a very rare visitor to British Columbia and Ontario (*ibid.,* 28:633, 680).

RED-BREASTED MERGANSER

Mergus serrator Linnaeus 1758

Other Vernacular Names: Fish Duck, Saw-bill.

Range: Breeds in Greenland, Iceland, the British Isles, northern Europe and
Asia from Scandinavia to Kamchatka, the Aleutian Islands, and from
Alaska eastward across nearly all of arctic Canada except the northern part
of Keewatin District and the arctic islands, south to northern British Columbia and Alberta, central Saskatchewan and Manitoba, southern Ontario,
the Great Lakes states, northern New York, New England, and the eastern
provinces of Canada to Newfoundland. Winters mostly on salt water, in
North America from southeastern Alaska south to Baja California, the Gulf
coast, the Atlantic coast from Florida to the Gulf of St. Lawrence, and inland in smaller numbers as far north as the Great Lakes.

North American subspecies:

M. s. serrator L.: Common Red-breasted Merganser. Breeds as indicated
above, except in Greenland.

M. s. schiøleri Salomonsen: Greenland Red-breasted Merganser. Resident
in Greenland.

Measurements (after Delacour, 1959):
   Folded wing: Males 224-260, females 217-230 mm.
   Culmen: Males 53-62, females 48-55 mm.
Weights: Nelson and Martin (1953) reported that eighteen males averaged 2.5 pounds (1,133 grams) and seventeen females averaged 2.0 pounds (907 grams), with maximums of 2.9 pounds (1,314 grams) and 2.8 pounds (1,268 grams), respectively. Schiøler (1926) reported that ten wintering adult males averaged 1,209.5 grams (2.67 pounds) and ten adult females averaged 959.5 grams (2.12 pounds).

IDENTIFICATION

In the Hand: The long, narrow, serrated bill with a hooked tip will distinguish this species from all other mergansers except the common merganser. In the red-breasted merganser the bill is distinctive in that (1) the nostrils are located in the basal third of the bill, (2) the feathering on the side of the upper mandible reaches considerably farther forward than that on the lower mandible, (3) the upper mandible is relatively longer and lower at the base than in other mergansers, at least six or more times as long as it is high at the base when measured from the cutting edge to the highest unfeathered point, and (4) the bill has a smaller, narrower nail at the tip. Both sexes are smaller than the common merganser, with adult males and females having maximum folded wing lengths of 260 and 230 mm., respectively.

In the Field: When in nuptial plumage, the male red-breasted merganser may be recognized by its green head, which extends backward into a shaggy double crest and is separated in front from a brownish breast by a white foreneck. The sides and flanks appear to be a light gray, bordered anteriorly with a black patch having regular white spots. The female is not nearly so "two-toned" as the female common merganser; her grayish body merges gradually with the brownish head, and neither the paler throat nor the lores are in strong contrast to the rest of the head. The female calls of the two species are very similar, but the courtship notes of the male red-breasted merganser are a somewhat catlike *yeow-yeow,* uttered during bizarre posturing. In flight, both sexes resemble the common merganser, but males exhibit a brownish breast band, while females appear to have a darker brown, less reddish head and neck color, which gradually merges with the grayish breast.

AGE AND SEX CRITERIA

Sex Determination: In adults, white middle and lesser coverts, and tertials that are either black or white margined with black indicate a male. First-year males begin to acquire malelike features about December, when black feathers appear on the head, mantle, and scapulars, while the white scapular feathers do not appear until the end of March.

Age Determination: First-year males are readily aged by their mostly grayish black tertials, which are narrow and have wispy tips, and the absence of pure white on the middle and lesser coverts. Adult females may be distinguished from first-year birds by tertials and greater tertial coverts that are smoothly rounded rather than narrow with wispy tips (Carney, 1964).

DISTRIBUTION AND HABITAT

Breeding Distribution and Habitat: The North American breeding distribution of this species is the most northerly and most extensive of any of the merganser species. It breeds in the Aleutian Islands from Attu to the Alaska Peninsula, as well as on Kodiak Island (Murie, 1959) and probably also on St. Lawrence Island (Fay, 1961). On the mainland of Alaska it has a wide occurrence throughout most of the state, although it is less frequent and perhaps is only an occasional breeder from Kotzebue Sound north and east along the Arctic coast (Gabrielson and Lincoln, 1959).

In Canada it breeds from the Arctic coast of the Yukon and Mackenzie District eastward across southern Keewatin District and southward to northern British Columbia, northern Alberta, central Saskatchewan, and virtually all of the more easterly provinces. It also breeds on southern Baffin Island (Godfrey, 1966), as well as along the coast of Greenland.

South of Canada, it breeds locally in northern Minnesota (Lee *et al.,* 1964a), uncommonly in northern Wisconsin (Jahn and Hunt, 1964), in northern Michigan (Zimmerman and Van Tyne, 1959), and locally in the northeastern states to Maine (Palmer, 1949). There have been a few isolated records of breeding farther south, such as in Pennsylvania (*Audubon Field Notes,* 22:584), North Carolina (*ibid.,* 10:377), and South Carolina (*ibid.,* 21:556).

The favored breeding habitat would seem to be inland freshwater lakes and streams that are not far removed from the coast. Deep, rock-lined lakes are seemingly favored over tundra ponds (Snyder, 1957), but the ground-nesting adaptations of this species allow it to nest in nonforested situations well away from a source of hollow trees. In northern Europe this species nests primarily in lakes and rivers having barren shores and clear waters, either among forests or in tundra zones. Areas having many available cavities, such as boulder-strewn areas, are rich in potential nest sites and thus tend to be favored (Hildén, 1964).

Breeding (hatched) and wintering (shaded) distributions of the
red-breasted merganser in North America.

Wintering Distribution and Habitat: In Alaska, red-breasted mergansers occur widely in the Aleutian Islands (Murie, 1959), and along the southern and southeastern coasts of Alaska they are also fairly common (Gabrielson and Lincoln, 1959). In Canada they winter along the entire coast of British Columbia, occur in small numbers on the Great Lakes, and extend from the St. Lawrence Valley to Newfoundland and the Maritime Provinces (Godfrey, 1966).

South of Canada, red-breasted mergansers winter along the Pacific coast from Puget Sound southward through Oregon and California to Mexico, where it is the commonest of the wintering mergansers (Leopold, 1959). Leopold reported seeing it along the Pacific coast and in the central highlands of northern Mexico, but not along the Caribbean coastline.

Along the Atlantic coastline, red-breasted mergansers are prevalent during winter from Maine southward at least as far as Georgia (Burleigh, 1958). They occur uncommonly from the Gulf coast of Florida (Chamberlain, 1960) westward through Louisiana and coastal Texas. In the Chesapeake Bay area they are frequent during the winter months, although larger numbers pass through on migration (Stewart, 1962).

Stewart reported that, in contrast to the freshwater tendencies of the common merganser, this species is characteristic of saline tidewaters, occurring all the way from open ocean through salt and brackish estuarine bays to fresh or slightly brackish waters, of which it makes only small usage. In marine habitats it tends to avoid deep or rough waters, preferring sheltered and relatively quiet areas where small fish are abundant and can be caught in shallow waters (Hildén, 1964).

GENERAL BIOLOGY

Age at Maturity: Sexual maturity probably occurs in two years, judging from plumage sequences (Dementiev and Gladkov, 1967). Some sexual display has been observed in first-year males.

Pair Bond Pattern: Pair bonds are renewed yearly, following a prolonged period of social display that begins on wintering areas. Pair bonds are relatively loose, and many instances of apparent polyandry and polygyny have been noted (Bauer and Glutz, 1969).

Nest Location: Unlike the two other North American mergansers, this species regularly nests away from trees. In Iceland, where trees of substantial size are lacking, red-breasted mergansers nest commonly. Bengtson (1970) noted that 63 percent of the 332 nests he found there were in holes or cavities, while 60 nests were under high shrubs, 49 under low shrubs, and 14 under sedge or tall forb cover. Bengtson reported a distinct island-nesting tendency for this species and a fairly close proximity of the nests to water (modal distances 10 to 30 meters). Hildén's (1964) study in the Valassaaret Islands included 238 nests of this species. He found the nests usually under boulders (39 percent), under dense juniper bushes (26 percent), or under *Hippophaë* thickets (15 percent). Unlike the common merganser, nesting occurs on both small islets and larger central islands, but the favored nesting substrate is associated with boulders. Islets with herbaceous vegetation are favored over those with grassy or wooded vegetation, apparently because of the presence of nesting lesser black-backed gulls (*Larus fuscus*). Curth (1954) reported that natural nesting cavities of this merganser average 27 centimeters wide and 7.8 centimeters deep. On the basis of studies of the use of nesting boxes, the preferred box dimensions are 17 to 23 centimeters high, 28 to 43 centimeters wide, and 42 to 50 centimeters long. The entrance hole should be 9 to 12.5 by 11.5 to 12.5 centimeters (Grenquist, 1958).

Clutch Size: Hildén (1964) reported that 144 clutches averaged 9.23 eggs, with a range of 6 to 17 and a mode of 9. Bengtson (1971) found an average clutch of 9.5 eggs for 158 first clutches in Iceland. Curth (1954) reported average clutch sizes for two different years of 9.8 and 9.9 eggs, excluding some abnormally large clutches that evidently resulted from dump-nesting. A sample of 27 renest clutches in Iceland averaged 6.2 eggs (Bengtson, 1972).

Incubation Period: Curth (1954) reported a mean incubation period of 31.8 days and an observed range of 29 to 35 days for wild birds. Slightly shorter periods have been estimated for artificially incubated eggs.

Fledging Period: Apparently quite variable, but one estimate is of 59 days (Bauer and Glutz, 1969).

Nest and Egg Losses: Hildén (1964) reported that among 67 clutches studied in a two-year period, 88 percent hatched, with six nests being taken by predators, one deserted, and one joint clutch with white-winged scoter eggs remaining unhatched. Although egg predators take many eggs during the egg-laying period, predation losses are evidently low once incubation begins. Curth (1954) reported much higher losses to predators, with as many as 30 percent of the nests being lost to common gulls (*Larus canus*). Ardamazkaja (cited in Bauer and Glutz, 1969) found that 91 percent of 790 nests near the Black Sea hatched during the years 1956 to 1961, with yearly variations of 57.2 to 95.8 percent. Hildén (1964) rather surprisingly found that in spite of their cavity-nesting or otherwise hiding their nests well, both red-breasted and common mergansers suffered as high or higher losses of eggs to predators (mostly crows) than did surface-nesting ducks.

Juvenile Mortality: Because of the prevalence of brood mergers in this species, average brood size counts are of little or no value in estimating pre-fledging losses. Hildén (1964) summarized past records of combined broods, which sometimes number from 30 to more than 60 ducklings in exceptional cases. Hildén's counts of total numbers of young in his study area over a three-year period indicated annual prefledging losses of 78, 84, and 92 percent. This seemingly high rate of juvenile mortality agreed well with an estimate of 86 percent for an earlier study. Hildén correlated yearly brood success with weather and judged that bad weather was an important factor in brood survival. Further, broods in sheltered bays survived severe weather better than those on the outer archipelago. The relatively great agility of the young seemingly reduced losses to predatory gulls, although the great black-backed gull (*Larus marinus*) was nevertheless considered to be a dangerous enemy.

Adult Mortality: Estimates of annual adult mortality rates are apparently unavailable for this species. Individuals known to have survived at least ten years have been reported (Bauer and Glutz, 1969).

Food and Foraging: Foods of the red-breasted merganser in North America have not yet received as much attention as might be desired. Cottam and Uhler (1936) examined 130 stomachs from a variety of locations. They reported the following relative abundance of foods: minnows, killifish, and sticklebacks, 34 percent; commercial and game fish, 14 percent; carp and suckers, 3 percent; unidentified fish, 25 percent; and crustaceans or miscellaneous, 23 percent. Munro and Clemens (1939) analyzed the foods of this species in British Columbia, where it is often considered a threat to salmon. On the basis of 77 specimens taken between November and January, it was found that the bird consumed primarily opaque salmon eggs, which are considered largely a waste product. Of 19 specimens taken from freshwater lakes and streams, sculpins (*Cottus*) were found in the largest number of stomachs (15), while salmonoid fry or fingerlings were present in only 3 specimens. Some sculpin eggs, insects, and annelid remains were also present. Among 15 specimens from salt water or estuaries, herring occurred with the greatest frequency (7 stomachs), sticklebacks were found in 3, sculpins in 2, while blennies and rock fish were present in 1 each. Crustacean remains were present in 5 specimens. Munro and Clemens believed that herring constitute the primary prey of red-breasted mergansers in salt water.

Munro and Clemens noted that while feeding on the coast, red-breasted mergansers often swim close to shore in single file, with their heads partly submerged. They are sometimes "parasitized" by gulls, which often try to steal fish that the mergansers bring to the surface. An example of cooperative foraging described by Des Lauriers and Brattstrom (1965) involved seven birds swimming with their heads partly submerged in water less than 24 inches deep. They moved in a loose line, and when one began to chase a fish the others joined in to form a semicircle around it until it was finally caught. Similar behavior has been noted in England (Hending *et al.,* 1963) among flocks feeding in turbid waters. There, groups of 7 to 24 birds dove in near synchrony, with most of the birds submerging within 2 or 3 seconds. The average diving duration was 17.4 seconds, the average diving pause 7.3 seconds, and the maximum observed diving duration 29 seconds.

Sociality, Densities, Territoriality: Availability of nesting cavities or suitably dense shrub cover probably determines the nesting distribution of this species, as well as such factors as nesting gull colonies and island sites. Bengtson (1970) reported a higher nesting density for this species on islands than on the mainland of Iceland. Excluding cavity nests, he noted a density of 23 per square kilometer on islands, as compared with 10 per square kilometer on the mainland. Since nearly 70 percent of the nests he found were in holes and cavities, a considerably higher overall nesting density was evidently present.

Interspecific Relationships: During winter there is probably little if any food competition between this species and the common merganser, since they tend to occupy saline and fresh waters, respectively. However, when both species are on fresh water, they seem to consume identical foods (Munro and Clemens, 1939).

A review by Mills (1962) suggests that the primary natural enemies of the red-breasted merganser are the great and lesser black-backed gulls, which consume both its eggs and ducklings. No doubt considerable destruction is caused by man, either through the misguided control efforts by fishermen or through the more pervasive and dangerous effects of pesticide accumulations on the bird's reproductive efficiencies.

General Activity Patterns and Movements: Red-breasted mergansers are necessarily daytime foragers, depending on their eyesight and underwater mobility for capturing prey. Nilsson (1965) reported that the population he studied gathered each evening at a communal roosting place on a small islet. Courtship activity was common there during evening and early morning hours. By an hour after sunrise, they had spread out over the entire area. While foraging they were frequently harassed by scavenging gulls, but were apparently always successful in evading them.

SOCIAL AND SEXUAL BEHAVIOR

Flocking Behavior: Red-breasted mergansers are relatively gregarious, and during migration as well as on wintering grounds they often occur in fairly large flocks. This no doubt is related in large part to the local concentrations of fish in suitable foraging areas, and perhaps also to the apparently greater efficiency of foraging in groups instead of individually. Munro and Clemens (1939) reported seeing flocks of 100 or more birds coming in to coastal British Columbia to forage on herring. Mills (1962) described winter flocks in Scotland of 30 to 400 birds, the latter groups apparently attracted to herring. With spring, these large flocks disperse toward their breeding grounds and no doubt gradually break up into pairs. Some summering flocks also occur locally in Scotland, which apparently represent molting accumulations.

Pair-forming Behavior: Social display related to pair-formation begins on the wintering areas. Display takes on a highly distinctive form in this species, with the males often circling around the females and periodically performing a complex and rather bizarre series of movements called the "knicks" display. Often, two males perform the display in synchrony or near synchrony, further adding to its complexity. From a resting posture, the male suddenly extends his neck and head diagonally upward, forming nearly a straight line. After a momentary pause, he pulls the head downward toward the water, simultaneously gaping, uttering a faint catlike call, and raising the folded wings while tilting the tail downward. The head is then retracted toward the shoulders, and the tail is more strongly down-tilted. Occasionally a male will also suddenly dash over the water in a hunched "sprint" posture, throwing up a spray of water to both sides. Apart from the weak call associated with the knicks display, the birds are otherwise nearly silent, adding further to the almost incredible activities. Females perform an infrequent but vigorous inciting movement, simultaneously uttering a harsh double note, but this display does not appear to be the primary stimulus for male display. Rather, it seems to prevent males from approaching the female too closely. A turning-of-the-back-of-the-head by males toward females has been reported by one observer (Curth, 1954), but in my experience, this does not appear to play a significant role in social display (Johnsgard, 1965).

Copulatory Behavior: Typically, copulation sequences are preceded by mutual drinking displays, followed by the assumption of a prone posture by the female. The male then performs a rather unpredictable series of drinking, preening, wing-flapping, and shaking movements. In my observations, the male always attempted to mount the female immediately after performing a rather rudimentary version of the knicks display (Johnsgard, 1965). After copulation, which lasts from 6 to 13 seconds, the male rotates while still grasping the female, performs a knicks display, and both birds then begin bathing (Nilsson, 1965).

Nesting and Brooding Behavior: Females begin to look for nest sites as long as two or three weeks before egg-laying begins and are especially active during early morning hours. Brooding females usually leave their nests only for short periods of 62 to 125 minutes, and even shorter periods are typical during rainy weather. The times of such departures from the nest vary greatly, but most often occur during the early morning hours. Apparently the females' food requirements are strongly reduced during incubation, and they will also drink salt water at such times. The young leave their nest site between 12 and 24 hours after the hatching of the last duckling. The family may move from two to five kilometers during their first few days, with the young sometimes riding on the back of the mother (Bauer and Glutz, 1969). Their cold-hardiness is greater than that of dabbling ducks, pochards, or scoters, and similar to that of eiders. Koskimies and Lahti (1964) found that three newly hatched red-breasted merganser ducklings retained their thermoregulation for at least three hours at a temperature of 0° to 2° Centigrade. However, prolonged periods of bad weather may greatly affect brood survival. Hildén (1964) noted this, and also reported on brood-merging tendencies in this species. He noted broods of as many as a hundred young with a single female. In some cases broods were observed to be escorted, at least temporarily, by two females.

Postbreeding Behavior: Males typically desert their mates early in incubation, and early observations of males apparently associated with broods have not been verified by more recent studies. Little information is available on postbreeding behavior and movements of red-breasted mergansers. There is no strong evidence that any substantial molt migration occurs, but very probably there is a general movement of males to brackish or saline waters prior to undergoing their flightless period. Hildén (1964) reported that, because of the species' sociality, small flocks were seen through the breeding season and it was difficult to determine the duration of the pair bonds. Drakes began to flock when the hens began incubation, and by late June flocks up to 30 were seen, including some presumably nonbreeding females. Most of these were gone by early July, suggesting a premolt migration by these birds.

COMMON MERGANSER (GOOSANDER)

Mergus merganser Linnaeus 1758

Other Vernacular Names: American Goosander, Fish Duck, Sawbill.

Range: Breeds in Iceland, central Europe, Scandinavia, Russia, Siberia to Kamchatka and some of the Bering Sea islands, and in North America from southern Alaska and the southern Yukon eastward across central Canada to James Bay and across the Labrador Peninsula to Newfoundland, southward in the western mountains to California, Arizona, and New Mexico, and northeastward to the Great Lakes, New York, and the New England states. Winters both on salt and fresh water, from the Aleutian Islands to southern California, from Newfoundland to Florida, and in the interior wherever large rivers or deep lakes occur.

North American subspecies:

M. m. americanus Cassin: American Merganser. Breeds in North America as indicated above.

Measurements (after Godfrey, 1966):

Folded wing: Males 267.5-281, females 236-274 mm.

Culmen: Males 54.5-59 mm., females not indicated (Delacour reported 45-50 mm. for *M. m. merganser*.)

Weights: Nelson and Martin (1953) reported that forty-five males averaged 3.5 pounds (1,588 grams) and twenty-nine females averaged 2.5 pounds (1,133 grams), with maximums of 4.1 pounds (1,859 grams) and 3.9 pounds (1,769 grams), respectively. Erskine (1971) noted that thirteen adult males averaged 1,709 grams (3.77 pounds) in November and thirteen adult females averaged 1,220 grams (2.69 pounds) in October. November averages for fourteen immatures of the respective sexes were 1,585 and 1,223 grams.

IDENTIFICATION

In the Hand: Immediately recognizable as a merganser on the basis of its long, cylindrical, serrated bill, only the red-breasted merganser has a culmen length as long as this species, from 45 to 60 mm. However, the bill differs in that it (1) has the nostril located in the middle third of the bill, (2) has the feathering on the side of the lower mandible reaching nearly as far forward as that on the side of the upper mandible, (3) has a relatively higher-based and shorter upper mandible that is usually no more than five times as long as high when measured from the mandible edge to the highest unfeathered area, and (4) has a larger, wider nail at its tip. Both sexes are larger than the red-breasted merganser, with adult males and females having minimum folded wing lengths of 280 and 250 mm., respectively.

In the Field: When in nuptial plumage, a male common merganser is unmistakable, with its dark greenish head with a bushy rather than a shaggy crest, its pure white to pinkish breast color, and the absence of gray or black on its sides. Females and immature males appear to have generally grayish to white bodies, strongly contrasting with their reddish brown heads and necks. A clear white throat and a white line between the eye and the base of the bill may be seen under favorable conditions. Sometimes the females utter harsh *karrr* notes, and during aquatic courtship the males produce a rather faint *uig-a* sound reminiscent of the twanging of a guitar string. In flight, a common merganser appears to be a very large, long-necked streamlined duck. It holds its head, neck, and body at the same level; both sexes exhibit a nearly pure white breast color and have almost entirely white underparts, including their underwing surface.

AGE AND SEX CRITERIA

Sex Determination: Adult males have white middle and lesser wing coverts and white tertials that are margined with black, rather than dark gray in these areas. First-year males reportedly also have the outer secondaries white and the inner ones gray (Bent, 1925), although more probably the reverse is true, with the outer gray secondaries conforming to the black outer secondaries of adult females. Erskine (1971) noted that not only are juvenile males larger than females, but also they have a distinctive pale patch, formed by several outer secondary coverts, on the wing.

Age Determination: Adult males can be distinguished from first-year ones by the latter's dark gray middle and lesser coverts and dark gray tertials. Adult females have solid gray, wider, and more rounded tertials and tertial coverts, while in immature females these feathers are narrower and have faded, wispy tips (Carney, 1964). Erskine (1971) reported that at least six females were found to breed at two years of age, but none were known to breed their first year. Males may, however, become fertile toward the latter part of their first year of life, and thus a fully developed penis structure may not indicate a bird older than one year. Immature birds have a well-developed bursa, which Erskine reported absent in adults. Additional age and sex criteria have been reported by Anderson and Timken (1971) who noted that the juvenile rectrices are lost by the end of November and that adults and second-year birds have red bills and/or feet while first-year birds are yellow to reddish orange in these areas.

DISTRIBUTION AND HABITAT

Breeding Distribution and Habitat: The North American breeding distribution of the common merganser, like that of the red-breasted merganser, is transcontinental in character but is essentially confined to forested regions.

In Alaska, the common merganser breeds chiefly in the southern coastal area, occurring west regularly as far as Prince William Sound. Broods have also been reported on Kodiak Island. Very few definite indications of breeding have been obtained for areas north of the Alaska Peninsula or in the interior, with Paxon Lake seemingly representing the northernmost location of known breeding (Gabrielson and Lincoln, 1959).

In Canada, breeding extends across the southern Yukon, southwestern Mackenzie District, and the wooded portions of British Columbia, the Prairie Provinces, and most of those parts of Ontario, Quebec, and Labrador south of the tree line, as well as in Newfoundland and the Maritime Provinces (Godfrey, 1965).

South of Canada, breeding occurs in Washington (Yocom, 1951), Oregon (Gabrielson and Jewett, 1940), and California (Grinnell and Miller, 1944). There is also an extension of the species' breeding range southward along the Rocky Mountains through Idaho, Montana, and Wyoming, with localized breeding as far south as Colorado (Bailey and Neidrach, 1967). It has also bred in Arizona (*Audubon Field Notes,* 11:423). East of the Great Plains, it also nests regularly in northern Minnesota (Lee *et al.,* 1964a), rarely

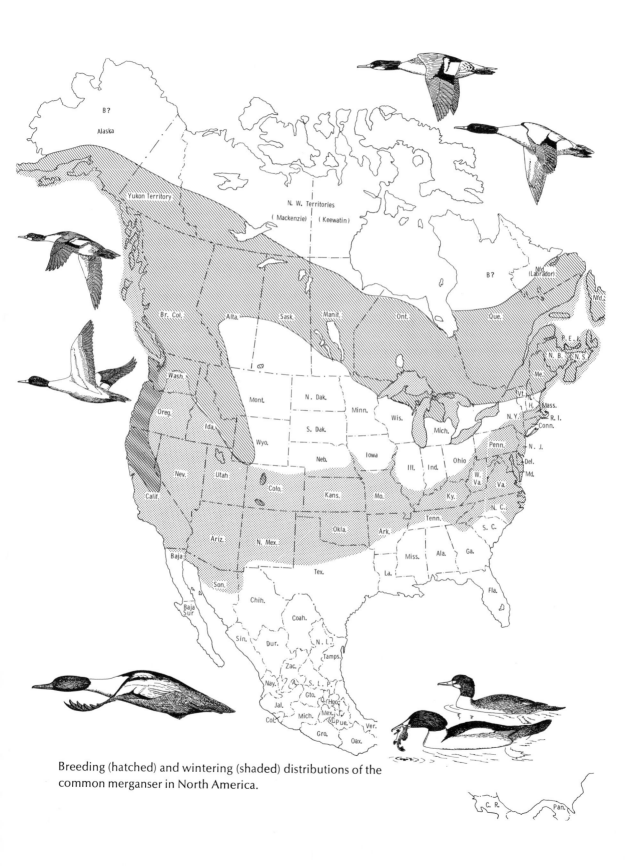

Breeding (hatched) and wintering (shaded) distributions of the common merganser in North America.

in Wisconsin (Jahn and Hunt, 1964), rather commonly in parts of Michigan (Parmelee, 1964; Zimmerman and Van Tyne, 1959), and in northern New England to Maine (Palmer, 1949). South of New England and northern New York there have been a few isolated breeding records, such as in western New York (*Audubon Field Notes,* 22:605), in Massachusetts (*ibid.,* 7:299; 8:335; 13:419), Connecticut (*ibid.,* 16:462), and even Virginia (*ibid.,* 19:531).

The preferred breeding habitat of this species consists of ponds associated with upper portions of rivers in forested regions and of clear freshwater lakes with forested shorelines. Clear water is needed for visual foraging by both adult and young birds. Hildén (1964) reported that this species is an inland rather than marine nester, breeding along extensive waters with barren shores and rivers with clear water, almost entirely within the forest zone. It is not socially attracted to gulls, and its nesting distribution seems primarily determined by nest site availability and landscape characteristics. Islands are favored breeding areas, especially if they are rather barren and boulder-covered, the boulders providing alternate nest sites if tree cavities are unavailable.

Wintering Distribution and Habitat: In contrast to the red-breasted merganser, this species preferentially seeks out fresh water during winter. It is found uncommonly in Alaska as far west as the Aleutians (Murie, 1959), and along coastal southeastern Alaska, where it varies from being common to plentiful (Gabrielson and Lincoln, 1959).

In Canada, it winters along coastal British Columbia, with small numbers found in the interior of that province and Alberta, on the Great Lakes, in southern Quebec, and along Newfoundland and the Maritime Provinces (Godfrey, 1966).

South of Canada, varying numbers of common mergansers may be found in winter on almost any large lake, reservoir, or river that remains partly ice-free all winter, southward as far as southern California, Texas, and the Carolinas. In the Chesapeake Bay region, they are common but locally distributed, with most of them occurring on fresh estuarine bays or bay marshes and a few ranging into slightly brackish estuarine bays or river marshes (Stewart, 1962). Very few common mergansers winter as far south as Mexico, and most of the records are from northern parts of that country (Leopold, 1959).

The most characteristic type of winter habitat consists of the mouths and the upper estuarine regions of rivers (Dementiev and Gladkov, 1967). Like red-breasted mergansers, this species needs relatively transparent waters for efficient foraging, and it congregates wherever fish are to be found in goodly numbers.

GENERAL BIOLOGY

Age at Maturity: Maturity is probably attained the second year of life (Dementiev and Gladkov, 1967; Erskine, 1971).

Pair Bond Pattern: Pair bonds are re-formed each winter, starting about November or December. The time of pair bond breakup is difficult to determine, but Hildén (1964) reported seeing pairs as late as early June. He did not observe any cases of males remaining with their mates after the young had hatched, although some early observations have suggested that this may sometimes occur. However, it appears that the male usually leaves the nesting area about the time the female begins to incubate (White, 1957).

Nest Location: Hildén's (1964) summary of the sites of 113 nests is probably representative, although trees large enough to support cavity nests were generally lacking from his study area. Of the total nests found, 68 percent were beneath boulders, 18 percent were in buildings, 13 percent were under dense, matlike junipers, and 1 percent were under *Hippophaë* bushes. The primary requirement appears to be concealment from above and associated darkness in the nest cavity. Common mergansers are apparently not attracted to gull colonies for nesting, and on large islands they tend to nest near shore on headlands. Islets located where waters become free of ice early in the spring season are also favored, according to Hildén. In Iceland, where this species is relatively rare, Bengtson (1970) noted that six of ten nests found were in holes, while two were under high shrubs and two were in other cover.

Where nests are located in trees, a variety of species are used, including oak, beech, chestnut, sycamore, basswood, willow, and alder (Bauer and Glutz, 1969). If artificial nesting boxes are used, their preferred dimensions are 23 to 28 centimeters wide and 85 to 100 centimeters high. The entrance should measure 12 by 12 centimeters and be located 50 to 60 centimeters above the base of the box (Grenquist, 1953).

Clutch Size: Hildén (1964) reported an average clutch size of 9.37 eggs for 35 clutches, with an observed range of 6 to 12 eggs and a modal clutch of 9 eggs. Von Hartmann (in Bauer and Glutz, 1969) reported a mean clutch size of 9.2 eggs for 104 Finnish clutches. The eggs are deposited daily (Bauer and Glutz, 1969).

Incubation Period: Probably 32 to 35 days, based on various estimates (Bauer and Glutz, 1969).

Fledging Period: From 60 to 70 days are required to attain fledging (Dementiev and Gladkov, 1967).

Nest and Egg Losses: Hildén (1964) reported that during a two-year period of study, 86 percent of twenty-nine nests hatched. When records of other nests studied were added, a total nesting success of 84 percent was determined for seventy-three nests. Considering total eggs, a hatching success rate of 77 percent was determined for this species. Crows and ravens were responsible for a high rate of egg losses prior to the onset of incubation, in spite of the fine concealment of most nests. This was attributed to the presence of conspicuous white down near the nest entrance and to the apparent memory that these predator birds have of nest sites that are used by mergansers year after year.

Juvenile Mortality: Relatively little information on prefledging losses of this species is available. Hildén (1964) noted that shortly after hatching their young, female common mergansers and their broods left his study area for unknown reasons. Some returned when the young were at least half grown, but the high mobility of this species' broods makes estimates of their numbers in an area very difficult.

Adult Mortality: The only estimate so far available of annual adult mortality is that of Boyd (1962), who calculated a 40 percent mortality rate for birds wintering in Britain.

GENERAL ECOLOGY

Food and Foraging: The controversies and emotions generated by the fish-eating tendencies of this species are considerable, and a judicious choice of references can allow the writer to cast the common merganser in almost any role that might be desired. Perhaps the fairest method is to consider the evidence on a region-by-region basis, since major regional and habitat differences in available food sources are obviously present.

In Alaska, British Columbia, and adjacent Washington, the primary concern has been the influence of common mergansers on the salmon and trout fisheries. Relatively few samples are available from Alaskan waters, but Fritsch and Buss (1958) examined 55 birds from Unakwik Inlet. Unidentified fish remains made up the largest single volumetric amount of foods, but of identified food materials various sculpins (Cottidae) made up the greatest volume (69 cubic centimeters), with the great sculpin (*Myoxocephalus*) adding another 61 cubic centimeters, shrimp totalling 54.5 cubic centimeters, and blennies (*Anoplorchus*) 14 cubic centimeters. Salmon eggs were present in trace amounts in 7 birds, and salmon fry were present in similar quantities in 3 birds. In British Columbia, Munro and Clemens (1937) examined the food taken by 363 common mergansers and found that in order of relative importance it consisted of freshwater sculpins, salmon eggs, salmonid fish (char, trout, salmon), sticklebacks, freshwater coarse fish, and various marine fish. These authors concluded that in British Columbia the common merganser did exert a significantly detrimental effect on salmon. Studies in Washington, as summarized by Meigs and Rieck (1967), indicate that local damage to trout fisheries can occur, particularly on trout-planted waters. These authors found that a juvenile bird consumed an average of 0.77 pounds of fish per day for 83 days, similar to an estimate by White (1937) that a young merganser daily consumes the equivalent of a third of its weight. More recent studies by White (1957) and by Latta and Sharkey (1966) suggest that food equal to about 20 to 28 percent of the body weight is consumed each day in older mergansers, but their birds did not maintain their original weight during the study periods.

Studies by White (1957) in the Maritime Provinces of Canada indicate a rather high depredation by the common merganser on salmon streams. Among samples of 724 common mergansers, salmon remains accounted for 5 to 91 percent of the fish remains and occurred in 45 to 96 percent of the stomachs examined. White estimated that a single merganser might consume 72 pounds of fish before attaining its full growth. Trout rivers in Michigan are sometimes utilized heavily by mergansers, according to Salyer and Lagler (1940), who examined 315 specimens from various parts of Michigan. They found that on trout streams, trout predominated in the merganser stomach samples, and judged that trout were preferentially selected from other available organisms in the streams. However, samples from nontrout waters indicated that in such areas the mergansers were innocuous and at times beneficial.

Mergansers collected in Minnesota, Nebraska, and South Dakota were examined by Timken and Anderson (1969). Among 222 birds, about 30 percent had food items present in their stomachs. Only 19 of 151 identified fish remains represented game species, and the most important food was gizzard shad (*Dorosoma*), which composed 37 percent of the total food weight. Freshwater drum (*Aplodinotus*) and white bass (*Roccus*) were next in importance; these three species made up about 60 percent of the total number of fish found. A similar finding was provided by Alcorn (1953), based on a sample of 110 stomachs from Nevada. Of a total of 267 fish present, 76 percent were various rough fish, mostly consisting of carp (*Cyprinus*). Heard and Curd (1959) likewise reported that 80 percent of the fish found in mergansers obtained from Lake Carl Blackwell, Oklahoma, were various rough or forage fishes. Huntington and Roberts (1959) found no evidence that the common merganser was a menace to sport fishing in New Mexico and correlated the amounts of various fish eaten with their availability as indicated by fisheries studies.

The general conclusion from most of these studies is that the common merganser is an opportunistic forager, feeding on such species as are fairly common and readily captured. In most cases these consist of rough fish rather than game fish, but in areas specifically managed for trout or salmon production, mergansers may well concentrate on this available supply of food. The maximum sizes of fish taken by mergansers are rather astonishing. Alcorn (1953) reported finding carp up to 12¾ inches long; Salyer and Lagler (1940) noted a case of a merganser with a 14-inch, 15-ounce brown trout; and Coldwell (1939) reported a 22-inch eel being eaten by a merganser. Wick and Rogers (1957) described a female merganser that had choked to death on a sculpin measuring 14.9 centimeters and weighing 64.3 grams. Latta and Sharkey (1966) judged that girth rather than length probably determined the maximum size of fish that could be swallowed. Captive birds seemed to prefer small trout over larger ones, and when given a choice of trout, sculpins, and creek chubs (*Semotilis*), they consumed all three species, with the sculpin in somewhat smaller numbers.

The only detailed study on duckling foods is that of White (1957), who analyzed the stomach contents of 118 ducklings. These included nearly 1,400 insects, of which more than 93 percent were mayflies. There were also over 300 fish present, 70 percent of which were species other than salmon or trout.

Mergansers catch their prey visually, and in clear water can see fish up to 10 feet away (White, 1937). They prefer to feed in fairly shallow waters from 1½ to 6 feet deep, and when diving for food generally remain under water for 10 to 20 seconds, but occasionally remain submerged up to 45 seconds (Salyer and Lagler, 1940). They have been reported to dive as deep as 30 feet (Heard and Curd, 1959). White (1957) described cooperative foraging by flocks of twenty or more mergansers, which would form a long line parallel to the shore of a river or shallow lake. With much wing-splashing the flock would advance, then suddenly the birds would dive and catch the fish that had been thus concentrated. Single flocks of as many as seventy birds were observed foraging by this method.

Sociality, Densities, Territoriality: Probably most mergansers breed in relatively well-isolated and well-separated situations, since an adequate supply of food for the female and developing young is required. Parmelee (1954) noted that one or two pairs along a sixteen-mile stretch of the Sturgeon River in Michigan seemed typical, although on some Lake Michigan islands a more concentrated nesting of this species, as well as of the red-breasted merganser, occurs. A comparable situation was described by Hildén (1964) in the Valassaaret group of islands of the Gulf of Bothnia. In 1962 this island group had an estimated breeding population of 34 pairs scattered over the six square kilometers of land area, or nearly 6 pairs per square kilometer. However, many of the tiny rocky islets supported nesting pairs, and thus nest site availability as well as proximity to suitable foraging areas were probably important factors determining distribution and density characteristics.

Interspecific Relationships: When both species are on fresh water, common and red-breasted mergansers have similar foraging tendencies and consume nearly identical foods. However, for most of the year these species are well separated ecologically from one another, and it is doubtful that much competition occurs. Double-crested cormorants also are freshwater fish-eaters, but are rather rarely found in association with common mergansers.

Egg predators such as crows and ravens, and duckling predators such as the larger gulls, no doubt account for substantial mortality to eggs and perhaps also broods; at least this is indicated by such studies as have been done (Hildén, 1964). Merganser ducklings seem more agile than those of most species in eluding predators and furthermore appear to be less sensitive to chilling effects of severe weather. Eagles, owls, minks, and loons were mentioned by White (1957) as possible enemies of merganser ducklings.

General Activity Patterns and Movements: Common mergansers are well known to be daytime foragers. Timken and Anderson (1969) reported that fall migrants in South Dakota seem to confine their feeding to morning hours, while during winter and spring they forage in the early morning and again in the late afternoon. A similar morning and afternoon foraging periodicity was noted by Salyer and Lagler (1940) in Michigan. According to White (1957), the most active period of feeding is just before twilight, and there is usually a resting period of at least two hours at midday. Nilsson (1966) mentioned that this species spent less time foraging than did common goldeneyes in the same locality.

SOCIAL AND SEXUAL BEHAVIOR

Flocking Behavior: During fall, the size of migrant flocks is usually rather small. Timken and Anderson (1969) indicated that groups of 8 or 9 birds were typical, and the groups never exceeded 30. Salyer and Lagler (1940) also mentioned that foraging is usually done in small flocks of fewer than 12 birds, with such groups often having two or three adult males and the rest females or femalelike immatures. These flocks do not appear to feed cooperatively, but probably the success of birds feeding in small groups is greater than that of single birds, since these are seen infrequently. Nilsson (1966) mentioned seeing aggression among feeding flocks and in one case observed a bird stealing a fish from another. As spring approaches, flock sizes further decrease, and many birds are then seen in pairs.

Pair-forming Behavior: Pair-forming displays may be seen in wintering areas and also among spring migrants. It is marked by a great deal of surface chasing among the males, somewhat resembling the "sprints" of the red-breasted merganser. The most common male display is a guitarlike note, uttered with the neck partly stretched and the head feathers fluffed. A second call, a bell-like note, is uttered during a sudden vertical stretching of the head and neck in a "salute" posture. Males also at times suddenly kick a jet of water backward some distance, but there is no associated head movement. The male also swims ahead of the female, with his tail cocked diagonally or flat on the water, and turns the back of the head toward the female, especially if she is inciting. The inciting behavior of this species is much like that of the red-breasted merganser. It consists of a loud, harsh call, repeated once or twice, and is associated with rapid forward swimming as each note is uttered (Johnsgard, 1965). Short display flights have been seen on a few occasions (Johnsgard, 1955); these terminate in a long, "skidding" stop near the courted females.

Copulatory Behavior: Copulation in this species is normally preceded by a mutual drinking display. The female then assumes a prone posture, after which the male performs a lengthy series of drinking, preening, shaking, and similar "comfort movements" that differ little if at all from their nondisplay counterparts (Johnsgard, 1965). Nilsson (1966) also noted that the male's precopulatory behavior was seemingly unritualized and involved preening, drinking, and bill-dipping movements. Mounting is not preceded by any displays, and, after treading, either the male immediately releases the female (Johnsgard, 1965) or the pair rotates in the water (Nilsson, 1966). In my observations, the male then swims away from the female, while uttering his courtship call repeatedly and keeping the back of his head oriented toward her. Nilsson observed only bathing after copulation.

Nesting and Brooding Behavior: Females remain fairly gregarious during the early stages of the nesting season, while they are searching for suitable nest sites, and in areas providing numerous suitable sites assemblages of nesting females may occur. The males may remain in the general vicinity of the nest during incubation and are sometimes also seen in the presence of broods, but they do not defend the young (Bauer and Glutz, 1969). Often, however, the males leave their mates and drift downstream, leaving the female and brood to forage in the upper reaches of the river (White, 1957). While incubating, females usually leave their nests for a short time each day, often between 7:00 a.m. and 2:00 p.m., for periods of 15 to 90 minutes.

After hatching occurs, the female typically remains in the nest for one and one-half to two days before leading the young to water. Several undocumented reports of females carrying young to water have occurred. The young are highly precocial, and broods are highly mobile, a situation enhanced by the tendency of the female to carry her brood on her back. While still fairly young the ducklings begin increasingly to shift for themselves and seem to survive fairly well without direct parental attention. Before the young have fledged, the female often deserts her brood to begin the postnuptial molt. At this time the ducklings often begin to gather into larger assemblages (Bauer and Glutz, 1969). An important facet of the habitat for flightless young is the presence of resting or roosting places closely adjacent to water at least two feet deep, where the birds can rapidly escape from danger (White, 1957).

Postbreeding Behavior: The presence of a molt migration has not been established for this species. However, White (1957) noted that most yearling females apparently leave the breeding streams before molting and that both adult and immature males apparently move out to sea to complete their molts. During the fall, aggregations of fairly large numbers of birds occur on favored foraging areas and a leisurely movement southward begins. The birds gradually move to larger lakes or other ice-free waters to spend the winter.

STIFF-TAILED DUCKS
Tribe Oxyurini

This bizarre group of diving ducks differs from the rest of the Anatidae in so many respects that by any standard it demands special attention. Of the eight species that are presently recognized, most are placed in the genus *Oxyura,* which name refers to the stiffened, elongated tail feathers typical of the group. In these species the tail feathers extend well beyond the rather short tail coverts and are usually narrow-vaned, so that the individual rectrices tend to separate when spread. The feet are unusually large, and the legs are placed farther to the rear of the body than in any other waterfowl tribe, increasing propulsion efficiency during diving but rendering the birds nearly helpless on land. This grebelike adaptation is paralleled by the evolution of numerous short, glossy body feathers, presumably increasing the effectiveness of water-proofing. In the typical stiff-tails the bill is rather short, broad, and distinctly flattened toward the tip, and virtually all the foraging is done under water. At least in the North American species of stiff-tails, most of the food taken is of vegetable origin. Nests of the typical stiff-tails are built above water, of reed mats or similar vegetation, and often a ramp leads from the nest cup to the water, providing easy access. The birds are quite heavy-bodied and have relatively short wings, so that flight is attained with some difficulty in most species. The masked duck is something of an exception to this point, since its combination of small body size and fairly long wings allows it to land and take off with surprising agility from water of moderate depth.

Only two species of stiff-tails have ever been reported from North America, and it is most unlikely that any others will ever occur here by natural means. The ruddy duck is much the more widespread and abundant of these, while the little-known masked duck barely reaches the Mexico–United States border as a breeding species. Indeed, the masked duck is the species most recently added to the list of known breeding North American waterfowl, since it was not until 1967 that firm evidence of its breeding in Texas was established.

MASKED DUCK

Oxyura dominica (Linnaeus) 1766

Other Vernacular Names: None in general use.

Range: Breeds from coastal Texas (rarely), southward through Mexico (probably breeding along the Gulf coast and in the southern interior), Central America, the West Indies, and the lowlands of South America from Colombia to northern Argentina. Probably resident in most areas; winter movements unreported.

Subspecies: None recognized.

Measurements (after Delacour, 1959):

Folded wing: Males 135-142, females 133-140 mm.

Culmen: Males 33-35, females 32-34 mm.

Weights: Very few weights are available. Weller (1968) reported that a male weighed 400 grams, and Hartman (1955) reported a male weighing 410 grams, and a female weighing 360 grams. Haverschmidt (1968) reported a female weight range of 298 to 335 grams. Ripley and Watson (1956) noted that two adult male and female specimens weighed 386 and 445 grams, respectively, while the corresponding respective weights of two immature birds were 387 and 275 grams. Seaman (1958) reported the weight of an adult female as 317 grams. Collectively these figures would indicate that males probably average about 390 grams (13.9 ounces) and females about 320 grams (11.4 ounces).

IDENTIFICATION

In the Hand: This tiny stiff-tailed duck might be confused only with the ruddy duck, from which it may be distinguished by the white wing speculum, the bill, which is shorter (culmen under 37 mm.) and does not widen appreciably toward the tip, the longer tail (at least 80 mm.), and the large nail, which is not recurved. Unlike the ruddy duck, the outer toe is shorter instead of longer than the middle toe.

In the Field: Although not particularly wary, masked ducks are usually extremely difficult to find in the field, since they usually inhabit marshes extensively overgrown with floating and emergent vegetation, in which the birds mostly remain. The male in nuptial plumage is unmistakable, with its black "mask," long and often cocked tail, and spotted cinnamon color, but most observations in the United States have been of females or femalelike males. These birds are remarkably similar to female ruddy ducks and require considerable care in identification. The white wing markings are never visible unless the bird flies or flaps its wings, both of which are infrequent. The best field mark is the strongly striped facial marking, which consists of three instead of two buffy areas, including a superciliary stripe, an upper cheek stripe, and a buffy cheek and throat area. Female ruddy ducks have only two buffy areas and completely lack any pale stripe above the eye. When the birds take off they rarely fly high, but usually skim the marsh vegetation, suddenly slowing and dropping vertically downward out of sight in the marsh. Both sexes are normally quiet, although some calls have been attributed to the male.

AGE AND SEX CRITERIA

Sex Determination: Although males in nuptial plumage may be readily recognized by their black "mask" and spotted rusty cinnamon body color, immature or nonbreeding males have a plumage pattern extremely similar to that of females, and internal examination may be needed to determine sex. The curiously spined penis structure typical of *Oxyura* also occurs in this species (Wetmore, 1965) and may provide for sexing live birds without actual examination of the gonads.

Age Determination: No information is available on the rate at which the adult plumage is attained, and the juvenal plumage so closely resembles that of the adult female that probably the only certain plumage criterion of immaturity is the presence of juvenal tail feathers. As in the ruddy duck, these rectrices usually have conspicuous bare shaft-tips with terminal enlargements marking the point where the downy tail feathers have broken off. Ripley and Watson (1956) stated that, as compared with adults, subadult specimens have noticeably wider and paler margins on the back and wing coverts and almost downlike feathers on the underparts, which produce a rather mottled effect.

DISTRIBUTION AND HABITAT

Breeding Distribution and Habitat: The North American distribution of this little-studied species is limited to Mexico and, in quite recent years, the coastal portions of Texas.

In Mexico, the masked duck has been reported from the freshwater marshes of Nayarit, Jalisco, Colima, Tamaulipas, and Veracruz, but at least until recently there were no definite Mexican breeding records (Leopold, 1959). However, Berrett (1962) reported the presence of several adults and a single young bird on a roadside pond near Villahermosa, Tabasco, and no doubt breeding also occurs elsewhere along the Caribbean coast if not elsewhere in Mexico.

In the United States, the masked duck has been suspected for some time of having bred in the Brownsville area of Texas, but it was not until 1967 that the first definite United States record of breeding was obtained. This occurred at the Anahuac National Wildlife Refuge, Chambers County, Texas, when five young birds were found, one of which seemed to be several weeks younger than the others, and three adult birds were seen in the vicinity. In the autumn of 1968 a second record was established when a nest with six eggs was found near Falfurrias, Brooks County, Texas (Johnsgard and Hagemeyer, 1969; *Audubon Field Notes,* 22:625). A male and three females or immatures were also seen in November 1968 at Flour Bluff, Texas, and a pair was thought to have nested that fall in the vicinity of the Welder Refuge (*Audubon Field Notes,* 23:78, 373, 496).

By 1969, the masked duck was seemingly established in southern Texas. There were five or six pairs at the Welder Wildlife Refuge that summer, the species was seen at Rockport until mid-July, and it again appeared at Anahuac Refuge in midsummer. No nests were found at Anahuac, but a female and eight young were observed there in late October 1969 (*ibid.,* 23:673; 24:67).

No definite records of breeding in Texas were obtained in 1970 or 1971. The occurrence of a hurricane there in early August 1970 caused extensive damage to coastal habitats of southern Texas (*ibid.,* 24:696) and may well have affected nesting success. Surprisingly, a pair was observed courting in May 1970 at Holly Beach, Louisiana, but no subsequent indication of nesting was found (*ibid.,* 24:692).

It would thus appear that at least several cases of successful nesting by this species occurred in Texas during the late 1960s, and it remains to be

● = Extralimital Specimen Records
○ = Extralimital Sight Records

Breeding distribution of the masked duck in North and Central America. Extralimital (non-Texas) U.S. records since 1950 are also indicated.

seen whether this will continue or will prove to have been a temporary phenomenon.

The breeding habitat of this species consists of tropicallike marshes or swamps, densely vegetated with emergent vegetation and usually having lily pads, water hyacinths, or other floating-leaf aquatic plants extensively covering the water surface. The birds are sometimes seen in mangrove swamps, but most of the few breeding records are from freshwater habitats.

Wintering Distribution and Habitat: Seasonal movements of this species have not been studied but are probably not great. They have been seen during Christmas counts at the Welder Wildlife Refuge near Sinton, Texas, where they also regularly occur during the breeding season. Habitats used at this time of year do not seem to differ from those used for breeding.

GENERAL BIOLOGY

Age at Maturity: Not yet reported.

Pair Bond Pattern: Probably monogamous, with temporary pair bonds. Apparent pair-forming behavior has been seen during spring. Broods in Texas have been seen being led by females or femalelike birds, without definite males in the vicinity.

Nest Location: In Panama, the nests are reported to be placed in rushes and are said to lack down (Phillips, 1926). However, Dale Crider (pers. comm.) found that "snowflake" down was typical of the nests he found in Argentina. A number of clutches have been collected in the rice plantations of Cuba; Bond (1961) noted that one of these that he observed was in a deep cup of rice stems and was placed just above the water level.

Crider (pers. comm.) found that in northern Argentina the nests were located in flooded rice fields, amid rice clumps beside deep water into which the female could readily escape. The nests were roofed over and basketball-like, with a lateral entry.

Clutch Size: Usually reported as 5 or 6 eggs (Phillips, 1926), or from 4 to 6 (Wetmore, 1965). However, Bond (1961) listed eight Cuban clutches containing between 8 and 18 eggs, which strongly suggests that dump-nesting may occur in areas of nesting concentrations. Dale Crider (pers. comm.) also found a high average clutch size of about 10 eggs in Argentina, but obvious dump-nesting often made the clutches larger, with one nest of 27 eggs found. Parasitism by black-headed ducks (*Heteronetta atricapilla*) was also frequent. According to Crider, the normal egg-laying rate was one egg per day. The eggs are similar in appearance to the eggs of ruddy ducks, but are distinctly smaller and have smooth rather than chalky surfaces. Bond (1958) reported their dimensions as 53.7 to 55.6 by 40 to 41.6 mm.

Incubation and Fledging Periods: Not yet definite, but Dale Crider (pers. comm.) judged the incubation period to be about 28 days.

Nest and Egg Losses: No specific information. Dale Crider (pers. comm.) found that the common caracara (*Caracara plancus*) was a major egg predator of most ducks in northern Argentina.

Juvenile and Adult Mortality: No specific information. Dale Crider (pers. comm.) found rather small brood sizes and judged that the piranha was probably the most serious enemy of ducklings of this and other species in northern Argentina.

GENERAL ECOLOGY

Food and Foraging: Phillips (1926) reported on foods found in Cuban specimens, which largely consisted of the seeds of smartweed (*Polygonum*), as well as small amounts of water lily (*Castalia*), rush (*Fimbristylis*), dodder (*Cuscuta*), and saw grass (*Cladium*). Three Cuban specimens mentioned by Cottam (1939) had virtually the same contents and no doubt represented the same specimens. Weller (1968) noted several types of seeds in the gizzard of a male that he collected. Dale Crider (pers. comm.) found that wild millet (*Echinochloa*) seeds were important foods in northern Argentina.

Masked ducks dive extremely well and virtually silently. They seem to remain under water for long periods, but frequently will emerge with only their heads above water, and then often remain hidden beneath a lily leaf. They apparently obtain essentially all of their food from vegetable sources, and the ponds that they typically inhabit are not very deep. Almost every pond or marsh on which I have observed masked ducks or on which masked ducks had been recently seen (in Jamaica, southern Texas, and Colombia) has also had common jacanas (*Jacana spinosa*) present. This would suggest the importance of floating-leaf plants as a basic part of the habitat requirements of masked ducks, either in conjunction with the associated foraging opportunities or in providing possible escape cover. Least grebes (*Podiceps dominicus*) have also been typical of these habitats, and the two species are rather similar in their diving characteristics and inconspicuous presence. To what extent the least grebe's foods might overlap with those of the masked duck is unknown. It is of interest that the shape of the masked duck's bill differs so strongly from that of the typical *Oxyura* species and more closely approaches those of *Anas* and *Aythya*. One might suppose that this difference may be related to a higher dependence on aquatic plants and a lower incidence of invertebrates, such as midge larvae, in the diet of this species.

Diving behavior of adults and young has been noted by Dirk Hagemeyer (*in litt.*). The brood he studied in 1967 always fed in a ditch about three feet deep. They would forage for about 15 to 30 minutes, then retire to the grassy shoreline to preen and rest for about 90 minutes. In ten dives that were timed on November 4, the young remained submerged from 15 to 17 seconds. The brood studied in 1969 foraged in the same ditch, but in water that was generally four to six feet in depth and locally up to eight feet deep. One adult was observed foraging for about 45 minutes in water approximately five to six feet deep. It remained submerged from 23 to 26 seconds during its foraging dives and had intervening rest periods of 9 to 12 seconds at the surface. In general, the birds preferred to remain around small areas of open water about three to four feet deep, and scarcely moved more than a few hundred feet over a period of several weeks.

Although some observers had stated that masked ducks can readily "leap" from the water into flight, this behavior is evidently not exactly comparable to the takeoff behavior of dabbling ducks. Dale Crider has informed me that he never saw such a leaping takeoff and that the birds always initially made a shallow dive under water and emerged in flight a foot or so ahead of the point of submergence. This interesting method of taking flight is no doubt related to the posterior location of the feet and the small surface area of the wings, which prevent their effective use in pushing the body out of the water directly. Crider found that in waters too shallow for the birds to dive into, they were unable to take flight directly and could be readily caught.

Sociality, Densities, Territoriality: No specific information, but probably comparable to the ruddy duck in these regards. The records of apparent dump-nests would suggest that females may sometimes nest in close proximity to others.

Interspecific Relationships: Masked ducks are sometimes found on the same ponds as ruddy ducks, but seemingly prefer more densely vegetated ones and do not need such large areas of open water for landing and taking off. Thus they probably compete little if at all with ruddy ducks. The importance of other potential competitors, predators, etc., still remains relatively unstudied, but Dale Crider (pers. comm.) reported that black-headed ducks, rosybill ducks (*Netta peposaca*), and fulvous whistling ducks were all common breeders in habitats used by masked ducks in northern Argentina.

General Activity Patterns and Movements: Phillips (1926) mentioned that masked ducks apparently feed by day and fly at night, a situation seemingly typical of stiff-tailed ducks. Dale Crider (pers. comm.) often noted masked ducks in flight when it was nearly too dark to see anything.

SOCIAL AND SEXUAL BEHAVIOR

Flocking Behavior: Most observers have reported that masked ducks are rarely seen in large groups; Phillips (1926) indicated that groups of 10 to 20 birds are unusually large. The largest number so far reported seen in the United States was a group of 13 present at the Welder Wildlife Refuge in December 1968 (*Audubon Field Notes,* 23:373).

Pair-forming Behavior: Almost nothing is known of the pair-forming displays of this species. Courtship has been reportedly seen during April in Texas (Davis, 1966) and during May in Louisiana (*Audubon Field Notes,* 24:692). Davis noted that the male's display was rather similar to that of the ruddy duck. Likewise, other observers have reported that the male cocks its tail, inflates its breast, thrusts its neck back and forth, and strikes the breast with its bill. Several sounds have been attributed by various observers to the male, including a repeated *kirri-kirro,* a cock pheasantlike response to diverse loud noises, and a dull, almost inaudible *oo-oo-oo* (Johnsgard and Hagemeyer, 1969). Females are said to utter repeated hissing noises. Dale Crider (pers. comm.) heard clucking sounds uttered by females and said that males apparently produce weak calls, which he was never able to hear, during their breast-beating display.

Copulatory Behavior: Not yet described.

Nesting and Brooding Behavior: Too few nests have been found in North America to provide any definite information on incubation behavior. The nests and young that have been seen in Texas have all occurred rather late in the year (September and October), and only femalelike birds have been found associated with broods. Current evidence suggests that in northern latitudes the male remains in breeding plumage through October and gradually becomes more femalelike during November and December. In Costa Rica and Panama the male's breeding plumage may be retained longer, at least by some birds (Johnsgard and Hagemeyer, 1969).

Dale Crider (pers. comm.) noted that in Argentina masked ducks were also fall-breeders, and nesting was associated with rising water levels in rice fields. Males remained in the vicinity of the nest until some time into incubation, but were never seen in association with broods. Considerable variation in the timing of the postnuptial molt was evident, since some flightless males were found while others were still in full breeding plumage. After the eggs had hatched, the broods were apparently often brought back to the nest site for night roosting. Molting of adults apparently occurred in natural ponds adjacent to the rice fields.

Postbreeding Behavior: Nothing is known of postbreeding movements. The brood found at Anahuac Refuge in 1967 was observed for about 45 days before it disappeared, the birds presumably having fledged. Masked ducks were not seen again on the refuge until the following summer (Johnsgard and Hagemeyer, 1969).

RUDDY DUCK

Oxyura jamaicensis (Gmelin) 1789

Other Vernacular Names: Butterball, Stiff-tail.

Range: Breeds from central British Columbia to southwestern Mackenzie District, across the Canadian prairies to the Red River valley of Manitoba, with sporadic breedings in southern Ontario and Quebec, and southward through the western and central United States to Baja California, coastal Texas, and occasionally eastward to the Great Lakes or beyond. Also breeds in the West Indies, the Central Valley of Mexico, and in various Andean lakes from Colombia to Chile. Winters in North America from British Columbia along the coast and to a limited extent inland through the western United States and south to Mexico and Central America, along the Atlantic coast from Massachusetts to Florida, in the West Indies, and along the Gulf coast.

North American subspecies:

O. j. jamaicensis (Gmelin): North American Ruddy Duck. Breeds in North America as indicated above. Regarded by the A.O.U. (1957) as *O. j. rubida* (Wilson).

Measurements (after Delacour, 1959):

Folded wing: Males 142-154, females 135-145 mm.

Culmen: Males 39-44, females 37-42 mm.

Weights: Nelson and Martin (1953) reported that twelve males averaged 1.3 pounds (589 grams), while seventeen females averaged 1.1 pounds (498 grams), Mumford (1954) found that ten males averaged 1.19 pounds

(539 grams), and six females averaged the same. Jahn and Hunt (1964) noted that eleven males averaged 1.06 pounds (481 grams), while three adult females averaged 1.19 pounds (539 grams). Maximum weights are 1.8 pounds (815 grams) for males, reported by Nelson and Hunt, and 1.75 pounds (794 grams) for females, reported by Mumford (1954).

IDENTIFICATION

In the Hand: Excepting the very rare masked duck, ruddy ducks can be easily distinguished from all other North American ducks by their long, narrow tail feathers and their short, wide, flattened bill. Ruddy ducks are the only North American species in which the nail of the bill is narrow and small on the upper mandible surface but wide and recurved below the tip. Ruddy ducks also differ from masked ducks in that they lack any white on the wings, the outer toe is as long or longer than the middle toe, and the bills are longer (culmen length 37 to 44 mm.).

In the Field: Except during fairly late spring and summer, ruddy ducks of both sexes are in a rather brownish and inconspicuous plumage. On the water they appear as very chunky diving ducks, with short necks and a long tail either held on the water surface or variably cocked above it. The whitish cheeks, which are streaked with brown in females, are the most conspicuous field marks at this time, but as spring progresses the male assumes an increasingly bluish bill and a more reddish body plumage, together with a contrasting black crown. Ruddy ducks seem to have greater difficulty in taking flight than any other North American duck, including the masked duck. They patter along the water for some distance before attaining their characteristic buzzing flight, with their short wings beating furiously to keep the bird aloft. Neither sex is highly vocal, but the female utters a rare squeaky threat call, and during display males produce a dull thumping noise that terminates in a weak croak.

AGE AND SEX CRITERIA

Sex Determination: Although the wings of males are slightly larger than those of females, they provide no definite sex clues. Thus, an entirely unmarked white cheek area or brownish red body feathers are the best plumage criteria of sex. Males in their first fall and winter of life are thus easily confused with females, but a folded wing measurement of more than 145 mm. would indicate a male.

Age Determination: Both sexes evidently retain their juvenal tail feathers until January or February, a surprisingly long time, so that notching at the tips of these feathers should provide a useful aging criterion through most of the first year (Bent, 1925). Further, the tertials of immature birds are straight rather than curved and drooping, the greater tertial coverts are somewhat squared rather than rounded at the tips, and the middle coverts are slightly rough and trapezoidal in shape rather than being smooth and rounded (Carney, 1964). Although the narrow juvenal tail feathers of *Oxyura* are not conspicuously notched, in young birds the terminal portion of the shaft is often wholly devoid of barbs near the tip.

DISTRIBUTION AND HABITAT

Breeding Distribution and Habitat: This strictly New World species has a North American breeding range that approaches those of the canvasback and the redhead, and, like the ranges of those species, tends to be disruptive and probably declining.

In Alaska a single definite record of a brood seen in the Tetlin area in 1959 constitutes the only known breeding, but adults or pairs have been seen from time to time (Hansen, 1960). Otherwise, the vicinity of Great Slave Lake would appear to be the northern breeding limit of this species, which increases in abundance southwardly through British Columbia, Alberta, Saskatchewan, and Manitoba. There are a few local and sporadic breeding records for southern Ontario and southern Quebec, but any breeding east of Manitoba is noteworthy (Godfrey, 1966).

In Washington, breeding is fairly regular throughout the eastern part of that state (Yocom, 1951). The birds also breed in shallow lakes and marshes of eastern Oregon (Gabrielson and Jewett, 1940) and in California (Grinnell and Miller, 1944), where they have nested as far south as the Salton Sea (*Audubon Field Notes,* 10:410). They also breed in the freshwater marshes of Baja California, as well as on the arid central uplands of Mexico south to the Valley of Mexico (Leopold, 1959). Limited breeding occurs along the southern coast of Texas (*Audubon Field Notes,* 15:480; 20:583; 22:625) and perhaps also in interior Texas, and there are also records of breeding in Kansas, New Mexico, Arizona, and Nevada. Along the Gulf and Atlantic coasts isolated breeding records have been obtained for Louisiana (*ibid.,* 23:634; 24:692), Florida (*ibid.,* 18:503; 19:535), South Carolina (*ibid.,* 13:410; 14:442), and New Jersey (*ibid.,* 11:398; 14:439). In New York ruddy ducks breed at Jamaica Bay and the Montezuma marshes (*ibid.,* 13:410; 19:540), and they have bred once or more in Indiana (*ibid.,* 7:311; 15:471), Wisconsin (Jahn and Hunt, 1964), and Michigan (Parmelee, 1954).

The heart of the ruddy duck's breeding range in the United States is in the

Breeding (hatched) and wintering (shaded) distributions of the ruddy duck in North America.

northern Great Plains, extending westward from Minnesota (Lee *et al.*, 1964a) and northwestern Iowa (Low, 1941) through the Dakotas, Nebraska, and the Salt Lake basin of Utah (Williams and Marshall, 1938), and northward through the grasslands of Montana to the Canadian border.

The breeding habitat of ruddy ducks consists of permanent freshwater or alkaline marshes having emergent vegetation and relatively stable water levels. Suitable nesting habitat must have open water in fairly close proximity to nesting cover, including emergent plants that provide accessibility as well as adequate cover density, and additionally can be bent down by the birds to form a nest platform, and with water passageways such as muskrat channels that will permit easy movement between the nest vicinity and open water (Bennett, 1938; Joyner, 1969).

Wintering Distribution and Habitat: Wintering in Canada is limited to small numbers in southern British Columbia and southern Ontario (Godfrey, 1966). Winter surveys in the United States and Mexico during the late 1960s indicated that over 60 percent of the wintering ruddy duck population occurred in the Pacific Flyway, with the Mississippi and Atlantic flyways each providing about 15 percent and the Central Flyway providing less than 10 percent. In the Pacific Flyway, ruddy ducks winter in Puget Sound and southward along the coastline of Washington, Oregon, and California, and in the Central Valley of California as well. They are largely confined to brackish bays and freshwater areas, and are rarely seen on the open ocean. They are abundant on the Pacific coast of Mexico during winter, where among diving ducks they are outnumbered only by the lesser scaup. Leopold (1959) mentioned seeing a flock of more than 107,000 in a single lagoon near Acapulco in 1952, and said they thrive in the brackish coastal marshes of Mexico. Relatively few occur on the Gulf coast of Mexico during winter, and even fewer are found in the interior.

On the Atlantic coast, ruddy ducks winter from Massachusetts southward, occurring as far south as Florida's Lake Okeechobee and on the Kissimmee River valley lakes (Chamberlain, 1960), as well as on brackish coastal marshes of the Gulf coast from Florida through Louisiana (Lowery, 1960) and Texas (Peterson, 1960). Ruddy ducks also winter in small numbers through the interior of these southern states, but not in the numbers typical of coastal situations.

In the Chesapeake Bay region, where ruddy ducks are abundant and their average wintering numbers represent about 50 percent of the Atlantic Flyway population, their ecological distribution is of interest. January counts for 1955 to 1958 indicated that slightly brackish estuarine bays supported 54 percent of the birds, brackish estuarine bays 41 percent, salt estuarine bays

5 percent, and fresh water estuarine bays 1 percent. They are usually not present on the coastal bays or ocean proper and apparently move to salt estuarine bays during the coldest weather (Stewart, 1962). It thus appears that ideal ruddy duck wintering habitat consists of brackish to slightly brackish estuaries or coastal lagoons of shallow depths. An abundance of submerged plants, small mollusks, and crustaceans no doubt also figures importantly in winter usage by ruddy ducks.

GENERAL BIOLOGY

Age at Maturity: McClure (1967) reported that captive-raised male ruddy ducks mature their first year, and although two females also were recorded as breeding their first year, they usually do not breed until their second year. Ferguson (1966) noted that two aviculturalists reported breeding in first-year birds, two in second-year birds, and one in third-year birds. It is presumed that first-year breeding is normal in wild ruddy ducks.

Pair Bond Pattern: Pair bonds are renewed each spring, after the males regain their nuptial plumage. Males probably remain sexually attracted to females for a relatively longer period than in most ducks, but desert them and leave the breeding area before the brood has fledged (Joyner, 1969).

Nest Location: Williams and Marshall (1938) reported that of fifty ruddy duck nests, 32 percent were in hardstem bulrush (*Scirpus acutus*), an amount well in excess of the plant's relative abundance. About the same number (30 percent) were in alkali bulrush (*S. paludosus*), a much more common species of bulrush. Twenty percent were in salt grass (*Distichlis*), a surprising number, considering that this is not a true emergent plant, and 14 percent were in cattails (*Typha*). In another Utah study, Joyner (1969) noted that three nests were in Olney bulrush (*S. olneyi*) or mixed bulrush-cattail stands, one each was in hardstem and alkali bulrush stands, one in a mixture of cattails and hardstem bulrushes, one in cattails, and two in salt grass.

Bennett (1938) found that 14 of 22 Iowa nests were in stands of round-stem bulrush (*S. occidentalis*), 6 were in mixed stands of this species and other emergents, 1 was in a stand of reeds (*Phragmites*), and 1 was in a mixture of several emergents and sedges. He believed that roundstem bulrush was favored for nesting because of the relative ease with which it can be bent over to form a nest. Low (1941) reported on 71 Iowa nests and concluded that nesting cover was determined not so much by preferences for specific plants as for cover type having a suitable water depth. A depth of 10 to 12 inches at the nest location was favored, with an observed range of 0 to 36 inches. Cover density at the nest site was dense in 63 percent of the nest sites and sparse in only 6 percent of the cases. Based on the total numbers of nests, lake sedge

(*Carex lacustris*) provided cover for the most, followed by hardstem bulrush and narrow-leaved cattail (*T. angustifolia*). On the basis of usage relative to available cover, the relative plant usage in decreasing sequence was: slender bulrush (*S. heterochaetus*), whitetop (*Fluminea*), hardstem bulrush, lake sedge, and narrow-leaved cattail. Low noted, as had Bennett, that river bulrush (*Scirpus fluviatilis*) was not used for nesting, probably because of its stiff, tough stalks.

Clutch Size: Low (1941) found an average clutch size of 8.1 eggs in seventy-one nests, Bennett (1938) noted an average clutch of 7.05 in eighteen nests, and Williams and Marshall (1938) found 158 eggs in nineteen nests, or 8.3 eggs per nest. Parasitic egg-laying no doubt influences average clutch size data and helps account for some unusually large clutches. The egg-laying rate is probably about one per day, with a day sometimes being skipped (Joyner, 1969).

Incubation Period: Low (1941) determined that four naturally incubated clutches hatched in 25 days and two in 26 days. Joyner (1969) indicated a 23- to 24-day incubation period. Eggs hatched in an incubator normally require only 21 days to hatch, but sometimes require up to 25 days (Hochbaum, 1944).

Fledging Period: Hochbaum (1944) considered that 52 to 66 days are probably required, based on field estimates.

Nest and Egg Losses: Low (1941) reported that water level fluctuations were the most serious source of nest and egg losses, with rises causing nest flooding and water level recessions causing nest desertion. Of 71 nests he studied, 4 were flooded, 12 deserted, 3 lost to predation by minks, and 52 (73 percent) were successfully terminated. Williams and Marshall (1938) reported a lower nesting success (38 percent) in Utah, with no losses due to predation but with 76 of 158 eggs lost from other factors such as desertion and flooding. This 52 percent hatching success compares with Low's (1941) estimate of a 71 percent hatching success.

Juvenile Mortality: Because of seemingly weak parental attachment, ruddy duck broods rarely retain their original composition for very long, and thus brood size counts fail to provide a suitable estimate of prefledging mortality. Joyner (1969) noted a tendency for abandoned ducklings to join with other ducklings, especially those somewhat older than themselves, and believed that because of their precocity they seem to survive well when separated from adult birds.

Postfledging mortality rates are not available, but age ratios of hunter-shot birds in Wisconsin (62 adults to 325 immatures) suggest a much higher vulnerability to hunters among immature than adult birds (Jahn and Hunt, 1964).

Adult Mortality: No estimates of annual adult mortality rates are available. In most areas the ruddy duck is not a favored game species and hunting mortality rates would appear low.

GENERAL ECOLOGY

Food and Foraging: Cottam's (1939) study of food volumes found in 163 adult ruddy ducks taken during nine months of the year is the most complete to date. He found plant foods to constitute over 70 percent by volume of the materials found, with pondweeds (Najadaceae) and sedges (Cyperaceae) accounting for nearly half of the total. Tubers, stems, and leaves of pondweeds, especially *Potamogeton* species, seem to be the favorite foods, while bulrushes (*Scirpus*) figured most prominently among the Cyperaceae represented. A surprising number and variety of insects are also consumed, especially during summer. Of these, the larvae of midges (Chironomidae) and horseflies (Tabanidae) are particularly important, perhaps because of their abundance in mud-bottom waters. Other aquatic and terrestrial insects are also sometimes eaten, even including such land-dwelling forms as locusts. Cottam found relatively few mollusks and correspondingly small amounts of crustaceans among the samples he examined. It seems probable that large samples from brackish-water wintering areas would have larger amounts of these materials present.

Stewart (1962) provided information on food contents of 35 ruddy ducks from the Chesapeake Bay region. He noted that the seeds, leaves, and stems of various submerged plants and that certain small mollusks and crustaceans were the principal foods present in these samples. The small bivalve macoma mollusks (*Macoma* spp.) the small *Mya* and *Mulinia* clams, the gastropod *Acteocina,* and various amphipod and ostracod crustaceans were represented frequently in these samples. Lynch (1968) mentioned that midge larvae are sometimes also eaten in the Chespeake Bay area.

Water depths favored and normal diving times have been rather little studied in this species. A few observations on captive ruddy ducks indicate average diving times of about 14 seconds with intervening pauses of 10 seconds and a maximum observed diving duration of 29 seconds (Johnsgard, 1967). These were in rather shallow and turbid ponds at the Wildfowl Trust and may not be typical of wild birds. The flattened bill of this species seems well developed for probing in muddy bottoms and sifting out small particles, and the slightly recurved nail may be useful in tearing leaves or stems from underwater plants.

Sociality, Densities, Territoriality: Low (1941) estimated that over 1,000 acres of nesting cover, the average nesting density was about one nest per 21 acres. In some areas the densities approached one nest per 10 acres, and the maximum observed density was on a 32-acre slough, with one per 2.4 acres. Williams and Marshall (1938) estimated an overall nesting density of 0.016 nests per acre on a total of 3,000 acres of potential nesting cover, with the highest observed density of two nests on 1.5 acres of hardstem bulrushes.

Stoudt (1969), in reviewing peak breeding densities of waterfowl on five prairie study areas in Canada and South Dakota, reported a range of ruddy duck densities of from less than one to twelve pairs per square mile.

To a greater degree than seems characteristic of other North American diving ducks, the ruddy duck does appear to occupy a defended territory during the breeding season. The performance of the "bubbling" display by paired males in the absence of their mates and often when other males come into view would at least lead the observer to believe that this display serves as a territorial pronouncement. Joyner (1969) believed that the male defends a small territory that may extend only ten feet or so around the nest entrance. He observed that apparent territories were spaced from 20 to 100 feet apart, with the distance of such spacing dependent on the presence or absence of channels through the emergent vegetation. The more this vegetation was disrupted by channels the closer the territories were situated.

Interspecific Relationships: Probably the presence of foreign eggs in ruddy duck nests contributes to nest desertion rates and thus nesting success in this species, although data are still inadequate on this point. Low (1941) noted that eleven (12.6 percent) of the ruddy duck nests he found had one to four redhead eggs present. None of the redhead eggs hatched, but the success of the ruddy duck nests was not mentioned. Perhaps the ruddy duck lays in the nests of others more often than it is parasitized by other species. Joyner (1969) noted mixed clutches involving the ruddy duck, cinnamon teal, mallard, and pintail, although it was in some cases impossible to determine the original "owner" of the nest. Low (1941) found ruddy duck eggs in the nests of redheads, canvasbacks, and western grebes, and Weller (1959) summarized additional cases of interspecific parasitism. The reproductive significance of such social parasitism is still uncertain, but a recent study indicates that ruddy ducks are less efficient social parasites than are redheads (Joyner, 1975).

General Activity Patterns and Movements: Phillips (1926) mentioned that the ruddy duck appears to be entirely a daytime forager, but apparently migrates only at night. No specific information is available on daily periodicities of behavior or local movements.

SOCIAL AND SEXUAL BEHAVIOR

Flocking Behavior: Although rarely associating with other species, the ruddy duck sometimes forms rather large flocks on migration and in favored wintering areas. The group of more than 107,000 seen by Leopold (1959) has been mentioned, and Stewart (1962) mentioned local counts of several thousand birds during winter and spring in the Chesapeake Bay area.

Pair-forming Behavior: In association with the relatively late assumption of the nuptial plumage by males, a relatively late period of pair formation is typical. Joyner (1969) apparently observed sexual display between April and late July, interpreting much of the later display as territorial proclamation or defense. He noted that this species normally begins prenuptial courtship on the breeding grounds, rather than while in wintering or migration areas. In Washington state, I (1955) saw no definite pair-forming behavior among wild birds and interpreted the male displays I saw in late May and June as territorial defense.

The most conspicuous of the male pair-forming or territorial-proclamation displays is the "bubbling" display (Johnsgard, 1965). This display, usually described as a beating of the bill on the inflated neck, has strong visual and acoustical characteristics that make it well adapted for a marshy habitat. Although it is often performed before females or other males, it is also frequently done by lone and seemingly resident birds, suggesting a territorial function. Males also swim before females, cocking their tails and exposing the white under tail coverts, often stopping momentarily to perform the bubbling display. Quick aggressive rushes over the water toward other birds, followed by an equally rapid return to the female, are also characteristic. A short display flight, or "ringing rush," is quite frequent and produces even more water noise than does the bubbling display. Females lack any definite inciting, but rather aggressively gape at any male that approaches too closely, seemingly including their mates. A squeaking noise often accompanies this gaping and is nearly the only sound that female ruddy ducks ever make. Males also have a very soft aggressive note and also a belchlike sound that terminates the bubbling display.

Copulatory Behavior: Few observations on copulation in ruddy ducks have been made, but I have observed several sequences (Johnsgard, 1965). The male approaches the female cautiously, periodically dipping his bill and flicking it laterally as it is retracted. Sometimes the female will assume a partially prone posture, but in most of the cases I have seen the male had suddenly mounted her without any obvious indication of readiness on the part of the female. During treading the female is almost entirely submerged, and as soon as it is terminated the male dismounts, faces the female and performs the bubbling display several times in quick succession. A lengthy preening period then follows.

Nesting and Brooding Behavior: Egg-laying begins as soon as a flimsy nest foundation has been laid. As the clutch increases in size, the nest is gradually enlarged, and often both an entrance "ramp" and an overhead cupola are added by manipulating the surrounding vegetation. There is usually little or no down present, and the nest may either have a well-developed bowl or be nearly flat on the nesting platform. Evidently incubation often begins before the last egg is deposited, since it is not uncommon for eggs with incompleted embryonic development to be still present at the time the female leaves with her brood. The incubation rhythm of the female is still unknown, but the occurrence of only slightly incubated eggs among hatched clutches suggests that the female leaves the nest for sufficiently long periods as to allow other females to lay their own eggs in the clutch.

Joyner (1969) noted that in Utah, broods hatched from as early as mid-May to early August, suggesting that renesting efforts may occur if initial nestings are unsuccessful. However, there is no evidence to support the frequently quoted belief that two broods are normally reared by this species in some parts of its range. Joyner found that male ruddy ducks were typically present with females leading broods, and he believed that they assisted in the defense of the ducklings. He saw drakes regularly following families until late June, while only one in twenty-two broods counted on July 10 was associated with a male adult. Fifteen of these broods were still being led by females. Most females left the area by late July, apparently moving to molting areas, although a few broods were still hatching at that time.

Postbreeding Behavior: Considering the limited flying abilities of ruddy ducks, it seems probable that adults do not move far from their breeding areas to undergo their molt. Yet there are few observations on ruddy ducks during this period. They probably are extremely secretive, inhabiting the densest cover in overgrown marshes. They no doubt normally undergo their flightless period at this time, but scattered reports of flightless ruddy ducks during winter and spring months suggest that an unusual molt pattern may be present. A double annual wing molt has been reported by Siegfried (1971) for at least one related species of *Oxyura* and may be true for others as well.

NAME DERIVATIONS

SOURCES

INDEX

Name Derivations

(Excluding extralimital species and most subspecies unless these are sometimes considered full species)

Aix — from Greek, a kind of waterfowl mentioned by Aristotle.

sponsa — from Latin: bethrothed, as if in wedding dress.

Anas — from Latin: a kind of duck.

acuta — from Latin, referring to the sharp tail of the male.

americana — of America. The derivation of the vernacular name wigeon is from the French *vigeon* and perhaps in turn from the Latin *vipio,* a kind of crane.

bahamensis — of the Bahama Islands.

carolinensis — of Carolina. The derivation of the vernacular name teal is unknown, but earlier English versions include "teale" and "tele."

clypeata — from Latin *clypeum:* shield-like, referring to the bill.

crecca — from Latin, formed like *crex,* to express the sound.

cyanoptera — from Greek *kuanos:* blue, and *pteron:* wing.

diazi — in honor of Augustin Diaz, Director of the Mexican Geographical and Exploring Commission, 1886.

discors — from Latin: discordant.

falcata — from Latin, referring to the sickle-shaped feathers of the male.

formosa — from Latin: beautiful.

fulvigula — from Latin *fulvus:* reddish, and *gula:* throat.

penelope — referring either to the mythological character Penelope, who was celebrated for her virtue, or more probably from the Latin *penelops,* a kind of duck mentioned by Pliny.

platyrhynchos — from Greek *platys:* broad, and *rhynchos:* bill. The vernacular name mallard is derived from the French *malart,* a male duck.

querquedula — from Latin: a kind of small duck.

rubripes — from Latin *ruber:* red, and *pes:* a foot, or red-footed.

strepera — from Latin *streperus:* noisy, obstreperous. The derivation of the vernacular name gadwall is unknown, the oldest known English variant being "gaddel."

Anser — from Latin, meaning a goose.

albifrons — from Latin *albus:* white, and *frons:* forehead.

caerulescens — from Latin: bluish.

canagicus — of the island of Kanaga or Kyktak (Aleutian Islands).

hyperborea — from Latin *hyperboreus:* beyond the north wind.

543

rossii — in honor of Bernard R. Ross, of the Hudson's Bay Company, who provided the specimens on which the species' name was based.

Aythya — from the Greek *aithuia,* a kind of water bird mentioned in Aristotle's Natural History.

affinis — from Latin: allied. The vernacular name scaup is from the Old French *escalope* and Old Dutch *schelpe,* and refers to the mollusks on which the birds sometimes feed.

americana — of America.

collaris — from Latin: collared.

fuligula — from Latin, diminutive of *fulix* or *fulica:* a coot, or perhaps from *fuligo:* soot.

marila — probably from the Greek *marile:* charcoal.

valisineria — after the wild celery *Vallisneria,* which in turn was named in honor of Antonio Vallisneri (1661–1730), Italian naturalist.

Branta — probably corrupted from *brenthos* or *brinthos,* the Aristotelian name of an unknown bird. The vernacular name brant (brent in Great Britain) may be similarly derived, or possibly is from the Welsh *brenig,* a limpet.

bernicla — apparently from the Old English *bernekke,* original meaning unknown.

canadensis — of Canada.

leucopsis — from Greek *leucos:* white, and *opsis:* appearance, referring to the white face. The vernacular name barnacle goose refers to the once-held belief that these birds originated from barnacles.

nigricans — from Latin: blackish.

Bucephala — from Greek: a broad forehead.

albeola — diminutive of Latin *albus:* white. The vernacular name bufflehead is a corruption of the earlier name "buffalo-headed duck."

clangula — diminutive of Latin *clangor:* a noise.

islandica — of Iceland. The vernacular name is in honor of Sir John Barrow (1764–1848), one-time secretary of the British Admiralty.

Cairina — supposed to be derived from Cairo, in Egypt, thus a misnomer for this American form.

moschata — from Latin *moschus:* musk. The vernacular name muscovy is a corruption of musk duck.

Camptorhynchus — from Greek *kamptos:* flexible, and *rhynchus:* beak, referring to the leathery bill.

labradorius — of Labrador.

Chen — from Greek: a goose. Here considered part of *Anser.*

Clangula — diminutive of Latin *clangor:* a noise.

hyemalis — from Latin, pertaining to *hiems,* winter or wintry. The vernacular name oldsquaw is based on the garrulous behavior of this species.

Cygnus — from Latin: a swan.

buccinator — from Latin: a trumpeter.

columbianus — of the Columbia River.

olor — from Latin: a swan.

Dendrocygna — from Latin *dendron:* a tree, and *cygnus:* a swan.

arborea — from Latin, pertaining to trees.

autumnalis — from Latin, meaning the period of harvest.

bicolor — from Latin: of two colors.

Histrionicus — from Latin, meaning histrionic and relating to histrio, a stageplayer.

Lampronetta — from Greek *lampros:* shining or beautiful, and *netta:* a kind of duck. Here considered part of *Somateria.*

Lophodytes — from Greek *lophos:* a crest, and *dutes:* a diver. Here considered part of *Mergus.*

Mareca — the Brazilian name for a kind of teal. Here considered part of *Anas.*

Melanitta — from *melas, melanos:* black, and *netta:* a duck. The vernacular name scoter is possibly from the Dutch word *koet,* or perhaps is a variant of "scout," which is in local use in Great Britain for scoters as well as guillemots and razorbill auks.

deglandi — in honor of Dr. C. D. Degland (1787–1865), French naturalist.

fusca — from Latin: dusky.

nigra — from Latin *niger:* black.

perspicillata — from Latin: conspicuous or spectacular.

Mergus — from Latin: a diver.

albellus — diminutive of Latin *albus:* white.

cucullatus — from Latin: wearing a hood.

merganser — from Latin *mergus:* a diver, and *anser:* a goose. The vernacular name goosander is probably from the Old Norse *Gas* and *ønd,* meaning goose-duck.

Oidemia — from Greek *oidema,* Latin *oedema:* a swelling, in reference to the shape of the bill. Here considered part of *Melanitta.*

Olor — from Latin: a swan. Here considered part of *Cygnus.*

Oxyura — from Greek *oxy:* sharp, and *oura:* tail, referring to the pointed rectrices.

dominica — of Santo Domingo.

jamaicensis — of Jamaica (from which the species was first described).

Philacte — from Greek *philos:* loving, and *akte:* the seashore. Here considered part of *Anser.*

Polysticta — from Greek *poly:* many, and *sticte:* spotted.

stelleri — in honor of G. W. Steller (1709–1746), German naturalist on Bering's expedition to the arctic for Russia.

Somateria — from Greek *soma, somatos:* the body, and *erion:* wool or down. The vernacular name eider is derived from the Icelandic *ejdar,* used there for the common eider.

fischeri — in honor of G. von Waldheim Fischer (1771–1853), Russian naturalist.

mollissima — superlative of Latin *mollis:* very soft.

spectabilis — from Latin, meaning conspicuous or spectacular.

Spatula — from Latin, meaning spoonlike. Here considered part of *Anas.*

Sources

Addy, C. E. "Atlantic Flyway." In Linduska (1964), pp. 167–184.

Ahlén, I., and A. Andersson. (1970). "Breeding ecology of an eider population on Spitsbergen." *Ornis Scandinavica,* 1:83–106.

Alcorn, J. R. (1953). "Food of the common merganser in Churchill County, Nevada." *Condor,* 55:151–152.

Aldrich, J. W., and others. (1949). "Migration of some North American waterfowl: A progress report on an analysis of banding records." U.S. Dept. of Interior, Fish and Wildlife Service, Special Scientific Report: Wildlife, No. 1, 48 pp.

Aldrich, J. W., and K. P. Baer. (1970). "Status and speciation in the Mexican duck (*Anas diazi*)." *Wilson Bulletin,* 82:63–73.

Alison, R. (1970). "The behaviour of the oldsquaw (*Clangula hyemalis*) in winter." M.S. thesis, University of Toronto, Toronto.

———. (1972). "The breeding biology of the oldsquaw (*Clangula hyemalis*) at Churchill, Manitoba." Ph.D. dissertation, University of Toronto, Toronto.

American Ornithologists' Union. (1957). *Check-list of North American birds.* 5th ed. Baltimore: Lord Baltimore Press, Inc.

Anderson, B. W., and R. L. Timken. (1971) "Age and sex characteristics of common mergansers." *Journal of Wildlife Management,* 35:388–393.

Anderson, W. (1957). "A waterfowl nesting study in the Sacramento Valley, California, 1955." *California Fish and Game,* 43:71–90.

———. (1960). "A study of waterfowl nesting in the Suisun marshes." *California Fish and Game,* 46:217–226.

———. (1965). "Waterfowl production in the vicinity of gull colonies." *California Fish and Game,* 51:5–15.

Atkinson-Willes, G. (ed.). (1963). *Wildfowl in Great Britain.* London: Monographs of the Nature Conservancy, No.3.

Atwater, M. G. (1959). "A study of re-nesting in Canada geese in Montana." *Journal of Wildlife Management,* 23:91–97.

Audubon, J. J. (1840–1844). *The birds of America.* Philadelphia: Chevalier.

Austin, G. T. (1969). "A record of the tufted duck for Connecticut." *Wilson Bulletin,* 81:332.

Bailey, A. M. (1948). "Birds of Arctic Alaska." Colorado Museum of Natural History, Popular Series, No. 8, pp. 1–317.

Bailey, A.M., and R. J. Niedrach. (1967). *A pictorial checklist of Colorado birds, with brief notes on the status of each species in neighboring states of Nebraska, Kansas, New Mexico, Utah and Wyoming.* Denver: Museum of Natural History.

Balham, R. W. (1954). "The behavior of the Canada goose (*Branta canadensis*) in Manitoba." Ph.D. dissertation, University of Missouri, Columbia.

Banko, W. E. (1960). "The trumpeter swan: Its history, habits, and population in the United States." U.S. Dept. of Interior, Fish and Wildlife Service, North American Fauna, No. 63. pp. 1–214.

Banko, W. E., and R. H. Mackay. "Our native swans." In Linduska (1964), pp. 155–164.

Bannerman, D. A. (1958). *Birds of the British Isles.* Vol.7. Edinburgh and London: Oliver & Boyd.

Barry, T. W. (1956). "Observations on a nesting colony of American brant." *Auk,* 73:193–202.

———. (1962). "Effect of late seasons on Atlantic brant reproduction." *Journal of Wildlife Management,* 26:19–26.

———. "Brant, Ross' goose, and emperor goose." In Linduska (1964), pp. 145–154.

———. (1967). "Geese of the Anderson River delta, Northwest Territories, Canada." Ph.D. dissertation, University of Alberta, Edmonton.

Bartonek, J. C., and J. J. Hickey (1969). "Food habits of canvasbacks, redheads and lesser scaups in Manitoba." *Condor,* 71:280–290.

Bartonek, J. C., and H. W. Murdy. (1970). "Summer foods of lesser scaup in subarctic taiga." *Arctic,* 23:35–44.

Bauer, K. M., and U. N. Glutz von Blotzheim. (1968). *Handbuch der Vögel Mitteleuropas.* Band 2. Frankfurt am Main: Akademische Verlagsgesellschaft.

———. (1969). *Handbuck der Vögel Mitteleuropas.* Band 3. Frankfurt am Main: Akademische Verlagsgesellschaft.

Beard, E. B. (1964). "Duck brood behavior at the Seney National Wildlife Refuge." *Journal of Wildlife Management,* 28:492–521.

Beckwith, S. L., and H. J. Hosford. (1955). "The Florida duck in the vicinity of Lake Okeechobee, Glades County, Florida." Presented at 9th Annual Conference, Southeastern Association of Game and Fish Commissioners, October 1955, 25 pp., processed.

———. (1957). "A report on seasonal food habits and life history notes of the Florida duck in the vicinity of Lake Okeechobee, Glades County, Florida." *American Midland Naturalist,* 57:461–473.

Beer, J. (1945). "Sex ratios of ducks in southwestern Washington." *Auk,* 62:117–124.

Bellrose, F. C., and E. B. Chase. (1950). "Population losses in the mallard, black duck and blue-winged teal." Illinois Natural History Survey, Biological Notes, No. 22, pp. 1–27.

Bellrose, F. C. and A. S. Hawkins. (1947). "Duck weights in Illinois." *Auk,* 64:422–430.

Bellrose, R. C., K. L. Johnson and T. U. Meyers. (1964). "Relative value of natural cavities and nesting houses for wood ducks." *Journal of Wildlife Management,* 28:661–676.

Bellrose, R. C., and F. B. McGilvrey. "Characteristics and values of artificial nesting cavities." In Trefethen (1966), pp. 125–131.

Bengtson, S. (1966). "Observations on the sexual behavior of the common scoter (*Melanitta nigra*) on the breeding grounds, with special reference to courting parties." In Swedish, with English summary. *Vår Fågelvärld,* 25:202–226.

———. (1966). "Field studies on the harlequin duck in Iceland." *Wildfowl Trust Annual Report*, 17:79–94.

———. (1970). "Location of nest-sites of ducks in Lake Mývatn area, north-east Iceland." *Oikos*, 21:218–229.

———. (1971). "Variation in clutch-size in ducks in relation to their food supply." *Ibis*, 113:523–526.

———. (1972a). "Reproduction and fluctuations in the size of duck populations at Lake Mývatn, Iceland." *Oikos*, 23:35–58.

———. (1972b). "Breeding ecology of the harlequin *Histrionicus histrionicus* (L.) in Iceland." *Ornis Scandinavia*, 3:25–43.

Bennett, J. L. (1938a). *The blue-winged teal, its ecology and management*. Ames: Collegiate Press, Inc.

———. (1938b). "Redheads and ruddy ducks nesting in Iowa." *North American Wildlife Conference Transactions*, 3:647–650.

Benson, D. A. (1968). "Species of waterfowl killed in Canada during the 1967–68 hunting season." Canadian Wildlife Service, Progress Notes, No. 7, pp. 1–3 plus tables.

———. (1969). "Waterfowl harvest and hunter activity in Canada during the 1968–69 hunting season." Canadian Wildlife Service, Progress Notes, No. 10, pp. 1–6 plus tables.

Benson, D., and F. C. Bellrose. "Eastern production areas." In Linduska (1964), pp. 89–98.

Benson, D., and L. W. DeGraff (1968). "Distribution and mortality of redheads banded in New York." *New York Fish and Game Journal*, 15:52–70.

Bent, A. C. (1923). "Life histories of North American wild fowl." Part 1. U.S. National Museum Bulletin, 126, pp. 1–244.

———. (1925). "Life histories of North American wild fowl." Part 2. U.S. National Museum Bulletin, 130, pp. 1–316.

Berrett, D. C. (1962). "The birds of the Mexican state of Tabasco." Unpublished Ph.D. dissertation, Louisiana State University, Baton Rouge.

Bezzel, E. (1959). "Beitrage zur Biologie der Geschlecter bei Entenvogeln." *Anzeiger der Ornithologischen Gesellschaft in Bayern*, 5:269–355.

Bjärvall, A. (1968). "The hatching and nest-exodus behaviour of mallard." *Wildfowl*, 19:70–80.

———. (1969). "Unusual cases of re-nesting mallards." *Wilson Bulletin*, 81:94–96.

Blurton, P. J. K. (1960). "Brent goose population studies, 1958–59." *Wildfowl Trust Annual Report*, 11:94–98.

Boase, H. (1959). "Notes on the display, nesting and moult of the mute swan." *British Birds*, 52:114–123.

Bolen, E. G. (1962). "Nesting of black-bellied tree ducks in Texas (*Dendrocygna autumanalis*)." *Audubon Field Notes*, 16:482–485.

———. (1964). "Weights and linear measurements of black-bellied tree ducks." *Texas Journal of Science*, 16:257–260.

———. (1967a). "Nesting boxes for black-bellied tree ducks." *Journal of Wildlife Management*, 31:794–797.

———. (1967b). "The ecology of the black-bellied tree duck in southern Texas." Ph.D. dissertation, Utah State University, Logan.

———. (1970). "Sex ratios in the black-bellied tree duck." *Journal of Wildlife Management*, 34:68–73.

———. (1971). "Pair-bond tenure of the black-bellied tree duck." *Journal of Wildlife Management*, 35:385–388.

———. (1971b). "Some views on exotic waterfowl." *Wilson Bulletin*, 83:430–434.

Bolen, E. G., and B. J. Forsyth. (1967). "Foods of the black-bellied tree duck in south Texas." *Wilson Bulletin,* 79:43–49.

Bolen, E. G., B. McDaniel, and C. Cottam. (1964). "Natural history of the black-bellied tree duck (*Dendrocygna autumnalis*) in southern Texas." *Southwestern Naturalist,* 9:78–88.

Bond, J. (1961). "Sixth supplement to the check-list of birds of the West Indies (1956)," pp. 1–12. Philadelphia: Academy of Natural Sciences.

———. (1971). *Birds of the West Indies.* 2d ed. Boston: Houghton Mifflin.

Borden, R., and H. A. Hochbaum. (1966). "Gadwall seeding in New England." *North American Wildlife and Natural Resources Conference Transactions,* 31:79–88.

Borrer, D. J. (1950). "A check-list of the birds of Ohio, with the migration dates for the birds of central Ohio." *Ohio Journal of Science,* 50:1–32.

Boyd, H. (1954). "White-fronted goose statistics." *Wildfowl Trust Annual Report,* 6:73–79.

———. (1956). "Statistics of the British population of the pink-footed goose." *Journal of Animal Ecology,* 25:253–273.

———. (1958). "The survival of Greenland white-fronted geese ringed in Greenland." *Dansk Ornithologisk Forenings Tidsskrift,* 52:1–8.

———. (1959). "The composition of goose populations." *Ibis,* 101:441–445.

———. (1961). "The flightless period of the mallard in England." *Wildfowl Trust Annual Report,* 12:140–143.

———. (1962). "Population dynamics and the exploitation of ducks and geese. In E. LeCren (ed.), *The exploitation of natural populations,* pp. 85–97. New York: Wiley.

———. (1964). "Barnacle geese caught in Dumfriesshire in February, 1963." *Wildfowl Trust Annual Report,* 15:75–76.

Brakhage, G. K. (1965). "Biology and behavior of tub-nesting Canada geese." *Journal of Wildlife Management* 29:751–771.

———. "Management of mast crops for wood ducks." In Trefethen (1966), pp. 75–80.

Brandt, H. (1943). *Alaska bird trails.* Cleveland: Bird Research Foundation.

Braun, E. L. (1950). *Deciduous forests of eastern North America.* Philadelphia: Blakiston Co.

Breckenridge, W. J. (1953). "Night rafting of American golden-eyes on the Mississippi River." *Auk,* 70:201–204.

Brooks, A. (1903). "Notes on the birds of the Cariboo District, British Columbia." *Auk,* 20:277–284.

———. (1920). "Notes on some American ducks." *Auk,* 37:353–367.

Burgess, H. H., H. H. Prince, and D. L. Trauger. (1965). "Blue-winged teal nesting success as related to land use." *Journal of Wildlife Management,* 29:89–95.

Burleigh, T. D. (1944). "The bird life of the Gulf Coast region of Mississippi." Louisiana State University, Museum of Zoology Occasional Papers, No. 20:329–490.

———. (1958). *Georgia birds.* Norman: University of Oklahoma Press.

Byrd, G. V., D. L. Johnson, and D. D. Gibson. (1974). "The birds of Adak Island, Alaska." *Condor,* 76:288–300.

Cain, B. W. (1970). "Growth and plumage development of the black-bellied tree duck, *Dendrocygna autumnalis* (Linnaeus)." *Texas A. and I University Studies,* 3:25–48.

Campbell, J. M. (1969). "The canvasback, common goldeneye and bufflehead in arctic Alaska." *Condor,* 71:80.

Carney, S. M. (1964). "Preliminary keys to waterfowl age and sex identification by means of wing plumage." U.S. Dept.

of Interior, Fish and Wildlife Service, Special Scientific Report: Wildlife, No. 82. 48 pp.

Carney, S. M., and A. D. Geis. (1960). "Mallard age and sex determination from wings." *Journal of Wildlife Management*, 24:372–381.

Carroll, J. J. (1932). "A change in the distribution of the fulvous tree duck in Texas." *Auk*, 49:343–344.

Carter, B. C. (1958). "The American goldeneye in central New Brunswick." Canadian Wildlife Service, Wildlife Management Bulletin, Series 2, No. 9. 47 pp.

Chamberlain, E. B. (1960). "Florida waterfowl populations, habitats and managements." Florida Game and Fresh Water Fish Commission, Technical Bulletin, No. 7, pp. 1–62.

———. (1967). "Progress report: Productivity study of whistling swans wintering in Chesapeake Bay." *Proceedings Annual Conference of Southeastern Association of Game and Fish Commissioners,* 20: 154–157.

Chapman, J. A. (1970). "Weights and measurements of dusky Canada geese wintering in Oregon." *Murrelet,* 51:34–37.

Chapman, J. A., C. J. Henry, and H. M. Wright. (1969). "The status, population dynamics and harvest of the dusky Canada goose." *Wildlife Monographs* 18. 48 pp.

Chattin, J. E. "Pacific Flyway." In Linduska (1964), pp. 233–252.

Cheng Tso-hsin. (1963). *China's economic fauna: Birds.* Peiping: Science Publishing Society. (Translated by Joint Publication Research Service, Washington, D.C., 1964.)

Childs, H. E., Jr. (1969). "Birds and mammals of the Pitmegea River region, Cape Sabine, northwestern Alaska." University of Alaska Biological Papers, No. 10. 74 pp.

Choate, J. S. (1967). "Factors influencing nesting success of eiders in Penobscot Bay, Maine." *Journal of Wildlife Management,* 31:769–777.

Coldwell, C. (1939). "The feeding habits of American mergansers." *Canadian Field-Naturalist, 53:53–55.*

Collias, N. E., and J. R. Jahn. (1959). "Social behavior and breeding success in Canada geese (*Branta canadensis*) under semi-natural conditions." *Auk,* 76:478–509.

Conover, H. B. (1926). "Game birds of the Hooper Bay region of Alaska." *Auk,* 43: 162–180.

Cooch, F. G. (1955). "Observations on the autumn migration of blue geese." *Wilson Bulletin,* 67:171–174.

———. (1957). "Mass ringing of flightless blue and lesser snow geese in Canada's eastern arctic." *Wildlife Trust Annual Report,* 8:58–67.

———. (1958). "The breeding biology and management of the blue goose *Chen caerulescens.*" Ph.D. dissertation, Cornell University, Ithaca.

———. (1961). "Ecological aspects of the blue-snow goose complex." *Auk,* 78: 72–79.

———. (1963). "Recent changes in distribution of color phases of *Chen c. caerulescens.*" *Proceedings XIII International Ornithological Congress,* 1962, vol. 2, pp. 1182–1194.

———. "Snows and blues." In Linduska (1964), pp. 125–133.

———. (1965). "The breeding biology and management of the northern eider (*Somateria mollissima borealis*) in the Cape Dorset area, Northwest Territories." Canadian Wildlife Service, Wildlife Management Bulletin, Series 2, No. 10. 68 pp.

Cooch, F., and J. P. Ryder. (1971). "The genetics of polymorphism in the Ross' goose (*Anser rossi*)." *Evolution,* 25: 461–470.

Cooch, F. G., G. M. Stirrett, and G. F. Boyer. (1960). "Autumn weights of blue geese (*Chen caerulescens*)." *Auk,* 77: 460–465.

Cottam, C. (1939). "Food habits of North American diving ducks." U.S. Dept. of Agriculture, Technical Bulletin, 643. 139 pp.

Cottam, C., and W. C. Glazener. (1959). "Late nesting of water birds in south Texas." *North American Wildlife Conference Transactions,* 24:382–395.

Cottam, C., and P. Knappen. (1939). "Food of some uncommon North American birds." *Auk,* 56:138–169.

Cottam, C., J. J. Lynch, and A. L. Nelson. (1944). "Food habits and management of American sea brant." *Journal of Wildlife Management* 8:36–56.

Cottam, C., and F. M. Uhler. (1936). "The role of fish-eating birds." *Progressive Fish Culturist,* 14:1–14.

Coulter, M. W. (1953). "Mallard nesting in Maine." *Auk,* 70:490.

———. (1954). "Some observations of mallards in central Maine." *Maine Audubon Society Bulletin,* 10:20–23.

Coulter, M. W., and W. R. Miller. (1968). "Nesting biology of black ducks and mallards in northern New England." Vermont Fish and Game Department Bulletin, No. 68–2. 74 pp.

Cowardin, L. M., C. E. Cummings, and P. B. Reed, Jr. (1967). "Stump and tree nesting by mallards and black ducks." *Journal of Wildlife Management,* 31: 229–235.

Craighead, J. J., and D. S. Stockstad. (1964). "Breeding age of Canada geese." *Journal of Wildlife Management,* 28:57–64.

Cronan, J. M., Jr. (1957). "Food and feeding habits of the scaups in Connecticut waters." *Auk,* 74:459–468.

Cunningham, E. R. (1969). "A three year study of the wood duck on the Yazoo National Wildlife Refuge." *Proceedings Annual Conference of the Southeastern Association of Game and Fish Commissioners,* 22:145–155.

Curth, P. (1954). "Der Mittelsager. Soziologie und Brutbiologie." *Neue Brehm-Bucherei,* Heft 126. Leipzig: A. Ziemsen Verlag.

Dane, B., C. Walcott, and W. H. Drury. (1959). "The form and duration of the display actions of the goldeneye (*Bucephala clangula*)." *Behaviour,* 14:265–281.

Dane, B., and W. G. van der Kloot. (1964). "An analysis of the display of the goldeneye duck (*Bucephala clangula* L.)." *Behaviour,* 22:282–328.

Dane, C. W. (1966). "Some aspects of breeding biology of the blue-winged teal." *Auk,* 83:389–402.

———. (1968). "Age determination of blue-winged teal." *Journal of Wildlife Management,* 32:267–274.

Dau, C. (1972). "Observations on the natural history of the spectacled eider (*Lampronetta fischeri*)." M.S. thesis, University of Alaska, College.

Davis, L. I. (1966). "Birds of the Rio Grande Delta region, an annotated check-list." Privately published (mimeo).

Dawson, W. L., and J. H. Bowles. (1909). *Birds of Washington.* Seattle: Occidental Publishing Company.

DeGraff, L. W., and R. Bauer. (1962). "Breeding American wigeon in New York." *Wilson Bulletin,* 74:101.

Delacour, J. (1954–1964). *The waterfowl of the world.* 4 vols. London: Country Life Ltd.

Delacour, J. and S. D. Ripley (1975). "Description of a new subspecies of the white-fronted goose *Anser albifrons.*" *American Museum Novitates,* 2565: 1–4.

Dementiev, G. P., and N. A. Gladkov. (eds.). (1967). *Birds of the Soviet Union.* Vol. 4. Translated from 1952

Russian edition, Israel Program for Scientific Translations. Washington, D.C.: U.S. Department of Interior and National Science Foundation.

Denson, E. P. (1970). "The trumpeter swan, *Olor buccinator:* A conservation success and its lessons." *Biological Conservation,* 2:253–256.

Des Lauriers, J. R., and B. H. Brattstrom. (1965). "Cooperative feeding behavior in red-breasted mergansers." *Auk,* 82: 639.

Dickey, D. R., and A. J. Van Rossem. (1923). "The fulvous tree-ducks of Buena Vista Lake." *Condor,* 25:39–50.

Dickinson, J. C., Jr. (1953). "Report on the McCabe collection of British Columbian birds." Harvard University, Museum of Comparative Zoology, Bulletin, 109:121–209.

Dillon, O. W., Jr. (1959). "Food habits of wild mallard ducks in three Louisiana parishes." *North American Wildlife Conference Transactions,* 24:374–382.

Dimmick, R. W. (1968). "Canada geese of Jackson Hole: Their ecology and management." Wyoming Game and Fish Commission, Bulletin 11. 86 pp.

Dirschl, H. J. (1969). "Foods of lesser scaup and blue winged teal in the Saskatchewan River delta." *Journal of Wildlife Management,* 33:77–87.

Drewien, R. C., and L. F. Fredrickson. (1970). "High density mallard nesting on a South Dakota island." *Wilson Bulletin,* 82:92–96.

Drewien, R. C., and P. F. Springer. (1969). "Ecological relationships of breeding blue-winged teal to prairie potholes." In *Saskatoon Wetlands Seminar,* Canadian Wildlife Service Report Series, No. 6, pp. 102–105.

Duebbert, H. F. (1961). "Recent brood records for the white-winged scoter in North Dakota." *Wilson Bulletin,* 73: 209–210.

———. (1966). "Island nesting of the gadwall in North Dakota." *Wilson Bulletin,* 78:12–25.

———. (1969). "High nest density and hatching success of ducks on South Dakota CAP land." *North American Wildlife and Natural Resources Conference,* 34:218–228.

Dwight, J., Jr. (1914). "The moults and plumages of the scoters—genus *Oidemia.*" *Auk,* 31:293–308.

Dwyer, T. J. (1970). "Waterfowl breeding habitat in agricultural and nonagricultural land in Manitoba." *Journal of Wildlife Management,* 34:130–136.

Dzubin, A. (1955). "Some evidences of home range in waterfowl." *North American Wildlife Conference Transactions,* 20:278–297.

———. (1959). "Growth and plumage development of wild-trapped juvenile canvasbacks." *Journal of Wildlife Management,* 23:279–290.

———. (1965). "A study of migrating Ross geese in western Saskatchewan." *Condor,* 67:511–534.

Dzubin, A., H. W. Miller, and G. V. Schildman. "White-fronts." In Linduska (1964), pp. 135–143.

Earl, J. P. (1950). "Production of mallards on irrigated land in the Sacramento Valley, California." *Journal of Wildlife Management,* 14:332–342.

Edwards, M. (1966). "Wintering of whistling swans with mute swans in Grand Traverse Bay." *Jack-Pine Warbler,* 44: 177.

Einarsen, A. S. (1965). *Black brant: Sea goose of the Pacific coast.* Seattle: University of Washington Press.

Elgas, R. (1970). "Breeding populations of tule white-fronted geese in northwestern Canada." *Wilson Bulletin,* 82: 420–426.

Ellarson, R. S. (1956). "A study of the old-squaw duck on Lake Michigan." Ph.D. dissertation, University of Wisconsin, Madison.

Ellig, L. J. (1955). "Waterfowl relationships to Greenfields Lake, Teton County, Montana." Montana Fish & Game Commission, Technical Bulletin, No. 1. 35 pp.

Elliot, J. J. (1961). "Recent history of the Barrow's goldeneye in New York." *Kingbird,* 11:131–136.

Emmons, J. (1970). "Gadwalls revisited." *Florida Wildlife,* 24(6):12–15.

Engeling, G. A. (1949). "The mottled duck, a determined nester." *Texas Game and Fish,* 7(8):6–7, 19.

———. (1950). "Nesting habits of the mottled duck (*Anas fulvigula maculosa*) in Colorado, Fort Bent and Brazoria Counties, Texas." M.S. thesis, Texas A. & M. College, College Station.

———. (1951). "Mottled duck movements in Texas." *Texas Game and Fish,* 9(5):2–5.

Erickson, R. C. (1948). "Life history and ecology of the canvas-back, *Nyroca valisineria* (Wilson), in southeastern Oregon." Ph.D. dissertation, Iowa State College, Ames.

Erskine, A. J. (1960). "A discussion of the distributional ecology of the bufflehead (*Bucephala albeola;* Anatidae:Aves) based on breeding biology studies in British Columbia." M.S. thesis, University of British Columbia, Vancouver.

———. (1961). "Nest-site tenacity and homing in the bufflehead." *Auk,* 78:389–396.

———. (1964). "Nest-site competition between bufflehead, mountain bluebird and tree swallow." *Canadian Field-Naturalist,* 78:202–203.

———. (1971). "Growth and annual cycle of weights, plumages and reproductive organs of goosanders in eastern Canada." *Ibis,* 113:42–58.

———. (1972). *Buffleheads.* Canadian Wildlife Service Monograph Series, Number 4. Ottawa: Information Canada.

Evans, M. (1970). "Wild swans at Slimbridge, 1969–70." *Wildfowl* 21:134–136.

Evans, R. D., and C. W. Wolfe. (1967). 'Waterfowl production in the Rainwater Basin of Nebraska." *Journal of Wildlife Management,* 31:788–794.

Evans, R. M. (1970). "Oldsquaws nesting in association with arctic terns at Churchill, Manitoba." *Wilson Bulletin,* 82:383–390.

Evenden, F. G., Jr. (1947). "The bufflehead nesting in Oregon." *Condor,* 49:169.

Fay, F. H. (1960). "The distribution of waterfowl to St. Lawrence Island, Alaska." *Wildfowl Trust Annual Report,* 12:70–80.

Fencker, H. (1950). "The Greenland white-fronted goose and its breeding-biology." *Dansk Ornithologisk Forenings Tidsskrift,* 44:61–65.

Ferguson, W. H. (1966). "Will my birds nest this year?" *Modern Game Breeding,* 2:18–20, 34–35.

Fisher, J., and R. T. Peterson. (1964). *The world of birds.* Garden City, N.Y.: Doubleday and Company.

Fleming, W. B. (1959). "Migratory waterfowl in Arizona. Arizona Game & Fish Department, *Wildlife Bulletin,* No. 5, pp. 1–74.

Foley, D. D. (1960). "Recent changes in waterfowl populations in New York." *Kingbird,* 10:82–93.

Freeman, M. M. R. (1970). "Observations on the seasonal behavior of the Hudson Bay eider." *Canadian Field-Naturalist,* 84:145–153.

Frith, H. C. (1967). *Waterfowl in Australia.* Honolulu: East-West Center Press.

Fritsch, L. F., and I. O. Buss. (1958). "Food of the American merganser in Unakwik Inlet, Alaska." *Condor,* 60: 410–411.

Gabrielson, I. N. and F. C. Lincoln. (1959). *The birds of Alaska.* Washington, D.C.: Wildlife Management Institute, and Harrisburg: Stackpole Company.

Gates, J. M. (1957). "Autumn food habits of the gadwall in northern Utah." *Proceedings, Utah Academy of Sciences, Arts and Letters,* 34:69–71.

———. (1962). "Breeding biology of the gadwall in northern Utah." *Wilson Bulletin,* 74:43–67.

Gehrman, K. H. (1951). "An ecological study of the lesser scaup duck (*Aythya affinis* Eyton) at West Medical Lake, Spokane County, Washington." M.S. thesis, Washington State University, Pullman.

Geis, A. D. (1959). "Annual and shooting mortality estimates for the canvas-back." *Journal of Wildlife Management,* 23: 253–261.

Geis, A. D., R. I. Smith, and J. P. Rogers. (1971). "Black duck distribution, harvest characteristics, and survival." U.S. Dept. of Interior, Fish and Wildlife Service, Special Scientific Report: Wildlife, No. 139. 241 pp.

Gibbs, R. M. (1961). "Breeding ecology of the common goldeneye, *Bucephala clangula americana, in Maine.*" M.S. thesis, University of Maine, Orono.

———. (1962). "Juvenile mortality of the common goldeneye, *Bucephala clangula americana,* in Maine." *Maine Field Naturalist,* 18:67–68.

Girard, G. L. (1939). "Notes on life history of the shoveller." *North American Wildlife Conference Transactions,* 4: 364–371.

———. (1941). "The mallard, its management in western Montana." *Journal of Wildlife Management,* 5:233–259.

Glazener, W. C. (1946). "Food habits of wild geese on the Gulf Coast of Texas." *Journal of Wildlife Management,* 10: 322–329.

Glegg, W. E. (1951). "On seven eggs attributed to the Labrador duck." *Ibis,* 93:305.

Glover, F. A. (1956). "Nesting and production of the blue-winged teal (*Anas discors* Linnaeus) in northwest Iowa." *Journal of Wildlife Management,* 20:28–46.

Godfrey, W. E. (1966). "The birds of Canada." National Museums of Canada, Bulletin No. 203, Biological Series No. 73, pp. 1–428.

Goochfield, M. (1968). "Notes on the status of the tufted duck (*Aythya fuligula*) in North America with a report of a new observation from Wyoming." *Condor,* 70:186–187.

Goodman, D. C., and H. I. Fisher. (1962). *Functional anatomy of the feeding apparatus in waterfowl (Aves: Anatidae).* Carbondale: Southern Illinois University Press.

Goodwin, C. E. (1956). "Black duck and mallard populations in the Toronto area." *Ontario Field Biologist,* 10:7–18.

Gorman, M. L. (1970). "The daily pattern of display in a wild population of eider duck." *Wildfowl,* 21:105–107.

Gorman, M. L., and H. Milne. (1972). "Creche behaviour in the common eider *Somateria m. mollissima L.*" *Ornis Scandinavica,* 3:21–25.

Grenquist, P. (1953). ("On the nesting of the goosander in bird-boxes.") Finnish, with English summary. *Soumen Riista,* 8:49–59.

———. (1958). ("A nesting box for the red-breasted merganser.") Finnish, with separate English summary. *Soumen Riista,* 12:94–99.

———. (1963). "Hatching losses of common goldeneye." *Proceedings XIII Interna-*

tional *Ornithological Congress,* 1962, vol. 2, pp. 685–689.

———. (1965). "Changes in abundance of some duck and seabird populations off the coast of Finland 1949–1963." *Finnish Game Research,* 27:1–114.

Grice, D., and J. P. Rogers. (1965). "The wood duck in Massachusetts." Massachusetts Division of Fisheries and Game, Final Report, Proj. No. W-19-R, p. 196.

Grieb, J. R. "Canada goose populations of the Central Flyway—their status and future." In Hine and Schoenfeld (1968), pp. 31–41.

———. (1970). "The shortgrass prairie Canada goose population." *Wildlife Monographs,* 22:1–48.

Grinnell, J., and A. H. Miller. (1944). "The distribution of the birds of California." Cooper Ornithological Club, *Pacific Coast Avifauna,* No. 27.

Griswold, J. (1965). "We raise the first trumpeter swans." *America's First Zoo,* 17(3):17–20.

Gross, A. O. (1944). "The present status of the American eider on the Maine coast." *Wilson Bulletin,* 56:15–26.

Guignion, D. (1969). "Clutch size and incubation of the American eider (*Somateria mollissima dresseri*) on Brandypot Island." *Naturaliste Canadien,* 95:1145–1152.

Guiguet, C. J. (1958). "The birds of British Columbia: Waterfowl." British Columbia Provincial Museum Handbook, No. 15, pp. 1–84.

Handley, C. O., Jr. (1950). "The brant of Prince Patrick Island, Northwest Territories." *Wilson Bulletin,* 62:128–132.

Hansen, H. A. (1960). "Changed status of several species of waterfowl in Alaska." *Condor,* 62:136–137.

———. (1961). "Loss of waterfowl production to flood tides." *Journal of Wildlife Management,* 25:242–248.

———. (1962). "Canada geese of coastal Alaska." *North American Wildlife and Natural Resources Conference Transactions,* 27:301–320.

Hansen, H. A., and U. C. Nelson. (1957). "Brant of the Bering Sea—Migration and mortality." *North American Wildlife Conference Transactions,* 22:237–254.

Hansen, H. A., and P. E. K. Shepherd, J. G. King, and W. A. Troyer. (1971). "The trumpeter swan in Alaska." *Wildlife Monographs,* 26:1–83.

Hanson, H. C. (1949). "Methods of determining age in Canada geese and other waterfowl." *Journal of Wildlife Management,* 13:177–183.

———. (1965). *The giant Canada goose.* Carbondale: Southern Illinois University Press.

Hanson, H. C., P. Queneau, and P. Scott. (1956). *The geography, birds and mammals of the Perry River region.* Montreal: Arctic Institute of North America.

Hanson, H. C., and R. H. Smith. (1950). "Canada geese of the Mississippi Flyway, with special reference to an Illinois flock." Illinois Natural History Survey, Bulletin 25(3):59–210.

Harmon, B. G. (1962). "Mollusks as food of lesser scaup along the Louisiana coast." *North American Wildlife and Natural Resources Conference Transactions,* 27:132–138.

Harris, S. W. (1966). "Summer birds of the lower Kashunuk River, Yukon-Kuskokwim Delta, Alaska." *Murrelet,* 47:57–65.

Harris, S. W., C. L. Buechele, and C. F. Yocom. (1954). "The status of Barrow's golden-eye in eastern Washington." *Murrelet,* 35:33–38.

Harris, S. W., and P. E. K. Shepherd. (1965). "Age determination and notes on the breeding age of black brant." *Journal of Wildlife Management,* 29:643–645.

Harrison, J. G., and M. A. Ogilvie. (1968). "Immigrant mute swans in south-east England." *Wildfowl Trust Annual Report*, 18:85–87.

Hartman, F. A. (1955). "Heart weights in birds." *Condor*, 57:221–238.

Hartman, F. E. (1963). "Estuarine wintering habitat for black ducks." *Journal of Wildlife Management*, 27:339–347.

Hartz, S. T. (1962). "The distribution of the fulvous tree duck." *Cassinia*, 46:10–12.

Harvey, J. M. (1971). "Factors affecting blue goose nesting success." *Canadian Journal of Zoology*, 49:223–234.

Hasbrouck, E. M. (1944a). "Apparent status of the European wigeon in North America." *Auk*, 61:93–104.

———. (1944b). "The status of Barrow's goldeneye in the eastern United States." *Auk*, 61:544–554.

Hatter, J. (1960). "Baikal teal in British Columbia." *Condor*, 62:480.

Haverschmidt, F. (1968). *Birds of Surinam*. Edinburgh: Oliver and Boyd.

Hawkins, A. "Mississippi Flyway." In Linduska (1964), pp. 185–207.

Heard, W. R., and M. R. Curd. (1959). "Stomach contents of American mergansers, *Mergus merganser* Linnaeus, caught in gill nets set in Lake Carl Blackwell, Oklahoma." *Oklahoma Academy of Science Proceedings*, 39:197–200.

Hending, P., B. King, and R. Prytherch. (1963). "Communal diving in turbid water by red-breasted mergansers." *Wildfowl Trust Annual Report*, 14:172–173.

Henny, C. J. and N. E. Holgerson. (1974). "Range expansion and population increase of the gadwall in eastern North America." *Wildfowl* 25:95–101.

Hester, F. E., and T. L. Quay. (1961). "A three-year study of the fall migration and roosting-flight habits of the wood duck in east-central North Carolina." *Proceedings 15th Annual Conference of Southeastern Association of Game and Fish Commissioners*, pp. 55–60.

Hibbard, E. A. (1971). "Additional information on the wood duck in North Dakota." *Prairie Naturalist*, 3:13–16.

Hickey, J. J. (1952). "Survival studies of banded birds." U.S. Dept. of Interior, Fish and Wildlife Service, Special Scientific Report: Wildlife, No. 15. 177 pp.

Higgins, F. K., and L. J. Schoonover. (1969). "Aging small Canada geese by neck plumage." *Journal of Wildlife Management*, 33:212–214.

Hildén, O. (1964). "Ecology of duck populations in the island group of Valassaaret, Gulf of Bothnia." *Annales Zoologici Fennici*, 1:1–279.

Hine, R. L., and C. Schoenfeld (eds.). (1968). *Canada goose management: Current continental problems and programs*. Madison: Dembar Educational Research Services, Inc.

Hochbaum, H. A. (1944). *The canvasback on a prairie marsh*. Washington, D.C.: Wildlife Management Institute, and Harrisburg: Stackpole Co.

———. (1955). *Travels and traditions of waterfowl*. Minneapolis: University of Minnesota Press.

Hoffmann, R. (1927). *Birds of the Pacific states*. Boston: Houghton Mifflin.

Hoffpauir, C. (1964). "Waterfowl." *Louisiana Wild Life and Fisheries Commission 10th Biennial Report*, 1962–1963, pp. 107–111.

Hoogerheide, C. (1950). "De Eidereenden, *Somateria mollissima* L., op Vlieland." *Ardea*, 37:139–160.

Hori, J. (1963). "Three-bird flights in the mallard." *Wildfowl Trust Annual Report*, 14:124–132.

Huey, W. S. (1961). "Comparison of female mallard with female Mexican duck," *Auk*, 78:428–431.

Hull, E. D. (1914). "Habits of the old-squaw (*Harelda hyemalis*) in Jackson

Park, Chicago." *Wilson Bulletin,* 26: 116–123.

Hunt, E. G., and W. Anderson. (1966). "Renesting of ducks at Mountain Meadows, Lassen County, California." *California Fish and Game,* 52:17–27.

Hunt, E. G., and A. E. Naylor. (1955). "Nesting studies of ducks and coots in Honey Lake Valley." *California Fish and Game,* 41:295–314.

Huntington, E. H. and A. A. Roberts. (1959). "Food habits of the merganser in New Mexico." New Mexico Department of Game and Fish, Bulletin No. 9, pp. 1–36.

Hyde, R. A. (1958). "Florida waterfowl band recoveries, 1920–1957." Florida Game and Fresh Water Fish Commission, Report on F.A. Project W-19-R, pp. 1–57.

Imhoff, T. A. (1962). *Alabama birds.* University: University of Alabama Press.

Irving, L. (1960). "Birds of Anaktuvuk Pass, Kobuk, and Old Crow." U.S. National Museum, Bulletin 217, pp. 1–409.

Jahn, L. R., and R. A. Hunt. (1964). "Duck and coot ecology and management in Wisconsin." Wisconsin Conservation Department, Technical Bulletin 33. pp. 1–212.

Jehl, J. R., Jr., and B. S. Smith. (1970). "Birds of the Churchill Region, Manitoba." Special Publication No. 1, Manitoba Museum of Man and Nature, Winnipeg. 87 pp.

Jewett, S. G., W. P. Taylor, W. T. Shaw, and J. W. Aldrich. (1953). *Birds of Washington State.* Seattle: University of Washington Press.

Johnsgard, P. A. (1955). "The relation of water level and vegetational change to avian populations, particularly water-fowl." M.S. thesis, Washington State University, Pullman.

———. (1959). "Evolutionary relationships among the North American mallards." Ph.D. dissertation, Cornell University, Ithaca.

———. (1960a). "Pair-formation mechanisms in *Anas* (Anatidae) and related genera." *Ibis,* 102:616–618.

———. (1960b). "A quantitative study of sexual behavior of mallards and black ducks." *Wilson Bulletin,* 72:133–155.

———. (1961a). "The sexual behavior and systematic position of the hooded merganser." *Wilson Bulletin,* 73:226–236.

———. (1961b). "Wintering distribution changes of mallards and black ducks." *American Midland Naturalist,* 66:477–484.

———. (1961c). "Evolutionary relationships among the North American mallards." *Auk,* 78:1–43.

———. (1964a). "Comparative behavior and relationships of the eiders." *Condor,* 66:113–129.

———. (1964b). "Observations on the biology of the spectacled eider." *Wildfowl Trust Annual Report,* 15:104–107.

———. (1965). *Handbook of waterfowl behavior.* Ithaca: Cornell University Press.

———. (1967a). "Sympatry changes and hybridization incidence in mallards and black ducks." *American Midland Naturalist,* 77:51–63.

———. (1967b). "Observations on the behavior and relationships of the white-backed duck and the stiff-tailed ducks." *Wildfowl Trust Annual Report,* 18:98–107.

———. (1968). *Waterfowl: their biology and natural history.* Lincoln: University of Nebraska Press.

Johnsgard, P. A., and I. O. Buss. (1956). "Waterfowl sex ratios during spring in Washington State and their interpretation." *Journal of Wildlife Management,* 20:384–388.

Johnsgard, P. A., and D. Hagemeyer. (1969). "The masked duck in the United States." *Auk,* 84:691–695.

Johnsgard, P. A., and J. Kear. (1968). "A review of parental carrying of young by waterfowl." *Living Bird,* 7:89–102.

Johnson, A. R., and J. C. Barlow. (1971). "Notes on the nesting of the black-bellied tree duck near Phoenix, Arizona." *Southwestern Naturalist,* 15:394–395.

Johnson, D. A. (1957). "Wyoming, duck factory of the plains." *Wyoming Wildlife,* 21(9):37–39.

Johnson, L. L. (1967). "The common goldeneye duck and the role of nesting boxes in its management in north-central Minnesota." *Journal of the Minnesota Academy of Science,* 34:110–113.

Johnson, O. W. (1961). "Reproductive cycle of the mallard duck." *Condor,* 63:351–364.

Johnston, R. F. (1964). "The breeding birds of Kansas." University of Kansas, *Publications of the Museum of Natural History,* 12:575–655.

Johnston, W. (1935). "Notes on the nesting of captive mute swans." *Wilson Bulletin,* 47:237–238.

Johnstone, S. T. (1957). "On breeding of whistling ducks." *Avicultural Magazine,* 63:23–25.

———. (1961). "Breeding the king eider, 1961." *Avicultural Magazine,* 67:196–197.

———. (1970). "Waterfowl eggs." *Avicultural Magazine,* 76:52–55.

Jones, H. L. (1966). "The fulvous tree duck in the East; its past and present status." *Chat,* 30:4–7.

Jones, R. D., Jr. (1964). "Age group counts of black brant in Izembek Bay, Alaska." *Wildfowl Trust Annual Report,* 15:147–148.

———. (1965). "Returns from Steller's eiders banded in Izembek Bay, Alaska." *Wildfowl Trust Annual Report,* 18:83–85.

———. (1970). "Reproductive success and age distribution of black brant." *Journal of Wildlife Management,* 34:328–333.

Jones, R. D., Jr., and D. M. Jones. (1966). "The process of family disintegration in black brant." *Wildfowl Trust Annual Report,* 17:75–78.

Joyner, D. E. (1969). "A survey of the ecology and behavior of the ruddy duck (*Oxyura jamaicensis*) in northern Utah." M.S. thesis, University of Utah, Salt Lake City.

———. (1975). "Nest parasitism and brood-related behavior of the ruddy duck (*Oxyura jamaicensis rubida*)." Ph.D. dissertation, University of Nebraska, Lincoln.

Kear, J. (1970). "Studies on the development of young tufted duck." *Wildfowl,* 21:123–132.

Kear, J., and P. A. Johnsgard. (1968). "Foraging dives by surface-feeding ducks." *Wilson Bulletin,* 80:231.

Keith, L. B. (1961). "A study of waterfowl ecology on small impoundments in southeastern Alberta." *Wildlife Monographs,* 6:1–88.

Keith, L. B., and R. P. Stanislawski. (1960). "Stomach contents and weights of some flightless adult pintails." *Journal of Wildlife Management,* 24:95–96.

Kenyon, K. (1961). "Birds of Amchitka Island, Alaska." *Auk,* 78:305–325.

———. (1963). "Further observations of whooper swans in the Aleutian Islands." *Auk,* 80:540–542.

Kessel, B., and T. J. Cade. (1958). "Birds of the Colville River, northern Alaska." *University of Alaska Biological Papers,* 2:1–83.

Kessel, B., H. K. Springer, and C. M. White. (1964). "June birds of the Kolomak River, Yukon-Kuskokwim Delta, Alaska." *Murrelet,* 45:37–47.

King, J. C. (1963). "Duck banding in arctic Alaska." *Journal of Wildlife Management,* 27:356–362.

———. (1970). "The swans and geese of Alaska's Arctic Slope." *Wildfowl*, 21: 11–17.

Kistchinski, A. A. (1971). "Biological notes on the emperor goose in north-east Siberia." *Wildfowl*, 22:29–34.

Kitchen, D. W., and G. S. Hunt. (1969). "Brood habitat of the hooded merganser." *Journal of Wildlife Management*, 33:605–609.

Klopman, R. B. (1958) "The nesting of the Canada goose at Dog Lake, Manitoba." *Wilson Bulletin*, 70:168–183.

———. (1962). "Sexual behavior in the Canada goose." *Living Bird*, 1:123–129.

Kortright, F. H. (1943). *The ducks, geese and swans of North America*. Washington, D.C.: Wildlife Management Institute.

Koskimies, L. (1955). "Juvenile mortality and population balance in the velvet scoter (*Melanitta fusca*) in maritime conditions." *Acta XI International Ornithological Congress* 1954, pp. 476–479.

———. (1957). "Nistortreue and Sterblichkeit bei einem marinen Bestand der Samtente." *Vogelwarte*, 18:46–51.

———. (1958). ("Juvenile mortality and its causes in the velvet scoter, *Melanitta fusca*.") *Suomen Riista*, 12:70–88. (In Finnish, with separate English summary.)

Koskimies, J., and L. Lahti. (1964). "Cold-hardiness of the newly hatched young in relation to ecology and distribution in ten species of European ducks." *Auk*, 81:281–307.

Koskimies, J., and E. Routamo. (1953). "Zur Fortpflanzungsbiologie der Samtente *Melanitta f. fusca* (L). 1. Allgemeine Nistokologie." *Papers on Game Research* (*Riistatietelliaia Julkaisuja*), 10:1–105.

Kossack, C. W. (1950). "Breeding habits of Canada geese under refuge conditions." *American Midland Naturalist*, 43:627–649.

Kozlik, F. M., A. W. Miller, and W. C. Rienecker. (1959). "Color-marking white geese for determining migration routes." *California Fish and Game*, 45:69–82.

Kurtz, H. L. (1940). "The diving ability of the black duck." *Journal of Wildlife Management*, 4:19–20.

Lack, D. (1968). *Ecological adaptations for breeding in birds*. London, Methuen and Co.

Lagler, K. F., and C. C. Wienert. (1948). "Food of the old-squaw in Lake Michigan." *Wilson Bulletin*, 60:118.

Larrison, E. J., and K. G. Sonnenburg. (1968). *Washington birds: Their location and identification*. Seattle: Seattle Audubon Society.

Latta, W. C., and R. F. Sharkey. (1966). "Feeding behavior of the American merganser in captivity." *Journal of Wildlife Management*, 30:17–23.

Lebret, T. (1961). "The pair formation in the annual cycle of the mallard, *Anas platyrhynchos* L." *Ardea*, 49:97–158.

Lee, F. W., *et al.* (1964a). "Waterfowl in Minnesota." Minnesota Department of Conservation Technical Bulletin, No. 7, p. 1–210.

———. (1964b). "Ducks and land use in Minnesota. Four studies." Minnesota Department of Conservation Technical Bulletin, No. 8, pp. 1–140.

Lemieux, L. (1959). "The breeding biology of the greater snow goose on Bylot Island, Northwest Territories." *Canadian Field-Naturalist*, 73:117–128.

Lensink, C. J. (1968). "Clarence Rhode National Wildlife Refuge." In U.S. Dept. of Interior, Fish & Wildlife Service, *Annual Report, 1968*.

Leopold, A. S. (1959). *Wildlife of Mexico: The game birds and mammals*. Berkeley: University of California Press.

Leopold, A. S., and R. H. Smith. (1953). "Numbers and winter distribution of Pacific black brant in North America." *California Fish and Game,* 39:95–101.

Leopold, F. "Experiences with home-grown wood ducks." In Trefethen (1966), pp. 113–123.

Lewis, H. F. (1937). "Migrations of American brant." *Auk,* 54:73–95.

Ligon, J. S. (1961). *New Mexico birds and where to find them.* Albuquerque: University of New Mexico Press.

Lind, H. (1959). "Studies on courtship and copulatory behavior in the goldeneye [Bucephala clangula (L.)]." *Dansk Ornithologisk Forenings Tidsskrift,* 53:177–219.

Lindsey, A. A. (1946). "The nesting of the New Mexican duck." *Auk,* 63:483–492.

Linduska, J. P. (ed.) (1964). *Waterfowl tomorrow.* Washington, D.C.: U.S. Department of the Interior, Bureau of Sport Fisheries and Wildlife.

Linsdale, J. M. (1951). "A list of the birds of Nevada." *Condor,* 53:228–249.

Lokemoen, J. T. (1966). "Breeding ecology of the redhead duck in western Montana." *Journal of Wildlife Management,* 30:668–681.

Longcore, J. R., and G. W. Cornwell. (1964). "The consumption of natural foods by captive canvasbacks and lesser scaups." *Journal of Wildlife Management,* 28:527–531.

Longhurst, W. M. (1955). "Additional records of tule geese from Solano County, California." *Condor,* 57:307–318.

Longwell, J. R., and V. Stotts. (1959). "Some observations on the recovery of diving ducks banded in the Maryland portion of Chesapeake Bay." Southeastern Association of Game and Fish Commissioners, *Proceedings 12th Annual Conference,* pp. 285–291.

Low, J. B. (1940). "Production of the redhead (*Nyroca americana*) in Iowa." *Wilson Bulletin,* 52:153–164.

———. (1941). "Nesting of the ruddy duck in Iowa." *Auk,* 58:506–517.

———. (1945). "Ecology and management of the redhead, *Nyroca americana,* in Iowa." *Ecological Monographs,* 15:35–69.

Lynch, J. J. (1943). "Fulvous tree-duck in Louisiana." *Auk,* 60:100–102.

———. (1968). "Values of the South Atlantic and Gulf Coast marshes and estuaries to waterfowl." In J. D. Newson (ed.), *Proceedings of the marsh and estuary symposium, Louisiana State University, Baton Rouge, 1967,* pp. 51–63.

Lynch, J. J., and J. R. Singleton. (1964). "Winter appraisals of annual productivity in geese and other water birds." *Wildfowl Trust Annual Report,* 15:114–126.

MacInnes, C. D. (1962). "Nesting of small Canada geese near Eskimo Point, Northwest Territories." *Journal of Wildlife Management,* 26:247–256.

———. (1963). "Interactions of local units within the Eastern Arctic population of small Canada geese." Ph.D. dissertation, Cornell University, Ithaca.

———. (1966). "Population behavior of Eastern Arctic Canada geese. *Journal of Wildlife Management,* 30:536–553.

MacInnes, C. D., and F. C. Cooch. (1963). "Additional eastern records of Ross' goose." *Auk,* 80:77–78.

MacInnes, C. D., and B. C. Lieff. "Individual behavior and composition of a local population of Canada geese." In Hine and Schoenfeld (1968), pp. 93–101.

Mackay, G. H. (1892). "Habits of the oldsquaw (*Clangula hyemalis*) in New England." *Auk,* 9:330–337.

Mackay, R. H. (1957). "Movements of trumpeter swans shown by band returns and observations." *Condor,* 59:339.

Madsen, F. J. (1954). "On the food habits of the diving ducks in Denmark." *Danish Review of Game Biology,* 2:157–266.

Maher, W. J. (1960). "Another record of the Baikal teal in northwestern Alaska." *Condor,* 62:138.

Maher, W. J., and D. N. Nettleship. (1968). "The pintail (*Anas acuta*) breeding at latitude 82° N. on Ellesmere Island, N.W.T., Canada." *Auk,* 85:320–321.

Manning, T. H. (1942). "Blue and lesser snow geese on Southampton and Baffin Islands." *Auk,* 59:158–175.

Manning, T. H., E. O. Höhn, and A. H. Macpherson. (1958). The birds of Banks Island." National Museums of Canada Bulletin No. 143:1–144.

Marshall, D. B. (1958). "The Pacific Flyway. Waterfowl in the Pacific Flyway of North America." *Wildfowl Trust Annual Report,* 9:128–142.

Marshall, I. K. (1967). "The effects of high nesting densities on the clutch size of the common eider, *Somateria mollissima* (L.)." (Abstract). *Journal of Ecology,* 55(3):59.

Martin, A. C., H. S. Zim, and A. L. Nelson. (1951). *American wildlife and plants.* New York: McGraw-Hill.

Martin, E. M., and A. O. Haugen. (1960). "Seasonal changes in wood duck roosting flight habits." *Wilson Bulletin,* 72:238–243.

Martin, F. (1964). "Behavior and survival of Canada geese in Utah." Utah State Department of Fish and Game, Publication No. 64–7, pp. 1–89.

McCartney, R. B. (1963). "The fulvous tree duck in Louisiana." M.S. thesis, Louisiana State University, Baton Rouge.

McClure, R. F. (1967). "Captive propagation of the American ruddy duck." *Modern Game Breeding,* 3(10):7–9, 29–31.

McGilvrey, F. B. (1966). "Nesting of hooded mergansers on the Patuxent Wildlife Research Refuge, Laurel, Maryland." *Auk,* 83:477–479.

———. (1967). "Food habits of sea ducks from the north-eastern United States." *Wildfowl Trust Annual Report,* 18:142–145.

———. (1968). "A guide to wood duck production habitat requirements." U.S.

Dept. of Interior, Bureau of Sport Fisheries and Wildlife Resources Publication No. 60.

McHenry, M. G. (1968). "Mottled ducks in Kansas." *Wilson Bulletin,* 80:229–230.

McKinney, F. (1953). "Incubation and hatching behaviour in the mallard." *Wildfowl Trust Annual Report,* 5:68–70.

———. (1959). "Waterfowl at Cold Bay, Alaska, with notes on the display of the black scoter." *Wildfowl Trust Annual Report,* 10:133–140.

———. (1961). "An analysis of the displays of the European eider *Somateria mollissima mollissima* (Linnaeus) and the Pacific eider *Somateria mollissima v. nigra* Bonaparte." *Behaviour,* Supplement VII. 123 pp.

———. (1965a). "Spacing and chasing in breeding ducks." *Wildfowl Trust Annual Report,* 16:92–106.

———. (1965b). "The displays of the American green-winged teal." *Wilson Bulletin,* 77:112–121.

———. (1965c). "The spring behavior of wild Steller eiders." *Condor,* 67:273–290.

———. (1967). "Breeding behaviour of captive shovelers." *Wildfowl Trust Annual Report,* 18:108–121.

———. (1970). "Displays of four species of blue-winged ducks." *Living Bird,* 9:29–64.

McKnight, D. B., and I. O. Buss. (1962). "Evidence of breeding in yearling female lesser scaup." *Journal of Wildlife Management,* 26:328–329.

McMahan, C. A. (1970). "Food habits of ducks wintering on Laguna Madre, Texas." *Journal of Wildlife Management,* 34:946–949.

Meanley, B., and A. G. Meanley. (1958a). "Nesting habitat of the black-bellied tree duck in Texas." *Wilson Bulletin,* 70:94–95.

———. (1958b). "Postcopulatory display in fulvous and black-bellied tree ducks." *Auk,* 75:96.

———. (1959). "Observations on the fulvous tree duck in Louisiana." *Wilson Bulletin,* 71:33–45.

Mendall, H. L. (1949). "Food habits in relation to black duck management in Maine." *Journal of Wildlife Management,* 13:64–101.

———. (1958). "The ring-necked duck in the Northeast." *University of Maine Bulletin,* 60(16), and *University of Maine Studies,* Second Series, No. 73:1–317.

Mickelson, P. G. (1973). "Breeding biology of cackling geese (*Branta canadensis minima* Ridgway) and associated species on the Yukon-Kuskokwim Delta, Alaska." Ph.D. dissertation, University of Michigan, Ann Arbor.

Miegs, R. C., and C. A. Rieck. (1967). "Mergansers and trout in Washington." *Proceedings 47th Annual Conference, Western Association of State Game and Fish Commissioners,* pp. 306–318.

Miller, A. W., and B. D. Collins. (1954). "A nesting study of ducks and coots on Tule Lake and Lower Klamath National Wildlife Refuges." *California Fish and Game,* 40:17–37.

Miller, H., and A. Dzubin. (1965). "Regrouping of family members of the white-fronted goose (*Anser albifrons*) after individual release." *Bird Banding,* 36:184–191.

Miller, H., A. Dzubin, and J. T. Sweet. (1968). "Distribution and mortality of Saskatchewan-banded white-fronted geese." *North American Wildlife and Natural Resources Conference Transactions,* 33:101–119.

Millais, J. G. (1913). *British diving ducks.* 2 vols. London: Longmans, Green and Co.

Minton, C. D. T. (1968). "Pairing and breeding of mute swans." *Wildfowl* 19:41–60.

Moisan, G., R. I. Smith, and R. K. Martinson, (1967). "The green-winged teal: Its distribution, migration and population dynamics." U.S. Dept. of Interior, Fish and Wildlife Service, Special Scientific Report: Wildlife, No. 100, pp. 1–248.

Monnie, J. B. (1966). "Reintroduction of the trumpeter swan to its former prairie breeding range." *Journal of Wildlife Management,* 30:691–696.

Morse, T. E., J. L. Jakabosky, and V. P. McCrow. (1969). "Some aspects of the breeding biology of the hooded merganser." *Journal of Wildlife Management,* 33:596–604.

Mosby, H. S. (ed.). (1963). *Wildlife investigational techniques.* 2d ed. Washington, D.C.: The Wildlife Society.

Mumford, R. E. (1952). "The hooded merganser in Indiana." *Indiana Audubon Quarterly,* 30:2–7.

———. (1954). "Waterfowl management in Indiana." Indiana Department of Conservation P.R. Bulletin No. 2, p. 1–99.

Munro, J. A. (1939). "Studies of waterfowl in British Columbia. Barrow's golden-eye, American golden-eye." *Transactions Royal Canadian Institute,* 22:259–318.

———. (1941). "Studies of waterfowl in British Columbia. Greater scaup duck, lesser scaup duck." *Canadian Journal of Research,* Sect. D, 19:113–138.

———. (1942). "Studies of waterfowl in British Columbia. Buffle-head." *Canadian Journal of Research,* Sect. D. 20:133–160.

———. (1944). "Studies of waterfowl in British Columbia. Pintail." *Canadian Journal of Research,* Sect. D, 22:60–86.

———. (1949). "Studies of waterfowl in British Columbia. Baldpate." *Canadian Journal of Research,* Sect. D, 27:289–307.

Munro, J. A., and W. A. Clemens. (1936). "Food of the American merganser (*Mer-*

gus merganser americanus) in British Columbia, Paper No. 3." *Canadian Field-Naturalist,* 50(3):34–36.

———. (1937). "The American merganser in British Columbia and its relation to the fish population." Biological Board of Canada, Bulletin, 55:1–50.

———. (1939). "The food and feeding habits of the red-breasted merganser in British Columbia." *Journal of Wildlife Management,* 3:46–53.

Munroe, B. L. J. (1968). "A distributional survey of the birds of Honduras." American Ornithologists' Union, Ornithological Monographs, No. 7, pp. 1–758.

Murie, O. J. (1959). "Fauna of the Aleutian Islands and Alaska Peninsula." U.S. Dept. of Interior, Fish and Wildlife Service, North American Fauna, No. 61, pp. 1–406.

Murray, L. H. (1958). "The black duck in Saskatchewan." *Blue Jay,* 16:109–111.

Musgrove, J. W., and M. R. Musgrove. (1947). *Waterfowl in Iowa.* 2d ed. Des Moines: State Conservation Commission.

Myres, M. T. (1957). "An introduction to the behavior of the goldeneyes: *Bucephala islandica* and *B. clangula* (Class Aves, Family Anatidae)." M.A. thesis, University of British Columbia, Vancouver.

———. (1959). "The behavior of the sea-ducks and its value in the systematics of the tribes Mergini and Somateriini, of the family Anatidae." Ph.D. dissertation, University of British Columbia, Vancouver.

———. (1959b). "Display behavior of bufflehead, scoters and goldeneyes at copulation." *Wilson Bulletin,* 71:159–168.

Nagel, J. (1965). "Field feeding of whistling swans in northern Utah." *Condor,* 67:446–447.

Naylor, A. E. (1960). "The wood duck in California with special reference to the use of nest boxes." *California Fish and Game,* 46:241–269.

Nelson, A. D., and A. C. Martin. (1953). "Gamebird weights." *Journal of Wildlife Management,* 17:36–42.

Nelson, H. K. (1952). "Hybridization of Canada geese with blue geese in the wild." *Auk,* 69:425–428.

Nelson, U. C., and U. A. Hansen. (1959). "The cackling goose—its migration and management." *North American Wildlife Conference Transactions,* 24:174–187.

Nilsson, L. (1965). ("Observations of the spring behaviour of the red-breasted merganser.") *Vår Fågelvärld,* 24:244–256. (In Swedish, with English summary.)

———. (1966). ("The behaviour of the goosander (*Mergus merganser*) in the winter.") *Vår Fågelvärld,* 25:148–160. (In Swedish, with English summary.)

———. (1969). ("The behaviour of the goldeneye *Bucephala clangula* in winter.") *Vår Fågelvärld,* 28:199–210. (In Swedish, with English summary.)

———. (1971). ("Migration, nest-site tenacity and longevity of Swedish goldeneye *Bucephala clangula.*") *Vår Fågelvärld,* 30:180–183. (In Swedish, with English summary.)

Odin, C. R. (1957). "California gull predation on waterfowl." *Auk,* 74:185–196.

Ogilvie, M. A. (1964). "A nesting study of mallard in Berkeley New Decoy, Slimbridge." *Wildfowl Trust Annual Report,* 15:84–88.

———. (1967). "Population changes and mortality of the mute swan in Britain." *Wildfowl Trust Annual Report,* 18:63–73.

Ohlendorf, H. M., and R. F. Patton. (1971). "Nesting record of the Mexican duck (*Anas diazi*) in Texas." *Wilson Bulletin,* 83:97.

Olney, P. J. S., and D. H. Mills, (1963). "The food and feeding habits of the goldeneye, *Bucephala clangula,* in Great Britain." *Ibis,* 105:293–300.

O'Neill, E. J. "Ross goose observations." *Condor,* 56:311.

Oring, L. W. (1964). "Behavior and ecology of certain ducks during the post-breeding period." *Journal of Wildlife Management,* 28:223–233.

———. (1966). "Breeding biology of the gadwall, *Anas strepera* Linnaeus." Ph.D. dissertation, University of Oklahoma, Norman.

———. (1968). "Growth, molts and plumages of the gadwall." *Auk,* 85:355–380.

———. (1969). "Summer biology of the gadwall at Delta, Manitoba." *Wilson Bulletin,* 81:44–54.

Parmelee, D. F. (1954). "Notes on the breeding of certain ducks and mergansers in Dickinson County, Michigan." *Jack-Pine Warbler,* 32:110–118.

Parmelee, D. F., and S. D. MacDonald. (1960). "The birds of west-central Ellesmere Island and adjacent areas." *National Museums of Canada Bulletin,* 169:1–101.

Parmelee, D. F., and H. A. Stephens, and R. H. Schmidt. (1967). "The birds of southeastern Victoria Island and adjacent small islands." *National Museums of Canada Bulletin,* 222:1–229.

Paynter, R. A., Jr. (1951). "Clutch-sizes and egg mortality of Kent Island eiders." *Ecology,* 82:497–507.

Pearse, T. (1945). "Mating of the Pacific harlequin duck." *Canadian Field-Naturalist,* 59:66–67.

Pearson, T. C., C. G. Brimley, and H. H. Brimley. (1919). *Birds of North Carolina.* Revised in 1959 by D. L. Wary and H. T. Davis. Raleigh: North Carolina Department of Agriculture.

Perrins, C. M., and C. M. Reynolds. (1967). "A preliminary study of the mute swan, *Cygnus olor.*" *Wildfowl Trust Annual Report,* 18:74–84.

Peterson, R. T. (1960). *A field guide to the birds of Texas.* Boston: Houghton Mifflin.

Pettingill, O. S., Jr. (1959). "King eider mated with common eider in Iceland." *Wilson Bulletin,* 71:205–207.

———. (1962). "A hybrid between a king eider and common eider observed in Iceland." *Wilson Bulletin,* 74:100.

Phillips, J. C. (1916). "Two problems in the migration of waterfowl." *Auk,* 33:22–27.

———. (1923–1926). *The natural history of the ducks.* 4 vols. Boston: Houghton Mifflin.

Player, P. V. (1971). "Food and feeding habits of the common eider at Seafield." *Wildfowl,* 22:100–106.

Ploeger, P. L. (1968). "Geographical differentiation in Arctic Anatidae as a result of isolation during the Last Glacial." *Ardea,* 56:1–159.

Pool, W. (1962). "Feeding habits of the harlequin duck." *Wildfowl Trust Annual Report,* 13:126–129.

Poston, H. J. (1969). "Relationship between the shoveler and its breeding habitat at Strathmore, Alberta." *Saskatoon Wetland Seminar,* Canadian Wildlife Service Report Series, No. 6, pp. 132–137.

Prince, H. H. (1968). "Nest sites used by wood ducks and common goldeneyes in New Brunswick." *Journal of Wildlife Management,* 32:489–500.

Raitasuo, K. (1964). "Social behaviour of the mallard in the course of the annual cycle." *Papers on Game Research (Riistatieteellisiä Julkaisuja)* 24:1–62.

Rapp, W. F., Jr., J. L. C. Rapp, H. E. Baumgarten, and R. A. Moser. (1971). "Revised check-list of Nebraska birds." Occasional Papers of the Nebraska Ornithologists' Union, No. 5a, second revised printing, pp. 1–35.

Raveling, D. G. (1968a). "Can counts of group sizes of Canada geese reveal population structure?" In Hine and Schoenfeld (1968), pp. 87–91.

———. (1968b). "Weights of *Branta canadensis interior* during winter." *Journal of Wildlife Management,* 32:412–414.

———. (1969a). "Social classes of Canada geese in winter." *Journal of Wildlife Management,* 33:304–318.

———. (1969b). "Preflight and flight behavior of Canada geese." *Auk,* 86:671–681.

Rawls, C. K., Jr. (1949). "An investigation of life history of the white-winged scoter (*Melanitta fusca deglandi*)." M.S. thesis, University of Minnesota, Minneapolis.

Reeves, H. M., H. H. Dill, and A. S. Hawkins. "A case study in Canada goose management: The Mississippi Valley population." In Hine and Schoenfeld (1968), pp. 150–165.

Reinecker, W. C. (1965). "A summary of band returns from lesser snow geese (*Chen hyperborea*) of the Pacific Flyway." *California Fish and Game,* 51: 132–146.

———. (1968). "A summary of band recoveries from redheads (*Aythya americana*) banded in northeastern California." *California Fish and Game,* 54:17–26.

Ringlegen, H. (1951). "Aus dem leben des Mittelsägers (*Mergus serrator* L.) I." *Vogelwelt,* 72:43–50.

Ripley, S. D., and G. E. Watson. (1956). "Cuban bird notes." *Postilla,* 26:1–6.

Roberts, T. S. (1932). *The birds of Minnesota.* 2 vols. Minneapolis: University of Minnesota Press.

Rogers, J. P. (1959). "Low water and lesser scaup reproduction near Erickson, Manitoba." *North American Wildlife Conference Transactions,* 24:216–224.

———. (1964). "Effect of drought on reproduction of the lesser scaup." *Journal of Wildlife Management,* 28:213–222.

Rogers, J. P., and J. L. Hansen. (1967). "Second broods in the wood duck." *Bird Banding,* 38:234–235.

Rogers, J. P., and L. J. Korschgen. (1966). "Foods of lesser scaups on breeding, migration and wintering areas." *Journal of Wildlife Management,* 30:258–264.

Rollin, N. (1957). "Incubation by drake wood duck in eclipse plumage." *Condor,* 59:263–265.

Rollo, J. D., and E. G. Bolen. (1969). "Ecological relationships of blue and green-winged teal on the high plains of Texas in early fall." *Southwestern Naturalist,* 14:171–188.

Rolnik, V. (1943). "Instructions for the incubation of eider duck eggs." *Journal of Wildlife Management,* 7:155–162.

Rosche, R. C. (1954). "Notes on some birds of Yellowstone National Park." *Wilson Bulletin,* 66:600.

Ryder, J. P. (1964). "A preliminary study of the breeding biology of Ross's goose." *Wildfowl Trust Annual Report,* 15:127–137.

———. (1967). "The breeding biology of Ross' goose in the Perry River region, Northwest Territories." Canadian Wildlife Service Report Series, No. 3, pp. 1–56.

———. (1969). "Nesting colonies of Ross' goose." *Auk,* 86:288–292.

———. (1970a). "A possible factor in the evolution of clutch size in Ross' goose." *Wilson Bulletin,* 82:5–13.

———. (1970b). "Timing and spacing of nests and breeding biology of Ross' goose." Ph.D. dissertation, University of Saskatchewan, Regina.

Salomonsen, F. (1950). *The birds of Greenland.* Part 1. Copenhagen: Ejnar Munksgaard.

———. (1965). "Tenth preliminary list of recoveries of birds ringed in Greenland." *Dansk Ornithologisk Forenings Tids-*

skrift, 59:92–103. (In Danish, with English summary.)

———. (1968). "The moult migration." *Wildfowl*, 19:5–24.

Salyer, J. C., II, and K. F. Lagler. (1940). "The food and habits of the American merganser, considered in relation to fish management." *Journal of Wildlife Management*, 4:186–219.

Schiøler, E. L. (1925–1926). *Danmarks Fugle*. 2 vols. Copenhagen: Gyldendelske.

Scott, D. (1967). "The Bewick's swans at Slimbridge, 1966–67." *Wildfowl Trust Annual Report*, 17:24–27.

Scott, P., and H. Boyd. (1957). *Wildfowl of the British Isles*. London: Country Life Ltd.

Scott, P., and the Wildfowl Trust. (1972). *The swans*. London: Michael Joseph.

Seaman, G. A. (1958). "Masked duck collected in St. Croix, Virgin Islands." *Auk*, 75:215.

Sedwitz, W. (1958). "Six years (1947–1952) nesting of gadwall (*Anas strepera*) on Jones Beach, Long Island, N.Y." *Proceedings Linnaean Society of New York*, No. 66–70:61–70.

Shepherd, P. E. K. (1962). "An ecological reconnaisance of the trumpeter swan in south central Alaska." M.S. thesis, Washington State University, Pullman.

Sheppard, R. W. (1949). "The American brant on the lower Great Lakes." *Canadian Field-Naturalist*, 63:99–100.

Sherman, G. R. (1965). "The form and duration of the male displays of the king eider (*Somateria spectabilis* Linnaeus)." M.S. thesis, University of Nebraska, Lincoln.

Sherwood, G. A. (1960). "The whistling swan in the west with particular reference to the Great Salt Lake Valley, Utah." *Condor*, 62:370–377.

———. (1965). "Canada geese of the Seney National Wildlife Refuge." Seney National Wildlife Refuge, 222 pp. (mimeo).

Shields, A. M. (1899). "Nesting of the fulvous tree duck." Cooper Ornithological Club Bulletin, 1:9–11.

Sibley, C. G. (1949). "The incidence of hybrids in migrant blue and snow geese in Kansas." *Condor*, 51:274.

Siegfried, W. R. (1971). "Double wing-moult in the Maccoa duck." *Wildfowl*, 21:122.

Sincock, J. L., M. M. Smith, and J. J. Lynch. "Ducks in Dixie." In Linduska (1964), pp. 99–102.

Singleton, J. R. (1953). "Texas coastal waterfowl survey." Texas Game and Fish Commission, F.A. Report, Series 11. 128 pp.

Sirén, M. (1951). "Increasing the goldeneye population with nest boxes." *Suomen Riista*, 6:83–101, 189–190. (In Finnish, with English summary.)

———. (1952). "Studies on the breeding biology of the goldeneye." *Papers on Game Research (Riistatieteellisia Jlkaisuja)*, 8:101–111. (In Swedish, with English summary.)

———. (1957a). "On the faithfulness of goldeneye to its nesting region and nesting site." *Soumen Riista*, 11:130–133. (In Finnish, with separate English summary.)

———. (1957b). "How goldeneye broods can be tied to one's own game grounds." *Suomen Riista*, 11:59–64. (In Finnish, with separate English summary.)

Skinner, M. P. (1937). "Barrow's goldeneye in the Yellowstone National Park." *Wilson Bulletin*, 49:3–10.

Sladen, W. J., and W. W. Cochran. (1969). "Studies of the whistling swan, 1967–1969." *North American Wildlife and Natural Resources Conference Transactions*, 34:42–50.

Smart, G. (1965). "Body weights of newly hatched Anatidae." *Auk*, 82:645–658.

Smith, A. G. (1971). "Ecological factors affecting waterfowl production in the Alberta Parklands." Bureau of Sport Fisheries and Wildlife, Fish and Wildlife Service, Washington, D.C., Research Publication, 98.

Smith, D. (1946). "The canvas-back in Minnesota." *Auk,* 63:73–81.

Smith, R. I. (1968). "The social aspects of reproductive behavior in the pintail." *Auk,* 85:381–396.

Snyder, L. L. (1957). *Arctic birds of Canada.* Toronto: University of Toronto Press.

Soper, J. D. (1942). "Life history of the blue goose *Chen caerulescens* (Linnaeus)." *Proceedings of the Boston Society of Natural History,* 42:121–225.

Sowls, L. K. (1955). *Prairie Ducks: A study of their behavior, ecology and management."* Washington, D.C.: Wildlife Management Institute and Harrisburg, Pa.: Stackpole Company.

Spencer, D. L., U. C. Nelson, and W. A. Elkins. (1951). "America's greatest goose-brant nesting area." *North American Wildlife Conference Transactions,* 15:290–295.

Spencer, H. E., Jr. (1953). "The cinnamon teal (*Anas cyanoptera* Vieillot): Its life history, ecology, and management." M.S. thesis, Utah State Agricultural College, Logan.

Sprunt, A., Jr., and E. B. Chamberlain. (1949). *"South Carolina bird life."* Columbia: University of South Carolina Press.

Sterling, T., and A. Dzubin. (1967). "Canada goose molt migrations to the Northwest Territories." *North American Wildlife and Natural Resources Conference Transactions,* 32:355–373.

Stewart, P. A. (1957). "Nesting of the shoveller (*Spatula clypeata*) in central Ohio." *Wilson Bulletin,* 69:280.

———. (1958). "Local movements of wood ducks (*Aix sponsa*)." *Auk,* 75:157–168.

Stewart, R. E. (1958). "Distribution of the black duck." U.S. Fish & Wildlife Service, Circular 51, pp. 1–8.

———. (1962). Waterfowl populations in the upper Chesapeake region. U.S. Dept. of Interior, Fish and Wildlife Service, Special Scientific Report: Wildlife, No. 65, pp. 1–208.

Stewart, R. E., and J. H. Manning. (1958). "Distribution and ecology of whistling swans in the Chesapeake Bay region." *Auk,* 75:203–211.

Stewart, R. E., A. D. Geis, and C. D. Evans. (1958). "Distribution of populations and hunting kill of the canvasback." *Journal of Wildlife Management,* 22:333–370.

Stewart, R. E., Jr. (1968). "Pond ecology and waterfowl production in relation to optimum water resource utilization in the Turtle Mountains of North Dakota." M.S. thesis, North Dakota State University, Fargo.

Stieglitz, W. O., and C. T. Wilson. (1968). "Breeding biology of the Florida duck." *Journal of Wildlife Management,* 32:921–934.

Stone, W. B., and A. D. Masters. (1971). "Aggression among captive mute swans." *New York Fish and Game Journal,* 17:50–52.

Stotts, V. (1935). "Black duck breeding study ends in the Kent Island area." *Maryland Tidewater News,* 12(4):1,4.

———. (1957). "The black duck (*Anas rubripes*) in the Upper Chesapeake Bay." *Proceedings 10th Annual Conference, Southeastern Association of Game and Fish Commissioners,* pp. 234–242.

———. (1958). "The time of formation of pairs in black ducks," *North American Wildlife Conference Transactions,* 23:192–197.

Stotts, V. D., and D. E. Davis. (1960). "The black duck in the Chesapeake Bay of Maryland: Breeding behavior and biology." *Chesapeake Science,* 1(3–4):127–154.

Stoudt, J. H. (1969). "Relationships between waterfowl and water areas on the

Redvers Waterfowl Study Area." In *Saskatoon Wetlands Seminar*, Canadian Wildlife Report Series, No. 6, pp. 123–131.

———. (1971). "Ecological factors affecting waterfowl production in the Saskatchewan Parklands." Bureau of Sport Fisheries & Wildlife, Fish and Wildlife Service, Washington, D.C. Resource Publication, 99.

Strohmeyer, D. L. (1967). "The biology of renesting by the blue-winged teal." Ph.D. dissertation, University of Minnesota, Minneapolis.

Sugden, L. G. (1963a). "Barrow's goldeneye using old crow nests." *Condor*, 65: 330.

———. (1963b). "A garganey duck in the wild in Alberta." *Blue Jay*, 21:4–5.

———. (1973). "Feeding ecology of pintail, gadwall, American wigeon and lesser scaup ducklings in southern Alberta." Canadian Wildlife Service Report Series, No. 24, 32 p.

Sutton, G. M. (1931). "The blue goose and lesser snow goose on Southampton Island, Hudson Bay." *Auk*, 48:335–364.

———. (1967). *Oklahoma birds*. Norman: University of Oklahoma Press.

Swanson, G. A., and J. C. Bartonek. (1970). "Bias associated with food analysis in gizzards of blue-winged teal." *Journal of Wildlife Management*, 34:739–746.

Swarth, H. S., and H. C. Bryant. (1917). "A study of the races of the white-fronted goose (*Anser albifrons*) occurring in California." *University of California Publications in Zoology*, 17: 209–222.

Tate, D. J. (1966). "Morphometric age and sex variation in the whistling swan (*Olor columbianus*)." M.S. thesis, University of Nebraska, Lincoln.

Teer, J. G. (1964). "Predation by long-tailed weasels on eggs of blue-winged teal." *Journal of Wildlife Management*, 28:404–406.

Tener, J. S., and A. G. Loughrey. (1970). "The migratory waterfowl program in Canada." *North American Wildlife and Natural Resources Conference Transactions*, 35:287–295.

Texas Game, Fish and Oyster Commission. (1945). *Principal game birds and mammals of Texas*. Austin: Published by the Commission.

Thompson, D.Q., and M.D. Lyons. (1964). "Flock size in a spring concentration of whistling swans." *Wilson Bulletin*, 76: 282–285.

Thompson, D. Q., and R. A. Person. (1963). "The eider pass at Point Barrow, Alaska." *Journal of Wildlife Management*, 27:348–356.

Timken, R. L., and B. W. Anderson. (1969). "Food habits of common mergansers in the northcentral United States." *Journal of Wildlife Management*, 33:87–91.

Todd, W. E. C. (1963). *Birds of the Labrador Peninsula and adjacent areas*. Toronto: University of Toronto Press.

Townsend, G. H. (1966). "A study of waterfowl nesting on the Saskatchewan River delta." *Canadian Field-Naturalist*, 80:74–88.

Trauger, D. L. (1971). "Population ecology of lesser scaup (*Aythya affinis*) in subarctic taiga." Ph.D. dissertation, Iowa State University, Ames.

Trauger, D., A. Dzubin, and J. P. Ryder, (1971). "White geese intermediate between Ross' geese and lesser snow geese." *Auk*, 88:856–875.

Trefethen, J. B. (ed.). (1966). *Wood duck management and research: a symposium. Theme: Emphasizing management of forests for wood ducks*. Washington, D.C.: Wildlife Management Institute.

Tuck, L. M. (1968). "Recent Newfoundland bird records." *Auk*, 85:304–311.

Uspenski, S. M. (1965). "The geese of Wrangel Island." *Wildfowl Trust Annual Report,* 16:126–129.

Vermeer, K. (1968). "Ecological aspects of ducks nesting in high densities among larids." *Wilson Bulletin,* 80:78–83.
———. (1969). "Some aspects of the breeding of the white-winged scoter at Miquelon Lake, Alberta." *Blue Jay,* 27:72–73.
———. (1970). "Some aspects of the nesting of ducks on islands in Lake Newell, Alberta." *Journal of Wildlife Management,* 34:126–129.
Vos, A. de (1964). "Observations on the behavior of captive trumpeter swans during the breeding season." *Ardea,* 52:166–189.

Wainwright, C. B. (1957). "Results of wildfowl ringing at Abberton Reservoir, Essex, 1949–1966." *Wildfowl Trust Annual Report,* 18:28–35.
Weier, R. W. "Survey of wood duck nest sites on Mingo Wildlife Refuge in southeast Missouri." In Trefethen (1966), pp. 91–108.
Weller, M. W. (1957). "Growth, weights and plumages of the redhead, *Aythya americana.*" *Wilson Bulletin,* 69:5–38.
———. (1959). "Parasitic egg laying in the redhead (*Aythya americana*) and other North American Anatidae." *Ecological Monographs,* 29:333–365.
———. (1964a). "The reproductive cycle." In Delacour, pp. 35–79.
———. (1964b). "Distribution and migration of the redhead." *Journal of Wildlife Management,* 28:64–103.
———. (1965). "Chronology of pair formation in some Nearctic *Aythya* (Anatidae)." *Auk,* 82:227–235.
———. (1967). "Courtship of the redhead (*Aythya americana*)." *Auk,* 84:544–559.
———. (1968). "Notes on some Argentine anatids." *Wilson Bulletin,* 80:189–212.

Weller, M. W., D. L. Trauger, and G. L. Krapu. (1969). "Breeding birds of the West Mirage Islands, Great Slave Lake, N.W.T." *Canadian Field-Naturalist,* 83:344–360.
Wetmore, A. (1965). "The birds of the Republic of Panamá. Pt. 1. Tinamidae (tinamous) to Rhynchopidae (skimmers)." *Smithsonian Miscellaneous Collections,* Vol. 150:1–483.
Wheeler, R. J. (1965). "Pioneering of the blue-winged teal in California, Oregon, Washington and British Columbia." *Murrelet,* 46:40–42.
Wheeler, R. J., and S. W. Harris. (1970). "Duck nesting and production in the Humboldt Bay area of California." *California Fish and Game,* 56:180–187.
White, C. M., and J. R. Haugh. (1969). "Recent data on summer birds of the upper Yukon River, Alaska, and adjacent parts of the Yukon Territory, Canada." *Canadian Field-Naturalist,* 83:257–271.
White, H. C. (1937). "Local feeding of kingfishers and mergansers." *Journal of the Biological Board of Canada,* 3:323–338.
———. (1957). "Food and natural history of mergansers on salmon waters in the Maritime Provinces of Canada." *Fisheries Research Board of Canada Bulletin,* 116:1–63.
Wick, W. Q., and R. G. Jeffrey. (1966). "Population estimates and hunter harvest of diving ducks in northeastern Puget Sound, Washington." *Murrelet,* 47:23–32.
Wick, W. Q., and H. E. Rogers. (1957). "An unusual merganser fatality." *Condor,* 59:342–343.
Wienmeyer, S. N. (1967). "Bufflehead food habits, parasites, and biology in northern California." M.S. thesis, Humboldt State College, Arcata.
Willey, C. H. (1968). "The ecological significance of the mute swan in Rhode Island." Presented at the Northeast Fish

and Wildlife Conference, Bedford, N.H., January 17, 1968. 23 pp. (mimeo).

Willey, C. H., and B. F. Halla. (1972). "Mute swans of Rhode Island." Rhode Island Department of Natural Resources, Wildlife Pamphlet No. 8, 47 p.

Williams, C. S. (1967). *Honker: A discussion of the habits and needs of the largest of our Canada geese.* Princeton, N.J.: D. Van Nostrand Co.

Williams, C. S., and W. H. Marshall. (1938). "Duck nesting studies, Bear River Migratory Bird Refuge, Utah, 1937." *Journal of Wildlife Management,* 2:29–48.

Williamson, F. S. L., M. C. Thompson, and J. Q. Hines. (1966). "Avifaunal investigations." In U.S. Atomic Energy Commission, *Environment of the Cape Thompson Region, Alaska,* pp. 437–480.

Wingfield, B., and J. B. Low. (1953). "Waterfowl productivity in Knudson Marsh, Salt Lake Valley, Utah." *Proceedings 33rd Annual Conference, Western Association of State Game and Fish Commissioners,* pp. 177–181.

Winner, R. W. (1959). "Field-feeding periodicity of black and mallard ducks." *Journal of Wildlife Management,* 23: 197–202.

———. (1960). "Fall and winter movements of black and mallard ducks." *Journal of Wildlife Management,* 24:332–335.

Wright, B. S. (1954). *High tide and an east wind: The story of the black duck.* Washington, D.C.: Wildlife Management Institute and Harrisburg: Stackpole Co.

Yocom, C. F. (1951). *Waterfowl and their food plants in Washington.* Seattle: University of Washington Press.

———. (1965). "Estimated populations of Great Basin Canada geese over their breeding range in western Canada and western United States." *Murrelet,* 46:18–26.

———. (1970). "Weights of ten species of ducks captured at Ohtig Lake, Alaska." *Murrelet,* 51:20–21.

———. (1972). "Weights and measurements of Taverner's and Great Basin Canada geese." *Murrelet,* 53:33–34.

Zimmerman, D. A., and J. Van Tyne. (1959). "A distributional check-list of the birds of Michigan." *University of Michigan Museum of Zoology Occasional Papers,* No. 608, pp. 1–63.

Index

English vernacular names of waterfowl indexed here are in general those used in this book for species or larger groupings. Vernacular names for subspecies are only indexed to those pages where they may be listed among the subspecies included in the species accounts. Pages that include the primary discussions of each species are indicated by boldface under the species' vernacular name and its scientific name. Species other than waterfowl are not indexed.